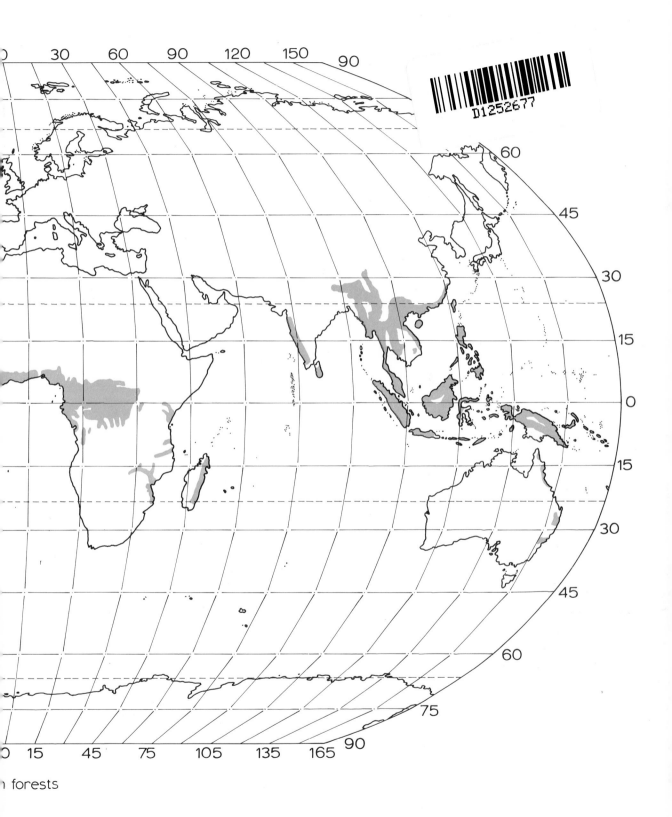

n forests

TROPICAL RAIN FOREST ECOSYSTEMS

STRUCTURE AND FUNCTION

ECOSYSTEMS OF THE WORLD

Editor in Chief:

David W. Goodall

CSIRO Division of Land Resources Management, Wembley, W.A. (Australia)

ECOSYSTEMS OF THE WORLD 14A

TROPICAL RAIN FOREST ECOSYSTEMS

STRUCTURE AND FUNCTION

Edited by

F.B. Golley

Institute of Ecology
University of Georgia
Athens, Ga. (U.S.A.)

ELSEVIER SCIENTIFIC PUBLISHING COMPANY

Amsterdam — Oxford — New York 1983

ELSEVIER SCIENTIFIC PUBLISHING COMPANY
1 Molenwerf
P.O. Box 211, 1000 AE Amsterdam, The Netherlands

Distributors for the United States and Canada:

ELSEVIER SCIENCE PUBLISHING COMPANY INC.
52 Vanderbilt Avenue
New York, N.Y. 10017, U.S.A.

Library of Congress Cataloging in Publication Data
Main entry under title:

Tropical rain forest ecosystems.

    (Ecosystems of the world ; 14A)
    Includes bibliographies and index.
    1. Rain forest ecology. I. Golley, Frank B.
II. Series.
QH541.5.R27T76   574.5'2642   81-7861
ISBN 0-444-41986-1 (v. 1)   AACR2

ISBN 0-444-41986-1 (Vol. 14A)
ISBN 0-444-41702-8 (Series)
ISBN 0-444-41810-5 (Set)

Printed in The Netherlands

PREFACE

The tropical rain forest will be treated in the *Ecosystems of the World* series in two parts. In this first part the authors focus on ecosystem structure and function. Part B, under the editorship of H. Lieth and M.J.A. Werger, will examine the rain forest environment, including soils, and biogeography, and will include regional studies. Part A has been under preparation for five years and some chapters were completed two or three years ago while others were written within weeks and months of the final deadline. This unevenness in timing means that some chapters are complete and up to date, while others touch the subject lightly. The editor has tried, within his own limits of knowledge, to bring all chapters up to a point where they contribute to the whole. Nevertheless, the disadvantage of uneven treatment remains in a contributed volume. Hopefully, this disadvantage is balanced by the advantage of a variety of experiences and a wider range of expertise which comes with many authors.

In this volume we will examine the rain forest using the ecosystem concept developed at the University of Georgia, Athens (Ga., U.S.A.) from the work of such ecologists as E.P. Odum, B.C. Patten, L. Pomeroy, R. Wiegert, D.C. Crossley, and the editor. Thus, ecosystem is not employed as a synonym of habitat, community, formation or some other descriptive term. Rather, it is a technical term in ecology which refers to a system of living and non-living components, interacting as a whole. There are other ecosystem concepts but this one serves to relate the various structural attributes of rain forests to their functional or dynamic properties. This integrated approach is useful in applied ecology as well as theoretical ecology. Certainly the authors of the chapters are not all interested in or even accepting of this point of view. In some instances their contributions take a very different direction, emphasizing the biological relationships of organisms without considering the ecosystem in which these relationships fit. This means that our book has two intersecting patterns. The basic theme is ecosystem structure and function. The minor theme serves to elucidate particular features of forest biology relating to structure and function and human use of forests. Thus, the various contributions fit into the overall scheme so that a whole pattern emerges. Unfortunately, the subject is too immature, or too complex, or the editor is too limited in ability to bring the volume to a conclusion where a grand theory of tropical forest structure and function can be identified and described. This is a matter for the future.

The original conception of this book was to bring in authors representing all of the various points of view in tropical forest studies. Unfortunately, this conception could not be carried out, and some authors had to cancel their participation almost at the last minute. For this reason the editor wrote several more chapters than he intended. Also, Norman Myers was enlisted as a contributor at a late date and was extremely cooperative in writing chapters on conservation and rates of forest destruction. Other colleagues contributed by reviewing chapters. I especially acknowledge with appreciation the comments of Francesco di Castri, Kermit Cromack, Ted St. John, and David Coleman. Finally, I am especially endebted to Gladys Russell, Institute of Ecology, University of Georgia, who typed, organized and otherwise assisted me in the editorial work, especially when I was located temporarily in Washington, D.C. Hopefully, this volume will contribute to man's understanding and use of this important ecosystem.

F.B. GOLLEY

University of Georgia
Athens, Georgia

LIST OF CONTRIBUTORS TO VOLUME 14A

HERBERT G. BAKER
Department of Botany
University of California
Berkeley, Calif. 94720 (U.S.A.)

KAMILJIT S. BAWA
Department of Biology
University of Massachusetts
Boston, Mass. 02125 (U.S.A.)

PATRICK S. BOURGERON
Natural Resource Ecology Laboratory
Colorado State University
Fort Collins, Colo. (U.S.A.)

FRANÇOIS BOURLIÈRE
15, Avenue de Tourville
75007 Paris (France)

EBERHARDT F. BRUNIG
Chair of World Forestry
University of Hamburg
Federal Research Center for Forestry and Forest
    Products
Leuschnerstrasse 91
D-2050 Hamburg 80 (Federal Republic of
    Germany)

JOHN F. EISENBERG
National Zoological Park
Smithsonian Institution
Washington, D.C. 20008 (U.S.A.)

JOHN EWEL
Botany Department
University of Florida
Gainesville, Fla. 32611 (U.S.A.)

GORDON W. FRANKIE
Department of Entomology
Texas Agricultural and Mechanical University
College Station, Texas 77843 (U.S.A.)

FRANK B. GOLLEY
Institute of Ecology
University of Georgia
Athens, Ga. 30602 (U.S.A.)

HAROLD HEATWOLE
Department of Zoology
University of New England
Armidale, N.S.W. 2351 (Australia)

DANIEL H. JANZEN
Department of Biology
University of Pennsylvania
Philadelphia, Penn. 19104 (U.S.A.)

CARL F. JORDAN
Institute of Ecology
University of Georgia
Athens, Ga. 30602 (U.S.A.)

ERNESTO MEDINA
Centro de Ecologia
IVIC
Caracas (Venezuela)

NORMAN MYERS
Upper Meadow
Old Road
Headington, Oxford (United Kingdom)

PAUL A. OPLER
Office of Endangered Species
Fish and Wildlife Department
U.S. Department of Interior
Washington, D.C. 20040 (U.S.A.)

DENIS F. OWEN
Biology Department
Oxford Polytechnic
Oxford (England)

CHRISTINE PADOCH
Institute of Environmental Science
University of Wisconsin
Madison, Wis. 53706 (U.S.A.)

P.B. TOMLINSON
Harvard Forest
Petersham, Mass. 01366 (U.S.A.)

ANDREW P. VAYDA
Department of Human Ecology
Cook College
Rutgers University
New Brunswick, N.J. 08903 (U.S.A.)

FRANK H. WADSWORTH
Institute of Tropical Forestry
Southern Forest Experiment Station
Forest Service, U.S. Department of Agriculture
Rio Piedras, P.R. 00928 (U.S.A.)

THOMAS M. YUILL
Department of Veterinary Science
University of Wisconsin
Madison, Wis. 53706 (U.S.A.)

CONTENTS OF VOLUME 14A

Chapter 1

INTRODUCTION

FRANK B. GOLLEY

The object of this book is to present selected data on the biology of tropical rain forests in the context of the ecosystem paradigm. These data are useful for the understanding and rational use of forests, and are especially important today when these forests are being so heavily exploited that they may disappear as large blocks of intact primary forest by the end of the century. The approximately 16 million square kilometers of potential tropical closed forest lands are being converted to other uses at a rate greater than 200 000 square kilometers per year (Myers, 1979). These conversion processes, in turn, have direct and immediate impacts on the human environment and may have long-term impacts on man's ability to sustain life in tropical regions. While each day spontaneous settlers, shifting cultivators and fuel wood harvesters, who are among the major contributors to forest conversion, continue to make their inroads to forests, governments and scientists meet, study, and plan on how to reduce or redirect this human impact and preserve what remains of the resource. In each case intelligent and effective discussion and planning is limited by gaps in our understanding of the tropical forest biome.

The fact that we have limited knowledge of tropical rain forests is not widely recognized or appreciated. A recent study by the National Academy of Sciences of the United States (NRC, 1980) states that only about one-sixth of the probable species of plants and animals living in the tropics have been collected, identified and named. Further, there are fewer than a dozen detailed ecosystem studies in the world's tropical forests comparable to those used as a basis for land planning and forest management in temperate and arctic regions.

While tropical biologists are actively publishing over 600 technical reports yearly, the numbers of biologists are far too few for the task at hand. A recent census of tropical ecologists (Yantko and Golley, 1978) describes the nature of the community trained to address tropical forest science. There are about 2000 to 3000 tropical ecologists worldwide. These scientists are concentrated in a few countries with well-developed science establishments. Of course, these are usually in developed nontropical areas. If the distribution of tropical ecologists was equal in all countries there would be no more than about 25 ecologists per country. This population is clearly inadequate to carry out research, teach the ecologists of the next generation, administrate the environmental agencies and monitor the state of the environment to protect human health. Turning to systematic biology, the NRC report also stated that there were probably no more than 1500 trained professional systematists in the world capable of dealing with the approximate three million tropical organisms.

For systematic biology and ecology the cadres of trained people are too few; while the data on tropical forests are too scattered and unfocused. Clearly research on tropical forests needs coordination and direction so that it can become the basis of an additive process leading toward rational management and public policy. We are hopeful that the ecosystem paradigm provides such a means to achieve coordination. Clearly as it is developed in this volume and in other recent summaries (UNESCO, 1978) it does not go far enough. We have not developed a grand synthesis of tropical forest biology nor can we present refined system models from which to predict cause and effect. Rather, in this volume we bring together a collection of individual and occasionally disparate approaches to tropical forest biology, linking them together under the concept of the ecosystem. Before we examine the flow of these ideas in the synopsis of individual chapters, we should examine more closely the ecosystem paradigm underlying this and other volumes in the *Ecosystems of the World* Series.

THE ECOSYSTEM

The word ecosystem refers to a system of living organisms interacting with the physical, chemical, biological and social environments. The idea of a system is important because it means that the complex of living organisms and environment interact together to form a whole. This whole system has distinct characteristics which separate it from other systems. The term ecosystem was coined by Tansley (1935), expanded by Evans (1956), and given wide usage by Odum (1953). According to Major (1969) the term expresses a very general concept inherent in the thought of many observers of natural history.

Ecosystems may occur at a variety of geographical and biological scales. For example, Evans (1956) extends the concept to each unit of a hierarchy of biological organization made up of the individual–population–community–biome–biosphere. At the largest scale of this system the biosphere interacts with the hydrosphere, lithosphere, and atmosphere to form the world ecosystem or ecosphere of planet Earth. The subdivision of the ecosphere is of special interest to ecologists and a very complex terminology and taxonomy has evolved to describe these subdivisions. From an ecological point of view the major factors used in the delimitation of subunits are the physical size of the unit, the importance of environmental features in organization and control of the unit and its biological complexity.

The environmental features of importance in ecosystem classification are related to the energy dynamics of the planet, as well as the planet's shape and rotation. In astronomical terms, two circles can be identified on the celestial sphere where the sun reaches its most northern or southern declination. These are located at 23 degrees, 27 minutes north and south of the equator. The northern circle is called the Tropic of Cancer and the southern the Tropic of Capricorn. The word tropic is derived from Latin *tropicus* meaning a turn of the sun and from Greek *tropikos* referring to the solstice. Our word tropics means a location within the two astronomical tropics. Tropical forest ecosystems, then, are those ecosystems occurring within the tropics which are dominated by trees. There are three main areas of forest corresponding to the three continents of Asia, Africa and Iberio-America. Each of these forest areas is widely separated from the others by oceans and arid lands.

Actually there are a great variety of tropical forest ecosystems, and these will be identified and discussed at length in Volume B. Tropical forest is used here to refer to those ecosystems where trees form a continuous canopy over the soil surface. Our definition separates forests from savanna and savanna woodland where the trees form a discontinuous canopy or occur as isolated clumps or even as isolated individuals. Savanna and savanna woodland are the subject of another volume in the *Ecosystems of the World* Series.

Ecosystem study involves the examination of the structure and function of different ecosystems and through their comparisons the development of general statements of ecosystem behavior. Structure refers to the quantity of energy and chemical elements, expressed in terms of biomass. Structure also includes the distribution of these attributes in time and space, as well as their distribution among living organisms. A structural analysis is static since it does not involve change in biomass or species variety over time. Temporal processes are part of the functional analysis of ecosystems. Function includes energy dynamics, nutrient cycling, ecological succession and similar dynamic processes. In most instances an ecosystem study focuses on a plot of forest, compares the structure and function on that site with other sites, and develops general statements about other, unstudied sites from these comparisons. Other, non-ecosystem studies may focus on an organism, or a community of organisms, on an environmental factor, such as soils, or on a biological process. These studies are not necessarily site specific. Thus, the ecosystem studies intersect with the general biological and environmental studies to form a complete description of the tropical forest.

THE HISTORICAL VIEWPOINT

Tropical forests have been studied from a variety of viewpoints, however, ecosystem studies *per se* are relatively recent. In temperate regions most ecosystem studies have been made within the last 50 years; in the tropics within the last 25 years. The International Biological Program (IBP) (1964–1974) gave ecosystem studies special impetus. However, well before IBP a joint Thai–Japanese group began ecosystem studies of tropical forest in Thailand, 1961–1962. These expeditions were led by Professors T. Kira, Osaka City University, and T. Shidei, Kyoto University. Their research has been presented mainly in the journal *Nature and Life in Southeast Asia*, published by the Japan Society for the Promotion of Science, Tokyo.

Following these Japanese–Thai studies and comparable work in temperate North American and European regions there was a convergence of activities in the Neotropics supported by the United States Atomic Energy Commission (now the Department of Energy) and under IBP auspices in the African and Asian tropics. In Puerto Rico Howard T. Odum, in 1963, began a study of the effects of gamma irradiation on tropical montane rain forest at El Verde in the Luquillo Mountains. This area has remained continuously in forest cover under protection and management first by the Spanish crown and later by the U.S. Forest Service. Odum's study involved scientists from many countries and universities, who investigated all aspects of forest structure and function, including the reaction of the forest to a 10 000 Ci ^{134}Cs/^{137}Cs source. The forest site was located at 424 m elevation and has many tabanuco trees (*Dacryodes excelsa*) in the canopy. While these studies have continued, the work to 1967 was published in Odum (1970).

At approximately the same time the Atomic Energy Commission, through a contract with Battelle Memorial Institute, Columbus, Ohio, U.S.A., supported other studies of tropical forests in the Republic of Panama and in Columbia. These joint U.S.–Panamanian–Colombian studies were designed to determine the feasibility of constructing a sea-level canal across the isthmus either in Panama or Colombia by nuclear excavation. A team from the University of Georgia, Athens, Georgia, U.S.A., subcontracted to study the forest ecology. In this instance a variety of forests were encountered but the type occupying the largest area of land was tropical moist forest. In contrast to El Verde in Puerto Rico where precipitation was in excess over evapotranspiration at all months, in the tropical moist forest in Darien, Panama, a distinct dry season occurs from approximately January to March. At this season some trees, including the emergent cuipo (*Cavanillesia platanifolia*), lose their leaves. These studies focused on mineral storages and fluxes between the various parts of the forest since an objective was to predict pathways and storage of radioactive products from the excavation. The study was completed in 1969 and was published in 1975 (Golley et al., 1975).

Other broad-scale ecosystem investigations have been recently completed or are underway in the New World tropics. In Panama, on Barro Colorado Island located in Gatun Lake, the Smithsonian Tropical Research Institute maintains a nature preserve that has an unusually fine and long-term collection of natural history and behavioral observations. Recently the STRI has established an ecosystem study which will utilize this foundation of biological information and will focus on the tropical forest structure and dynamics. In Costa Rica a consortium of universities and research organizations called The Organization for Tropical Studies (OTS) has operated a comparative ecosystem study for many years. The OTS program has emphasized a comparison of the biology of the dry deciduous forest (a savanna woodland forest) and the rain forest. In Mexico ecologists under the leadership of Arturo Gómez-Pompa have carried out studies on a variety of ecosystems at Jalapa. These investigations have focused on the processes of secondary succession, although they also have a practical bent with focus on the coffee plantation ecosystem and other agro-ecosystems. And in Brazil, at Manaus, a team under the leadership of Harold Sioli from the Max Planck Institute of Germany and more recently sponsored by INPA, Brazil, have made a great variety of studies of forests and waters. Many of their papers are referred to in this volume and are published in Acta Amazonica of INPA.

Further north, within the U.S. have been two team projects on tropical ecosystems. Under IBP auspices Dieter Muller Dombois and associates have studied the biology of Hawaii tropical forest systems. These comparative studies have developed a great deal of basic biological information, as well as emphasizing the impacts of introduced herbivores on the survival of native vegetation. Finally, in Florida a team of ecologists led by Ariel Lugo and Samuel Snedaker, formerly of the University of Florida, have investigated the productivity and comparative dynamics of the mangrove forests on the Florida coast. Mangrove forest is a peculiar variant of tropical forest which occurs on the sea–land margin. It is discussed in a geographical and botanical context in Volume 1 of the *Ecosystems of the World* Series (Chapman, 1977).

In Africa three ecosystem projects have been carried out under IBP auspices. Prof. G. Lemée and his colleagues in 1966 began a study of the subequatorial rain forest in Ivory Coast (Lemée, 1975). This program of the French Office de Recherche Scientifique et Technique Outre-Mer (ORSTOM) considered the forest structure and function, including water balance, productivity and mineral cycling. Two locations with different soils were compared. In both cases the mean precipitation was over 1700 mm per year and was concentrated into two rainy seasons. The other two ecosystem studies in Africa were located in woodland or savanna areas and will be treated in detail in other volumes. However, for completeness, they deserve mention here. The first was also under IBP and also was a French ORSTOM project. Prof. Maxime Lamotte organized a large team effort focused on the savanna ecosystems of Ivory Coast. These studies have yielded a tremendous body of data and are continuing under Ivory Coast and French direction. The second is located in Miombo Woodland, the forest type characteristic of many parts of the African continent. Prof. Francois Malaisse of the University of Zaire at Lubumbashi has organized a team to study the botany and zoology of the Miombo ecosystem. These studies are also continuing.

In Asia two ecosystem studies have been developed under IBP. A joint Malaysia/United Kingdom and Japanese study was organized at Pasoh forest, Malaysia. These studies have focused on several aspects of the structure and function of this dipterocarp forest and were published as an issue of the *Malaysian Nature Journal* (Volume 30, 1978). The second study is located near Varanasi, India, in dry deciduous forest. Prof. R. Misra and his colleagues (Singh and Misra, 1978) at Banares

Hindu University have concentrated mainly on the production ecology of the forests, grasslands and agricultural ecosystems at this site.

In response to the need for information, the desperate problems of some tropical forest regions, and the relative lack of active ecosystem programs in tropical forests, the UNESCO organized a new program following the termination of the IBP. This program is called Man and the Biosphere (MAB) and has the objective of not only studying ecosystem structure and function but also of focusing on human activities in relation to ecosystem stability. That is, MAB seeks to go beyond IBP by putting man within the ecosystem. MAB is divided into fourteen international themes or subdivisions, the first of which concerns tropical and subtropical forests. At this time MAB 1 has a number of pilot projects active in tropical forests. One of these is located in Venezuela, in the Amazon near San Carlos de Rio Negro. A Venezuelan–German–U.S. research team is comparing the structure and function of forests growing on the two dominant soils, a podzol sand and a laterite. These baseline studies are the basis for examination of the problems involved with conversion of natural forest to agriculture and to forestry. Another pilot project is located at Tai forest, Ivory Coast and is studied by an Ivory Coast–French–Italian team. In this instance baseline studies are used for evaluation of forestry, agriculture and settlement schemes. Other projects are organized in the Asian tropics. These include an Indonesian project on East Kalimantan and a Papua New Guinea study of the Gogol Valley, which both deal with the ecological and social problems of logging a forest and resettlement of forest inhabitants. In Malaysia and Thailand studies are directed at forest structure and function, while in the Philippines the problems of river basin development and coastal zone management are under study. The location of MAB tropical forest projects showing cooperation by countries is shown in Fig. 1.1. Quite clearly a decisive shift in scientific attention toward tropical forests has occurred recently due to the leadership of UNESCO.

This capsule history of ecosystem research in rain forest ignores the studies of individual ecosystem processes and the hundreds of years of natural history and biological research which provide the understanding of mechanisms of rain forest structure and function. These studies have been and

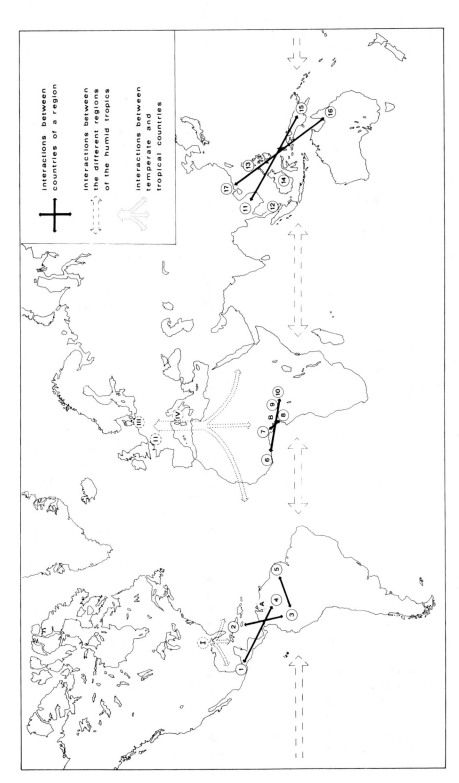

Fig. 1.1. The international network of MAB projects in the humid tropics (from Di Castri and Hadley, 1979). Key to locations as follows: Sites of pilot projects: *1* = Jalapa and other sites, Mexico; *2* = Sierra del Rosario, Cuba; *3* = Iquitos, Peru; *4* = San Carlos de Rio Negro, Venezuela; *5* = Oyapok, French Guyana; *6* = Tai forest, Ivory Coast; *7* = Omo and other sites, Nigeria; *8* = Makoko, Gabon; *9* = Basse Lobaye, Central African Republic; *10* = Yangambi, Zaire; *11* = Sakaerat, Thailand; *12* = Pasoh and other sites, Malaysia; *13* = Puerto Galera–Agno River, the Philippines; *14* = east Kalimantan, Indonesia; *15* = Gogol, Papua New Guinea; *16* = north Queensland, Australia; *17* = Tinhu Mountains, China. Examples of cooperating institutions in temperate countries: *I* = Institute of Ecology, Athens, Ga. U.S.A.; *II* = Office de Recherche Scientifique et Technique Outre-Mer (ORSTOM), France; *III* = Institute of World Forestry, Hamburg–Reinbek, Federal Republic of Germany; *IV* = Department of Microbiology, University of Rome, Rome, Italy. Examples of collaborating institutions in developing countries playing regional or international role: *A* = Centro Internacional de Ecologia Tropical (CIET) at Caracas, Venezuela; *B* = Centre Régional de Documentation at Yaoundé, Cameroun.

remain highly vigorous and will be cited as appropriate in the following chapters. However, as mentioned above, they have a different focus and objective than ecosystem investigations, which seek to understand the structure and function of communities and larger landscape units. The focus of the ecosystem studies, as defined in this volume, is on the rain forest community. However, where possible, the observations of the forest community are interpreted within the context of watersheds or landscapes. Further, the mechanistic explanations of ecosystem structure and function usually employ data on physiology, behavior, genetics and basic biology. For this reason, the present volume examines the rain forest from all of these different points of view. Hopefully this organization will provide the breadth and depth to understand the complex ecological patterns characteristic of this ecosystem.

In the past there have been relatively few attempts to develop an integration of rain forest ecology — the complexity of species and structure tends to frustrate general interpretation. Paul Richards' classic, *The Tropical Rain Forest* (Richards, 1964) is probably the main treatment in the English language. Recently Whitmore (1975) has published a modern synthesis of the information on forests in the Asian region. Further, UNESCO, UNEP and FAO, as part of the MAB activity, have prepared a state of knowledge report on the world tropical forest resource (UNESCO, 1978). In the present volume we have not tried to develop an integrated description of rain forest, as, for example, in a system model. Rather, we have imposed an artificial and abstract order on the various presentations, organizing them into structural sections, functional studies, basic studies of physiology and behavior, and consideration of human applications of rain forest.

SYNOPSIS

The volume begins with the structure of tropical forests considered from a biological point of view. There are estimated to be about 3 million species of tropical organisms, as compared with only 1.5 million in temperate regions (Sohmer, 1978). There are roughly three times as many known species of animals as of plants and the vast majority of these

animals are insects. This biological richness can be analyzed from a spatial or horizontal point of view, as when successive samples of plant stems or animals are collected and compared, as well as from a cross-sectional view. A cross-section of the tropical forest reveals a variety of strata, with associated flora and fauna (see Chapter 3).

The uninterrupted extent of tropical forest and biological richness of the forest (at least of plants, Prance, 1977) is greatest in South America. The biological richness is a function of the evolutionary history of the forest plants and animals and the change in land and climate. Raven and Axelrod (1974) suggest that the angiosperms and other groups of plants probably originated in a tropical setting in western Gondwanaland (Africa) when it was a continent and then migrated to what has become South America, India and Australia. The observed species richness in Southeast Asia, which is the most taxonomically diverse tropical forest area in the world, may reflect survival of taxa which migrated into this relatively isolated, equable and diverse area.

The analysis of species richness from the taxonomic and biogeographical point of view will be discussed only briefly since it will be treated in Part B. This analysis will begin with a discussion of the basic architectural form of the trees, which are the dominant feature of rain forests. The basic, inherited pattern of tree architecture can be described by a limited series of architectural models. As the trees grow they encounter environmental constraints which alter their shape from the basic model form. The eventual result is a complex pattern of forest on the vertical and horizontal scale. The biomass of forests, which is the basis of the energy and chemical inventories, depends upon these patterns. These features of rain forests are developed in three chapters. Chapter 2 is a condensed description of the architectural models of trees. Chapter 3 briefly describes the vertical and horizontal patterns, with a discussion of a pattern in an African forest. Chapter 4 discusses the vertical and horizontal pattern of forests using examples from Asia and America and then describes patterns of biomass.

Examination of the fauna of tropical forests is more difficult from a structural viewpoint, largely because of the great variety of taxa and the fact that animals live upon and within the plants and move from one type of organism to another. Thus, animals are best examined by taxa, by habits, and by habitat. This is the focus of a rather extensive discussion in Chapter 5. The consideration of the density of animals (Chapter 6) is difficult. There are few studies of faunal abundance and relatively few studies of animal density. Thus, Chapter 6 can only briefly treat density and biomass of animals. These chapters provide the basis for the final structural chapter (Chapter 7) which is concerned with the storage of energy and nutrient elements in the biomass. The chapters in the section on forest structure provide a view of ecosystems dominated by trees, with a rich variety of fauna and flora, distributed in the vertical dimension over several strata and in the horizontal dimension over environmental gradients of slope, soil and water. These data form the basis for considering the dynamic relationships between structural components.

In the section on rain forest function we will examine two kinds of dynamic phenomena. In the first, function refers to the flux of energy and minerals between forest components, the dynamic response of the compartments in organic production and decomposition, and the response of the entire system in ecological succession. The second set of phenomena are concerned with the interactions between taxa, as in feeding and in pollination. In the first instance we focus on the physical or chemical flux between structural elements; in the second on the biological interactions. Both types of functional analyses are required for a complete description of rain forest dynamic behavior.

With this background we naturally turn to questions of why and how the structural and functional attributes work as they do. To answer such questions, it is necessary to explore some of the extensive physiological and behavioral knowledge of tropical species. This is accomplished through chapters on adaptation to moisture stress and temperature in plants and animals, and on animal behavior.

The final section concerns man's use of and interaction with tropical forest. A variety of human populations have adapted their life style to live within these systems, and it is important for modern man to understand their modes of adaptation. However, modern man also looks on these forests as resources upon which to build modern societies. We are concerned with the way timber is produced in natural and managed forest, the conservation of forests and new, often imaginative methods of conserving yet also utilizing their resources. It has been stated that the tropical forest is fast disappearing (Gómez-Pompa, et al., 1972) and we must understand the rates of exploitation so that conservation can be successful. Further, use of the forest by man is strongly controlled by disease organisms. These relationships must be examined in detail. Finally, we must explore in a synthetic fashion the future of this important natural resource both in terms of its use and preservation.

In all the sections we have requested that authors present concepts and general principles which are supported by appropriate data. We have not asked for encyclopedic treatment of each subject. In some chapters the information base is very rich, in others there are relatively little data from which to derive concepts and, thus, the treatment is uneven. Clearly there are a variety of ways to organize the subject; the particular organization used here reflects the editor's personal bias, the structure of his concept of ecology, and his belief that an integration of basic and applied approaches is essential to understand and to use resources. I hope that this volume will contribute to the conservation of a precious natural resource.

REFERENCES

Bates, H.W., 1892. *The Naturalist on the River Amazons.* Murray, London.

Chapman, V.J., 1977. *Wet Coastal Ecosystems.* Ecosystems of the World, 1. Elsevier, Amsterdam, 428 pp.

Di Castri, F. and Hadley, M., 1979. Research and training for ecologically-sound development: problems, challenges, and strategies. In: *Fifth Int. Symp. Tropical Ecology, Kuala Lumpur, 1979* (mimeograph).

Evans, F.C., 1956. Ecosystems as the basic unit in ecology. *Science*, 123: 1127–1128.

Golley, F.B., McGinnis, J.T., Clements, R.G., Child, G.I. and Duever, M.J., 1975. *Mineral Cycling in a Tropical Moist Forest Ecosystem.* University of Georgia Press, Athens, Ga., 248 pp.

Gómez-Pompa, A., Vazquez-Yanes, C. and Guevara, S., 1972. The tropical rain forest: a nonrenewable resource. *Science*, 177: 762–765.

Lemée, G., 1975. Recherches sur l'écosystème de la forêt subéquatoriale de basse Côte d'Ivoire. *Terre Vie*, 29: 169–264.

Major, J., 1969. Historical development of the ecosystem concept. In: G.M. van Dyne (Editor), *The Ecosystem Concept in Natural Resource Management*. Academic Press, New York, N.Y., pp. 9–22.

Myers, N., 1979. *The Sinking Ark*. Pergamon Press, Oxford.

NRC (National Research Council), 1980. *Research Priorities in Tropical Biology*. National Academy of Sciences, Washington, D.C.

Odum, E.P., 1953. *Fundamentals of Ecology*. Saunders, Philadelphia, Pa., 574 pp.

Odum, H.T. and Pigeon, R.F. (Editors), 1970. *A Tropical Rain Forest. A Study of Irradiation and Ecology at El Verde, Puerto Rico*. U.S. Atomic Energy Commission, Washington, D.C., 1678 pp.

Prance, G.T., 1977. Floristic inventory of the tropics: Where do we stand? *Ann. Mo. Bot. Gard.*, 64: 659–684.

Raven, P.H. and Axelrod, D.I. 1974. Angiosperm biogeography and past continental movements. *Ann. Mo. Bot. Gard.*, 61: 539–673.

Richards, P.W., 1964. *The Tropical Rain Forest: An Ecological Study*. Cambridge University Press, Cambridge, 450 pp.

Singh, K.P. and Misra, R., 1978. *Structure and Functioning of Natural, Modified and Silvicultural Ecosystems of Eastern Uttar Pradesh*. Technical Report, Oct. 1975–Oct. 1978. UNESCO MAB, Banares Hindu University, Varanasi.

Sohmer, S.H., 1978. Tropical biology. In: *Environmental Biology Program Report, NSF, 2, No. 4*. National Science Foundation, Washington, D.C., pp. 5–10.

Tansley, A.G., 1935. The use and abuse of vegetation concepts and terms. *Ecology*, 16: 284–307.

UNESCO, 1978. *Tropical Forest Ecosystems: A State-of-Knowledge Report Prepared by UNESCO, UNEP and FAO*. *Nat. Resour. Res.*, 14: 683 pp.

Whitmore, T.C., 1975. *Tropical Rain Forests of the Far East*. Clarendon Press, Oxford, 281 pp.

Yantko, J. and Golley, F.B., 1978. A census of tropical ecologists. *Bioscience*, 28: 260–264.

Chapter 2

STRUCTURAL ELEMENTS OF THE RAIN FOREST

P.B. TOMLINSON

INTRODUCTION

Structural analyses of tropical rain forest may proceed to different levels of resolution. This account deals mainly with the major tropical rain forest components, i.e. trees, and attempts to establish the immediately obvious processes involved in their development. An analysis of the architecture of individual trees provides the analytical tool for the assessment of plant interaction. This assessment of gross morphological diversity is a resumé of the approach adopted by Hallé et al. (1978). Detailed morphological accounts of the biological constituents of rain forest plants are found in Schnell (1970), Whitmore (1975), Longman and Jeník (1974). Only the above-ground parts are considered in any detail. The architecture and interaction of root systems in the rain forest have been summarized recently by Jeník (1978).

A preliminary structural analysis of the vertical dimensions of the forest recognizes a limited number of *synusiae*, or aggregations of taxa with a common life-form:

(1) Canopy trees (including stranglers, cf. Richards, 1957)
(2) Understorey trees
(3) Shrubs
(4) Lianes or woody climbers (might include stranglers)
(5) Understorey herbs
(6) Vascular epiphytes
(7) Vascular parasites
(8) Vascular saprophytes

Each of these may be capable of further biological subdivision, e.g., the lianes according to their method of climbing, or the epiphytes according to their water economy, or the herbs according to their method of vegetative spread.

ARCHITECTURE

Following Hallé and Oldeman (1970) and Hallé et al. (1978) it is recognized that each individual species has a precise and genetically determined growth plan or *architectural model*, while the expression of this growth plan at any one developmental stage may be said to represent the *architecture* of the plant. These concepts differ from those implied in the general terms life-form or growth habit in that the latter are both static concepts and refer to the end-product — e.g. herb, shrub, or tree, with an implication of size. Size is not involved in the recognition of an architectural model, which is an abstraction whose dynamic expression is the architecture of the tree at any developmental stage. Giant forest trees and small herbs may have the same growth plan although the final expression of this leads to ecologically important differences in size. Most living organisms have a precisely determined form so that the concept of architectural model, here considered in relation to trees, is universally applicable. It has been used or implied in the description of other groups of plants (e.g. lianes by Cremers, 1973, 1974; herbs by Jeannoda-Robinson, 1977; sea grasses by Tomlinson, 1974; rhizomatous plants by Bell and Tomlinson, 1980).

The architectural continuum

Hallé and Oldeman (1970) initially found that by using a set of simple and readily observed growth characteristics it was possible to categorize all trees as belonging to 21 different architectural models. Examination of a wider range of species, over a greater geographic area (Hallé, 1974) and with some extension of the criteria used, has subsequently added only two new models (Hallé et al., 1978). The 23 architectural models now defined seem an acceptable and manageable number of points of reference considering that it encompasses the total diversity of tree forms. The system of nomenclature adopted, which names the defined models after people, is discussed and defended by Hallé et al. (1978). It is clear that if a different set of growth criteria were used, or more refined methods of analysis were admitted, a different and more elaborate set of reference points could be established (e.g. Serebryakova, 1971).

There is a continuum of developmental possibilities and, thus, many species cannot be fitted with certainty into one of the defined tree models. However, since many trees do exhibit the same basic growth plan, there are pronounced aggregations around particular syndromes of developmental characteristics on this continuum. The architectural continuum is therefore not uniform. The implication of this distribution, in ecological terms, is that certain combinations of growth features (other than those which are mutually antagonistic or exclusive) are adaptive. This is an aspect of tree morphology which needs to be elaborated more precisely and in quantitative terms. A good start has been made by Horn (1971), Fisher and Honda (1977, 1979), Givnish (1978), and Fisher (1978), who have all taken the topic of crown shape beyond physiognomic appearance.

However, a description of forest structure by the naming of its constituent tree models is not in itself a very useful exercise — there seems to be only a limited correlation between architecture and vegetation type — because the genetically expressed growth parameters must be understood in an ecological context (Ashton, 1978).

Reiteration

Methods by which the architectural model of a tree may be established have been described by Hallé et al. (1978). The best source of information is cultivated or plantation-grown plants where development may proceed with a minimum of disturbance. In contrast, in natural environments the tree may or may not *conform* to its architectural plan, depending on the extent to which the plan is disrupted by stressful circumstances, as by storm or predator damage, or by crown interaction. Following Oldeman (1974) we have to add the concept of *reiteration*, or growth response to environmental circumstances, to our analysis of tree architecture. Reiteration may be traumatic, as when broken limbs are restored, or adaptive, as when existing axes are reorientated. The normal reiterative response is for resting meristems, which are not expressed in the architectural model, to develop and in doing so they more or less repeat the architecture of the crown of the tree. The simplest and most familiar expression of this is the substitution of a damaged leader by a latent meristem, but the kinds of growth response encompassed in the concept of reiteration are many and varied. In many conifers reiteration is partial, since only part of the original model is repeated as, for example, the plagiotropic branches in *Araucaria* (Veillon, 1978). The reiterative ability of a tree is probably as important an ecological parameter as architecture itself, if not greater, but varies enormously. At one end of the scale there is no possibility of reiteration, as with single-stemmed palms in which the embryonic shoot apical meristem persists without vegetative branching throughout the total life span of the tree (as in Holttum's and Corner's models), while at the other end of the scale, in temperate trees which exhibit Rauh's model, the reiterative capacity of the tree is high because of the existence of numerous reserve meristems. In *Rhizophora* (Attims's model) reiteration from dormant lateral meristems is limited because reserve meristems have a short life span. Reiteration is much less a feature of crown development in conifers compared with most angiosperms since production and persistence of reserve meristems is limited (cf. Edelin, 1977).

If the reiterative ability of most trees is their most important adaptive feature, this does not minimize the importance of an initial understanding of architectural processes since it is only through a knowledge of the architectural model of a tree that the phenomenon of reiteration can be assessed. The growth plan must be understood before it can be seen to have been disrupted. In certain trees, the distinction between model-conforming and reiterated specimens may be hard to discern, partly through lack of precision in the definition of the model. Such trees may in fact be successful because the plasticity which is the essence of reiterative ability is carried over into the architectural plan itself. More developmental information about the biological class of trees with "mixed axes" (see below) is badly needed.

Summary of architectural tree models

The 23 models in Hallé et al. (1978) may be briefly presented in summary form in such a way as to indicate the main diagnostic features used (Fig. 2.1). Explanation of the terms used is given in the glossary.

A. Unbranched trees; examples: single-stemmed palms, many tree ferns — 2 models (Holttum's, Corner's).

B. Single-trunked trees, the trunk a linear sympodium; examples: many cycads — 1 model (Chamberlain's).

C. Trees branching by true dichotomy, very rare; examples: *Hyphaene* spp. (Palmae) — 1 model (Schoute's).

D. Trees with only basal branching; examples: multiple-stemmed palms — 1 model (Tomlinson's)

E. Trees with determinate branched axes arising from a basal rhizome system; examples: bamboos — 1 model (McClure's).

F. Trees with all branching below a terminal inflorescence; examples: cassava (Euphorbiaceae, many Apocynaceae, Araliaceae) — 1 model (Leeuwenberg's).

G. Trees as in F, but with secondary erection of certain branches as successive trunk modules; examples: *Hura crepitans* (Euphorbiaceae), *Ochroma lagopus* (Bombacaceae) — 1 model (Koriba's).

H. Trees with sympodial trunks, branches either monopodial or sympodial; examples: *Theobroma cacao* (Sterculiaceae), *Alstonia boonei* (Apocynaceae) — 2 models (Nozeran's, Prévost's).

I. Trees with monopodial, rhythmically growing trunks, branches plagiotropic in various ways; examples: *Fagraea crenulata* (Loganiaceae), *Terminalia catappa* (Combretaceae), *Araucaria heterophylla* (Araucariaceae) — 3 models (Fagerlind's, Aubréville's, Massart's).

J. Trees with continuous monopodial growth of trunk, continuous or diffuse branching; examples: *Rhizophora* spp. (Rhizophoraceae). *Gossypium* spp. (Malvaceae), *Castilla elastica* (Moraceae), *Coffea* spp. (Rubiaceae), *Pandanus* spp. (Pandanaceae) — 5 models (Attims's, Pettit's, Roux's, Cook's, Stone's).

K. Trees with rhythmic growth of trunk and rhythmic branching; examples: *Mangifera indica* (Anacardiaceae), *Hevea brasiliensis* (Euphorbiaceae) — 2 models (Scarrone's, Rauh's).

L. Trees with mixed axes; examples: *Bougainvillea* spp. (Nyctaginaceae) *Strychnos variabilis* (Loganiaceae), *Delonix regia* (Leguminosae) — 3 models (Champagnat's, Mangenot's, Troll's).

In preliminary descriptions the examples chosen are, where possible, likely to be commonly cultivated or commercially important species which can serve as reference points, but this kind of introduction needs amplification by analysis of forest-grown species. It should be noted that dicotyledons encompass the totality of tree architectural diversity, with the majority of species in the more elaborately branched models, especially those with pronounced differentiation of branches. Monocotyledons, by virtue of the restrictions placed on their growth because of the usual absence of a secondary vascular cambium, exemplify the models with more limited branching ability and differentiation. *Pandanus* is exceptional in this respect. Conifers have a very restricted range of architectural possibilities, since they largely belong to three developmentally related models, Attim's, Massart's and Rauh's. Gymnosperms may never develop mixed axes. This may be accounted for in three general ways: (1) absence of distichy; (2) progressive differentiation of axes of progressively higher orders; and (3) limited ability for sympodial growth.

It should again be emphasized that since architectural analysis is likely to be unfamiliar to many readers, categorization of a given species by the Hallé and Oldeman system is not always a prime objective; the main value is the close scrutiny of overall growth patterns which the approach requires. If an observer is dissatisfied with his ability to fit a given species into a given growth model, the exercise will serve the purpose of making a careful

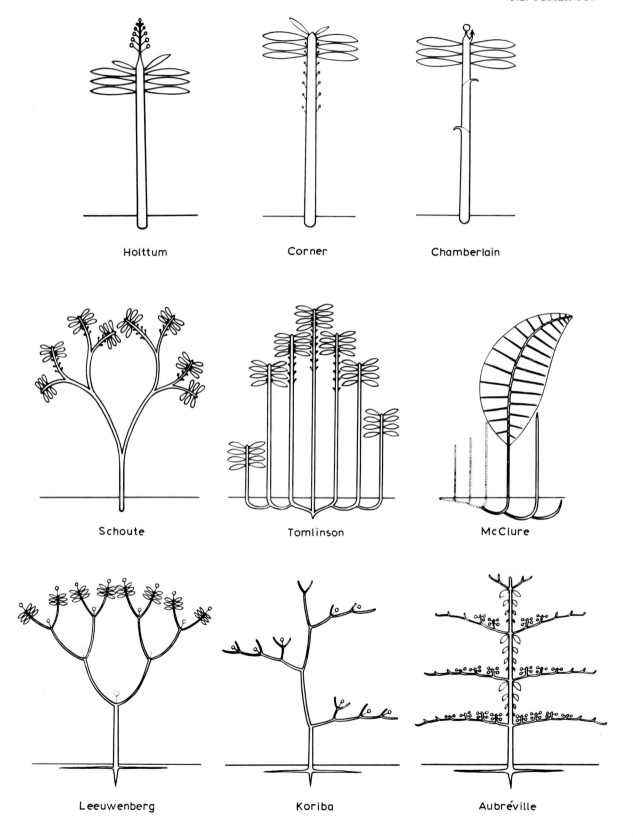

Holttum   Corner   Chamberlain

Schoute   Tomlinson   McClure

Leeuwenberg   Koriba   Aubréville

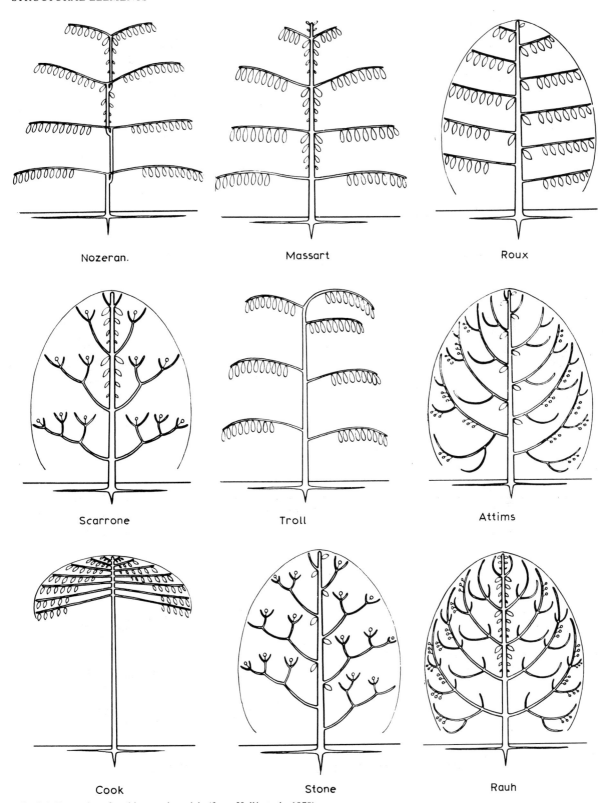

Fig. 2.1. Examples of architectural models (from Hallé et al., 1978).

inventory of simple growth characteristics which are ecologically important, and possibly demonstrate the extent to which reiteration can and does occur.

PRIMARY MERISTEMS

Axis meristems are the ultimate constructional units of the forest, since they are the centers of actual or potential growth of trees. Among these, the shoot apical meristem may be the most important forest component since it represents, to greater or lesser degree, the potential for further development of the whole plant. It is only by exploitation of the structural framework established by these primary meristems that the secondary (thickening) meristems, where they exist, can achieve their effect in providing mechanical support and renewable conducting tissues. They in turn provide the bulk of forest biomass.

Primary meristems may be categorized as follows:

I. *Seed meristems*
   (1) Dormant, a period normally considered short in tropical trees.
   (2) Active, as in germinating or viviparous seeds (cf. De Vogel, 1980).
II. *Vegetative meristems*
   (1) Shoot meristems: (a) active and producing orthotropic axes, typically trunks; (b) active and producing plagiotropic axes, typically branches; (c) inactive, i.e. resting, dormant or otherwise inhibited (in the several meanings of these terms).
   (2) Root meristems (further breakdown is desirable but not feasible with present knowledge, cf. Jeník, 1978).
III. *Reproductive meristems*, i.e. flower buds or their differentiated precursors.

One could extract a view of the actual and potential growth processes of the forest from a knowledge of the number, distribution and potential behavior of the total population of primary meristems, as suggested by Oldeman (1974) in his recognition of "infrastructural sets". Quantification, however, requires a more precise demographic analysis of a forest plot than seems possible with current resources. Comparative analysis of this kind would give a measure of the total regenerative ability of forest types and their ability to respond to change and recover from gross destruction. Mangrove communities seem particularly deficient in this respect. Studies of Gill and Tomlinson (1971) have shown that this characteristic is probably one reason for the susceptability of mangroves to defoliation by herbicides (Walsh et al., 1973).

At a simpler level, the study of individual bud structure, physiology and response still remains a basic feature of the forest inventory.

BUD MORPHOLOGY

A bud as a shoot apical meristem and its immediate derivatives representing an "unextended, partly developed shoot" (Romberger, 1963) is a more or less recognizable morphological entity. Plants with thick stems (pachycaulous axes) and short internodes (as for example, palms) have less discrete buds than the more precisely circumscribed units in slender-stemmed (leptocaulous) plants where internodal extension separates precursors and derivatives. The discreteness of buds is therefore sometimes related to the method of shoot extension, but such morphological niceties are lost on herbivores, which appreciate buds as localized nutritional centers. Structural features of both active and inactive buds are related in part to protection against predators and pathogens, as well as minimizing drying and insolation. When the bud is massive, as in palms, the large number of crown leaves and their woody leaf bases constitute an immediate armor, facilitated by the basal growth of individual leaves, but with frequent additional devices, notably spines. *Pandanus* even has spiny leaf margins. Cycads often have spiny bud scales.

In dicotyledons, bud-scales, representing modified leaves. leaf bases, stipules or prophylls are the most common protective organs. They are characteristic of almost all primary lateral meristems and, even in tropical trees, of many terminal meristems on shoots with rhythmic growth. Prophyllar buds, i.e. lateral buds subtended by prophylls, can be important as the precursors of secondary bud complexes.

Both active and inactive terminal meristems can have protective envelopes of great diversity, as follows:

I. *Structural envelopes*
  (1) Bud-scales.
  (2) Stipules, which may be lateral (e.g. Cunoniaceae, Magnoliaceae), interpetiolar (e.g. Rubiaceae) or adaxial (e.g. Erythroxylaceae). These may be further categorized as conspicuous (e.g. up to 30 cm long in *Cecropia*) or inconspicuous (5 mm long or less).
  (3) Grooved leaf bases, as in Guttiferae, Avicenniaceae, Dilleniaceae.
  (4) Enlarged or tubular leaf bases, especially prominent in the ochrea of Polygonaceae.
II. *Trichomes.* These may constitute the sole covering of buds (e.g. Sapotaceae), but otherwise supplement structural organs.
III. *Exudates.* Mucilages, varnishes, resins and latex are common as envelopes.

None of these features is mutually exclusive and many may be combined. One may categorize as "wet" buds those in which liquid exudate accumulates in a cavity formed by structural members, the exudate apparently derived from glandular hairs (colleters) which normally line the stipules (e.g. Rubiaceae, Rhizophoraceae). Minute lateral stipules cannot be dismissed as insignificant since they may be the source of exudates and they contribute a proportionally greater bulk to bud construction than other appendages because they develop precociously. However, the idea that the bud is necessarily close-packed is contradicted by tropical examples. In many Rhizophoraceae (Tomlinson and Wheat, 1979), the abundant free space between adjacent lateral primordia in terminal buds is filled by colleter-originated mucilage (possibly polysaccharides). In *Rhizophora stylosa* the exudate is sugary (a galactose) and its function as a bird-attracting device has been observed by Primack and Tomlinson (1978).

Exudates may also appear from ephemeral glands on the margins of the young leaf primordia themselves, as in many Euphorbiaceae. This is one reason why such leaves have marginal irregularities when they are mature.

The biochemical defenses of woody plants are highly relevant to a discussion of bud protection, although not immediately obvious. Phenolics ("tannins") are most prevalent, but the analysis of alkaloids, saponins and other physiologically active plant substances remains little explored at an ecological level (but cf. Feeny, 1976; McKey et al., 1978). To what extent toxic compounds are localized in tropical woody plants remains little investigated, but sometimes there is histological evidence, as in the accumulation of tannins in the lateral stipules within terminal buds (e.g. *Trema*, Ulmaceae). This might render such organs unpalatable and indigestible; herein might be one function of "vestigial" stipules.

EXTENSION GROWTH

The periodicity and rate of extension growth is the result of bud activity, and hence of the primary organization of the shoot system. Two contrasted states may be recognized.

(1) *Rhythmic (episodic) growth*, with alternate periods of quiescence and activity. The level at which a bud has been dormant is usually reflected in some morphological discontinuity in the resulting shoot (bud-scale scars, reduced leaves, congested internodes, branches; sometimes all four together). This produces shoots with an articulated morphology. Bud composition normally fluctuates during cycles of activity, which may be correlated with seasonal climatic changes.

(2) *Continuous growth*, with continuous or potentially continuous growth, with no bud dormancy. Consequently there is no morphological discontinuity along a shoot which has a non-articulated construction. Bud composition is constant.

To what extent growth rhythms in tropical trees are endogenous, are the result of correlated feedback mechanisms or are climatically induced remains little investigated. The above contrasted categories, therefore, do not cover all possibilities, especially if a potentially ever-growing tree has growth rhythms imposed by climatic factors. Palms probably come closest to the ever-growing category since they have a potentially constant rate of appendage production, modified only by environmental factors and without internal meristem interactions. In mangrove Rhizophoraceae rate of expansion of leaf pairs is moderated by climatic factors and internal growth correlations. Such trees contrast in the extreme with the deciduous temperate trees (Tomlinson, 1980).

AXIS DIFFERENTIATION

A central feature of canopy structure in a forest is the division of labor between axes. This differentiation may be the result of primary processes, relating to special properties of the parent meristem at the time of initiation, or of secondary processes, when axes become differentiated (often forming complexes) as a result of interaction between other axes. Apical control, or acrotony, versus basitony are the most familiar examples of this interaction in temperate trees, but much greater complexity exists in tropical trees. We can tabulate in a somewhat arbitrary way the various possibilities open to vegetative meristems for the expression of their growth potential.

I.   *Long-shoots.* Leafy axes with elongated internodes which contribute the major architectural features of the tree.
      A.   Simple axes, in which the developmental potential of the meristem is predominantly either orthotropic or plagiotropic and leads to either trunk or branch.
           (1)   *Orthotropic shoots*, axes with erect orientation, radial symmetry i.e. spiral or decussate phyllotaxis, with little secondary leaf orientation; typically "trunks".
           (2)   *Plagiotropic shoots*, axes with suberect or horizontal orientation, dorsiventral symmetry in distichous phyllotaxis common, with considerable leaf reorientation; typically "branches".
      B.   Mixed axes; the developmental potential of the meristem changes during its growth expression so, in the simplest example, the axis is basally orthotropic, but distally plagiotropic, the former part of the trunk, the latter a branch. Growth in height is then achieved by superposition of successive axes with this mixed potential. This type of tree growth is little understood, but it seems common, as in many Leguminosae.
II.   *Short-shoots.* Leafy axes with congested internodes which do not contribute to the overall architecture of the tree, although they may be quite long-lived.
      A.   Lateral short-shoots, originating from

axillary meristems and involving some form of apical control.
      B.   Terminal short-shoots, originating from terminal meristems by apposition growth, mostly obvious in the lateral branch complex of the *Terminalia*-type representing Aubréville's model (see Fisher, 1978).

Short-shoots are frequently sexually specialized in that only they produce flowers.

The continuum of developmental possibilities between these categories is well-filled. However, it is true to say that differentiated axes are less clearly circumscribed in trees where differentiation is the result of growth correlation, as in the least specialized of the Hallé–Oldeman models.

Inflorescences, flowers (angiosperms) and cones (gymnosperms) are the most highly specialized shoot units in woody plants. Two basic processes contrast the distribution of sexual units, once the tree has reached reproductive maturity.

(1) Shoots determinate by sexuality, i.e. the flowering process influences crown structure directly, sympodial (substitution) growth is a major branching response.

(2) Shoots not determinate by sexuality, i.e. reproductive units are lateral and do not influence crown structure directly, growth is monopodial and there is no sexually determined substitution growth.

The situation in nature is more diverse than this simple sub-division suggests, since in pseudomonopodial growth, as for example in many Annonaceae, the inflorescence is morphologically terminal, but displaced so early into a lateral position that the resultant shoot is biologically of the second kind. The main consideration then becomes an appreciation of total crown organization and the effect of sexuality. Cauliflory and ramiflory are extreme examples in which flowering would seem to proceed independently of crown development. Otherwise flowering and vegetative shoot extension are highly interdependent processes.

Contrasted crown structures which result from different flower positions are shown between Fagerlind's and Aubréville's models, as illustrated in Hallé et al. (1978) in Fig. 2.2.

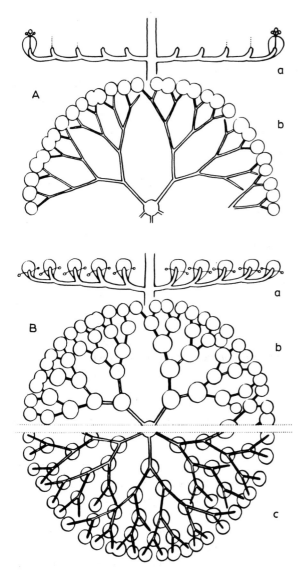

Fig. 2.2. Diagrammatic comparison between a tier of branches in two models. A. Fagerlind's model, tier in side view (a), and from above (b). Newly initiated leafy rosettes are restricted to the periphery of the tier because each meristem is determinate via terminal flowering. B. Aubréville's model, tier in side view (a), from above (b), and from below (c). The meristems are indeterminate, since flowering is lateral, and each continues to produce a leafy rosette so that the photosynthetic surface is more extensive. (From Hallé et al., 1978).

BRANCHING

Vegetative meristem proliferation in forest trees results in the elaboration of a branch system. The diversity of branch expression contributes to the complexity of the canopy, but general principles can be perceived.

In geologically early vegetation types, dichotomous branching (equal division of an apical cell or meristem) was a dominant developmental process. This method of branching has been almost (but not quite) superseded in modern trees by lateral branching from meristems in the axils of leaves, which results in greater control of branch development. The precision and versatility of branching in modern trees is one of the major features accounting for their ecological success. Essential facts can be summarized as follows (see also Tomlinson, 1978; Hallé et al., 1978).

Architectural expression

In an architectural context, two types of branching can be recognized in a tree.

(1) *Serial branching* — branching under direct genetic control and inherent in the architectural model, i.e. shown by a tree which conforms to its model. This kind of branching may be said to be "deterministic".

(2) *Reiterative branching* — branching which is a direct response to environmental factors, mostly typically when a tree is damaged mechanically or by herbivores so that the genetic growth plan is disrupted. The original model-conforming architecture is now disrupted; there is substitution within the crown of reiterated branch complexes. Normally these repeat the tree model, either wholly or partially, with the usual exception of the root system. This kind of branching may be said to be "opportunistic".

These contrasted generalized categories have been perceived elsewhere in the description of methods of branching in the rhizome system of plants (Bell and Tomlinson, 1980).

For a tree, it is clear that the crown is made up of a series of successive complexes as the initial model-conforming tree responds to environmental fluctuations.

Developmental expression

Two contrasted branching processes can be distinguished in the above-ground parts of woody plants.

Syllepsis. The lateral branch develops contemporaneously with the parent axis without an intervening period of rest. The morphologically visible consequence of this is that the base of the sylleptic branch lacks reduced or scale-like prophylls, the first leaf (or leaf pair) is a more or less normally developed foliage leaf and the first internode below it (or them) is extended as a hypopodium. In many examples this means that a distinct unbranched leader is absent.

Prolepsis. The lateral branch develops after a period of rest (dormancy, correlative inhibition, etc.) and so is not contemporaneous in development with the parent axis. The morphologically visible consequence is that the base of a proleptic branch has reduced prophylls (bud-scales), congested basal internodes (no hypopodium) represented by their scars if the branch grows out, with a gradual transition to normal foliage leaves. The morphological consequence of this, especially seen in temperate trees, is that there is an unbranched leader. Branch meristems then grow out in the second season of their production.

Normally these two contrasted kinds of morphology are sufficiently clear that they will indicate the previous developmental history of a branch system. The use of these terms in this contrasted sense (see Tomlinson and Gill, 1973; Hallé et al., 1978) is a simplification of their older limited application which was based on a geographically restricted study of tree development (Späth, 1912).

In the architecture of a given tree, branching may be exclusively by syllepsis (as in Attims's, Roux's and Cook's models) or exclusively by prolepsis, as in temperate examples of Rauh's model, or by a combination of the two methods where, as in Nozeran's model, plagiotropic axes originate by syllepsis, orthotropic axes, which constitute new trunk units, originate by prolepsis.

In contrast, where reiterative branching occurs from dormant buds, the outgrowing shoot is inevitably proleptic. There is a strong correlation between syllepsis and plagiotropy, on the one hand, and between prolepsis and orthotropy on the other, but the subject remains little investigated experimentally.

The existence of contrasted meristem types produced during primary growth demands a causal explanation in structural terms. In some examples, e.g. Myrsinaceae, with intermittent branching, a single axillary meristem can have contrasted developmental possibilities, i.e. it may exhibit either syllepsis or prolepsis and the difference is determined relatively late in the development of the bud (Wheat, 1980). In contrast the same leaf axil may support alternative shoot types, as in *Rhizophora* where a leaf pair which produces a sylleptic vegetative branch or inflorescence, can also support a dormant bud. Close juxtaposition of developmentally contrasted shoot types within a single leaf axil is not readily accounted for according to simple theories of apical dominance.

Numbers of meristems

As we have seen, the total numbers of meristems produced by a tree and the number which persist as "reserve buds" is not easily determined. Morphological examination of developing shoots shows, however, that the number of lateral meristems produced during primary growth varies widely in trees. In an idealized condition each leaf subtends a single meristem and any not utilized in architectural ramification can persist as reserve meristems. In many trees, and especially conifers, fewer than this ideal number is generated since only a proportion of leaf axils subtend meristems; in conifers most lateral meristems function early and reserve meristems are often so few that such trees uncommonly sprout belatedly (Edelin, 1977).

In contrast many dicotyledonous trees produce supernumerary buds in each leaf axil, most typically in a serial arrangement one above the other, less commonly in horizontal or lateral series and large numbers of potential reserve meristems may be developed. These primary bud complexes may be supplemented by secondary proliferation. A random sample of cultivated and native woody plants (representing 82 dicotyledonous families) in south Florida showed that 37% produce supernumerary buds (L.E. Newstrom, pers. comm.). Vines have a disproportionately higher tendency to produce supernumerary buds.

Any mechanism for building up of reserve meristems is offset by their rate of mortality. Presumably the population of buds reaches some constant value but the size of this population can only be indicated, either by observation of damaged and fallen trees, or by experimental manipulation.

Cataclysmic events, such as frosts or inundation which defoliate trees, may provide dramatic evidence of the ability or otherwise of a tree to regenerate from reserve meristems. In *Rhizophora mangle* it is known that lateral reserve meristems live for only three to four years (Gill and Tomlinson, 1971), so that when a mangrove forest is defoliated by frost or hurricane the fact that this species does not sprout from older wood is very evident. In the same environment *Avicennia* and *Laguncularia* show a marked tendency to develop epicormic sprouts.

It should be clear that these structural features, together with a complex of physiological factors, are ecologically important as they determine the rapidity and effectiveness of crown repair.

Branch complexes

Aggregations of axes which interact mutually so that the assemblage functions as a unit are readily recognized in trees; indeed most major branch systems function in this way, but have a diversity of origins. The term "module" has been used to refer to axis units which are the product of activity of a single meristem which is determinate, normally by flowering. On this basis, many trees may be said to have "modular construction" (Prévost, 1978). However, the term module has already found a variety of applications (cf. Harper and Bell, 1979) and may refer to different structural units. In the simplest possible configuration, the tree is entirely made up of orthotropic modules, as in Leeuwenberg's model; otherwise modules may be recognized as units of construction of major branch complexes, as in Scarrone's and Aubréville's models. The important consideration is that trees are capable of analysis in terms of units larger than the basic elements of stem and leaf. These units normally elaborate a branch complex by sympodial growth, of which there may be two main types.

These two possibilities are visually contrasted in Hallé et al. (1978, fig. 43).

Plagiotropy by substitution. A common method for development of a plagiotropic branch complex is by repeated substitution of a terminal inflorescence. Such systems may have great regularity because the number of parts in each module can be very strict, the ultimate being a reduction to a single foliage leaf, its associated internode and the terminal inflorescence, as can be seen in many Piperaceae. Such a system is very tightly programmed since only one active leaf-producing meristem exists at the periphery of the complex.

Plagiotropy by apposition. Aubréville's model illustrates precisely an alternative method of sympodial growth, in which the terminal meristem of each unit is not determinate but is displaced by the continuing lateral meristem. The residual parent meristem functions indefinitely as a short-shoot, retains an erect orientation and produces lateral inflorescences. The complex therefore retains a continuing ability to produce foliage leaves and flowers which is not found in substitution growth.

The most familiar examples of this kind of growth is shown by species of *Terminalia* and the construction has been repeatedly referred to as "*Terminalia*-branching", but is widespread among tropical trees, either in Aubréville's model where apposition growth is a strongly expressed genetic property of the tree, or is exhibited in the distal parts of plagiotropic complexes, where the condition is gradually imposed by interaction among shoots (cf. Fig. 2.3, from Hallé et al., 1978).

Only recently has *Terminalia*-branching been subjected to precise quantitative analysis (Fisher, 1978) and on this basis it has been possible to demonstrate that the net result is a ramifying system of axes which minimizes path length and mutual shading of leaves within the complex, while presumably maximizing photosynthetic efficiency (Fisher and Honda, 1977, 1979).

REPRODUCTIVE POTENTIAL

The production of new seed meristems and their ultimate recruitment into the forest population is an important though indirect aspect of forest construction, but one which can only be mentioned briefly here and in relation to tree architecture.

Fruits and seeds

In many trees, as determined by their architectural model, the position of flowers (and hence ultimately of fruits) is not influenced by the architecture. The most extreme expression of this prin-

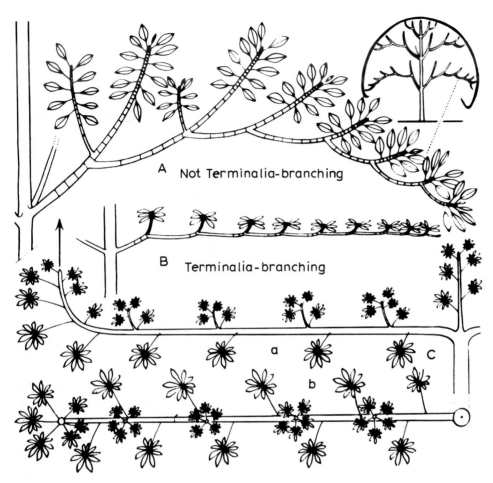

Fig. 2.3. Orthotropy and plagiotropy in branches. A. Orthotropic branch complex. All axis are morphologically equivalent to the trunk but not functionally so. B. *Terminalia*-branching. Modular branch with plagiotropy by apposition. C. Secondary and reversible plagiotropy in a branch of *Ceiba pentandra*. Lateral view (a) and from above (b). (From Hallé et al., 1978).

ciple is found in cauliflorous or ramiflorous species. Here the controlling factor may be the initial position of flowers in relation to a pollinator (as in the long pendulous inflorescences of bat-pollinated flowers in *Kigelia*) supported by the thicker branches. Most cauliflorous trees have massive fruits (as in species of *Artocarpus*, *Couroupita*, *Kigelia*, *Omphalocarpon*, *Theobroma*), requiring massive support.

In trees with lateral inflorescences, flowering does not determine architecture, but architecture influences the number of axes which are capable of generating flowers. In trees with terminal inflorescences, branching is dependent on a previous flowering; the simplest example is Leeuwenberg's model, where all axes fork below terminal inflo-

rescences. One can grasp intuitively that these elementary differences can lead to different reproductive capabilities. In the simplest situation, Holttum's model, representing all uniaxial monocarpic trees, has a "big-bang" effect, since reproduction is a unique event in the life cycle of the plant. In contrast, Corner's model is also uniaxial, but with lateral sexual branches so that the plant is capable of producing seeds at a steady rate throughout most of its life span. The palms *Corypha* and *Cocos* illustrate these contrasted behaviors.

In branched trees, with their open growth, such contrasts are less striking but are likely to exist. On this basis, periodicity of extension growth, position of flowers and architecture are all part of this aspect of forest biology. Observations which determine average phenologies for different species in forest tracts are but a preliminary to a full demographic assessment, as pointed out by Janzen (1978).

Seedlings and germination

Although seedlings of forest trees are relatively easily studied, it is only recently that comprehensive efforts to initiate comparative studies have been attempted (e.g. Ng, 1978; De Vogel, 1980). The general conclusion is that, whereas epigeal germination, where the cotyledons are brought above the surface of the ground, is relatively a uniform morphological process, hypogeal germination, where the cotyledons are below ground, is morphologically diverse and a more elaborate categorization is possible. The result is to demonstrate a surprising biological diversity of establishment procedures in forest trees which reflects the importance of this phase in the life cycle. Biological differences in some instances relate directly to the size of a seed and hence to its dispersibility.

The special requirement of monocotyledons for establishment growth is discussed later.

SECONDARY MERISTEMS IN FOREST STRUCTURE

Although the bulk of standing forest biomass is generated by the secondary vascular cambium of trees, it is remarkable that this tissue has been little investigated in tropical trees. The few comments here relate to aspects of secondary growth which contribute to evident features of forest structure and whose significance may be more or less evident.

Reaction anatomy

Tension and compression wood play a major role in determining the form of trees, since the final orientation of branches in most trees seems dependent on its development. The subject is presently under survey (J.B. Fisher, pers. comm.) and is of economic importance because reaction wood strongly influences the quality of the resulting timber.

Two of the models in Hallé and Oldeman's system are defined by secondary orientation of axes. In Koriba's model, in which construction is modular, trunk segments are derived from branch axes by erection of one of a tier of branches developing below the inflorescence which terminates the previous module. That reaction wood is responsible for this change seems clear, but published evidence has only been provided for *Hura crepitans* (Tomlinson, 1978). Similarly Troll's model accommodates those trees with essentially plagiotropic axes which are secondarily erected, again presumably by reaction wood. The tree is developed both by this process of secondary erection and by superposition of successive axes. No anatomical documentation of this process has been provided but is obviously important because a large number of species have been assigned to this model (Hallé et al., 1978).

Periodicity of cambial activity

It is a familiar generalization about tropical trees that since they live in relatively non-seasonal climates in which annual climatic fluctuations may be small, they have not evolved dormancy mechanisms which strongly influence growth periodicity. However extreme this generalization may be, it is clear that there is not the same precise correlation between extension and radial growth which characterizes most temperate trees. The obvious consequence is the absence or weak development of growth rings in tropical woody plants which eliminates the method for reliable and facile age determination of tropical trees, a fact which is so detrimental to tropical ecology and population biology.

To what extent cambial activity is periodic in tropical trees remains insufficiently investigated to allow helpful generalizations to be made, despite the work which has been done (e.g., Coster, 1927–1928; Alvim, 1964; Lawton and Lawton, 1971; Amobi, 1974). The subject has been reviewed by Fahn et al. (1981).

One approach to the problem requires continued recording of diameter increase over extended periods, for which there is an array of very sensitive devices (Breitsprecher and Hughes, 1975), complemented by anatomical observations of progressive changes in the cambial zone. A major research effort is needed in this direction (Berlyn and Bormann, 1981).

Trunk irregularities

Variations from the normal tapered cylindrical form of tree trunks which increases the surface area of the cambium are especially common in tropical trees and provide a physiognomically distinctive feature which has generated an extensive literature. Most obvious and familiar are the buttressed trunk bases of many tropical trees, which are particularly striking when the buttresses are narrow and plank-like. The transition from this to the tree form characteristic of wet soils in the tropics in which aerial roots develop stilts or "flying buttresses" may or may not be abrupt (see many illustrations in Corner, 1978).

Fluted trunks form a variant on the above scheme, are less common and have received little attention. The extreme form is to be found in fenestrated trunks of a few tropical trees (e.g. *Minquartia guianensis*, fig. 80 in Hallé et al., 1978). In discussing the high frequency of such elaborated trunks in tropical trees, Smith (1972) has suggested that they exist because they are adaptively neutral in a tropical environment. In this they may parallel the architectural richness of tropical trees generally. However, it is a dangerous argument to dismiss such a striking range of physiognomies as non-adaptive because no better explanation of their existence has been found.

Bark structure

In dicotyledonous trees bark texture and appearance is determined by a combination of the histological features of the phellogen or cork cambium and the method of circumferential expansion of the cork cambium itself. This, combined with bark color and presence of latex provides a range of diagnostic features evident when the trunk is slashed, upon which tree identification by tropical foresters is much dependent. The importance of this character has led to some study of bark anatomy (e.g. Whitmore, 1963; Parameswaran, 1971) but no comprehensive treatise has been produced. In particular the rate of biomass loss via the phellogen does not seem to be included in most productivity studies, but may be appreciable. In mangrove communities tidal run-off carries an evident scum of dead cells which are the products of pneumatophore lenticel tissue, continually eroded and renewed to maintain open gas channels.

Anomalous secondary thickening

Variations in the radial increment derived from a secondary vascular cambium from the norm represented by the typical dicotyledonous tree are conspicuous in tropical forests. The development of a trunk which is not a uniformly tapered cylinder has been mentioned. More extreme forms include dissected steles, polyxylic steles and steles with included phloem, many of which result from successively produced cambia. Such abnormalities certainly categorize specialized biological groups within the forest (notably lianes) where functional advantages seem obvious. But trees of normal physiognomy may show included phloem (e.g. *Avicennia*, *Pisonia*) and the adaptive significance of the anomaly is not immediately explicable. A field-orientated study of the many variants on the usual bidirectional vascular cambium would be very worthwhile.

WOODY PLANTS WITHOUT SECONDARY GROWTH

Palms, pandans and tree-ferns constitute a special biological group within the rain forest in which trunk development is determined by primary growth alone. They have a distinctive physiognomy — they are pachycaulous, not or little-branched and have tufted crowns of large, usually compound leaves. Cycads with manoxylic stem structure and a few dicotyledons with limited or anomalous cambial activity mimic this growth form (Holttum's, Corner's, Chamberlain's, Schoute's and, to a certain extent, Stone's model).

Since a number of these forms are probably recent in their evolutionary origin (e.g. monocotyledonous trees) while others are clearly ancient (e.g. cycads), it is evident that they represent one extreme variant of the continuing evolutionary experimentation by plants in the tree habit. They further depict the tropical forest as an acceptable milieu for botanical diversity.

The growth form of palms is readily explicable in relation to the growth-limiting characteristics of plants without secondary vascular and mechanical tissues (Schoute, 1903; Holttum, 1953) and such plants provide excellent examples of the way in which anatomy, physiology, development and morphology may be understood in terms of the architecture of the plant as an integrated whole. Primary thickening growth of the type exhibited by palms produces massive axes with short internodes, the leaves large and usually compound, aggregated into a crown of fixed size. The axis remains unbranched, because the mechanical and transport capacity of the trunk is fixed and cannot support or supply an enlarging crown. Such plants, if they branch at all, either produce branches at the base, with independent root systems (Tomlinson's model) or if they branch distally, as in *Pandanus*, have either progressively narrower branches, or branches of limited number and size, or have aerial roots which by-pass the trunk.

The seedling axis of such plants is a potential bottleneck, since the maximum trunk diameter can be reached only gradually (by establishment growth, Tomlinson and Zimmermann, 1967). Consequently juvenile stages in such plants are often complex and remarkably specialized (Tomlinson and Esler, 1973). From this it is clear that an understanding of the ecological role of these plants must be based on a detailed morphological analysis of all ontogenetic stages, perhaps to a greater extent than other forest components.

ROOT SYSTEMS

If the forest canopy is the most obvious part of the forest ecosystem, it still is only the superstructure of which the foundations are to be sought within the substrate. But we know little of root systems and only a few general comments are made here.

Root architecture

Jeník (1978) has recently made an attempt to categorize root systems of tropical woody plants, largely on the basis of his own observations. He recognizes 25 types, based on taxonomic examples. However, his categorization is entirely morphological because we still are so ignorant of root development in woody plants that a dynamic assessment which takes into account growth expression is not yet possible. Features which are considered are: presence or absence of secondary thickening; the extent to which the root system is adventitious, with the monocotyledons exhibiting

one extreme; the extent to which there is differentiation between orthotropic and plagiotropic roots; and the place of origin of roots. It is clear from extreme examples that the ecotope can influence root structure strongly, as in the high incidence of stilt-roots and pneumatophores in swamp forest (both fresh and salt water), or of aerial roots in "elfin-forest" (Gill, 1969).

Aerial roots

The high incidence of aerial root systems in plants of tropical rain forests is a consequence of the warm and usually moist atmosphere and the great diversity of biological types, notably epiphytes. Given the relative suitability of the tropical climate or microclimates for above-ground root growth, aerial roots have a diversity of functions. For some plants they exist for physio-mechanical reasons, as with stilt-palms and pandans, essentially by-passing the basal trunk bottleneck of the cone-shaped seedling axis. In others they appear to provide stability in insecure substrates, as with stilt roots (and possibly some buttresses) in swamp forest (Corner, 1978), or they represent a mechanism for developing an above-ground aerating system in anaerobic substrates as with the pneumatophores of fresh-water and mangrove communities. Here it is of interest to see how the same functional objective is achieved by quite different developmental pathways (cf. *Rhizophora* and *Sonneratia* or *Avicennia*; e.g. Gill and Tomlinson, 1976, 1977). Aerial roots within a single individual may show marked dimorphism, as between anchoring and feeding roots in root climbers from several unrelated families (e.g. *Freycinetia* of the Pandanaceae, many Araceae, Cyclanthaceae and some Ericaceae). The highly specialized aerial root system of strangling epiphytes progressively provides initial anchorage, subsequent feeding and final support.

A general commentary on the diversity of aerial roots is provided by Gill and Tomlinson (1976).

Mycorrhizal associations

Symbiotic or mutualistic associations between root systems of trees and soil microorganisms probably constitute the most significant aspect of forest dynamics and the subject is receiving increasing emphasis (e.g. Janos, 1975). In this instance the investigator is less concerned with the gross aspects of root morphology than with the behavior of the ultimate ramifications of the root system. It is probably here, in the ability of the tree to extract a share of the limited supply of soil nutrients that competition between species and individuals is at its most severe. The continued recycling of nutrients is dependent on a high mycorrhizal efficiency. Certainly this is the least obvious component of forest structure but by no means the least significant.

LEAVES

If the shoot apical meristem is a suitable unit for developmental analysis of forest structure, the leaf is the most obvious gross photosynthetic unit. Much of the architectural diversity is related to alternative mechanisms for rendering the display of leaf units the most efficient, and a particularly striking example has been analyzed in *Terminalia catappa* (Aubréville's model) by J.B. Fisher (Fisher, 1978; Fisher and Honda, 1977, 1979). Attention has also turned to the size and shapes of individual leaves themselves (Givnish and Vermeij, 1977). Many authors have commented on the uniformity of leaf shape in the tropical forest, without commenting on the diversity of ways in which these units may be displayed, for which tree architecture provides an initial level of analysis.

Leaf longevity

The evergreen aspect of the rain forest obscures the diverse rates at which individual species may produce leaves and the life span of leaves once produced. Evergrowing trees may maintain a relatively constant canopy because rate of production and leaf fall are synchronous, the simplest example being provided by palms. The extreme contrast is the deciduous condition, rare in non-seasonal forest but sometimes adopted in a response to flooding. Where growth is intermittent, trees may synchronize leaf loss and renewal completely, in the type of flushing described graphically by Longman and Jeník (1974) as "leaf-exchanging". It is clear that the method of leaf renewal has much less influence on the aspect of the canopy in an evergreen forest

than in a deciduous hardwood forest, but the method of leaf renewal may have important survival value for the individual tree.

Compound leaves and phyllomorphic branches

A question considered recently by Givnish (1978) is the adaptive significance of compound leaves, leading him to conclude that the compound leaf may be seen as a relatively large "throw-away" unit which allows a tree to adjust its photosynthetic display with a minimum disturbance to its overall architecture. This concept may be confirmed by the remarkable parallelism between compound leaves and determinate branches in some highly specialized tropical trees, representative of Cook's model. In these examples the tree, which is morphologically branched monopodially, mimics an unbranched tree because the branch axes are not a permanent feature of the plant. In some ways the biological reverse of this is found in trees with indeterminate short-shoots (which may be either terminal or lateral) because these units function as leaf-generating centers of considerable longevity. The approach here seems to be the reverse of throwaway structures — that is, permanent centers for the supply of photosynthetic units with a fixed position in the architecture of the tree.

CONCLUDING REMARKS

The reductionist approach adopted in this brief outline leaves undescribed many of the aspects of forest structure in which the ecologist has most interest — succession, sylvigenetic cycles, forest mosaics on the larger scale, stratification, competitive ability and gap dynamics on the smaller scale. Approaches to these questions using architectural criteria have been made by Oldeman (1974; see also Hallé et al., 1978, pp. 209–385). This kind of approach demonstrates the importance of preliminary morphological analysis, because morphology is the visible expression of the developmental success of a tree species in the highly competitive environment of the forest. From the morphological analysis can be derived a very useful description (Fig. 2.4) which is basic to studies of animal distribution, physiology of trees and production ecology.

Fig. 2.4. Profile of a forest plot 20 × 30 m at Montagne La Fumée, Eperon Sud, Saül, French Guiana (from Hallé et al., 1978, p. 347).

GLOSSARY

apposition growth, growth resulting in branching by displacement of a continued active terminal meristem by a more vigorous lateral — that is, no meristem abortion involved (cf. *substitution growth*).

bud complex, a group of closely juxtaposed buds; may be either *primary* e.g. a series of buds all of the same branch order developed within a single leaf axil, or *secondary*, the products of repeated branching producing an aggregate of buds belonging to several branch orders.

cauliflory, production of flowers on the trunk.

hypopodium, the part of a branch which is localized between its origin and its first leaf; usually long in sylleptic branches, it remains very short in proleptic ones.

mixed axes, axes in which there is a programmed change in orientation during ontogeny, e.g. from orthotropy to plagiotropy or vice versa.

monopodium, an axis established by a single indeterminate meristem — that is, branches remain subordinate; hence *monopodial growth*, growth by continuous activity of a single meristem.

orthotropy, gravitational response which produces a vertical axis, hence *orthotropic shoot* with the complex of characters resulting from this response — that is, radial symmetry and vertical orientation (cf. *plagiotropy*).

phyllotaxis, the primary arrangement of leaves on stems: *decussate*, successive pairs of leaves at right angles; *distichous*, leaves alternate, but restricted to a single plane; *spiral*, leaves alternate, but radially arranged — that is, forming a helix.

plagiotropy, gravitational response which produces an oblique or horizontal axis, hence *plagiotropic shoot* with the complex of characters resulting from this response — that is, dorsiventral symmetry and horizontal orientation (cf. *orthotropy*).

prolepsis, development of a lateral branch only after a period of dormancy as a lateral bud; hence *proleptic branch*, a branch developed by prolepsis.

prophylls, the first leaves (or leaf) on a branch, commonly reduced morphologically, e.g. as a scale leaf. Usually a pair inserted laterally in dicotyledons, single and inserted adaxially in monocotyledons.

pseudomonopodial branching, branching which is morphologically sympodial, by periodic abortion of the terminal bud, but this is obscured by the development of a lateral bud immediately below the dead terminal scar; the axis superficially appears to be a monopodium.

ramiflory, production of flowers on older branches.

substitution growth, growth resulting in branching by replacement of a terminal meristem which is determinate either by abortion or, most usually, by becoming a flower or inflorescence (cf.. *apposition growth*).

supernumerary buds, buds additional to the minimal one in the axil of a leaf.

syllepsis, development of a lateral branch without a period of dormancy — that is, contemporaneous with its parent axis; hence *sylleptic branch*, a branch developed by syllepsis.

sympodium, a single axis formed by a series of lateral meristems in sequence; *sympodial growth*, growth from successive lateral meristems.

REFERENCES

Alvim, P. de T., 1964. Tree growth periodicity in tropical climates. In: M.H. Zimmermann (Editor), *The Formation of Wood in Forest Trees*. Academic Press, New York, N.Y., pp. 479–495.

Amobi, C.C., 1974. Periodicity of wood formation in some trees of lowland rainforest in Nigeria. *Ann. Bot. (Lond.), N.S.*, 37: 211–218.

Ashton, P.S., 1978. Crown characteristics of tropical trees. In: P.B. Tomlinson and M.H. Zimmermann (Editors), *Tropical Trees as Living Systems*. Cambridge University Press, Cambridge, New York, N.Y., pp. 591–615.

Bell, A.D. and Tomlinson, P.B., 1980. Adaptive architecture in rhizomatous plants. *Bot. J. Linn. Soc.*, 80: 125–160.

Berlyn, G. and Bormann, F.H. (Editors), 1981. *Age and Growth Rate Determination For Tropical Trees: New Research Directions. Proceedings of a Workshop Sponsored by the National Research Council Commission on Natural Resources, Harvard Forest, Petersham, Mass., 1980. Yale Forest. Bull.* 94: 137 pp.

Breitsprecher, A. and Hughes, W., 1975. A recording dendrometer for humid tropical environments. *Biotropica*, 7: 90–99.

Corner, E.J.H., 1978. The freshwater swamp-forest of South Johore and Singapore. *Gard. Bull. (Singapore), Suppl.*, 1: 266 (pl. 40).

Coster, C.H., 1927–28. Zur Anatomie und Physiologie der Zuwachszonen und Jahresringbildung in den Tropen. *Ann. Jard. Bot. Buitenzorg*, 37: 49–160; 38: 1–144.

Cremers, G., 1973. Architecture de quelques lianes d'Afrique tropicale. 1. *Candollea*, 28: 249–280.

Cremers, G., 1974. Architecture de quelques lianes d'Afrique tropicale. 2. *Candollea*, 29: 57–110.

De Vogel, E.F., 1980. *Seedlings of Dicotyledons. Structure, Development, Types. Descriptions of 150 Woody Malesian Taxa*. Centre for Agricultural Publishing and Documentation, Wageningen, 465 pp.

Edelin, C., 1977. *Images de l'architecture des conifères*. Thesis, Université des Sciences et Techniques du Languedoc, Montpellier, 255 pp.

Fahn, A., Burley, J., Longman, A., Mariaux, A. and Tomlinson, P.B., 1981. Possible contributions of wood anatomy to the determination of the age of tropical trees. In: G. Berlyn and F.H. Bormann (Editors), *Age and Growth Rate Determination For Tropical Trees: New Research Directions. Yale Forest. Bull.*, in press.

Feeny, P., 1976. Biochemical coevolution between plants and their insect herbivores. In: L.E. Gilbert and P.H. Raven (Editors), *Coevolution of Animals and Plants*. University of Texas Press, Austin, Texas, London, pp. 3–19.

Fisher, J.B., 1978. A quantitative study of *Terminalia* branching. In: P.B. Tomlinson and M.H. Zimmermann (Editors), *Tropical Trees as Living Systems*. Cambridge University Press, Cambridge, New York, N.Y., pp. 285–320.

Fisher, J.B. and Honda, H., 1977. Computer simulation of branching pattern and geometry in *Terminalia* (Combretaceae), a tropical tree. *Bot. Gaz.*, 138: 377–384.

Fisher, J.B. and Honda, H., 1979. Branch geometry and effective leaf area: a study of *Terminalia*-branching pattern. 1. Theoretical trees. 2. Survey of real trees. *Am. J. Bot.*, 66: 633–644; 645–655.

Gill, A.M., 1969. The ecology of an elfin forest in Puerto Rico. 6. Aerial roots. *J. Arnold Arbor.*, 50: 197–209.

Gill, A.M. and Tomlinson, P.B., 1971. Studies on the growth of red mangrove (*Rhizophora mangle* L.). 3. Phenology of the shoot. *Biotropica*, 3: 109–124.

Gill, A.M. and Tomlinson, P.B., 1976. Aerial roots: an array of forms and functions. In: J.G. Torrey and D.T. Clarkson (Editors), *The Development and Function of Roots.* Academic Press, New York, N.Y., pp. 237–260.

Gill, A.M. and Tomlinson, P.B., 1977. Studies on the growth of red mangrove (*Rhizophora mangle* L.). 4. The adult root system. *Biotropica*, 9: 145–155.

Givnish, T.J., 1978. On the adaptive significance of compound leaves, with particular reference to tropical trees. In: P.B. Tomlinson and M.H. Zimmermann (Editors), *Tropical Trees as Living Systems.* Cambridge University Press, Cambridge, New York, N.Y., pp. 351–380.

Givnish, T.J. and Vermeij, G.J., 1977. Sizes and shapes of liane leaves. *Am. Nat.*, 110: 743: 778.

Hallé, F., 1974. Architecture of trees in the rain forest of Morobe District, New Guinea. *Biotropica*, 6: 43–50.

Hallé, F. and Oldeman, R.A.A., 1970. *Essai sur l'architecture et la dynamique de croissance des arbres tropicaux.* Masson, Paris, 178 pp.

Hallé, F., Oldeman, R.A.A. and Tomlinson, P.B., 1978. *Tropical Trees and Forests. An Architectural Analysis.* Springer-Verlag, Berlin, 441 pp.

Harper, J.L. and Bell, A.D., 1979. The population dynamics of growth form in organisms with modular construction. In: R.M. Anderson et al. (Editors), *Population dynamics, 20th Symposium of the British Ecological Society, London,* pp. 29–52.

Holttum, R.E., 1953. Growth habits in monocotyledons: Variations on a theme. *Phytomorphology*, 5: 399–413.

Horn, H.S., 1971. *The Adaptive Geometry of Trees.* Princeton University Press, Princeton, N.J., 140 pp.

Janos, D.P., 1975. Effects of vesicular arbuscular mycorrhizae on lowland tropical rain forest trees. In: F.E. Sanders, B. Mosse, P.B. Tinker (Editors), *Endomycorrhizas.* Academic Press, London, pp. 437–446.

Janzen, D.H., 1978. Seeding patterns of tropical trees. In: P.B. Tomlinson and M.H. Zimmermann (Editors), *Tropical Trees as Living Systems.* Cambridge University Press, Cambridge, New York, N.Y., pp. 83–128.

Jeannoda-Robinson, V., 1977. *Contribution à l'étude de l'architecture des herbes.* Thesis, Université des Sciences et Techniques du Languedoc, Montpellier, 76 pp.

Jenik, J., 1978. Roots and root systems in tropical trees: Morphologic and ecologic aspects. In: P.B. Tomlinson and M.H. Zimmermann (Editors), *Tropical Trees as Living Systems.* Cambridge University Press, Cambridge, New York, N.Y., pp. 232–349.

Lawton, J.R. and Lawton, J.R.S., 1971. Seasonal variations in the secondary phloem of some forest trees from Nigeria. *New Phytol.*, 70: 187–196.

Longman, K.A. and Jenik, J., 1974. *Tropical Forest and Its Environment.* Longman, London, 205 pp.

McKey, D., Waterman, P.G., Mbi, C.N., Gartlan, J.S. and Struhsakerg, T.T., 1978. Phenolic content of vegetation in two African rain forests: ecological implications. *Science*, 202: 61–64.

Ng, F.S.P., 1978. Strategies of establishment in Malayan forest trees. In: P.B. Tomlinson and M.H. Zimmermann (Editors), *Tropical Trees as Living Systems.* Cambridge University Press, Cambridge, New York, N.Y., pp. 129–162.

Oldeman, R.A.A., 1974. *L'architecture de la forêt guyanaise.* *Mém. O.R.S.T.O.M.*, No. 73: 204 pp.

Parameswaran, N., 1971. Über die Struktur der tropischen Baumrinde und ihre Verwertungsmöglichkeiten. *Forstarchiv*, 41: 193–198.

Prévost, M.-F., 1978. Modular construction and its distribution in tropical woody plants. In: P.B. Tomlinson and M.H. Zimmermann (Editors), *Tropical Trees as Living Systems.* Cambridge University Press, Cambridge, New York, N.Y., pp. 223–231.

Primack, R.B. and Tomlinson, P.B., 1978. Sugar secretions from the buds of *Rhizophora*. *Biotropica*, 10: 74–75.

Richards, P.W., 1957. *The Tropical Rain Forest: An Ecological Study.* Cambridge University Press, Cambridge, 450 pp.

Romberger, J.A., 1963. Meristems, growth and development in woody plants. *U.S. Dep. Agric. For. Serv. Tech. Bull.*, 1293.

Schnell, R., 1970. *Introduction à la Phytogéographie des pays tropicaux, I. Les flores — les structures.* Gauthier-Villars, Paris, 499 pp.

Schoute, J.C., 1903. Die Stammesbildung der Monokotylen. *Flora (Jena)*, 92: 32–48.

Serebryakova, T.I., 1971. Types of major cycle and structure of aerial shoots in flowering plants. *Byull. Mosk. Ova. Ispyt. Prir., Otd. Biol.*, 76(1): 105–119 (in Russian).

Smith, A.P., 1972. Buttressing of tropical trees: A descriptive model and a new hypothesis. *Am. Nat.*, 106: 32–46.

Späth, H., 1912. *Die Johannistriebe.* Parey, Berlin.

Tomlinson, P.B., 1974. Vegetatiive morphology and meristem dependence — the foundation of productivity in seagrasses. *Aquaculture*, 4: 107–130.

Tomlinson, P.B., 1978. Branching and axis differentiation in tropical trees. In: P.B. Tomlinson and M.H. Zimmermann (Editors), *Tropical Trees as Living Systems.* Cambridge University Press, Cambridge, New York, N.Y., pp. 187–107.

Tomlinson, P.B., 1980. *The Biology of Trees Native to Tropical Florida.* P.B. Tomlinson, Petersham, Mass., 480 pp.

Tomlinson, P.B. and Esler, A.E., 1973. Establishment growth in woody monocotyledons native to New Zealand. *N.Z. J. Bot.*, 11: 627–644.

Tomlinson, P.B. and Gill, A.M., 1973. Growth habits of tropical trees: Some guiding principles. In: B.J. Meggers, E.S. Ayensu and W.D. Duckworth (Editors), *Tropical Forest Ecosystems in Africa and South America: A Comparative Review.* Smithsonian Institution Press, Washington, D.C., pp. 129–143.

Tomlinson, P.B. and Wheat, D.W., 1979. Bijugate phyllotaxis in Rhizophoreae (Rhizophoraceae). *Bot. J. Linn. Soc.*, 78: 317–321.

Tomlinson, P.B. and Zimmermann, M.H., 1967. Anatomy of the palm *Rhapis exelsa*. III. Juvenile phase. *J. Arnold Arbor.*, 47: 301–312.

Veillon, J.-M., 1978. Architecture of the New Caledonian species of *Araucaria*. In: P.B. Tomlinson and M.H. Zimmermann (Editors), *Tropical Trees as Living Systems*. Cambridge University Press, Cambridge, New York, N.Y., pp. 233–245.

Walsh, G.E., Barrett, R., Cook, G.H. and Hollister, T.A., 1973. Effects of herbicides on seedlings of the red mangrove, *Rhizophora mangle* L. *Bioscience*, 23: 361–364.

Wheat, D.W., 1980. Sylleptic branching in *Myrsine floridana* (Myrsinaceae). *Am. J. Bot.*, 67: 490–499.

Whitmore, T.C., 1963. Studies in systematic bark morphology. III. Bark taxonomy in Dipterocarpaceae. *Gard. Bull. (Singapore)*, 19: 321–371.

Whitmore, T.C., 1975. *Tropical Rain Forests of the Far East*. Clarendon Press, Oxford, 282 pp.

Chapter 3

SPATIAL ASPECTS OF VEGETATION STRUCTURE

PATRICK S. BOURGERON

INTRODUCTION

In the previous chapter the architectural analysis of rain forest trees provided an individualistic view of structure. The individual trees have a basic inherited, ground plan or design which is altered through their interaction with other plants, with animals, and the environment. In this chapter we will consider the structure of the forest as a whole, focusing on both the vertical elements which are the results of the architectural design features described in Chapter 2, and the horizontal element. Some of these features will be developed further in Chapter 4 which is concerned with the forest biomass.

In the broadest sense, there are two approaches to the study of vertical and horizontal structure of a forest. Forests may be described qualitatively or in quantitative terms. Qualitative descriptions have been concerned mainly with the stratification or the patterning of trees in the vertical and horizontal dimension. Floristic descriptions of the forest can also be included here. There are many examples of this approach, as for example Aubréville (1950–1951), Richards (1952), Guillaumet (1967), Guillaumet and Kahn (1978, 1979), Kahn (1978), Lescure (1978), and Bourgeron and Guillaumet (1981).

The quantitative approaches to forest structure have been initially developed largely for temperate vegetation. In tropical biology such approaches have been mainly due to the work of foresters. More recently ecologists have begun to develop mathematical models and a variety of statistical tools to deal with the more structurally complex and species-rich tropical rain forest. Mathematical models have been developed to determine relation-

ships between diameter, height and crown width (Pierlot, 1966, 1968; Rollet and Caussinius, 1969; and Caussinius and Rollet, 1970). Brunig in Chapter 4 presents further data on these relationships, and other examples may be found in Dawkins (1958), Schulz (1960), Wyatt-Smith (1960), White (1963), Ashton (1964), Veillon (1965), Pierlot (1966, 1968), Rollet (1969a, b, 1974), Chapman and White (1970), Hamilton (1975), Bouxin (1977) and Huttel (1977). A mathematical approach to species–area relationships in the tropical rain forests also has been developed by Rollet (1969a), Godron (1970, 1971), and Poissonet (1971) from only the French literature. Multivariate methods, which have been proven of value both in the field and at the theoretical level by Ashton (1964), Greig-Smith et al. (1967), Webb et al. (1967a, b, 1970, 1972), Austin and Greig-Smith (1968) and Williams et al. (1969a, b), are commonly used for the analysis of tropical forest communities (Austin et al., 1972; Bouxin, 1976; and Bourgeron, 1981). Biomass studies, which are discussed more fully in the following chapters, have also been conducted at the community level by Ogawa et al. (1965), Veillon (1965), Golley et al. (1969), Hozumi et al. (1969), Ovington and Olson (1970), Fittkau and Klinge (1973), Klinge and Rodrigues (1974), and Bernhard-Reversat et al. (1975). And finally, some multidisciplinary projects have used both qualitative and quantitative approaches, for example Odum and Pigeon (1970) in Puerto Rico, Paijmans (1970) in New Guinea, Holdridge et al. (1971) in Costa Rica, and Knight (1975) in Panama.

In these various quantitative and qualitative studies the students of tropical rain forest have begun from a variety of points of view, which led to two opposite assertions on the structure of tropical forests: (1) there is one vast plant community, in which local variations are fortuitous, and (2) observed patterns are related to highly precise habitat requirements of species, whose associations form patches of a mosaic (see Whitmore, 1975). This dichotomy is attributable to the fact that, in contrast to much temperate vegetation, the tropical forest still exists in places as vast undisturbed landscapes. Therefore, the outcome of the study depends on the answers to the following questions which must be addressed. Where does the ecologist begin his work in such an unfamiliar, and complex system? How many plots or transects are required to describe the structure of the forest of the Congo (Zaire) basin or the Amazon? At the largest scale we speak of the tropical rain forest as a global formation and contrast data from this formation with that of temperate forests, grasslands, tundras and oceans. Yet our understanding of the global character of the formation comes from relatively few widely separated studies and a larger number of observations by biological explorers.

Other ecologists have approached the tropical rain forest with a more restricted focus. At a medium scale the forest of a region, a state, or a small river basin is examined using the familiar techniques of forest inventory and sampling. In these studies ecologists have recognized structural and functional differences over slopes and over soil catenas. For example, Huttel and Bernhard-Reversat (1975) in Banco, Ivory Coast, showed that the forest on the top of hillocks differed in structural features from that on slopes and in valleys. Brunig (1974) has also described the change in vegetation structure on transects which cover differences in geology, soils and topography in Sarawak and Brunei. In these and other cases, the species each are distributed over continua of environmental conditions making boundaries between ecological communities difficult to recognize. Yet, a plot placed in the typical example of a recognizable type of vegetation — high forest or riverine forest, for example — can be shown to differ in significant respects from other sample plots.

Then finally, on a small scale, tropical ecologists frequently find considerable heterogeneity of structure from small plot (100 m^2) to plot within a single type of community. In some forests, this fine-grained heterogeneity is due to different ages and

succession of the vegetation occupying places in the forest where large trees have fallen. Gap formation caused by the fall of canopy trees which pull associated trees tied together by lianas all to the ground create conditions for rapid plant succession. Where tree fall is relatively frequent the forest appears to be a mosaic of patches each derived from gaps formed at different times. This concept of the tropical forest as a mosaic is not novel. Aubréville (1938) noted: "Si bien qu'en prospectant le long d'une piste, on ne peut pas apercevoir certaines espèces dominantes dans la région qui se groupent en dehors de l'itinéraire suivi. [While doing research on a line, one may not observe certain dominant species in the region which occur in groups off of the transect route.]" Aubréville (1938) compared the occurrence of dominant species to the spots on the skin of the panther. Watt (1947) referred to Aubréville's interpretation of this phenomenon, known as the mosaic or cyclical theory of regeneration (Richards, 1952), in the discussion of his view of pattern and process developed for temperate vegetation. Also, Jones (1955, 1956), Schulz (1960), Richards (1964), Guillaumet (1967), and Whitmore (1975) described this phenomenon in different tropical rain forests.

A recent study in the dry forest in Costa Rica by Hubbell (1979) describes this small-scale pattern in considerable detail. While the dry forest differs from rain forest, especially in a smaller number of species, it does represent a general pattern of tropical forest structure. Hubbell has examined the generalization that most tropical tree species occur at low adult densities, with the adults thinly and evenly distributed through space. This phenomenon of low density and uniform dispersion has been hypothesized as due to predation of seeds near the parent tree (Janzen, 1970) which would reduce the local density of a species and allow invasion of the area by other species, thus causing increased diversity. Hubbell's study was made on 13.44 ha of forest. He found 135 species of woody plants with stem diameters ≤ 2 cm dbh, including 87 overstorey and understorey trees, 38 shrubs and 10 vines. Careful study of the actual distribution of adults and juveniles on the plot showed that the trees were not uniformly distributed. Indeed, of 114 species with at least two individuals in the mapped area, 102 exhibited significant clumping. Because of the clumped distribution Hubbell found that many species were rare when half the area was examined, but were common when the entire area was studied.

Considering the hypothesis that tree distribution is due to seed predation, Hubbell tested the hypothesis that adult and juvenile densities decline exponentially away from the average adult. For the 30 most common species the prediction did not hold; the average adult is located in a clump of adults and juveniles. And actually in this case the distant juveniles suffer greater losses than those nearer the clump center. The nearest neighbor in these clumps or patches of a species averages 40 m and a four-fold increase in area only results in a 2.3-fold increase in number of adults. These patterns apparently are also related to the type of seed dispersal — the juvenile survival is more strongly skewed to the point of propagule origin for mammal dispersed seeds than for wind or bird dispersed seeds. Rare species showed a much lower rate of establishment than did common species suggesting that rarity is associated with a very slow per capita rate of juvenile establishment. Hubbell comments after reviewing these data "the observed clumped dispersion pattern of dry forest tree species is just what one would expect if the forest is essentially a palimpsest of small, regenerating light gaps of different ages."

Although a review of the different classifications of plant communities, and hence, of the concept of plant community itself, is not within the scope of this chapter (the reader can refer to Van Der Maarel, 1976, and to Whittaker, 1978a), we must understand how relative is recognition of communities in the field. Identification of plant communities results from a process of interaction between the phytosociologist and the vegetation (Whittaker, 1962, 1978a), a process which is in part subjective. Field recognition depends on the strategy of classification chosen, and choice of a strategy also is subjective. Whittaker's (1978b) statement, "Community-types are not natural but arbitrary units in the sense that their extensional definitions are strongly influenced if not wholly determined by phytosociologists' choices of characteristics by which communities are to be classified", must be kept in mind in any analysis of structure of tropical rain forest. Nevertheless, we will proceed using the ecological community as the basic element in the discussion.

VERTICAL DISTRIBUTION

A particularly striking feature of tropical rain forests (especially the lowland evergreen tropical rain forest) is the great number of individuals and their complex pattern of distribution between the ground and the canopy. Quickly, vehement discussion arises about the interpretation of this observation, as expressed by that unfortunate word, stratification. Discussions of stratification seem to result in endless debate, and while it is wise to stay away from such unfruitful discussions, it cannot be denied that the vertical distribution of plants in the tropical rain forests is a central problem of the structure of these communities and of their regeneration.

Background

Three characteristics of the tropical rain forests make the study of vertical patterns more important in these forests than in temperate forests: (1) the high diversity of species of any size; (2) the generally impressive number of individuals regardless of the species at any level beneath the canopy; (3) the height of the tallest trees. These characteristics are illustrated in Figs. 3.1 and 3.2.

The diversity of tropical forests is well known. For example, in the Amazon forest on an area of 10 ha there may be as many as 400 species of trees. Ashton (1964) has plotted the relationship of number of species and area surveyed in several forests in Southeast Asia. All of his curves continue to rise at the largest sample sizes. Relatively few of the species encountered in these forests are well known. Indeed, in some forests as many as one-half of the trees have not been named and examined by competent taxonomists.

The vegetation itself is organized in a complex pattern from the soil to the top of the canopy. Some ecologists (for example, Richards, 1963) identify three layers of tree leaves and branches corresponding to emergent trees, the main canopy and a third subcanopy at lower height. These layers produce the ragged or uneven canopy top one observes when flying over tropical forest. Below the trees are other layers representing an underbrush or shrub zone, a ground flora, and several layers of roots. In nutrient-poor soils there may be a thick mat of roots on the soil surface. Some trees have deep tap

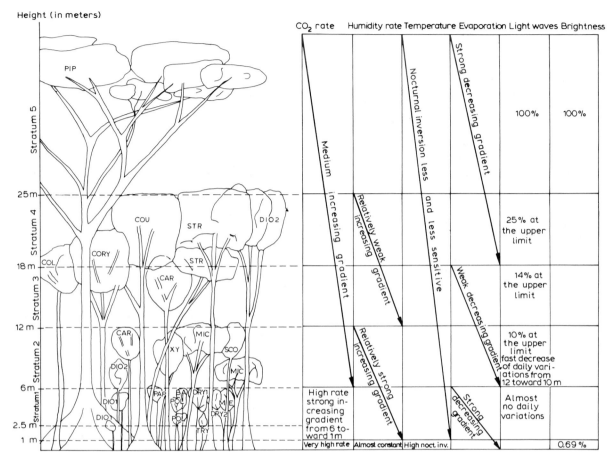

Fig. 3.1. Profile of one of twenty stands studied in Tai forest (Ivory Coast). The dotted lines show the limits of the strata recognized after description of the stand (method of description of Guillaumet and Kahn, 1979). Vegetation below 2.5 m has not been studied in details for allowing recognition of different layers. Therefore, the dotted line at 1 m corresponds to a particular level of bioclimatic factors (data from Cachan and Duval, 1963). The table of variations of the bioclimatic factors has been compiled from Cachan and Duval (1963). Species: *BA* = *Baphia nitida*; *CAR* = *Carapa procera*; *COL* = *Cola nitida*; *CORY* = *Corynanthe pachysceras*; *COU* = *Coula edulis*; *DIO 1* = *Diospyros mannii*; *DIO 2* = *Diospyros sanzaminika*; *DIO 3* = *Diospyros soubreana*; *DRY 1* = *Drypetes gilgiana*; *DRY 2* = *Drypetes principum*; *ME* = *Memecylon lateriflorum*; *MIC* = *Microdesmis puberula*; *PAR* = *Parinari aubrevillei*; *PIP* = *Piptadeniastrum africanum*; *POL* = *Polyalthia oliveri*; *SCO* = *Scotellia coriacea*; *STR* = *Strombosia glaucescens*; *TRY* = *Trichoscypha oba*; *XY* = *Xylopia quintasii*. (Figure from Bourgeron and Guillaumet, 1981.)

roots or other forms of roots that penetrate to the interface between the parent material and the soil.

The height of rain forest averages generally about 50 m, with emergent trees in certain areas reaching 70 to 80 m height. One of the tallest trees recorded was a *Koompassia excelsa* of 84 m height (Foxworthy, 1927). Maximum height of the forest is obtained on well-drained, fertile soils where the rainfall is about 2000 mm. Very wet, infertile, or mountainous sites have forests with less stature.

There are three definitions of stratification which express these characteristics:

(1) Stratification of species — that is, the aggre-

gation of the mature height of species, regardless of the frequency of their occurrence (e.g. Sawyer and Lindsey, 1971).

(2) Stratification of individuals — that is, the aggregation of all tree heights, mature and immature (e.g. Grubb et al., 1963).

(3) Stratification of leaf mass — that is, the aggregation of intra-individual strata of many individuals focusing on only one component of the vegetation (e.g. MacArthur and MacArthur, 1961; Odum et al., 1963).

Often, there is an inadequate distinction between these three types of stratification when one ex-

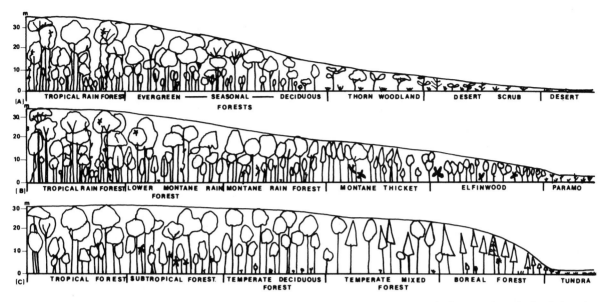

Fig. 3.2. Profile diagrams for three ecoclines. A. Along a gradient of increasing aridity from rain forest to desert in South America. B. Along a gradient of increasing altitude from rain forest to paramo in South America. C. Along a latitudinal gradient from tropical seasonal forest to the tundra. Levels a and b1 for studying horizontal distribution of vegetation (see p. 38) are appropriate for studying such ecoclines. In this Chapter, interests focus on the distribution of vegetation lying in, approximately, the left third part of ecoclines A and C, and the left two thirds of ecocline B. (After Whittaker, 1975.)

amines the actual vegetation in the field. Thus, Paijmans (1970) defined stratification as the stratification of individuals (p. 85), but later referred to the stratification of the leaf mass (p. 86).

There is also the usual dichotomy between qualitative and quantitative approaches. The most famous qualitative tool is the profile-diagram (Davis and Richards, 1933, 1934). Studies using this approach include Davis and Richards (1933, 1934), Richards (1952), Cain and Castro (1959), Guillaumet (1967), Huttel (1969), Paijmans (1970), Holdridge et al. (1971), Oldeman (1974a, b, 1978), Rollet (1974) and Hallé et al. (1978). There are also quantitative methods which explore the relationship between height and number of individuals. For instance, Godron (1971) described a method based on levels of maximum density determined by sampling at arbitrarily chosen distances above the ground. Unfortunately this technique does not give a realistic idea of the volume occupied at a certain level by the trunks, the main branches, and the crowns of the trees. In this kind of method, dependence on density makes the results suspect. Studies using this approach include Grubb et al. (1963), Odum et al. (1963), Paijmans (1970),

Soriano-Ressy et al. (1970), Holdridge et al. (1971), Sawyer and Lindsey (1971), Rollet (1974). Brünig in Chapter 4 discusses some of these methods and describes some of his own findings.

As a result of the complexity of the phenomenon and the lack of comparability of definition and methods, there is no definitive answer to the question of the existence of stratification in the tropical rain forests. There are those who do not see any evidence of stratification, regardless of the definition used (e.g. Cain and Castro, 1959; Schulz, 1960; Grubb et al., 1963; Paijmans, 1970; Godron et al., 1971; Holdridge et al., 1971), and those who describe and find a regular pattern of vertical distribution (e.g. Davis and Richards, 1933, 1934; Richards, 1952; Jones, 1955; Webb, 1959; Odum et al., 1963; Oldeman, 1974a, b, 1978; Hallé et al., 1978; Bourgeron and Guillaumet, 1981). However, among the authors describing a pattern of vertical distribution, there is little unity on their meaning or definition of the phenomenon. Thus, recently, Hallé et al. (1978) took special care to separate their view of stratification from those of previous works (pp. 333–335 in Hallé et al., 1978). Nevertheless, their conception is no more and no less than the stratification of species, when they assert that (p. 335) "... in certain plots, there are demonstrable horizontal sets composed of trees of the present[1]."

Moreover, it very often appears that the recognition of stratification is a conceptual choice, an "act of faith," made prior to working in the forest (Oldeman, 1978; Bourgeron and Guillaumet, 1981). It can be noted that the same study could serve both points of view, depending on the author's personal opinion.

A model of stratification

In this complex situation Bourgeron and Guillaumet (1981) have developed an approach to the problem of stratification which is based on the concepts of plant architecture described in the previous chapter, especially on the idea of re-iteration. Reiteration means the development of shoots outside of the usual architectural model due to environmental factors — that is, it is an opportunistic process (Hallé et al., 1978; Oldeman, 1978). If reiteration does not occur, the tree will stay in a suppressed state. Thus, the ecological potentialities of a tree differ, depending on whether the tree is mature or is a tree of the future, which can still reiterate, grow, and occupy more space. Re-iteration is related to energy level (Hallé et al., 1978; Oldeman, 1978), and to heredity, as well as to interactions between neighboring individuals of the same height (Fig. 3.3). Therefore, tree architecture can be considered a function of inherited capacity to reiterate, the interactions between neighbors, and the sharing of resources (e.g. space and light). Hopefully this model builds on a sound theoretical base of plant design but also considers the actual response of plants to their environment through the process of reiteration. Applying a method of tropical rain forest description (Guillaumet and Kahn, 1978, 1979), based on these concepts of plant architecture, and using the results of a detailed bioclimatic study (Cachan, 1963; Cachan and Duval, 1963), Bourgeron and Guillaumet (1981) described five strata between 2.5 m above the ground and the highest trees in the Tai forest (southwestern Ivory Coast). The central idea was that the trees of the same stratum are under the influence of the same set of environmental constraints. Thus, a stratum is both the set of trees at a certain level and the set of environmental factors at

this level. Recognition of strata is the result of analyzing descriptions and relevés on a series of homogeneous plots, and not from a preconceived pattern of vertical distribution.

Fig. 3.1 shows a stratification profile for the Tai Forest, Ivory Coast, as defined by Bourgeron and Guillaumet (1981), and the variations of the principal bioclimatic factors (the graphs are compiled from Cachan and Duval, 1963). Comparison of the figure and graph shows that there is a relationship between the stratification in the forest and the bioclimatic factors. It is important to note that, in this model, (1) the set of environmental factors at a certain level, and not a single factor, is considered, (2) the daily and seasonal variations are so important that trees of different strata may come under similar environmental conditions, but not at the same moment of the day or the year, and (3) that the relative importance of the bioclimatic factors differ depending on the set considered.

Ecological meaning of this for an individual can be seen by following on Fig. 3.1 the growth of a theoretical tree. From the ground to 1 m, the environmental characteristics are a high level of CO_2, high humidity (above 90%), a temperature up to 6°C colder than outside the forest cover, and a strong nocturnal inversion of temperature, practically no light, and less than 1% luminosity. Above 1 m (stratum 1), the principal differences with the ground layer involve temperature, and a lower influence of nocturnal inversion of temperature. Stratum 2 differs from stratum 1 in the variations of light and CO_2 level. In stratum 3, higher temperature and strong daily variations of light are found. In stratum 4, all the factors vary strongly, and finally, in stratum 5 (the emergents), conditions are comparable to those in open-fields, although there are two main differences in the life history of trees which reached stratum 5, and those grown in an open-field. First, the emergents have to grow under forest conditions [which influence the shape of trees, as has been discussed by Oldeman (1974a, b, 1978) and Hallé (1978)] until they reach stratum 5, and second, there is high humidity from

---

[1] A tree of the present is a tree which has reached its maximal expansion (Oldeman, 1974a, b, 1978; Hallé et al., 1978) — that is, a mature tree.

Fig. 3.3. Profile in the Tai forest (Ivory Coast). The photograph has been taken from a clean-cut field open a few days before. It appears that the emergents (here four *Parinari aubrevillei*, approximately 55 m high) do not form a continuous canopy. The continuous canopy is at about 25 m high, below this level the term closed forest can be applied. On the other hand, it is interesting to see four emergents so close to each other. That is in contrast with the hypothesis that emergents should be rare and spaced.

evaporation of the forest beneath the emergents. Fig. 3.4 shows what a seedling may "see" from the soil (see legend).

It is important to note that considering the sets of trees of the present as the backbone of the forest, and the trees of the future as merely growing when it is possible to replace a dead tree of the present

(Newman, 1954; Hallé et al., 1978) tends to de-emphasize the interactions existing between individuals at a certain level of their aerial system. Regardless of what happens at the level of the root systems (Longman and Jeník, 1974; Kahn, 1978), the trees of the present and of the future can compete directly at the level of their aerial systems.

Fig. 3.4. View of the understorey of the Tai forest (Ivory Coast) along a gentle slope. Characteristics of tropical rain forests which led to defining this vegetation as "exuberant" appear: many individuals of many species without any apparent vertical distributional pattern. It must be noted that the image of "closed forest" below the continous canopy (Fig. 3.3) must be pondered, and that the canopy can be more heterogeneous than it seems at first hand.

Illustration of this point can be found in Oldeman (1974a, pp. 78, 98, and 118).

Origin and maintenance of stratification

One of the main criticisms of the concept of stratification is that it is a "static, typologic concept of forest structure which gives no recognition to the dynamic nature of the canopy" (Whitmore, 1978). It is also hard to believe that a given pattern of stratification is a finality always reached regardless of local factors and unexpected disturbances. Stratification as defined above avoids these two problems. First, the recognition of strata results

from field work, and review of collected data, whatever the observer's opinion. Second, the dynamics of growth in the forest is conserved. For instance, we can assume that in the absence of catastrophes the trees of the future will grow up and contribute to the vertical structure. The phenomenon of suppression is too poorly known to accept Hallé et al.'s (1978) conclusion that "as long as the homeostatic state of the plot is maintained, the set of the future does not move and just survives" (p. 341). Moreover, death of some trees in the understorey or of trees in the canopy, or any local non-catastrophic disturbance creating heterogeneities at the scale of one individual, allows

Fig. 3.5. Two overstorey trees competing for space (*Chrysophyllum taiense* on the left, *Xylopia villosa* on the right). Both trees are approximately 30 m high, therefore above the continuous canopy. They are rooted at about only 3 m from each other. It is clear that, independently of what happened at the level of their root systems, their aerial systems reflect the sharing of space. Each portion of space is "filled", but the trees "manage" to occupy this space in such a way that they hardly overlap directly. The size of the trees are such that one can assume safely that no one will be excluded by competition. This demonstrates the dependence of architecture on interactions between neighbors, and also that coexistence may be achieved through different ways. (Photograph of Tai forest, Ivory Coast.)

growth to occur (Fig. 3.5). But it must be kept in mind that at the time the observer works, such heterogeneities are not visible. That is, the gap opened by a falling branch is filled by other branch(es), the fallen leaves have been replaced, and so forth. In the event of a drastic change, as most often caused by a tree fall resulting in a gap, succession phenomena occur, and a new building phase begins (Oldeman, 1974a, b, 1978; Hartshorn, 1978; Whitmore, 1978; Bourgeron and Guillaumet, 1981).

Thus, stratification depends on both en-

vironmental and biological factors, including inter- and intra-specific competition. Stratification is related to the diversification of sets of environmental factors (Bourgeron and Guillaumet, 1981), as it increases in complexity during sylvigenesis (e.g. Oldeman, 1974a, p. 125; 1978, p. 548). Adaptation to the shady understorey leads to the building of the strata (see mechanisms of distribution of layers of leaves in Horn, 1971). So, unsurprisingly, as noted by Richards (1952) and Oldeman (1974a), stratification is most apparent in undisturbed forests. Any important disturbance breaks the current state, and a new building phase starts. Thus, vertical distribution for individuals in the tropical rain forests follows a complex vertical gradient. That suggests that stratification has different causes which lead to the building of an original local pattern of vertical distribution, rather than having one single explanation. This is in agreement with Smith's (1973) formal review and discussion of the hypotheses on the origin of stratification, which stated that stratification involves many interacting factors.

HORIZONTAL DISTRIBUTION

Study of horizontal distribution can be conducted at several levels:

(a) At the interregional level, as by Whitmore (1975, pp. 181–186), whose interest is the comparison between formations of different regions such as Burma, Sri Lanka, and India.

(b) At the regional level — that is, within a geographical region. In this case, two sublevels must be considered: (1) variations within the entire geographical region which is covered by the forest — that is, the whole southwestern Ivory Coast; (2) variations within a very small area arbitrarily delimited, or corresponding to a natural unity (such as the drainage basin of a small river), as in Bouxin (1976, 1977), Huttel (1977) and Bourgeron (1981).

Distinction between these levels and sublevels is much more than of academic interest. Levels a and b1 recover the notion of distribution of the vegetation along a complex horizontal gradient (Whittaker, 1975, 1978a), as shown in Fig. 3.2. In this case, data collected at different points on a complex gradient are used to identify and describe the gradient. Level b2 focuses on analyzing data from the same point, or from a very small segment of the complex gradient cited above, with the interest of precisely defining the factors controlling the distribution of the vegetation at a microscale. If levels a and b1 are suitable for the classification of different types of vegetation, and for a general study, level b2 is indispensable for understanding intimate mechanisms of such phenomena as succession, which is of great interest for the long-term exploitation and conservation of the tropical rain forests (for example, see the study at a microscale of Webb et al., 1972).

Background

Qualitative descriptions of variation within the tropical rain forest started as early as 1908 with Chevalier, who travelled extensively through large parts of the African equatorial forests. Later, interest in the correlation of these variations with site factors developed, e.g. Richards (1952). Evidence of the dependence of vegetation on these site factors exists in many published works. For example, Black et al. (1950) showed, by comparison of plots of one hectare, that in the Brazilian Amazonian forest, near Tefé and Belém, periodically inundated *igapo* forests have fewer species, with strong species dominance, than the dry, never inundated, *tierra firme* forests, where the distribution of individuals among species is more regular and equal. Schulz (1960) stated that in the northern Surinam rain forest it is possible to distinguish geographic regions within the forest, with the vegetation on the mesic sites having approximately the same group of leading species. Differences in such an important life feature as phenology as well as floristics, dbh distribution and other abiotic and biotic features have been found between wet forests and dry forests in Costa Rica (Holdridge et al., 1971; Sawyer and Lindsey, 1971; Gordon et al., 1974). Guillaumet (1967) described the variation in the vegetation from north to south in the forests of the southwestern Ivory Coast.

In most of these cases, ecologists conclude that there is some relationship between the horizontal distribution of vegetation and environmental factors. For instance, Grubb and Whitmore (1966) pointed out that the distribution of lowland, lower, and upper montane forests in Ecuador is controlled by the frequency of fog, exposure to high wind, and soil factors. Webb et al. (1970) showed that the physiognomic-structural features of forests, as for instance the type of tree branching and the bark characteristics, change along an altitudinal gradient in eastern Australia. In fact, Webb and his co-workers found that these physiognomic-structural features are almost as efficient as floristics for the numerical classification of this vegetation. Austin et al. (1972) showed that, in the lowland forest of Brunei, vegetation is determined by soil texture and possibly by periodicity of flooding. Complexity of the species–habitat relationships is fully exhibited by the study of succession of Webb et al.

(1972). They showed that, by studying a same plot (20 × 40 m) in south Queensland (Australia) for twelve years after clearing, factors controlling the distribution of the vegetation changed. For the first year, the pattern of distribution was temporal. Then it shifted to a spatial pattern, related to microsite differences. Yet, at twelve years, the patchy structure was again unrelated to microsite differences with patches exhibiting quantitative rather than qualitative differences. For the reader's reference, many studies of the horizontal distribution of the tropical forests can be found in, among others: Black et al. (1950), Pires et al. (1953), Jones (1955), Dawkins (1958), Schulz (1960), Ashton (1964), Poore (1964, 1968), Nicholson (1965), Webb and Tracey (1965), Grubb and Whitmore (1966), Pierlot (1966), Guillaumet (1967), Webb et al. (1967a, b, 1970, 1972), Rollet (1969a, b), Tracey (1969), Williams et al. (1969b), Holdridge et al. (1971), Austin et al. (1972), Gray (1975), Hamilton (1975), Knight (1975), Bouxin (1976, 1977), Huttel (1977), Bourgeron (1981).

Interpretation

Review of this literature leads to the following general conclusions about horizontal vegetation structure of rain forests as related to environment.

(a) On a large geographic scale, vegetation is influenced by the effect of altitude (e.g. Grubb and Whitmore, 1966; Rollet, 1969b; Chapman and White, 1970; De Milde and Groot, 1970; Webb et al., 1970; Holdridge et al., 1971; Whitmore, 1975), which has been compared to the effect of the latitude (Whittaker, 1975). Factors controlling the altitudinal distribution are temperature (e.g. Good, 1947; Grubb and Whitmore, 1966; Webb et al., 1970) and moisture (e.g. Webb et al., 1970), although no clear hierarchy between environmental factors has been established.

(b) On a small scale, the local gentle topography seems to control at least partly the horizontal distribution (e.g. Nicholson, 1965; Austin and Greig-Smith, 1968; Webb et al., 1970; Austin et al., 1972; Bouxin, 1976; Huttel, 1977; Bourgeron, 1981), although all the studies do not lead their authors to this conclusion (e.g. Poore, 1968; Lawton, 1978). Water availability is sought as the first factor, of which topography and soil depth would be only the agents (Lind and Morrison,

1974). But interrelations between environmental factors is far from simple (Webb et al., 1970; Bouxin, 1976).

(c) Some forest areas are obviously different and are related to obvious environmental conditions. These include swampy and regularly flooded areas (Black et al., 1950; Pires et al., 1953; Guillaumet, 1967; Brunig, 1973; Whitmore, 1975; Huttel, 1977).

Unfortunately, it seems that each new work gives a new example which does not match the theory one would like to build from the previous works. The best one can do is to follow Webb et al.'s (1972) conclusion that tropical forests must be considered on two levels of organization. First, vegetation occurs in a framework, which can be a geographical or ecological unit. Then, within this framework, the vegetation is considered as a series of patches composed of species occurring probabilistically. This view is exactly that of the community mosaic discussed earlier. Few studies of ecosystem function are developed from the mosaic viewpoint. In the future ecologists might be expected to fit the sampling and study areas for functional studies more closely to this mosaic structure of the tropical forest.

Study of the horizontal distribution of vegetation, coupled with the study of the vertical distribution, leads to a concern for the distribution and abundance of species. This topic is called species diversity and while it is the subject of full development in Part B of this volume, it is of such importance that it is worthy of being briefly treated independently here.

DIVERSITY

Another form of structure expressed in the horizontal and vertical dimension focuses on the floristic composition of the vegetation. The dominance of the life forms of plants by trees, the large number of different species and the abundance of lianas, epiphytes and epiphyllae create a rich and diverse flora. Thus, a central question of tropical forest community analyses has been: why are there so many species in these forests? The problem can be formulated precisely: "Are there any discoverable general laws governing the composition and structure of many-species communities, and if so what are they?" (Pielou, 1975). The tropics, or more precisely the tropical rain forests, are at the core of almost all the hypotheses of diversity by virtue of the large number of species existing in these communities.

Background

Several aspects of diversity must be considered:

(a) richness — that is, the number of species in the community,

(b) evenness — that is, the distribution of individuals among species, also called equitability (Lloyd and Ghelardi, 1964).

Therefore, diversity has been understood either as richness-diversity (*sensu* Whittaker, 1972, 1977), or heterogeneity-diversity (*sensu* Peet, 1974).

Another aspect of diversity is the scale:

(a) diversity within the community, or within habitat: alpha diversity (MacArthur, 1965; Whittaker, 1972, 1977).

(b) diversity between habitats — that is, the extent of changes in species composition or the turnover along a gradient: beta diversity (MacArthur, 1965; Whittaker, 1972, 1977).

(c) diversity in the whole landscape: gamma diversity (Whittaker, 1972, 1977).

The different aspects of diversity have been reviewed by Whittaker (1972, 1977) and Peet (1974). In this discussion diversity is understood primarily as richness-diversity, and only secondarily as heterogeneity-diversity.

Observations and hypotheses

Generalizations and hypotheses are based on the fact that diversity increases towards the tropics, i.e. along the latitudinal gradient, called by Whittaker (1975) the master gradient. The major generalizations are:

(1) Alpha, beta, and gamma diversity are higher in the tropics (especially the humid tropics) than in temperate regions.

(2) Species number correspond to habitat complexity, and the tropics are thought as more complex than temperate regions.

(3) Tropical species are generally distributed more patchily than temperate species.

(4) Tropical species have smaller niche width than temperate species.

There are a variety of hypotheses to explain these diversity patterns. The first is the stability and predictability hypothesis (e.g. Connell and Orias, 1964; MacArthur, 1965, 1972; Pielou, 1975). A relation of cause to effect has been represented as (Pielou, 1975):

environment stability $\rightarrow$ community stability $\rightleftarrows$ high diversity

Predictability is related to the variance of the period and amplitude of environmental fluctuations. There are many counterexamples to this hypothesis, including: (1) low diversity in stable environments (Whittaker, 1965; Holdridge et al., 1971); and (2) high diversity in unstable and unpredictable environments (e.g. Whittaker and Niering, 1965; Whittaker, 1972, 1977; Naveh and Dan, 1973).

The second hypothesis is the environmental heterogeneity hypothesis (e.g. MacArthur, 1964, 1965; Karr, 1968, 1975; Karr and Roth, 1971; Ricklefs, 1977). In this hypothesis a high level of heterogeneity in soils, microclimate, water levels or other key environmental factors creates conditions for a large number of species to coexist in the same community. Again the argument is not completely convincing. For example, edaphic heterogeneity in tropical rain forests appears to be similar to that in temperate forests and does not explain the high diversity of species. Even if it is possible to understand stratification as an evolved characteristic allowing the maintenance of a high diversity (e.g. Ricklefs, 1977), this hypothesis does not explain the origin of diversity in the tropical rain forests.

The productivity hypothesis (Connell and Orias, 1964) argues that primary productivity is positively correlated with diversity. High productivity provides resources for a larger number of species to coexist than in less productive systems. This hypothesis has been rejected because there is sometimes a negative correlation between diversity and productivity (e.g. Williams, 1964; Whiteside and Harmsworth, 1967; McNaughton, 1968). Furthermore, Willson (1973) pointed out that the productivity per day of tropical rain forests is not higher than the productivity of temperate forests (see also Chapter 8). Rollet (1978) has also stated that diversity is higher on sites of medium nutrient richness than on too poor or too rich sites.

The predation and competition hypothesis (Paine, 1966) states that diversity is maintained at a high level by predation and/or competition. Ecologists exploring this hypothesis include Connell (1961, 1970, 1971, 1975), Harper (1969), Janzen (1970), Dayton and Hassler (1972), Menge and Sutherland (1976). Grime (1973) and Connell (1978) introduced the notion of intermediate disturbances as a factor favoring high diversity. Thus, the supposed relationship has an optimum point where diversity is maximum, while predation or other factors are at a median position.

An optimum pattern is also observed in stands occurring in intermediate positions which have a higher diversity than stands on extreme positions in the tropical rain forests (e.g., Black et al., 1950; Pires et al., 1953; Brunig, 1973; Bouxin, 1976; Huttel, 1977; Rollet, 1978). Terborgh (1973) generalized that diversity is higher on mesic habitats of wide areal extent (called "core" habitats) than in some more particular habitats such as swamps in limited areal extent (called "peripheral" habitats). However, there are examples that contradict the assumption that diversity should be higher at the center of a gradient than at its ends (see discussion in Whittaker, 1977).

A conceptual framework

Thus, no theory adequately explains forest diversity. However, some points can be clarified in the light of the recent literature. All of the hypotheses of diversity have been built with the assumption that communities exist in, or tend towards, a competitive equilibrium, as a consequence of the principle of exclusion of Gause (1934). The fact that communities reach a competitive equilibrium has been denied by many authors (among the most recent: Grubb, 1977; Wiens, 1977; Connel, 1978; Huston, 1979). The state communities eventually reach, from which they do not depart, and which is not the competitive equilibrium, has been called a dynamic equilibrium (Huston, 1979). This dynamic equilibrium can be understood as maintained in different ways. One way is that species having apparently the same niche in a community may avoid exclusion for some values in the frequencies of population reduction and growth rates (Huston, 1979). In Huston's model, five species are related by a set of Lokta-Volterra's equations. Instead of the competitive exclusion expected, Huston increased

diversity by periodically reducing populations, and by changing the growth rate (r) of the species. Fig. 3.6 shows Huston's contour map exhibiting the relations, between the frequency of population reduction and growth rate, which prevents competitive equilibrium from occurring, and thus, increases diversity.

Another way to understand the dynamic equilibrium is provided by Whittaker and Goodman's (1979) model. This model describes the distribution of carrying capacity (K) of a species along a microsite gradient as a function of the level of pressure of the environment (harsh, intermediate, and benign). The response of the population depends on r, K, and the environmental pressure. It appears that species evolve mechanisms buffering them from environmental fluctuations, which allow

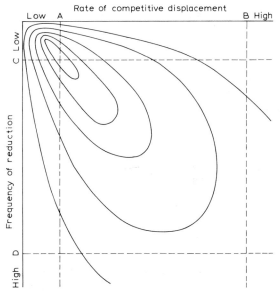

Fig. 3.6. Generalized contour map of the dynamic equilibria between the rate of competitive displacement and the frequency of population reduction. The rate of competitive displacement is directly proportional to the growth rate. Diversity is represented by the contour lines, with the highest diversity within the inner ellipsoid (in the upper left corner). The dotted lines show the predicated changes in diversity for one parameter held constant, and the other varying. Diversity is increased at some intermediate frequencies of population reductions. Low frequencies allow species to reach the competitive equilibrium, so diversity is decreased. Too high frequencies do not allow populations to recover from reductions, and this decreases diversity. At very low growth rates, diversity decreases because species disappear. At too high growth rates, diversity decreases because competitive equilibrium is reached. (After Huston, 1979.)

the coexistence of competitors by existence of subtle differences in the ecotopes. Two examples of such coexistence are (Whittaker and Levin, 1977):

(1) Two competing species reproducing at different times, during different conditions of the external environment, can maintain populations although they reproduce in the same part of the mosaic.

(2) Two competing species can maintain populations if each utilizes for its maximum growth or population increase a different part of the fluctuation.

In turn, the community is buffered from variation in its composition by these different mechanisms evolved by its species when the environment fluctuates (Whittaker and Levin, 1977, p. 125, 2.7; Whittaker and Goodman, 1979).

The concepts developed above allow us to understand more clearly the tropical rain forest. For instance, in the Tai forest (Bourgeron, 1981), the vegetation has been studied on a small geographical unit (part of a drainage basin), with a gentle undulating topography (ranging from 30 to 40 m in the vertical dimension). Classification and ordination gave the following results: (1) the vegetation is strongly homogeneous (Fig. 3.7A), but (2) the vegetation is also under the influence of the slope, and, with almost the same importance, the density of the continuous canopy (Fig. 3.7A and B) which conditions the bioclimatic factors in the understorey. Three types of population distribution have been observed:

(1) Species are rare. Approximately 60% of all the species found in the twenty study plots are rare. They occur in a few plots ($\leq 20\%$ of all the plots sampled), with generally a very small population size (≤ 10 individuals) in each plot the species is present.

(2) Species (approximately 25% of the total) are found in a majority of plots ($\geq 75\%$ of all the study plots), but with a small population size (≤ 15 individuals) in each plot the species occurs in.

(3) Species (15% of the total) are present in 75% or more of all the study plots, but with a fairly big population size (always >15 individuals, but generally >25 individuals) in each plot the species is present.

Type 1 species are specific to one kind of habitat (which corresponds to a position along the slope, see legend of Fig. 3.7). Type 1 species of the same

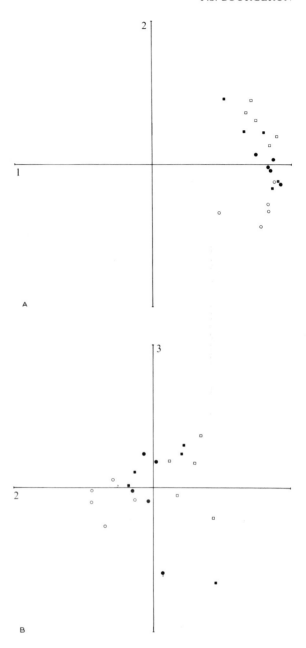

Fig. 3.7. Stand ordination by standardized Principal Component Analysis. The sites were located along five slopes on the following sites: top sites (□), strong slope sites (■), slope middle sites (●), slope bottom sites (○). The polarity of the variables on component 1 (Fig. 3.7A) suggests the homogeneity of the vegetation. However, two factors appear to control the distribution of the vegetation. Component 2 (Figs. 3.7A and B) is clearly related to the position of the stands along the slope. Component 3 (Fig. 3.7B) is related to the density of the foliage continuum (between 17 and 25 m) which corresponds to stratum 4 (Fig. 3.1). (Figure from Bourgeron, 1981.)

habitat overlap widely, but only a few of the available species occur in the same plot. Competitive exclusion is avoided (a) by the fact that only a few of the available species occur in the same plot, and (b) by the small population size of each one of the species growing in the same plot.

Types 2 and 3 species occur in at least three types of habitat. Differences in the distribution of species are quantitative.

A series of conclusions can be drawn from this study:

(1) First, data of Tai forest confirm Webb et al.'s (1972) conclusion that species are distributed within a framework in a fairly patchy way. In Tai forest the framework is the drainage basin.

(2) This apparent patchiness (expressed by the fact that only a few of all the available species of type 1 occur in the same plot, and by the quantitative differences in the distribution between species of type 2 or type 3) can be interpreted as the result of subtle ecotope differences evolved by competing species (Whittaker and Levin, 1977; Whittaker and Goodman, 1979).

(3) Consequently, there is no need to hypothesize that the niche width of tropical species should be small. Indeed, Knight (1975) showed that species in Barro Colorado Island, Panama, might have broader niche widths than temperate species.

It is then possible to generalize that the apparently overlapping species of the tropical rain forests avoid exclusion by different responses of their populations to the environment. Competitive equilibrium is prevented partly by low or fairly intermediate growth rates and the small population size of most species (Fedorov, 1966). Finally, population reductions can be understood as the result of seed predation (see Janzen, 1970, for instance), periodic floods or relative dryness killing seedlings, and other factors.

CONCLUSION

Although this chapter has only been concerned with vegetation, it is obvious that animals are part of the system through complex processes of co-evolution. There is actually an increasing number of studies reported on these plant–animal interactions (see Chapters 11 and 12). Besides the reductions of plant populations needed for coexistence of competing species, achieved through predation (e.g. Jansen, 1970), the plant–animal interactions can lead to sophisticated life cycles for plant species. For instance, seeds of *Samanea dinklagei* (a forest species of the southwestern Ivory Coast) need to be ingested by elephants. Similarly, another species of the southwestern Ivory Coast, *Massularia acuminata*, has been shown to be dependent for successful germination on ingestion of seeds by elephants: almost all the ingested seeds germinate as compared to only 10% of the non-ingested seeds. However, while the chances of germination of the seeds of these two species are considerably improved by ingestion by elephants, survival of the seedlings depends on the site factors.

In conclusion, spatial distribution of plants in the tropical forests is the result of complex processes. Both vertical and horizontal distributions, visible expression of the organization of species in the communities, facilitate the coexistence of a high number of species, and are the product of evolution of communities. Origin of these structures is still unclear, as is also the problem of evolution of taxa in geological times, and, hence, the origin of diversity. The only thing one can safely state is that diversity begets diversity, i.e. that diversity is a self-augmenting evolutionary process (Whittaker, 1975, p. 103).

ACKNOWLEDGEMENTS

This chapter was partially supported by an Ohio State University postdoctoral fellowship. I thank Dr. D. Crawford, R. Mitchell, E. Rudolph, and B.A. Schaal for reading and commenting the manuscript. Special thanks are due to Dr. Frank B. Golley who largely contributed to improve this paper by reviewing, editing and criticizing the different drafts. The photographs were provided by Rebecca Bourgeron.

REFERENCES

Ashton, P.S., 1964. Ecological studies in the mixed dipterocarp forests of Brunei State. *Oxford For. Mem.*, No. 25: 75 pp.

Aubréville, A., 1938. La forêt coloniale: les forêts de l'Afrique occidentale frangaise. *Ann. Acad. Sci. Colon.*, 9: 1–245.

Aubréville, A., 1950–1951. Le concept d'association dans la forêt dense équatoriale de la Basse Côte d'Ivoire. *Mém. Soc. Bot. Fr.*, pp. 145–148.

Austin, M.P. and Greig-Smith, P., 1968. The application of quantitative methods to vegetation survey. II. Some methodological problems of data from rain forest. *J. Ecol.*, 56: 827–844.

Austin, M.P., Ashton, P.S. and Greig-Smith, P., 1972. The application of quantitative methods to vegetation survey. III. A reexamination of rain forest data from Brunei. *J. Ecol.*, 60: 305–324.

Bernhard-Reversat, F., Huttel, C. and Lemée, G., 1975. Recherches sur l'écosystème de la forêt subéquatoriale de basse Côte d'Ivoire. *Terre Vie*, 29: 169–264.

Black, G.A., Dobzhansky, Th. and Pavan, C., 1950. Some attempts to estimate species diversity and population density of trees in Amazonian forests. *Bot. Gaz.*, 111: 413–425.

Bourgeron, P.S., 1981. Diversity pattern in the Tai forest (Ivory Coast). *J. Afr. Ecol.*, in press.

Bourgeron, P.S. and Guillaumet, J.L., 1981. A descriptive model of stratification in the Tai forest (Ivory Coast). *Candollea*, in press.

Bouxin, G., 1976. Ordination and classification in the upland Rurege forest (Rwanda, Central Africa). *Vegetatio*, 32: 97–115.

Bouxin, G., 1977. Structure de la strate arborescente dans un site de la forêt de montagne du Rwanda (Afrique Centrale). *Vegetatio*, 33: 65–78.

Brunig, E.F., 1973. Species richness and stand diversity in relation to site and succession of forests in Sarawak and Brunei (Borneo). *Amazoniana*, 4: 293–320.

Brunig, E.F., 1974. *Ecological Studies in the Kerangas Forests of Sarawak and Brunei*. Borneo Literature Bureau, Sarawak.

Cachan, P., 1963. Signification écologique des variations microclimatiques verticales dans la forêt sempervirente de Basse Côte d'Ivoire. *Ann. Fac. Sci. Dakar*, 8: 89–155.

Cachan, P. and Duval, J., 1963. Variations microclimatiques verticales et saisonnières dans la forêt sempervirente de basse Côte d'Ivoire. *Ann. Fac. Sci. Dakar*, 8: 5–87.

Cain, S.A. and Castro, B.M.O., 1959. *Manual of Vegetation Analysis*. Harper, New York, N.Y., 325 pp.

Caussinius, H. and Rollet, B., 1970. Sur l'analyse, au moyen d'un modèle mathématique, des structures par espèces des forêts denses humides. *C.R. Acad. Sci. Paris*, 270: 1341–1344.

Chapman, J.D. and White, F., 1970. *The Evergreen Forests of Malawi*. Oxford Commonwealth Forest Institute, Oxford.

Chevalier, A., 1908. La forêt vierge de la Côte d'Ivoire. *La Géographie*, 12: 201–210.

Connell, J.H., 1961. The influence of interspecific competition and other factors on the distribution of the barnacle *Chthamalus stellatus*. *Ecology*, 42: 710–723.

Connell, J.H., 1970. A predator–prey system in the marine intertidal region. I. *Balanus glandula* and several predatory species of Thais. *Ecol. Monogr.*, 40: 49–78.

Connell, J.H., 1971. On the role of natural enemies in preventing competitive exclusion in some marine animals and in rain forest trees. In: P.J. den Boer and G.R. Gradwell (Editors), *Dynamics of Populations*. Proc. Adv. Study Inst. Oosterbeek, 1970. Pudoc, Washington, pp. 298–312.

Connell, J.H., 1975. Producing structure in natural communities. In: M.L. Cody and J.M. Diamond (Editors), *Ecology and Evolution of Communities*. Harvard University Press, Cambridge, Mass., pp. 460–491.

Connell, J.H., 1978. Diversity in tropical rain forest and coral reefs. *Science*, 199: 1302–1310.

Connell, J.H., and Orias, E., 1964. The ecological regulation of species diversity. *Am. Nat.*, 98: 399–414.

Davis, T.A.W. and Richards, P.W., 1933. The vegetation of Morabelli Creek, British Guiana. An ecological study of a limited area of tropical rain forest. I. *J. Ecol.*, 21: 350–384.

Davis, T.A.W. and Richards, P.W., 1934. The vegetation of Morabelli Creek, British Guiana. An ecological study of a limited area of tropical rain forest. II. *J. Ecol.*, 22: 106–155.

Dawkins, H.C., 1958. *The Management of Natural Tropical High Forest With Special Reference to Uganda*. Oxford Forest Institute, Oxford, 155 pp.

Dayton, P.K. and Hessler, R.R., 1972. Role of biological disturbances in maintaining diversity in the deep sea. *Deep-Sea Res.*, 19: 199–208.

De Milde, R. and Groot, D., 1970. *Inventory of the Ebini-Italu Area*. U.N. Dep. For. Ind. Dev. Surv., Techn. Rep. No. 9: 106 pp.

Fedorov, A.A., 1966. The structure of the tropical rain forest and speciation in the tropics. *J. Ecol.*, 54: 1–11.

Fittkau, E.K. and Klinge, H., 1973. On biomass and trophic structure of the central Amazonian rain forest ecosystem. *Biotropica*, 5: 2–14.

Foxworthy, F.W., 1927. Commercial Timber Trees of the Malaya Peninsula. *Malay. For. Rec.*, 3: 419–432.

Gause, G.F., 1934. *The Struggle for Existence*. Williams and Wilkins, Baltimore, Md., 163 pp.

Gordon, M., 1970. Un modèle pour la courbe aire-espèces. *Nat. Can.*, 97: 491–492.

Godron, M., 1971. Comparaison d'une courbe aire-espèces et de son modèle. *Oecol. Plant.*, 6: 189–195.

Golley, F.B., McGinnis, J.T., Clements, R.G., Childs, G.Y. and Duever, M.J., 1969. The structure of tropical forests in Panama and Columbia. *Bioscience*, 19: 693–696.

Good, R., 1947. *The Geography of Flowering Plants*. Longman, London, 518 pp.

Gordon, W., Herbert, G.B. and Opler, P.A., 1974. Comparative phenological studies of trees in tropical wet and dry forests in the lowlands of Costa Rica. *J. Ecol.*, 62: 881–919.

Gray, B., 1975. Size composition and regeneration of *Araucaria* stands in New Guinea. *J. Ecol.*, 63: 273–289.

Greig-Smith, P., Austin, M.P. and Whitmore, T.C., 1967. Quantitative methods in vegetation survey. I. Association analysis and principal component ordination of rain forest. *J. Ecol.*, 55: 483–503.

Grime, J.P., 1973. Control of species density in herbaceous vegetation. *J. Environ. Manage.*, 1: 151–167.

Grubb, P.J., 1977. The maintenance of species richness in plant communities: the importance of the regeneration niche. *Biol. Rev.*, 52: 107–145.

Grubb, P.J. and Whitmore, T.C., 1966. A comparison of montane and lowland rain forest in Ecuador. II. The climate and its effects on the distribution and physiognomy of the forests. *J. Ecol.*, 54: 303–333.

Grubb, P.J., Lloyd, J.R., Pennington, T.D. and Whitmore, T.C., 1963. A comparison of montane and lowland rain forest in Ecuador. I. The forest structure physiognomy and floristics. *J. Ecol.*, 51: 564–599.

Guillaumet, J.L., 1967. Recherches sur la végétation et la flore de la région du Bas-Cavally (Côte d'Ivoire). *Mém. O.R.S.T.O.M.*, 20.

Guillaumet, J.L. and Kahn, F., 1978. Les diagnoses de la végétation. In: *Recherche d'un langage transdisciplinaire pour l'étude du milieu naturel (Tropiques humides)*. O.R.S.T.O.M., Paris.

Guillaumet, J.L. and Kahn, F., 1979. Descriptions des végétations forestières tropicales, approche morphologique et structurale. *Candollea*, 34: 109–131.

Hallé, F., 1978. Architectural variation at the specific level in tropical trees. In: P.B. Tomlinson and M.H. Zimmerman (Editors), *Tropical Trees as Living Systems*. Cambridge University Press, Cambridge, pp. 209–221.

Hallé, F., Oldeman, R.A.A. and Tomlinson, P.B., 1978. *Tropical Trees and Forests: An Architectural Analysis*. Springer-Verlag, Heidelberg, 441 pp.

Hamilton, A.C., 1975. A quantitative analysis of altitudinal zonation in Uganda forests. *Vegetatio*, 30: 99–106.

Harper, J.L., 1969. The role of predation in vegetational diversity. *Brookhaven Symp. Biol.*, 22: 48–62.

Hartshorn, G.S., 1978. Tree falls and tropical forest dynamics. In: P.B. Tomlinson and M.H. Zimmermann (Editors), *Trees as Living Systems*. Cambridge University Press, Cambridge, pp. 617–638.

Holdridge, L.R., Grenke, W.C., Hatheway, W.H., Liang, T. and Tosi, J.A., Jr., 1971. *Forest Environments in Tropical Life Zones: A Pilot Study*. Pergamon Press, Oxford.

Horn, H.S., 1971. *The Adaptive Geometry of Trees*. Princeton University Press, Princeton, N.J., 144 pp.

Hozumi, K., Yoda, K., Kokawa, S. and Kira, T., 1969. Production ecology of tropical rain forest in southwestern Cambodia. I. Plant biomass. *Nature Life S.E. Asia*, 6: 1–51.

Hubbell, S.P., 1979. Tree dispersion, abundance, and diversity in a tropical dry forest. *Science*, 203: 1299–1303.

Huston, M., 1979. A general hypothesis of species diversity. *Am. Nat.*, 113: 81–101.

Huttel, C., 1969. *Rapport d'activité pour l'année 1968*. O.R.S.T.O.M., Adiopodoumé, 37 pp.

Huttel, G., 1977. *Etude de quelques caractéristiques structurales de la végétation du bassin versant de l'Audrenisrou*. O.R.S.T.O.M., Adiopodoumé, 33 pp.

Huttel, C., and Bernhard-Reversat, F., 1975. Recherches sur l'écosystème de la Forêt subéquatoriale de Basse Côte d'Ivoire. V. Biomasse végétale et productivité primaire, cycle de la matière organique. *Terre Vie*, 29: 203–228.

Janzen, D.H., 1970. Herbivores and the number of tree species in tropical forests. *Am. Nat.*, 109: 501–578.

Jones, E.W., 1955. Ecological studies in the rain forest of southern Nigeria. IV. The plateau forest of the Okomu forest reserve. Part 1. The environment, the vegetation types of the forest and the horizontal distribution of species. *J. Ecol.*, 43: 564–594.

Jones, E.W., 1956. Ecological studies in the rain forest of southern Nigeria. IV. The plateau forest of the Okomu forest reserve. Part 2. The reproduction and history of the forest. *J. Ecol.*, 44: 83–117.

Kahn, F., 1978. *Architecture et dynamique spatiale racinaire chez les plantes ligneuses des zônes forestières tropicales humides*. O.R.S.T.O.M., Adiopodoumé, 38 pp.

Karr, J.R., 1968. Habitat and avian diversity on strip-mined land in east-central Illinois. *Condor*, 70: 348–357.

Karr, J.R., 1975. Production, energy pathways, and community diversity in forest birds. In: F.B. Golley and E. Medina (Editors), *Tropical Ecological Systems: Trends in Terrestrial and Aquatic Research*. Ecological Studies, Il. Springer-Verlag, Heidelberg, pp. 161–176.

Karr, J.R. and Roth, R.R., 1971. Vegetation structure and avian diversity in several New World areas. *Am. Nat.*, 105: 423–435.

Klinge, H. and Rodrigues, W.A., 1974. Phytomass estimation in a central Amazonian rain forest. In: H.E. Young (Editor), *IUFRO Biomass Studies*. University of Maine, Orono, Me., pp. 339–350.

Knight, D.H., 1975. A phytosociological analysis of species-rich tropical forest on Barro Colorado Island, Panama. *Ecol. Monogr.*, 45: 259–284.

Lawton, R.M., 1978. A study of the dynamic ecology of Zambian vegetation. *J. Ecol.*, 66: 175–198.

Lescure, J.P., 1978. An architectural study of the vegetation's regeneration in French Guiana. *Vegetatio*, 37: 53–60.

Lind, E.M. and Morrison, M.E.S., 1974. *East African Vegetation*. Longman, London, 258 pp.

Lloyd, M. and Ghelardi, R.J., 1964. A table for calculating the 'equitability' component of species diversity. *J. Anim. Ecol.*, 33: 217–225.

Longman, K.A. and Jeník, J., 1974. *Tropical Forest and Its Environment*. Longman, London, 205 pp.

MacArthur, R.H., 1964. Environmental factors affecting bird species diversity. *Am. Nat.*, 98: 287–397.

MacArthur, R.H., 1965. Patterns of species diversity. *Biol. Rev.*, 40: 410–533.

MacArthur, R.H., 1972. *Geographical Ecology: Patterns in the Distribution of Species*. Harper and Row, New York, N.Y., 269 pp.

MacArthur, R.H. and MacArthur, J.W., 1961. On bird species diversity. *Ecology*, 42: 594–598.

McNaughton, S.J., 1968. Structure and function in California grasslands. *Ecology*, 49: 962–972.

Menge, B.A. and Sutherland, J.P., 1976. Species diversity gradients: synthesis of the role of predation, competition, and temporal heterogeneity. *Am. Nat.*, 110: 315–359.

Naveh, Z. and Dan, J., 1973. The human degradation of Mediterranean landscapes in Israel. In: F. di Castri and H.A. Mooney (Editors), *Mediterranean Type Ecosystems: Origin and Structure*. Ecological Studies, 7. Springer-Verlag, Heidelberg, pp. 373–390.

Newmann, I.V., 1954. Locating strata in tropical rain forest. *J. Ecol.*, 42: 218–219.

Nicholson, D.I., 1965. A study of virgin forest near Sandakan North Borneo. In: *Symposium on Ecological Research in Humid Tropics Vegetation*. UNESCO, Paris, pp. 67–87.

Odum, H.T. and Pigeon, R.F. (Editors), 1970. *A Tropical Rain Forest: A Study of Irradiation and Ecology at El Verde, Puerto Rico*. U.S. Atomic Energy Commission, Washington, D.C., 1678 pp.

Odum, H.T., Copeland, B.J. and Zimmerman, R.Z., 1963. Direct and optical assay of leaf mass of the lower montane rain forest of Puerto Rico. *Proc. Natl. Acad. Sci.*, 49: 429–439.

Ogawa, H., Yoda, K., Ogino, K. and Kira, T., 1965. Comparative ecological studies on three main types of forest vegetation in Thailand. II. Biomass. *Nature Life S.E. Asia*, 4: 49–80.

Oldeman, R.A.A., 1974a. L'architecture de la forêt guyanaise. *Mém. O.R.S.T.O.M*, 73: 204 pp.

Oldeman, R.A.A., 1974b. Ecotopes des arbres et gradients écologiques en forêt guyanaise. *Terre Vie*, 28: 387–520.

Oldeman, R.A.A., 1978. Architecture and energy exchange of dicotyledonous trees in the forest. In: P.B. Tomlinson and M.H. Zimmermann (Editors), *Tropical Trees as Living Systems*. Cambridge University Press, Cambridge, pp. 535–560.

Ovington, J.D. and Olson, J.S., 1970. Biomass and chemical content of El Verde lower montane rain forest plants. In: H.T. Odum and R.F. Pigeon (Editors), *A Tropical Rain Forest: A Study of Irradiation and Ecology at El Verde, Puerto Rico*. U.S. Atomic Energy Commission, Washington, D.C., pp. 453–457.

Paijmans, K., 1970. An analysis of four tropical rain forest sites in New Guinea. *J. Ecol.*, 57: 77–101.

Paine, R.T., 1966. Food web complexity and species diversity. *Am. Nat.*, 100: 65–76.

Peet, R.K., 1974. The measurement of species diversity. *Annu. Rev. Ecol. Syst.*, 5: 285–307.

Pielou, E.C., 1975. *Ecological Diversity*. Wiley–Interscience, New York, N.Y., 165 pp.

Pierlot, R., 1966. Structure et composition des forêts denses d'Afrique centrale, spécialement celles du Kivu. *Acad. R. Sci. Outremer, N.S.*, 16: 363 pp.

Pierlot, R., 1968. Une technique d'étude de la forêt dense en vue de son aménagement: la distribution hyperbolique des grosseurs. *Bull. Soc. R. For. Belg.* 75: 122–130.

Pires, J.,M., Dobzhansky, Th., and Black, G.A., 1953. An estimate of the number of species of trees in an Amazonian forest community. *Bot. Gaz.*, 113: 467–477.

Poissonet, P., 1971. Relation entre le nombre d'espèces par échantillon et la taille de l'échantillon dans une phytocénose. *Oceol. Plant.*, 6: 289–296.

Poore, M.E.D., 1964. Integration in the plant community. *J. Ecol.*, 52 (Suppl.): 213–226.

Poore, M.E.D., 1968. Studies in Malaysian rain forest. I. The forest on Triassic sediments in Jenjka forest reserve. *J. Ecol.*, 56: 143–196.

Richards, P.W., 1952. *The Tropical Rain Forest: An Ecological Study*. Cambridge University Press, Cambridge, 450 pp.

Richards, P.W., 1964. The upland forests of Cameroon mountains. *J. Ecol.*, 51: 529–554.

Ricklefs, R.E., 1977. Environmental heterogeneity and plant species diversity: a hypothesis. *Am. Nat.*, 111: 376–381.

Rollet, B., 1969a. La regéneration naturelle en forêt dense humide sempervirente de plaine de la Guyane vénézuelienne. *Bois. For. Trop.*, 124: 19–38.

Rollet, B., 1969b. *Etudes quantitatives d'une forêt dense humide sempervirente de plaine de la guyane vénézuelienne*. Thesis, University of Toulouse, Toulouse, 473 pp.

Rollet, B., 1974. *L'architecture des forêts denses humides sempervirentes de plaines*. Centre Technique Forestier Tropical, Nogent-sur-Marne, 298 pp.

Rollet, B., 1978. Organization. In: *Natural Resources Research, Tropical Forest Ecosystems*. UNESCO, Paris, pp. 112–142.

Rollet, B. and Caussinius, H., 1969. Sur l'utilisation d'un modèle mathématique pour l'étude des structures des forêts denses humides sempervirentes de plaine. *C.R. Acad. Sci. Paris*, 268: 1853–1855.

Sawyer, J.O. and Lindsey, A.A., 1971. Vegetation of the life zones in Costa Rica. *Ind. Acad. Sci. Monogr.*, 2: 214 pp.

Schulz, J.P., 1960. *Ecological Studies on Rain Forest in Northern Suriname*. Van Eedenfonds, Amsterdam, 267 pp.

Smith, A.P., 1973. Stratification of temperate and tropical forests. *Am. Nat.*, 107: 671–683.

Soriano-Ressy, M., Desmarais, A.P. and Perez, J.W., 1970. A comparison of environments of rain forests in Dominica, British West Indies, and Puerto Rico. In: H.T. Odum and R.F. Pigeon (Editors), *A Tropical Rain Forest: A Study of Irradiation and Ecology at El Verde, Puerto Rico*. U.S. Atomic Energy Commission, Washington, D.C., pp. 326–349.

Terborgh, J., 1973. On the notion of favorableness in plant ecology. *Am. Nat.*, 107: 481–501.

Tracey, J.G., 1969. Edaphic differentiation of some forest types in eastern Australia. I. Soil physical factors. *J. Ecol.*, 57: 805–816.

Van der Maarel, E., 1976. On the establishment of boundaries of plant communities. *Ber. Dtsch. Bot. Ges.*, 89: 415–443.

Veillon, J.P., 1965. Variación altitudinal de la masa forestal de los bosques primarios en la vertiente nor occidental de la cordillera de los Andes, Venezuela. *Turralbia*, 15: 216–224.

Watt, A.S., 1947. Pattern and process in the plant community. *J. Ecol.*, 35: 1–22.

Webb, L.J., 1959. A physiognomic classification of Australian rain forest. *J. Ecol.*, 47: 551–570.

Webb, L.J. and Tracey, J.G., 1965. Current quantitative floristics studies in Queensland tropical rain forest. In: *Symposium on Ecological Research in Humid Tropics Vegetation*. UNESCO, Paris, pp. 257–261.

Webb, L.J., Tracey, J.G., Williams, W.T. and Lance, G.N., 1967a. Studies in the numerical analysis of complex rain forest communities. I. A comparison of methods applicable to site species data. *J. Ecol.*, 55: 171–191.

Webb, L.J., Tracey, J.G., Williams, W.T. and Lance, G.N., 1967b. Studies in the numerical analysis of complex rain forest communities. II. The problems of species sampling. *J. Ecol.*, 55: 525–538.

Webb, L.J., Tracey, J.G., Williams, W.T. and Lance, G.N., 1970. Studies in the numerical analysis of complex rain forest communities. V. A comparison of the properties of floristic and physiognomic structural data. *J. Ecol.*, 58: 203–232.

Webb, L.J., Tracey, J.G. and Williams, W.T., 1972. Regeneration and pattern in the subtropical rain forest. *J. Ecol.*, 60: 675–695.

White, H.H., Jr., 1963. Variation of stand structure correlated with altitude in the Luquillo mountains. *Caribb. For.*, 24: 46–52.

Whiteside, M.C. and Harmsworth, R.V., 1967. Species diversity in Chydorid (Claclocera) communities. *Ecology*, 48: 664–667.

Whitmore, T.C., 1975. *Tropical Rain Forests of the Far East*. Clarendon Press, Oxford, 282 pp.

Whitmore, T.C., 1978. Gaps in the forest canopy. In: P.B. Tomlinson and M.H. Zimmermann (Editors), *Tropical Trees As Living Systems*. Cambridge University Press, Cambridge, pp. 639–655.

Whittaker, R.H., 1962. Classification of natural communities. *Bot. Rev.*, 28: 1–239.

Whittaker, R.H., 1965. Dominance and diversity in land plant communities. *Science*, 147: 250–260.

Whittaker, R.H., 1972. Evolution and measurement of species diversity. *Taxon.*, 21: 213–251.

Whittaker, R.H., 1975. *Communities and Ecosystems*. Macmillan, New York, N.Y., 2nd ed., 385 pp.

Whittaker, R.H., 1977. Evolution of species diversity in land communities. *Evol. Biol.*, 10: 1–67.

Whittaker, R.H., 1978a. Direct gradient analysis. In: R.H. Whittaker (Editor), *Ordination of Plant Communities*. Junk, The Hague.

Whittaker, R.H., 1978b. Approaches to classifying vegetation. In: R.H. Whittaker (Editor), *Classification of Plant Communities*. Junk, The Hague, pp. 1–31.

Whittaker, R.H. and Goodman, D., 1979. Classifying species according to their demographic strategy. I. Population fluctuations and environmental heterogeneity. *Am. Nat.*, 113: 185–200.

Whittaker, R.H. and Levin, S.A., 1977. The role of mosaic phenomena in natural communities. *Theor. Popul. Biol.*, 12: 117–139.

Whittaker, R.H. and Niering, W.A., 1965. Vegetation of the Santa Catalina mountains, Arizona. II. A gradient analysis of the South slope. *Ecology*, 42: 429–452.

Wiens, J.A., 1977. On competition and variable environments. *Am. Sci.*, 65: 592–597.

Williams, L.G., 1964. Possible relationships between plankton–diatom species numbers and water quality estimates. *Ecology*, 45: 809–823.

Williams, W.T., Lance, G.N., Webb, L.J., Tracey, J.G. and Connell, J.H., 1969a. Studies in the numerical analysis of complex rain forest communities. IV. A method for the elucidation of small-scale forest pattern. *J. Ecol.*, 57: 635–654.

Williams, W.T., Lance, G.N., Webb, L.J., Tracey, J.G. and Dale, M.B., 1969b. Studies in the numerical analysis of complex rain forest communities. III. The analysis of successional data. *J. Ecol.*, 57: 515–535.

Willson, M.F., 1973. Tropical plant production and animal species diversity. *Trop. Ecol.*, 14: 62–65.

Wyatt-Smith, J., 1960. Stems per acre and topography. *Malay. For.*, 23: 57–58.

Chapter 4

VEGETATION STRUCTURE AND GROWTH

EBERHARD F. BRUNIG

ELEMENTS OF STRUCTURE

Any forest stand can be regarded as a porous, heterogenous semi-transparent and semi-permeable layer through which a variety of exchanges of energy and matter operate between the atmosphere and the ground. Consequently, the geometric or architectural stand structure has an important effect on the intensity and pattern of physical and chemical exchanges between stand, soil and atmosphere (Baumgartner, 1969), and determine the resources available to the various trophic sectors of the ecosystem (Brunig, 1970a). As we have seen, the architectural structure of single trees and of natural forest stands also reflect the effects of climatic and edaphic site conditions in terms which may be interpreted as physio-ecological adaptations to growth-affecting site influences. Variation of structural elements within and between stands of forests is due to differences in floristic (kind, number and proportion of species), geometric (architectural features, physiognomy) and biochemical structure. These differences are associated with differences of site conditions, dynamics of regeneration, growth and succession and of biotic impacts (Brunig, 1971; Brunig et al., 1979).

Within-stand diversity of structure is greatest when growth factors of the sites are available in balanced and moderate amounts or under conditions near optimum. Within-stand diversity is smallest but between-stand diversity greatest if sites are less favorable due to deficiencies or excesses of growth factors. The effects of even small differences of edaphic and climatic factors between sites are evidenced by relatively large differences in floristic and geometric structure. The subject has recently been reviewed by Ashton and Brunig (1975) and

Whitmore (1975, 1977) mainly on evidence from Southeast Asia.

Features of tree architecture relevant to the theme are leaf anatomy, shape, color and orientation (Gates, 1965, 1968; Gates and Johnson, 1979; Karschon and Pinchas, 1969), crown architecture (Brunig, 1970a, 1974, 1976a; Horn, 1971; Hallé et al., 1978) and the ratios of tree height/stem diameter and size of live crown to tree height and stem diameter (Brunig, 1970a, 1976a; McMahon, 1975). Features of stand stature and architecture which are similarly assumed to be relevant in this respect are kind of species, species richness, species diversity, leaf area projection, crown area projection, stand basal area and phytomass, aerodynamic roughness of the canopy, and reflectivity of the canopy.

For purposes of analysis and comparison, several of these features may be quantitatively expressed in direct simple terms of dimension and dimension ratios, or in dimensionless parameters such as the various kinds of species diversity indices or the estimator of the aerodynamic canopy surface roughness.

The diameter (d) and cross-sectional or basal area (g) of a tree stem at breast height are easy to measure and basal area is a convenient indicator of a tree's share in the phytomass of the stand and, less reliably, of its contribution to stand productivity. The specific relationship between basal area and volume or phytomass of trees is ideally straight-linear (see Ovington, 1962, 1965; Ovington et al., 1967). Deviation from the straight-line is due to additional differences in tree shape, mainly involving its height (h) and crown size (diameter and length of crown). Preliminary results from phytomass studies in the San Carlos Amazon Rainforest

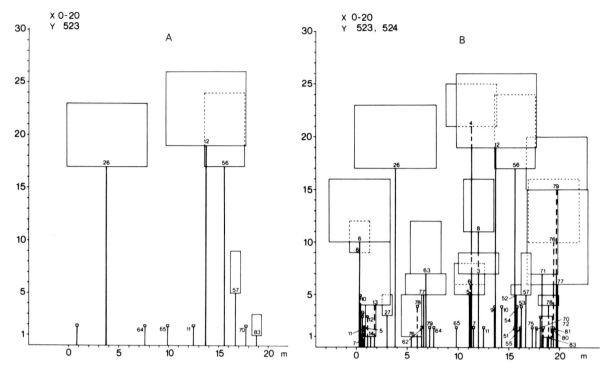

Fig. 4.1. The effect of viewing the forest in successively added 1 m wide transects in the Amazon lowland forest at San Carlos de Rio Negro, Venezuela. A. Transect at X 0–20 m and Y 523 in forest association N, cunuri–yaguacana–tamacuari forest with simple structure, the 1 m strip shows marked stratification into distinct canopy layers, Y 523 gaps are few, regeneration is slow and in small gaps usually from intermediate size classes. B. As before in A, but a further 1 m wide strip (Y 524) is added with the result that the stratification disappears. C. Transect at X 120–140 and Y 526 in the more species-rich forest association K, cunuri–yevaro–piapoco transition to

Ecosystem MAB Project indicate that phytomass regressions most closely fit the data if tree height and a crown volume estimator (crown width × crown length) are included as independent variables. Common regressions for all sites and species are then feasible, provided broad differences in specific phytomass density are considered (Brunig, et al., 1979). The species name, the parameters d, h and crown size and the coordinates of the tree positions are sufficient data to describe stand architecture adequately for most ecological purposes (Brunig and Synnott, 1977).

Radiation, temperature and precipitation are chief determinants of forest ecosystem structure and physiognomy. Within one bioclimatically uniform life zone, physical and chemical soil properties are the chief modifiers of the structure of mature natural forest. Within edaphically homogenous units, additional variation of stocking levels, regeneration and growth and therefore structure is introduced by the effects of extreme climatic events

and of phasic development. The additional variation due to extreme, mostly unfavorable, and sometimes destructive climatic events, such as drought, persistent flooding or periods of frequent lightning strikes may be substantial.

This discussion of forest structure which builds on ideas introduced in Chapters 2 and 3 will be based on a variety of data, but especially data from forest stands in Southeast Asia (Sarawak and Borneo) and the Amazon (San Carlos de Río Negro, Venezuela).

VERTICAL STRUCTURE

The vertical profile of mature humid tropical forest is characterized by the predominance of phanerophytes and the relative rarity or absence of other life forms. In mature humid tropical forest, the typical emergent tree on mesic sites has a hemispherical crown with sympodial branching

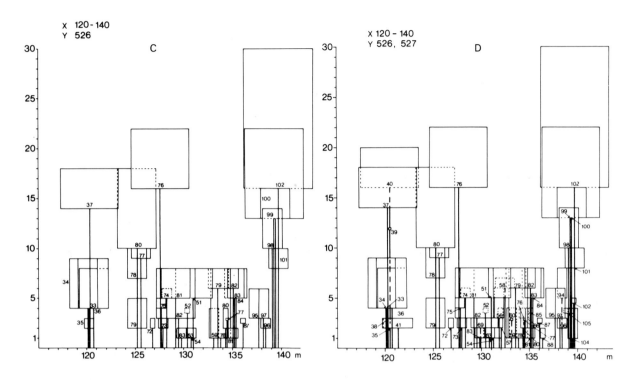

I, yevaro–hiua–cunuri forest with complex structure characterized by numerous moderately large gaps with vigorous regeneration from seedlings, the profile shows distinct layering in relation to the regeneration cycle. D. The addition of a second 1 m wide strip (Y 527) does not obscure the layering at this scale of gap regeneration. Layering will be obscured if more strips are added, but drawing becomes impossible unless the smallest size classes are excluded (compare Fig. 4.10), or only the bigger trees are successively added (e.g. Brunig, 1966, 1968 and 1974).

and notophyll, sclerophyll, coriaceous often pachyphyll leaves which are usually bunched and upright or pendulous. Crowns in the intermediate layers (under-canopy) are narrower, leaves predominantly mesophyll and more mesophytic, and branching and leaf pattern more diffuse. The leaves are arranged as in many other forest formations, in a manner which exhibits a more or less well-defined stratification in respect to leaf mass, leaf area index, leaf size, leaf shape and anatomy and species composition (Ashton, 1964a, 1973; Brunig, 1971, 1974; Klinge, 1973, 1979). Differences between leaves of canopy layers may mainly concern anatomical features, as in Andean cloud forest in Venezuela (Roth and Merida de Bifano, 1971), or be macroscopically noticeable as marked differences in shapes and sizes.

The number of possible strata increases with stand height and species richness. Their distinctiveness increases with decreasing species richness. Therefore, stratification is usually more easily rec-

ognized on less favorable sites, in certain stages of phasic development (usually very early and very late phases) and on smaller unit areas. The latter involves the danger that layering evident in stand profiles is in fact an artifact caused by narrowly slicing the complex population into narrow transects (Fig. 4.1).

The tendency to layer formation may be also enhanced by poor seed dispersal capacity of the tree species which would favor clumping of species and persistence of occupation of a microsite by a species which may be, or in the course of evolution become, specially adapted to the particular conditions of such a microsite. It has also been suggested that these layers provide effective walk and flight paths for predators, pollinators and dispersers (Smith, 1973) which would work towards stabilizing layering tendencies.

Trees in the top canopy have lower h/d ratios, indicating that they are less slender and more plump than trees in the lower stories. The ratio of

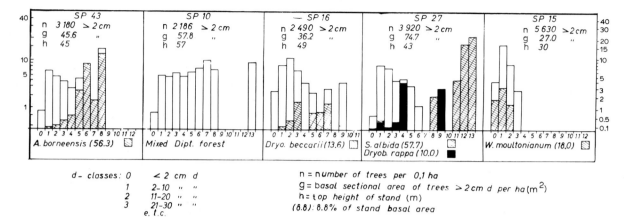

Fig. 4.2. Distribution pattern of basal area densities in 10 cm diameter classes in selected stands in Sarawak and Brunei representing the range of variation in dry-land forests. Sample plot 43: *Agathis* (?) *dammara* kerangas forest on giant podzol, Similajau Forest Reserve. SP 10: Oxisol, Sempadi Forest Reserve. SP 16: *Dryobalanops beccarii–Shorea flava* kerangas forest on medium Spodosol on moderate scarp-slope, Bako N.P. SP 27: *Shorea albida–Dryobalanops rappa* kerapah forest on shallow, wet peat over sandy Spodosol, Badas. SP 15: *Whiteodendron moultonianum–Dacrydium beccarii–Cotylelobium burckii* kerangas on shallow Spodosol on gentle dip-slope, Bako N.P.B. The units on the vertical scale are m^2 ha^{-1}.

crown sectional area to stem basal area declines with tree size. As a result top canopy trees are several times more wind-firm than trees in the under-canopy (Brunig, 1974; Brunig and Heuveldop, 1976).

Tendency to layer formation and the shape of the stand curves (number of trees versus stem diameter or tree height) are interdependent, the shape of the curves being determined by the rates of recruitment, growth and mortality. In stands with a balanced vertical structure, the logarithm of number of trees plotted over diameter class may form a straight line (Poore, 1967). Stand curves for physiognomically different forest types, whole forest associations, formations at various levels of classification, and lastly of regions, differ in the inclination by which the lines slope towards the larger size classes (Rollet, 1974, figs. 27–31). Deviation from the straight line occurs if layering and aggregation are caused by successional processes or site effects, as described by Brunig (1968, 1974) from kerangas forests, by Anderson (1961a) from peat-swamp forests in Sarawak and Brunei, and by Ashton (1964a) from dipterocarp forests in Brunei.

The vertical structure of stands can be represented by illustration, either depicting the stand naturalistically along real transects of varying width (Brunig, 1968, 1976b; Lamprecht, 1969; Rollet, 1974), or as idealized standardized profile

(Holdridge, 1970; Murphy and Uhl, 1979), by pictorial symbols (Dansereau, 1951; Addor et al., 1970) or by numerical parameters (Klinge, 1973, 1979; Brunig, 1976b; Brunig et al., 1979), the choice of method depending on the purpose.

Rollet (1974), ch. 5 in UNESCO, 1978) in a review of profile preparation reproduced a large proportion of the then available naturalistic profiles of various authors from Africa, America and Asia and added the results of his own survey of seasonal tropical humid evergreen forest in Imataca, Venezuela. While these profiles are very instructive, it seems questionable that further standardization beyond certain conventions of measures, area sizes and tree sizes and normalization of tree shapes for convenience would serve much purpose. Profiles cannot replace statistical parameters to characterize and compare forest structure. The main use of profiles is, and most likely will remain, the illustrative characterization of actual stand structure, particularly its range of variation due to gap, building and mature phases, chance pattern of aggregation and dispersion, and microsite differences.

Vertical structure may also be represented by the proportion of the basal area in each layer of the canopy. For example, Klinge (1973) reports basal area of 30.7 m^2 ha^{-1} from a central Amazonian rain forest area near Manaus. The emergent trees of the A layer contribute 7.1 m² ha⁻¹, main canopy trees (B layer) 14.6 m² ha⁻¹, the C layer 7 m² ha⁻¹ and the ground layers D and E each only 1 m² ha⁻¹. These basal area proportions vary between forests on different sites or in different phases of development. Maxima may occur in the A layer, as in single dominant forests such as the *Shorea albida* forests on peat and *Agathis dammara* forests on Spodosols in Borneo (Brunig, 1968, 1974 and 1976b).

Mixed dipterocarp forest of Southeast Asia has a fairly even distribution of basal area. However, aggregation of emergent species, such as *Dryobalanops* spp., may cause a relative increase of

density in the largest diameters similar to the *Shorea albida* and *Agathis* forests, and a higher total density per hectare. The rapid decline of basal area density as in sample plot *15* (Fig. 4.2) is also characteristic of the *cunuri* forest association in the MAB Amazon Ecosystem Project area at San Carlos, but for a higher total basal area stocking level. The bi-modal stand curve of basal area density illustrated by sample plot *27* in Bornean *Shorea albida kerangas* forest is at San Carlos represented by the complex *yevaro* forest associations. The yevaro forest is not only very similar to the *Agathis/Shorea albida* and *Dryobalanops beccarii* forest types in Bornean kerangas forests in structure, but also in its ecology. The bi-modal stand curve in the complex, species-richer *yevaro–hiua* forest association is shown in Fig. 4.3 (stratum I in the 50 × 50 m block *31*). It contrasts strongly to the steeply declining stand curve in the simple *cunuri–piapoco* forest association (stratum N in block *25*).

HORIZONTAL STRUCTURE

The patterns of vertical and horizontal stand architecture and their variations are interdependent and affected by the same factors and processes. The hypothetical ideal rain forest with random distribution of species and individuals of all sizes is modified by the often interacting effects of seasonal or irregular climatic events, geomorphological processes, biotic agents and competition including allelopathic interactions between species and between mature mother trees and their regeneration (Ashton and Brunig, 1975; Whitmore, 1977).

Reports on variation within and between stands are almost exclusively related to floristic variation or at best to such simple indicators of differences in stand structure as number of trees, tree heights and diameters, and rarely to basal area, volumes and phytomass. The data are usually obtained in small (0.1–0.5 ha), subjectively selected plots or transects. Rarely is the distribution pattern of number of trees, trees of certain species and basal areas recorded and comparisons are usually made on a plot basis without regard to patterns and variances. The reasons are that the data collecting and analysis of pattern and variances are time-consuming and difficult to interpret in terms of ecological and

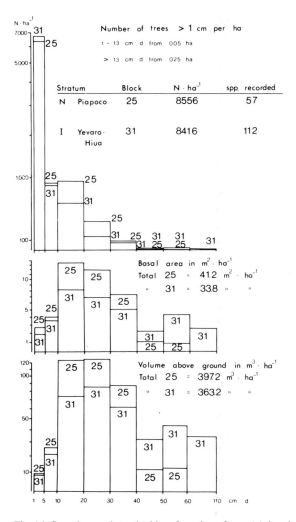

Fig. 4.3. Superimposed stand tables of number of trees (*n*), basal area (*g*) and stand volume (*v*) per hectare in simple structured cunuri–piapoco association on medium deep humus podzol (block *25*) and in the complex-structured yevaro–hiua association (block *31*).

silvicultural significance. A brief review of the situation is given in chapter 5 of UNESCO (1978). The proposed standard method for MAB ecosystems studies (Brunig and Synott, 1977) includes the survey and analysis of spatial patterns which may shed further light on this yet dimly understood feature of tropical forest stands.

Variation in volume and phytomass at a small scale of space in mature forest stands is often the result of regeneration patterns and population dynamics of the species present. The variation of structural features at this scale has been studied on edaphically heterogenous sites in a 20-ha kerangas and dipterocarp forest area in Sabal Forest Reserve, and along several site gradients in Brunei and Sarawak, and in a 10-ha area with corresponding forests on oligotrophic soils in the MAB Amazon Ecosystem Project near San Carlos de Rio Negro, Venezuela. The results and comparisons showed that in both regions there exists a similar pattern of wide variation of such structural parameters as number of trees, stand tables, basal areas and phyto-volume per unit area which was only very loosely related to microrelief and soil differences (Brunig, 1973a, Brunig et al., 1979). Minor differences between the regions may be related to the differences in evolutionary history. These data will be examined in detail since they were obtained with the same methods and are comparable, and also represent forests on two different continents.

The range of basal area variation between quadrats of 20×20 m in Sabal Forest Reserve lies in the order of 1 to 7, with a normal distribution about the mean [$g = 32.5$ m^2 ha^{-1} $\pm 26.3\%$ (st. dev.), trees > 10 cm diameter]. Analysis of variance showed that in spite of the normal distribution two significantly different populations were involved which could be defined as kerangas ($g = 32.8$ m^2 ha^{-1} $\pm 25\%$) on Spodosols and mixed dipterocarp forest ($g = 29.5$ m^2 ha^{-1} $\pm 39.4\%$) on Oxisols. Further subdivision of vegetation within these forest types did not produce meaningful results probably because variation at this small scale is overridingly random and possibly controlled by regeneration patterns.

At a medium scale, basal area densities and phyto-volume vary widely between stands which occupy different positions along catenas or ecological gradients. Determination of differences, however, is not an easy matter because the great within-stand variation at small scale poses a serious problem to sampling (see Brunig and Synott, 1977). At this scale most tree species or species groups are closely associated with specific types of geologic substrate, soil and site, and these together in turn determine stand stature and growing-stock densities. Therefore, variation of stand architecture at this scale will generally be closely related to variation of site conditions.

In the MAB Amazon Ecosystems Project near San Carlos tree frequencies, basal area densities and their stand tables vary between the association groups which were distinguished within the kerangas-type forest by the nearest neighbor monothetic divisive classification program FANTASMB (Brunig, 1976b; Brunig et al., 1979). There are also differences between these and the *tierra firme* forest which has been studied by Murphy and Uhl (1979). Table 4.1 gives a sample of basal area data from extensive area surveys in the Venezuelan Amazon and northern Borneo on Oxisols (climatic climax mixed dipterocarp and tierra firme forest) and on a variety of oligotrophic soils. The mean basal area for trees above 10 cm diameter on three tierra firme sites on Oxisols is 27.8 m^2 ha^{-1}, which is only little more than half the value of the well-stocked mixed dipterocarp forest in Sarawak (50 m^2 > 10 cm diameter) and a little less than the values reported by Klinge (1977: 30.7 m^2) and Takeuchi (1961/1962: 33.2 m^2), from tierra firme forest near Manaus, Brazil. The value is also low in comparison to the kerangas-type forest in the area (Table 4.1), but larger than the basal area density measured by Veillon (cit. in Brunig et al., 1979, table 5) in Zona alta forest on nearby Oxisols. Correspondingly low is the biomass which Jordan and Uhl (1978) measured as 391 t ha^{-1}.

The data from Sarawak were selected from Brunig (1966, table 16) to illustrate the range of basal area density over 2.5 cm diameter between mixed dipterocarp forest (sample plot *10*), single-dominant peat-swamp forest (sample plot *27*), single dominant forest on xeric, medium deep sandy kerangas Spodosols (sample plot *28*), on alternately waterlogged and dry peaty *kerapah* (sample plot *29*), on a "giant podzol" (sample plot *47*) and finally on a shallow Spodosol (sample plot *15*). The *yevaro* associations (H–K) correspond structurally to the *Agathis* forest with the exception that densities above 40 cm diameter are lower and densities in the lower size classes are

TABLE 4.1

Mean stocking densities of number of trees (n) and basal area (g) per hectare in humid tropical forests

Location and forest type or association	Diameter class (cm)						Basal area (m²)	Source
	1–9	10–19	20–29	30–39	>40	total		
Sarawak and Brunei								
SP 10, mixed dipterocarp	1878[1]	279	109	64	82	2412	54.8	
SP 27, *Shorea albida* PSF	3825[1]	385	59	69	74	4412	74.5	
SP 28, *Shorea albida* kerangas	2555[1]	277	79	44	64	3019	29.9	
SP 29, *Shorea albida* kerapah	7116[1]	247	49	0	49	7461	16.9	
SP 47, *Agathis* kerangas	5520[1]	613	124	79	99	6435	54.8	
SP 5, mixed kerangas	2231[1]	383	94	35	22	2755	25.7	
SP 4, *Gymnostoma* kerapah	1745[1]	494	208	133	5	2585	36.0	Brunig (1966, 1970a)
SP 15, *Dacrydium* kerapah	4705[1]	860	64	5	0	5634	27.0	
1–57 kerangas forest	–	–	–	–	–	–	36.5 (±1.601)	
San Carlos								
Tierra firme	not. m.	504	226	→	31	729	27.8	Murphy and Uhl (1979)
H. yevaro–hiua yevaro–cunuri	10 678	665	181	64	46	11 634	38.3	
I. yevaro–hiua	7267	1887	151	56	44	8361	37.5	
J. yevaro–macure	13 996	3006	206	51	9	16 385	38.4	
K. yevaro	10 870	783	230	75	33	12 011	41.9	
L. yucito–piapoco	9045	1880	192	26	2	11 128	34.7	Brunig et al. (1979)
M. yucito	6594	1215	234	65	11	8119	36.3	
N. piapoco	8375	770	256	66	20	9485	39.7	
O. mixed	646[2]	520	197	86	28	10 000	33.5	
P. bana alta	1508[2]	931	170	20	6	10 000	30.8	
Q. bana baja	17 704	482	19	0	0	18 205	19.7	
H–Q. caatinga	–	–	–	–	–	–	35.6	
British Guiana								
Morabukea	not rec.	141	168	→	60	309	–	Davis and Richards (1933)
Nigeria								
Mixed forest	not rec.	294	229	→	46	523	–	
Pantropical	not rec.	not. rec	101	42	54	(198)	32.2	Dawkins (1958, 1959)[3]

[1]2.6–10 cm only; [2]5–10 cm only; [3]girth limits in feet, only approximate diameter limits in cm (see Rollet, 1974, tab. 93).
In the San Carlos forest, yevaro, hiua, cunari, macure, yucito, piapoco are vernacular names of trees used temporarily until the reference collections have been determined by the herbarium at the Caracas Botanic Garden. Bana means open, low woodland and scrub on infertile soil.

higher in the Amazon. This appears to be a general feature (see Rollet, 1974, fig. 30) and also applies to the comparison between mixed dipterocarp and tierra firme forests (Table 4.1). All the compared associations occur on soils which for plant growth are very similar.

The mixed kerangas (sample plot *5*) and the *Gymnostoma* kerapah (sample plot *4*) agree reasonably well with the various *yucito–piapoco* associations (L–Q), especially to L and N which includes the *cunuri* consociation. Again, the site conditions and soil types correspond very closely between

Borneo and the Amazon. The *Dacrydium* forest (sample plot 15) is intermediate between high and low *bana* (P and Q). These associations again agree well in site and soil conditions.

This brief and tentative comparison shows that forest types on similar sites in Borneo and in Amazonia have similar basal area densities (Table 4.1). It also shows the great range of variation between forest association and site type units. This agrees with the results of Rollet's most intensive study of tropical forest structure (Rollet, 1974, esp. figs. 19–31).

The pantropical mean basal area density of Dawkins (1958, 1959) (33 m^2) is rather lower than the figure for mixed dipterocarp forest (which with 54.8 m^2 is fairly representative for mature mixed dipterocarp forest on fertile, deep soils) even if 20% are added to the pantropical mean for the unrecorded diameter classes below 20 cm which are not included. The pantropical mean is fairly close to the San Carlos mean for the kerangas-type forests (35.6 m^2) and to the Bornean mean for kerangas and kerapah (36.5 ± 1.601 m^2).

CANOPY STRUCTURE

In all areas of tropical humid evergreen forest, different mature forest stands often vary markedly in the stature, physiognomy and architectural structure of their trees, in pattern of distribution of individual trees and species, and as a result in canopy architecture and general stand structure. The variation of tree physiognomy and stand structure in a mature forest stand is closely related to site and phasic development.

Variation at medium scale in mature tropical humid evergreen forest is easily recognizable by variation of canopy aspect on aerial photographs on a wide range of scales and films. The corresponding variation of site conditions is also often clearly noticeable, especially in hill country. Examples are shown in Fig. 4.4. The marked differences in canopy texture and tone indicate differences of vegetation structure which are related to major differences of site and substrate (Brunig, 1969b).

The relationship between landform, soil and vegetation structure is well illustrated by the common catena: hydromorphic, relatively rich alluvial soils, red-yellow loam soils on slopes, and xeric

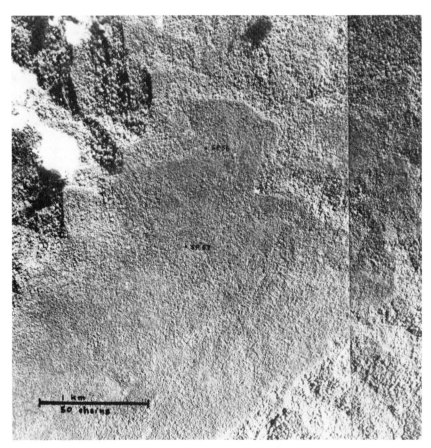

Fig. 4.4. Kerangas and kerapah forest on a sandstone plateau in Sarawak, Borneo. Cuesta catena formation is noticeable in the top-left corner. The forest types are lowland to submontane mixed dipterocarp forest with coarse canopy aspect on scarp-slopes, kerangas on dip-slopes and kerapah with peat bog formation on level parts of the plateau. Merurong Plateau, 700 m altitude.

oligotrophic sandy Spodosols and related soils on flat hilltops, terraces and mounds. An example is shown in Fig. 4.5 from the Melinau–Ingei watershed in Mulu National Park, Sarawak. The more favorable sites (nos. *1, 5–7, 13, 15, 16, 18*) carry species-rich, complex and tall stands with mesophyllous (leaf surface area 50–182 cm^2), big crowns and aerodynamically rough canopy surface. The more unfavorable sites (nos. *2–4, 8–12, 14, 17*) are occupied by relatively species-poor, simple stands with distinct layer formation and distinctly xeromorphic, coriaceous to pachyphyll, and sparser leafage. The leaves are mostly microphyll (leaf surface area from 2.25 to 20.25 cm^2) and leptophyll (leaf surface area less than 0.25 cm^2, needle- or

scale-like), usually steeply inclined, and contain much tannins and pigments (Brunig, 1966, 1970a, b, 1974). The crowns are small, the canopy low and aerodynamically smooth. The sites are often flat or almost flat, the soils extremely poor in minerals, they are physically or physiologically shallow and either poorly or excessively drained (Spodosols in nos. *8, 9, 11, 12, 14*; oligotrophic peats in nos. *2* and *10*; limestone with acid raw humus in no. *17*). Accordingly the diversity (*I.D.*) and the kind and richness of species composition vary, as indicated in the diagram.

A similar trend of decreasing complexity and height of the canopy occurs along the gradient of decreasing humidity poleward from the climatic

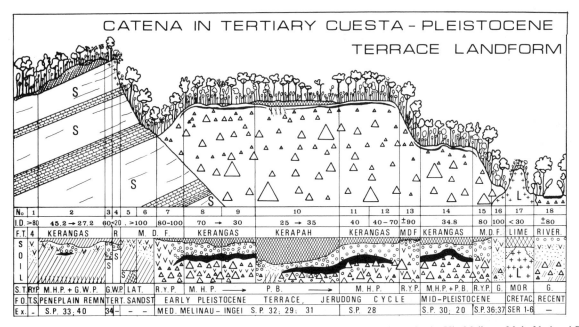

Fig. 4.5. Relationship between substrate, floristics and other features of the mature forest in the Ulu Melinau, Mulu National Park, Sarawak. Schematic, based on sample plot data.

Legend: *I.D.* = McIntosh Index of Diversity. *F.T.* = general forest type: 4 = *M.D.F.*; *R* = vegetation on rock edge; *M.D.F.* = mixed dipterocarp forest; LIME = limestone vegetation; RIVER = alluvial vegetation. *S.T.* = soil type according to the FAO soil survey: *R.Y.P.* = red-yellow podzolic loam; *M.H.P.* = medium-deep sandy humus podzol; *G.W.P.* = grey-white podzolic sandy clay; *LAT* = clayey latosol; *P.B.* = peat bog; *G.* = alluvial clayey gley; *MOR* = dry acid mor on limestone rock. FO = geologic formation, parent material (Tertiary sandstone). *Ex.* = number of sample plot used as example to draw the profile transect.

Typical species in the successively numbered zones are: *1* = various Dipterocarpaceae; *2* = *Casuarina nobilis, Dacrydium elatum, Tristania obovata, Combretocarpus rotundatus, Shorea revoluta, S. coriacea, S. ovata, Cotylelobium malayanum, Dipterocarpus crinitus, Agathis borneensis*; *3* = *Dryobalanops beccarii*; *4* = *Podocarpus* sp.; *5* = *Dryobalanops aromatica* with various Dipterocarpaceae; *6* = *Shorea hypochra*; *7* = *Shorea revoluta, S. ovata, Upuna borneensis, Dipterocarpus lowii*; *8* = *Agathis borneensis, Dipterocarpus borneensis, D. pachyphyllus, Shorea scabrida*; *9* = *Casuarina nobilis, Dacrydium beccarii* var.*, Shorea scabrida*; *10* = *Shorea albida, Gonystylus* spp.*, Combretocarpus rotundus, Cratoxylon glaucum, Palaquium* spp.*, Calophyllum* spp.; 11 and 12 as in 8 and 9; *13* = *Shorea revoluta, S. ovata, S. ochracea, S. parvifolia, Dipterocarpus crinitus, D. pachyphyllus, Dryobalanops beccarii, Eugeissona utilis*; *14* = *Shorea albida, Copaifera palustris, Engelhardtia serrata, Santiria rubiginosa, Hopea pentanervia, Calophyllum* spp.*, various Sapotaceae*; *15* = *Shorea revoluta, Dipterocarpus lowii, Shorea ovata*; *16* = *Alstonia spathulata*; *17* = *Casuarina nobilis (? sumatrana), Vatica* spp.*, specialised limestone flora*; *18* = *Shorea seminis*, various Dipterocarpaceae, *Eusideroxylon melangagai, Octomeles sumatrana*.

equator (Ashton, 1967; Webb, 1959, 1968) and with increasing altitude within the area of humid tropical evergreen forest (Ashton, 1964a; Brunig, 1966, 1974; Martin, 1977; Whitmore, 1977).

The change of tree stature, crown geometry and canopy architecture along a seral sequence of stands on different soil and site types is shown by an example from Sarawak of a typical catena from mesic red-yellow Oxisols to oligotrophic shallow Spodosols (Fig. 4.6). Similar changes of vegetation occur along gradients of peat bog development on inland plateaus and terraces with extremely oligo-

trophic and xeric sites (Fig. 4.7) and along the gradient of phasic communities in the deltaic peat-swamp forests (Anderson, 1961a; Brunig, 1970a) (Fig. 4.8).

Analogous changes occur along similar site gradients in the Amazon Basin in the lowlands and on sandstone plateaus and hills adjacent to the basin. Fig. 4.9 gives an aerial view of part of the forest in the MAB Amazon Ecosystem Project area at San Carlos de Rio Negro covering the gradient yevaro–cunuri–bana. The profiles of the three associations are reproduced in Fig. 4.10 and show

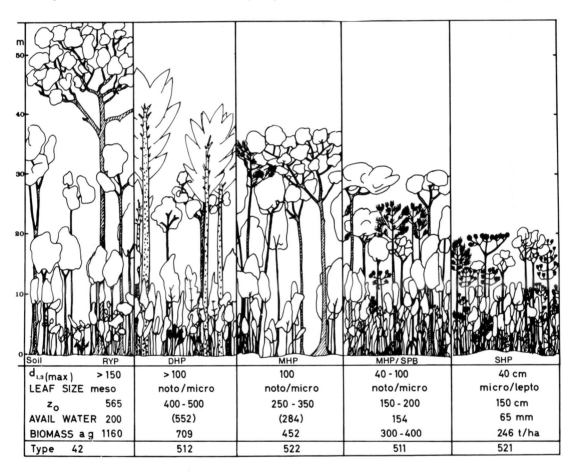

Soil	RYP	DHP	MHP	MHP/SPB	SHP
$d_{1,3}$ (max)	> 150	> 100	100	40 - 100	40 cm
LEAF SIZE	meso	noto/micro	noto/micro	noto/micro	micro/lepto
z_0	565	400 - 500	250 - 350	150 - 200	150 cm
AVAIL WATER	200	(552)	(284)	154	65 mm
BIOMASS a g	1160	709	452	300 - 400	246 t/ha
Type	42	512	522	511	521

Fig. 4.6. Change of stand architecture along a common vegetation and soil catena in Sarawak, Borneo. The tree stature (height and max. diameter, and stand diameter) and stand biomass decrease and the crown architecture (leaf size, crown shape and the estimator z_0 of the aerodynamic roughness of the canopy, acc. to Brunig, 1970a) change from more mesic (left) to more xeric sites (right). Forest types (Brunig, 1969b) are: *42* = mixed dipterocarp forest on Oxisol; *512–521* = various types of kerangas and kerapah with *Agathis dammara* dominant in *512* on a "giant podzol", *522* mixed kerangas on medium deep Spodosol, *511* kerangas with abundant *Shorea albida* and *Gymnostoma nobile* on Spodosol/Tropaquod and *521 Dacrydium–Gymnostoma* forest on shallow Spodosol. The water availability (in brackets) indicates that this amount is not really available to the trees as a result of the lack of roots in much of the soil space, especially in the giant podzol. This catena is frequently found on large Quaternary terraces throughout Sarawak. The leptophyllous trees are *Gymnostoma nobile* and *Dacrydium beccarii*, the trees with "flame-like" crown *Agathis dammara*. Profiles from sample plot data for all trees > 1 cm *d*.

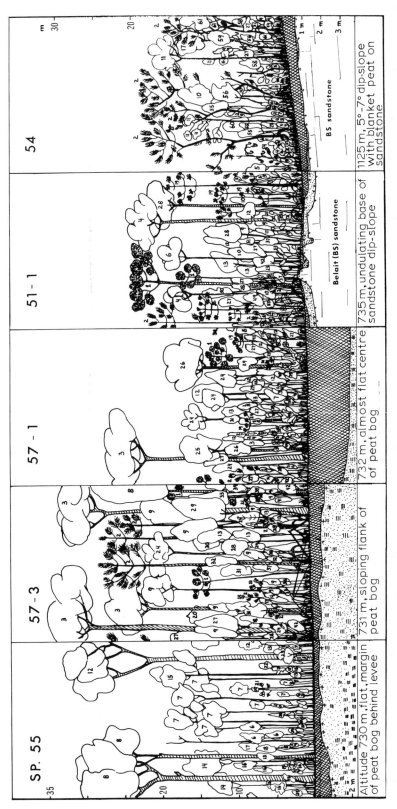

Fig. 4.7. Variation of forest stature and architecture along a gradient of peat bog development on a Tertiary sandstone plateau. Main emergent species are *Shorea albida* and *Combretocarpus rotundatus* in SP 55 to 57–1; *Dacrydium beccarri*, *Gymnostoma nobile* and *Tristania* spp. in SP 51–1 and 54. Merurong Plateau, Sarawak.

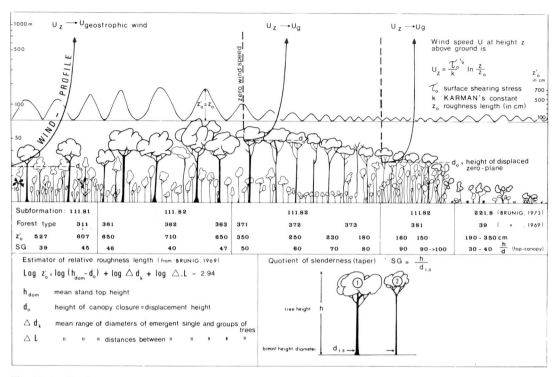

Fig. 4.8. Profile through the whole sequence of phasic community development in the peat-swamp forests of Sarawak. Forest types: *311* = mixed *Gonystylus bancanus* forest; *361–363* = *Shorea albida* association (tree form 1); *371–373* = *Shorea albida* consociation (tree form 2); *381* = *Shorea albida* pole forest (*padang alan bunda*), *39* = open padang (similar to bana, but on deep peat). The wavy line above the canopy symbolizes the size of aerodynamic roughness z_0 of the canopy below.

the same kind of change of canopy structure which occurs under similar conditions in Borneo. In all cases tree form changes along with the other features of stand architecture and is in a consistent manner correlated to site changes, both in the examples from the Amazon Basin and Borneo.

Tree shape varies both with canopy structure and with age and social position of the tree. It can be an important indicator of the vigor, social status and ecological and mechanical resistance of a tree. Parameters which are suitable criteria in this respect are the tree height/breast-height diameter (h/d) ratio, the crown diameter/breast-height diameter ratio and the crown sectional area/basal area (a_k/g) ratio. The regression line of h over d is generally curvilinear, the value of the ratio generally decreasing in the larger trees and the line becoming almost level in the diameter range of the A-level trees, but the scatter of the usually few individuals in the A-layer is usually wide.

Rollet (1974) reproduces scatter diagrams of tree frequencies in 2-m height and 5-cm diameter classes of 15 443 trees from twenty transects of 0.25 ha (5×500 m) each, from Africa (6), America (3) and Asia (11) (Rollet, 1974, tables 26–29). The data scatter from Brazil and Venezuelan Guyana (3 transects) is remarkably narrow and heights are lower than in Africa (Gabon 4 and Ivory Coast 2) and Asia (Malaya 2, Borneo 4, Sumatra 2, Mindanao 2). The Asian scatter diagram shows taller trees in all size classes and the absolutely tallest trees. The difference is in the range of 10% over Africa and 20% over America. The latter height difference is in the order of the differences between the various oligotrophic forest associations at San Carlos and the corresponding kerangas and kerapah forests in Sarawak and Brunei. This feature may be general and is difficult to explain. The cause may be partly related to the more extreme oligotrophy of the Amazon soils, but perhaps more likely to the history of the flora and vegetation in relation to the more disruptive geologic and climatic history of the Amazon Basin (UNESCO, 1978, chapter 3).

Fig. 4.9. Large-scale photograph of part of the MAB Amazon Forest Ecosystem Project area with complex aerodynamically rough and optically and floristically diverse yevaro forest to the left, a belt of simple, smooth and uniform cunuri forest in the centre leading into low closed bana woodland to the right. The photograph covers approximately 240 × 240 m.

In the MAB Amazon Ecosystem Project San Carlos de Rio Negro a preliminary evaluation of the computer print-out of structural parameters for all trees above 1 cm diameter along two transects (Y 520–530 m and Y 570–580) produced some interesting results (Fig. 4.11 and Table 4.2). The trend of the values of the h/d ratios reflects the structural and ecological gradient from the complex yevaro forest association through the simple cunuri forest association to open, shrubby bana. The values of the mean h/d ratios per stand are somewhat higher in the more complex, taller and probably more vigorous and productive yevaro associations (I–K) than in the cunuri consociations (L–N). This is due to the slender form of the trees in

the intermediate and bottom layers of the yevaro forest, while the large emergents have very low h/d ratios between 45 and 60 (Fig. 4.11). This decline of h/d ratio from about 200 to 220 in the 1-cm diameter class through 100 to 120 at 15 cm, 90 at 20 cm to below 60 in the emergent layer accords with the hypothetical "reiteration" model of Hallé et al. (1978, fig. 84) and is an important adjustment to the stresses to which a tree is exposed in the main canopy (Brunig, 1970b, 1976a). The main canopy trees in Fig. 4.11 show the h/d ratios for individual trees in three major association groups yevaro (I, H, K), cunuri (L, N) and bana (P, Q). the highest h/d values, that is the most slender trees, are in the diameter classes below 20 cm and associated

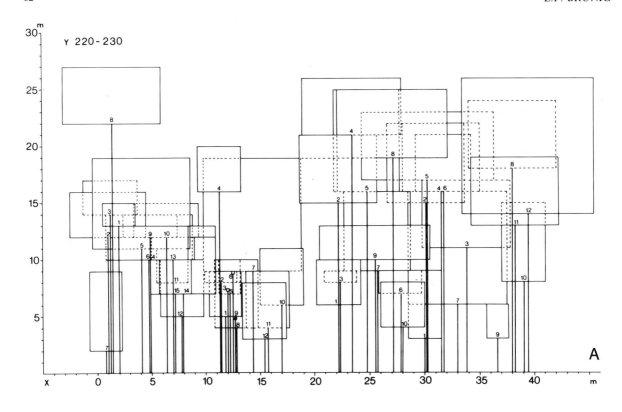

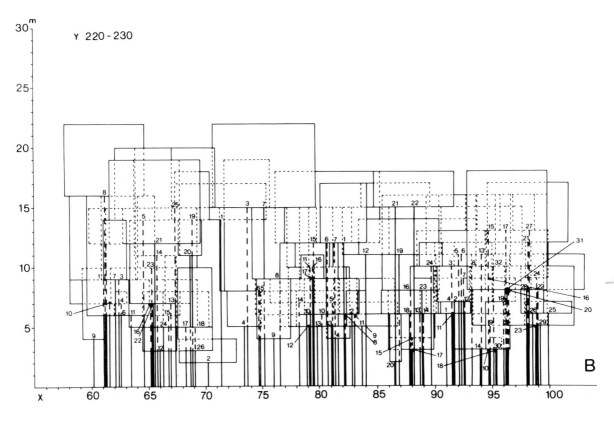

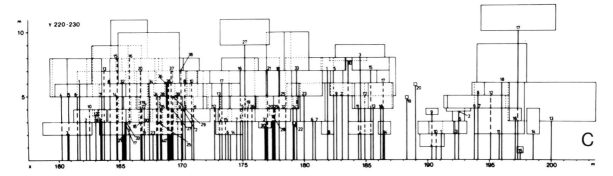

Fig. 4.10. Schematic profiles of stands along the gradient from more mesic caatinga associations N/O and M to "xeric" bana association Q in the MAB Amazon Forest Ecosystem Project at San Carlos de Rio Negro, Venezuela. The profiles are 10 × 40 m and include all trees >5 cm *d*. Crown size is indicated by squares of crown length and crown diameter. The numbers are the serial numbers of the trees in the field list. Broken lines: parts of trees hidden by trees in front. A. X 0–40, Y 220–230: yaguacana–seje association (N) with some yaguacana–cunuri association (O) to the right, 39 individuals, 21 species. B. X 0–40, Y 220–230: yaguacana–cunuri–tamacuari association (M) with transition to yucito–media luna high bana association (P) at the right, 99 individuals, 31 species. C. X 0–40, Y 220–230; yucito–media luna–cupi low bana association (Q), 111 individuals, 20 species. (For vernacular names of trees, see note to Table 4.1.)

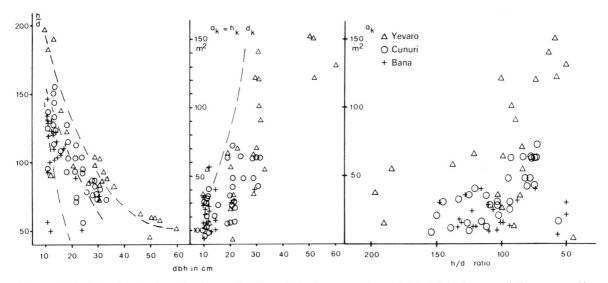

Fig. 4.11. Left: *h/d* ratio (slenderness) of trees of different bole diameter of breast height (*d*) in three associations yevaro–hiua, cunuri–piapoco and bana; broken lines indicate the means of each association. Middle: the crown-sectional area on *d*. The broken line shows the trend to greater wind firmness in the A/B-layer, especially in the exposed emergent layer of the canopy (from Brunig, 1977). Right: crown-sectional area over *h/d* ratio. The yevaro–hiua associations have on average larger crowns for the same *h/d* ratio (degree of slenderness) than the cunuri–piapoco association and the bana woodland. Exceptions are senescent trees (lower right-hand corner). (For vernacular names of trees, see note to Table 4.1.)

with small-crowned under-canopy trees in the tall forest associations. The lowest *h/d* ratio, in other words the most sturdy, wind-resistant tree shape, are characteristic of the top-canopy trees in the complex, aerodynamically rough yevaro association and in the low and irregular bana. In the latter, lower height reduces exposure, and variation

of the main canopy is consequently much larger than in the yevaro forest associations because the *h/d* ratio is not as critical for survival. The cunuri consociation shows the same pattern of relatively great slenderness combined with medium to low aerodynamic roughness as the structurally corresponding *padang alan bunga* (*Shorea albida*) con-

TABLE 4.2

The mean height/stem diameter ratio (h/d) and crown-sectional area/basal area ratio (a_k/d) in various forest associations in the MAB Amazon Ecosystem Project at San Carlos de Rio Negro (Venezuela)

Associations (incl. transitions)	h/d		a_k/d	
	520	570	520	570
I	–	195	–	8803
H	222	–	7120	–
J/K	–	215	–	4768
K	218	–	4945	–
L/N	–	178	–	3934
N	181	–	3288	–
Mean	210	195	5286	6463

Associations: I and H: complex, tall yevaro–hiua association; J and K: transitional associations; L and N: simple structured cunuri–yucito–piapoco associations, transects Y 520–530, 570–580.

sociation in peat swamp and the *Dacrydium beccarii–Gymmostoma nobile* forest types in kerangas in Sarawak.

Generally, the regression line of crown diameter (d_k) or crown-sectional area (a_k) over breast height diameter (d) is curvilinear, declining with increasing diameter, but the relationship seems somewhat more complex than the regressions of tree height on d and of h/d on d (Dawkins, 1963; Francis, 1966). This is possibly a consequence of more diverse and more effective influences of neighboring trees and other environmental factors on crown diameter growth than on tree height growth. The h/d and d_k/d ratios together are useful variables for the assessment of possible growing rates and yields for silvicultural planning (Dawkins, 1959; Brunig, 1977; Adlard, 1978; Alder et al., 1978; Alder and Schneider, 1979) and for the structural and ecological characterization of forest types and strata.

In the example of the Amazonian forest on oligotrophic soils at San Carlos, trees with the same h/d ratio have larger crowns in the yevaro associations (Fig. 4.11, center) and crown size increases more rapidly with decreasing h/d ratio in topcanopy trees than in the cunuri consociations. There is no relationship between crown area and h/d ratio in the bana. The three association groups are clearly structurally distinguished, especially the taller, more complex, more diverse and more dynamic yevaro forests. The complex yevaro asso-

ciations also have larger amounts of fallen and standing dead wood which supports the hypothesis that this association possesses a higher productivity and turnover rates of organic matter as a result of its structure and site which can support more intensive exchange with the environment.

A still better measure of the form of the tree and the ecological status of a stand with respect to vigor and stability is the relationship between crown size (crown sectional area) and h/d ratio (Fig. 4.11, right). This expresses the relationship between crown-sectional area as productive impact zone of the tree and the breast-height diameter or, better, the h/d ratio as combined measure of the mechanical stability and the capacity of the support and supply system of the tree. These relationships and their significance are discussed in more detail elsewhere.

In Fig. 4.11 the yevaro and cunuri associations form two structurally very distinctive groups. The yevaro forest combines larger crowns with lower h/d ratios, while the cunuri forest for the same h/d ratio has smaller crowns. In both association groups crown size increases with decreasing slenderness, but more rapidly in the yevaro association. There is no such trend in the bana. This decrease of the ratios of specific crown volumes, leaf area and leaf mass to stem basal area or stem volume with increasing tree size seems to be a general feature in tropical humid evergreen forests, which has been reported by Las Salas (1973) from evergreen forest in Colombia and by Ogawa et al. (1965) from deciduous forest in Thailand. Consequently, trees in the A/B-layers of the canopy would have crown volumes, leaf areas, leaf biomass and crown phytomass values which are absolutely large, but smaller in relation to the tree stem basal area and total phytomass. As an example, Klinge (1973) gives data on crown area, fresh leaf weight and basal area of a tierra firme stand near Manaus which show the following relations. The A/B tree strata (h 16.7–35.4 m) contribute 25.7% to the stand crown projection area of 7 ha ha^{-1}, 50.5% to the fresh leaf mass of the stand of 18.2 t ha^{-1} and 70.7% to the stand basal area of 30.7 m² ha^{-1}. Klinge (1977) observed "that specific leaf area in canopy species decreases with increasing breast height diameter, cunuri being a typical example. This generalization does not hold for 'yaguacana' (*Eperua leucantha*)".

The normalized crown-sectional area ($a_k = d_k \cdot l_k$)

expresses crown size by the two easily measured or visually estimated parameters crown length and crown width. It is superior to crown diameter alone as a physiological and ecological indicator. In spite of its usefulness and easy measurement it has been rarely used by foresters or ecologists in the tropics. Recently it has proved very useful in the MAB Amazon Ecosystem Project for structural characterization of associations, leaf area and leaf biomass analyses and for ecological interpretation of stand structure. The mean ratios of the vertical crown-sectional area (a_k) to stem basal area (g) is largest in the yevaro type (I) and declines to the cunuri consociation (L, N) (Table 4.1). That means, crowns are relatively much larger, especially in the emergent layer, in relation to the sectional area of the supporting stem, but they are smaller in relation to the total volume of the tree support system and its biomass (Brunig et al., 1979, fig. 14). While static properties are not impaired (see also right-hand side of Fig. 4.11), the demand on water supply per stem-sectional area unit will in the emergents of the complex yevaro association most probably be larger. In this situation a very large stand crown volume would be a risky proposition. It may be significant that the total crown-sectional area per unit ground area of the stands does not increase from the intermediate cunuri consociation (N) to the "mesic" yevaro association group (I, H, K) (Fig. 4.12). With the existence of a common leaf biomass regression on d and a_k this means that the stands do not carry a leaf mass in proportion to their total biomass. Leaf mass in the less complex cunuri consociation group also seems to approach asymptotically an upper limit, as previously reported by Ogawa et al. (1965) from Thailand. Further statistical analysis will bring more light on this intriguing question.

The interrelationships of structural features are illustrated by the simultaneous change of n, g and v, mean and top stand-height and height of tallest tree and of mean crown-sectional areas per tree and per unit ground area along the same transects Y 520–530 m and Y 570–580 m (Fig. 4.12). The association symbols are not the same as in Table 4.1, because the transects were classified separately. H and I are simple-structured forest types and are most probably early (H) and late (I) phases of the same vegetation/site complex. The two associations are very intricately mixed and therefore have been

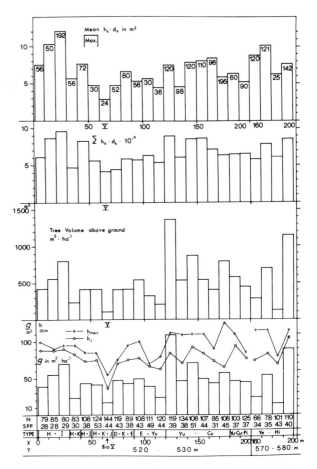

Fig. 4.12. Variation of structural parameters along a 10 m wide transect in the MAB Amazon Forest Ecosystem Project at Y 520–530 m (X 0–200 m) and Y 570–580 m (X 160–200 m). Legend: g = basal area in m² ha⁻¹; h_t = mean height of five tallest trees in 10 × 10 m quadrat; h_{max} = height of tallest tree; tree volume, estimated as sum of $(0.5\, g \cdot h)$ multiplied by 100; sum of $(h_k \cdot d_k)$ per ha illustrating the crown-sectional area per unit ground area; mean $h_k \cdot d_k$ is the mean crown-sectional area in m² per quadrat illustrating crown size variation, numbers are the sectional area of the largest crown in the quadrat in m².

lumped in the association plot map. The 240 m long transect in Fig. 4.12 starts in this mixed association H/I of simple-structured forest, traverses a very heterogenous forest zone in which biomass plot V is located and enters the more complex yaguacana/cunuri association beyond X 100. From X 180 follows a transitional zone which is characterized by the presence of *piapoco* which leads into association I which is complex yevaro/hiua forest on mesic, deep-rooted soils from X 160–200 in Y 570–580.

The distributions in Fig. 4.12 show the following features:

(1) The basal area (bottom) varies very strongly between different phases of stand development at small scale (e.g. biomass plot V) particularly within the more dynamic and complex associations to the right.

(2) The maximum tree height and the mean top height in the quadrats first decrease toward the more heterogenous (transitional) forest and then increase from left to right. At the same time the differences between the two parameters and their variability increases. This agrees with the increasing aerodynamic roughness and complexity of the canopy on the more mesic sites to the right.

(3) The tree volume ($h \cdot g \cdot 0.5$) per quadrat varies accordingly more than g or h and also increases slightly to the right.

(4) The total sectional area of leafed crowns per quadrat varies much less than the previous parameters. This was contrary to expectation. We would have expected that the crown-sectional area and consequently the volume of the leafed crowns and leaf mass per unit ground area would vary in relation to site variation even more than wood volume. But in fact the opposite is true and crown size (top) and crown-sectional area per hectare (second row) vary less than basal area and wood volume and do not differ much between the various association/site complexes.

This would mean, that the taller, more complex and aerodynamically rough, and probably more dynamic and productive associations to the right of the transect operate with a crown volume and possibly leaf area and leaf mass which on the average is not much larger per unit ground area or less per unit phytomass than those in the simple, uniform, aerodynamically smooth and apparently more static and less productive forest associations on the left. The ecological advantage would be that interception of precipitation is accordingly not much, if at all, increased (Brunig et al., 1978). This may be a critical advantage on these soils during irregularly occurring periods of drought (Brunig, 1969a, 1970a, b). The greater growth rates would then be achieved by greater efficiency and by greater intensity of exchange processes rather than by increasing the crown size and leaf mass. The verification of this hypothesis requires further investigation at San Carlos and in other areas of the humid tropical evergreen forest.

A parameter which is more difficult to measure

but very useful as an indicator of the ecological conditions in a forest ecosystem is its aerodynamic canopy surface roughness. This roughness can be estimated by the dimensionless parameter z_0 which is computed from wind profile data. The roughness parameter z_0 is related to the height and surface architecture of the forest canopy which can be expressed in terms of tree top height above a "closed canopy plane", crown and crown-group diameters, distances between these roughness elements, and the variances of these parameters. It is possible to obtain these quantitative basic data from ground surveys or from aerial photo-interpretation, or better by a combined survey, and to compute a value for each stand which indicates the relative position or rating of this stand in relation to aerodynamic roughness, keeping in mind that it is not the real z_0 parameter which is being calculated, because the real parameter depends among other factors on wind speed. This calculated indicator of the aerodynamic properties of a forest stand has a number of important aspects (Brunig, 1970a).

Firstly, the geometric canopy surface architecture determines the rates of incoming radiation which are intercepted, reflected and re-intercepted, and thereby the net radiation for individual trees and for the canopy. Canopies with greater aerodynamic roughness would, under otherwise equal conditions, absorb and exchange more energy. Secondly, greater irregularity and height variation of the canopy surface and consequently increased aerodynamic roughness means greater turbulence from free and forced convection. Increased turbulence in turn reduces atmospheric resistance to heat and vapor fluxes from the plant surface. Consequently, a greater amount of sensible and latent heat can be dissipated per unit area and time. Generally, greater aerodynamic surface roughness will tend to increase the ratio evaporation: incident net radiation. The tendency to increased turbulent exchange from free convection would be enhanced by greater differences in the optical properties of the tree crowns, which is a typical feature of the more complex and species-rich stands on mesic sites which can be easily recognized on black-and-white and colored aerial photographs. The effect of size, orientation and spacing of leaves on radiation interception, convective heat exchange and turbulence at a small scale is well known and has been exhaustively treated (Brunig, 1970a, b; Gates, 1965, 1968; Medina et al., 1978; Gates and Johnson, 1979).

Together with declining complexity and decreasing aerodynamic roughness of the canopy along the ecologic gradient of increasing oligotrophy and adversity of water regime goes an increase of sclerophylly and generally of xeromorphic features. This trend is visually more pronounced in Southeast Asia as a result of the presence on extremely oligotrophic sites of very small leafed, locally dominant species of such genera as *Gymnostoma*, *Casuarina*, *Podocarpus* and *Dacrydium* which have no physiognomic equivalent in the Amazon Basin (Brunig, 1966, 1974; Brunig et al., 1979). But scleromorphy and xeromorphic adaptations to adverse site conditions are otherwise structurally and possibly physiologically and biochemically the same and follow the same basic principles of water and nutrient economy in forests in Southeast Asia and in the Amazon Basin (Brunig, 1970a, 1971; Medina et al., 1978; Brunig et al., 1979). This xeromorphic diminution of leaf sizes and the tendency to upright or pendulous orientation and bunching of leaves and twigs also affects the aerodynamic roughness of the tree crown and has important physio-ecological implications, which have been discussed by Brunig (1966, 1970a, b, 1974, 1976b).

In agreement with expectations from theory, canopy surface features of humid tropical evergreen forest have been observed to change along ecological gradients in a consistent and meaningful manner. Examples from Southeast Asia are shown in Figs. 4.5 to 4.7 and from the Amazon Basin in Fig. 4.10. The simultaneous change of tree stature, canopy roughness expressed as z_0 (in cm), of leaf size and crown architecture and of above-ground biomass along the gradient of declining water availability is easily recognized. The simultaneous change of aerodynamic roughness and of the h/d ratio of trees in the A/B-layer along a gradient of phasic change of vegetation and soil is shown in Fig. 4.4. It is relevant that windthrow together with lightning gaps are particularly common in an area of relatively rough canopy and high h/d ratios. The combination of great aerodynamic roughness and therefore increased exposure of trees to eddies and slender bole shape, which reduces resistance to bending and swaying, produces a high suscepti-

bility to windthrow (Brunig, 1973b).

We may conclude that there are good reasons to hypothesize that the physiognomic features of the stands, the stature and shape of the trees and with this growth rates, stand dynamics and regeneration patterns are so designed that the risks of damage to the stand are contained within certain limits which ensure survival of the system at reasonable rates of activity. But much more research has to be done before we understand the interrelationships between stand structure, reproduction pattern and site conditions and the effects of changes in stand structure on stand dynamics and micro-climate within and immediately above the stand.

PHYTOMASS

Methodological problems of phytomass assessment

Reliable sufficient and representative data on total phytomass of stands or forest types are few in tropical humid evergreen forest. Each forest association/site unit has a typical phytomass which varies within the type, in accordance with phasic development and micro-site differences at small scale of variation. The ranges and variances of total and fractional phytomass between quadrats of 100 and 1000 m^2 is large in relation to the mean values. If phytomass is estimated by quadrat harvesting in preference to allometric estimates, the phytomass plot data must be supplemented with information on the pattern of variance within the vegetational unit concerned.

Methods and problems of phytomass sampling are described and discussed by Golley in UNESCO (1978, ch. 10); where he emphasizes the need to supplement intensive plot studies by extending the data base on the variation of forest structure and phytomass by surveying a larger tract surrounding the plot. Allometric regressions derived from sample trees are recommended for phytomass estimations. Such methods have been successfully used in tropical forest by Ogawa et al. (1965) in Thailand, Las Salas (1973) in seasonal evergreen lowland forest in Colombia, Jordan and Uhl (1978) in tierra firme forest on Oxisols in the MAB Amazon Ecosystem Project near San Carlos. The regression which achieved the most significant correlation to tree dry weight used $d^2 h$ and specific density as independent variables, but as Golley observes "the actual allometric relationship must be established for each forest because the relationship between d, h, volume and weight are influenced by site conditions (UNESCO, 1978 p. 237). Further studies of phytomass relationships in the yevaro, cunuri and bana association groups showed that the addition of crown-sectional area to $d^2 h$ as an independent variable improves the fit considerably (R^2 increases from 0.7 to 0.98) and makes the regression applicable to structurally very different associations.

A particularly troublesome problem of phytomass sampling is the assessment of the heart rot and hollowness which represents only a small fraction of the phytomass but varies strongly between different forest types and sites, and causes a considerable loss of commercial value of tropical forests (Panzer, 1971).

For broad assessments, the product basal area $\times$ total height $\times 0.5$ (Brunig, 1966) or 0.526 (Dawkins, 1959) gives a reasonable estimate of total tree and diameter class volume which can be converted to an approximate estimate of phytomass if the specific density of the timber is known, and lumping leaves and bark which contribute only a small proportion in mature high forest. The degree of stratification of the stand into diameter or height classes depends on the stand structure. A study in various communities of *Shorea albida* in kerangas and peat-swamp forests in Sarawak showed that the h/d ratio and stem taper and consequently the diameter/volume ratio vary strongly between communities. In addition, the same species produces timber of significantly different specific density and defectiveness (hollowness) on different sites in peat swamps and in kerangas or in different phasic communities. The same basal area and height values are therefore associated with different stand volumes and phytomass values and the volume estimator (basal area $\times 1/2$ tree height) is subject to considerable bias if the diameter classes are very wide. If a standardized mean canopy height is chosen for rapid assessments, the product stand basal area $\times$ mean stand height will give too high estimates for plots with a steeply declining stand curve and few emergents. The estimates will be too low in stands with a markedly bi-modal stand curve. In "normal stands" the deviations of the estimates are within $\pm 15\%$ of actually measured volumes.

Phytomass or plant biomass data from humid tropical forests are relatively rare and available data are point data and not representative. My statement of 1973 that "data on total basal area, volume or weight of the trees in virgin stands of the predominantly evergreen ombrophilous nonseasonal tropical forest are rare" is still valid. The information from forest inventories is generally restricted to commercial stem volumes. This volume represents between 10 and 50% of the total volume above ground. There are only a few cases in which total biomass was determined on small plots. The biomass was either directly measured or estimated from parameters with which biomass is correlated [a review for Amazonia is given by Klinge (1973) and Klinge et al. (1974); for Southeast Asia see Kira and Shidei (1967), Surianegara (1965), Kira (1969), Hozumi et al. (1969), Bullock (1973), Brunig (1974); data from Africa are available in Dawkins (1963), Hopkins (1963), Muller and Nielsen (1965, probably secondary forest), and Bernhard-Reversat et al (1973)].

Phytomass estimates

The estimates of the pantropical average phytomass in the rainforest vary widely and their reliability is rather poor. Estimates range from 300 to 650 t ha^{-1} total dry matter or 135 to 290 t ha^{-1} carbon (45%), averaging conservatively at about 200 t ha^{-1} carbon or about 450 t ha^{-1} dry matter. Rollet (1974; also in UNESCO, 1978, p. 129) calculated a pantropical mean above-ground phytovolume of stands for all trees higher than 4 m of 570 m^3 ha^{-1} $\pm 10.6\%$ ($p = 0.05$) from twenty plots of 0.25 ha each, which would indicate a dry matter value somewhat below the pantropical average above.

As we have seen, structural parameters of trees and stand vary widely within mature forest types between different soil/landform units, altitudes and regions. The phytomass varies accordingly. Knowledge of this variation is still inadequate. Estimates of global mean and total phytomass at the present state of knowledge are little more than reasoned guesses.

Brunig and Klinge (1977), in a comparison between Amazonian and Bornean phytomass structure, reports from a 0.2-ha sample plot in tierra firme forest a total phytomass of 1033 t ha^{-1}

fresh weight, of which 25% were below and 75% above the soil surface. The 75% above-ground fraction is to 76% (57% of total above-ground phytomass) composed of A/B-layer trees and to 88% (66% of total) of A/B/C-layer trees, the rest being undergrowth, ground vegetation, lianas and epiphytes. They cite an average fresh weight of 770 t ha^{-1} from structure data given by six authors for central Amazonian "tierra firme" forest. This value is of the same order as the mean fresh phytomass weight calculated from sample plots in kerangas forest on Spodosols in Sarawak and Brunei, indicating the relatively poor stocking in the Amazon basin.

The phytomass of sample plots representing fully stocked mature stands in various types of kerangas forest in Sarawak and Brunei ranges in the order of 1:10 from about 195 t ha^{-1} dry matter (of this 215 m^3 ha^{-1} or approximately 50% wood volume over 5 cm diameter above ground) to 1415 t ha^{-1} in highly agglomerated stands on "giant podzol". A value of 1158 t ha^{-1} was measured in the *Shorea albida* consociation in the peat swamps. Both values are considerably higher than the stocking in the previously quoted sample plot 10 in mixed dipterocarp forest on granodiorite with 54.8 m^2 ha^{-1} basal area (2 cm d), 55.5 m^2 ha^{-1} total basal area (65 m top height), and an estimated 1160 t ha^{-1}

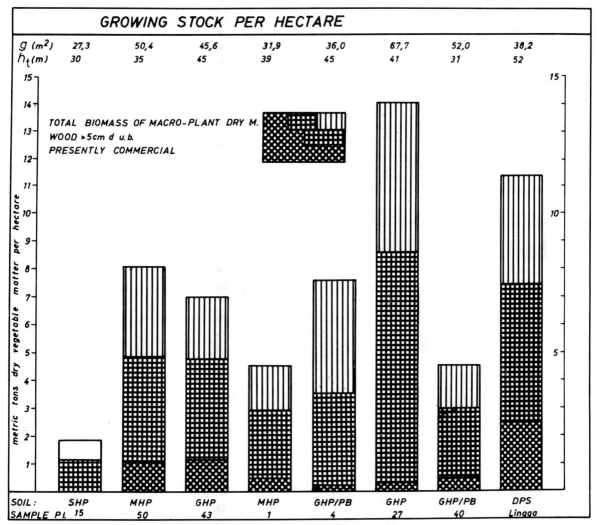

Fig. 4.13. Variation of total phytomass of trees > 1 cm d in sample plots of mature humid tropical forest on different sites and soils in Sarawak. HP = humus podzol; S = shallow; M = medium; G = groundwater; PB = peatbog; DPS = deep peat swamp; h_t = mean top height of the A-layer trees; g = basal area in m^2 ha^{-1}.

dry matter. This stocking is well above the hypothetical pantropical average for closed humid high forest.

The lowest phytomass, particularly of the above-ground fraction in mature natural forest types in Borneo, occur in stunted, open forests and woodlands on certain extremely unfavorable sites in kerangas and kerapah, in some types of mountain ridge forest and in the last stages of phasic peat-swamp development. Total phytomass in these scrubby stands may be less than 100 t ha^{-1} and a large proportion of this may be roots, especially on Tropaquods. The range of forest type/site unit related phytomass variation in Borneo is shown in Fig. 4.13.

Similar conditions and biomass values, allowing for the described tree height difference between Borneo and Amazonia, were reported by Klinge from certain high forest and bana woodland types near San Carlos de Rio Negro. In an extreme case of shrubby, open bana, roots presented as much as 80% of the phytomass, while the root fraction was 60% in the closed, tall bana and 20% in the high forest stands. The mean root phytomass of the high cunuri forest association was 132 t ha^{-1} which is above the values of 55 t ha^{-1} reported by Stark from tierra firme forest nearby (Klinge, 1977, 1979; Klinge and Herrera, 1978). The tierra firme forest on Oxisols in the area has a total living phytomass of 391 t ha^{-1} dry matter with a tree basal area of 33.6 m^2 ha^{-1} and a tree above-ground phytomass of 335 t ha^{-1}, and an average specific wood density of 0.96 g cm^{-3} (Jordan and Uhl, 1978). This forest with its relatively low basal area density, stature and phytomass appears to be rather typical of forests on Oxisols in tropical America and agrees well with Klinge's data from central Amazonia and Las Salas' data from Colombia. In comparison with Southeast Asia, the phytomass stocking of this tierra firme forest is low and corresponds rather more with kerangas on Spodosols and less with mixed dipterocarp forest on Oxisols, except that the growing stock in the tierra firme forest is physiognomically very different from kerangas.

Las Salas (1973), in a study of the dynamics of natural lowland rain forest and the changes induced by man in several types of seasonal rain forest at Carare, Colombia, assessed the phytomass by means of single tree and 10 × 10 m quadrat measurements. He found considerable differences between types. In a transition from low terrace to undulating hill country, the above-ground tree phytomass was 323 t ha^{-1} dry matter (basal area 31.6 m^2 ha^{-1}) plus 4.1 t ha^{-1} undergrowth. The tree biomass was composed of 248 t ha^{-1} stems, 49.6 t ha^{-1} branches, 17.2 t ha^{-1} twigs and 7.0 t ha^{-1} leaves. Stocking was lower on the terraces with 185 t ha^{-1} total phytomass, of this 167.5 trees (17.9 m^2 ha^{-1}).

MEANS TO FUNCTIONAL-ECOLOGICAL INTERPRETATION; GAPS OF KNOWLEDGE

The precarious condition and vulnerability of the tropical humid forest ecosystem has been described by many authors. There is a general consensus that the architecture of individual trees and the structure of the whole stand are somehow related to the functionality and stability of the forest ecosystem. But there have been few observational and hardly any experimental studies of these important questions until very recently. Most quoted opinions are based on circumstantial evidence and, while they serve well to state hypotheses for further research, are not yet filling the wide gap of knowledge in this field.

Stand height and diameter curves

The remarkable and general difference between Borneo and Amazonia in the height of the tallest, emergent trees and also of the main canopy height in stands with smooth, dense and distinct canopy cannot be explained. Present climatic conditions are similar. Soil fertility may be generally lower in the Amazon Basin, but differences between the same soil may be expected to be slight. The question, therefore, must remain unanswered except by the hypothesis that differences may be due to a different evolutionary history. Otherwise, the trend of stand height over site conditions is similar, except that the Amazon Basin has no equivalent to the very tall, even canopy with high albedo of the *Shorea albida*, *S. pachyphylla*, and *Dryobalanops rappa* consociations of the Sarawak peat swamps.

The biological interpretation of stand tables of whole stands and of individual species is difficult and pitfalls are many (Brunig, 1966, 1974, 1976b). It is not surprising, therefore, that "authors have mostly been in search of a mathematical representation which would fit their data ... and generally did not look for biological interpretations" (UNESCO, 1978, p. 115). This situation will not change until we know more about the growth physiology and autecology of individual species and have observed actual performance of species in the field under natural and modified conditions.

Tree shape

Tree height, stem diameter, crown geometry and crown size vary between layers within stands and between forest association/site units in the same manner in Borneo and Amazonia. In the absence of experimental evidence, the causal factors are not known. The hypothesis is that tree shapes are so designed that the use of available resources, especially light and water, is maximized within the limitations of risk of damage from drought, overheating and windthrow, but there is little experimental data available yet on the physioecological significance of tree architecture and its variation with species, genotype, age and social position. Research in this area with fast-growing and early maturing species is urgently needed.

Stand density

Humid tropical forest types on similar, very oligotrophic sites in the neotropics and in Borneo have similar basal area densities and variation patterns of stocking in relation to phase and site variations. The apparent exception is the mixed dipterocarp forest which not only possesses taller stature but also a greater basal area density than the corresponding tierra firme forest types.

The described gradients of basal area, volume, phytomass and crown volume can possibly be explained in terms of a compromise between maximizing production and filtering efficiency on one hand and adjusting leaf mass and supporting stem volume to the fluctuations of the radiation, temperature, moisture and wind regimes of the site in order to reduce risk of damage. Again, evidence of scientific research has only begun to be produced by current tropical forest ecosystem research projects.

Species richness and diversity

Fittkau (1973) argues in analogy to some aquatic systems that the tropical rain forest acts as a nutrient filter the more efficiently the greater is its richness of tree species. If this is true and generally applicable, the remarkable similarity of tree species richness and diversity of forest associations on practically identical sites in Borneo and Amazonia could in part be explained. The number of tree species on any site increases, during stand development, to the limit which is possible under the given conditions of variability of site, and it stays at that level until catastrophic events interfere (Brunig, 1973c). The greater the variability of growth-affecting site factors, the greater is the number of specific situations to which species can adapt. Consequently, more species can be accommodated and, each having a narrow space to compete in, the greater will be species diversity. We conclude that the greater the number of environmental factors which act effectively on the plant populations, the less one factor dominates, the richer and more diverse will be the stand. Conversely, if this range of effectiveness is restricted by adverse site conditions, such as regular or occasional physiologically effective severe and prolonged droughts or waterlogging, the smaller will be the number of species and the lower will be the diversity. In the latter case, salvaging nutrients from throughfall would be less efficient. Consequently, additional nutrient-preserving devices would be necessary in the humid tropical climate. Such devices could be sclerophyllous, pachyphyllous and coriaceous leaves, or the slowing of the decomposing processes in the litter by biochemical means. Very high tannin contents of tree leaves in kerangas, which may retard litter decomposition by masking proteins, and the response of *Gymnostoma nobile* to fertilizing by reducing this content have been reported in detail elsewhere (Brunig, 1966). Species with high concentrations of nonhydrolyzable polyphenols tend to mor formation, thereby conserving nutrients and providing a convenient medium for the development of a dense superficial root mat to salvage released and incoming nutrients. It may be significant that among kerangas species with only moderately aggressive tannins are *Agathis dammara*, which develops a very intensive, deep root system and prefers deep soils, *Ploiarium alternifolium*, which prefers sites with impeded drainage, and *Shorea albida*, which grows on deep peats or on relatively deep, but never on shallow-xeric, kerangas soils.

The consistent feature of decline in species diversity and the increasing steepness of the species dominance curve to the more unfavorable soils (Brunig, 1973a) may be a side-effect of these biochemical devices towards increasing species dominance. Experimental evidence is lacking except in the case of *Shorea albida* which showed a strong allelopathic effect on *Gonystylus bancanus*, reducing the net photosynthesis rate of this competing species by components in its litter and mor, and thereby establishing its dominance.

Canopy structure

A tall, irregularly broken, aerodynamically rough and multi-layered canopy produces greater air turbulence and more rapid heat and vapor transfers both within the canopy and between canopy and atmosphere. Rough canopies also intercept and absorb solar radiation more effectively than smooth surfaces; as a result, exchange intensities for radiation, heat, gasses and water vapor are greater. A closed, uniform, aerodynamically smooth canopy has lower absorption and exchange intensities and the individual trees are less exposed to radiation and wind. Smaller tree stature and sclerophyllous, often steeply inclined and highly reflectant leaves further reduce radiation and heat load and the probability of damaging water deficiency and overheating. Loomis and Williams (1969) and Loomis et al. (1967) incorporated canopy characteristics (e.g. light extinction coefficients and leaf angles) in models of light distribution and stand production, and concluded that, other factors being constant, greatest efficiency will be obtained at low leaf angles and LAI (leaf area index) values when light intensities are low, and at high leaf angles and LAI values when light intensities are high. Humid tropical forest geometry conforms with this pattern.

A complex vertical structure with continuous leafage from top to bottom certainly reduces the impact of rain on the soil by means of continuous interception. The total amount of throughfall in humid and wetter areas is only slightly reduced even by a dense, complex canopy and this reduction may be ecologically less insignificant than the reduction in the kinetic energy of the impact of rain drops. In simple-structured canopies with sparse leafage in the under-canopy and undergrowth, common on extremely oligotrophic sites with un-

favorable water regime, a thick litter, mor and peat layer and dense root mat may compensate for the lower nutrient salvaging capacity of the canopy.

Tree form, canopy structure and the resistance of trees and stands to drought, wind, storm and diseases are closely interrelated. Consequently, variation of canopy structure in mature humid tropical forests should be associated with site gradients related to radiation, temperature, wind and moisture regimes and the stability and dynamics of the ecosystem. The available observations in Borneo and Amazonia show that tree shape and canopy structure and mortality patterns change with site gradients of moisture and nutrients which corroborates the hypotheses. In turn, stand architecture affects site climate in a very complex manner, but experimental evidence is yet rare and is just beginning to be produced by current humid tropical forest ecosystem studies which include catenas involving distinct site and vegetation structure gradients related to water and nutrient supplies.

CONCLUSION

Baumgartner and Brunig (ch. 1 in UNESCO, 1978) concluded their review of the biospheric role of tropical forest: "very little research has been carried out in natural and modified tropical forests on the interrelations between floristic and architectural structure, the fractioning of matter and energy, and their relevance to ecosystem stability and functioning. Available information refers to one or few factors, but the interrelationships and interactions are usually omitted." Particularly urgently needed is knowledge on those structure-dependent processes which are most likely to spawn biospheric effects which have a wide horizontal range. Examples are the role of forests of different structure in storing, cycling and releasing carbon dioxide, water and energy in various forms. Suspicion is mounting that tropical forests play a vital role in maintaining world climate by their effect on the atmospheric carbon, water, thermal energy and wind systems. But as long as the fundamental physical, chemical and physiological processes within the tropical forest ecosystems and the interactions and interdependencies between them and tree and stand architecture are poorly understood, any assessment of the effects of changes of forest architecture on the environment and on the level of sustainable biologic and economic productivity of the forests will remain guesswork. Under such conditions, forecasts of long-term trends of the condition of the biosphere at any level remain speculative.

REFERENCES

Addor, E.E., Qushing, W.N. and Grabau, W.E., 1970. A procedure for describing the geometry of plants and plant assemblages. In: H.T. Odum and R.F. Pigeon (Editors), *A Tropical Rainforest. A Study of Irradiation and Ecology at El Verde, Puerto Rico.* U.S. Atomic Energy Commission, Washington, D.C., pp. B151–B167.

Adlard, P.G., 1978. Estimation of tree competition and cooperation in forest stands. In: E.F. Brunig (Editor), *Transactions of the International MAB–IUFRO Workshop on Tropical Rainforest Ecosystems Research.* Chair for World Forestry, Hamburg–Reinbek, Spec. Rep. No. 1, pp. 160–172.

Alder, D. and Schneider, T.W., 1979. A stand growth model as a tool in studying management options for MAB-rainforest ecosystem projects and for temperate forests. In: S. Adisaemarto and E.F. Brunig (Editors), *Transactions of the Second International MAB–IUFRO Workshop on Tropical Rainforest Ecosystems Research.* Chair for World Forestry, Hamburg–Reinbek, Spec. Rep. No. 2, pp. 128–165.

Alder, D., Synnott, T.J. and Smith, J.P., 1978. GROPE: A standardised growth projection method for tropical rainforest. In: E.F. Brünig (Editor), *Transactions of the International MAB–IUFRO Workshop on Tropical Rainforest Ecosystems Research.* Chair for World Forestry, Hamburg–Reinbek, Spec. Rep. No. 1, pp. 263–270.

Anderson, J.A.R., 1961a. *The Ecology and Forest Types of the Peatswamp Forests of Sarawak and Brunei in relation to Their Silviculture.* Thesis, University of Edinburgh, Edinburgh, 117 pp.

Ashton, P.S., 1964a. Ecological studies in the mixed dipterocarp forests of Brunei State. *Oxford For. Mem.,* No. 25: 75 pp.

Ashton, P.S., 1964b. A quantitative phytosociological technique applied to tropical mixed rainforest. *Malay. For.,* 27(3): 304–317.

Ashton, P.S., 1967. Climate versus soils in the classification of Southeast Asian tropical lowland vegetation. *J. Ecol.,* 55(3): 67–68.

Ashton, P.S., 1973. *Report on Research Undertaken During the Years 1963–1967 on the Ecology of Mixed Dipterocarp Forest in Sarawak.* Inst. South East Asian Biology, University of Aberdeen, Aberdeen, 412 pp. (mimeograph).

Ashton, P.S., 1978. Crown characteristics of tropical trees. In: P.B. Tomlinson and M.H. Zimmermann (Editors), *Tropical Trees As Living Systems.* Cambridge University Press, Cambridge, pp. 591–615.

Ashton, P.S. and Brünig, E.F., 1975. The variation of tropical moist forest in relation to environmental factors and its relevance to land-use planning. *Mitt. Bundesforschungsanst. Forst-Holzwirtsch.,* 109: 59–86.

Baumgartner, A., 1969. Meteorological approach to the exchange of CO_2. *Photosynthetica,* 3(2): 127–149.

Baumgartner, A. and Brunig, E.F., 1978. Tropical forests and the biosphere. In: UNESCO, *Tropical Forest Ecosystems. A State of Knowledge Report Prepared by UNESCO, UNEP, FAO. Nat. Resour. Res.,* 14: 33–60.

Bernhard-Reversat, F., Huttel, Ch. and Delaunay, G., 1973. Productivité primaire en forêt tropicale pluvieuse de Côte d'Ivoire. *Rapp. Lab. Ecol. Vég.,* Orsay.

Brunig, E.F., 1966. *Der Heidewald von Sarawak and Brunei — Eine Studie seiner Vegetation und Ökologie.* Habil-Schrift, University Hamburg, Hamburg, 137 pp.

Brunig, E.F., 1968. Der Heidewald von Sarawak und Brunei. *Mitt. Bundesforschungsanst. Forst-Holzwirtsch.,* No. 68, Vol. I: 152 pp., Vol. II: 431 pp.

Brunig, E.F., 1969a. On the seasonality of droughts in the lowlands of Sarawak (Borneo). *Erdkunde,* 23(2): 127–133.

Brunig, E.F., 1969b. Forest classification in Sarawak. *Malay. For.,* 32(2): 143–179.

Brunig, E.F., 1970a. Stand structure, physiognomy and environmental factors in some lowlands forests in Sarawak. *Trop. Ecol.,* 11(1): 26–43.

Brunig, E.F., 1970b. On the ecological significance of drought in the equatorial wet evergreen (rain) forest of Sarawak (Borneo). In: I.R. Flenley (Editor), *The Water Relations of Malesian Forests. Dep. Geogr., Univ. Hull, Misc. Ser.,* No. 11: 66–96.

Brunig, E.F., 1971. *Forstliche Produktionslehre.* Europ. Univ. Schriften, Reihe Forst-Holzwirt., No. 1. Verlag Peter Lang, Frankfurt, 328 pp.

Brunig, E.F., 1973a. Biomass diversity and biomass sampling in tropical rainforest. In: *IUFRO Biomass Studies, IUFRO S. 4.01.* College of Life Science and Agriculture, University of Maine, Orono, Me., pp. 269–293.

Brunig, E.F., 1973b. Some further evidence on the amount of damage attributed to lightning and wind-throw in *Shorea albida* forest in Sarawak. *Commonw. For. Rev.,* 52(3): 260–265.

Brunig, E.F., 1973c. Sturmschäden als Risikofaktor bei der Holzproduktion in den wichtigsten Holzerzeugungsgebieten der Erde, 1. *Mitt. Bundesforschungsanst. Forst-Holzwirtsch.,* 93: 17–33.

Brunig, E.F., 1973d. Sturmschäden als Risikofaktor bei der Holzproduktion in den wichtigsten Holzerzeugungsgebieten der Erde, 2. *Forstarchiv,* 44(7): 137–140

Brunig, E.F., 1974. *Ecological Studies in the Kerangas Forests of Sarawak and Brunei.* Borneo Literature Bureau, Sarawak Forest Department, Kuching, 237 pp.

Brunig, E.F., 1976a. Tree form in relation to environmental conditions: an ecological view-point. In: M.G.R. Cannel and F.T. Last (Editors), *Tree Physiology and Yield Improvement.* Academic Press, London, pp. 139–156.

Brunig, E.F., 1976b. Classifying for mapping of kerangas and peatswamp forest as examples of primary forest types in Sarawak (Borneo). In: P.S. Ashton (Editor), *The Classification and Mapping of Southeast Asian Ecosystems. Dep. Geogr., Univ. Hull, Misc. Ser.,* No. 17: 57–75.

Brunig, E.F., 1977. Ökologische Stabilität von forstlichen Monokulturen als Problem der Bestandesstruktur. In: P. Müller (Editor), *Verhandlungen der Gesellschaft für Ökologie, Göttingen 1976.* The Hague, 622 pp.

Brunig, E.F. and Heuveldop, J., 1976. Structure and functions in natural and man-made forests in the humid tropics. In: *XVI IUFRO World Congress, Oslo*, pp. 500–511.

Brunig, E.F. and Klinge, H., 1977. Comparison of the phytomass structure of tropical rainforest stands in Central Amazonas, Brazil, and in Sarawak, Borneo. In: *Essays Presented to E.J.H. Corner for His 70th Birthday. Gard. Bull. (Singapore)*, 1977: 81–101.

Brunig, E.F. and Synnott, T.J., 1977. An outline for a basic interdisciplinary research program with emphasis on a common approach to research methodology and measurement techniques. With contributions by P.G. Adlard, D. Alder, G. Aubert, J. Heuveldop and H. Klinge. In: E.F. Brunig (Editor), *Transactions of the International MAB–IUFRO Workshop on Tropical Rainforest Ecosystems Research*. Chair of World Forestry, Hamburg–Reinbek, Spec. Rep. No. 1, pp. 265–331 [2nd ed., 1978, pp. 276–342.]

Brunig, E.F., Herrera, R., Heuveldop, J., Jordan, C. Klinge, H. and Medina, E., 1977. The international Amazon Project coordinated by Centro de Ecologia, Instituto Venezolano de Investigaciones Cientificas: organization and recent advances. In: E.F. Brünig (Editor), *Transactions of the International MAB–IUFRO Workshop on Tropical Rainforest Ecosystems Research*. Chair of World Forestry, Hamburg–Reinbek, Spec. Rep., No. 1, pp. 104–126.

Brunig, E.F., Heuveldop, J., Smith, J.P. and Alder, D., 1978. Structure and functions of a rainforest in the International Amazon Ecosystem Project: floristic stratification and variation of some features of stand structure and precipitation. In: J.S. Singh and B. Gopal (Editors), *Glimpses of Ecology. Professor R. Misra Commemoration Volume*. International Scientific Publications, Jaipur, Prakash. pp. 125–144.

Brunig, E.F., Alder, D. and Smith, J.P., 1979. The International MAB Amazon Rainforest Ecosystem Pilotproject at San Carlos de Rio Negro: Vegetation classification and structure. In: S. Adisoemarto and E.F., Brünig, *Transactions of the Second International MAB–IUFRO Workshop on Tropical Rainforest Ecosystem Research*. Chair of World Forestry, Hamburg–Reinbek, Spec. Rep., No. 2, pp. 67–100.

Bullock, J.A., 1973. *Terrestrial Productivity of Lowland Rainforest, the Pasoh Project*. Malay. Comm I.B.P., Kuala Lumpur 10 pp. (stencilled).

Dansereau, P., 1951. Description and recording of vegetation upon a structural basis. *Ecology*, 32: 172–229.

Davis, T.A.W. and Richards, P.W., 1933. The vegetation of Morabelli Creek, British Guiana. An ecological study of a limited area of tropical rain forest. I. *J. Ecol.*, 21: 350–384.

Dawkins, H.C., 1958. *The Management of Natural Tropical High Forest With Special Reference to Uganda*. Imperial Forestry Institute, Oxford, Inst. Pap., No. 34, 155 pp.

Dawkins, H.C., 1959. The volume increment of natural tropical high-forest and limitations on its improvement. *Emp. For. Rev.*, 38(96): 175–180.

Dawkins, H.C., 1963. *The Productivity of Tropical High Forest Trees and Their Reaction to Controllable Environment*. Thesis, University of Oxford, Oxford.

Fittkau, E.J., 1973. Artenmannigfaltigkeit amazonischer Lebensräume aus ökologischer Sicht. *Amazoniana*, 4(3): 321–340.

Francis, E.C., 1966. Crowns, boles and timber volumes from aerial photographs and field surveys. *Commonw. For. Rev.*, 45: 32–66.

Gates, D.M., 1965. Energy, plants and ecology. *Ecology*, 46: 1–13.

Gates, D.M., 1968. Energy exchange and ecology. *Bioscience*, 18: 90–95.

Gates, D.M. and Johnson, H., 1979. The role of pubescence on the light climate of tree leaves. In: H. Mayer, G. Gietl and G. Enders (Editors), *Universitätsschriften Fakultät für Physik, Meteorologisches Institut. Wiss. Mitt. München*, No. 35: 11–25.

Hallé, F., Oldeman, R.A.A. and Tomlinson, P.B., 1978. *Tropical Trees and Forests. An Architectural Analysis*. Springer-Verlag, Berlin, 441 pp.

Holdridge, L.R., 1970. A system for representing structure in tropical forest associations. In: H.T. Odum and R.F. Pigeon (Editors), *A Tropical Rainforest. A Study of Irradiation and Ecology at El Verde, Puerto Rico*. US Atomic Energy Commission, Washington, D.C., pp. B147–B150.

Hopkins, B., 1963. Biological productivity in Nigeria. *Sci. Assoc. Nigeria Proc.*, 6: 20–28.

Horn, H.S., 1971. *Adaptive Geometry of Trees*. Princeton University Press, Princeton, N.J., 144 pp.

Hozumi, K., Yoda, K. and Kira, T. 1969. Production ecology of tropical rain forest in southeastern Cambodia. I. Plant biomass (with Kokawa, S.). II. Photosynthetic production in an evergreen seasonal forest. *Nature Life S.E. Asia*, 6: 1–5; 57–81.

Jordan, C.F. and Uhl, C., 1978. *Biomass of "Tierra Firme" Forest of the Amazon Basin Calculated by a Refined Allometric Relationship. Annual Report, Nutrient + Dynamics of a Tropical Rainforest Ecosystem and Changes in the Nutrient Cycle Due to Cutting and Burning*. Institute of Ecology, University of Georgia, Athens, Ga., 35 pp.

Karschon, R. and Pinchas, L., 1969. Leaf temperatures in ecotypes of *Eucalyptus camadulensis* Dehn. *Beih. Z. Schw. Forstver.*, 46: 261–269.

Kira, T., 1969. Primary productivity of tropical rainforest. *Malay. For.*, 32(4): 375–384.

Kira, T. and Shidei, T., 1967. Primary production and turnover of matter in different forest ecosystems of the western Pacific. *Jap. J. Ecol.*, 17(2): 70–87.

Klinge, H., 1973. Struktur und Artenreichtum des Zentralamazonischen Regenwaldes. *Amazoniana*, 4(3): 283–292.

Klinge, H., 1977. *Biomass Studies in Amazon Caatinga near San Carlos de Rio Negro, Territory, Venezuela*. Mimeographed Research Report.

Klinge, H., 1979. *Die Phytomasse der hohen und niederen amazonischen Caatinga bei San Carlos de Rio Negro, Territorio Federal Amazonas, Venezuela*. Mimeographed Research Report, 22 pp.

Klinge, H. and Herrera, R. 1978. Biomass studies in Amazon Caatinga forest in southern Venezuela. 1. Standing crop of composite root mass in selected stands. *Trop. Ecol.*, 19: 93–110.

Klinge, H., Rodrigues, W.A., Brunig, E.F. and Fittkau, E.J., 1974. Biomass and structure in a Central Amazonian rainforest. In: E. Medina and F. Golley (Editors), *Trends in Tropical Ecology*. Springer-Verlag, Heidelberg, pp. 115–122.

Lamprecht, H., 1969. Über Strukturanalysen im Tropenwald. *Beih. Z. Schw. Forstverein*, 46: 51–61.

Las Salas, G. de, 1973. Eigenschaften und Dynamik eines Waldstandortes im Grenzbereich des immergrünen tropischen Regenwaldes im mittleren Magdalenental (Kolumbien). *Göettinger Bodenkundl. Ber.*, 27: 1–206.

Loomis, R.S. and Williams, W.A., 1969. Productivity and the morphology of crop stands: Patterns with leaves. In: R.C. Dinauer (Editor), *Physiological Aspects of Crop Yield*. Am. Soc. Agron. Crop Sci., pp. 27–45.

Loomis, R.S., Williams, W.A. and Duncan, W.G., 1967. Community architecture and the productivity of terrestrial plant communities. In: A. San Pietro, F.A. Greer and T.J. Army (Editors), *Harvesting the Sun*, Academic Press, New York, N.Y., pp. 291–308.

McMahon, T.A., 1975. The mechanical design of trees. *Sci. Am.*, 233(1): 92–102.

Martin, P.J., 1977. *The Altitudinal Zonation of Forests Along the West Ridge of Gunang Muln*. Sarawak Forest Department, Kuching, 76 pp.

Medina, E., Sobrado, M. and Herrera, R., 1978. Significance of leaf orientation for leaf temperature in an Amazonian sclerophyll vegetation. *Radiat. Environ. Biophys.*, 1978: 1–10.

Muller, D. and Nielsen, J., 1965. Production brute, pertes par respiration et production nette dans la forêt ombrophile tropicale. *Forstl. Forsögsvaes. Dan.*, 29: 69–160.

Murphy, P.G. and Uhl, C., 1979. Composition, structure and regeneration of a tierra firme forest of the Amazon basin of Venezuela. In: Institute of Ecology, *Annual Report and Budget Request on the Study of Nutrient Dynamics of a Tropical Rainforest Ecosystem and Changes in the Nutrient Cycle due to Cutting and Burning*. University of Georgia, Athens, Ga., 87 pp.

Ogawa, H., Ogino, K., Shidei, T., Rateenawongse, D. and Apasuti, C., 1965. Comparative ecological studies on three main types of forest vegetation in Thailand. I. Structure and floristic composition. *Nature Life S.E. Asia*, 4: 13–48.

Ovington, J.D., 1962. Quantitative ecology and the woodland ecosystem concept. In: J.B. Cragg (Editor), *Advances in Ecological Research. I.* Academic Press, New York, N.Y., pp. 103–192.

Ovington, J.D., 1965. Organic production, turnover and mineral cycling in woodlands. *Biol. Rev.*, 40: 295–336.

Ovington, J.D., Forrest, W.G. and Armstrong, J.S., 1967. Tree biomass estimation. In: H.E. Young and C.D. Monk (Editors), *Symp. Primary Productivity and Mineral Cycling in Natural Ecosystems*. Ecol. Soc. Am. — Am. Assoc. Adv. Sci., 13 Annu. Meet., 1967, New York City. University of Maine Press, Orono, Me., pp. 4–31.

Panzer, K.F., 1971. Erkennung und Bewertung von Stammfäule an tropischen Bäumen. *Mitt. Bundesforschungsanst. Forst-Holzwirtsch.*, No. 82: 233–240.

Poore, M.E.D., 1967. The concept of association in tropical rainforest. *J. Ecol.*, 55(3): 46–47.

Rollet, B., 1974. *L'architecture des forêts denses humides sempervirentes de plaine*. Centre Technique Forestier Tropical, Nogent-sur-Marne, 298 pp.

Roth, I. and Merida de Bifano, T., 1971. Morphological and anatomical studies of leaves of the plants in a Venezuelan cloud forest. I. *Acta Biol. Venez.*, 7(2): 127–155.

Smith, A.P., 1973. Stratification of temperate and tropical forests. *Am. Nat.*, 107(957): 671–683.

Surianegara, I., 1965. The primary productivity of selected forests in Indonesia. *Rimba Indonesia*, 10(4): 246–256.

Takeuchi, M., 1961/62. The structure of the Amazonian vegetation. III. Campina forest in the Rio Negro region. IV. High campina forest in the upper Rio Negro. *J. Fac. Sci., Univ. Tokyo, Sect. III, Bot.*, 8: 27–37; 279–288.

UNESCO, 1978. *Tropical Forest Ecosystema. A State of Knowledge Report Prepared by UNESCO, UNEP, FAO. Nat. Resour. Res.*, 14: 683 pp.

Webb, L.J., 1959. A physiognomic classification of Australian rain forests. *J. Ecol.*, 47: 551–570.

Webb, L.J., 1968. Environmental relationships of the structural types of Australian rainforest vegetation. *Ecology*, 49(2): 296–311.

Whitmore, T.C., 1975. *Tropical Rain Forest of the Far East*. Clarendon Press, Oxford, 281 pp.

Whitmore, T.C., 1977. Modes of variation in the composition of Tropical Lowland Evergreen Forest in the Southeast Asian archipelago and their correlation with the environment. *Mitt. Bundesforschungsanst. Forst-Holzwirtsch.*, 115: 130–152.

Chapter 5

ANIMAL SPECIES DIVERSITY IN TROPICAL FORESTS

FRANÇOIS BOURLIÈRE

INTRODUCTION

When the first naturalist explorers entered the rain forests of the tropics they were impressed at once by the bewildering richness of the fauna. Alfred Russel Wallace (1878), whose first-hand experience of both the South American and Eastern tropics was unmatched at that time, has summarized their amazement in two classic sentences:

"Animal life is, on the whole, far more abundant and varied within the tropics than in any other part of the globe, and a great number of peculiar forms are found there which never extend into temperate regions. Endless eccentricities of form and extreme richness of colour are its most prominent features, and these are manifested in the highest degree in those equatorial lands where the vegetation acquires its greatest beauty and fullest development."

A century later, ecologists are still asking the fundamental questions of the origins and the causes of such an impressive species diversity and are still arguing about the meaning of the endless variety of form, of function and of behavior of tropical rain forest animals. The chapters devoted to this problem in recent ecology textbooks (MacArthur, 1972; Ricklefs, 1973; Pianka, 1974, to quote but a few of them) afford ample proof that these questions are far from settled.

Furthermore, the word diversity is not given the same meaning by those belonging to different ecological schools of thought. For most it means simply the number of species in different communities — that is, the species richness of faunas at different study sites. Others consider that the term diversity should be restricted to measures or indices that include the relative abundance of each species — a kind of measurement difficult, if not impossible, to make in many tropical forest conditions or for a variety of animal groups. However, since species number is certainly an indicator of diversity in the common usage of the word and since it is always correlated with indices taking into account relative abundance, the number of species can be used as a measure of diversity (Whittaker, 1977; Connell, 1978). Species richness and species diversity will therefore be considered as synonymous in the present chapter.

SPECIES RICHNESS: THE FACTS

Species richness of some well-known tropical study sites

The number of species of all the major groups of terrestrial vertebrates so far known to live (or to have recently lived) on ten tropical study sites is given in Table 5.1. Sites 1 to 7 are located in lowland rain forest areas of the eastern and western hemispheres, site 8 is in the Western African "forest–savanna mosaic", and sites 9 and 10 in two different kinds of African savannas. The vertebrate fauna of all these sites may be considered to be adequately studied, more or less continuous collecting having been done in them for a number of years, if not decades. However the totals given are not necessarily final, some animals (e.g. bats, amphisbaenids, canopy lizards and amphibians) being notoriously difficult to capture.

The overall species richness of the lowland tropical forest sites, as compared with that of the two savanna sites, stands out quite clearly. The only exception is that of the two forests located on the island-continents of New Guinea and Madagascar,

TABLE 5.1

Species richness of vertebrates (fish excluded) in ten well-investigated tropical study sites

Study sites	Mean annual rainfall (mm)	Altitude (m)	Surface area (km^2)	Number of mammal species[1]	Number of bird species[2]	Number of reptile species	Number of amphibian species	Sources
Lowland rain forest								
1. Barro Colorado island, Panama	2600	164	14.8	97(46)	366(83)	68	32	1
2. Kartabo, Guyana	2500	10	0.6	73(12)	464(21)	93	37	2
3. Pasoh forest, west Malaysia	1900	75–150	7.8		212(21)	>20	25	3
4. Bukit Langan forest, west Malaysia	c.2300	c.40	6.4	>90(40)	>119	50	23	4
5. Makokou area Gabon	1730	500	2000	119(30)	342(59)	63	38	5
6. Gogol Forest study sites, Papua New Guinea	3800	40–60	10.0	27	162	34	23	6
7. Analamazoatra (Perinet) forest, east Madagascar	1708	900	8.0	29(9)	73	>47	54	7
Forest–savanna mosaic								
8. Lamto, Ivory Coast	1300	110	2000	128(32)	263(64)	63	38	8
Savannas								
9. Serengeti National Park, Tanzania	500–1000	1200–1700	25 000	130(25)	381(79)	61	23	9
10. Fété Olé Sahelian savanna, north Senegal	213	40	100	36(5)	112(36)	13	8	10

[1]Number of bats indicated in parentheses following the total; [2]number of long-range migrants indicated in parentheses following the total.

Sources: 1 = Koford et al. (1977), Willis and Eisenmann (in press), Myers and Rand (1969); 2 = Beebe (1925); 3 = E.R. Wells (pers. comm.); 4 = Lim Boo Liat et al. (1974); 5 = A. Brosset (pers. comm.); 6 = D. Liem (pers. comm.); 7 = Eisenberg and Gould (1970), supplemented by R. Albignac and R.L. Peterson, Benson et al. (1976–77), A. Domergue and R. Blommers-Schlösser (pers. comm.); 8 = Lamotte (1978), supplemented by H. Heim de Balsac, V. Aellen, D. Thomas, F. de Vree and G. Bellier (pers. comm.); 9 = A.R.E. Sinclair, J. Verschuren and D.A. Kreulen (pers. comm.); 10 = Bourlière (1978).

the vertebrate faunas of which are impoverished compared with those of the neighbouring large continental areas. As expected, the species richness of the African forest–savanna mosaic is quite similar to that of the lowland rain forest.

The totals given in Table 5.1 do not necessarily represent the highest number of sympatric species known for the taxonomic group considered. For instance, Pearson et al. (1977) report a grand total of 488 bird species (61 of them being long-range migrants) on their 15 km^2 study area at Limoncocha, northeast Ecuador (altitude: 300 m; mean annual rainfall: 2978 mm). Lloyd et al. (1968) have collected 87 non-riparian species of reptiles (40 lizards and 47 snakes) on 50 km^2 of lowland rain forest at Nanga Tekalit, Sarawak. Crump (1974) has found 81 species of anuran amphibians

on a 3-km^2 study area at Santa Cecilia, northeast Ecuador (altitude: 340 m; mean annual rainfall: 4279 mm). These figures probably represent world records.

Similar quantitative data are much scarcer for invertebrates. A total of 550 species of butterflies have been collected at Ega on the Amazon (Bates, 1863), 400 species at Kartabo, Guyana (Beebe, 1925), c. 392 at Lamto, Ivory Coast (R. Vuattoux, pers. comm., 1979), 350 at Guayabetal, Colombia (Legg, 1978), 269 at Barro Colorado, Panama (Huntington, 1932 and later records), c. 265 at Tafo, Ghana (Legg, 1978), 131 at Elundu, Zaire (Cook, 1978), and c. 125 at Analamazoatra, Madagascar (P. Viette, pers. comm., 1979).

Eighty-five species of termites have been reported from Kartabo (Beebe, 1925), 52 from Pasoh forest, west Malaysia (Abe and Matsumoto, 1979), 43 from Barro Colorado Island, Panama (Snyder and Zetek, 1934), and 43 from 1.5 ha of southern Cameroon rain forest (Collins, in Woods and Sands, 1978). There are 50 species of termites in the forest savanna mosaic of Lamto (Josens in Lamotte, 1978), 39 in the Cap Vert area, Senegal (Roy-Noël, 1974) but 23 only on the 7 ha of southern Guinean savanna of Nigeria studied by Woods (Woods and Sands, 1978), and 23 at Fété Olé, northern Senegal (Lepage in Bourlière, 1978).

Data on ants are much scarcer: 96 species at Kartabo (Beebe, 1925) and 45 at Lamto (Lévieux in Lamotte 1978).

Other insect groups well known for their species richness in lowland rain forests of the tropics are the Buprestidae, Cerambycidae, Lucanidae, Brenthidae, Cetoniidae, Scolytidae and Dynastinae among Coleoptera, the Pseudophyllinae among the Orthoptera, the Fulgoridae and Membracidae among the Homoptera, and the Drosophilidae and mosquitoes among the Diptera.

There are however some exceptions to what is too often considered as general rule. Owen and Owen (1974) have reported that the Ichneumonidae, parasitoid members of the Order Hymenoptera, were apparently more abundant in temperate than in tropical localities — a fact already noticed by Paulian (1949) in his pioneer studies of the lower Ivory Coast forest. Species of the grass-feeding Acridinae among the Orthoptera, and of the dung beetles (Scarabeinae) or the detritivorous Tenebrionidae among the Coleoptera are also far less numerous in tropical forests than in the open savannas.

The levels of animal species diversity in tropical forests

Species diversity can be defined on several spatial scales, from a restricted micro-habitat such as a clump of epiphytes to a whole region. The surface area of each rain forest study site mentioned in Table 5.1 — a few square kilometres at the most — is intermediate between these two extremes and corresponds to what the average human observer would call a landscape. Within such a landscape a number of different communities coexist and are more or less rich in species, homogeneous in composition, and independent from each other.

Hence the necessity to distinguish different levels of animal species diversity (Whittaker, 1960, 1977; MacArthur, 1965).

The richness in species of a sample representing a particular taxonomic community regarded as homogeneous despite its internal pattern is called an *alpha* or *within-habitat diversity*. This is the most widely used diversity measure and Whittaker (1977) contends that "diversity in this sense seems biologically the most appropriate definition of species diversity". The species richness of a landscape which includes more than one kind of community is called a *gamma* or *landscape diversity*. As pointed out by Pielou (1974), alpha and gamma diversities measure the same thing and differ only in that the first applies to homogeneous and the second to heterogeneous collections. The *beta diversity*, *between-habitat diversity* or *species-replacement* is a different concept. It measures the extent of change in species composition among different communities in a landscape, or along an environmental gradient. Ways of measuring these three kinds of diversity are given by Pielou (1974, 1975).

Still other types of diversity have been distinguished, for instance the regional diversity for broader geographic areas like islands or mountain ranges including differing landscapes, or at the other extreme, the point diversity for a well-defined microhabitat within a community. The former is of particular importance for the biogeographer, the latter for those ecologists who deal with communities of small animals with restricted means of dispersal. As rightly pointed out by Harper (1977), each category of organisms defines, so to speak, the scale of its environment, and the bird's-eye view of a tropical rain forest has very little to do with that of a tree frog, a scale insect or an earthworm.

The above-mentioned levels of animal species diversity are particularly important to keep in mind in the case of tropical forests for two reasons.

First, none of the study sites mentioned in Table 5.1 can be considered to be made up of an homogeneous environment, despite the fact that most of these areas were selected for study because they were in extensive stands of "primary" forest, not recently modified by man's presence. For example, most of them include at least a small clearing around the research station. The forest itself is not all mature and includes some second growth. Flooded forest is present in many sites,

together with some riverine vegetation and wetlands. Figures given in Table 5.1 thus obviously
correspond to gamma or landscape diversities.
Examples of alpha or within-habitat diversities for
two of the same study sites are given by Pearson
(1977) who found 254 and 154 species of birds, at
Limoncocha (Ecuador) and M'Passa (Gabon) respectively, on 15-ha sampling areas of uniform
forest habitats.

That adjacent habitats in a same study site can
have very different alpha diversities is particularly
obvious in the case of rather sedentary animals, like
amphibians and many reptiles. Inger and Colwell
(1977) have, for instance, compared species richness for these two classes of vertebrates in three
adjacent areas of broad-leaf evergreen forest, deciduous dipterocarp forest and agricultural land on
the grounds of the Sakaerat Experiment Station,
northeast Thailand (altitude: 200 m; mean annual
rainfall: 1500 mm). The evergreen forest yielded 77
species of amphibians and reptiles, the deciduous
forest 67, and the agricultural lands only 55. There
was however much taxonomic overlap among the
three communities: 15 of the 24 species of frogs, 10
of the 31 species of lizards and 6 of the 47 species of
snakes were collected in all three habitats.

Similar differences, though less obvious, can
even be found between the more mobile bird
communities. During an intensive banding programme carried out near Belem in the Lower
Amazon (altitude: 20 m; mean annual rainfall:
2800 mm), in which mist nets were stretched out
from 0.22 up to 22 m above the ground, Lovejoy
(1974) netted 104 species in his *tierra firme* rain
forest study area, 125 species in a nearby *varzea* or
riverine swamp forest subject to tidally induced
flooding, and 127 species in the *igapo* or permanent
swamp forest.

The second characteristic which makes the distinction between the different kinds of diversity
particularly important in tropical forests is their
extreme structural heterogeneity, within as well as
between habitats. This is mostly due to their
incredible floristic richness and the fact that lowland evergreen forests are seldom dominated by a
single or a few big-tree species. When 2773 tree-
sized individuals with a trunk girth greater than
91 cm, and representing 375 species, are found
packed on a 23-ha quadrat in Malaysia (Poore,
1968), the more likely pattern of species distri-

bution is a broad mixture where every individual
appears to be distributed at random. Besides trees
of all ages and shapes, numerous other plant life-
forms occur in greater abundance in rain forests
than elsewhere. Such is the case of stranglers,
lianas, vines, epiphytes, "mobile creepers"
(Oldeman, 1974a), ant-plants, pitcher-plants, etc.
As mentioned by Longman and Jenik (1974) the
spatial distribution of rhizophere and phyllosphere
is very different in a temperate forest and in a
tropical one. In the latter soil pockets can be found
at any height above the ground, and the same
happens for water which may form small "hanging
aquaria" in suitable tree hollows or in some epiphytes. Such a diversity of microsites is usually
inhabited by specialized communities of small animals. For instance, in the water trapped at the leaf
base of Jamaican epiphytic bromeliads, Laessle
(1961) has found 68 different species of living
organisms, many of them restricted to that very
special habitat. Most tropical forests can therefore
be considered as a patchy mosaic of habitats, a
"harlequin environment" as Harper (1977) put it.

SPECIES RICHNESS: THE MECHANISMS

Is it possible, on the basis of the scanty available
knowledge, to find out an answer to the important
questions: "how can so many animal species coexist
in small areas of tropical rain forest?" and "do they
indeed share the spectrum of available resources?".
Obviously no single answer is likely to be the only
possible one at the present time, especially perhaps
because this "spectrum of resources" needs to be
more carefully defined and quantitatively studied,
at least over a whole annual cycle, and preferably
several. Environmental resources indeed are not
limited to the abundance, availability and nutritional value of food. They also include "shelter"
— that is, the existence of adequate breeding or
nesting sites, not to mention roosts, sleeping trees
and refuge areas. However meagre our present
knowledge of these aspects of tropical biology may
be, the importance of some factors nevertheless
stands out clearly.

Time partitioning

The simplest mechanism which permits two species or groups of species to live sympatrically or

even syntopically without competing for food and shelter with others, is to be active at different times of the day. This is actually what happens in many animal groups. At M'Passa, northeast Gabon, Charles-Dominique (1975) found that competition for the same food categories was avoided between mammals and birds as a result of their different times of activity: 96% of the bird species are diurnal, whereas 70% of the mammal species are nocturnal (Fig. 5.1). A similar situation exists between butterflies and moths, and in many other insect groups.

A more refined analysis of the diurnal activity rhythm of nine sympatric species of squirrels at M'Passa has shown that the four largest species have shortened activity cycles. This behavior tends to reduce competition with the other smaller species of squirrels during the final few hours of daylight (Emmons, 1975). Different species of tropical bats also differ from one another in their pattern of

nightly activity, and this applies to insectivorous species (Brown, 1968) as well as to nectarivorous (Heithaus et al., 1975) and frugivorous species (Bonaccorso, 1975).

Space partitioning

The more or less complex vertical "layering" of tropical forests has many consequences for the animal members of their communities. The microclimate of the canopy is very different from that of the undergrowth (Cachan, 1963), and the morphology as well as the orientation of branches, the density of foliage, and the kinds and abundance of food items are very different in different layers. This will necessarily influence the vertical distribution of the various trophic categories of consumers.

In the mature lowland rain forest of Finca La Selva, northeast Costa Rica, for instance, Slud (1960) noted that the more common canopy birds are the wholly or partly frugivorous toucans, cotingas, parrots and cacique birds, whereas woodpeckers, woodhewers, large trogons, jacamars and puffbirds are mostly found in the middle forest stratum (15–25 m). The understorey is the domain of most hummingbirds, antbirds, manakins, flycatchers and tanagers; tinamous, the great curassow (*Crax rubra*), ground doves and many wrens remain on the forest floor or close to it. Vultures, swifts and a few hawks are commonly seen above the canopy.

To study more thoroughly the influence of forest stratification upon bird distribution, ornithologists have more recently devised objective methods to quantify foliage density, substrate stability and frequency of sun-lit patches, and to correlate these factors with species richness and foraging techniques. Such is the case, for instance, of the MacArthur and Horn (1969) method of leaf density measurement, which enables the observer to estimate the total sum of leaves at different heights above the ground and draw "mean foliage profiles" (Fig. 5.2). Contrary to what happens in temperate latitudes, the expected correlation between foliage complexity and number of bird species has not been found in lowland tropical evergreen forests (Orians, 1969; Lovejoy, 1974; Pearson, 1975).

Some degree of vertical stratification has also been found among arboreal mammals in most types

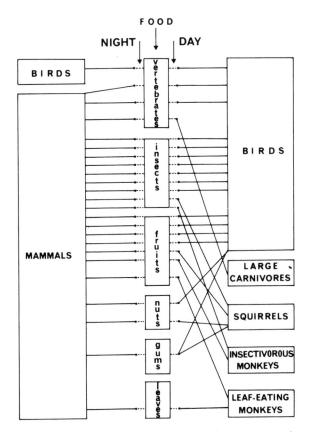

Fig. 5.1. Time partitioning of food resources between sympatric species of mammals and birds in the rain forest of northeast Gabon (after Charles-Dominique, 1975).

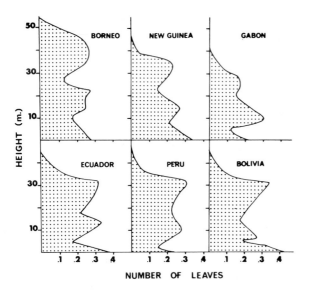

Fig. 5.2. The mean foliage profile in six different rain forests plots, as measured by Pearson (1977).

of tropical forests. In the Krau Game Reserve, western Malaysia, two gibbons (*Hylobates lar* and *H. syndactylus*) and two langurs (*Presbytis obscurus* and *P. melalophus*) spend most of their total daytime in the canopy, though the latter species is less often seen in the upper canopy. Among the two sympatric macaque species, *Macaca fascicularis* is far more arboreal than *M. nemestrina*, despite the fact that both species feed in higher strata than those preferred for travel (Mackinnon and Mackinnon, 1978). Similar preferential uses of definite forest layers have also been found among the sympatric monkeys of M'Passa (Gautier-Hion, 1978) and of the Kibale forest, western Uganda (Struhsaker, 1978). In all cases, however, there were considerable overlaps in feeding heights for all pair combinations of species. The eight sympatric species of squirrels inhabiting the mature forest of M'Passa also have some specific preferences for

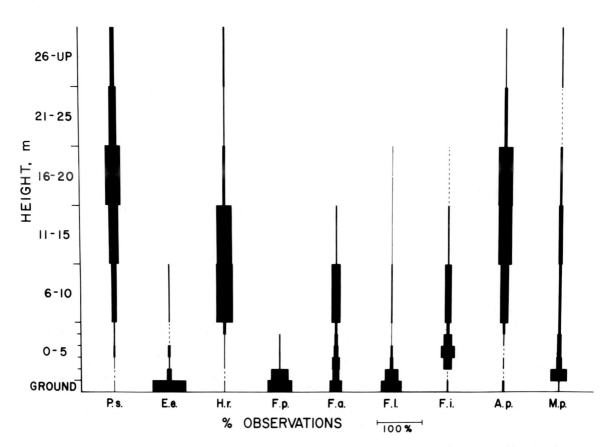

Fig. 5.3. Vertical height distribution of nine species of sympatric rain forest squirrels in northeast Gabon, arranged in order of decreasing body size: *Protoxerus strangeri* (*P.s.*), *Epixerus ebii* (*E.e.*), *Heliosciurus rufobachium* (*H.r.*), *Funisciurus pyrrhopus* (*F.p.*), *F. aneryth-rus* (*F.a.*), *F. lemniscatus* (*F.l.*), *F. isabella* (*F.i.*), *Aethosciurus poensis* (*A.p.*) and *Myosciurus pumilio* (*M.p.*). (After Emmons, 1975.)

feeding and moving at different heights (Emmons, 1975; see Fig. 5.3). Even tropical bats can display preferential "cruising altitudes" when searching for their prey (Bonaccorso, 1979).

Vertical stratification is also well known among tropical forest invertebrates, particularly mosquitoes (Haddow et al., 1947; Mattingly, 1957) and termites (Abe and Matsumoto, 1979; Fig. 5.4).

Part of the species richness of tropical forests can therefore be correlated with the layered structure of the vegetation. This diversity however can also be ascribed in part to the heterogeneity of the forest on the horizontal plane. Constant changes take place within the forest: old trees die and tall ones are killed by lightning strikes, or uprooted by hurricanes and landslides. Natural clearings created by such tree falls are the starting point of new regeneration cycles: pioneer species appear rapidly, seedlings and saplings previously stunted by shade start growing again, and new seeds are deposited by birds and mammals. In this way these small gaps fill up gradually and the animal component of the community changes at the same time. Tree falls may be frequent in some tropical forests. Oldeman (1974b), for example, found that "gaps" due to tree falls may represent up to 90 to 95% of some forested areas in French Guiana. No wonder that tropical forests have been regarded as actual mosaics of regeneration cycles, a large part of the ecosystem being in a state of non-equilibrium. This situation certainly contributes to their high animal species richness (Connell, 1978).

Resource partitioning

Food

It may be appropriate, before discussing the role of food specialization as a factor of animal species diversity, to call to mind some basic facts about food resources. That everything green is not edible, and that every fruit is not palatable is self-evident. Yet, the differences in nutritional value of the various food items for the different taxonomic categories of animals are still too often underrated.

Fig. 5.4. Vertical stratification of termite nests in Pasoh Forest, west Malaysia. Abbreviations: Rhinotermitidae (*RHI*): *Sch* = *Schedorhinotermes*; *Par* = *Parrhinotermes*; *Cop* = *Coptotermes*. Amitermitinae (*AMI*): *Ami* = *Amitermes*; *Mcc* = *Microcerotermes*. Termitinae (*TER*): *Ter* = *Termes*; *Per* = *Pericapritermes*; *Dic* = *Dicuspiditermes*; *Pro* = *Procapritermes*; *Hom* = *Homallotermes*. Macrotermitinae (*MAC*): *Mac* = *Macrotermes*; *Odo* = *Odontotermes*; *Mic* = *Microtermes*. Nasutitermitinae (*NAS*): *Hos* = *Hospitalitermes*; *Lon* = *Longipeditermes*; *Nas* = *Nasutitermes*; *Lac* = *Lacessititermes*; *Bul* = *Bulbitermes*. (After Abe and Matsumoto, 1979.)

Hladik (1977) has shown how dissimilar the protein, sugar and fat contents of fruits eaten by monkeys in Gabon, Panama and Sri Lanka can be. Snow (1976) recorded that the fleshy parts of some Trinidad fruits eaten by specialized fruit-eating birds contain up to 14% of protein and 39% of fat (dry weight), whereas succulent fruits consumed by man do not usually contain more than 6% proteins and a trace of fat. The role of "secondary substances", toxic and repulsive, as well as attractive and stimulating, is still not clear. That dipterocarp fruits are seldom, if ever, eaten by any vertebrate in western Malaysia, despite the fact that most southeast Asian forest trees belong to this plant family is quite astonishing and calls for further investigation (Medway, 1972). Animals may also seek in plant products something else besides nutrients, for instance the carotenoids that they cannot synthesize and which play such an important role in their displays and warning colorations (Rothschild, 1975; Snow, 1976).

Whether or not the abundance of food may be a limiting factor for animal populations in tropical forests is another point which needs clarifying. This is obviously not the case, on a short-term basis, at the times or places where a certain type of food is temporarily superabundant — when large trees bear fruits, or when there is a flush of young leaves. But what happens during the "lean periods" of the yearly cycle, most tropical forest production being more or less seasonal? Much depends obviously on the ability of the consumer species to move (and how far), or to change their food habits for a time. It is, therefore, dangerous to generalize.

That the year-long food production of a forest might be limiting on a long-term basis is suggested however in some instances. That the arboreal primate biomass is much higher in some undisturbed forest areas in Africa (Struhsaker, 1975) or Sri Lanka (Eisenberg et al., 1972) than on Barro Colorado Island, Panama, might well be explained by a lasting competition with the impressive biomass of sloths living on the island (Eisenberg and Thorington, 1973). Pearson (1977) has also raised the possibility of competition between fruit-eating birds and monkeys, or even squirrels to explain some striking inter-continental differences in species richness of these three taxonomic groups in otherwise similar environments.

A number of recent field studies of tropical forest mammals have firmly documented the fact that, at least in some sympatric groups of taxonomically related animals, the available food resources were rather neatly partitioned through specific food preferences and feeding "strategies" (see Chapter 12 for a full discussion of this problem).

In northeast Gabon, for example, the five sympatric species of nocturnal prosimians avoid any competition by partitioning both food and space (Charles-Dominique, 1977). In the canopy, one species is predominantly insectivorous, whereas another is mainly folivorous, and the third eats large amounts of plant gums. In the undergrowth, one prosimian is mostly frugivorous and the other insectivorous. Furthermore, the hunting technique of the lorisines differs from that of galagines. While the slow-moving potto (*Perodicticus potto*) and angwantibo (*Arctocebus calabarensis*) find out their prey by smell and select mainly slow-moving (and even repulsive for us!) insects, the two canopy bush babies (*Galago demidovii* and *Euoticus elegantulus*) specialize on more active insects which they sometimes catch when they take flight, propelling their body forward whilst maintaining a grasp on the branch with their hind feet.

Competition between the four mammalian consumers of social insects living in the same area is avoided in much the same way. The nocturnal and terrestrial aardvark (*Orycteropus afer*), a very efficient burrower, feeds upon termites, destroying most of the nests it visits — a hunting technique which calls for a very large home range. The giant pangolin (*Manis gigantea*), also nocturnal and terrestrial, is not as powerful a digger; it cannot destroy a whole termite colony in a single visit and only takes a part of its population. It therefore can be satisfied with a smaller home range. Out of the two species of arboreal pangolins, the long-tailed one (*M. tetradactyla*) is nocturnal and smaller than the other, and feeds upon arboreal ant nests. As for the last species, the tree pangolin (*M. tricuspis*), it is a nocturnal generalist which feeds upon both termites and ants, and spends part of its activity time at ground level (Pagès, 1970).

The three small ungulates living in the undergrowth of the same Gabonese forest avoid competition in also combining food specialization with time and space partitioning. While the water chevrotain (*Hyemoschus aquaticus*) is semi-aquatic, nocturnal and mostly frugivorous (Dubost, 1978), the

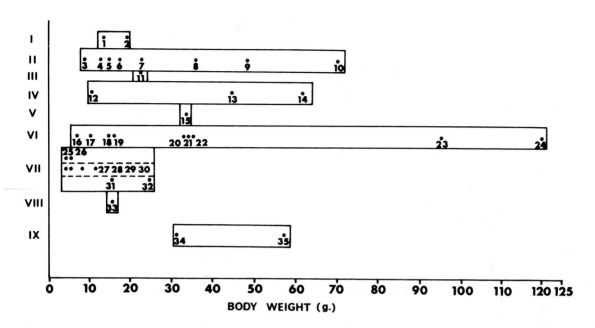

Fig. 5.5. The mean body weights (indicated by numbers *1–35*) of the 35 sympatric species of Barro Colorado bats belonging to different feeding guilds. These are numbered *I–IX*, as follows: *I* = ground storey frugivores: *II* = canopy frugivores; *III* = scavenging frugivores; *IV* = nectar-fruit omnivores; *V* = sanguivores; *VI* = gleaning carnivores; *VII* = slow-flying hawking insectivores; *VIII* = fast-flying hawking insectivores; *IX* = piscivores. Dashed lines separate members of different families that belong to a same feeding guild. (After Bonaccorso, 1975.)

blue duiker (*Cephalophus monticola*) is terrestrial, diurnal and mainly frugivorous, and the Bates' pygmy antelope (*Neotragus batesi*) is terrestrial, active both by day and by night, and totally folivorous (Feer, 1978).

The comprehensive study of the nine sympatric species of squirrels of northeast Gabon made by Emmons (1975) led her to the conclusion that the niches of the seven species co-occuring in dry mature forest are mostly separated by differences in body size. Each species belongs to a different size class, and there is an alternation of body weight class and foraging level such that there are a large, a medium and a small terrestrial species, and a large, a medium, a small and a tiny arboreal species. Body size appears to operate in partitioning nuts and seeds along a spectrum of both size and hardness — a mechanism of very general importance among terrestrial vertebrates. There are also some differences in species preferences and feeding techniques.

Maximal diversity among mammals is found in ground-living rodents and in bats. The communities formed by neotropical bats are by far the most complex assemblages of sympatric mam-

malian species occurring anywhere in the world, 35 to 50 species being commonly found coexisting within an area of a few square kilometres in the forests of tropical America. Thirty-five species of bats were thus found on Barro Colorado in 1973 by Bonaccorso (1979). They were divided by him into nine feeding "guilds", that is groups of species exploiting the same class of environmental resources in a similar manner: canopy frugivores, groundstorey frugivores, scavenging frugivores, nectar–pollen–fruit–insect omnivores, sanguivores, gleaning carnivores, slow-flying hawking insectivores, fast-flying hawking insectivores, and piscivores. Within each of these guilds, which contained from one to nine species, each one tended to specialize in food particles proportional in size to its body weight. When bats belonging to a same guild were very similar in size, they generally fed on different taxa, or similar taxa from different microhabitats, sometimes at different hours (Fig. 5.5).

The situation is very similar in birds. Thus, Pearson (1975) recognized seven feeding guilds in some lowland tropical forests of Amazonia: insect gleaners, salliers, snatchers, peckers and probers, hoverers, fruit-eaters, and army-ant followers. Each of these guilds includes many species of different families spread along a gradient of weight classes.

The more species-rich a taxonomic group, the less known are generally its feeding habits. This explains why we remain so ignorant about food partitioning in most insects and other invertebrate groups. Moreover, the situation is further complicated by the fact that many holometabolous insects have larvae that feed at one trophic level and adults that feed at another. The relative proportion of monophagous versus polyphagous species also varies a great deal in different groups.

Breeding sites

Species richness in tropical forests is enhanced as well by the great diversity of microsites which can be used for breeding purposes. Birds of the lowland rain forest not only build nests of a much more varied architecture than those of more open habitats, but they place them in much more diverse locations. This is true both of New World (Koepcke, 1972) and Old World species (Brosset, 1974).

This diversity in breeding behaviour applies also to the amphibians. Crump (1974) goes so far as to write that the most impressive aspects of their diversity in her Ecuadorian forest site was their "bizarre" modes of reproduction. The 74 species she observed during her field work on a 3-km^2 study area had ten different kinds of egg-laying behaviour: (1) eggs deposited in ditches, puddles, swamps or ponds; (2) eggs laid in tree cavities; (3) eggs deposited in a basin constructed on ground by the male; (4) eggs laid on vegetation above water; (5) eggs deposited in foam nests on or near water; (6) eggs laid on land, the tadpoles being carried to water on the dorsum of an adult; (7) eggs deposited in foam nests and larvae developing within them; (8) eggs laid out of the water, with direct development; (9) eggs carried in depressions on the dorsum of an aquatic female, and developing directly; and (10) eggs attached to the dorsum of a terrestrial female by "gills" and developing directly. The majority of these species were opportunistic feeders. Crump considered that it is the partioning of breeding sites which allows the coexistence of so many anuran species in so small an area, none of the species being distributed uniformly within its available habitats. Furthermore, the maximum

number of species breeding at one place synchronously was ten, temporal partitioning complementing breeding site partitioning.

Mutualism and co-evolution

The bewildering animal richness so characteristic of most tropical forests implies increased interspecific competition, increased specialization for resources use, and narrowing of the ecological niches of the species belonging to the same guild. On the other hand, the strong predation pressure which manifests itself so often in tropical forest ecosystems, can also promote prey diversity by lowering the population densities of the prey species, and thus may allow the local coexistence of species which would otherwise be eliminated by competitive exclusion (see discussion in Ricklefs, 1973; or Pianka, 1974).

The interactions between coexisting species in rich tropical communities are not all of a competitive and antagonistic nature, however. In the humid tropics, where environmental conditions are much more predictable than anywhere else, many species with similar or complementary requirements tend to occur together extensively, and thus to become a consistent part of each other's environment (Ricklefs, 1973). This leads to a kind of interaction which occurs far less frequently in nontropical environments, a strong interdependence or even a close association with mutual benefits. It has long been noticed that the importance of such mutualistic interactions increased from temperate to tropical climates, and that they were most numerous in the warm evergreen forests. For example, there are no obligate ant–plant mutualisms north of 24°N, no nectarivorous or frugivorous bats north of 32 to 33°N, and no euglossine orchid bees north of 24°N (Orians et al., 1974). These mutual plant-–animal associations can lead to strong interdependence and coevolution.

Association and cooperation can also occur between animal species of different, or even similar, taxonomic categories. One of the oldest examples of such inter-specific animal associations is that of the mixed-species flocks of insectivorous birds that often (but not always) follow army ants or driver ant swarms. Their importance has been well documented in tropical rain forests of both the New and the Old World (Moynihan, 1962; Brosset,

1968; Croxall, 1976). Within these flocks, two categories of birds are usually found, regular and occasional members, the latter including some wintering migrants (Willis, 1966). There are at least two major possible advantages in these associations. The most likely is that mixed flocking helps the birds in locating appropriate food items and serves as an efficient way of finding areas of high food density in a patchy environment. The varied responses of insects on being disturbed coupled with the different and fairly specialized feeding techniques of the regular flock members ensure benefit for all and avoid competition. Birds may also gain protection from predators, although that has not yet been supported by actual observations.

Similar inter-specific associations occur in monkeys (Gautier and Gautier-Hion, 1969; Gartlan and Struhsaker, 1972; Gautier-Hion and Gautier, 1974, 1979). Some of them are very transitory, but others can last for weeks or even months. Associated species, however, spend the nights in separate sleeping trees, though very close to each other. These mixed groups can involve species belonging to different genera, but also sympatric members of the same genus having rather similar diets, and being not too different in body size. Here again the main advantage for mixed-groups members appears to be to make easier the location of patchily distributed food sources and the detection of predators. A monospecific group of similar size might well offer the same benefits to its members, but at the cost of a stringent social hierarchy which would imply a greater energy expenditure for its enforcement.

The best examples of elaborate coevolved mutual associations are found among insects. There is no need here to describe once more the *Heliconius–Passiflora–Anguria* system, so masterfully studied by Gilbert (1975). In this case, the mutualism between insect and plant influences the rate, intensity and richness of coevolution between the insect, its preys, its competitors, its predators and its mutualistic associates. Extreme specialization also plays an important role in mimicry relationships, best developed in the humid tropics.

REGIONAL DIFFERENCES IN ANIMAL SPECIES DIVERSITY

Although all tropical forests are richer in animal species than more open tropical habitats, not all of them are rich to the same extent, as shown for instance by the New Guinea and Madagascar study sites of Table 5.1. A number of factors may explain these regional differences.

Regional differences in physiognomy of the trees and dependent synusiae

There are some striking differences between the various forest areas in this respect, even though their foliage diversity may be comparable. This is exemplified by Pearson's (1977) study of six similar-sized plots in uniform lowland rain forest habitats undisturbed by man's activities in Ecuador, Peru, Bolivia, Gabon, Borneo and New Guinea. The number of bird species seen, and their foraging techniques, were very different in the six plots studied. In many ways they could be related to differences in the physiognomy of the forest vegetation. Tree-sized palms and cycads are common in roughly similar numbers on all the plots, except Borneo which has few, and Gabon which has none. Trees are taller in Borneo, and to some extent also in New Guinea, than elsewhere. The number of epiphytes is the greatest on the Ecuador and Borneo plots and the smallest on the Gabon plot. The amount and spatial arrangement of the available micro-habitats (habitat heterogeneity) is consequently not comparable in all these lowland rain forest areas.

Historical factors

Some of the above-mentioned regional differences can also be ascribed to the historical factors responsible for the different spectrum of plant and animal species found in the localities studied. Pearson's New Guinea plot with no primates and only a few relatively uncommon marsupial frugivores such as tree kangaroos (*Dendrolagus* sp.) had the greatest number of fruit-eating bird species. The abundance of frugivorous mammals, primates and squirrels on his Gabon and Borneo plots parallels the low numbers of fruit-eating birds in these areas. The absence of ant-following birds in Borneo and

New Guinea coincides with the lack of insect-raiding ants in diurnal columns in those parts of the World. This emphasized the limitations of taxon-oriented studies of species richness and the need to undertake more ecosystem-oriented long-term studies.

History enters the picture still in another way, through the differences of historical geography between different tropical forests areas, particularly through their different degree of ecological fragmentation during the Pleistocene (Karr, 1976; Pearson, 1977). Modern taxonomic and biogeographic studies have suggested that more "forest refuges" were present in South America during the interpluvials than in Africa (Haffer, 1969; Laurent, 1973; Vanzolini, 1973). and this might be one of the major explanations of the greater species richness of the neotropics in most taxa, as compared to Africa. Moreover, within the limits of a same continent, or even within a same large forest block, species richness can vary a great deal according to the past history of the study area — whether or not it corresponds to one former forest refuge particularly. It is worthy of notice that the greatest species richness for birds (Pearson, 1975, 1977) and anuran amphibians (Crump, 1974) have been found at Limoncocha and Santa Cecilia, Ecuador, study sites located in the postulated Napo refuge, the largest and apparently the most persistent of the South American "forest islands".

Physiographical factors

Physiography by itself, as well as through the changes it imposes upon vegetation, explains also some of the observed regional differences in forest species diversity.

The extent of available land area is an important variable to take into consideration, as well as the distance from the nearest continental mass. During his extensive survey of New Guinea satellite islands Diamond (1973) has shown, for instance, that bird species richness was higher on large islands than on small ones, and higher on islands near a large land mass than on remote islands. Furthermore, on a given small island the existing fauna was in a state of dynamic equilibrium resulting from a delicate balance between immigration and extinction, as postulated by MacArthur and Wilson (1967). On Karkar Island off New Guinea, 62% of the bird species present fifty years previously had disap-

peared at the time of Diamond's visit, having been replaced in the meantime by an approximately equal number of new immigrant species. Whether such a mechanism operates for less easily dispersed animals than birds or insects, for example, non-flying mammals, land reptiles or amphibians, still remains to be established however.

Sometimes the low species diversity of island animal communities can be compensated by a higher population density of the established species. An example of such density compensation is that of the avifauna of Puercos Island in the Pearl Archipelago (Archipiélago de las Perlas), off Panama, studied by MacArthur et al. (1972). The total bird fauna is very poor, twenty species only having been found resident in the partly deciduous tropical forest of the island. But the total bird population density was as high as that of the mainland, if not higher. Three-quarters of the island birds were obviously recent over-water colonists, representing a highly non-random sample of the mainland avifauna. So-called niche shifts between island and mainland birds of the same species included habitat expansions and wider ranges of vertical foraging strata. Density compensation on islands is not an absolute rule however — even among birds. Summed population density on islands may sometimes be comparable to, or less than on the mainland.

Changes of animal species richness with altitude may be explained to a great extent by the associated changes in vegetation and food resources. However, on some isolated mountains, the "island effect" may play an important role, as in paramo-dwelling birds (Vuilleumier, 1970). Within a given taxonomic group the influence of altitude upon species diversity may be different in the various trophic categories. The changes in bird species richness taking place along an Andean elevational gradient (from 500 m to >3500 m) as studied by Terborgh (1977) in the Cordillera Vilcabamba, Peru, illustrate this point. In progressing upwards from lowland rain forest to montane rain forest, cloud forest, and to elfin forest, Terborgh found a gradual trend toward decreasing canopy stature and reduced number of plant strata. On the whole, the number of resident bird species declined with forest stature. However, the rate of change in number with altitude of each of the three major trophic subdivisions of the avifauna was strikingly

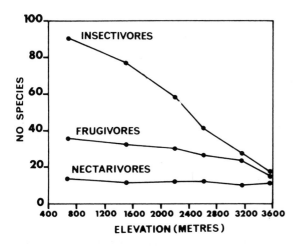

Fig. 5.6. Altitudinal changes in species richness in three guilds of syntopic birds in the Cordillera Vilcabamba, Peru. (After Terborgh, 1977.)

different (Fig. 5.6): the number of insectivores decreased 5.2-fold from the bottom to the top of the gradient, frugivores decreased by a factor of 2.3, and nectarivores showed no change. As Terborgh put it, this is a good demonstration that diversity is a complex community phenomenon, not just a number which can be "explained" with one or another competing hypothesis.

CONCLUSIONS

Obviously much remains to be done to understand better the mechanisms which permit the increased animal species richness in tropical forests compared to temperate ones. The different contributory variables overlie in an intricate mosaic and their relative importance is hard to appreciate. It is still too early to try and rank the respective roles of habitat, food and time partitioning, although Schoener (1974) did make such an attempt. We need more facts, obtained by standardized sampling methods, better techniques of density estimation, and also a much better knowledge of the life-histories and dispersal mechanisms of the organisms concerned. The comparison of species diversities of a large number of different taxonomic categories must be undertaken on the same study plots, located in largely undisturbed communities. The observational method alone may not be capable of answering some of the most pertinent

questions raised. It will have to be complemented by an experimental approach, to study the ways and means through which animal species diversity changes in tropical forests under stress. Opportunity should be taken, for instance, to study the long-term effects of selective logging or tree-poisoning on species richness. The establishment of large, physiognomically uniform, tree plantations of native or exotic species (teak, rubber, eucalypts, tropical pines, etc.) provides another opportunity to study the ways native animals adapt themselves to simplified or "artificial" forest conditions. So far not enough attention has been given to the possibilities offered for ecological research by some large development schemes in the tropics.

REFERENCES

Abe, T. and Matsumoto, T., 1974. Distribution of termites in Pasoh forest reserve in West Malaysia. In: *IBP Synthesis Meeting, Kuala Lumpur, 12–18 August 1974*.

Abe, T. and Matsumoto, T., 1979. Studies on the distribution and ecological role of termites in a lowland rain forest of West Malaysia (3). Distribution and abundance of termites in Pasoh Forest Reserve. *Jap. J. Ecol.*, 29: 337–351.

Bates, H.W., 1863. *The Naturalist on the River Amazons.* Murray, London.

Beebe, W., 1925. Studies of a tropical jungle. One quarter of a square mile of jungle at Kartabo, British Guyana. *Zoologica (N.Y.)*, 6: 1–193.

Benson, C.W., Colebrook-Robjent, J.F.R. and Williams, A., 1976–77. Contribution à l'ornithologie de Madagascar. *Oiseau R.F.O.*, 46: 103–134, 209–242, 367–386; 47: 41–64, 167–190.

Bonaccorso, F.J., 1979. Foraging and reproductive ecology in a Panamanian bat community. *Bull. Fla. State Mus., Biol. Sci.*, 24: 359–408.

Bourlière, F., 1978. La savane sahélienne de Fété Olé, Sénégal. In: M. Lamotte and F. Bourlière (Editors). *Structure et fonctionnement des écosystèmes terrestres.* Masson, Paris, pp. 187–229.

Brosset, A., 1968. La vie sociale des oiseaux dans une forêt équatoriale du Gabon. *Biol. Gabonica*, 5: 29–69.

Brosset, A., 1974. La nidification des oiseaux en forêt gabonaise: architecture, situation des nids et prédation. *Terre Vie*, 28: 579–610.

Brown, J.H., 1968. Activity patterns of some neotropical bats. *J. Mammal.*, 49: 754–757.

Cachan, P., 1963. Signification écologique des variations microclimatiques verticales dans la forêt sempervirente de basse Côte d'Ivoire. *Ann. Fac. Sci. Univ. Dakar*, 8: 89–155.

Charles-Dominique, P., 1975. Nocturnality and diurnality. An ecological interpretation of these two modes of life by an analysis of the higher vertebrate fauna in tropical forest ecosystems. In: W.P. Luckett and F.S. Szalay (Editors),

Phylogeny of Primates. Plenum Press, New York, N.Y., pp. 69–88.

Charles-Dominique, P., 1977. *Ecology and Behavior of Nocturnal Primates, Prosimians of Equatorial West Africa.* Duckworth, London, 277 pp.

Connell, J.H., 1978. Diversity in tropical rain forests and coral reefs. *Science*, 199: 1302–1310.

Cook, L.M., 1978. Zaire butterflies and faunal diversity in the tropics. *Biol. J. Linn. Soc.*, 10: 349–360.

Croxall, J.P., 1976. The composition and behaviour of some mixed-species bird flocks in Sarawak. *Ibis*, 118: 333–346.

Crump, M.L., 1974. Reproductive strategies in a tropical Anuran community. *Univ. Kansas Mus. Nat. Hist., Misc. Publ.*, 61: 1–68.

Diamond, J.M., 1973. Distributional ecology of New Guinea birds. *Science*, 179: 759–769.

Dubost, G., 1978. Un aperçu sur l'écologie du Chevrotain africain *Hyemoschus aquaticus* Ogilby, Artiodactyle Tragulidé. *Mammalia*, 42: 1–62.

Eisenberg, J.F. and Gould, E., 1970. Appendix A. *Smithson. Contrib. Zool.*, 27: 127.

Eisenberg, J.F. and Thorington, R.W., Jr., 1973. A preliminary analysis of a neotropical mammal fauna. *Biotropica*, 5: 150–161.

Eisenberg, J.F., Muckenhirn, N. and Rudran, R., 1972. The relationship between ecology and social structure in primates. *Science*, 179: 863–874.

Emmons, L.H., 1975. *Ecology and Behavior of African Rainforest Squirrels.* Thesis, Cornell University, Ithaca, N.Y., 269 pp.

Feer, F., 1978. *Données écologiques sur le Néotrague de Bates Neotragus batesi du Nord-Est du Gabon.* Thesis, Université de Paris, Paris.

Gartlan, J.S. and Struhsaker, T.T., 1972. Polyspecific associations and niche separation of rain forest anthropoids in Cameroon, West Africa. *J. Zool.*, 168: 221–266.

Gautier, J.P. and Gautier-Hion, A., 1969. Les associations polyspécifiques chez les Cercopithecidae du Gabon. *Terre Vie*, 23: 164–201.

Gautier-Hion, A., 1978. Food niches and coexistence in sympatric primates in Gabon. In: D.J. Chivers and J. Herbert (Editors), *Recent Advances in Primatology, 1. Behaviour*, Academic Press, London, pp. 269–286.

Gautier-Hion, A. and Gautier, J.P., 1974. Les associations polyspécifiques de Cercopithèques du plateau de M'Passa (Gabon). *Folia Primatol.*, 22: 134–177.

Gautier-Hion, A. and Gautier, J.P., 1979. Niche écologique et diversité spécifique chez les Cercopithèques forestiers. *Terre Vie*, 33: 493–507.

Gilbert, L.E., 1975. Ecological consequences of a coevolved mutualism between butterflies and plants. In: L.E. Gilbert and P.H. Raven (Editors), *Coevolution of Animals and Plants.* The University of Texas Press, Austin, Texas, pp. 210–240.

Haddow, A.J., Gillett, J.D. and Highton, R.B., 1947. The mosquitoes of Bwamba County, Uganda. V. The vertical distribution and biting cycle of mosquitoes in rain forest, with further observations on microclimate. *Bull. Entomol. Res.*, 37: 301–330.

Haffer, J., 1969. Speciation in Amazonian forest birds. *Science*, 165: 131–137.

Hallé, F. and Oldeman, R.A.A., 1970. *Essai sur l'architecture et la dynamique de croissance des arbres tropicaux.* Masson, Paris, 178 pp.

Harper, J.L., 1977. *Population Biology of Plants.* Academic Press, New York, N.Y., 892 pp.

Heithaus, E.R., Fleming, T.H. and Opler, P.A., 1975. Foraging patterns and resource utilization in seven species of bats in a seasonal tropical forest. *Ecology*, 56: 841–854.

Hladik, C.M., 1977. *Le régime alimentaire des primates et son adaptation aux ressources du milieu forestier.* Thesis, Université de Paris, Paris, 224 pp.

Huntington, E.I., 1932. A list of the Rhopalocera of Barro Colorado Island, Canal Zone, Panama. *Bull. Am. Mus. Nat. Hist.*, 63: 191–230.

Inger, R.F. and Colwell, R.K., 1977. Organization of contiguous communities of amphibians and reptiles in Thailand. *Ecol. Monogr.*, 47: 229–253.

Karr, J.R., 1976. Within- and between-habitat avian diversity in African and Neotropical lowland habitats. *Ecol. Monogr.*, 46: 457–481.

Koepcke, M., 1972. Über der Resistenzformen der Vogelnester in einem begrenzten Gebiet des tropischen Regenwaldes in Peru. *J. Ornithol.*, 113: 138–160.

Koford, C., Smythe, N., Hayden, J. and Bonaccorso, F.J., 1977. *Checklist of Mammals of Barro Colorado Island* (mimeographed).

Laessle, A.M., 1961. A micro-limnological study of Jamaican bromeliads. *Ecology*, 42: 499–517.

Lamotte, M., 1978. La savane préforestière de Lamto, Côte d'Ivoire. In: M. Lamotte and F. Bourlière (Editors), *Structure et fonctionnement des écosystèmes terrestres.* Masson, Paris, pp. 231–311.

Laurent, R.F., 1973. A parallel survey of equatorial amphibians and reptiles in Africa and South America. In: B.J. Meggers et al. (Editors), *Tropical Forest Ecosystems in Africa and South America: A Comparative Review.* Smithsonian Press, Washington, D.C., pp. 259–266.

Legg, G., 1978. A note on the diversity of world Lepidoptera (Rhopalocera). *Biol. J. Linn. Soc.*, 10: 343–347.

Lim Boo Liat, Muul, I. and Chai Kah Sin, 1974. *Zoonotic Studies of Small Animals in the Canopy Transect at Bukit Langan Forest Reserve, Selangor, Malaysia.* Paper presented at the IBP Synthesis Meeting, Kuala Lumpur, 12th–18th August 1974.

Lloyd, M., Inger, R.F. and King, F.W., 1968. On the diversity of reptile and amphibian species in a Bornean rain forest. *Am. Nat.*, 102: 497–515.

Longman, K.A. and Jenik, J., 1974. *Tropical Forest and Its Environment.* Longman, London, 205 pp.

Lovejoy, T.E., 1974. Bird diversity and abundance in Amazon forest communities. *Living Bird*, 13: 127–191.

MacArthur, R.H., 1965. Patterns of species diversity. *Biol. Rev.*, 40: 510–533.

MacArthur, R.H., 1972. *Geographical Ecology. Patterns in the Distribution of Species.* Harper and Row, New York, N.Y., 269 pp.

MacArthur, R.H. and Horn, H.S., 1969. Foliage profile by vertical measurements. *Ecology*, 50: 802–804.

MacArthur, R.H. and Wilson, E.O., 1967. *The Theory of Island Biogeography.* Princeton University Press, Princeton, N.J., 203 pp.

MacArthur, R.H., Diamond, J.M. and Karr, J.R., 1972. Density compensation in island faunas. *Ecology*, 53: 330–342.

Mackinnon, J.R. and Mackinnon, K.S., 1978. Comparative feeding ecology of six sympatric primates in West Malaysia. In: D.J. Chivers and J. Herbert (Editors), *Recent Advances in Primatology, 1. Behaviour.* Academic Press, London, pp. 305–321.

Mattingly, P.F., 1957. Studies on West African mosquitoes. I. The seasonal distribution, biting cycle and vertical distribution of four of the principal species. *Bull. Entomol. Res.*, 47: 149–168.

Medway, Lord, 1972. Phenology of a tropical rain forest in Malaya. *Biol. J. Linn. Soc.*, 4: 117–146.

Medway, Lord and Wells, D.R., 1971. Diversity and density of birds and mammals at Kuala Lompat, Pahang. *Malay. Nat. J.*, 24: 238–247.

Moynihan, M., 1962. The organisation and probable evolution of some mixed species flocks of neotropical birds. *Smithson. Misc. Coll.*, 143: 1–140.

Myers, C.W. and Rand, A.S., 1969. Checklist of amphibians and reptiles of Barro Colorado Island, Panama, with comments on faunal change and sampling. *Smithson. Contrib. Zool.*, 10: 1–11.

Oldeman, R.A.A., 1974a. L'architecture de la forêt guyanaise. *Mém. ORSTOM*, No. 73: 204 pp.

Oldeman, R.A.A., 1974b. Ecotopes des arbres et gradients écologiques verticaux en forêt guyanaise. *Terre Vie*, 28: 487–520.

Orians, G.H., 1969. The number of bird species in some tropical forests. *Ecology*, 50: 783–801.

Orians, G., et al., 1974. Tropical population ecology. In: G. Farnworth and F.B. Golley (Editors), *Fragile Ecosystems. Evaluation of Research and Applications in the Neotropics.* Springer-Verlag, Heidelberg, pp. 5–65.

Owen, D.F. and Owen, J., 1974. Species diversity in temperate and tropical Ichneumonidae. *Nature*, 249: 583–584.

Pagès, E., 1970. Sur l'écologie et les adaptations de l'Oryctérope et des pangolins sympatriques du Gabon. *Biol. Gabonica*, 6: 27–92.

Paulian, R., 1949. *Un naturaliste en Côte d'Ivoire.* Stock, Paris, 217 pp.

Pearson, D.L., 1975. The relation of foliage complexity to ecological diversity of three Amazonian bird communities. *Condor*, 77: 453–466.

Pearson, D.L., 1977. A pantropical comparison of bird community structure on six lowland forest sites. *Condor*, 79: 232–244.

Pearson, D.L., Tallman, D. and Tallman, E., 1977. *The Birds of Limoncocha, Napo Province, Ecuador.* Instituto Linguistico de Verano, Quito, 15 pp.

Pianka, E.R., 1974. *Evolutionary Ecology.* Harper and Row, New York, N.Y., 356 pp.

Pielou, E.C., 1974. *Population and Community Ecology: Principles and Methods.* Breach, New York, N.Y., 424 pp.

Pielou, E.C., 1975. *Ecological Diversity.* Wiley-Interscience, New York, N.Y., 162 pp.

Poore, M.E.D., 1968. Studies in Malaysian rain forest. I. The forest on the Triassic sediments in Jengka Forest Reserve. *J. Ecol.*, 56: 143–196.

Ricklefs, R.E., 1973. *Ecology.* London, Nelson, 861 pp.

Rothschild, M., 1975. Remarks on carotenoids in the evolution of signals. In: L.E. Gilbert and P.H. Raven (Editors), *Coevolution of Animals and Plants.* University of Texas Press, Austin, Texas, pp. 20–50.

Roy-Noël, J., 1974. Recherches sur l'écologie des Isoptères de la presqu'île du Cap Vert, Sénégal. *Bull. Inst. Fondam. Afr. Noire, Ser. A*, 36: 291–609.

Schoener, T.W., 1974. Resource partitioning in ecological communities. *Science*, 185: 27–39.

Slud, P., 1960. The birds of Finca "La Selva", Costa Rica; A tropical wet forest locality. *Bull. Am. Mus. Nat. Hist.*, 121: 49–148.

Snow, D., 1976. *The Web of Adaptations: Bird Studies in the American Tropics.* Quadrangle. New York, N.Y., 176 pp.

Snyder, T.E. and Zetek, J., 1934. The termite fauna of the Canal Zone and its economic significance. In: C.A. Kofoid (Editor), *Termites and Termite Control.* University of California Press, Stanford, Calif., pp. 186–203.

Struhsaker, T.T., 1975. *The Red Colobus Monkey.* Chicago University Press, Chicago, Ill., 311 pp.

Struhsaker, T.T., 1978. Food habits of five monkey species in the Kibale forest, Uganda. In: D.J. Chivers and J. Herbert (Editors), *Recent Advances in Primatology, 1. Behaviour.* Academic Press, London, pp. 225–248.

Terborgh, J., 1977. Bird species diversity on an Andean elevational gradient. *Ecology*, 58: 1007–1019.

Thiollay, J.M., 1970. Recherches écologiques dans la savane de Lamto (Côte d'Ivoire): le peuplement avien. Essai d'étude quantitative. *Terre Vie*, 24: 108–143.

Vanzolini, P.E., 1973. Paleoclimate, relief, and species multiplication in equatorial forests. In: B.J. Meggers et al. (Editors), *Tropical Forest Ecosystems in Africa and South America: A Comparative Review.* Smithsonian Press, Washington, D.C., pp. 255–258.

Vuilleumier, F., 1970. Insular biogeography in continental regions. The northern Andes of South America. *Am. Nat.*, 104: 373–388.

Wallace, A.R., 1878. *Tropical Nature and Other Essays.* Macmillan, London, 356 pp.

Whittaker, R.H., 1960. Vegetation of the Siskiyou Mountains, Oregon and California. *Ecol. Monogr.*, 30: 279–338.

Whittaker, R.H., 1972. Evolution and measurement of species diversity. *Taxon*, 21: 213–251.

Whittaker, R.H., 1977. Evolution of species diversity in land communities. In: M.K. Hecht, W.C. Steere and B. Wallace (Editors), *Evolutionary Biology*, 10, Plenum Press, New York, N.Y., pp. 1–67.

Willis, E.O., 1966. The role of migrant birds at swarms of army ants. *Living Bird*, 5: 187–231.

Willis, E.O. and Eisenmann, E., in press. *A Revised List of Birds of Barro Colorado Island, Panama.*

Woods, T.G. and Sands, W.A., 1978. The role of termites in ecosystems. In: M.V. Brian (Editor), *Production Ecology of Ants and Termites.* Cambridge University Press, Cambridge, pp. 245–292.

Chapter 6

THE ABUNDANCE AND BIOMASS OF FOREST ANIMALS

DENIS F. OWEN

The diversity of animal species has been discussed in Chapter 5; here the object will be to discuss the quantity of faunal biomass in tropical forests and its distribution among the various elements of the fauna.

METHODS AND RESULTS

Rain forest is not the easiest of ecosystems from which to obtain estimates of total animal biomass: the structural complexity and diversity of species tends to discourage rather than encourage undertaking the notoriously tedious task of estimating biomass. Nevertheless, in the report on the El Verde forest in Puerto Rico (Odum and Pigeon, 1970) various investigators make a brave attempt to estimate biomass, the results of which are summarized in the last chapter of the report (Odum, 1970). To find out how abundant animals are in a given area requires the use of various techniques and different sorts of expertise. Odum et al. (1970) explain how biomass was determined at El Verde:

Larger, visible animals such as snails, frogs, and resting insects were picked from trunks and limbs of trees from around a specially constructed "tree house" thus ensuring that canopy species were included as well as those nearer the ground. Trees were felled and the leaves and branches searched, although of course individuals able to fly after being disturbed must have escaped. Animals associated with bromeliads, palm crowns, lianas, and tree ferns were counted separately. Estimates of numbers of night-flying insects and bats were obtained by counting individuals picked up by flash spotlight at regular (timed) intervals. Birds were counted in the early morning when they make most

noise and are thus easier to locate, and representative species were collected and weighed. Traps set for small mammals produced only *Mus musculus* and *Rattus rattus*, both introduced species and strange inhabitants of rain forest, but it must be remembered that Puerto Rico is an island with a relatively poor fauna, and like many islands has experienced more than its share of introductions and extinctions brought about by man. Ground-dwelling and litter animals were removed from quadrats to a depth of 10 cm below the soil surface, and small soil animals were extracted by using standard apparatus.

The results indicate a total biomass of 11.8 g m^{-2} dry weight, a remarkably low figure compared to 42 405 g m^{-2} of living and dead plant material. The most important animals are earthworms with 4.2 g m^{-2} dry weight. This estimate of total biomass may be compared to 21.0 g m^{-2} for Amazonian *tierra firme* forest (Fittkau and Klinge, 1973), 7.68 g m^{-2} for *miombo* woodland (Malaisse et al., 1972), and 6.4 g m^{-2} for a red mangrove swamp (Golley et al., 1962).

Even though the various estimates are similar, there is little doubt that the El Verde rain forest figure is an underestimate. The list of 1200 species of insects collected at El Verde from 1963 to 1967 (Drewry, 1970) is surely only a small fraction of the total species in the area: many of the families listed contain fewer species than occur in an English suburban garden. It is the flying insects in particular that have been missed; it is possible to sample flying insects quantitatively, but the appropriate techniques were not used at El Verde. Other groups that must have been underestimated are animals, chiefly insects, that feed internally in leaves, stems, roots, and wood. But even if the biomass at El

Verde is ten times the published estimate it is still very low compared to that of the vegetation. And this is the general observation of tropical forest faunas — high diversity and low densities and biomass.

Many zoologists and naturalists have independently arrived at this conclusion. For example, Elton (1973) reported on brief visits to forests in Brazil and to Barro Colorado Island, Panama, during which he checked for himself the low densities and high diversities of invertebrates. Using a variety of simple techniques, including sweep-netting, tree-trunk brushing, and suction trapping, he obtained semi-quantitative information which, he claimed, supported the view that invertebrates occur at low densities, and also that most of them are small. For the "field layer" (from near ground level to about 2 m) he suggested that a figure of 1 to $2\,m^{-3}$ is a reasonable estimate of abundance. He noted that there are exceptions, chiefly certain species of ants, Diptera, and isopods, which may be locally very abundant. Although generally scarce he found predators (especially spiders) remarkably frequent compared to the densities of their presumed prey, and was astonished to find widespread leaf damage but little or no evidence of leaf-eaters such as lepidopteran caterpillars.

Elton goes on to review evidence obtained by other observers and collectors, starting with Bates (1863) who spent eleven years collecting and recording in the Amazons, and concluding with a discussion of the results of sweep sampling in forest in Costa Rica (Janzen and Schoener, 1968). It would be easy to dismiss Elton's observations as being based on inadequate sampling for too short a time, and on unfamiliarity with the forest fauna; however, it is not the information collected but the impressions formed and the questions asked and answered that are important in his paper. In particular he proposes that the low population density of most forest species is an evolutionary adaptation to intense predation and/or that the commoner species are nocturnal. He draws attention to the extraordinary adaptations for defense (camouflage, mimicry, keeping still, etc.), noting that there is no point in an animal looking more like a twig than one twig looks like another, and remarks that offensive adaptations are equally spectacular "... we [must] imagine a great many defence codes made and then the codes broken, until those lines of evolutionary adaptation simply cannot be developed any further. There would seem to be three possible further directions to take: (a) extinction; (b) change to nocturnal habits ...; (c) to live at very low population density." Which means that if an animal has to be diurnal then it must also occur at low density.

Hairston et al. (1960) picked out the primary consumers (animals feeding on living plant material) as being unusual, noting that only exceptionally do their numbers (as a trophic level) anywhere near match what might be expected from the biomass of their potential food. They concluded that in terrestrial ecosystems (but not in the ocean) primary consumers are predator-limited, in contrast to decomposers and secondary to nth order consumers which are food-limited. Hairston et al. (1960) generalized about all terrestrial ecosystems; Elton (1973) is concerned only with rain forest where the arrangement, if indeed it exists, seems best developed.

However, the matter may be more complex than Elton imagined. For example, Golley (1977), in a short-term study of soil, litter, and understorey insects in the oligotrophic Amazon forest at San Carlos de Rio Negro, Venezuela, suggests that litter faunas may not be reduced in abundance in tropical compared to temperate sites while the soil and understorey insects do illustrate the general pattern. Also Fleming (1975), studying small mammals in American temperate and tropical forests, and Karr (1975) measuring bird biomass in Illinois, U.S.A., Liberia and Panama found low or no clear differences between populations and standing crop biomass of animals on temperate versus tropical sites. Finally Wolda (1978), in a detailed study of insect abundance, concluded that tropical forest insects also do not fluctuate more or less in abundance from year to year than temperate species. Rather, fluctuation in insect abundance is a function of climatic stability; populations fluctuate widely where climate fluctuates widely regardless of latitude. Quite clearly the general patterns of abundance depend upon the habitat, and the group of organisms under study.

A further example, which illustrates the problems of sampling and the temporal as well as spatial dynamics of animals is shown by the Ichneumonidae. The Ichneumonidae are parasitic on the larvae and pupae of insects with a complex metamorphosis, especially Lepidoptera, Diptera, Neuroptera, Coleoptera, and Symphyta. There are more ichneumonids than all the species of vertebrates put together and in few groups of animals can there remain so many undescribed species: a random sample from any rain forest area in the world would produce more undescribed than described species.

Large samples of ichneumonids were obtained from four sites, two tropical and two temperate, by using Malaise traps, the most effective method of sampling a flying insect community (Townes, 1972a). All four sites are in areas much disturbed and altered by human activities: the two tropical sites are gardens within the forest region and can roughly be classified as extended forest edge enriched with introduced plants; one of the temperate sites (Leicester, England) is also an enriched garden, whereas the other is in agricultural land along a small stream. The four samples are analyzed in Table 6.1. The differences in sample size do not necessarily reflect differences in abundance: much depends on habitat and the efficiency of the traps in different situations. The number of species recorded in each of the four samples is astonishing, and as shown in Table 6.1 the relative rarity of most of them is emphasized by the number taken once only and by the absence of really common species. The information theory index of diversity, H, enables comparison between the four samples. The values of H for Freetown and Leicester are not significantly different but all other paired samples are different from each other at the 1% level. The value of H is significantly smaller for the Kampala than for the Leicester and the Skåne samples and is smaller for Freetown than for Skåne. Thus, there is no evidence for the expected greater diversity in the two tropical localities; indeed all four samples

might be regarded as typical of the tropics. A large (but, especially for the tropical species, unknown) proportion of the species parasitize Lepidoptera caterpillars. There is no doubt about the greater diversity of Lepidoptera in the tropics: there are more than 300 species of butterflies in the Freetown area and only 21 at Leicester. Butterflies comprise only a fraction of the total species of Lepidoptera but probably reflect the situation for the remainder.

The explanation of the high diversities and apparently low population densities in both tropical and temperate ichneumonids is probably associated with the fact that each species tends to be niche-specific rather than host-specific (Townes, 1972b). In the parasite–host relationships discussed here there may be no more niches in the tropics than in the temperate region. To what extent might this apply to other groups of animals?

The parasitic larvae of ichneumonids are dependent mainly on primary consumers. How can the low biomass of rain forest primary consumers (Odum, 1970) be explained? As already mentioned, Elton thinks that predators control numbers well below the level set by the availability of food and/or most of the consumers are nocturnal. However, there is another explanation which has the advantage of making fewer assumptions: the consumers are present, both by day and by night, but are difficult to find. Let me elaborate with an example.

The Freetown Peninsula in Sierra Leone occupies an area of 456 km². It is mountainous and forested, although much of the forest has been cleared on level ground and on slopes that are not too steep for cultivation. The climate is seasonal with a dry season from about November to March, followed by severe thunderstorms in April and May, then a very wet rainy season from June to September which ends with more thunderstorms.

TABLE 6.1

Two tropical and two temperate samples of Ichneumonidae compared (from Owen and Owen, 1974)

	Sample size	Species	Diversity index, H, and s.e.	Species taken once	Commonest species (%)
Kampala, Uganda	2268	293	4.524 ± 0.032	116	10.1
Freetown, Sierra Leone	1979	319	4.934 ± 0.029	117	4.9
Leicester, England	2495	326	4.937 ± 0.024	122	3.2
Skåne, Sweden	10 994	758	5.481 ± 0.014	203	5.5

Virtually all forms of plant and animal life in the forest show seasonal patterns of abundance which in one way or another are associated with rainfall.

During four years (1966–1970) and three visits (in 1972) I observed and collected butterflies in the forest and formed conclusions, some of them admittedly tentative, that have a bearing on the question of low population density yet are evidence of the normal level of forest leaf consumption. I recorded 319 species of butterflies, many of them infrequently, but a substantial number abundant for at least short periods of the year. The caterpillars of all but a few (which are predators of Homoptera) are primary consumers; most feed on leaves, but there are also flower- and seed-feeders. As in all rain forests there is conspicuous stratification: entire genera are restricted to the ground layer where the adults feed from fallen fruit, others occur from 3 to 5 m and are chiefly nectar-feeders, and some occur in the canopy where they are presumed to be nectar-feeders. I made no attempt to estimate abundance (although relative abundance was an easy matter for some genera), which in any case would be extremely difficult for such a mobile and patchily distributed group of insects, but the common observation of twenty or more individuals of perhaps six species of large butterflies feeding from fallen fruit in an area of no more than 1 m^2 is suggestive of considerable biomass. Moreover the presence of 319 species of butterflies probably means that there are about fifty times as many moths (some known to be very large), mostly nocturnal, and almost all with leaf-feeding caterpillars.

In this forest (as in others) it is easy to form the impression that this or that species is rare but such an impression would in many instances be wrong. Even though many species may be found at all times of the year, there is a marked tendency for each to reach a short and sharp seasonal peak, the timing of which differs between species and to some extent between years. *Acraea quirina* occurs relatively infrequently throughout the year but in May or June (depending on the timing of the onset of the rains) the gregarious caterpillars swarm on the new leaves of two species of understorey shrubs, *Rinorea elliotii* and *R. subintegrifolia*. Within about two weeks virtually all new leaves are eaten or holed but the caterpillars quickly pupate and the forest is soon flooded with adult butterflies. What is inter-

esting is that for ten or eleven months of the year caterpillars cannot be found and butterflies are scarce, but the holed leaves of *Rinorea* shrubs remain as evidence of what has happened. Many similar examples could be cited. In each the holing of the leaves takes place very quickly and for most of the year no caterpillars are to be found.

Equally striking are the rarer butterflies. In four years I found only one individual of *Pseudaletis leonis*, a conspicuous black and white mimetic lycaenid. Then in October and November 1972, I collected 12 from an area of a few square meters at the edge of the secondary forest. Another large mimetic lycaenid, *Mimacraea neurata*, is hardly ever seen, yet in March 1972 I watched an individual on five consecutive days as it circled round and round a tree at a height of 3 to 6 m. I collected and killed the butterfly on 8 March and by 13 March another appeared at the same place and behaved in the same way. This too was collected and was replaced by a third on 17 March which was also collected to be immediately replaced by a fourth. Despite careful searching no other individuals were seen in the vicinity. The lesson here is that removal results in almost immediate replacement, but where did the replacements come from? Evidently conspicuous animals like butterflies are easily overlooked.

These observations suggest that rain forest butterflies are strongly "pulsed" and that each species is abundant as a caterpillar or adult for very short periods. Assuming that moths and grasshoppers are similarly pulsed, the presence of leaf damage in the apparent absence of consumers is readily explained especially as many trees retain their leaves for twelve months or more.

These various observations illustrate some of the key problems in estimating the abundance and biomass of forest animals. First, the source of the forest food webs, the green leaves, are located high in the canopy — in contrast, for example, with a tropical grassland and savannah, even though the amount of green food is roughly similar. This means, of course, that the fauna consuming green leaves must be climbers, small in body size and weight, and/or capable of flight, as well as having the adaptations needed for a diet of vegetation which may contain a variety of chemicals which are toxic. Sutton and Hudson's (1980) recent paper illustrates this vertical distribution of flying insects in a rain forest in Zaïre (Fig. 6.1). There is a marked concentration of insects in and above the canopy, over a wide range of orders. As the leaves fall to the forest floor they then form a more accessible resource to soil and litter organisms. And as a consequence, the soil fauna biomass in tropical forests may be as much as four times the herbivore biomass (Table 6.2).

The second problem concerns the grouping of the fauna into categories such as herbivores, predators, saprovores and so on. These categories are meant to subdivide the very diverse forest fauna into manageable units, which have functional significance. However, the actual operation consists of identification and sampling of species populations, each of which has special and characteristic behavior which control their susceptibility and access to sampling, and then the grouping of the populations into units which have some paramount

feature in common. The theories which have been developed to explain why these collections behave in certain ways and why they are diverse or abundant often ignore these operational problems. All forest animals cannot be treated as one unit, nor can herbivores or predators. The trophic groupings of herbivore, carnivore and saprovore are useful when the forest energy or mineral dynamics are analyzed. However, some other system might be more realistic. For example, Gilbert (1980) has suggested that tropical forest animals can be organized into four functional groups. The first is made up of organisms in food webs or food chains which have co-evolved to form relatively distinct and separate units. The second group consists of those species that link up a variety of webs. These linking animals collect food from many different species. The third grouping is named keystone mutualists by Gilbert. Keystone mutualists are species which provide food, shelter, habitat and resources for many other species. Certain large trees may be keystone mutualists in the forest. The final grouping consists of the ants which form a mosaic in horizontal and vertical space (Leston, 1978). Ants are both antagonistic to and supportive of other organisms. The survival of a tree seedling, for example, may depend upon its development in a cell of the ant mosaic where the ants use and protect that tree species. While these groupings have special advantages for an ecological study, the zoologist most commonly focuses on a specific group of animals and restricts this study taxonomically. This approach capitalizes on our knowledge of the life history and habits of the faunal element and results in accurate information. However, seldom are enough zoologists assembled at one site for a sufficiently long period to provide knowledge of the entire fauna. Rather, the forest ecologist is left with the problem of combining studies from many forests into a general description for a given site, as for example in Golley et al. (1973).

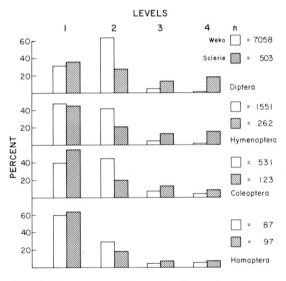

Fig. 6.1. The percentage of the catch of insects in sticky traps at two sites in Zaïre at four canopy levels: 1 is above the canopy, 2 is at the canopy, 3 is intermediate and 4 is at ground level. Data redrawn from Sutton and Hudson (1980).

TABLE 6.2

Biomass (kg ha^{-1}) of the fauna of several tropical forests

	Soil fauna	Herbivores	Carnivores	Authors
Amazon lowland rain forest	165	30	15	Fittkau and Klinge (1973)
Lower montane rain forest	80	25	10	Odum et al. (1970)
Red mangrove forest	52	8	4	Golley et al. (1962)

The third problem concerns the size of the fauna. As mentioned, various observers of tropical forest insect fauna (Janzen and Schoener, 1968; Golley, 1977; Elton, 1973) have suggested that tropical forest insects are smaller in size than temperate forest insects. For example, Elton showed that 62–78% of the insects in his sweep samples were under 3 mm body length and Janzen and Schoener (1968) found 63% under 3 mm in length. Each forest has a theoretical faunal biomass spectrum but as far as I know this spectrum has not been described for any tropical or temperate forest. We would assume that the spectrum would have several peaks, representing the insects and large vertebrates and in tropical forests the vertebrate peaks would be much reduced in size, while the insect peak would be strongly skewed to the left of the distribution. These spectra would, I feel, provide a much more useful description of the faunal biomass than the familiar pyramid of number or biomass.

Finally, the secondary or higher order consumers may form different patterns from the herbivores and saprovores in tropical forest communities. Birds, reptiles, and amphibians are secondary and higher order consumers or (for some birds) fruit-eaters, and in rain forests in particular are highly opportunistic moving from food source to food source. Many species of forest mammals (including a majority of the bats) are also secondary or higher order consumers, but the larger species (where present) are mostly leaf- or fruit-eaters. In the Tano Nimri Forest, Ghana, a biomass of 72 kg km^{-2} is estimated for ten species of primary consumer (three ungulates and seven primates); the leaf-eating black colobus monkey (*Colobus polykomos*), is the commonest species with a density of 3.6 kg km^{-2} and a biomass of 36 kg km^{-2} (Bourlière, 1963). On Barro Colorado Island, Panama, Montgomery and Sunquist (1975) reported that the arboreal mammal fauna of sloths and howler monkeys weighed 53 kg ha^{-1}. These figures are probably among the highest that can be expected for a community of primary consumer forest mammals, and contrast markedly with biomasses of 25 000 kg km^{-2} reported for grass-feeding mammals in the African savannah. Few rain forests support populations of big mammals: the Budongo in Uganda is exceptional because it has both a resident and migratory population of elephants which are severely damaging the trees (Laws et al., 1975). The migrants move in

from surrounding savannah during the dry season and then move out again when the rains return; but the whole balance of elephant numbers in this part of Uganda has been upset because of enforced restriction of ancient migration routes.

Acting in a contrasting way is the effect of the stable environmental factors within the forest on the fauna. For example, Happold (1975, 1977) studying the small rodent fauna of western Nigeria showed that the forest fauna was made up of six species with an average density of 25.3 ± 17.2 ha^{-1}, while the savannah fauna comprised nine species with a density of 47.8 ± 29.3 animals ha^{-1}. A detailed study of rodents in the Gambari forest from 1968 to 1975 showed relatively less variation in numbers from year to year than at Wytham Woods, England, in a temperate forest environment.

CONCLUSIONS

Thus, in summary, apart from a few estimates, what seems to be missing in rain forest ecology are reliable assessments of primary consumer biomass, density, and diversity. The birds, reptiles, amphibians, and parasitic and predatory insects and other invertebrates are really of secondary importance. My guess is that plant-feeding insects are much more abundant than is often thought; many (like the wood-borers) are difficult to find and even more difficult to sample quantitatively. What we do not know is whether the diversity and abundance of animals in 1 m^3 of foliage in one year is the same in rain forest as it is in temperate woodland. Nor do we have comparable figures for 1 m^3 of wood or dead vegetation. Nevertheless, it seems reasonable to conclude that the "importance" of rain forest animals lies more in their role as "shunters" of materials and energy than as primary consumers. Yet as in all ecosystems dead plant material does not accumulate in rain forest: everything is decomposed; but what is the "importance" of animals (termites, earthworms and others) as decomposers when compared to that of bacteria and fungi?

The real problem is that so many animals are mobile or hard to find. Although it is possible to obtain detailed information on diversity at different levels in the forest (e.g. Haddow et al., 1961), estimates of abundance and biomass remain elusive. The figures in Table 6.1 show that in one group of animals high diversity and (presumably) low population density can occur at both low and high latitudes. Sampling of ichneumonids has continued at the Leicester site and the number of species recorded now stands at 529, more than a quarter of the British list. The method used covers an area of 2.6 m² to a height of 1.1 m. No bait or other attractant is used. Can anyone produce a comparable figure for rain forest? Maybe by standing still and looking carefully a better impression of animal life can be obtained than by moving around.

I wonder if the apparent rarity of forest animals is perhaps an illusion arising from unfamiliarity and technical difficulty in finding, let alone estimating the abundance of, animals in a complex ecosystem. It is easy to form the impression that snakes are uncommon in African forests but to see snakes you have to be a skilled snake-watcher. My impression is that collectors and taxonomists with specialized knowledge are quite good at finding specimens in those groups with which they are familiar, while more broadly based ecologists fare less well.

REFERENCES

Bates, H.W., 1863. *The Naturalist on the River Amazons.* Murray, London.

Bourlière, F., 1963. Observations on the ecology of some large African mammals. *Afr. Ecol. Human Evol.*, 36: 43–54.

Diamond, J.M., 1973. Distributional ecology of New Guinea birds. *Science*, 179: 759–769.

Drewry, G.E., 1970. A list of insects from El Verde, Puerto Rico. In: H.T. Odum and R.F. Pigeon (Editors), *A Tropical Rain Forest: A Study of Irradiation and Ecology at El Verde, Puerto Rico.* U.S. Atomic Energy Commission, Washington, D.C., pp. 129–150.

Elton, C.S., 1973. The structure of invertebrate populations inside Neotropical rain forest. *J. Anim. Ecol.*, 42: 55–104.

Fittkau, E.J. and Klinge, H., 1973. On the biomass and trophic structure of the Central Amazonian rain forest ecosystem. *Biotropica*, 5(1): 2–14.

Fleming, T., 1975. The role of small mammals in tropical ecosystems. In: F.B. Golley, L. Petrusewicz and L. Ryszkowski (Editors), *Small Mammals, the Productivity and Population Dynamics.* Cambridge University Press, Cambridge, pp. 269–298.

Gilbert, L.E., 1980. Food web organization and the conservation of neotropical diversity. In M.E. Soulé and B.A. Wilcox (Editors) *Conservation Biology. An Evolutionary–Ecological Perspective.* Sinauer Association, Sunderland, 355 pp.

Golley, F.B., 1977. Insects as regulators of forest nutrient cycling. *Trop. Ecol.*, 18(2): 116–123.

Golley, F.B., Odum, H.T. and Wilson, R., 1962. A synoptic study of the structure and metabolism of a red mangrove forest in southern Puerto Rico in May. *Ecology*, 43: 9–18.

Golley, F.B., McGinnis, J.T., Clements, R.G., Child, G.I. and Duever, M.J., 1975. *Mineral Cycling in a Tropical Moist Forest Ecosystem.* University of Georgia Press, Athens, Ga.

Haddow, A.J., Corbet, P.S., Gillett, J.D., Dirmhirn, I., Jackson, T.H.E. and Brown, K.W., 1961. Entomological studies from a high tower in Mpanga Forest, Uganda. *Trans. R. Entomol. Soc. Lond.*, 113: 24–368.

Hairston, N.G., Smith, F.E. and Slobodkin, L.B., 1960. Community structure, population control, and competition. *Am. Nat.*, 94: 421–425.

Happold, D.C.D., 1975. The effects of climate and vegetation on the distribution of small rodents in Western Nigeria. *Z. Säugetierkd.*, 40: 221–242.

Happold, D.C.D., 1977. A population study on small rodents in the tropical rain forest of Nigeria. *Terre Vie*, 31: 385–458.

Janzen, D.H. and Schoener, J.W., 1968. Differences in insect abundance and diversity between wetter and drier sites during a tropical dry season. *Ecology*, 49: 96–110.

Karr, J., 1975. Production, energy pathways, and community diversity in forest birds. In: F.B. Golley and E. Medina (Editors), *Tropical Ecological Systems.* Springer-Verlag, Berlin, pp. 161–176.

Laws, R.M., Parker, I.S.C. and Johnstone, R.C.B., 1975. *Elephants and Their Habitats: the Ecology of Elephants in North Bunyoro, Uganda.* Clarendon Press, Oxford.

Leston, D., 1978. A neotropical ant mosaic. *Ann. Entomol. Soc. Am.*, 71(4): 649–653.

Malaisse, F., Alexandre, J., Freson, K., Goffinet, G. and Malaise-Mousset, M., 1972. The miombo ecosystem: a preliminary study. In: P.M. Golley and F.B. Golley (Editors), *Tropical Ecology, With An Emphasis on Organic Production.* University of Georgia Press, Athens, Ga., 418 pp.

Montgomery, G.G. and Sunquist, M.E., 1975. Impact of sloths on neotropical forest energy flow and nutrient cycling. In: F.B. Golley and E. Medina (Editors), *Tropical Ecological Systems.* Springer-Verlag, Berlin, pp. 69–98.

Odum, H.T., 1970. Summary: an emerging view of the ecological system at El Verde. In: H.T. Odum and R.F. Pigeon (Editors), *A Tropical Rain Forest: A Study of Irradiation and Ecology at El Verde, Puerto Rico.* U.S. Atomic Energy Commission, Washington, D.C., pp. I. 191–I. 289.

Odum, H.T. and Pigeon, R.F. (Editors), 1970. *A Tropical Rain Forest: A Study of Irradiation and Ecology at El Verde, Puerto Rico.* U.S. Atomic Energy Commission, Washington, D.C., 1678 pp.

Odum, H.T., Abbott, W., Selander, R.K., Golley, F.B. and Wilson, R.F., 1970. Estimates of chlorophyll and biomass of the Tobonuco Forest of Puerto Rico. In: H.T. Odum and R.F. Pigeon (Editors), *A Tropical Rain Forest: A Study of Irradiation and Ecology at El Verde, Puerto Rico.* U.S. Atomic Energy Commission, Washington, D.C., pp. 3–18.

Owen, D.F. and Owen, J., 1974. Species diversity in temperate and tropical Ichneumonidae. *Nature*, 249: 583–584.

Sutton, S.L. and Hudson, P.J., 1980. The vertical distribution of small flying insects in the lowland rain forest of Zaire. *J. Linn. Soc. (Zool.)*, 68: 111–123.

Townes, H., 1972a. A light-weight Malaise trap. *Entomol. News*, 83: 239–247.

Townes, H., 1972b. Ichneumonidae as biological control agents. *Proc. Tall Timbers Conf. Ecol. Anim. Control Habitat Manage.*, 3: 235–248.

UNESCO, 1978. *Tropical Forest Ecosystems, A State of Knowledge Report. Nat. Resour. Res.*, 14: 683 pp.

Wolda, H., 1978. Fluctuations in abundance of tropical insects. *Am. Nat.*, 112(988): 1017–1045.

Chapter 7

THE ABUNDANCE OF ENERGY AND CHEMICAL ELEMENTS

FRANK B. GOLLEY

INTRODUCTION

In the previous chapters the structure of tropical forests was described in terms of its architectural and biological dimensions. These chapters describe a system in which a large variety of biological species coexist, usually at low population densities, and form a forest characterized by great height, great weight, and a complex distribution of plants and animals vertically and horizontally. In this chapter we turn from the complex biological structure and examine some of the forest's physical and chemical attributes. In this change of focus we begin to directly apply the ecosystem concept.

The tropical forest is treated initially as a black box (Fig. 7.1). The rich biological complexity discussed above is ignored and the living materials are treated as living or dead protoplasm. Then this undifferentiated forest black box will be subdivided (Fig. 7.1) into functional groups. In some cases, we will separate primary producers from decomposers, in other instances, we will subdivide primary producers into leaves and stems. Finally, we will subdivide the functional groups into the individual species which make up the leaves and stems, and plants and animals which have occupied our attention above. The reason we do this is two-fold. First, we have adopted the point of view that a tropical rain forest is an object of study. That is, the forest is an ecosystem with its own characteristics. These characteristics are partly the additive features of its parts and are partly special features that are unique to it as an ecosystem. The energy and nutrient content of an ecosystem is the sum of the energy and nutrient contents of its parts. The processing of energy and nutrients through the ecosystem is not the sum of the energy and nutrient flows of each

species, as we shall discuss in the next section. Therefore, to relate the functional system properties of the forest to its structural properties, we must treat the structure initially as a functional unity without considering all its biological dimensions.

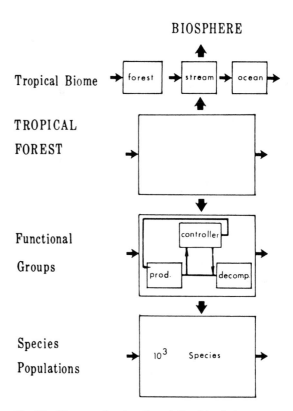

Fig. 7.1. Diagram showing the relationships between populations, functional groups, tropical forest ecosystems, and the tropical biome. Beginning at the top of the figure, the forest biome consists of forests linked to streams and to the oceans. The forest ecosystem can be analyzed into functional groups and into species populations depending upon the type of study and the degree of detail needed. (From Golley, 1975.)

The second reason for this approach is practical. A rain forest ecosystem probably contains thousands of species. Only part of these species are known to science and only a few taxonomists can identify or name the specimens collected in the usual study. It is no exaggeration to state that there are few, if any, sites in tropical rain forest where the fauna and flora are as well known as in the temperate forest stands studied under the International Biological Program. Hopefully this situation will change, but at present the ecosystem ecologists cannot develop adequate biological detail in their studies due to inadequate taxonomic information and expertise.

Therefore, the mechanistic study of the rain forest ecosystem as a processor of solar energy into heat and work, and of atmospheric and soil nutrient inputs into outputs to the atmosphere and hydrosphere requires that we treat the structure of the system as energy and chemical elements. As ecosystems have developed over geological and successional time they tend to reach a steady state of energy and chemical content. That is, ecosystems do not grow indefinitely larger, although they appear to grow indefinitely more complex. The steady state quantity tends to be that of the natural, undisturbed rain forest stand discussed in this volume. Unfortunately, we do not know how these steady state quantities vary over time and space. Therefore, we must assume that the data reported for forest stands, unless otherwise indicated, represent the storage of energy and elements of a steady state rain forest in dynamic equilibrium with its environment. With this assumption, the data on the storage or standing crop of energy and chemical elements can be used to compare and differentiate rain forest ecosystems. And later, when we turn to forest function, these data will be contrasted with the flux of energy and nutrients to and from the ecosystems.

The methodology required to establish the storage of chemical elements and energy in a forest stand is conceptually simple but technically difficult. It is necessary to collect samples that are representative of the forest components being described and submit these to chemical analysis. Obtaining an adequate sample of components such as leaves, or stems, or herbivores in a stand that may weigh hundreds of metric tons per hectare is obviously a problem. Usually the ecologist samples

a plot of forest which is a representative prism from the mineral soil to the atmosphere above the canopy. This prism is similar to the pedon of the soil scientist or the landscape prism of the geochemist. Techniques to determine the energy content of biological material are well described, for example in Paine (1971). Techniques to measure the concentrations of chemical elements in forest soil and water samples are also well described in standard chemical handbooks. However, ecologists are less cognizant of the procedures required to assure the accuracy and precision of their data. These problems are discussed briefly in Golley (1980) and in Fortescue (1980). Then, the total quantities of energy or chemical elements in the forest are calculated by multiplying the biomass of each component by its respective energy content or chemical concentration and summing the quantities from all components. These values represent the storage within the component of interest in the forest system model or within the forest as a whole.

THE ENERGY VALUE OF TROPICAL FOREST

There have been a large number of caloric determinations made on ecological samples, especially through the work of the International Biological Program. Examples relating to forests, animals and bacteria can be found in Ovington and Heitkamp (1960), Slobodkin and Richman (1961), Hough (1969), Madgwick (1970) and Prochazka et al. (1970). Wiegert (1976) is the source for background papers in ecological energetics. However, almost all of these studies have focused on non-tropical materials. Thus, it is appropriate to ask if the energy contents of tropical and temperate biota should differ in significant ways?

The energy content of a sample depends upon its organic constitution. The compounds which make up organic tissues differ in their energy content. For example, starch, cellulose, and sugars typically have energy values from 14.6 to 17.5 kJ g^{-1} while proteins have values from 12.9 to 27.2 and fats have values up to 38.3 (Lieth, 1975), Golley (1961) suggested that since alpine or arctic plants must store energy as fats and other compounds to cope with periods of cold, while tropical vegetation does not cope with cold temperatures and, therefore, does not store fats, we would anticipate that tropical forests would have lower caloric values than arctic or alpine tundra vegetation. Golley (1961) compared the energy contents of plants from tundra to rain forest (Table 7.1) and found that there was a gradient of decreasing energy per gram from the tundra to the tropical forest. A later study of vegetation in Panama (Golley, 1969) supported these findings.

However, this pattern may not be found in all cases, because in tropical forests energy is expended on production of defensive compounds, attractants and a range of chemical compounds which support the mutualistic relationships of the tropical biota. Howard-Williams (1974) on sterile sands in the Amazon found much higher caloric values in rain forest litter than were found by Golley in a more equable habitat in Puerto Rico. Howard-Williams explains these differences as due to the low nutrient availability in the soil which limits growth, causing photosynthate to be channeled into production of high energy compounds such as waxes, resins and fats. These compounds could protect the leaves from herbivory. Where tropical forests store these high energy compounds their caloric values will reflect these storages.

Energy content may also vary significantly between types of tropical forests and between components within a forest, as has been found repeatedly in temperate forests. In Panama four forests on a transect from the mountains to the coast provided a comparison of quite different tropical communities (Golley, 1969). A summary of these data (Table 7.2) illustrates a pattern of energy contents across forests and compartments. The premontane forest occurred at the highest elevation. The tropical moist forest occupies the undulating uplands between mountains and the riverine lowlands. Mangrove forests form a fringe along the coastline. Mangrove forests had the highest energy values for leaves, stems and litter, and shared the highest value for fruits with tropical moist forest. Premontane forest roots had the highest energy value. Among forest components stems had the highest energy values in three forests and fruits had the highest value in the fourth.

These observations parallel those made in temperate forests. For example, seeds and fruits often have the highest values since high energy compounds may be stored in these organs. Madgwick (1970) showed in *Pinus virginiana* male flowers and mature leaves (20.94 and 20.94 kJ g^{-1}) had the highest energy content, as compared to branches (20.18), bole wood (19.81) and bole bark (19.56). Jordan (1971) also found this pattern for various tropical species in montane rain forest in Puerto Rico. He showed that leaves contained a higher

TABLE 7.1

Energy values (kJ g^{-1}) in ecological communities (from Golley, 1961)

Community	Number of samples	Energy value
Tropical rain forest (Puerto Rico)	15	16.30
Mangrove forest (Puerto Rico)	11	15.63
Spartina marsh, Ga. (U.S.A.)	14	17.01
Broomsedge field, S.C. (U.S.A.)	143	16.34
Herb old field, S.C. (U.S.A.)	35	17.47
Grass old field, Mich. (U.S.A.)	115	17.05
Pine stand (England)	14	20.02
Alpine meadow, N.H. (U.S.A.)	3	19.68
Alpine heath, N.H. (U.S.A.)	2	20.02

1 kcal = 4.18 kJ.

TABLE 7.2

Energy values (kJ g^{-1}) of forests and forest components in the Republic of Panama (from Golley, 1969)

Component	Premontane forest	Tropical moist forest	Riverine forest	Mangrove forest
Canopy leaves	17.13	16.09	17.26	17.47
Stems	17.43	17.55	17.76	18.14
Fruit	16.76	18.01	15.67	17.97
Litter	16.72	16.92	16.67	17.30
Roots	17.38	16.55	17.09	16.84

1 kcal = 4.18 kJ.

content of energy (17.2 kJ g^{-1}) than did stems (16.59–16.97) and roots (14.79).

Thus far we have not considered taxonomic differences in energy content. A frequency distribution of energy values in taxa would show a wide range across organisms. However, there would be two distinct peaks in the distribution. One peak at about 16.7 kJ g^{-1} would represent plants and another at about 21 kJ g^{-1} would represent animals. In the Cummins and Wuycheck (1971) compendium on caloric values the grand mean for primary producers is 19.56 kJ g^{-1} ash-free, for detritus consumers 20.44, and for macroconsumers 24.32. Correcting the energy value per gram of biomass by the quantity of ash in the sample will increase the energy value. However, within a taxon caloric value can change remarkably depending upon the season, reproduction and other biological conditions. A change of 2 kJ g^{-1} is not unusual and therefore mean values for taxa have limited general use.

Tropical forest plant taxa show variation in caloric content equal to or greater than that of species elsewhere. For example, the energy value of stem wood ranged from 14.6 kJ g^{-1} for *Sloanea buteriana* in Puerto Rico (Jordan, 1971) to 21.3 for *Eusideroxylon zwargeri* in Indonesia (Hadi et al., 1979). In contrast, Ovington and Heitkamp (1960) in a variety of English tree species found that stem wood varied from 19.2 to 20.0 kJ g^{-1}, and Ovington and Lawrence (1967) showed that stems in a Minnesota environment ranged from 18.8 to 19.6 kJ g^{-1}. These taxonomic differences become important in studies of biomass of biofuel systems and energy plantations (Perera, 1979), and in studies of the energy dynamics of ecosystems (Odum, 1970).

To summarize, the energy value of biotic components of a forest depends upon the chemical composition of that component. Organisms do not expend energy to manufacture, store, and protect high energy compounds unless there is an advantage for them to do so. Tropical vegetation parts that are susceptible to herbivory, such as leaves and flowers, store defensive compounds and if these are high energy compounds, then the energy content of the leaf or flower would be higher than usual for this type of tissue. Similarly where the tropical vegetation does not have an advantage in storing high energy compounds, then its caloric values

would be lower than those of arctic or alpine plants. Arctic conditions frequently require that organisms living there store high energy materials during their life cycle. In tropical forests high energy compounds may or may not be an advantage and the energy contents vary as a consequence. For this reason, energy content might be a more interesting parameter to measure in tropical forests than in temperate or alpine habitats.

CHEMICAL ELEMENTS

Analysis of the nutrient elements is more complex than the energy analysis. Theoretically all of the naturally occurring elements could occur in tropical forest organic tissues. According to Bowen (1966), 26 elements are essential for some organisms. These elements are carbon, hydrogen, nitrogen, oxygen, phosphorus, sulfur, aluminum, boron, barium, bromine, calcium, chlorine, cobalt, copper, iron, iodine, potassium, magnesium, manganese, molybdenum, sodium, selenium, silicon, tin, vanadium, and zinc. A study of the standing crop of each of these nutrient elements is a large task. Not only are special analytical methods required for some of the elements, but they also interact with each other so that they influence the behavior and abundance of other elements, as well as the analytical determinations.

Here our interest is to examine the quantities of some of the most abundant elements stored in the forest system at an instant of time. These patterns may be expressed in two ways. First, the concentrations of a chemical element, expressed usually as a percent or as parts per million (p.p.m.), in a tissue gives a measure of the strength or relative content of that element. Concentrations can be compared in tissues to determine which is rich or poor in that particular chemical element. Second, the concentrations can be multiplied by the biomass to give the total amount or inventory of that element stored in the forest. These data are required for nutrient cycling studies. Thus, in this chapter we will be concerned both with concentrations (expressed as p.p.m.) and inventories (usually expressed as kg ha^{-1}).

The chemical content of a forest is the result of two inputs. One input which is usually the largest and most important overall comes from the soil.

The second input, which is especially important for elements with a gaseous phase, comes from the atmosphere. We predict that the abundances of the chemicals in the forest are organized in a unique way for each stand. That is, each forest has a formula which will state how abundant each element is in that biota. We do not yet have such formulas calculated but the idea of a formula expresses one of the goals of this type of research.

We further suggest that this formula is the result of four sets of chemical separations. First, the physical–chemical nature of elements influences their abundance one to another. For example, elements with an odd number of electrons in the outer ring are less abundant than those with even numbers of electrons. Second, the geochemical processes of earth formation and erosion cause the physical–chemical abundances in the mother rock to be altered in ways unique to particular geochemical environments. Third, the biota has special chemical requirements so that it develops a chemical constitution different from its geochemical substrate. And further, the interaction of the ecological community with its environment creates special mechanisms and processes to fit the biotic requirements to the geochemical environment under different physical environments of light, temperature and water. Thus, the chemical formula of the tropical forest is a function of physical-chemical,

geochemical, biochemical and ecochemical processes. The ultimate task of ecological chemistry or biogeochemistry is to account for each of these separations in explaining the chemical abundances in a given system. At this time we are very far from this objective.

Biomass

While the biomass for forests was discussed in Chapter 4, we will summarize some data here as basis for later discussions of the inventory of chemical elements. Biomass (dry weight) varies greatly from forest to forest (Table 7.3). Our present estimates are difficult to interpret because of different methods used and different sizes of samples and plots.

Nevertheless, there are broad trends and these are especially evident when data have been collected by the same group of investigators. For example, the Japanese ecologists have established a relationship between forest biomass and altitude in Asia (Fig. 7.2). These data show that across an altitudinal gradient from the lowlands of Southeast Asia to the mountains in Nepal and Japan there are two peaks of biomass. One peak is at the lowland rain forest zone (S, S, and K in Fig. 7.2) and the second is at evergreen conifer forest zone between 2500 and 2900 m altitude. However, leaf biomass

TABLE 7.3

Biomass (ton dry weight ha^{-1}) for selected tropical forests

Forest and locality	Biomass			Authority
	stem	leaf	roots	
Riverine (Panama)	1163	11.3	12	Golley et al. (1975)
Banco forest (Ivory Coast)	504	9.0	49	Huttel and Bernhard-Reversat (1975)
Pasoh forest (Malaysia)	467	8.2	–	Kato et al. (1978)
Rain forest (Brazil)	370	10.0	~40	Klinge (1972)
Tropical moist (Panama)	355	11.3	10	Golley et al. (1975)
Mangrove (Panama)	159	3.5	190	Golley et al. (1975)
Tropical rain (Thailand)	323	7.8	31	Kira et al. (1964)
San Carlos rain forest (Venezuela)	317	8.2	56	Jordan (1980)
Evergreen seasonal (Kampuchea)	314	8.4	32	Hozumi et al. (1969)
Rain forest (Colombia)	314	9.0	–	Las Salas (1978)
Lower montane (Puerto Rico)	269	8.1	71	Odum et al. (1970)
Premontane wet (Panama)	258	10.5	13	Golley et al. (1975)
Heath forest (Kampuchea)	145	7.7	19	Hozumi et al. (1969)
Dry deciduous forest (India)	73	5.0	21	Singh and Misra (1978)
Swamp forest (Kampuchea)	11	2.1	4	Hozumi et al. (1969)

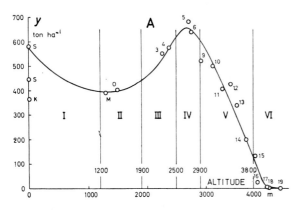

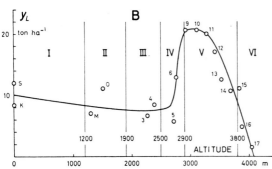

Fig. 7.2. Change with altitude of total biomass (y, t ha^{-1}) and leaf biomass (y_L) on an area basis (from Yoda, 1968).

alone does not show two peaks across the gradient (Fig. 7.2). Forests have similar leaf biomass up to 2500 m, then leaf biomass for evergreen coniferous forests at high altitudes increases to a peak and then falls (Fig. 7.2). Similar gradients may be recognized for other environmental factors. The large range of biomass shown in Table 7.3 for different stands represents adaptations to various environmental conditions. The highest biomass, in Riverine forest in Panama, occurs on highly fertile, flat bottom-lands along rivers. Low biomass is found in flooded or very dry habitats.

Table 7.3 shows clearly the differences in biomass between forest components. Stem weights are much larger than root weights, which, in turn, are larger than leaf weights. While these relationships are obvious, they are exceedingly important when the inventory of nutrients is calculated. The stem nutrient content tends to dominate that of all other components in the forest.

The data presented in Table 7.3 are for the dry weight biomass of forests. In some cases we must also know the fresh weight or the amount of water contained in the biomass. This is especially important when we are concerned with the forest water cycle. Klinge et al. (1975) provided data on the fresh weight of a central Amazonian forest in Brazil (Table 7.4). These data can be directly compared with those for Brazilian rain forest in Table 7.3, showing that about two-thirds of the fresh weight is made up of water. This conclusion is supported by Golley et al. (1975) who determined the percent water content of tropical moist forest in Panama (Table 7.5). Fruits and flowers contained the largest content of water (80%), followed by leaves (65%), roots (60%) and stems (50–60%). Samples from the wet and dry season also differed significantly (Table 7.5) with more water in the biomass during the wet season. Daubenmire (1972) similarly described the expansion and contraction of tree stems in the wet and dry season in Costa Rica due probably to the differential quantities of water in the tissues. The litter showed significant seasonal differences in water content, as well.

Carbon

Deevey (1970) describes the average abundance of chemicals in a representative sample of the biosphere. Of the more than one hundred chemical elements that might occur in the biota, the most important are carbon, hydrogen, oxygen, nitrogen, sulfur, and phosphorus. Generally, carbon makes up from 45 to 50% by dry weight of plant material. Since increased global carbon dioxide level in the atmosphere has been recognized as an environmental problem, a variety of ecologists have been interested in calculating the quantities of carbon stored in forests. Tropical forests often contain large quantities of living biomass (Table 7.3), and therefore, they can serve as important stores of carbon. In addition, carbon is stored in dead material in litter and fallen tree trunks, in surface soils, and as refractory material in deep soils. Schlesinger (1977) has summarized the various studies of soil detritus in the tropics and calculates that an average of 10.4 kg carbon is stored per square meter, with a coefficient of variation of 44%. This average can be compared to temperate forests (11.8) and boreal forests (14.9). The lower value for tropical forests is probably due to the higher decomposition rates observed.

TABLE 7.4

Biomass of fresh material in a central Amazonian rain forest (metric tons ha^{-1}) (from Klinge et al., 1975)

Leaf matter		
Dicotyledonous trees above 1.5 m height	14.1	
Palms above 1.5 m height	0.34	
Plants below 1.5 m height	0.6	
Total leaf matter of dicotyledonous trees and palms	18.1	
Branches and twigs		
Dicotyledonous trees above 1.5 m height	202.2	
Plants below 1.5 m height	0.2	
Total branches and twigs	202.4	
Stems		
Dicotyledonous trees above 1.5 m height	465.5	
Palms above 1.5 m height	2.1	
Plants below 1.5 m height	0.6	
Total stems	468.2	
Other plants (total biomass):		
Lianas	46.0	
Epiphytes	0.1	
Parasites	0.1	
Total other plants	46.2	
Total aerial biomass		743.9
Root mass		
Fine roots	49.0	
Other roots	206.0	
Total root mass	255.0	255.0
Total biomass		989.9

TABLE 7.5

Percent water content of tropical moist forest vegetation; values represent averages with one standard error in parentheses (from Golley et al., 1975)

Compartment	Dry season, February	Wet season, September
Overstorey leaves	63.2(3.2)	69.9(1.5)
Understorey leaves	64.3(2.5)	73.8(1.3)
Overstorey stems	48.4(0.4)	66.7(7.9)
Understorey stems	54.2(0.3)	65.3(1.7)
Overstorey fruits and flowers	88.8(2.4)	76.8(4.9)
Understorey fruits and flowers	80.1(8.4)	85.4(2.0)
Litter	20.9(0.5)	72.4(0.6)
Roots	60.3(1.7)	61.8(2.9)

Other elements

Measurements of those elements other than carbon, hydrogen and oxygen require a variety of special analytical techniques. Of all the chemical elements that might occur in organic matter, only about five or six are routinely determined. These are usually the elements that are required in large amounts for plant growth: nitrogen, phosphorus, potassium, calcium, and magnesium. However, in ecological surveys up to twenty elements may be examined (see for example, Golley et al., 1975; and Geisler and Schneider, 1976).

As mentioned above, the study of chemical abundance in tropical forests is based on a prism of vegetation and soil which is usually less than one hectare in the horizontal dimension and extends from the top of the canopy to a meter or so in the soil. Elemental concentrations in samples of biomass and soil are multiplied by the biomass or bulk density to give the inventory of that element in the prism. The biomass samples may represent the combined vegetation, the components of the forest, the species in the forest, or the component parts of a species. In each case the forest inventory is reconstructed by adding up the sums representing all of the parts. The forest prism is considered representative of a stand, a forest type, or a geographic region and usually comparisons between elemental concentrations or inventories are used to show how forests differ or are similar. At present the data are so limited that these comparisons are mainly descriptive. Eventually, however, we may be able to predict the chemical constitution of the landscape and explain how this constitution has evolved. Given these considerations, we will discuss in this section the chemistry of whole forests, components and species.

As we would anticipate, the concentrations of the elements are not the same (Table 7.6). The elements with highest concentrations are usually nitrogen, calcium, magnesium, potassium, phosphorus, sodium, and aluminum. This group does not necessarily represent those elements that are most

TABLE 7.6

Comparison of elemental concentrations for two forests in Panama to illustrate the differences in elemental abundance in the forest biomass (from Golley et al., 1975)

Element	Concentration (p.p.m.)	
	tropical moist	premontane wet
N	14 000	15 000
Ca	17 800	10 500
K	11 000	8300
Mg	2000	2700
P	1200	1000
Na	200	1800
Al	1050	1549
B	22	23
Ba	66	113
Co	41	50
Cs	18	30
Cu	8	10
Fe	176	511
Mn	63	352
Mo	4.2	6.9
Ni	130	23
Pb	36	44
Sr	90	136
Ti	9	25
Zn	27	43

abundant in the lithosphere and atmosphere (Table 7.7). Rather, it represents the selective uptake and retention by tropical forest biota. The elements present in smaller concentrations (Table 7.6) also may be taken up and held at levels above that present in the forest environment. In other cases there may be discrimination against an element by the biota. Relatively little is known about the requirements, concentration or discrimination for chemical elements by non-cultivated tropical plants.

The data in Table 7.6 also indicate that forests may differ in chemical concentrations. The tropical moist forest in Table 7.6 grows on level plains in the Darien Province of the Republic of Panama. Premontane wet forest grows on low mountains bordering the tropical moist forest. The soils of these two forests are quite different. Tropical moist forest grows on soils derived from sedimentary deposits and is rich in calcium and magnesium. Premontane wet forest grows on soils derived from basalts. Presumably these different environments are reflected in the chemical concentrations of the vegetation. Tropical moist forest has higher concentrations of calcium and potassium, while the premontane wet forest has higher concentrations of aluminum, iron, manganese and other trace elements. The two forests are similar in the concentrations of nitrogen, phosphorus, and a few other elements. These data illustrate a typical pattern found in biogeochemical studies. Depending upon the specific chemical element, forests may be similar or different in chemical constitution. Within a limited geographic region the forests usually do not display wide and consistent differences for all the elements. Indeed, if the forest biomass of two forests is similar, there must be a minimal standard elemental complement associated with that biomass. While elements may compensate for the abundance or deficit of one or another essential chemical, there is a minimal level that must be maintained if that biomass is to survive.

There has been very little study of the interaction of elements within tropical forests. Golley and Richardson (1977) examined the interrelationships of the elements in Table 7.6 (excluding nitrogen) for forests on a continuum across the Darien Province in Panama. Besides tropical moist and premontane wet forest, the continuum included riverine forest

TABLE 7.7

Abundance of selected elements in the four parts of the ecosphere (from Fortescue, 1980); data for the biosphere are based on those for angiosperms (from Bowen, 1966) (in p.p.m.)

Element	Lithosphere	Hydrosphere marine	Atmosphere	Biosphere (angiosperms)
O	456 000	857 000	231 500	410 000
Si	273 000	3	–	200
Al	83 600	0.01	–	550
Fe	62 200	0.01	–	140
Ca	46 600	400	–	18 000
Mg	27 640	1350	–	3200
Na	22 700	10 500	–	1210
K	18 400	380	–	14 000
H	1520	108 000	0.035	55 000
P	1120	0.07	–	2300
Mn	1060	0.002	–	630
Ba	390	0.03	–	14
S	340	885	–	3400
C	180	28	460	454 000
N	19	0.5	755 100	30 000
Pb	13	0.00003	–	2.7

and mangrove. Nine stands were studied. Two stands represented tropical moist forest in two seasons. Four stands represented young second-growth forest in the tropical moist forest region. All of these stands were within a few kilometers of each other. The other three forests were represented by a single stand. Golley and Richardson (1977) used the statistical technique of factor analysis (Nabholz and Richardson, 1975) to show common patterns of correlations between elemental abundances. This statistical study showed that there were few common patterns of abundance among similar types of forests, among similar ages of forest, or between different types and ages of forest. This result was unexpected. It was anticipated that similar types of forest would show common patterns of abundance. The results may reflect the variability in concentrations of the samples for the forests or it may reveal a level of complexity that has not been explored.

In another study by the same authors the chemical concentrations across a transect in Colombia were examined (Golley et al., 1978). In this case data were available for the bed rock and from soils and organic samples of leaves, epiphytes and litter collected at six locations. The samples were tested for correlations between biotic material and soils — that is, for a significant location effect. In no case

did concentration in vegetation correlate significantly with soil concentrations. However, soils appeared to closely follow bed rock chemistry. The authors concluded that in this geographic region soils and bed rock chemistry were related, while vegetation and soil chemistry were only poorly correlated.

When we expand the region of interest beyond the few hundred kilometers in the Panama or Colombia example to a continent, patterns of forest chemistry emerge. The best example of a biogeochemical survey of this broad type is that of Furch and Klinge (1978) for the Amazon Basin. The Amazon is divided into a series of ecological regions on the basis of water chemistry (Fittkau, 1971). There are four subregions (Fig. 7.3). The central region is characterized by waters which are very low in chemical elements, low in soil nutrients, and low in vegetation concentrations. The Peripheral subregions are richer in chemical elements, with highest concentrations occurring in the Western Peripheral subregion. Comparison of some of the alkali (Li, Na, K, Rb, Cs) and alkali earth metals (Be, Mg, Ca, Sr, Ba) in leaves (Table 7.8) shows how the central Amazon subregion vegetation is deficient in calcium especially, and also potassium. This pattern is also observed for the mineral soil and the drainage water (Fig. 7.4). The

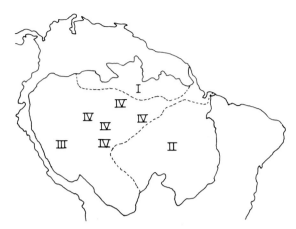

Fig. 7.3. Ecological subregions of Amazonia: *I* = Northern Peripheral Amazonia; *II* = Southern Peripheral Amazonia; *III* = Western Peripheral Amazonia; *IV* = Central Amazonia. (From Furch and Klinge, 1979.)

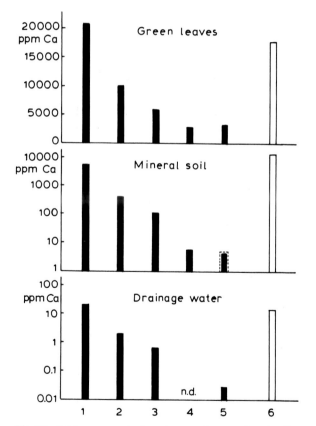

Fig. 7.4. Calcium concentrations in green leaves, mineral soil and drainage water of five forest ecosystems of northern South America: *1* = tropical moist forest (Panama); *2* = montane forest (Puerto Rico); *3* = tall Amazon caatinga (Venezuela); *4* = evergreen rain forest (Colombia); *5* = seasonal evergreen rain forest (Brazil); *6* = world average. (From Furch and Klinge, 1979.)

tropical moist forest of Panama discussed above is near the world average for calcium, while Amazon forests are much lower. Thus, a regional comparison of chemical composition in tropical forests reveals patterns that reflect the geochemistry of the landscape.

While these various observations appear to be contradictory they actually reflect different scales of distribution. At the broad regional or continental scale, a relatively limited set of samples shows patterns which correlate with the broad patterns of geology and geochemistry. As the geographic scale is reduced and the numbers of samples per area is increased, it appears that for certain elements the vegetation concentrations diverge from the soil or rock concentrations — that is, it appears that the biota becomes decoupled from the substrate chemically. Probably Panama, Colombia and the Amazon represent these points on a curve (Fig. 7.5) which describes the relation of chemical concentration and the substrate. It is important to emphasize again that this hypothetical curve may differ for each element so that at one site the biota may reflect an abundance of an element in the substrate and also a limited supply of another element. In order to survive, the organisms must obtain some specified level of nutrient supply. If that supply is inadequate in the substrate, the biota must evolve methods of concentrating and storing this element. These adaptations will be discussed more fully in Chapter 9. I know of no sites where lack of an element prevents all growth of tropical vegetation. However, low nutrient levels coupled

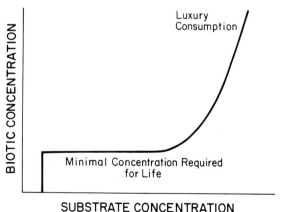

Fig. 7.5. Hypothetical relationship between chemical concentration of vegetation and substrate for a specific element.

TABLE 7.8

Alkali- and alkali-earth metals in leaves of primary and secondary vegetation in northern South America (from Furch and Klinge, 1979).

Forest type, locality and soil	Ecological subregion	Concentration (p.p.m.)							Source
		Na	K	Cs	Mg	Ca	Sr	Ba	
Primary vegetation									
Tropical moist forest[1], Panama. residual soil	Extra-Amazonia	150	15 250	27	2800	20 900	97	115	Golley et al. (1975)
Montane forest, Puerto Rico, residual soil	Extra-Amazonia	2000	10 400	n.d.	3700	10 100	n.d.	n.d.	Ovington and Olson (1970)
Evergreen rainforest[3], Colombia, alluvial soil	Extra-Amazonia	5	5270	n.d.	1670	3070	n.d.	n.d.	Fölster et al. (1976)
Tropical rainforest[2], Peru	Western Peripheral Amazonia	188	14 018	n.d.	3456	14 286	n.d.	n.d.	Stark (1971)
Tropical rainforest[3] (Amazon caatinga), Venezuela, sandy podzol:	Northern Peripheral Amazonia								
tall caatinga		n.d.	8400	n.d.	1080	6020	n.d.	n.d.	Herrera and Klinge (unpubl. data)
low caatinga		n.d.	9311	n.d.	1741	8562	n.d.	n.d.	
Climax vegetation[3] Surinam, laterite	Northern Peripheral Amazonia	500	14 250	n.d.	3150	5000	n.d.	n.d.	Stark (1970)
Dimorphandra sp., Surinam, podzol	Northern Peripheral Amazonia	500	1548	n.d.	2400	8000	n.d.	n.d.	Stark (1970)
Seasonal evergreen rainforest, Manaus, Oxisol	Central Amazonia								
general average		1500	4000	n.d.	2500	3500	56	5	Klinge (1976), Furch (unpubl.)
young leaves		203	8375	n.d.	2267	2613	n.d.	n.d.	Stark (1971)
old leaves		296	6208	n.d.	2493	3450	n.d.	n.d.	Stark (1971)
Climax vegetation[3], Manaus, podzol	Central Amazonia	240	6500	n.d.	2200	2500	n.d.	n.d.	Stark (1970)
Secondary vegetation									
Surinam[3], laterite	Northern Peripheral Amazonia	350	3250	n.d.	3575	10 515	n.d.	n.d.	Stark (1970)
Surinam[3], podzol	Northern Peripheral Amazonia	350	1950	n.d.	2950	4750	n.d.	n.d.	Stark (1970)

[1] Overstorey and understorey trees, mean; [2] young leaves; [3] general average; n.d. = no data.

with lack of water or other factors may restrict growth and development of vegetation.

These findings mean that the forest inventories of elements also will differ. Such differences are illustrated by data on the storage of abundant elements in several neotropical forests (Herrera et al., 1978) (Table 7.9). In this example, the Puerto Rican premontane forest had especially elevated quantities of potassium, calcium and magnesium, while the tall Amazonian caatinga and the seasonal evergreen forest in Brazil had highest nitrogen levels. In fact, some differences between forests were a factor of ten. These differences reflect variation in biomass (Table 7.3) and in chemical concentrations. In either case, wide differences are observed between types of forest adequate to account for the variation shown in the Table. For this reason, data on comparative inventories in forests are of relatively little interest, except in ecosystem modelling where the inventory is a measure of the quantity of that element stored in the biota. The storages of elements can be contrasted to the cycling rates into or out of the forest or its components. The division of elemental storage by the rate of cycling is turnover, which is a valuable index to ecosystem function.

In these studies we have considered forest chemistry as a whole stand property. However, examination of the forest components also show important differences in chemical concentration and inventory. In general, fruits, flowers, bark and leaves have higher concentrations of essential elements than do stems and roots. An example from the tropical moist forest in Panama (Table 7.10) illustrates the usual pattern. In a detailed statistical examination of Panama vegetation, Golley and Richardson (1977) found considerable commonality among the elements when analyzed by compartments. For example, in leaves phosphorus, potassium, copper, zinc and magnesium acted as a common group as did calcium, strontium, barium, and boron. These groupings were thought to represent enzyme systems in the leaves in the first case and the structural cellular component in the leaves in the second. In the litter the calcium-dominated complex was also identified, and in addition a complex of molybdenum, magnesium, iron, manganese, copper, and aluminum. This latter group probably represented soil which had become mixed with litter through the activities of the fauna.

These latter findings were especially interesting because, as mentioned above, analysis of the chem-

TABLE 7.9

Inventory of elements in the vegetation and surface soil (kg ha^{-1}) (from Herrera et al., 1978)

Forest	N	P	K	Ca	Mg
Tropical moist (Panama)	1360	670	1010	2420	1140
Montane (Puerto Rico)	5600	186	3455	26 269	2685
Tall Amazon caatinga (Venezuela)	8235	–	733	913	376
Evergreen (Colombia)	6763	299	428	551	204
Seasonal evergreen (Brazil)	12 200	216	562	528	298

TABLE 7.10

Chemical concentration (p.p.m.) in forest compartments in tropical moist forest, Panama (from Golley et al., 1975)

Compartment	N	Ca	K	Mg	P
Overstorey leaves	20 000	21 200	14 300	2700	2200
Understorey leaves	21 000	10 600	16 200	2900	2400
Overstorey stems	5000	10 800	12 100	1000	500
Understorey stems	7000	11 400	12 500	1600	800
Fruits and flowers	14 000	6300	17 400	2200	2200
Litter	17 000	26 100	2400	1400	1500
Roots	8000	14 800	7600	2200	1100

istry of these different forest stands showed few cases where elements occurred at similar abundances. Even two stands of tropical moist forest several kilometers from each other had statistically different abundances (Golley and Richardson, 1977). Further, second-growth sites in the tropical moist forest area only contained one group of elements (Al, Mo, Ba and Ti) which had a common level of abundance with the mature forest, probably reflecting soil material mixed with vegetation samples of litter. In contrast, leaves, litter and stems did have many similar abundances between them, even when leaves were from forests as diverse as premontane wet forest and mangrove forest. In this case, the biochemical controls on elemental distribution and abundance override the geochemical controls. Clearly the chemical storages in tropical forests are very complex and further support the point made earlier that tropical rain forest cannot be treated as a single ecological entity.

In all of the above studies the vegetation has been treated as a unit of study. Those ecologists who have examined the chemistry of tropical forest species also have found that the taxonomic differences between species can be significant. We assume that these plants have evolved and have become adapted to specific chemical environments. The nutrient requirements and the elemental composition of a species reflects its history. Any one forest is composed of many species with different histories. While the species in a forest have the same environment and must cope with approximately the same abundances in the soil and atmosphere, each, depending upon its historical background, probably reacts to these sources a little differently. These speculations are borne out by Tanner (1977) who examined species growing on four different sites and found that for most elements a species had a characteristic chemical composition but that the species differed from each other. Jordan (1977) examining six species in the montane forest of Puerto Rico also found that each species had a characteristic composition independent of site, as long as the sites were within the same soil type. Ovington and Olson (1970) reported, but did not analyze, a large set of chemical values for different species in these same Puerto Rican forests.

The extant data strongly suggest that species have a characteristic chemical composition; do individuals of different species sharing the same soil prism have similar chemical constitutions? Recently, Golley and Klinge (unpublished) have examined this question on a 5×50 m transect near Manaus, Brazil. In this analysis the chemistry of leaves, stems and roots was examined. Each individual tree was located on the transect and a comparison was made of the chemistry of members of the same species located at some distance from each other compared to nearest neighbors of different species. Nearest neighbors shared the same site with the root systems in the same area of soil. These comparisons showed that among leaves (Table 7.11) the least essential or unessential elements (Pb, Ni) usually occurred at similar concentrations in nearest neighbors, while certain essential elements (Mg, Mn, Na, Ca) occurred at similar concentrations in individuals of the same species. Clearly, the species behaved very dif-

TABLE 7.11

Distribution of elements in leaves among rain forest species, showing elements exhibiting most similar concentrations between nearest neighbor or another individual of the same species

Species	Nearest neighbor	Ind. of the same species
Protium heptaphyllum	Pb	Ca, Mg
Micrandra sclerocyathium	–	Mn, Na
Licania heteromorpha	Ni	–
Eschweilera odora	Pb	K, Mg, Mn
Eschweilera wachenhemii	–	Mn, Na
Nemaluma engleri	Ca, Cd	–
Rinorea macrocarpa	–	Al, B, Ca, Mg, Mn, Na, Pb, Pt, Si

ferently. *Rinorea macrocarpa* showed many similarities among elements within individuals of that species, while *Licania heteromorpha* showed none. However, over all species 78% of the comparisons in leaves and 63% in stems showed the species effect on concentration of elements was of *greater* significance, while the location effect was significant in only 20% of the comparisons.

These analyses of the patterns of nutrient storage in tropical forest vegetation have emphasized the differences between locations, components and taxa. Comparative data are becoming available in adequate amounts so that investigators can begin to form hypotheses for field testing. The great weakness in the subject is that almost nothing is known about the nutrient requirements of tropical forest species and, therefore, it is not possible to evaluate nutrient levels in the soil as adequate or inadequate for plant growth directly and to devise mechanistic explanations of the observed patterns. This is an important area for research by physiological ecologists. Finally, it is also important to expand the number of elements that are examined, since the abundances are interrelated. This advance will await better and more versatile analytical tests.

REFERENCES

Bowen, H.J.M., 1966. *Trace Elements in Biochemistry.* Academic Press, London, 241 pp.

Cummins, K.C. and Wuycheck, J.C., 1971. Caloric equivalents for investigators in ecological energetics. *Ver. Theor. Angew. Limnol.*, 18: 1–158.

Daubenmire, R., 1972. Phenology and other characteristics of tropical semideciduous forest in NW Costa Rica. *J. Ecol.*, 60: 147–170.

Deevey, E.S., Jr., 1970. Mineral cycles. *Sci. Am.*, 223: 149–158.

Fittkau, E.J., 1974. Zur ökologischen Gliederung Amazoniens. 1. Die erdgeschichtliche Entwicklung Amazoniens. *Amazoniana*, 5(1): 77–134.

Fölster, H. and Las Salas, G. de, 1976. Litterfall and mineralization in three tropical evergreen forest stands, Colombia. *Acta Cient. Venez.*, 27: 196–202.

Fortescue, J.A.C., 1980. *Environmental Geochemistry, A Holistic Approach.* Ecological Studies 35. Springer-Verlag, Berlin, 347 pp.

Furch, K. and Klinge, H., 1978. Toward a regional characterization of the biogeochemistry of alkali- and alkali-earth metals in northern South America. *Acta Cient. Venez.*, 29: 434–444.

Geisler, R. and Schneider, J., 1976. The element matrix of Amazon waters and its relationship with the mineral content of fishes. *Amazoniana*, 6(1): 47–65.

Golley, F.B., 1961. Energy value of ecological materials. *Ecology*, 42: 581–584.

Golley, F.B., 1969. Caloric value of wet tropical forest vegetation. *Ecology*, 50: 517–519.

Golley, F.B., 1975. Productivity and mineral cycling in tropical forests. In: *Productivity of World Ecosystems*, NAS Symposium. Washington, D.C., pp. 106–115.

Golley, F.B., 1980. Analytical demands in ecological mineral cycling investigations. In: *International Winter Conf. on Developments in Atomic Plasma Spectrochemical Analyses, 1980, San Jose, Puerto Rico.*

Golley, F.B. and Richardson, T., 1977. Chemical relationships in tropical forests. *Geo-Eco-Trop.*, 1: 35–44.

Golley, F.B., McGinnis, J.T., Clements, R.G., Child, G.I. and Duever, M.J., 1975. *Mineral Cycling in a Tropical Moist Forest Ecosystem.* University of Georgia Press, Athens, Ga.

Golley, F.B., Richardson, T. and Clements, R.G., 1978. Elemental concentrations in tropical forests and soils of northwestern Colombia. *Biotropica*, 10(2): 144–151.

Hadi, S. et al., 1979. Penggunaan Kayu bakar dan limbah pertanian di Indonesia (Laporan perkembangan). In: *Kertas kerja untuk Lokakkarya Energi Komite Nasional WEC.* Badan Litbang Pertanian. Lombaga Paneli tian Hasil Hutan, Bogor.

Herrera, R., Jordan, C.F., Klinge, H. and Medina, E., 1978. Amazon ecosystems, their structure and functioning with particular emphasis on nutrients. *Interciencia*, 3(4): 223–231.

Hough, W.A., 1969. Caloric value of some forest fuels of the Southern United States. *U.S. Dep. Agric. For. Ser. Res., Note* SE–120.

Howard-Williams, C., 1974. Nutritional quality and calorific value of Amazonian forest litter. *Amazoniana*, 1: 67–75.

Hozumi, K., Yoda, K., Kokawa, S. and Kira, T., 1969. Production ecology of tropical rain forests in southwestern Cambodia. 1. Plant biomass. *Nat. Life S.E. Asia*, 6: 1–51.

Huttel, C. and Bernhard-Reversat, F., 1975. Recherches sur l'écosystème de la forêt subéquatoriale de basse Côte-d'Ivoire. 5. Biomasse végétale et productivité primaire. Cycle de la matière organique. *Terre Vie*, 29: 203–228.

Jordan, C.F., 1971. Productivity of a tropical forest and its relation to a world pattern of energy storage. *J. Ecol.*, 59: 127–142.

Jordan, C.F., 1980. Nutrient cycling in an Amazonian rain forest (in manuscript).

Kato, R., Tadaki, Y. and Ogawa, H., 1978. Plant biomass and growth increment studies in Pasoh Forest. *Malay. Nat. J.*, 30(2): 211–224.

Kira, T., Ogawa, H., Yoda, K.A. and Ogino, K., 1964. Primary production by a tropical rain forest of southern Thailand. *Bot. Mag. Tokyo*, 77: 428–429.

Klinge, H., 1972. Biomasa y materia organica del suelo en el ecosistema de la pluviselva Centro Amazonica. In: *IV. Congreso Latinoamericano de suelos Caracas*, 22 pp. (mimeograph).

Klinge, H., 1976. Bilanzierung von Hauptnährstoffen im Ökosystem tropischer Regenwald (Manaus) — vorläufige Daten. *Biogeographica*, 7: 59–77.

Klinge, H., Rodrigues, W.A., Brunig, E. and Fittkau, E.J., 1975. Biomass and structure in a central Amazonian rain forest. In: F.B. Golley and E. Medina (Editors), *Tropical Ecological Systems*. Springer-Verlag, Berlin, pp. 115–122.

Las Salas, G. de, 1978. El ecosistema forestal Carare–Opon. *CONIF, Ser. Tecn.*, No. 8.

Lieth, H., 1975. Measurement of caloric values. In: H. Lieth and R. Whittaker (Editors), *Primary Productivity of the Biosphere*. Springer-Verlag, Berlin, pp. 119–129.

Madgwick, H.A.I., 1970. Caloric values of *Pinus virginiana* as affected by time of sampling, tree age, and position in stand. *Ecology*, 51: 1094–1097.

Nabholz, V. and Richardson, T.H., 1975. Factor analysis: an exploratory technique applied to mineral cyclings. In: F.G. Howell, J.B. Gentry, M.H. Smith (Editors), *Mineral Cycling in Southeastern Ecosystems*. USERDA, Tech. Inf. Center, pp. 126–141.

Odum, H.T., 1970. Summary: an emerging view of the ecological system at El Verde. In: H.T. Odum and R.F. Pigeon (Editors), *A Tropical Rain Forest: A Study of Irradiation and Ecology at El Verde, Puerto Rico*. U.S. Atomic Energy Commission, Washington, D.C., pp. 191–289.

Odum, H.T., Abbott, W., Sealander, R.K., Golley, F.B. and Wilson, R.F., 1970. Estimates of chlorophyll and biomass of the Tabunuco forest of Puerto Rico. In: H.T. Odum and R.F. Pigeon (Editors), *A Tropical Rain Forest: A Study of Irradiation and Ecology at El Verde, Puerto Rico*. U.S. Atomic Energy Commission, Washington, D.C., pp. 13–19.

Ovington, J.D. and Heitkamp, D., 1960. The accumulation of energy in forest plantations in Britain. *J. Ecol.*, 48: 639–646.

Ovington, J.D. and Lawrence, D.B., 1967. Comparative chlorophyll, and energy studies of prairie, savannah, oakwood and maise field ecosystems. *Ecology*, 48: 515–524.

Ovington, J.D. and Olson, J.S., 1970. Biomass and chemical content of El Verde lower montane rain forest plants. In: H.T. Odum and R. Pigeon (Editors), *A Tropical Rain Forest: A Study of Irradiation and Ecology at El Verde, Puerto Rico*. U.S. Atomic Energy Commission, Washington, D.C., pp. 53–75.

Paine, R.T., 1971. The measurement and application of the calorie to ecological problems. *Annu. Rev. Ecol. Syst.*, 2: 145–164.

Perera, W.R.H., 1979. *Biofuel Systems and Plantations — Energy Forms: Their Environmental Implications*. Environment and Policy Institute, East-West Center, Hawaii, 87 pp.

Prochazka, G.J., Payne, W.J. and Mayberry, W.R., 1970. Calorific content of certain bacteria and fungi. *Bacteriology*, 104: 646–649.

Schlesinger, W.H., 1977. Carbon balance in terrestrial detritus. *Annu. Rev. Ecol. Syst.*, 8: 51–81.

Singh, K.P. and Misra, R., 1978. *Structure and Functioning of Natural, Modified and Silvicultural Ecosystems of Eastern Uttar Pradesh*. Banares Hindu University, Varanasi.

Slobodkin, L.B. and Richman, S., 1961. Calories/gm. in species of animals. *Nature*, 191(4785): 299.

Stark, N., 1970. The nutrient content of plants and soils from Brazil and Surinam. *Biotropica*, 2: 51–60.

Stark, N., 1971. Nutrient cycling II. Nutrient distribution in Amazonian vegetation. *Trop. Ecol.*, 12: 177–201.

Tanner, E.V.J., 1977. Four montane rain forests of Jamaica: a quantitative characterization of the floristics, the soils, and the foliar mineral levels, and a discussion of the interrelations. *J. Ecol.*, 65: 883–918.

Wiegert, R.G., 1976. *Ecological Energetics*. Benchmark Papers in Ecology No. 4. Dowden, Hutchinson and Ross, Stroudsburg, Pa.

Yoda, K., 1968. A preliminary survey of the forest vegetation of eastern Nepal. III. Plant biomass in the sample plots chosen from different vegetation zones. *J. College Arts Sci., Chiba Univ., Nat. Sci. Ser.*, 5(2): 277–302.

Chapter 8

PRODUCTIVITY OF TROPICAL RAIN FOREST ECOSYSTEMS AND THE IMPLICATIONS FOR THEIR USE AS FUTURE WOOD AND ENERGY SOURCES

CARL F. JORDAN

INTRODUCTION

The florid descriptions of tropical vegetation in novels and the popular press would certainly lead the reader to expect that tropical forests are a virtual uncontrolled frenzy of growth. The naive layman might even be concerned about entering the Amazon forest, for fear that some snake-like vine would snare him as he walked along a jungle path. Indeed, even among professional ecologists, there is almost unanimous agreement that productivity in tropical forests is higher than in any other forest type of the world. Murphy (1975) states, "Forests receiving abundant year-round rainfall and lacking distinct seasonality in leaf fall are, on the average, the most productive of any of the terrestrial ecosystems measured to date. Total annual net primary production averages 2400 g m^{-2} yr^{-1}. The maximum value is 3210 g m^{-2} yr^{-1} for lowland forest in Sarawak." Lugo et al. (1973) say, "Tropical ecosystems are more productive than their temperate counterparts. Tropical forests as a whole, with a mean annual net primary production of 2160 g m^{-2}, exceed temperate forests, averaging 1300 g m^{-2} yr^{-1}, by a factor of 1.7, and boreal forests, averaging only 800 g m^{-2} yr^{-1} by a factor of 2.7." In a recent review of Lugo et al., Murphy (1977) concluded that their estimates of tropical productivity were around 3000 g m^{-2} yr^{-1} too low.

According to Golley and Lieth (1972), "Tropical forests have an average net primary productivity of 2530 g m^{-2} yr^{-1}, ranging from 520 to 4840 g m^{-2} yr^{-1}. There seems little doubt that on the average tropical forests are more productive than temperate forests." Rodin and Bazilevich (1967) calculate the annual productivity of tropical rain forests to be between 2700 and 3450 g m^{-2} yr^{-1} and they

conclude that this "indicates a very high rate of annual organic matter increment in the tropical and subtropical belts, considerably greater than in the plant communities of temperate latitudes." Whittaker and Likens (1975) also rank tropical rain forests as first in rate of production among natural terrestrial ecosystems, with a normal range of 1000 to 3500 g m^{-2} yr^{-1}.

A few reviewers consider productivity in tropical forests significantly higher than the above figures. Westlake (1963) suggested that the range of productivity of tropical forests to be 2600 to 5200 g m^{-2} yr^{-1}. On the basis of available solar radiation, Brünig (1968) calculated the "maximum potential gross assimilation rates" in tropical forests to be between 5600 and 8900 g m^{-2} yr^{-1}, and concluded that "The average potential productivity of the vegetation in the tropical rain forest is several times greater than in continental boreal coniferous forests on comparable average productive forest sites."

The consequence of the high estimates of forest productivity, quite expectedly, is the impression that tropical forests are a vast reservoir of wood production. Thus, Brunig (1968) states, "Worldwide planning of forestry production in the future will have to consider the relatively high potential of the Tropical Rain forest area for inexpensive timber production. The rapid expansion of international transport facilities and relative cheapness of sea-transport and the rising demands in regions which border the potential producing areas add to the potential importance of the tropics as timber producing area."

It is not surprising then, that politicians, industrial entrepreneurs, and national planners in tropical countries are basing plans for future development in part upon a supposedly high potential for plant productivity of tropical ecosystems. For example, in the February 11, 1977 issue of *Science* (volume 195, p. 564), the following news item appeared: "An energy strategy based on biomass is a natural for Brazil, says Jose Goldemberg, director of the physics institute at the University of Sao Paulo, and coordinator of an academic energy policy group. We have lots of land, lots of water, and an ideal climate for growth." Indeed, even influential scientists in the United States believe vegetative growth in the tropics represents a tremendous potential. Abelson (1975) quotes a figure for manioc production of $5000 \, \text{g m}^{-2} \, \text{yr}^{-1}$. Since manioc is a principal crop in the Amazon Basin, he suggests that large plantations of this crop could represent an energy alternative for Brazil.

Directors of multinational corporations also are convinced that tropical rain forest ecosystems have a tremendous exploitable potential. The following quotation appeared in *Time* magazine, November 15, 1976, page 59, regarding Daniel Ludwig, of National Bulk Carriers, Inc.: "In 1967, Ludwig paid $3 million to a group of Brazilian families for a 4650-sq-mi [$12\,044 \, \text{km}^2$] swatch of rain forest in Brazil's remote Amazon region. He then set in motion a bold plan for developing the tract, which is almost the size of the state of Connecticut, to help meet the future world shortages of food, lumber, and wood pulp for paper-making that he expects."

However, not all scientists share the opinion that tropical vegetation represents a great potential for cheap and rapid production of wood and/or energy. Whitmore (1975), after a comparison of herbaceous growth versus woody growth in tropical rain forests, dissents from the view that tropical forests have higher production rates than temperate forests. He states, "We can note that the luxuriousness and appearance of unbridled growth given by the vegetation of the perhumid tropics does not therefore arise from an intrinsically higher growth rate than exists amongst temperate species. The unfamiliar life-forms of palm, pandan, the giant monocotyledonous herbs, and the abundant climbers make a vivid impression of "vegetative frenzy" on the botanist brought up in a temperate climate. The appearance of rapid growth of pioneer trees of forest fringes and clearings, which forms the other part of the impression, does not result, as far as we yet know, from a particularly efficient dry-weight

production or energy conversion, but arises from the architecture of the tree, which results from the capacity for unrestricted elongation of internodes and production of leaves in the continually favourable climate."

Kato et al. (1974), after studying the production of the Pasoh forest in Malaysia, also had doubts about the supposed high wood production in tropical forests. They state, "The amount of evidence is too scarce, but these [their] figures seem to show that the traditional belief in the high rate of wood production by tropical rain forests is most probably an illusion."

Leigh (1975), in his review and comparison of wood production in tropical and temperate areas, concluded that while wood production varied greatly from year to year, "rates are roughly comparable for tropical and climax temperate forest".

In a series of studies (Jordan, 1971a, b; Jordan and Murphy 1978), I have provided evidence that not only is rate of wood production not higher in tropical forests, but that actually the efficiency of wood production is higher in temperate zones.

What is the basis of this apparent disagreement between those who claim productivity of tropical forests is higher than temperate forests and those who claim it is not? Before resolving the contradiction, I will define some of the terms used in studies of forest productivity, and then discuss some of the environmental factors which affect forest production.

DEFINITIONS OF PRODUCTIVITY AND METHODS OF MEASUREMENT

Gross photosynthesis is the rate at which plants transform carbon dioxide from the atmosphere into simple sugars. At the same time that photosynthesis is occurring, simple sugars are being oxidized in the plant, yielding life-sustaining energy in a process called respiration. During the daytime, the rate of carbon fixation is usually greater than respiration. The difference between the two rates is called net photosynthesis:

$$GP - R = NP$$

where GP is gross photosynthesis, R is respiration, and NP is net photosynthesis. Net photosynthesis is usually measured by enclosing a leaf or a plant in a chamber and measuring the change in the carbon dioxide content of the air passing through the chamber with a gas analyzer (Woodwell and Botkin, 1970). If the plant in the chamber is subjected to a dark period, the carbon dioxide content in the chamber increases, since respiration is occurring but not photosynthesis. It was once believed that gross photosynthesis could be calculated by assuming dark respiration to be the same as light respiration. For example, for light–dark intervals of 12 h, it was thought that:

$$GP_{24\,h} = NP_{24\,h} + 2(R_{dark,\,12\,h})$$

However, it has been recently discovered that light respiration, or photorespiration is much higher than dark respiration (Zelitch, 1971). While light respiration has been measured in the laboratory, techniques are not yet available for field measurements, and consequently we have no reliable measurement of gross photosynthesis in natural ecosystems.

Net primary production is the term commonly used in ecology to designate productivity of some or all the plants in an ecosystem. The term is conceptually similar to net photosynthesis, but there is an important difference: Net photosynthesis is usually given in grams of carbon assimilated per unit of plant per hour or per minute; net primary production is usually given in grams, kilograms, or tons of dry weight produced per unit ecosystem per year or per growing season, and includes the nutrient elements assimilated by the plant, as well as the net carbon fixation.

While the plants in an ecosystem are producing leaves, fruits, flowers and wood, consumers are eating part of this organic matter. Some of the organic matter consumed by herbivores is respired away, and some is transformed into the biomass of the consumers. When the leaves, etc., fall to the forest floor, some is respired by the decomposers and some is transformed into the biomass of the decomposers. Net primary production minus respiration of consumers and decomposers equals net ecosystem production:

$$NPP - (R_h + R_d) = NEP$$

where NPP is net primary production, R_h and R_d

are respiration of herbivores and decomposers, and NEP is net ecosystem production.

If net ecosystem production is greater than zero, some or all parts of the ecosystem are getting larger. This usually happens during the process of succession. If net ecosystem production is less than zero, some or all parts of the ecosystem may be getting smaller. This could occur in a mature forest where heavy shade, seed predation, or other causes prevent establishment of seedlings, yet occasionally dead trees fall over. It also could occur after some sort of disaster such as a hurricane that knocks down many forest trees, resulting in a lower rate of net primary production and a higher rate of decomposer respiration.

There have been two notable attempts to measure tropical net ecosystem production by measuring gas exchange in a portion of the entire forest. In one attempt, a forest "prism" was enclosed in a giant cylinder, 20 m across and 23 m high (Odum and Jordan, 1970). In the other, the "Mean Windfile Approach", an array of sensors were placed throughout the forest to quantify carbon dioxide flux, but the forest was otherwise undisturbed (Lemon et al., 1970). A critique of the methods has been given by Ordway (1969). In the giant cylinder, turbulence at the top of the cylinder caused by wind results in irregular flows through the top of the cylinder. Nevertheless, Murphy (1975) found that the empirical results of the giant cylinder experiment compared favorably with other independent measurements of net ecosystem production. The Mean Windfile Approach works well in a homogeneous stand such as a crop of corn, but the heterogeneity of a forest stand results in irregular profiles that are difficult to quantify on an area basis (Ordway, 1969).

Gas exchange measurements are expensive and complicated to carry out. Consequently there have not been enough to give us any picture of global or regional patterns of productivity.

However, there is another measurement which is simple and cheap to make, and which has been used throughout the world as an index of total net primary productivity. This is to collect the "small litter" usually consisting of leaves, fruit, flowers, and fine twigs. Based on the litter and total net production data of Bray and Gorham (1964), Murphy (1977) calculated that annual net productivity averaged about 3 times annual litter production. However, based upon the litter and wood production data presented by Jordan and Murphy (1978) and Tables 8.1 to 8.5 below, net primary production ranges from 1.3 times litter production in the tropics to 4 times litter production in the northern latitudes.

Although wood production is more difficult to measure than litter fall, there have been several estimates of net primary production in temperate zones by analyzing tree rings and lengths of twigs between annual whorls (Whittaker and Woodwell, 1968). Since tree rings are caused by differential growth rates caused by seasonality, this method cannot be used in the continuously wet tropics. It would seem that it might be applicable in the seasonally dry tropics. However, experienced tropical foresters (F.H. Wadsworth, pers. comm.) suggest that misleading discontinuous rings often occur in the trees of these regions.

There has been a relatively simple study of wood production in the tropics using aluminum band dendrometers (Jordan, 1971b). In this method, changes in tree diameters were measured, diameters were correlated with biomass, and changes in wood biomass were calculated. The major problem with this method was that the aluminum bands frequently broke and had to be replaced, resulting in interruptions in the growth record.

FACTORS WHICH AFFECT PRIMARY PRODUCTIVITY

A primary objective of this chapter is to compare forest productivity in tropical and temperate ecosystems. However, there are many factors which influence productivity, and which could obscure the effect of latitude on productivity. Before temperate–tropical comparisons are made, it is necessary to consider these factors.

TABLE 8.1

Rates of wood and litter production in broad-leaved mesic forests where radiation balance at the earth's surface is between 25 and 40 kcal cm^{-2} yr^{-1} (104–167 kJ cm^{-2} yr^{-1})

Author	Forest	Production (g m^{-2} yr^{-1}) wood	litter	
Aaltonen (1948)[1]	birch, Finland	–	190	*Betula* sp.
Viro (1955)	birch, Finland	–	180	*Betula* sp.
Viro (1955)	birch, Finland	–	150	*Betula* sp.
Jenny et al. (1949)	birch, Calif. mts.	–	80	*Betula* sp.
Bonnevie-Svendsen and Gjems (1957)	beech, Norway	–	280	*Fagus* sp.
Mork (1942)	birch, Norway	–	190	*Betula* sp.
Andersson and Enander (1948)[1]	poplar, Sweden	–	190	*Populus* sp.
Knudsen and Mauritz-Hansson (1939)[1]	birch, Sweden	–	170	*Betula* sp.
Lindquist (1964)[1]	angiosperms, Sweden	–	280	
Andersson (1973)	beech, Sweden	1420	480	*Fagus* sp.
Andersson (1973)	beech, Sweden	1390	390	*Fagus* sp.
Andersson (1973)	beech, Sweden	900	330	*Fagus* sp.
Andersson (1973)	basswood, Sweden	1440	80	*Tilia* sp.
Rodin and Bazilevich (1967)	birch, Moscow, U.S.S.R.	390	370	*Betula* sp.
Rodin and Bazilevich (1967)	birch, Novosibirsk, U.S.S.R.	540	520	*Betula* sp.
Rodin and Bazilevich (1967)	birch, Novosibirsk, U.S.S.R.	550	270	*Betula* sp.
Dylis (1971)	northern hardwood, Moscow, U.S.S.R.	835	242	
Nihlgard and Lindgren (1977)	beech, Sweden	1310	480	*Fagus* sp.
Andersson (1971)	deciduous, Sweden	1320	70	
Boysen-Jensen (1932)[2]	ash, Denmark	410	330	*Fraxinus* sp.
Möller (1945)[2]	beech, Denmark	740	390	*Fagus* sp.
Möller (1945)[2]	beech, Denmark	960	390	*Fagus* sp.
Thamdrup (1973)	beech, Denmark	1354	407	*Fagus* sp.
		$\bar{X} = 968 \pm 399$	$\bar{X} = 281 \pm 133$	

[1] In: Bray and Gorham (1964). [2] In: Kira et al. (1967).

Secondary succession

In forest areas where land has been cleared for agricultural or forestry purposes, the processes of secondary succession begin shortly after the land is abandoned. In temperate areas, net production is low at first while plants become established in the area if succession is starting from plowed fields (Odum, 1969). Net production increases as the vegetation becomes larger and leaf area index increases (Odum, 1969). As the forest reaches maturity, Odum claims that net productivity drops, but it drops only in the sense that total biomass of the forest is not increasing, because old trees are dying and falling over. Younger trees filling in the gaps could keep the net primary production relatively high. Only in a completely stagnant even-aged forest would net production drop, and then it

would not drop to zero, since the forest still would be producing leaves. Net ecosystem production, however, could drop to zero.

Odum's (1969) generalizations concerning low productivity during the early years of succession were drawn chiefly from studies in temperate areas where grasses and herbs were the first invaders, and tree species became established only later in succession. However, in the wet tropics, early stages of succession are characterized by a very dense undergrowth (Budowski, 1963). This is in agreement with my own observations on secondary succession in a Puerto Rican rain forest following radiation damage (Jordan, 1971b). Within two years after radiation ceased, tree seedlings were becoming established, and yearly changes in standing crop were equal to those in the adjacent closed forest. Ewel (1971) found that in Panama, leaf production

TABLE 8.2

Rates of wood and litter production in broad-leaved mesic forests where radiation balance at the earth's surface is between 40 and 50 kcal cm^{-2} yr^{-1} (167–209 kJ cm^{-2} yr^{-1})

Author	Forest	Production (g m^{-2} yr^{-1})		
		wood	litter	
Bray and Gorham (1964)	northern hardwoods, Toronto, Ont.	–	430	
Coldwell and DeLong (1950)[1]	maple, Montreal, Que.	–	340	*Acer* sp.
Coldwell and DeLong (1950)[1]	beech, Montreal, Que.	–	220	*Fagus* sp.
Coldwell and DeLong (1950)[1]	birch, Montreal, Que.	–	170	*Betula* sp.
Coldwell and DeLong (1950)[1]	poplar, Montreal, Que.	–	170	*Populus* sp.
Reiners (1972)	oak, Minnesota	423	467	*Quercus* sp.
Ovington et al. (1963)	oak, Minnesota	–	354	*Quercus* sp.
Alway et al. (1933)[1]	maple, Minnesota	–	220	*Acer* sp.
Hole and Nielsen (1964)[1]	oak, Wisconsin	–	620	*Quercus* sp.
Murphy et al. (1974)	aspen, Wisconsin	–	232	*Populus* sp.
Murphy et al. (1974)	maple, Wisconsin	–	263	*Acer* sp.
Loucks (1973)	oak, Wisconsin	392	319	*Quercus* sp.
Loucks (1973)	oak, Wisconsin	354	410	*Quercus* sp.
Chandler (1941)[1]	northern hardwoods, New York	–	305	
Scott (1955)[1]	northern hardwoods, Connecticut	–	210	
Polster (1950)	beech, Germany	1100	320	*Fagus* sp.
Ehwald (1957)[1]	beech, Germany	910	350	*Fagus* sp.
Polster (1950)	birch, Germany	660	200	*Betula* sp.
Polster (1950)	oak, Germany	800	240	*Quercus* sp.
Ebermayer (1876)[2]	beech, Germany	850	450	*Fagus* sp.
Danckelmann (1887)[1]	beech, Germany	–	417	*Fagus* sp.
Medwecka-Kornas et al. (1973)	oak, Poland	373	398	*Quercus* sp.
Whittaker et al. (1974)	northern hardwoods, low elev.	719	399	
Whittaker et al. (1974)	northern hardwoods, mid elev.	658	374	
		$\bar{X} = 658 \pm 248$	$\bar{X} = 328 \pm 111$	

[1]In: Bray and Gorham (1964). [2]In: Rodin and Bazilevich (1967).

TABLE 8.3

Rates of wood and litter production in broad-leaved mesic forests where radiation balance at the earth's surface is between 50 and 60 kcal cm^{-2} yr^{-1} (209–250 kJ cm^{-2} yr^{-1})

Author	Forest	Production (g m^{-2} yr^{-1})		
		wood	litter	
Tarsia (1973)	poplar, Italy	1205	637	*Populus* sp.
Rodin and Bazilevich (1967)	aspen, Voronezh, U.S.S.R.	1450	340	*Populus* sp.
Rodin and Bazilevich (1967)	aspen, Voronezh, U.S.S.R.	410	480	*Populus* sp.
Rodin and Bazilevich (1967)	oak, Dubrava, U.S.S.R.	200	330	*Quercus* sp.
Rodin and Bazilevich (1967)	oak, Dubrava, U.S.S.R.	320	358	*Quercus* sp..
Rodin and Bazilevich (1967)	oak, Dubrava, U.S.S.R.	200	400	*Quercus* sp.
Rodin and Bazilevich (1967)	oak, Dubrava, U.S.S.R.	40	384	*Quercus* sp.
Remezov and Bykova (1953, in Bray and Gorham, 1964)	poplar, Voronezh, U.S.S.R.	–	430	*Populus* sp.
Sviridova (1960, in Bray and Gorham, 1964)	poplar, Voronezh, U.S.S.R.	–	530	*Populus* sp.
Ehwald (1957, in Bray and Gorham, 1964)	beech, Switzerland	–	225	*Fagus sp.*
Whittaker (1966)	angiosperms, Tennessee	1014	320	
Whittaker (1966)	tulip trees, Tennessee	2408	410	*Liriodendron* sp.
Reichle et al. (1973a)	tulip trees, Tennessee	346	372	*Liriodendron* sp.
Blow (1955, in Bray and Gorham, 1964)	oaks, Tennessee	–	290	*Quercus* sp.
DeSelm et al. (1964, in Bray and Gorham, 1964)	oaks, Tennessee	–	450	*Quercus* sp.
Olson (1964, in Bray and Gorham, 1964)	tulip trees, Tennessee	–	470	*Liriodendron* sp.
Olson (1964, in Bray and Gorham, 1964)	oak, Tennessee	–	500	*Quercus* sp.
Ovington (1956)	angiosperms, England	369	137	
Ovington (1965)	oak and chestnut, England	260	–	*Quercus* sp. *Castanea* sp.
Ovington and Madgwick (1959)	birch, England	730	170	*Betula* sp.
Ohmasa and Mori (1937, in Bray and Gorham, 1964)	hardwood, Japan	–	223	
Jaro (1958, in Bray and Gorham, 1964)	locust, Hungary	–	265	*Robinia* sp.
Jaro (1958, in Bray and Gorham, 1964)	beech, Hungary	–	330	*Fagus* sp.
Jaro (1958, in Bray and Gorham, 1964)	angiosperms, Hungary	–	378	
Jaro (1958, in Bray and Gorham, 1964)	oak, Hungary	–	402	*Quercus* sp.
Rodin and Bazilevich (1967)	"lime forest", Armenia, U.S.S.R.	440	291	
Rodin and Bazilevich (1967)	"lime forest", Armenia, U.S.S.R.	150	452	
Whittaker and Woodwell (1969)	oaks, Long Island, New York	783	406	*Quercus* sp.
Satoo (1970)	poplar, Japan	560	220	*Populus* sp.
Satoo (1970)	deciduous forests, Japan	466	236	
Miller (1971)	beech, New Zealand	285	600	*Nothofagus* sp.
Hughes (1971)	alder-birch, England	426	273	*Alnus* sp. *Betula* sp.
Carlisle et al. (1966)	oak, England	–	382	*Quercus* sp.
Denaeyer and Duvigneaud (1973)	oak, Belgium	919	524	*Quercus* sp.
Duvigneaud and Denaeyer (1967)	oak–birch, Belgium	448	270	*Quercus* sp., *Betula* sp.
Witkamp and Van der Drift (1961, in Bray and Gorham, 1964)	oak–birch, The Netherlands	–	370	*Quercus* sp., *Betula* sp.
		$\bar{X} = 610 \pm 537$	$\bar{X} = 367 \pm 116$	

was highest during the first two years of succession, stem production was highest during the interval of 2 to 4 years, and root production was highest in the 4 to 6 year interval. At another site in Panama, a 6 year old secondary successional stand had a leaf area index equal to that of the surrounding mature forest (Golley et al., 1975). It is probable that this rapid production of leaf biomass during early secondary succession in the wet tropics led early observers to believe that productivity of tropical forests in general is higher than in temperate zones.

Succession in the dry tropics contrasts sharply with that in the wet tropics. In the dry tropics, total productivity is lower, and ground cover is patchy in contrast to a more uniform coverage in wet areas. Sprouting is more important in dry forests, seasonal changes in growth are greater, and susceptibility to climatic variations is greater (Ewel, 1977).

Nutrients and organic matter

Due to the well-known responses of agricultural crops to fertilizer, we almost take it for granted that natural forests growing on fertile soil will grow more rapidly than forests growing on poor soils. This may be the case, but there is very little evidence for it because it is very difficult to find two forests with the same species, water and light regime, yet growing on soils of different fertility. Some evidence is provided by Duvigneaud et al. (1971) who studied the production of seven different oak forests located on soils of different fertility in Belgium, and found that productivity was generally positively correlated with soil fertility, and in the tropical Cerrado of Brazil, Goodland and Pollard (1973) found that the gradient from stands of small, widely scattered trees to well-developed woodland parallels a soil fertility gradient.

TABLE 8.4

Rates of wood and litter production in broad-leaved mesic forests where radiation balance at the earth's surface is between 60 and 70 kcal cm^{-2} yr^{-1} (250–290 kJ cm^{-2} yr^{-1})

Author	Forest	Production (g m^{-2} yr^{-1})		
		wood	litter	
Metz (1952, in Bray and Gorham, 1964)	angiosperms, South Carolina	–	530	
Metz (1952, in Bray and Gorham, 1964)	angiosperms, South Carolina	–	470	
Metz (1952, in Bray and Gorham, 1964)	angiosperms, South Carolina	–	510	
Ashton (1964, in Bray and Gorham, 1964)	*Eucalyptus*, Victoria	–	810	*Eucalyptus* sp.
Kimura (1960, in Kira et al., 1967)	broad-leaved evergreen, Japan	920	1140	
Kirata (1965, in Kira and Shidei, 1967)	broad-leaved evergreen, Japan	–	600	
Webb (1964, in Bray and Gorham, 1964)	subtropical rain forest, New South Wales	–	720	
Webb (1964, in Bray and Gorham, 1964)	subtropical rain forest, New South Wales	–	730	
Webb (1964, in Bray and Gorham, 1964)	warm temperate rain forest, New South Wales	–	450	
Webb (1964, in Bray and Gorham, 1964)	warm temperate rain forest, New South Wales	–	590	
Webb (1964, in Bray and Gorham, 1964)	warm temperate rain forest, New South Wales	–	680	
Webb (1964), in Bray and Gorham, 1964)	wet sclerophyll, New South Wales	–	600	
Cromack and Monk (1975)	hardwood, North Carolina	–	437	
Tsutsumi (1971)	broad-leaved, Japan	–	510	
Garg and Vyas (1975)	deciduous, India	–	400	
Subba Rao et al. (1972)	sal, India	–	1094	*Shorea* sp.
Subba Rao et al. (1972)	teak, India	–	777	*Tectona* sp.
Bandhu (1973)	deciduous, India	–	772	
Ramm (1975)	deciduous, India	423	450	
Misra (1972)	deciduous, India	930	620	
		$\bar{X} = 758 \pm 290$	$\bar{X} = 644 \pm 204$	

Evidence which is currently being gathered in a nutrient-poor region of the Amazon Basin indicates that forest trees in low fertility sites have evolved mechanisms to conserve nutrients, thereby minimizing the effect of low nutrient levels in soils (Herrera et al., 1978). The most important of these mechanisms is a root mat 10 to 30 cm in depth which covers the surface of the mineral soil and acts as an ion exchange column for nutrients which reach the forest floor (Stark and Jordan, 1978). Rates of nutrient loss from this ecosystem (Jordan, 1978) are considerably lower than from other ecosystems on more fertile soil (Likens et al., 1977). Leaf litter production in this forest, while some-

TABLE 8.5

Rates of wood and litter production in broad-leaved mesic forests where radiation balance at the earth's surface is greater than 70 kcal cm^{-2} yr^{-1} (290 kJ cm^{-2} yr^{-1})

Author	Forest	Production (g m^{-2} yr^{-1})		
		wood	litter	
Golley et al. (1975)	tropical moist, Panama	–	1135	
Golley et al. (1975)	pre-montane, Panama	–	1048	
Golley et al. (1975)	riverine, Panama	–	1161	
Jenny et al. (1949)	broad-leaved, Colombia	–	1011	
Zonn and Cheng-Kwei (1962, in Rodin and Bazilevich, 1967)	rain forest, southeast China	–	1160	
Bernhard-Reversat et al. (1972)	evergreen forest, Ivory Coast	–	820	
Nye (1961)	moist tropical, Ghana	1120	1052	
Rozanov and Rozanov(1964, in Rodin and Bazilevich, 1967)	bamboo, Burma	700	–	*Oxytenanthera* sp.
Jordan (1971b)	rain forest, Puerto Rico	486	547	
Kira et al. (1967)	tropical rain forest, Thailand	533	2322	
Jenny et al. (1949)	rain forest, Colombia	–	852	
Laudelout and Meyer (1954)	mixed forest, Zaïre	–	1232	
Klinge and Rodrigues (1968)	rain forest, Brazil	–	730	
Mitchell (1964, in Bray and Gorham, 1964)	secondary forest, Malaya	–	830	
Mitchell (1964, in Bray and Gorham, 1964)	secondary forest, Malaya	–	1050	
Mitchell (1964, in Bray and Gorham, 1964)	secondary forest, Malaya	–	1440	
Mitchell (1964, in Bray and Gorham, 1964)	dipterocarp, Malaya	–	1090	*Dryobalanops* sp.
Mitchell (1964, in Bray and Gorham, 1964)	dipterocarp, Malaya	–	770	*Dryobalanops* sp.
Mitchell (1964, in Bray and Gorham, 1964)	sal, Malaya	–	1480	*Shorea* sp.
Mitchell (1964, in Bray and Gorham, 1964)	sal, Malaya	–	1020	*Shorea* sp.
Wanner (1970)	rain forest, north Borneo	–	1070	
Wanner (1970)	rain forest, Java	–	810	
Muller and Nielsen (1965, in Kira et al., 1967)	tropical seasonal, Ivory Coast	900	440	
Hopkins (1966)	tropical seasonal, Nigeria	–	720	
Edwards (1977)	tropical montane, New Guinea	–	635	
Dilmy (1971)	tropical rain forest, Sumatra	580	–	
Dilmy (1971)	tropical montane, Sumatara	1240	–	
Haines and Foster (1977)	tropical moist, Panama	–	1110	
Medina and Zelwer (1972)	montane, Venezuela	–	780	
Klinge and Rodrigues (1968)	tropical rain forest, Mañaus	–	730	
Kira (1974)	tropical rain forest, Malaysia	640	1055	
Anonymous (1975)	evergreen, Ivory Coast	400	1000	
Muller and Nielsen (1965, in Kira et al., 1967)	tropical rain forest, Ivory Coast	750	210	
Klinge (1974)	tropical rain forest, Manaus	–	670	
Klinge (1974)	tropical rain forest, Belem	–	900	
Cornforth (1970)	evergreen seasonal forest, Trinidad	–	700	*Mora* sp.
		$\bar{X}=734\pm275$	$\bar{X}=957\pm362$	

what lower than other tropical forests, is within the range of many temperate forests on fertile soil (Jordan, 1978), indicating that the low nutrient level may not seriously affect productivity under natural conditions. However, the studies initiated by Herrera et al. (1978) are showing that, when the forest and its root mat are destroyed during agricultural or forestry operations, productivity decreases rapidly due to leaching of nutrients.

While there are many site to site variations within each latitudinal zone, the problem of nutrient retention, in general, is more severe in tropical areas, for two reasons. First, the continual high temperatures result in continual high rates of microbial activity, litter decomposition, and consequent high potential for leaching, especially in the humid tropics (Olson, 1963; Jenny et al., 1949). Second, large areas such as the Amazon Basin in South America are geologically very old and highly weathered (Fittkau et al., 1975) in contrast to many temperate areas which have been recently glaciated, a process which exposed new bedrock. Weathering of the newly exposed bedrock often provides a source of nutrients for ecosystems. Golley (1975) has hypothesized that these temperate–tropical differences have resulted in two important tropical–temperate differences in structure and function. In the tropical regions, the greatest percentage of nutrients are incorporated in the living biomass, while in temperate regions, exchange on the mineral soil is a more important form of nutrient storage. In tropical regions, cycles of nutrients are more rapid, resulting in a greater stability of the cycles (Jordan et al., 1972).

Soil organic matter is an important contributor to soil fertility in any latitude, not only because of its nutrient content, but also because of its ability to adsorb dissolved nutrients. However, its importance in the tropics may be particularly important because of the generally lower exchange capacity and higher potential leaching rates of tropical soils. Nye and Greenland (1960) have documented rapid decreases in agricultural productivity in many tropical soils, and correlated the decrease with the destruction of the soil organic matter.

Mycorrhizae have been hypothesized to play a critical role in the cycling of nutrients in some tropical forests, thereby maintaining their productivity (Went and Stark, 1968). However, Jordan and Herrera (1981) hypothesized that mycorrhizae

and direct cycling of nutrients are not so much an important characteristic of tropical ecosystems as they are of oligotrophic ecosystems. The reason they have been associated more with tropical forests is that oligotrophic forests are more common in tropical areas. However, in the temperate zone, it is well known that mycorrhizae play an important role in the nutrition of pines (Wilde, 1968) and that pines often grow in nutrient-poor environments in the temperate region (Monk, 1966).

Water availability and seasonality

Many workers have shown a general correlation between rainfall and tree growth in tropical forests. Lack of water will cause the slowing down or cessation of growth, and radial growth is especially sensitive to water supply in the form of rainfall, soil moisture and internal water potential (Hopkins, 1970). Daubenmire (1972) in Costa Rica using a dendrometer to measure radial growth of trees found that, in 12 of the 25 species studied, growth was confined to the rainy season, while the other species continued growth for a month or two into the dry season.

However, observations on leaf flushing in Costa Rica (Daubenmire, 1972) and twig elongation in Nigeria (Hopkins, 1970) have shown that it is not the coming of the rains which actually triggers the growth. In many species, growth began in advance of the rainy season. Daubenmire believes the cause of the onset of growth in Costa Rica is photoperiod, and Hopkins thinks the cause in Nigeria is minimum night temperature as well as photoperiod. Since keying the initiation of growth of tropical trees to an unusual rain storm during the middle of the dry season could be disastrous, initiation of growth during a photoperiod that was correlated with the onset of the usual rainy season apparently has been the best evolutionary strategy.

In some regions of the tropics, there is virtually no dry season (Walter, 1971) and the vegetation type is evergreen forest. In regions where the dry season is a few months or less, the vegetation is usually forest, soil conditions permitting, and the trees are often dry season deciduous. In regions where the dry season approaches half of the year, the vegetation type is open woodland or savannah (Malaisse, 1974). In Puerto Rico, Weaver (1978) compared diameter growth on wet and dry sites, and found that growth rates were up to fifteen times higher on the wet sites. In dry forest types the trees are smaller, often scrubby, canopy cover is incomplete, and productivity is lower than in the closed evergreen forest. In these forests, fire, as well as low rainfall may be a cause of the low biomass and low productivity.

Temperature and photosynthetically active radiation

It might seem almost beyond question that greater amounts of photosynthetically active radiation and higher temperatures would result in higher ecosystem productivity. It is difficult to obtain evidence for this however, because it is almost impossible to find natural ecosystems that occur along a gradient of radiation while all other environmental components remain constant. The decreasing amounts of productivity and smaller forest stature that one encounters upon ascending tropical mountains has been attributed by Grubb (1977) to be due to decreased temperature and solar radiation. However, there is doubt as to whether the effect is direct or indirect. Leigh (1975) attributes the decreased productivity to decreased transpiration rates on mountain tops, which he believes slows the movement of nutrients up through the trees. Lower rates of transpiration are caused by higher humidities, which are caused in turn by lower temperatures. Grubb (1977) argues against this transpiration theory, and says that humus accumulation on mountain tops results in low nutrient availability because high acidity with consequent aluminum toxicity in the humus lowers production. Wanner et al. (1973), however, show that at least in some regions in Southeast Asia, humus is oxidized as rapidly on mountains as in the lowlands, indicating that there should be no difference in humus accumulation.

Along a gradient of decreasing latitude, the annual amount of photosynthetically active radiation available to plants increases. The reviews in the first section of this paper conclude that net primary productivity is higher in the tropics. The implicit assumption by the authors of those reviews was that although other environmental variables such as nutrients and moisture affect forest productivity, these factors affect the data from temperate forests to the same extent as from tropical

forests, and in a statistical sense the only variable which changes along the latitudinal gradient is solar radiation.

Although net primary production is higher in latitudes with greater solar radiation, the distribution of the productivity between woody and non-woody tissues varies, and this distribution is important from the point of view of the wood-using industry. This subject will be dealt with in a following section.

Root production

One of the most difficult production parameters to measure is root growth. While many ecosystem productivity studies give estimates of root production, most of these estimates are based on some sort of index such as a root–shoot biomass ratio. A summary of root production estimates on this basis by Bray (1963) shows that ratios of most trees vary between 0.1 and 0.2, and that there is no difference between temperate and tropical trees. Many of these root production estimates may be seriously in error. Harris and Todd (1972) found that seasonal root sloughing and die-off caused annual root production to be several times higher than estimates based on annual changes in root biomass. They found that when production of these sloughed-off rootlets was taken into account, annual root production in a mesophytic hardwood forest in Tennessee was 584 g m^{-2}. Since aboveground wood production in this same forest was 334 g m^{-2} yr^{-1} (Reichle et al., 1973b), the root–shoot production ratio is 1.7.

Coleman (1976) reviews recent work in root productivity, and points out that not only is production and sloughing of rootlets important, but also root exudates represent an important energy drain from trees. Coleman concluded that in most ecosystems, root production actually is greater than above-ground production.

While there have been several attempts to estimate tropical root biomass (Jenik, 1971; Santantonio et al., 1977; Klinge, 1973), there have been no generally known published reports of tropical root production on an ecosystem scale. However, as part of the San Carlos project in the Amazon Territory of Venezuela (Medina et al., 1977) we have been able to measure directly the growth of roots which form a root mat on top of the mineral soil in that region (Jordan and Escalante, 1980). The root growth in the San Carlos forest averaged 201 g m^{-2} yr^{-1}. A preliminary estimate of above-ground wood production for the same forest is 600 g m^{-2} yr^{-1}, yielding a root–shoot production ratio of about 0.33.

Primary consumers

Short-term primary productivity of forests can be severely reduced when an unusual outbreak of herbivorous insects occurs (Franklin, 1970). However, usually no more than 5 to 10% of the area of the living leaves is consumed by insects, and in fact, it has been hypothesized that sometimes phytophagous insects actually stimulate growth by increasing the rate of nutrient cycling and by eliminating old senescent trees (Mattson and Addy, 1975).

Jordan and Herrera (1978) have found in comparing nutrient cycles in tropical and temperate forests, that when making comparisons of the structure and function of ecosystems, comparison of oligotrophic versus eutrophic ecosystems yields more useful generalizations than comparison of temperate versus tropical ecosystems. For example, based on studies of missing leaf area of fresh leaves, it appears that grazing insects consume about the same proportion in temperate forests on fertile soil (5–8%, Franklin, 1970) as in tropical forests on fertile soil (3–8%, Odum, 1970). In contrast, in an oligotrophic tropical forest in the Amazon Basin, Jordan and Uhl (1978) found less than 2% insect consumption of the leaves. They concluded that relatively high levels of secondary plant compounds and sclerophyllous leaves were nutrient conserving mechanisms in oligotrophic forests.

Biochemical differences

Within the past decade, it has been discovered that certain non-tree species, many of which grow in the tropics, fix carbon much more efficiently than others (Black, 1971). The more efficient biochemical pathway is called the C_4-dicarboxylic acid cycle. As a result of higher efficiency of carbon fixation, net primary productivity of these C_4 plants is higher.

Sugar cane (*Saccharum officinarum*) is one of the most important crop plants that has the C_4 cycle. Sugar cane grows primarily in tropical and sub-tropical areas, and average agricultural productivity figures for the tropics are often high because of sugar cane. High productivity data based upon sugar cane cannot, however, be used to predict potential productivity of tree species in the tropics.

RESOLUTION OF THE CONTRADICTION

Data treatment

Now that we have defined the terms used by production ecologists, and examined the factors which influence ecosystem production, we can resolve the apparent disagreement presented in the first section, regarding whether productivity in tropical forests is higher than in temperate forests.

I have summarized 139 studies of wood and litter production in Tables 8.1–8.5. Data are broken down into litter production and wood production. For wood production data, most of the studies cited include root production estimates. Even when root production was estimated, it is likely that the total yearly root production was much greater than estimated, due to the large amount of roots which die and slough off annually. In some studies, shrub production was included in the wood production, in others it was not. For litter production, the usual case was for litter to include leaves, fruits, and flowers. In some cases, twigs also were counted as part of the litter. Tree fall data were not included either as litter fall, since tree fall represents wood production, nor as wood production, since in the general scheme of forest productivity, its productive capacity presumably is compensated by the saplings which replace it.

The data are classified into five groups, to show differences in wood and litter production between high latitude and tropical forests. Classification according to latitude is not really satisfactory for showing temperate–tropical differences. For example, England and Canada have the same latitudes, but wholly different climates and different plant associations, due to the warming influence on England of the Atlantic Gulf Stream. A much better classification is according to radiation balance at the earth's surface (Budyko, 1974), because the redistribution of heat at the earth's surface is accounted for. Budyko (1974, p.155) presents a world map showing isolines of radiation balance.

The ecosystems in Tables 8.1–8.5 were classified according to whether their annual radiation balance, as shown on the map, was between 104 and 167 kJ cm^{-2} yr^{-1} (subtundra), 167 and 209 (northern hardwoods), 209 and 250 (mid-temperate hardwoods), 250 and 290 (south temperate and subtropical) and above 290 (tropical).

When we are comparing temperate and tropical ecosystems, what we really are intending to compare is ecosystems with a low radiation balance, that is, ecosystems that have a low amount of solar energy available for growth, and those with a high radiation balance, that is, ecosystems that have a high amount of solar energy available for growth (Jordan and Murphy, 1978). When we compare productivity in high radiation balance and low radiation balance ecosystems, all the other factors discussed in previous sections must be held constant, or the results will be confounded. This is impossible to do perfectly, but to minimize the effects of variables other than the radiation balance, I eliminated many of the available data according to the following criteria:

Only forests having a continuous canopy were included in the analysis. It would be inappropriate to include open, savanna-type stands because the production characteristics of trees occurring under these conditions would be expected to differ from those of trees in a closed forest situation. I did not exclude forests containing pioneer tree species as long as the forests were considered to have a continuous canopy. From the continuous canopy stage onward, stage of secondary succession should not greatly affect net primary productivity, except in the unusual case of a stagnant, even-aged "climax" forest, because as large trees become senescent and die, younger, more vigorous trees take their place, thus maintaining the net primary productivity of the ecosystem. Since none of the data appeared to be from stagnant forests, all data from closed forests were considered.

Data from mountain top forests were excluded. There is no doubt that productivity of these forests is lower than low altitude forests. The only question is whether the low productivity is due to low sunshine, low transpiration, or low nutrient levels.

Variation in water supply is a factor which tends to obscure the relationship between light available during the growing season, and production. To minimize this factor, I used data only from mesic forests. In most cases, the growing season of high latitude mesic forests is limited by temperature, but I have included data from several lower latitude forests where the growing season is limited by a dry season. Forests which become dormant or semi-dormant during a dry season can still be considered mesic if there is abundant water during the non-dormant season. In contrast, savanna-type forests which may be limited by moisture during the growing season are not included in the data.

Soil fertility is another factor which causes differences in production. There is no way to know how this factor influenced the data, but there is no reason to suspect that it affected data from tropical forests to a different degree than it did data from temperate forests.

Because there are few, if any, primarily gymnosperm forest communities in the tropics, we have used data only from primarily angiosperm forests. In doing so, I eliminated a variable (different major taxa) which might tend to obscure comparisons.

There are two more criteria which can be used in excluding certain studies from inclusion in the comparisons: One is the quantity of data, and the other is the quality of that data. An example of differences in quantity of data is the litter fall studies in the tropics. In some studies, data were collected for only a few months, while in others results were based on a year or more of collection. Examples of differences in quality are the various amounts of effort used in estimating root growth. Further, there are also disagreements among scientists as to which methods are most satisfactory. For example, some ecologists say dendrometer studies of tropical tree growth are poor because the screws may affect diameter growth at the critical point. Others reject permanent diameter tapes because of breakage and slippage. Ordinary diameter measurements are almost impossible to duplicate because of the irregularity of the trunks.

While there may be some agreement between scientists on which are good studies and which are poor studies, any division along the continuum from good to bad studies would be arbitrary. For this reason, the only criterion that I have used in selecting data is that it has been published. This strategy could cause inaccuracies in calculated production averages. Since there is no absolute standard against which to judge the averages, we cannot know if there are inaccuracies. However, the principal theme of this chapter is a comparison of productivity rates in various latitudinal zones. If there are errors in the data due to underestimates of root production for example, the comparisons will not be affected if the errors occur with the same frequency in the data from various latitudes.

This is the basic assumption underlying the comparisons presented here: although there probably are errors in the data, the errors are of equal average magnitude, and are equally distributed in the data from the various regions of the world.

Results of comparisons

Rates of litter production are lowest in regions with lowest radiation balance (Table 8.1: $\bar{X} = 281$ g m^{-2} yr^{-1}), and rates increase with increasing radiation balance. Highest rates are in the tropics (Table 8.5: $\bar{X} = 957$ g m^{-2} yr^{-1}). An analysis of variance of the rates of litter fall showed that there were significant differences between the five regions at the 99.95% level of confidence. The F ratio was 50.98, with 4 and 130 degrees of freedom. However, analysis of variance of the rates of wood production showed no difference between any regions at the 90% level of confidence. The ratio was 1.68 with 4 and 55 degrees of freedom.

These results show that net primary productivity, which is the sum of wood production and litter production, is highest in tropical regions, and is lower in regions with lower radiation balance at the earth's surface. This confirms the results of Golley and Lieth (1972), Lugo et al. (1973), Murphy (1975), Whittaker and Likens (1975) and others. However, Jordan (1971a, b), Kato et al. (1974), Leigh (1975) and Whitmore (1975), who were considering wood production, and questioned higher production in the tropics, were right also.

Foresters and users of wood products, as well as politicians and planners, are concerned with the rate at which tropical forests can produce wood, not litter. They have been misled into believing that tropical forests have a tremendous potential for wood production, on the basis of estimates of total net primary productivity which includes litter production. Published values of the extremely high rates of sugar cane production (Westlake, 1963) also possibly have misled non-biologists into believing that the tropics have high values for wood production. As mentioned above, sugar cane is an unusual plant with a much higher photosynthetic efficiency than all trees, and most other herbaceous plants (Black, 1971). Further, sugar cane can only be raised on fertile, well-watered flat or rolling terrain.

PLANTATIONS

The data presented so far show that productivity of wood in natural tropical forests is not higher than productivity of wood in natural temperate forests. But what about plantations? There are two important questions regarding tropical forest plantations.

(1) Is productivity higher in tropical plantations than in natural tropical forests? Brunig (1977) states, "The tropical moist forest is widely considered by politicians, industrial entrepreneurs, and pioneer farmers to be an unproductive asset that is going to waste, one that should be mined, if possible, and replaced by more productive agri- and silvicultural ecosystems".

(2) Is productivity higher in tropical plantations than in temperate planatations? This is a question that multinational corporations must weigh when they have the option of establishing plantations in the tropics where productivity may or may not be higher than in the temperate zone, or establishing in the temperate zone where the infra-structure for processing wood products already exists, and where the distance to the market for the wood products is usually much shorter.

In this section, I present some data on productivity of tropical tree plantations, and attempt to make a comparison between tropical plantations, natural tropical forests, and temperate plantations. It might seem that comparisons of wood productivity in plantations of temperate and tropical zones would be easier than comparisons of natural forests, because in plantations records of harvest and age of trees are usually recorded. However, the fact is that it is almost impossible to make meaningful comparisons between any two plantations, regardless of their location, because the plantation records are of yield only. There is generally no available information on the investment involved in establishing and caring for the plantation, and these investments can differ greatly. For example, in some areas, seeds are simply broadcast into logged-over areas. In other areas, seedlings are planted in the soil, following site preparation. However, the amount of site preparation can vary greatly, from simply burning piled slash to intensive plowing and cultivation. In some cases, seedlings are inoculated for mycorrhiza and treated for prevention against other types of fungi. In some cases, there is irrigation of the seedlings. In others, planting is done only after a period of rainfall, meaning that expensive equipment and labor must be on stand-by until conditions are right. After seedling establishment, there are often pesticide spraying programs and fertilizer applications. Many intensively cultivated plantations have available expensive fire suppression programs. In some regions, plantations are thinned to prevent stagnation of growth by overcrowding.

These differences between plantation management techniques in various regions certainly could cause large differences in yield. For meaningful comparisons of plantation productivity, there should be, for all sites, estimates of costs, either in terms of dollars, or of energy, for site preparation and plantation maintenance. However, since such

estimates are generally not available, I will assume that errors due to different amounts of energy supplements are evenly distributed, and therefore the relative differences between latitudes are not affected.

The average production of wood in plantations of the tropics and subtropics was 1193 ± 741 g m^{-2} yr^{-1} (Table 8.6). This value is higher than the average wood production in natural tropical humid forest given in Table 8.5 (734 ± 275 g m^{-2} yr^{-1}), but since the variance around the average for the plantations is large, the difference is not statistically different. Clearly, further measurements of growth rates in plantations are necessary before we can say that destruction of the natural tropical forests and replacement with plantations is worthwhile.

How do the values for wood production in tropical plantations compare with values for temperate plantations? Art and Marks (1971) have listed 89 values of net annual primary production of forest plantations in temperate zones throughout the world. The average value is 1343 ± 894 g m^{-2} yr^{-1}. Plantations in the temperate zone average higher in their production than tropical plantations,

TABLE 8.6

Wood production in tropical plantations

Author	Species	Location	Number of Stands	Production (g m^{-2} yr^{-1})	
				range	average
Lamb (1968)	*Gmelina arborea*	Malawi	several	425–1277	851
Lamb (1968)	*Gmelina arborea*	Sierra Leone	4	483–622	552
Synnott and Kemp (1976)	*Aucoumea* sp.	Gabon	several		1000
Grijpma (1969)	*Eucalyptus deglupta*	New Guinea	4	1184–2960	2072
Grijpma (1967)	*Anthocephalus cadamba*	Java	several	520–840	680
Semana (1978)	five tropical exotics	Philippines	several	1330–2800	2065
Wadsworth (1960)	various	tropical humid	15	156–2500	549
Wadsworth (1960)	various	subtropical very wet	3	1008–5905	2737
Wadsworth (1960)	various	tropical dry	5	300–705	472
Wadsworth (1960)	various	subtropical humid	7	225–1700	1070
Anonymous (1976a)	*Pinus patula*	Kenya	1	250–1250	750
Anonymous (1976b)	*Pinus patula*	Uganda	1	250–1250	750
Heuveldop and Castillo (1977)	*Pinus caribaea*	Venezuela	1	420–560	490
Liegel (1976)	*Pinus caribaea*	Puerto Rico	3	1100–2950	2025
Lamb (1973)	*Pinus caribaea*	thirteen Caribbean countries	13	140–5120	1840

Average of the fifteen above averages 1193 ± 741

although again the differences are not significant due to high standard deviations.

Other observations tend to confirm that wood production in tropical plantations may not be unusually high. In Venezuela, an area of seasonal tropical forest was cleared and planted with exotic hardwoods because it was felt that there was great potential for pulp wood production in the region. Eight years after planting, Tillman (1975) assessed the conditions of the various crops, as follows: "Of the seven *Eucalyptus* species, there are only three species left, all having very poor and sickly appearance. All have some features in common: the crowns are fairly poor, the size of the trees within plots is very unequal, many have grown rapidly in height but put on very little diameter, trunks tend to be forked, and at the time of observation, trees were suffering from severe insect and fungus attacks." A plantation of *Grevillea robusta* was defoliated by leaf-eating ants. Plantations of *Gmelina arborea*, and *Anthocephalus cadamba* were in better condition, but growth had stopped because the canopies had closed, and there was need of silvicultural thinning. Tillman (1975) concluded her assessment of the plantations as follows: "The success of clear cutting and replacing natural forests with more productive exotic plantations has till now proved to be so insecure that these operations cannot be recommended."

Dawkins (1958) has discussed theoretically the maximum rates of production in tropical plantations, and concluded that low growth rates in tropical plantations are a result of high requirements for light and space by the crowns of tropical species. This is another way of stating my hypothesis (Jordan, 1971b) that tropical trees are less efficient in relation to available light than temperate trees.

In the forestry literature, there are occasionally reports of some phenomenal rates of growth of tropical plantation species. For example, Wycherley (1962) reports that in Malaya, *Ochroma lagopus* grew to a height of 14.5 m and a diameter of 0.6 m in three years. However, the common name of this species is balsa, and its specific gravity is perhaps less than 15% of many tropical hardwood species. It is clear that this phenomenal growth is simply volume growth. Biomass production could well be less than for other species in the natural forest.

Finally, since dipterocarps comprise an impor-

tant wood source in the Far East, an opinion regarding their productivity is relevant here. "The dipterocarps, in well managed selectively logged stands in the Philippines can yield only 100 to 150 m^3 per ha in 35 years, or 2.9 to 4.3 m^3 per ha per year, or about 1.3 to 1.9 dry metric tons per ha per year [130–190 g m^{-2} yr^{-1}]" (Semana, 1978).

The evidence certainly does not show that productivity of tropical plantations is greater, on the average, than productivity of temperate plantations. The idea that plantations of exotic tropical species can solve future wood and energy needs more cheaply and easily than temperate plantations most definitely needs further analysis.

CONCLUSION

High levels of foliage production in the tropics have caused estimates of overall forest productivity to be high. This has led to the false impression among some scientists that levels of wood production are also high, relative to temperate forests.

The major point of this chapter is that rates of wood production in the tropics, whether the forests are natural or plantations, are not higher than in the temperate zone. It is a fallacy that the high amounts of sunshine in the tropics automatically make the tropics an ideal location for establishing energy and wood plantations. On the average, wood production is not greater than in the temperate regions.

Before more capital is invested in tropical plantations, and before more natural tropical forests are destroyed, the costs of establishing an infrastructure for wood production and processing in tropical countries must be carefully analyzed. If it is marginally economical to use forests for energy and wood in the temperate zone, where processing infra-structure, market, and distribution already exist, how economical can it be in the tropics?

ACKNOWLEDGEMENT

I thank Drs. Peter Murphy and Frank Wadsworth for helpful discussions and critical review of the manuscript.

REFERENCES

Aaltonen, V.T., 1948. *Boden und Wald*. Paul Parey, Berlin, 457 pp.

Abelson, P.H., 1975. Energy alternatives for Brazil. *Science*, 189: 417.

Alway, F.J., Methley, W.J. and Younge, O.R., 1933. Distribution of volatile matter, lime, and nitrogen among litter, duff, and leaf mould under different forest types. *Soil Sci.*, 36: 399–407.

Andersson, F., 1971. Methods and preliminary results of estimation of biomass and primary production in a south Swedish mixed deciduous woodland. In: P. Duvigneaud (Editor), *Productivity of Forest Ecosystems, Proceedings of the Brussels Symposium*. UNESCO, Paris, pp. 281–287.

Andersson, F., 1973. IBP studies on plant productivity of South Swedish Ecosystems. In: D.E. Reichle, R.V. O'Neill and J.S. Olson, *Modeling Forest Ecosystems. Report of International Woodlands Workshop, International Biological Program/PT Section. Report EDFB-IBP-73-7, UC-48-Biology and Medicine*. Oak Ridge National Laboratory, Oak Ridge, Tenn., pp. 11–26.

Andersson, S.O. and Enander, J., 1948. Om produktionen av lovforna och dennas sammansättning i ett mellansvenskt aspbestand. *Sven. Skogsvårdsfören. Tidskr.*, 46: 265–270.

Anonymous, 1975. Recherches sur l'écosystème de la forêt subéquatoriale de basse Côte-d'Ivoire. *Terre Vie*, 29: 169–264.

Anonymous, 1976a. *Permanent Sample Plot Growth Trends For P. patula in Kenya*. Research project R 3142, Working paper No. 8. Unit of Tropical Silviculture, Oxford University, Oxford, 8 pp.

Anonymous, 1976b. *Permanent Sample Plot Growth Trends For P. patula in Uganda*. Research project R 3142, Working paper No. 1. Unit of Tropical Silviculture, Oxford University, Oxford, 9 pp.

Art, H.W. and Marks, P.L., 1971. A summary table of biomass and net annual primary productivity in forest ecosystems of the world. In: *Forest Biomass Studies. Section 25, Growth and Yield, 15th I.U.F.R.O. Congress, Gainesville, Fla.* College of Life Sciences and Agriculture, Orono, Me., pp. 3–32.

Bandhu, D. 1973. Chakia project, tropical deciduous forest ecosystem. In: D.E. Reichle, R.V. O'Neill and J.S. Olson, *Modeling Forest Ecosystems. Report of International Woodlands Workshop, International Biological Program/PT Section. Report EDFB-IBP-73-7, UC-48-Biology and Medicine*. Oak Ridge National Laboratory, Oak Ridge, Tenn., pp. 39–62.

Bernhard-Reversat, F., Huttel, C. and Lemée, G., 1972. Some aspects of the seasonal ecological periodicity and plant activity in an evergreen rain forest of the Ivory Coast. In: P.M. Golley and F.B. Golley (Editors)), *Tropical Ecology with An Emphasis on Organic Production*. University of Georgia, Athens, Ga., pp. 217–234.

Black, C., 1971. Ecological implications of dividing plants into groups with distinct photosynthetic reproduction capacities. *Adv. Ecol. Res.*, 7: 87–114.

Blow, F.E., 1955. Quantity and hydrologic characteristics of litter under upland oak forests in eastern Tenn. *J. For.*, 53: 190–195.

Bonnevie-Svendsen, C. and Gjems, O., 1957. Amount and chemical composition of the litter from larch, beech, Norway spruce, and Scots pine stands and its effect on the soil. *Medd. Nor. Skogsforsoksv.*, 48: 111–174.

Boysen-Jensen, P., 1932. *Die Stoffproduktion der Pflanzen*. Gustav Fischer, Jena.

Bray, J.R., 1963. Root production and the estimation of net productivity. *Can. J. Bot.*, 41: 65–72.

Bray, J.R. and Gorham, E., 1964. Litter production in forests of the world. *Adv. Ecol. Res.*, 2: 101–157.

Brunig, E.F., 1968. On the limits of vegetable productivity in the tropical rain forest and the boreal coniferous forest. *J. Indian Bot. Soc.*, 46: 314–322.

Brunig, E., 1977. The tropical rain forest — A wasted asset or an essential biospheric resource? *Ambio*, 6: 187–191.

Budowski, G., 1963. Forest succession in tropical lowlands. *Turrialba*, 13: 42–44.

Budyko, M.I., 1974. *Climate and Life*. Academic Press, New York, N.Y., 508 pp.

Carlisle, A., Brown, A.H.F. and White, E.J., 1966. Litter fall leaf production and the effects of defoliation by *Tortrix viridana* in a sessile oak (*Quercus petraea*) woodland. *J. Ecol.*, 54: 65–85.

Chandler, R.F., 1941. The amount and mineral nutrient content of freshly fallen leaf litter in the hardwood forests of central New York. *J. Am. Soc. Agron.*, 33: 859–871.

Coldwell, B.B. and DeLong, W.A., 1950. Studies of the composition of deciduous forest tree leaves before and after partial decomposition. *Sci. Agric.*, 30: 456–466.

Coleman, D.C., 1976. A review of root production processes and their influences on soil biota in terrestrial ecosystems. In: J.M. Anderson and A. Macfadyen (Editors), *The Role of Terrestrial and Aquatic Organisms in Decomposition Processes. The 17th Symposium of the British Ecological Society*. Blackwell, Oxford, pp. 417–434.

Cornforth, I.S., 1970. Leaf fall in a tropical rain forest. *J. Appl. Ecol.*, 7: 603–608.

Cromack, K. and Monk, C., 1975. Litter production, decomposition, and nutrient cycling in a mixed hardwood watershed and a white pine watershed. In: F.G. Howell, J.B. Gentry and M.H. Smith (Editors), *Mineral Cycling in Southeastern Ecosystems*. ERDA, Washington, D.C. pp. 609–624.

Danckelmann, B., 1887. Streuertragstafel für Buchen- und Fichtenhochwaldungen. *Z. Forst Jagdwes.*, 19: 577–587.

Daubenmire, R., 1972. Phenology and other characteristics of tropical semi-deciduous forest in north-western Costa Rica. *J. Ecol.*, 60: 147–170.

Dawkins, H.C., 1958. The volume increment of natural tropical high-forest and limitations on its improvements. In: *Pointe Noire Conference of 1958*, Item C.2.

Denaeyer, S. and Duvigneaud, P., 1973. The mixed forest of Virelles–Blaimont in Haute, Belgium. In: D.E. Reichle, R.V. O'Neill and J.S. Olson, *Modeling Forest Ecosystems. Report of International Woodlands Workshop, International Biological Program/PT Section. Report EDFB-IBP-73-7, UC-48-Biology and Medicine*. Oak Ridge National Laboratory, Oak Ridge, Tenn., pp. 71–85.

Dilmy, A., 1971. The primary productivity of equatorial forests in Indonesia. In: P. Duvigneaud (Editor), *Productivity of*

Forest Ecosystems. Proceedings of the Brussels Symposium, UNESCO, Paris, pp. 333–337.

Duvigneaud, P. and Denaeyer, S., 1967. Biomasses, productivity, and mineral cycling in deciduous mixed forests in Belgium. In: H.E. Young (Editor), *Symposium on Primary Productivity and Mineral Cycling Ecosystems.* University of Maine, Orono, Me., pp. 167–186.

Duvigneaud, P., Kestemont, P. and Ambroes, P., 1971. Productivité primaire des forêts temperées d'essences feuillues caducifoliées en Europe occidentale. In: P. Duvigneaud (Editor), *Productivity of Forest Ecosystems. Proceedings of the Brussels Symposium.* UNESCO, Paris, pp. 259–270.

Dylis, N., 1971. Primary production of mixed forests. In: P. Duvigneaud (Editor), *Productivity of Forest Ecosystems. Proceedings of the Brussels Symposium.* UNESCO, Paris, pp. 227–232.

Edwards, P.J., 1977. Studies of mineral cycling in a montane rain forest in New Guinea. II. The production and disappearance of litter. *J. Ecol.,* 65: 971–992.

Ehwald, E., 1957. Über den Nährstoffkreislauf des Waldes. *Dtsch. Akad. Landwirtsch. Tagungsber.,* 6: 1–56.

Ewel, J., 1971. Biomass changes in early tropical succession. *Turrialba,* 21: 110–112.

Ewel, J., 1977. Differences between wet and dry successional tropical ecosystems. *Geo-Eco-Trop.,* 1: 103–117.

Fittkau, E., Junk, W., Klinge, H. and Sioli, H., 1975. Substrate and vegetation in the Amazon region. In: *Berichte der Internationalen Symposien der Internationalen Vereinigung für Vegetationskunde, Vegetation and Substrat, Rinteln, 1969,* pp. 73–90.

Franklin, R.T., 1970. Insect influences on the forest canopy. In: D.E. Reichle, (Editor), *Analysis of Temperate Forest Ecosystems.* Ecological Studies 1. Springer-Verlag, Berlin, pp. 86–99.

Garg, R.K. and Vyas, L.N., 1975. Litter production in deciduous forest near Udaipur (South Rajasthan), India. In: F.B. Golley and E. Medina (Editors), *Tropical Ecological Systems.* Ecological Studies 11. Springer-Verlag, Berlin, pp. 131–135.

Golley, F.B., 1975. Productivity and mineral cycling in tropical forests. In: *Proceedings of a Symposium presented at the Fifth General Assembly of the special Committee for the I.B.P.* National Academy of Sciences, Washington, D.C., pp. 106–115.

Golley, F.B. and Lieth, H., 1972. Bases of organic production in the tropics. In: P.M. Golley and F.B. Golley, (Editors), *Tropical Ecology with An Emphasis on Organic Production.* University of Georgia, Athens, Ga., pp. 1–26.

Golley, F.B., McGinnis, J.T., Clements, R.G., Child, G.I. and Duever, M.J., 1975. *Mineral Cycling in a Tropical Moist Forest Ecosystem.* University of Georgia Press, Athens, Ga., 248 pp.

Goodland, R. and Pollard, R., 1973. The Brazilian cerrado vegetation: a fertility gradient. *J. Ecol.,* 61: 219–224.

Grijpma, P., 1967. *Anthocephalus cadamba,* a versatile, fast growing industrial tree species for the tropics. *Turrialba,* 17: 321–329.

Grijpma, P., 1969. *Eucalyptus deglupta* Bl. una especie forestal prometedora para los tropicos humedos de America Latina. *Turrialba,* 19: 267–283.

Grubb, P.J., 1977. Control of forest growth and distribution on wet tropical mountains. *Ann. Rev. Ecol. Syst.,* 8: 83–107.

Haines, B. and Foster, R.B., 1977. Energy flow through litter in a Panamanian forest. *J. Ecol.,* 65: 147–155.

Harris, W.F. and Todd, R.E., 1972. Forest root biomass production and turnover. *Eastern Deciduous Forest Biome Memo Rep.,* No. 72–156 (Oak Ridge National Laboratory, Oak Ridge, Tenn.

Herrera, R., Jordan, C., Klinge, H. and Medina, E., 1978. Amazon ecosystems. Their structure and functioning with particular emphasis on nutrients. *Inter Ciencia,* 3: 223–232.

Heuveldop, J. and Castillo, C., 1977. Unpublished data on the production of *Pinus caribaea* near Uverito, Estado Monagas, Venezuela.

Hopkins, B., 1966. Vegetation of the Olokemeji forest reserve, Nigeria. IV. The litter and soil with special reference to their seasonal changes. *J. Ecol.,* 54: 687–703.

Hopkins, B., 1970. Vegetation of the Olokemeji forest reserve, Nigeria VI. The plants of the forest site with special reference to their seasonal growth. *J. Ecol.,* 58: 765–793.

Hughes, M.K., 1971. Tree biocontent, net production and litter fall in a deciduous woodland. *Oikos,* 22: 62–73.

Jaro, Z., 1958. Alommennyisegek a magyar erdokben. *Erdeszeti Kut.,* 1: 151–162.

Jenik, J., 1971. Root structure and underground biomass in equatorial forests. In: P. Duvigneaud (Editor), *Productivity of Forest Ecosystems. Proceedings of the Brussels Symposium.* UNESCO, Paris, pp. 323–331.

Jenny, H., Gessel, S.P. and Bingham, F.T., 1949. Comparative study of decomposition rates of organic matter in temperate and tropical regions. *Soil Sci.,* 68: 419–432.

Jordan, C.F., 1971a. A world pattern in plant energetics. *Am. Sci.,* 59: 425–433.

Jordan, C.F., 1971b. Productivity of a tropical forest and its relation to a world pattern of energy storage. *J. Ecol.,* 59: 127–142.

Jordan, C.F., 1978. *Nutrient Dynamics of a Tropical Rain Forest Ecosystem and Changes in the Nutrient Cycle Due to Cutting and Burning.* Annual Report to U.S. National Science Foundation. Institute of Ecology, University of Georgia, Athens, Ga., 207 pp.

Jordan, C.F. and Escalante, G., 1980. Root productivity in an Amazonian rain forest. *Ecology,* 61: 14–18.

Jordan, C.F. and Herrera, R., 1981. Biogeochemical cycles and tropical forests. *Am. Nat.,* 117: 167–180.

Jordan, C.F. and Murphy, P.G., 1978. A latitudinal gradient of wood and litter production, and its implication regarding competition and species diversity in trees. *Am. Midl. Nat.,* 99: 415–434.

Jordan, C.F. and Uhl, C., 1978. Biomass of a "tierra firme" forest of the Amazon Basin calculated by a refined allometric relationship. *Oecol. Plant.,* 13: 387–400.

Jordan, C.F., Kline, J.R. and Sasscer, D.S., 1972. Relative stability of mineral cycles in forest ecosystems. *Am. Nat.,* 106: 237–253.

Kato, R., Tadaki, Y. and Ogawa, H., 1974. Plant biomass and growth increment studies. In: *IBP synthesis Meeting, Kuala Lumpur, 1974* (mimeograph).

Kimura, M., 1960. Primary production of the warm temperate laurel forest in the southern part of Osumi Peninsula,

Kyusha, Japan. *Misc. Rep. Res. Inst. Nat. Res. (Tokyo)*, 52–53: 36–47.

Kira, T., 1974. Primary productivity of Pasoh forest. In: *IBP Synthesis Meeting, Kuala Lumpur, 1974* (mimeograph).

Kira, T. and Shidei, T., 1967. Primary production and turnover of organic matter in different forest ecosystems of the western Pacific. *Jap. J. Ecol.*, 17: 70–87.

Kira, T., Ogawa, H., Yoda, K. and Ogina, K., 1967. Comparative ecological studies on three main types of forest vegetation in Thailand IV. Dry matter production with special reference to the Khao Chong rain forest. *Nat. Life S.E. Asia*, 5: 149–174.

Klinge, H., 1973. Root mass estimation in lowland tropical rain forests of Central Amazonia, Brazil. I. Fine root masses of a pale yellow latosol and a giant humus podzol. *Trop. Ecol.*, 14(1): 29–38.

Klinge, H., 1974. Litter production on tropical ecosystems. In: *IBP Synthesis Meeting, Kuala Lumpur, 1974* (mimeograph).

Klinge, H. and Rodrigues, W., 1968. Litter production in an area of Amazonian tierra firme forest. Part I. Litter-fall, organic carbon and total nitrogen contents of litter. *Amazonia*, I: 287–302.

Knudsen, F. and Mauritz-Hansson, H., 1939. Om produktionen av lovforna och dennas sammansättning i ett mellansvenskt björkbestand. *Sven. Skogsvårdsfören. Tidskr.*, 37: 399–347.

Lamb, A.F.A., 1968. *Fast Growing Timber Trees of the Lowland Tropics. No. 1.* Gmelina arborea. Commonwealth Forestry Institute, Department of Forestry, University of Oxford, Oxford, pp. 12–13.

Lamb, A.F.A., 1973. *Fast Growing Timber Trees of the Lowland Tropics.* Pinus Caribaea. Vol. I. Unit of Tropical Silviculture, Department of Forestry, Oxford, 254 pp.

Laudelout, H. and Meyer, J., 1954. Les cycles d'éléments minérales et de matière organique en forêt équatorial Congolaise. *Trans. Fifth Int. Congr. Soil Sci.*, 2: 267–272.

Leigh, E.G., 1975. Structure and climate in tropical rain forest. *Annu. Rev. Ecol. Syst.*, 6: 67–86.

Lemon, E., Allen, L.H. and Muller, L., 1970. Carbon dioxide exchange of a tropical rain forest. Part II. *BioScience*, 20: 1054–1059.

Liegel, L., 1976. *Results of Triangular Spacing Trials on Three Different Soils in Puerto Rico.* Draft No. 1. Institute of Tropical Forestry, Rio Piedras, Puerto Rico.

Likens, G.E., Bormann, F.H., Pierce, R.S., Eaton, J.S. and Johnson, N.M., 1977. *Biogeochemistry of a Forested Ecosystem.* Springer-Verlag, Berlin, 146 pp.

Loucks, D.L., 1973. IBP-Eastern deciduous forest biome — Lake Wingra Basin oak forests. In: D.E. Reichle, R.V. O'Neill and J.S. Olson, *Modeling Forest Ecosystems. Report of International Woodlands Workshop, International Biological Program/PT Section. Report EDFB-IBP-73-7, UC-48-Biology and Medicine.* Oak Ridge National Laboratory, Oak Ridge, Tenn., pp. 133–138.

Lugo, A. et al., 1973. Tropical ecosystem structure and function. In: E. Farnworth and F.B. Golley (Editors), *Fragile Ecosystems.* Springer-Verlag, Berlin, pp. 67–111.

Malaisse, F.P., 1974. Phenology of the Zambezian woodland area with emphasis on the miombo ecosystem. In: H. Lieth (Editor), *Phenology and Seasonality Modeling.* Ecological Studies 8. Springer-Verlag, Berlin, pp. 269–286.

Mattson, W.J. and Addy, N.D., 1975. Phytophagous insects as regulators of forest primary production. *Science*, 190: 515–522.

Medina, E. and Zelwer, M. 1972. Soil respiration in tropical plant communities. In: P.M. Golley and F.B. Golley (Editors), *Tropical Ecology with An Emphasis on Organic Production.* University of Georgia, Athens, Ga., pp. 245–269.

Medina, E., Herrera, R., Jordan, C. and Klinge, H., 1977. The Amazon Project of the Venezuelan Institute for Scientific Research. *Nat. Resour.* 13(3): 4–6.

Medwecka-Kornas, A., Lomnicki, A. and Bandola-Ciolczyk, E., 1973. Energy flow in the deciduous woodland ecosystem, Ispina project, Poland. In: D.E. Reichle, R.V. O'Neill and J.S. Olson, *Modeling Forest Ecosystems. Report of International Woodlands Workshop, International Biological Program/PT Section. Report EDFB-IBP-73-7, UC-48-Biology and Medicine.* Oak Ridge National Laboratory, Oak Ridge, Tenn., pp. 144–150.

Metz, L.J., 1952. Weight and nitrogen and calcium content of the annual litter fall of forests in the South Carolina Piedmont. *Proc. Soil Sci. Soc. Am.*, 16: 38–41.

Miller, R.B., 1971. Forest productivity in the temperate-humid zone of the southern hemisphere. In: P. Duvigneaud (Editor), *Productivity of Forest Ecosystems. Proceedings of the Brussels Symposium.* UNESCO, Paris, pp. 299–308.

Misra, R., 1972. A comparative study of net primary productivity of dry deciduous forest and grassland of Varanasi, India. In: P.M. Golley and F.B. Golley (Editors), *Tropical Ecology with An Emphasis on Organic Production.* University of Georgia, Athens, Ga., pp. 279–293.

Möller, C.M., 1945. Untersuchungen über Laubmenge, Stoffverlust, und Stoffproduktion des Waldes. *Forstl. Forsogvæs. Dan.*, 17: 1–287.

Monk, C., 1966. An ecological significance of evergreenness. *Ecology*, 47: 504–505.

Monk, E., 1942. Om strofallet i vare skoger. *Medd. Nor. Skogforsoksv.*, 29: 297–365.

Muller, D. and Nielsen, J., 1965. Production brute, pertes par respiration et production nette dans la forêt ombrophile tropicale. *Forstl. Forsögväs Dan.*, 29: 60–160.

Murphy, P.G., 1975. Net primary productivity in tropical terrestrial ecosystems. In: H. Leith and R. Whittaker (Editors), *Primary Productivity of the Biosphere.* Springer-Verlag, Berlin, pp. 217–231.

Murphy, P.G., 1977. Rates of primary productivity in tropical grassland, savanna and forest. *Geo-Eco-Trop.*, 1: 95–102.

Murphy, P.G., Sharitz, R.R. and Murphy, A..J., 1974. Leaf-litter production in the aspen and maple–birch forest types and the contribution by individual tree species. In: T. D. Rudolph (Editor), *The Enterprise Radiation Forest, Pre-irradiation Ecological Studies.* U.S. Atomic Energy Commission, TID-26113, Washington, D.C., pp. 115–118.

Nihlgard, B. and Lindgren, L., 1977. Plant biomass, primary production and bioelements of three mature beech forests in South Sweden. *Oikos*, 28: 95–104.

Nye, P.H., 1961. Organic matter and nutrient cycles under moist tropical forest. *Plant Soil*, 13: 333–346.

Nye, P.H. and Greenland, D.J., 1960. *The Soil Under Shifting Cultivation.* Commonwealth Bureau of Soils, Harpenden, Tech. Comm. No. 51, 156 pp.

Odum, E.P., 1969. The strategy of ecosystem development. *Science*, 164: 262–270.

Odum, H.T., 1970. Holes in leaves and the grazing control mechanism. In: H.T. Odum and R.F. Pigeon (Editors), *A Tropical Rain Forest: A Study of Irradiation and Ecology at El Verde, Puerto Rico*. U.S. Atomic Energy Commission, Washington, D.C., pp. 169–180.

Odum, H.T. and Jordan, C.F., 1970. Metabolism and evapotranspiration of the lower forest in a giant plastic cylinder. In: H.T. Odum and R.F. Pigeon (Editors), *A Tropical Rain Forest: A Study of Irradiation and Ecology at El Verde, Puerto Rico*. U.S. Atomic Energy Commission, Washington, D.C., pp. I165–I190.

Ohmasa, M. and Mori, K., 1937. The amount of fall and decomposition of the leaf litter of the forest trees of Japan. *Bull. For. Exp. Stn. Tokyo-Fu*, 3: 39–101.

Olson, J.S., 1963. Energy storage and the balance of producers and decomposers in ecological systems. *Ecology*, 44: 322–331.

Ordway, D.E., 1969. An aerodynamicist's analysis of the Odum cylinder approach to net CO_2 exchange. *Photosynthetica*, 3: 199–209.

Ovington, J.D., 1956. The form, weights, and productivity of tree species grown in close stands. *New Phytol.*, 55: 289–304.

Ovington, J.D., 1965. Organic production, turnover, and mineral cycling in woodlands. *Biol. Rev. (Cambridge)*, 40: 295–336.

Ovington, J.D. and Madgwick, H.A.I., 1959. The growth and composition of natural stands of birch 1. Dry matter production. *Plant Soil*, 10: 271–283.

Ovington, J.D., Heitkamp, D. and Lawrence, D.B., 1963. Plant biomass and productivity of prairie, savanna, oakwood and maize field ecosystems in central Minnesota. *Ecology*, 44: 52–63.

Polster H., 1950. *Die physiologischen Grundlagen der Stofferzeugung im Walde*. Bayerischer Landwirtschaftsverlag, Munich, 96 pp.

Ramm, S.S., 1975. Primary production and nutrient cycling in tropical deciduous forest ecosystem. *Trop. Ecol.*, 16: 140–146.

Reichle, D.E., O'Neill, R.V. and Olson, J.S., 1973a. *Modeling Forest Ecosystems. Report of International Woodlands Workshop, International Biological Program/PT Section. Report EDFB-IBP-73-7, UC-48-Biology and Medicine*. Oak Ridge National Laboratory, Oak Ridge, Tenn., 339 pp.

Reichle, D.E., Dinger, B.E., Edwards, N.T., Harris, W.F. and Sollins, P., 1973b. Carbon flow and storage in a forest ecosystem. In: G.M. Woodwell and E.V. Pecan (Editors), *Carbon and the Biosphere. Proc. of the 24th Brookhaven Symposium in Biology*. U.S. Atomic Energy Commission, Washington, D.C., pp. 345–365.

Reiners, W.A., 1972. Structure and energetics of three Minnesota forests. *Ecol. Monogr.*, 42: 71–94.

Remezov, N.P. and Bykova, L.N., 1953. Uptake and cycle of nitrogen and ash elements in aspen stands. *Pochvovedenie*, 8: 28–41.

Rodin, L.E. and Bazilevich, N.I., 1967. *Production and Mineral Cycling in Terrestrial Vegetation*. Oliver and Boyd, Edinburgh, 288 pp. (translation).

Rozanov, B.G. and Rozanova, I.M., 1964. The biological cycle of nutrient elements of bamboo in the tropical forests of Burma. *Bot. Zh.*, 49(3) (in Russian).

Santantonio, D., Hermann, R.K. and Overton, W.S., 1977. Root biomass studies in forest ecosystems. *Pedobiologia*, 17: 1–31.

Satoo, T., 1970. A synthesis of studies by the harvest method: Primary production relations in the temperate deciduous forests of Japan. In: D.E. Reichle (Editor), *Analysis of Temperate Forest Ecosystems*. Springer-Verlag, Berlin, pp. 55–72.

Scott, D.R.M., 1955. Amount and chemical composition of the organic matter contributed by overstory and understory vegetation to forest soil. *Yale University, Sch. For. Bull.*, 62: 73 pp.

Semana, J.A., 1978. Fast-growing plantation hardwoods for pulp and paper production. In: *International Conference on Improved Utilization of Tropical Forests, Forests Products Laboratory, U.S. Forest Service, Madison, Wis., 1978* (mimeograph).

Stark, N. and Jordan, C.F., 1978. Nutrient retention by the root matt of an Amazonian rain forest. *Ecology*, 59: 434–437.

Stark, N. and Spratt, M., 1978. Root biomass and nutrient storage in rain forest oxisols near San Carlos de Rio Negro. *Trop. Ecol.*, 18: 1–9.

Subba Rao, B.K., Dabral, B.G. and Panda, S.K., 1972. Litter production in forest plantation of chir (*Pinus roxburghii*), Teak (*Tectona grandis*), and Sal (*Shorea robusta*) at New Forest, Dehra Dun. In: P.M. Golley and F.B. Golley (Editors), *Tropical Ecology with An Emphasis on Organic Production*. University of Georgia, Athens, Ga., pp. 235–243.

Sviridova, L.K., 1960. Role of improvement cuttings in raising forest soil fertility. *Pochvovedenie*, 4: 68–72.

Synnott, T.J. and Kemp, R.H., 1976. Choosing the best silvicultural system. *Unasylva*, 28: 74–79.

Tarsia, N., 1973. Italian IBP "Cesurni" experimental area. In: D.E. Reichle, R.V. O'Neill and J.S. Olson, *Modeling Forest Ecosystems. Report of International Woodlands Workshop. International Biological Program/PT Section. Report EDFB-IBP-73-7, UC-48-Biology and Medicine*. Oak Ridge National Laboratory, Oak Ridge, Tenn., pp. 226–230.

Thamdrup, H.M., 1973. The Danish IBP woodland project. In: D.E. Reichle, R.V. O'Neill and J.S. Olson, *Modeling Forest Ecosystems. Report of International Woodlands Workshop, International Biological Program/PT Section. Report EDFB-IBP-73-7, UC-48-Biology and Medicine*. Oak Ridge National Laboratory, Oak Ridge, Tenn., pp. 231–250.

Tillman, E., 1975. *Assessment of Experimental Tree Plantations in Venezuela*. Working document No. 2. Rep. de Venezuela, Ministerio de Agricultura y Cria., Caracas.

Tsutsumi, T., 1971. Accumulation and circulation of nutrient elements in forest ecosystems. In: F. Duvigneaud (Editor), *Productivity of Forest Ecosystems, Proceedings of the Brussels Symposium*. UNESCO, Paris, pp. 543–552.

Viro, P.J., 1955. Investigations on forest litter. *Commun. Inst. For. Fenn.*, 45: 65.

Wadsworth, F.H., 1960. *Datos de crecimiento de plantaciones forestales en Mexico, Indias Occidentales y Centro y Sur America*. Segundo Informe Anual de la Seccion de

Forestacion, Comite Regional sobre Investigacion Forestal, Comision Forestal Latinamericana, Organizacion de las Naciones Unidas para la Agricultura y la Alimentacion, Centro Tropical de Investigaciones Forestales, Servicio Forestal, Rio Piedras, Puerto Rico.

Walter, H., 1971, *Ecology of Tropical and Subtropical Vegetation*. Oliver and Boyd, Edinburgh, 539 pp.

Wanner, H., 1970. Soil respiration, litter fall and productivity of tropical rain forest. *J. Ecol.*, 58: 543–547.

Wanner, H., Soerohaldoko, S., Santosa, N.P.D., Panggabean, G., Yingchoi, P. and Nguyen-Thi-Tuyet-Hoa, 1973. Die Bodenatmung in tropischen Regenwäldern Südost-Asiens. *Oecologia*, 12: 289–302.

Weaver, P.L., 1978. *Long-term Periodic Annual dbh Increment in Several Natural Forests of the Commonwealth of Puerto Rico*. Ecosystems Management, Institute of Tropical Forestry, Rio Piedras, Puerto Rico (mimeograph).

Went, F.W. and Stark, N., 1968. Mycorrhiza. *BioScience*, 18: 1035–1039.

Westlake, D.F., 1963. Comparison of plant productivity. *Biol. Rev.*, 38: 385–425.

Whitmore, T.C., 1975. *Tropical Rain Forests of the Far East*. Clarendon Press, Oxford, 282 pp.

Whittaker, R.H., 1966. Forest dimensions and production in the Great Smoky Mountains. *Ecology*, 47: 103–121.

Whittaker, R.H. and Likens, G., 1975. The biosphere and man. In: H. Lieth and R. Whittaker (Editors), *Primary Productivity of the Biosphere*. Springer-Verlag, Berlin, pp. 305–328.

Whittaker, R.H. and Woodwell, G.M., 1968. Dimension and production relations of trees and shrubs in the Brookhaven forest, New York. *J. Ecol.*, 56: 1–25.

Whittaker, R.H. and Woodwell, G.M., 1969. Structure, production and diversity of the oak–pine forest at Brookhaven, New York. *J. Ecol.*, 57: 155–174.

Whittaker, R.H., Bormann, F.H., Likens, G.E. and Siccama, T.G., 1974. The Hubbard Brook ecosystem study: forest biomass and production. *Ecol. Monogr.*, 44: 233–252.

Wilde, S.A., 1968. Mycorrhizae and tree nutrition. *BioScience*, 18: 482–484.

Witkamp, M. and Van der Drift, J., 1961. Breakdown of forest litter in relation to environmental factors. *Plant Soil*, 15: 295–311.

Woodwell, G.M. and Botkin, D.B., 1970. Metabolism of terrestrial ecosystems by gas exchange techniques: the Brookhaven approach. In: D.E. Reichle (Editor), *Analysis of Temperate Forest Ecosystems*. Ecological Studies 1. Springer-Verlag, Berlin, pp. 73–85.

Wycherley, P.R., 1962. Growth of balsa trees *Ochroma lagopus* Sw. at the Rubber Research Institute experiment station. *Malay. For.*, 25: 140–149.

Zelitch, I., 1971. *Photosynthesis, Photorespiration and Plant Productivity*. Academic Press, New York, N.Y., 270 pp.

Zonn, S.V. and Cheng-Kwei, L., 1962. Dynamics of the decomposition of litters and seasonal variations of their ash composition in two types of tropical biogeocoenoses. *Soobshch. Lab. Lesoved., Akad. Nauk. S.S.S.R.*, 21 (in Russian).

Chapter 9

NUTRIENT CYCLING AND NUTRIENT CONSERVATION

FRANK B. GOLLEY

INTRODUCTION

The object of this chapter is to examine the rates of nutrient cycling and the evolution of nutrient conservation mechanisms in tropical forests. Tropical forests are chosen as a subject of special enquiry since they often have a large biomass per unit area (Rodin and Bazilevich, 1967) and a greater variety of species (Richards, 1964) compared to other forests and vigorous biological activity usually can take place throughout the year. The large biomass and species variety led residents from temperate climates to conclude that tropical forests were highly productive and that the soils and climate would support productive agriculture and forestry. These expectations have seldom been realized in tropical wet and moist forest regions, although even today the popular press continues to state that the tropical forests are among the few remaining regions of the world available for agricultural expansion. Through the work of scientists such as Nye and Greenland (1960) it has been widely recognized by soil scientists and ecologists that the luxuriant and tall tropical forests may grow on relatively nutrient poor, highly weathered substrates. In these situations tropical forests have evolved mechanisms to efficiently utilize the nutrients in the soil solution as well as those entering the forest from the atmosphere and to recycle nutrients. While all forests have mechanisms to conserve nutrients, we speculate that these mechanisms are most highly developed in tropical forests, especially those growing on nutrient-poor substrates. Tropical forests, then, are an especially interesting community type in which to study nutrient cycling and nutrient conservation.

The term nutrient cycling or biological cycling is defined as "the uptake of elements from the soil and the atmosphere by living organisms, biosynthesis involving the formation of new complex compounds, and the return of elements to the soil and atmosphere with the annual litter fall of part of the organic matter or with the death of organisms in the biogeocoenosis" (Rodin and Bazilevich, 1967). Through the biological cycle the biota acts upon the lithosphere, hydrosphere and atmosphere. "Living matter basically affects the entire chemistry of the earth's crust, imparting direction to the geochemical history of almost all the elements in it" (Vernadsky, 1934, quoted by Rodin and Bazilevich, 1967).

The rates of nutrient cycling are controlled by the chemical sources in the atmosphere and soil, by the energy to power biological processes and the environment which influences water availability, the rates of evapotranspiration, and the speed of biological activities, and by the structure of the biological community and populations. An ecosystem may be open in the sense that nutrients easily move from the sources to the biota and back to the sources throughout the year. Other ecosystems are described as closed. Closed nutrient cycles are characterized by movement of elements within the biota with little loss, and, of course, little uptake, from the sources. Where the sources are limited we might expect that the cycles will be closed. Closed cycles imply nutrient conservation since it is the adaptation for conservation or closure which prevents loss of elements from the biotic components to the environment. Here we are not concerned with the question of whether systems are open or closed but, rather, with the mechanisms that might be used in nutrient conservation if the sources of nutrients are limited and if environmental factors promote leakage or loss of chemicals from the biota. Conventional wisdom dictates that in tropical forests both of these conditions hold.

The mechanisms of uptake, storage, transfer and loss of elements in the forest are ultimately explained by the collective behaviors of the species of living organisms making up the forest community. Taking a temporal view, in the history of these biological species the chemical environment must play a role. The biological organism requires a variety of chemical elements for the construction of its protoplasm but, in addition, it undoubtedly reflects to some degree the peculiar geochemical characteristics of its center of origin. Thus, as discussed in Chapter 7 we expect each species to have a chemical signature which reflects the geochemical environment of its origin, the biological requirements of the protoplasm and the chemical environment where it presently occurs. Over the history of the earth the species have migrated extensively and each stand of forest must include species with a variety of chemical histories. For this reason, the chemistry of a stand only partly reflects the chemistry of the substrate. It is not clear which of the separations, physical, chemical, geochemical, biochemical, or ecochemical are most important in controlling the stand chemistry. Golley and Richardson (1977)

used factor analysis techniques on data obtained in a variety of tropical forest stands in Panama (Golley et al., 1975) to examine these separations. In their analysis the effect of location produced very little organization of the chemical abundances in the forest biomass, while a biological separation into components such as leaves, stems, fruits, roots and litter resulted in a variety of factors which could be interpreted from previous knowledge of plant physiology. It was concluded that biological constraints overrode geochemical factors in governing the distribution and abundance of elements in the stands examined from Panama. This conclusion was supported by further studies in northwest Colombia (Golley et al., 1978). Thus, the biological structure of the forest ecosystem probably plays a key role in its nutrient cycling and conservation.

NUTRIENT REQUIREMENTS

We know little about the nutrient requirements of the tropical forest vegetation. If an ecosystem is in a dynamic steady state the input of chemical elements to the vegetation should equal the output from the biota. If the ecosystem is growing then input should equal output plus storage in the

TABLE 9.1

Output of selected elements from tropical forests (kg ha^{-1} yr^{-1}); output includes the flux due to litterfall, fall of dead trees, and throughfall combined

Forest	Output (kg ha^{-1} yr^{-1})					Author
	N	P	K	Ca	Mg	
Tropical moist forest (Panama)	–	12	197	298	35	Golley et al. (1975)
Ombrophile forest (Ivory Coast)						Bernhard-Reversat (1975)
Banco Plateau	213	10	88	84	85	
Banco talweg	218	24	251	116	77	
Banco framiré (*Terminalia ivorensis*)	187	22	108	90	49	
Yapo forest	126	10	108	124	39	
Yapo framiré	127	7	123	144	32	
La Selva (Costa Rica)	150	–	32	140	–	Gessel et al. (1979)
Palo Verde (Costa Rica)	110	–	80	360	–	Gessel et al. (1979)
Kade (Ghana)	248	14	293	317	71	Nye (1961)
Rain forest (Puerto Rico)	–	–	139	63	16	Jordan et al. (1972)
Heterogene forest (Zaire)	224	7	48	105	53	Laudelout and Meyer (1954)
Brachystegia (Zaïre)	223	9	62	91	44	Laudelout and Meyer (1954)
Macrolobium (Zaïre)	154	9	87	84	49	Laudelout and Meyer (1954)
Parasoleraie	140	4	104	124	43	Laudelout and Meyer (1954)

biomass. Output is commonly measured by litter fall, fall of dead trees, and throughfall. Root death should also be included but it is exceedingly difficult to measure. The absolute rates of nutrient output vary for different chemical elements and for different forests (Table 9.1).

It is difficult to relate the rates shown in Table 9.1 to the information on nutrient requirements of crop plants or forest plantations. Lane and Levins (1977) point out that Liebig's Law of the Minimum is inappropriate to apply to the community. Their assertion is partly based on the fact that nutrients act synergistically and that the members of the biota interact with each other in the transfer and storage of elements. Indeed, there may be physical linkage between individuals of different species through root grafts (Bormann, 1966) and fungal connections (Hayman, 1978). Obviously, the network of nutrient transfers in ecosystems is not conducive to single causal explanations.

A further problem is that the enrichment experiments of the physiologist use a parameter such as production or growth as the output to describe the response to alteration of the nutrient supply to the plant. It is quite likely that communities will respond to fertilization by increased production, but production is not an appropriate parameter for evaluation of chemical control of communities. Production may vary widely from year to year and the community may survive using stored production from previous periods of time. Community survival is a more appropriate parameter in such an analysis, yet survival in relation to nutrient supply probably operates at time sequences that are not readily studied. Since the communities present in the landscape have, by definition, survived, we can assume that these communities are adapted to their chemical environment.

While we may conclude that often the community develops in concert with the chemical environment of the substrate, there may be instances where the biotic demands do not fit the available element supply in the abiotic compartments of the ecosystem. The two cases appropriate to forests are: (1) the case where the vegetation originally fitted the substrate but where weathering processes have gradually decreased supplies of available elements through leaching and transport, and (2) a landscape where the forest biota has a chemical history different from the substrate and

gradually invades a nutrient-poor substrate by developing mechanisms to conserve nutrients. Either case may be detected by a deflected succession to another steady state system after the forest stand is destroyed or to unusually slow rates of recovery of the steady state or both.

Our conclusion, then, is that community survival is probably seldom affected solely by nutrient availability, even though nutrient enrichment may result in change in structure and/or function of the system. However, on obviously nutrient-poor substrates, a community may exist which has a biomass, species diversity and productivity well beyond what would be expected from a knowledge of nutrient availability and plant response to nutrient supply. The adaptive mechanisms of the species in the community which survives in these latter types of habitats are grouped here under the category of nutrient conservation mechanisms.

NUTRIENT CONSERVATION

Nutrient conservation can involve storage of nutrients in the biotic components or control of the movement of nutrients between components. A convenient guide to examine these patterns is a linear nutrient cycling model used by Golley et al. (1975) (Fig. 9.1) to describe the nutrient dynamics in tropical forest in Panama. This model identifies some of the functional components of the forest ecosystem and the more important pathways between components. It does not account for species differences in nutrient storage or transfer. Conservation mechanisms might evolve wherever there is a nutrient transfer between compartments; however, it is likely that conservation would be especially valuable where transfers occur between biotic and abiotic compartments. Our analysis will progress through the model beginning with the leaf.

The leaf

It is well known that nutrients can leach from leaves under the influence of rainfall. These potentially mobile nutrients are in the translocation fluids in the leaf and move to the leaching solution by diffusion and mass flow (Tukey, 1971). Hydrogen ions in the rain water are exchanged for cations absorbed on exchange sites in the leaf tissue. Tukey

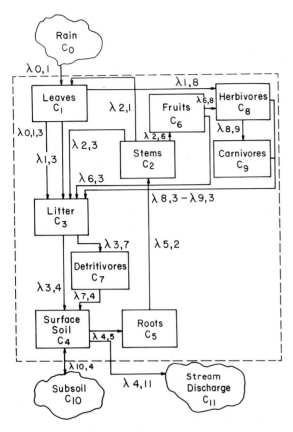

Fig. 9.1. A diagrammatic model of a tropical forest ecosystem, depicting nine organic compartments and illustrating the flow of mineral elements through the system. The compartments are labeled as C_1, C_2 ... C_{11}. C_0, C_{10} and C_{11} are external to the organic system. Transfers between compartments are identified by a λ, with subscripts indicating the compartment the flow was from and the compartment the flow goes to.

and Tukey (1962) state that sodium and manganese are easily leached, calcium, magnesium, sulfur, potassium and strontium–yttrium are moderately easily leached and iron, zinc, phosphorus and chloride are difficult to leach from leaves. Leachability of nutrients is influenced by the wettability of the leaf surface which is in turn a function of the presence of waxes, hairs, drip tips and other leaf morphological characteristics. In addition, the age of the leaf and the type of plant influence loss rates of nutrients from the leaf surfaces.

It is also well known that nutrients leach from leaves under natural forest conditions. Bernhard-Reversat (1975) shows in rain forest leaves in the Ivory Coast that the relationship between nutrients

leached from leaves and the amount of rainfall differs for the various elements. For phosphorus, potassium at one site and magnesium the rate of loss tends to become constant at between 200 and 400 mm over a four weeks observation period (Fig. 9.2). In contrast, sodium, potassium at another site, and calcium exhibit a continuous increase in loss of nutrients with amount of rainfall. These data, together with the data on leaching from leaves under laboratory conditions, would lead us to expect that there might be a direct relationship between leaching in vegetation throughfall and the quantity of rainfall for certain elements.

A relationship between throughfall concentrations and amount of rainfall should be especially evident for a highly mobile element such as potassium. I have compared the ratio of potassium in the throughfall to the potassium content of rainfall and graphed this ratio against the amount of annual rainfall. We would expect that the ratio would decrease with increasing rainfall but there is no direct relationship. The failure to show a relationship may be due to the fact that the elements

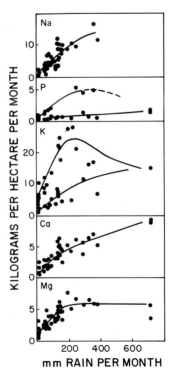

Fig. 9.2. The quantities of selected elements (kg ha^{-1} month^{-1}) in throughfall as a function of the monthly rainfall (mm month^{-1}) in two Ivory Coast forests (from Bernhard-Reversat, 1975).

are often attached to particulate matter which is washed out of the atmosphere early in a rain storm, and thus, the input of an element may be related more to the number and intensity of storms than the total rainfall amount. Further, field data on rainfall and the chemistry of throughfall is often crude and very limited. Thus, we feel that lack of a trend in these data is a result of deficiencies in the data and not good evidence of nutrient conservation. However, if the mean values of rainfall and the proportion of potassium in throughfall to rainfall for temperate and tropical forests are compared (Table 9.2) a difference between forest types is apparent. As expected the precipitation in tropical forests is about double that in temperate forests. However, the ratio of potassium in throughfall to rainfall is slightly lower in tropical forests suggesting that nutrients such as potassium may be conserved at the leaf surface in tropical forests. Jordan et al. (1979) recently have actually demonstrated that nutrients in the rainfall of Amazonian rain forest were scavenged by the canopy.

What nutrient conservation mechanisms could evolve in leaves to reduce loss of nutrients through leaching? These mechanisms might involve anatomical, physiological, and/or ecological features of leaves. Richards (1964) reviews the information on gross anatomy of leaves in tropical rain

forest. He shows that there is a dominance of entire sclerophyllous leaves belonging to the mesophyll size class of Raunkiaer (area 2025–18 255 mm^2), with entire leaf margin and often an acuminate or drip tip. Leaf texture is hard, often leathery, the upper surface glabrous and often highly polished, with any hairiness confined to the lower surface. Leaf shape varies with stratum of the forest. Canopy leaves are smaller, thicker and more leathery in texture. Lower strata leaves more frequently have acuminate tips. Shape also varies with leaf age. Juvenile leaves often are larger, divided or compound and possess a drip tip. Finally, Richards points out that leaf shape differs in various tropical forests. For example, as altitude increases there is a marked increase in the percentage of small leaves and a decrease in the percentage of leaves with entire margins.

Richards reports that there have been numerous authors who have regarded the leaf morphology of tropical trees as related to rapid draining of rain water from the leaves. Since leaching of the leaf is directly related to the wettability of the leaf surface, which in turn is a function of hairiness, waxes and other impermeable layers or shape, these morphological features can conceivably be adaptations to reduce nutrient loss through leaching. And, indeed, Tanner (1977) has shown that the con-

TABLE 9.2 The ratio of potassium in throughfall as compared to rainfall for tropical and temperate forests

	Rainfall (mm)	Ratio	Author
Rain forest			
Amazon	2800	1.63	Herrera (1979)
Panama	1937	5.27	Golley et al. (1973)
Puerto Rico	3080	7.5	Jordan et al. (1972)
Ivory Coast	2095	8.8	Bernhard-Reversat (1975)
Ghana	1664	13.58	Nye (1961)
$\bar{X}$	2314	9.93	
Temperate forest			
Beech	800	6.89	Nihlgard (1970)
Oak	1700	10.47	Carlisle et al. (1967)
Beech	1100	6.05	Mayer and Ulrich (1974)
Broadleaf forest	1796	12.07	Iwatsubo and Tsutsumi (1967)
Coweeta (N.C., U.S.A.)	2080	6.49	Best and Monk (1975)
Pine Hardwood	1168	19.9	Wells et al. (1972)
$\bar{X}$	1440	10.3	

centration of nutrients in the foliage of montane forest in Jamaica is inversely related to the coriaceousness of the leaves.

Physiological mechanisms of nutrient conservation might either limit the movement of ions to the translocation fluid or from the exchange sites in the leaf or actively move elements from the leaf into the other plant tissues. It is well known that elements may be transported from leaves to other tissues (Stenlid, 1958). Temperature, oxygen and age of tissue influence the transport rate. Low temperatures and oxygen deficiency inhibit transport. Mature leaves are more likely to lose elements than are young leaves, probably because of the high demand for cations in the growing tissues and the lower concentrations in the translocation fluid. Elements such as calcium, strontium and magnesium move in relatively small amounts once fixed in the leaf. In contrast, potassium and phosphorus are readily moved from leaves to other tissues (Tukey, 1970). In field studies, ^{137}Cs also was shown to be translocated out of the leaves in a *Liriodendron* forest over the summer (Olson, 1966). In this example, translocation downward was several times the loss by litterfall. The foliage content of ^{137}Cs decreased over four months from 124 mCi to 58.5 mCi. A total of 4.5 mCi was lost in rain and 12 mCi was moved in litterfall. The difference of 49 mCi was presumably lost by downward translocation. Further, Edwards (1977) studied leaf weight in a New Guinea rain forest before and after abscission and found that loss of weight before leaf fall varied for species but in general was about 10% less than the original dry weight of the leaves. This difference is probably due to resorption of nutrients from the leaf.

Mitchell et al. (1975) also have shown that nitrogen in a deciduous forest at Coweeta, North Carolina (U.S.A.), is recycled from the leaves to the stems and branches. Quantitatively this internal recycling accounted for 51 kg ha^{-1} yr^{-1} transferred from leaves to branches. These authors point out that this pathway of translocation decreases the need for newly acquired nitrogen each spring when growth is resumed.

Ecological mechanisms involve colonization of the leaf surface by a community of organisms called the epiphyllae. The epiphyllae include algae, lichens, fungi, and various animals, all of which form a dense mat on the leaf surface. Leaves of tropical trees may live a year or more and often develop epiphyllae. It has been shown that the epiphyllae can fix nitrogen (Harrelson, 1970; Foreman, 1975) and possibly make nitrogen directly available to the leaf itself. Presumably epiphyllae also change the wetting characteristics of the leaf surface and alter the water movement over the leaf. Witkamp (1970) has shown that nuclide retention on tropical forest leaves in Puerto Rico with epiphyllae was 1.7 to 20 times greater than those from which the epiphyllae were removed. Thus, epiphyllae may effectively reduce the leaching of nutrients from leaves as well as collecting nutrients from the atmosphere.

Leaf fall

Once the leaf becomes senescent an abscission layer forms and the leaf falls to the forest floor. Even though the leaf has lost part of its chemical inventory through leaching, translocation and other processes, it still retains a substantial nutrient content. Indeed, in studies of litter fall compared to other pathways of nutrient flow to the soil, litter fall is usually the greatest flux (for example, see Golley et al., 1975), even for elements such as potassium which are highly mobile in throughfall.

Nutrient conservation could be effected by a delay in litter fall, or reduction in the litter decomposition rate (Witkamp and Ausmus, 1975). In tropical forests the potential for detrital decays exceeds the annual input creating conditions where litter-feeding populations are limited and where elements may cycle more than once a year. Litter falling to the ground also may be trapped in a canopy where decay is relatively slow and nutrient materials might be released at relatively slower rates than if the material were on the soil surface. As far as I know there are no data on the amounts of leaf or flower-fruit material trapped in the canopy but my observations in many forests suggest that the quantities might be significant. Clearly the more complex canopy with an abundance of vines should hold more material than monospecific or even-aged stands.

In evergreen stands leaves remain on the trees for longer periods than in deciduous forests and the evergreen condition has been proposed as a nutrient conservation adaptation (Monk, 1966). The evergreen stand requires less nutrients and energy to rebuild the leaf mass and the fall of leaves throughout the year provides a continuous source for tree uptake and growth. Further, tropical evergreen forests have larger quantities of leaves than temperate deciduous forests per area of the stand, while wood mass is about the same (Jordan, 1971). This means that the flux via leaf fall is even greater in tropical compared to temperate forests systems.

Once leaves strike the ground they are subject to decomposing organisms which break down the organic constituents, incorporate the nutrients within the saprovore tissues and ultimately release the matter as various ions, CO_2, water and so on. The rate of litter decomposition has been calculated by Olson (1963) (Fig. 9.3) for a variety of forests. The decomposition rate factor, k, is very high for tropical forests and very low for pine forests in temperate mountains. These rates are a function of such primary environmental features of the forest floor habitat as moisture and temperature, as well as the type of leaf material. For example, sclerophyllous leaves may decompose more slowly than non-sclerophyllous leaves. Cromack and Monk (1975) studying leaf decomposition in hardwood forest at Coweeta, North Carolina (U.S.A.) states that, "in forest ecosystems characterized by cycling low levels of nitrogen and phosphorus, the sclerophyll index can be considered an index to slower organic matter decomposition rates and release

rates of such nutrients as nitrogen and phosphorus."

Since the organic materials in the litter quickly lose the soluble chemical compounds, they actually have a relatively homogeneous chemical structure dominated by cellulose and lignin-like materials. The homogeneity of the litter, in turn, suggests that the variety of decomposer organisms feeding on litter may be less than the variety of organisms feeding directly on the living herbage. My unpublished studies in the forest at San Carlos de Rio Negro (Venezuela) suggest that this is indeed the case (Table 9.3). Kitazawa (1971) reports that the biomass of soil fauna is least in tropical as compared to other forests and "that the role of the soil fauna is relatively small." Further, we might expect that the saprovore organisms are also more similar from one forest to another than are herbivorous organisms. Kitazawa (1971) states, "there is a conspicuous diversity of species in the tropical region, nevertheless the numbers of major taxonomic and life form groups are nearly the same in every type of forest ecosystem from alpine to equatorial."

There is an exception to the pattern shown by leaf litter fall in the stem and wood litter. In this case the material is not leached to the same extent as leaves before falling to the ground. Indeed, the upright decaying stump may be invaded by a

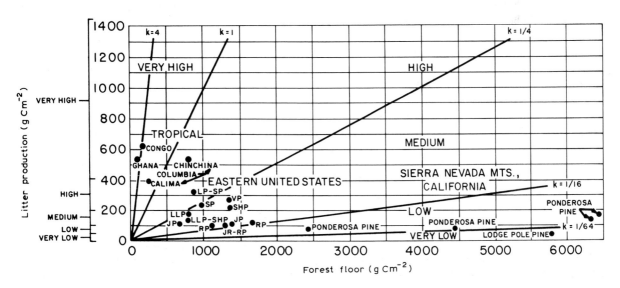

Fig. 9.3. Estimates of the decomposition rate factor, k, for evergreen forests, from the ratio of annual litter production to approximate steady state accumulation of the forest floor. Legend: LLP = long leaf pine; SHP = slash pine; SP = short leaf pine; LP = long leaf pine; VP = Virginia pine; JP = jack pine; and RP = red pine. (From Olson, 1963.)

TABLE 9.3

Relation of number of taxa to number of individuals captured in the canopy, understorey, litter and soil in two Amazonian forests growing on differing soils

	Podzol			Laterite			% Taxa in common
	taxa	individuals	taxa/ind.	taxa	individuals	taxa/ind.	
Canopy	35	86	0.41	45	104	0.43	14
Understorey	45	75	0.60	45	55	0.82	12
Litter	57	634	0.09	57	465	0.12	12
Soil	22	150	0.15	23	235	0.10	33

variety of organisms that fix nitrogen and store other nutrients in their galleries (Janzen, 1976). When wood falls to the ground a whole new decomposer fauna and flora is involved and the turnover can be highly different depending upon the environment, the species, and the physical location of the wood relative to the soil surface. Further, Edwards (1977) observed that branchwood and possibly stem wood tends to decay in place, while twigs and leaves fall intact to the forest floor. Decay in place may be an important feature of wood decomposition in tropical forests.

The litter provides the source of organic carbon which is important in maintaining the exchange capacity of the surface soil horizon in many soils. Organic carbon enters the soil from the litter and from decaying roots. Part of the carbon is oxidized or lost by leaching. The remainder is incorporated in the soil humus. The humus is itself subject to oxidation through the action of microorganisms but its rate of destruction is less than the fresh litter. According to Nye and Greenland (1960) the proportions of fresh material converted to soil humus in tropical forest will probably lie between 1/10 and 1/5 of the total input. Under moist lowland evergreen or semideciduous tropical forests Nye and Greenland (1960) report a standing crop in the soil of about 67 000 kg ha^{-1} (60 000 lbs per acre) of carbon. A recent presentation (Schlesinger, 1977) states that the mean soil carbon content for tropical forests is 10.4 kg m^{-2}, which is above Nye and Greenland's observation. Even higher levels may occur in highland areas, in tropical lowland podzols, and on some recent volcanic soils.

It is rather obvious that an adaptive mechanism to increase the soil carbon in the surface soil and therefore increase the capacity of this stratum to hold and exchange nutrients would be of advantage

to the community. We might expect to find selection for chemical characteristics of the leaves which balance the factors promoting breakdown of organic matter and those that retard decomposition and maintain organic matter in the soil. The two-phased curves of litter decomposition observed by Golley et al. (1975) and Witkamp and Olson (1963) suggest that there are, indeed, two general classes of materials in the litter reflecting the balance between conservation and breakdown. In the opposite direction the decomposition of organic matter and the release of CO_2 can react with soil water to form carbonic acid. The production of carbonic acid may occur at natural pH levels in tropical forest soils (Johnson et al., 1975) and increase leaking of cations from the soil.

Nitrogen may also be conserved in tropical forests through control by soil and litter pH and tannin levels (Jordan et al., 1979). In temperate forests nitrogen may be conserved by inhibition of nitrification from ammonia to nitrate. Nitrates are more easily leached from the soil than ammonium ions. Experiments by the above investigators in the Amazonian rain forest showed relatively low numbers and activity of nitrifying bacteria.

Root uptake and loss

Once the organic materials are decomposed the elements are available for leaching out of the root zone in soil water or for uptake by roots. The uptake must satisfy the demand for leaf, fruit and flower production, growth of wood, consumption by herbivores and replacement of trees dying in the stand. All of these demands must be met by input from the substrate except those obtained from atmospheric inputs.

Odum (1970) has focused on the uptake of

nutrients in his examination of nutrient cycling in the El Verde forest on Puerto Rico. He argues from an analysis of meteorologic evidence that uptake is a function of evapotranspiration, which is, in turn, a function of the moisture content of the air in and above the canopy. Dry air during the tropical dry season or due to particular air mass or meteorologic conditions causes more water to be transpired and more water carrying nutrients to be moved from soil water, through the roots and stems to the leaves. As a consequence of this relationship, Odum speculates that continental forests experiencing drier air are taller, have fewer epiphytes and other adaptive mechanisms to moisture excess. In contrast, mountain forests, especially elfin forests, are short, heavily laden with epiphytes, have stilt roots to raise the trees above the sodden soil and have root mats to collect nutrients. In the latter case, air moisture is too great to allow adequate transpiration, which reduces uptake of nutrients and causes a reduction in biomass, nutrient storage and cycling rates.

Root distribution in the substrate is also not constant with depth. There are generally conceived to be three general types of root systems; a well-developed tap root, well developed laterals, and some combination of taproot and lateral roots. Numerous studies have shown that in tropical forests the mass of surface roots declines with depth (Fig. 9.4). Surface roots are associated with recycling of materials from litter, while deep roots function in bringing elements from the subsoil. An extreme example is observed on laterite soils in the Amazon, where surface roots form a mat 20–30 cm deep on top of the soil surface. Stark and Jordan (1978) have shown that this root mat intercepts a very large proportion of the elements which come from the litter in throughfall. Indeed, these roots act as a chemical ion exchange column or filter in these ecosystems.

Root uptake is also enhanced by mycorrhizal associations. These fungi act to increase the surface area of the root, improve the uptake kinetics of the feeder roots, and in some cases form a living connection between the root and litter (Went and Stark, 1968). The vesicular–arbuscular mycorrhizae, especially those of the *Endogone* genus, are almost universally present in all soils in association with a wide variety of plants of different taxonomic groups. The relationship between fungi and plant is

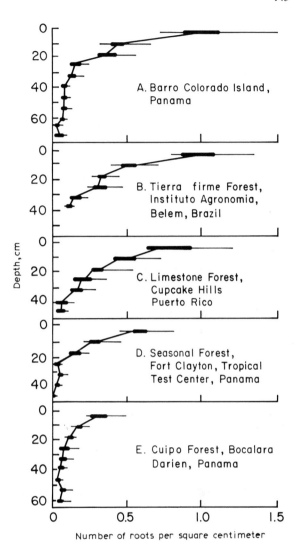

Fig. 9.4. A description of root distribution with depth in a variety of tropical forests. The number of roots on a square centimeter column are from the forest floor to water or to the point where no roots were observed. (From Odum and Pigeon, 1970.)

obligate as far as the endophyte is concerned, but even so they display a remarkable lack of host/endophyte specificity. Within the Angiospermae a few families display ectomycorrhizal infections but as a group they mainly form vesicular–arbuscular infections. Apparently there has been coevolution between host and fungi from a time very early in the evolution of the land flora, which took place about 400 million years ago on the border of the Silurian and Devonian eras (Nicholson, 1975). Some of the earliest land plant fossils appear to have hyphae and vesicles of endophytes associated with them. As new plants evolved, mycorrhiza coevolved and became both wide-spread and relatively non-specific.

Endomycorrhiza are especially important in the phosphorus nutrition of the host. Nicholson (1975) has suggested that in "virgin" soils blue green algae together with heterotrophic prokaryotes could have fixed atmospheric nitrogen so that nitrogen would not be in short supply when land plants evolved. In contrast, phosphorus is in relatively short supply since it is rarer than certain other essential elements for physical-chemical reasons and has also been lost or immobilized from soils through geochemical processes. Under such conditions any relationship between the evolving land plants and endophytes which would ameliorate phosphorus as a limit to plant growth would be of survival value. Thus, "as nodulation has evolved as a mechanism for nitrogen fixation, vesicular-arbuscular mycorrhizae may have been evolved as a means for the more efficient extraction of phosphorus from the pedosphere" (Draft and Nicholson, 1969).

Nutrient conservation adaptations are especially important at the litter–soil–root interface since it is here that chemical elements can be easily lost from the ecosystem in soil water. Clearly the development of the root–fungi interaction is an evolutionary advantage to the plant and has probably been selected for since essentially all forest trees have some type of mycorrhizal relationship. The pattern of root distribution in the soil is also clearly a mechanism that has been selected for conservation reasons.

In tropical forests most mycorrhizae are of the vesicular–arbuscular type. Surveys to describe mycorrhiza–plant relationships have shown that most, if not all trees, have these fungal associates; the earliest of these descriptions was by Janse (1896), who reported 69 of 75 species of woody plants with mycorrhizal infection in Java. Janos (1975) has shown mycorrhizae increased seedling growth in a variety of tropical forest species.

Stems and branches

In forests the stem and branch biomass is large relative to any other organic compartment. These stems and branches also turnover very slowly since the life span of trees may be several hundred years. The consequence of large storage and low turnover is a damping or buffering effect on the nutrient cycles (Golley et al., 1975; Klinge, 1976). It appears that forests that occur in potentially high turnover environments, such as the tropics, have a relatively large percentage of the element content of the system stored in the biotic compartments as compared to the soil (Table 9.4). This relationship is especially true for elements in high demand and/or potentially those at high risk of loss of elements from the system, for example, potassium and phos-

TABLE 9.4

Percent of the total inventory contained in the biotic compartments of tropical forest ecosystems in Panama (from Golley et al., 1975)

Forest type	Element												
	P	K	Ca	Mg	Na	Co	Cs	Cu	Fe	Mn	Pb	Sr	Zn
Second growth													
2 yr. July harvest	54	48	1	1	>1	6	12	>1	5	1	8	3	3
2 yr. Oct. harvest	70	63	2	2	3	11	10	2	13	2	16	5	1
4 yr. July harvest	79	49	3	4	1	21	22	5	15	1	34	5	>1
6 yr. July harvest	82	58	17	5	2	24	16	3	15	2	20	8	6
Tropical moist													
Rio Sabana	89	89	12	16	2	59	*	20	38	38	*	19	12
Rio Lara	88	90	20	13	26	67	53	18	43	55	46	24	4
Premontane wet	96	85	48	22	47	57	66	7	14	10	75	70	59
Riverine	99	97	61	35	14	92	81	48	84	13	53	63	82
Mangrove	75	97	32	89	75	53	10	37	37	17	58	35	34

*Not determined.

phorus in Table 9.4. There are two features of the soil that influence this interpretation. The inventory of the soil depends upon the depth of soil used in the analysis. The depth should include the region where the majority of roots are concentrated. Further, the humus in the soil influences the available chemical inventory as mentioned earlier.

Rain water moves over the branches and stems, as well as the leaves. This flow of water is termed stemflow and it may amount to 5 to 10% of the water reaching the forest floor. Stemflow also leaches nutrients from the branches and bark, removes attached particles and flows over a variety of epiphytes. Possibly the most significant aspect of stemflow is that the water containing nutrients is directed down the stem to the roots around the trees.

Herbivores

Tukey and Morgan (1963) and Tukey (1970) have shown that injured leaves lose more nutrients from leaching than uninjured leaves. Besides abrasion from storms, leaves are typically injured through feeding by herbivores. A variety of studies have shown that about 8 to 10% of the leaf surface in forests is consumed annually by insect herbivores. Most of these studies have been in temperate forests, but tropical estimates (for example Edwards, 1977; and Odum and Ruiz-Reyes, 1970) support the generalization. Where the herbivores' consumption exceeds these rates, for example, where insects defoliate the trees, an increased rate of cycling of nutrients and increased plant productivity may be observed (Crossley et al., 1977), although there must be some point where herbivory reduces plant production, as seen in agricultural situations.

Over the millions of years of plant evolution, the plants have evolved a variety of morphological, physiological, biochemical and ecological adaptations to counter injury by animal feeding. These same mechanisms have, in turn, been used by animals as a means of locating and using the desired plant species for food, shelter or to satisfy other demands. Thus, there has been coevolution between plants and animals leading to a restriction of the plant–animal relationship with development of some rather complex and subtle interactions on nutrient cycling. For example, Owen (1976) sug-

gests that the larvae of the butterfly *Acraea pentapolis*, which feed on the leaves of the umbrella tree (*Musanga cercopiodes*) may cause an increase in the nutrient cycling rate. Chewed and damaged leaves drop from the tree out of sequence and earlier than undamaged leaves. These leaves decompose earlier, possibly making nutrients available for special plant requirements such as fruit formation. In this example, the insect feeding may affect the phenology of the host plant. Janzen discusses these matters in more detail in Chapter 11.

Montgomery and Sunquist (1975) examined the role of two-toed and three-toed sloths (*Choloepus hoffmanni* and *Bradypus infuscatus*) on nutrient cycling in a tropical forest in Panama. These mammals crop the trees intensively. For example, sloths used 25% of the trees on the study area and removed 1.6% of the annual leaf production (but one tree may lose as much as 20% of its leaves to sloths). The sloths, in turn, defecate on the ground beneath the tree where the fecal matter slowly decomposes and the nutrients can then be returned by invasion of tree roots into the fecal mass. Sloth feces thus form a stable and long term source of nutrients, selectively returning nutrients to the very trees they consume.

Haines (1975) has also shown how another animal, the leaf cutting ant *Atta colombica*, accumulates nutrients through its activity in tropical forests. These ants harvest leaves and transport them to underground fungus colonies. The degraded materials are then dumped in refuse heaps. These refuse dumps are, in turn, heavily invaded by roots which recycle the nutrients.

It is obvious that the injury and consumption of leaves of forest trees by herbivores could be a significant flux of nutrients in the system with the chance that nutrients could be lost from the dung, frass or bodies of dead animals and leached from the system. Beside the evolution of chemical or morphological features that directly reduce feeding by animals, such as phenolic compounds (McKey et al., 1978), the resources for animal growth and reproduction might be altered so that herbivore fauna is reduced in density or in size. As discussed elsewhere, it has been shown by Elton (1973), Janzen and Schoener (1968) and Golley (1977) that the insect herbivore fauna is on the average smaller in size in tropical forests than in temperate forests. While this effect may be due to multiple factors, one consequence of reduced size is lowered intake of the plants by the animals. The diversity of tropical forest insects is also greater than that of temperate forest insects, but at this time the evidence does not show any consistent difference in density.

Species differences in nutrient uptake

These discussions have been developed from the point of view of an ecosystem model; they have ignored differences between species. In tropical forests the different species of trees at a site also have different concentrations of elements in their leaves or stems (Tanner, 1977). These species differences may be genetic since in Jamaica Tanner (1977) showed that species able to grow in all four forest types investigated had approximately constant levels of nutrients in the foliage, with the exception of potassium and magnesium. As discussed earlier, a plant species has a characteristic chemical constitution which reflects its history and special growth requirements. At a finer level of detail ecosystem analysis should consider these species differences in nutrient uptake, storage and loss. For example, Chenery and Sporne (1976) have shown that aluminum accumulation occurs in tropical woody families with primitive characteristics more frequently than more advanced families. In order to survive in an environment with high aluminum content in the soil these plants have apparently evolved to tolerate aluminum in their tissues. This type of relationship probably will influence the patterns of nutrient cycling in forests.

SIGNIFICANCE OF CONSERVATION MECHANISMS

The preceding section was designed to show that a variety of conservation adaptations are possible in tropical forests. However, these observations only provide the potential and not the actual array of adaptation utilized in a given forest stand. In a metaphorical sense, a forest has a variety of strings to pluck, any combination of which might result in a melody. We can visualize a matrix of types of forests and conservation mechanisms. If we could substantiate the use of a particular mechanism in a given forest we could obtain a pattern of adaptation for the entire array of forests. Presumably forests growing on impoverished substrates might show

more adaptive conservation mechanisms than those growing on rich substrates (Jordan and Herrera, 1979). Unfortunately the data are relatively sparse, and therefore, I will examine several forest sites for which relatively large data sets exist and use these to explore the actual patterns of adaptation to nutrient supply.

Tropical moist forest in Panama

Nutrient cycling in tropical moist forest in Darien Province, Panama, was studied by Golley et al. (1975). This study focused on the inventories of elements in the biomass and soil with relatively less attention to the transfer rates between compartments. The forest was assumed to be at or near steady state and the cycles were calculated from the measured loss rates from the biota to the soil, the measured rain input and river discharge output. Species chemistry was not determined. This forest occurs in a region with a strong three-month long dry season (January–March) and on soils that are derived from calcareous shales. Rainfall is about 1900 mm per year.

Comparison of the inventory in the surface soil and the annual transfer from biota to soil via litterfall and throughfall (Table 9.5) shows that phosphorus and potassium are transferred at rates that are a high percentage (over 50%) of the soil inventory. Further, the input and output of phosphorus and potassium are balanced but the cycling rates are many times the input–output rates (Fig. 9.5). In contrast, calcium, magnesium and other elements are lost as a relatively low percentage of the soil inventory (Table 9.5) and are lost from the system at relatively high percentages compared to the amounts cycling. Comparison of the biotic and soil inventory shows that phosphorus and potassium occur at high percentages in the vegetation (Table 9.4).

These data show that phosphorus and potassium are concentrated in the biota, cycle at relatively high rates between biota and soil, are in relatively short supply in the soil, and are balanced for the whole system with respect to their input and output. Other elements do not exhibit similar patterns, being either abundant in the substrate or cycling at relatively low rates (Table 9.5). We conclude that among the elements studied phosphorus and potassium might be limiting to the system and adap-

TABLE 9.5

Summary of mineral cycling dynamics in tropical moist forest (from Golley et al., 1975)

Element	Soil inventory (kg ha^{-1})	Annual loss from vegetation to soil (kg ha^{-1} yr^{-1})	Loss as percent of inventory	Discharge from soil (kg ha^{-1} yr^{-1})
P	22	12	54.5	0.7
K	353	197	55.8	9.3
Ca	22 166	298	1.3	163.2
Mg	2256	35	1.6	43.6
Na	1121	27	2.4	92.5
Co	7	1.2	17.1	0.7
Cu	7	0.4	.1	0.4
Fe	26	4.9	18.8	10.1
Mn	31	0.8	< .1	0.3
Sr	79	1.1	1.4	0.4
Zn	134	0.9	< .1	0.6

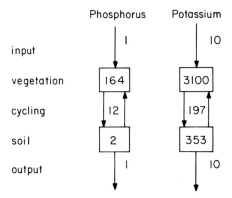

Fig. 9.5. The input–output dynamics of a tropical moist forest in Panama. The flow of phosphorus and potassium are shown in kg ha^{-1} yr^{-1} through vegetation, cycling between vegetation and soil and out of the soil in ground water. Storage in vegetation and soil are in kg ha^{-1} (data from Golley et al., 1975).

tations to sequester or recycle phosphorus and potassium may have evolved in this forest.

Unfortunately, data were not collected to specifically examine nutrient conserving mechanisms. Given the form of the model the important fluxes are from leaves to litter. For phosphorus the flux is 75% of the inventory in the leaves; for potassium the flux is 41% of the leaf inventory. No root mats were observed in this forest. Mycorrhizæ probably occur but in 1966 when the study was carried out these ecologists were unaware of their significance in nutrient cycling. The leaf morphology was typical of tropical forests generally and epiphyllae occurred on leaf surfaces. In the absence of direct observation we suspect that the concentration of

elements in non-mobile stems is the major conservation mechanism used in these forests and that mycorrhizae and feeder roots beneath the litter result in relatively efficient recycling of the essential elements.

Montane forest in Puerto Rico

The montane forest in Puerto Rico has been studied in great detail by a research team directed by H.T. Odum. This research has been reported in Odum and Pigeon (1970) and the mineral cycling data in Jordan et al. (1972). The Puerto Rican forest called El Verde forest is located at 424 m elevation and receives about 3000 mm of rainfall annually. While there is considerable variation in climate the monthly evapotranspiration never exceeds monthly precipitation.

In this forest rain input is less than loss to streams for potassium, calcium, magnesium and sodium, but is approximately in balance for strontium, copper, and manganese. The storage in the biota in relation to storage in the soil is greater for calcium, potassium, sodium, manganese and copper but is lower for magnesium, iron and strontium (Table 9.6). The percentage of the biotic storage that cycles per year to the soil in litterfall, throughfall and stemflow is from 7 to 20% for all elements except potassium (83%) and copper (75%). Further, the percentage of the soil inventory being taken up by the roots per year ranges from 5 to 34% for all elements except potassium (439%) and copper

TABLE 9.6

Mineral cycling data for a montane forest in Puerto Rico (from Jordan et al., 1972).

Element	Compartmental content (kg ha^{-1})				Flux (kg ha^{-1} yr^{-1})					
	leaves	litter	soil	wood	in via rain	in via rock weathering	leaf and litter fall	stem flow and through-fall	soil to wood	runoff from soil
Ca	55	11	176	380	21.8	21.3	49.9	13.00	59.3	43.1
K	24	1	31	143	18.2	2.6	2.1	136.8	135.7	20.8
Mg	26	6	155	95	4.9	10.1	12.0	4.3	15.6	15.0
Na	21	1	156	218	57.2	7.3	4.2	26.0	20.8	64.5
Fe	1.3	23.6	28.5	9.6	0.0	0.10	1.10	1.09	2.24	0.10
Mn	3.4	0.6	3.4	15.2	0.04	0.00	2.26	0.16	0.33	0.04
Cu	0.08	0.10	0.19	0.59	0.68	0.00	0.05	0.47	0.42	0.68
Sr	0.39	0.12	8.86	4.17	0.14	0.02	0.33	0.10	0.41	0.16

(221%) (Table 9.6). Clearly in the El Verde forest potassium and copper could be limiting since these elements cycle at rapid rates, do not have large inputs in rainfall, nor occur in large excess in the soil. Nutrient conservation mechanisms might have evolved for conservation of these and other elements.

Odum (1970) in his chapter on mineral cycling homeostasis summarizes the results of the El Verde study. Mechanisms of conservation cited in the chapter include extensive epiphyllae especially on shade leaves, a mat of surface roots at the soil surface, storage in the biotic compartments and a good fit between the saturation constants of the air and ecosystem mineral cycling functions. The adaptations are apparently directed towards specific elements. For example, Witkamp (1970) showed that epiphyllae caused an increase in retention of radionuclides applied to leaves in the order $Cs > P > Mn > Sr$. Phosphorus was shown by Luse (1970) to be lost mainly in leaf fall and to be taken up very efficiently by the roots, probably by mycorrhizae. Potassium is very mobile and is probably even more efficiently cycled at the soil surface to the root mat. Kline (1970) analysed the half life of ^{144}Ce, ^{95}Zr, ^{95}Nb, ^{137}Cs and ^{54}Mn in leaves in the forest and found that the leaf half time (250 days) was most similar to the radioactive half life (314 days) for ^{54}Mn, the only essential element tested, indicating that leaf turnover was the predominate agent of

removal from the canopy and understorey. In contrast, the leaf half time for ^{137}Cs (450 days) deviated strongly for the radioactive half life (10 900 days) indicating that this element is far from being in a steady state nutrient cycle. However, manganese had still not achieved steady state after the major input five years previously. Control is at the litter–soil interface; uptake of ^{137}Cs, ^{144}Ce, and ^{95}Zr–^{95}Nb was essentially negligible.

San Carlos de Río Negro

A pilot tropical forest ecosystem project of UNESCO's Man and Biosphere Program has been operated by Venezuelan ecologists, assisted by ecologists from the U.S.A. and Federal Republic of Germany, at San Carlos on the Río Negro in the Amazon forest of Venezuela. There are a variety of forest ecosystems in the San Carlos area. Most intensive research has been on the Amazon caatinga, growing on quartz sand and the *tierra firme* forest on lateritic clay soils. Cycling data have been obtained from a variety of studies of processes, with a synthetic report on the caatinga by Herrera (1979). These studies are important since they represent an extreme condition of low nutrient availability in the soil (Herrera et al., 1970). Thus, they represent an oligotrophic condition to contrast with the eutrophic conditions in Puerto Rico and Panama in the sense of Jordan and Herrera (1979).

Herrera's (1979) detailed study was carried out on a forest growing on a Spodosol with very low total or exchangeable nutrient supply (Table 9.7). The input–output dynamics of this forest show that it is in balance, and depends largely on rain input to compensate for the small losses from the system (Table 9.8). Storage in the biomass is significant especially in the root biomass and in litter, a condition quite different from the other forests (Table 9.9). In these circumstances, a highly developed root mat and litter layer occurs on the soil surface and effectively captures nutrients in water falling on the surface (Stark and Jordan, 1978), as well as providing a habitat for mycorrhizal fungi and other organisms which take up nutrients and recycle them (Herrera et al., 1978). Other nutrient

TABLE 9.7

Inventory of elements in the soil under caatinga forest at San Carlos de Rio Negro in kg ha^{-1} (from Herrera, 1979)

Horizon	Depth (cm)	C	N	P	K	Ca	Mg
0 + A^1	0–21	56 900	1600	47	141	263	31
A$_2$	21–40	10 900	121	27	6	27	0.4

TABLE 9.8

Summary of nutrient transfer rates among ecosystem compartments, in kg ha^{-1} yr^{-1} (from Herrera, 1979).

Flows	N	P	K	Ca	Mg
Rainfall	21.2	16.7	18.0	16.0	3.1
Throughfall	25.2	5.5	29.5	6.0	4.1
Fine litterfall	42.1	2.6	27.3	31.0	8.8
Treefall	2.1	0.3	1.6	1.6	0.3
Root renewal	225.0	17.1	89.1	50.4	37.3
Uptake by vegetation	273.2	8.8	129.5	73.0	47.4
Leaching at 12 cm	15.3	21.2	26.0	21.2	4.4
Streamflow discharge	8.2	16.0	3.5	2.8	0.6

TABLE 9.9

The elemental content of forest compartments at San Carlos de Rio Negro (from Herrera, 1979)

Compartments	Dry weight (kg ha^{-1})	Nutrient content (kg ha^{-1})				
		N	P	K	Ca	Mg
Leaves	7032	72	4	40	17	17
Stems	178 200	264	28	281	222	36
Roots	132 000	834	69	327	244	142
Fine litter	6590	52	3	6	33	16
Dead timber	15 202	80	2	4	34	6
Surface soil						
0–21 cm	493 500	715	21	64	119	14
21–40 cm	1 713 800	70	15	5	15	0
Subsoil						
40–75 cm	6 072 500	0	18	4	61	4
Total (incl. soil 0–40)		2087	142	727	684	231

conserving mechanisms demonstrated to occur in these forests include the depression of nitrifying bacteria by low pH and high concentrations of tannins (Jordan et al., 1979), nutrient scavenging by the canopy of nutrients exiting the system in rain and dust (Jordan et al., 1979), epiphyllae and sclerophyll leaves (Medina et al., 1978; Herrera, 1979).

These three neotropical tropical forests represent some of the differences observed in nutrient cycling. The geological substrates of each are quite different, the soils, therefore, are different and the cycling patterns for certain elements such as calcium (Table 9.10) and magnesium are different. Note for example that while calcium is lost from all systems, the amount lost in the Panama forest is large. However, the ratio of the amount cycled to that stored is relatively similar in San Carlos, the nutrient-poor site, and Panama. On the other hand, for elements such as nitrogen, phosphorus and potassium (Table 9.10) the patterns have substantial similarity. For these elements the biological features of the forest control the chemical patterns more than geological features, a conclusion also drawn by Golley et al. (1978) from a chemical reconnaissance of a transect in Colombia. In all the forests the ratio of the quantities cycling to that stored in the biomass is less than 15% and the ratio of the input from rainfall to that stored is less than 5% except at San Carlos where the substrate is unusually deficient in nutrients. Storage in the biomass clearly has a strong buffering influence on the impact of environmental disturbances.

These considerations of the nutrient cycling rates and adaptations for conservation of nutrients lead to the following sets of questions regarding nutrient cycling in tropical forests:

First, are there sufficient nutrients in rainfall to satisfy the demands of the biota, assuming nutrient conservation mechanisms are capable of holding nutrients once they enter the system?

As we have seen, during a single year, rainfall nutrient quantities are often less than the quantities cycled and much less than the amounts stored in the biomass of mature forests. However, the input quantities could over tens to hundreds of years (Table 9.11) equal the storage in biomass. Since ecological succession in tropical forest may require

TABLE 9.11

The relation of rain input of elements to the biotic inventory of mature tropical moist forest (kg ha^{-1})

Element	Biotic inventory	Rain input	Years of input to equal inventory
P	164	1	164
K	3103	9.5	327
Ca	4103	29	141
Mg	429	4.9	88
Na	55	31	2
Co	12	2	6
Cu	2	0.5	3
Fe	18	3	6
Mn	29	0.4	73
Sr	21	0.1	210
Zn	8	0.9	9

TABLE 9.10

Comparison of nutrient cycling data for three neotropical forests (data from Golley et al., 1975; Jordan et al., 1972; and Herrera, 1979); data in kg ha^{-1} or kg ha^{-1} yr^{-1}; cycling is the quantity in throughfall, litterfall and stem flow

		Biotic storage	Rain input	Output	Diff. in to out	Ratio input/ storage	Cycling	Ratio cycling/ storage
Nitrogen	San Carlos	1170	21	15	+6	0.02	69	0.06
	El Verde	1230	14	29	−15	0.01	160	0.13
Phosphorus	San Carlos	101	17	21	−5	0.17	8	0.08
	Panama	164	1	1	0	0.01	12	0.07
Potassium	San Carlos	648	18	26	−8	0.03	58	0.09
	Panama	3103	10	10	0	0.003	197	0.06
Calcium	San Carlos	483	16	21	+5	0.03	39	0.08
	Panama	4103	29	163	+134	0.01	298	0.07
	El Verde	435	22	43	+21	0.05	63	0.14

hundreds of years and the age of a single individual tree may be hundreds of years, it is not unreasonable to conclude that rain input alone could supply the nutrient supply to the forest.

The above conclusion seems unreasonable since our experience, especially in agriculture, suggests that the soil is the prime source of nutrients for plant growth. Soils do contain large sources of specific nutrients and, together with rainfall inputs, supply adequate nutrients to the soil solution where root uptake takes place. But it is not reasonable to couch the comparison in an either/or context. Soil and atmospheric inputs are acting in concert. There may very well be in most situations adequate nutrient resources available to the biota but the ability of the biota to utilize these resources may be limited by environmental factors.

Thus, we conclude that nutrient conservation may be required for reasons of environmental limits to uptake as well as poor nutrient supply. Odum (1970) has emphasized control of uptake by transpiration pumping controled in turn by air moisture. Other authors have emphasized control of recycling in the root–litter–leaf pathway. Conservation might be focused on solving problems in either the uptake or loss part of this system.

Therefore, we can ask:

Can the vegetation pump enough water to satisfy the nutrient demand? Transpiration requires both adequate soil water and dry air at the leaf surface. If both of these conditions are in the proper relationship then the transpiration pump can function efficiently. These conditions are found especially on large land masses where relatively dry air movements occur intermixed with rainy periods — a dry–wet season environment. They do not hold where the dry season is very pronounced nor where the air moisture is excessive, such as in mountain areas on islands. Odum (1970) has discussed these relationships with special regard to forests on Puerto Rico. He finds taller forests, deeper roots, and less epiphytes where the environmental conditions promote adequate transpiration. Jordan and Kline (1977) examined transpiration of the trees at San Carlos de Río Negro using tritium. Their studies indicated that transpiration was related to sapwood area independent of tree species or soil type. These data tend to support the Odum hypothesis.

A further question is, can leaching of nutrients from the living tissues be reduced? Yes, we have accounted for a variety of mechanisms to reduce leaching of nutrients. These include morphological, physiological and ecological adaptations of the leaves, storage of the nutrients in the slower turning over trunks and branches, and chemical adaptations to reduce herbivory. We also find that decomposition can be retarded to reduce leaching from the dead organic matter. Rate of decomposition can be controlled, in part, by the chemistry of the organic material and the timing of the loss of plant parts.

Clearly, there are many alternatives for the adaptation of the species to balance their demands for nutrients, the nutrient supply and the environmental controls on supply and/or demand.

CONCLUSION

In this chapter we have explored the mechanisms for nutrient conservation in forest vegetation by evaluating various anatomical, physiological, biochemical and ecological mechanisms that are known to influence nutrient flux, biomass flux or storage, or other dynamic features of the vegetation related to its chemistry. These examples do not prove that they are used for nutrient conservation, only that they could be selected through evolution if nutrients were limited in the environment of that species. There is relatively poor evidence that nutrients are limiting to a forest community — most studies of forest production show that the observed differences in production are due mainly to temperature, water and solar energy. Indeed, J.R. Kline (pers. comm.) has argued that forests are usually decoupled from their nutrient supply in the soil and can satisfy their needs by recycling and atmospheric input. Of course, this pattern itself could be interpreted as an adaptation to poor nutrient supply.

Possibly the most convincing experience is that in certain environments with a poor nutrient supply in the substrate, such as podzolic sands and laterite clays in the Río Negro region of the Amazon forest, the vegetation exhibits a relatively large number of the possible adaptations listed here. In less extreme environments fewer adaptations are observed. Thus, experience suggests that adaptation to poor nutrient supply is important, even though the hard data are unconvincing. Obviously a number of hypotheses can be suggested for testing by careful experimentation in the field.

REFERENCES

Bernhard-Reversat, F., 1975. Recherches sur l'écosystème de la forêt subéquatoriale de basse Côte-d'Ivoire. VI. Les cycles des macroéléments. *Terre Vie*, 29: 229–254.

Best, G.R. and Monk, C.D., 1975. Cation flux in hardwood and white pine watersheds. In: F.G. Howell, J.B. Gentry and M.H. Smith (Editors), *Mineral Cycling in Southeastern Ecosystems*. USERDA, Tech. Inf. Center, pp. 847–861.

Bormann, F.H., 1966. The structure, function, and ecological significance of root grafts in *Pinus strobus* L. *Ecol. Monogr.*, 36: 1–26.

Carlisle, A., Brown, A.H.F. and White, E.J., 1967. The nutrient content of tree stem flow and ground flora litter and leachates in a sessile oak (*Quercus petraea*) woodland. *J. Ecol.*, 55: 615–627.

Chenery, E.M. and Sporne, K.R., 1976. A note on the evolutionary status of aluminum-accumulators among dicotyledons. *New Phytol.*, 76: 551–554.

Cromack, K. and Monk, C.D., 1975. Litter production, decomposition and nutrient cycling in a mixed hardwood watershed and a white pine watershed. In: F.G. Howell, J.B. Gentry and M.H. Smith (Editors), *Mineral Cycling in Southeastern Ecosystems*. USERDA Symposium Series (Conf. 740513), pp. 609–694.

Crossley, D.A., Monk, C.D., Todd, R.L., Waide, J.B., Swank, W.T., Wallace, J.B. and Webster, J.R., 1977. *Effect of Perturbation on Nutrient Circulation in Forested Watershed Ecosystems at Coweeta*. Report on Grant BMS74-12088 AO1 to the NSF (mimeograph).

Draft, M.J. and Nicholson, T.H., 1969. Effect of *Endogone* mycorrhiza on plant growth. II. Influence of soluble phosphate on endophyte and host in maize. *New Phytol.*, 68: 945–952.

Edwards, P.J., 1977. Studies of mineral cycling in a montane rain forest in New Guinea II. The production and disappearance of litter. *J. Ecol.*, 65: 971–992.

Elton, C.S., 1973. The structure of invertebrate populations inside neotropical rain forest. *J. Anim. Ecol.*, 42: 55–104.

Foreman, R.T.T., 1975. Canopy lichens with blue-green algae: a nitrogen source in a Colombian rain forest. *Ecology*, 56: 1176–1184.

Gessel, S.P., Cole, D.W., Johnson, D. and Turner, J., 1979. The nutrient cycles of two Costa Rican forests. In: *Actas del IV Symposium Internacional de ecologia tropical, 11, Panama*, pp. 623–645.

Golley, F.B., 1977. Insects as regulators of forest nutrient cycling. *Trop. Ecol.*, 18(2):116–123.

Golley, F.B. and Richardson, T., 1977. Chemical relationships in tropical forests. *Geo-Eco-Trop*, 1(1): 35–44.

Golley, F.B., McGinnis, J.T., Clements, R.G., Child, G.I. and Duever, M.J., 1975. *Mineral Cycling in a Tropical Moist Forest Ecosystem*. University of Georgia Press, Athens, Ga., 248 pp.

Golley, F.B., Richardson, T. and Clements, R.G., 1978. Elemental concentrations in tropical forests and soils of northwestern Colombia. *Biotropica*, 10(2): 144–151.

Grubb, P.J., 1977. Control of forest growth and distribution on wet tropical mountains: with special reference to mineral nutrition. *Annu. Rev. Ecol. Syst.*, 1977: 83–107.

Haines, B., 1975. Impact of leaf-cutting ants on vegetation development at Barro Colorado Island. In: F.B. Golley and E. Medina (Editors), *Tropical Ecological Systems*. Springer-Verlag, Berlin.

Harrelson, M.A., 1969. *Tropical Epiphyllae and Nitrogen Fixation*. Dissertation, University of Georgia, Athens, Ga., 103 pp.

Hayman, D.S., 1978. Endomycorrhizae. In: Y.R. Dommergues and S.V. Krupa (Editors), *Interactions Between Non-Pathogenic Soil Microorganisms and Plants*. Elsevier, Amsterdam, pp. 401–442.

Herrera, R.A., 1979. *Nutrient Distribution and Cycling in an Amazon Caatinga Forest on Spodosols in Southern Venezuela*. Thesis, University of Reading, Reading, 244 pp.

Herrera, R.A., Jordan, C.F., Klinge, H. and Medina, E., 1978a. Amazon ecosystems: their structure and functioning with particular emphasis on nutrients. *Interciencia*, 3(4): 223–231.

Herrera, R., Merida, T., Stark, N., and Jordan, C.F., 1978b. Direct phosphorus transfer from leaf litter to roots. *Naturwissenschaften*, 65: 208.

Iwatsubo, G. and Tsutsumi, T., 1967. On the amount of plant nutrients supplied to the ground by rainwater in adjacent open plot and forests. *Bull. Kyoto Univ. For.*, 39: 110–124.

Janos, D.P., 1975. Effects of vesicular–arbuscular mycorrhizae on lowland tropical rain forest trees. In: F.E. Sanders, B. Mosse and P.B. Tinker (Editors), *Endomycorrhizas*. Academic Press, London, pp. 437–446.

Janse, J.M., 1896. Les endophytes radicaux de quelques plantes Javanaises. *Ann. Jard. Bot. Buitenzorg*, 14: 53–212.

Janzen, D.H., 1976. Why tropical trees have rotten cores. *Biotropica*, 8: 110.

Janzen, D.H. and Schoener, T.W., 1968. Differences in insect abundance and diversity between wetter and drier sites during a tropical dry season. *Ecology*, 49(1): 96–110.

Johnson, D.W., Cole, D.W. and Gessel, S.P., 1975. Processes of nutrient transfer in a tropical rain forest. *Biotropica*, 7(3): 208–215.

Jordan, C.F., 1971. A world pattern in plant energetics. *Am. Sci.*, 59: 425–433.

Jordan, C.F. and Herrera, R., 1979. Tropical forests: are nutrients really critical? *Am. Nat.*, in press.

Jordan, C.F., Kline, J.R. and Sasscer, D.S., 1972. Relative stability of mineral cycles in forest ecosystems. *Am. Nat.*, 106(948): 237–253.

Jordan, C.F., Golley, F., Hall, J. and Hall, J., 1979. Nutrient scavenging of rainfall by the canopy of an Amazonian rain forest. *Biotropica*, in press.

Jordan, C.F., Todd, R.L. and Escalante, G., 1979. Nitrogen conservation in a tropical rain forest. *Oecologia*, 39: 123–128.

Kitazawa, Y., 1971. Biological regionality of the soil fauna and its function in forest ecosystem types. In: P. Duvigneaud (Editor), *Productivity of Forest Ecosystems. Proceedings of the Brussels Symposium*: UNESCO, Paris, pp. 485–498.

Kline, J.R., 1970. Retention of fallout radionuclides by tropical forest vegetation. In: H.T. Odum and R.F. Pigeon (Editors), *A Tropical Rain Forest. A Study of Irradiation and Ecology at El Verde, Puerto Rico*. U.S. Atomic Energy Commission, Washington, D.C., pp. H191–H198.

Klinge, H., 1976. Bilanzierung von Hauptnährstoffen im Ökosystem tropischer Regenwald (Manaus). Vorläufige Daten. *Biogeographica*, 7: 59–77.

Lane, P. and Levins, R., 1977. The dynamics of aquatic systems. 2. The effects of nutrient enrichment on model plankton communities. *Limnol. Oceanogr.*, 22(3): 454–471.

Laudelout, H. and Meyer, J., 1954. Les cycles d'éléments minéraux et de matière organique en forêt équatoriale congolaise. *Trans. Fifth Int. Congr. Soil Sci.*, 2, pp. 267–272.

Luse, R.A., 1970. The phosphorus cycle in a tropical rain forest. In: H.T. Odum and R.F. Pigeon (Editors), *A Tropical Rain Forest. A Study of Irradiation and Ecology at El Verde, Puerto Rico*. U.S. Atomic Energy Commission, Washington, D.C., pp. H161–H166.

Mayer, R. and Ulrich, B., 1974. Conclusions on the filtering action of forests from ecosystem analysis. *Oecol. Plant.*, 9(2): 157–168.

McKey, D., Waterman, P.G., Mbi, C.N., Gartlan, J.S. and Struhsaker, T.T., 1978. Phenolic content of vegetation in two African rain forests: ecological implications. *Science*, 202: 61–64.

Medina, E., Sobrado, M. and Herrera, R., 1978. Significance of leaf orientation for leaf temperature in an Amazonian sclerophyll vegetation. *J. Rad. Environ. Biophys.*, 15: 131–140.

Mitchell, J.E., Waide, J.B. and Todd, R.L., 1975. A preliminary compartment model of the nitrogen cycle in a deciduous forest ecosystem. In: F.G. Howell, J.B. Gentry and M.H. Smith (Editors), *Mineral Cycling in Southeastern Ecosystems*. USERDA, Tech. Inf. Center, pp. 41–57.

Monk, C.D., 1966. An ecological significance of evergreenness. *Ecology*, 47(3): 504–505.

Montgomery, G.G. and Sunquist, M.E., 1975. Impact of sloths on neotropical forest energy flow and nutrient cycling. In: F.B. Golley and E. Medina (Editors), *Tropical Ecological Systems*. Springer-Verlag, Berlin, pp. 69–98.

Nicholson, T.H. 1975. Evolution of vesicular–arbuscular mycorrhizas. In: F.E. Sanders, B. Mosse and P.B. Tinker (Editors), *Endomycorrhizas*. Academic Press, London, pp. 25–34.

Nihlgard, B., 1970. Precipitation, its chemical composition and effect on soilwater in a beech and a spruce forest in south Sweden. *Oikos*, 21: 208–217.

Nye, P.H., 1961. Organic matter and nutrient cycles under moist tropical forest. *Plant Soil*, 13(4): 333–346.

Nye, P.H. and Greenland, D.J., 1960. *The Soil Under Shifting Cultivation*. Commonwealth Bureau of Soils, Harpenden, Tech. Comm. 51, 156 pp.

Odum, H.T., 1970. *Summary: An emerging view of the ecological system at El Verde*. In: H.T. Odum and R.F. Pigeon (Editors), *A Tropical Rain Forest. A Study of Irradiation and Ecology at El Verde, Puerto Rico*. U.S. Atomic Energy Commission, Washington, D.C., pp. I191–I289.

Odum, H.T. and Pigeon, R.F., 1970. *A Tropical Rain Forest. A Study of Irradiation and Ecology at El Verde, Puerto Rico*. U.S. Atomic Energy Commission, Washington, D.C., 1678 pp.

Odum, H.T. and Ruiz-Reyes, J., 1970. Holes in leaves and the grazing control mechanism. In: H.T. Odum and R.F. Pigeon (Editors), *A Tropical Rain Forest. A Study of Irradiation and Ecology at El Verde, Puerto Rico*. Washington, D.C., pp. I69–I80.

Olson, J.S., 1963. Energy storage and the balance of producers and decomposers in ecological systems. *Ecology*, 44: 322–331.

Olson, J.S., 1965. Equations for cesium transfer in a *Liriodendron* forest. In: R.D. Hungate (Editor), *Radiation and Terrestrial Ecosystems*. Pergamon Press, Oxford, pp. 1385–1392.

Owen, D.F., 1976. *Animal Ecology in Tropical Africa*. Longman, London, 2nd ed.

Richards, P.W., 1964. *The Tropical Rain Forest: An Ecological Study*. Cambridge University Press, Cambridge, 450 pp.

Rodin, L.E. and Bazilevich, N.I., 1967. *Production and Mineral Cycling in Terrestrial Vegetation*. Oliver and Boyd, Edinburgh, 288 pp.

Schlesinger, W.H., 1977. Carbon balance in terrestrial detritus. *Annu. Rev. Ecol. Syst.*, 8: 51–81.

Stark, N.M. and Jordan, C.F. 1978. Nutrient retention by the root mat of an Amazonian rain forest. *Ecology*, 59(3): 434–437.

Stenlid, C., 1958. Salt losses and redistribution of salts in higher plants. In: W. Ruhland (Editor), *Encyclopedia of Plant Physiology*, Springer-Verlag, Berlin, pp. 615–637.

Tanner, E.V.J., 1977. Four montane rain forests of Jamaica: a quantitative characterization of the floristics, the soils and the foliar mineral levels, and a discussion of the interrelations. *J. Ecol.*, 65: 883–918.

Tukey, H.B., Jr., 1970. Leaching of metabolites from foliage and its implication in the tropical rain forest. In: H.T. Odum and R.F. Pigeon (Editors), *A Tropical Rain Forest. A Study of Irradiation and Ecology at El Verde, Puerto Rico*. U.S. Atomic Energy Commission, Washington, D.C., pp. H155–H160.

Tukey, H.B., Jr., 1971. Leaching of substances from plants. In: T.F. Preece and C.H. Dickinson (Editors), *Ecology of Leaf Surface Microorganisms*. pp. 67–80.

Tukey, H.B., Jr. and Morgan, J.V., 1963. Injury to foliage and its effect upon the leaching of nutrients from above ground plant parts. *Physiol. Plant.*, 16: 557–564.

Tukey, H.B., Jr. and Tukey, H.B., 1962. The loss of organic and inorganic materials by leaching for leaves and other above ground plant parts. In: *Radioisotopes in Soil–Plant Nutrition Studies*. International Atomic Energy Agency, Vienna, pp. 289–302.

Vernadsky, V.I., 1934. *Studies in Geochemistry*. Nauka, Leningrad, 2nd ed. (in Russian).

Wells, C.A., Whigham, D. and Lieth, H., 1972. Investigation of mineral nutrient cycling in an upland Piedmont forest. *J. Elisha Mitchell Sci. Soc.*, 88(2): 66–78.

Went, F.W. and Stark, N., 1968. Mycorrhiza. *Bioscience*, 18: 1035–1039.

Witkamp, M., 1970. Mineral retention by epiphyllic organisms. In: H.T. Odum and R.F. Pigeon (Editors), *A Tropical Rain Forest. A Study of Irradiation and Ecology at El Verde, Puerto Rico.* U.S. Atomic Energy Commission, Washington, D.C., pp. H177–H179.

Witkamp, M. and Ausmus, B.S., 1975. Processes in decomposition and nutrient transfer in forest systems. In: J.M. Anderson and A. Macfadyen (Editors), *The Role of Terrestrial and Aquatic Organisms in Decomposition Processes.* Blackwell, Oxford, pp. 375–396.

Witkamp, M. and Olson, J., 1963. *Breakdown of Confined and Nonconfined Oak Litter.* Oak Ridge National Laboratory, Oak Ridge, Tenn. (mimeograph).

Chapter 10

DECOMPOSITION

FRANK B. GOLLEY

INTRODUCTION

Decomposition refers to the physical and chemical processes involved in reducing dead organic matter in vegetation and animals to their elemental chemical constituents. Certainly for the vast bulk of forest organic matter decomposition is a two-stage process. First, particles ranging in size from a flower part to the bole of a large tree must be broken down into small pieces which can be chemically reduced. Second, usually through organismal activities these small pieces of organic matter are further reduced and mineralized to release the basic constituents of proteins, carbohydrates, lipids and minerals which can be consumed, absorbed by organisms or washed out of the system. In tropical forests, decomposition usually occurs in the soil or on the soil surface, although a relatively large percentage of trees and branches begin decay in the standing position (Edwards, 1977).

Studies of organic decomposition have been especially active in forests only within the last ten to fifteen years through the International Biological Program, and are still in their infancy in tropical forests. This is because the soil–litter system is difficult to observe directly and many of the important steps in decomposition involve microorganisms, especially fungi. Most ecologists are unfamiliar with the biology and the techniques to study the biology of microorganisms and fungi, especially in the field. Further, almost all studies thus far have dealt with decomposition of plant organic matter. Forest animal carcass decay has been poorly studied everywhere.

THE DIMENSIONS OF THE PROBLEM

In previous chapters we have presented data on the organic biomass and rates of litterfall in tropical forest. Jenny et al. (1949), in a classical paper, made the initial comparisons of decomposition in tropical and temperate environments. Sanchez (1976) surveyed these and more recent data. In general tropical forests produce about five tons of dry organic matter per hectare per year as the input to the decomposer system. This input is much greater than is typical of temperate forests (which is about $1 \ t \ ha^{-1} \ yr^{-1}$). The conversion of this fresh organic matter to humus occurs at a rate of from 30 to 50% per year. Of course, leaves may decay much more rapidly than branches and boles. Leaf decay may occur in three to six months under conditions of high temperature and rainfall (Golley et al., 1975).

Turning to the residue of decomposition, the soil organic matter, Sanchez (1976) reported that the percent organic matter in topsoil is similar in temperate and tropical soils. African, Puerto Rican and Hawaiian soils are reported to contain over 3% organic matter in the upper 15 to 30 cm. Several randomly chosen profiles in Brazil and Zaïre contained from 0.98 to 2.13% in the upper 15 cm. Sanchez explains the similarity in temperate and tropical soils as due to the following: First, there is no direct relationship between soil color and percent organic matter. Black soils do not necessarily have more organic matter than red soils. Second, in some tropical soils allophane reacts with organic radicals to form complexes resistant to mineralization. In these soils organic matter tends to accumulate. Other chemical processes are involved surely and these are under active study by soil scientists (for example, Young and Spycher, 1979).

Schlesinger (1977) also reviews data on soil carbon, and while his data support the conclusions of Sanchez, Schlesinger concludes the opposite. Schlesinger converts the percent organic matter data of the agronomist to quantities of carbon and also has tried to calculate the organic matter in the entire profile (to 1 m depth) not just in the plow zone. He finds that organic carbon in tropical forest soils averages 10.4 kg C m^{-2} and ranges from 3.7 to 20.5 kg C m^{-2}, with a coefficent of variation of 44%. In contrast, temperate forests average 11.8 kg C m^{-2}, range from 5.6 to 24.0 kg C m^{-2} and have a coefficient of variation of 35%. Clearly, the average organic carbon content in the two types of forest soils does not differ significantly.

The rates of breakdown of soil organic matter is about 2 to 5% per year (Sanchez, 1976), although soils high in allophane, clay, or oxides may have lower rates. The rate of soil organic matter decomposition in temperate forests is much lower (0.4–1%); the temperate–tropical difference is mainly due to temperature.

Schlesinger (1977) has reviewed the data on the rate of CO_2 evolution for tropical forest soils. These data have been obtained by a variety of techniques and are influenced by a number of contributory factors. They include, for example, the respiration of roots and of soil organisms. Daily rates of soil CO_2 loss range from 0.3 to 0.8 g C m^{-2} in Puerto Rico (Odum et al., 1970) to 2.4 to 16.7 g C m^{-2} in Costa Rica (Schulze, 1967). Annual release, calculated from daily measurements, ranges from 405 to 2117 g C m^{-2}. Schlesinger (1977) finds a linear relation between soil CO_2 release and latitude. The difference between this relationship and that for litterfall and latitude gives an estimate of the organic matter or carbon derived from roots and soil organisms and respiration of roots and soil organisms. In forests the carbon loss in soil respiration is 2.5 times the carbon input in aboveground litterfall.

Meentemeyer (1978) also considers the broad trends of decomposition. Since temperature and moisture are prime controls on decomposition processes, he has modeled rates of litter decomposition against actual evapotranspiration. The Thornthwaite method was used to calculate actual evapotranspiration. The relationship is linear over a span of climates ranging from arctic to tropical

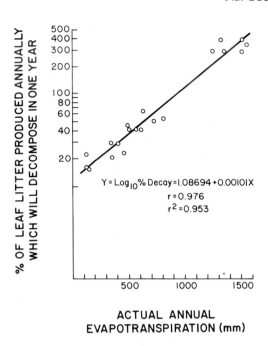

Fig. 10.1. The relationship between the percentage of annual litter production decomposing in a year to the annual evapotranspiration (according to Meentemeyer, 1978).

(Fig. 10.1). The correlation coefficient (0.976) gives one confidence in the prediction.

Annual and daily rates of litterfall and organic matter decomposition ignore the temporal patterns which these processes exhibit. These patterns reflect the environmental variation in the region since litterfall and decomposition are influenced by wind, rain and temperature. In forests which have adjusted to a dry season, often litterfall is maximum during this dry period (Golley et al., 1975). Similarly, litter decay is low during a dry season and is rapid during the wet season (Madge, 1965).

These data illustrate the dimensions of the decomposition process. The remainder of this chapter will be concerned with the organisms and processes which cause organic matter to be broken down with release of CO_2 and other gases and various minerals.

Besides carbon, nitrogen, sulfur and possibly phosphorus also have a gaseous phase. The nitrogen cycle is well known. The nitrogen reservoir is in the atmosphere but is not available directly to the vegetation. Rather, the gaseous nitrogen is converted into forms that can be assimilated by nitrogen-fixing organisms. In the decomposition process proteins in the dead plants and animals are broken down into urea or to ammonia and then can be further converted to nitrites or nitrates which can be lost to the atmosphere by denitrification. As Ellenberg (1971) pointed out, most ecosystems are fairly economic in nitrogen cycling although denitrification may be more important than currently realized (Bremner and Blackmer, 1979). Relatively little nitrogen is lost in ground water and that lost as a gas is returned through rainfall. For example, at San Carlos de Rio Negro, Venezuela, Jordan et al. (1979) reported an annual input of nitrogen to the forest floor of 85 kg ha^{-1}, and a loss as nitrates in streams of 2 kg ha^{-1}. Inhibition of conversion of ammonium ions (NH_4–N) to nitrate (NO_3–N) is probably due to low pH (4.5) and high concentrations of tannins in the litter and soil acting upon nitrifying bacteria. Maintenance of nitrogen in the form of ammonium ions, which can be taken up by plant roots and is not easily lost in ground water, is a conservative strategy for the forest ecosystem.

Herrera (1979) has proposed a gaseous phase of phosphorus, phosphine gas, as an answer to an imbalance in the phosphorus cycle at the forest near San Carlos de Rio Negro. In this case phosphorus is reduced to phosphine gas, escapes to the atmosphere where it is reoxidized and reenters the system in rainfall. The organisms and mechanisms involved in this cycle are unknown.

The sulfur cycle is also poorly known for tropical forests, although Johnson et al. (1977) discussed the role of sulfate concentrations in soils at Finca La Selva, Costa Rica. Their studies show a relatively highly acid rain probably from Irazu Volcano with the pH rising to near 6 in the soil solution.

BIOLOGICAL ROLE IN DECOMPOSITION

The dead organic matter that must be decomposed is high in carbon and energy, but relatively poor in nutrients. The nutrients released from the decomposing material must be adequate to support the activity and growth of the decomposer populations and plant uptake. As we have seen in some tropical forests with low nutrient reserves in the soil, the decomposer populations are a key to the efficient recycling of nutrients from the vegetation

and animals back to the vegetation (Chapter 9). There is also evidence (e.g. Cole et al., 1978) that similar recycling mechanisms occur within the soil subcommunity. Nutrients are insufficient to drive decomposer populations with a simple passthrough of chemical elements from the substrate, back to the substrate. Rather, for example, populations of bacteria take up phosphorus and hold it, while bacterial grazers such as protozoa and nematodes release inorganic phosphorus into the rhizosphere where plant uptake can occur. Thus, there is a complex mechanism of storage and release that can be triggered possibly by the roots and the environment. These processes depend upon a proper relationship between the carbon required for energy of metabolism and growth of the organisms and the particular element under study. Gosz et al. (1973) showed that there is probably an optimum level for each C:element ratio.

The various organisms active in decomposition can be divided taxonomically and ecologically into groups or components. These include bacteria, fungi, protozoa, nematodes, oligochaetes, micro- and macro-arthropods, and other animals. As far as I know there has been no soil system study in a tropical forest that deals with all of these groups simultaneously and which is concerned about their role in the ecosystem. Rather most studies focus on one group of organisms and are usually only concerned with describing their numbers and biomass. There is another collection of studies which, stimulated by the comparative ecosystem program of the IBP, compare characteristics of decomposer organisms in a variety of systems. They are quite useful since they show how tropical forest organisms may differ from those of temperate or coniferous forests. Kitazawa's (1971) comparison of the soil fauna is a useful place to begin.

Kitazawa divided the soil fauna into mesofauna consisting of Nematoda, Enchytraeidae, Acari, Collembola and Diptera larvae and the macrofauna consisting of larger organisms (Tables 10.1 and 10.2). These Tables present some of his data which provide a comparison of tropical and temperate forests. The major point is that "there is a conspicuous diversity of species in the tropical region; nevertheless the numbers of major taxonomic and life form groups are nearly the same in every type of forest ecosystem from alpine to equatorial." However, considering the biomass of

TABLE 10.1

Number and biomass of mesofauna in several ecosystem types (data from Kitazawa, 1971)

Mesofauna	Subalpine coniferous forest	Temperate deciduous forest	Tropical highland forest	Tropical rain forest
Nematoda				
number (10^5 m^{-2})	2.13	4.13	0.59	0.41
fresh weight (g m^{-2})	0.21	0.41	0.06	0.04
Enchytraeidae				
number (10^5 m^{-2})	1.03	2.22	0.32	0.10
fresh weight (g m^{-2})	1.13	2.45	0.35	0.11
Acari				
number (10^5 m^{-2})	0.53	0.16	0.13	0.07
fresh weight (g m^{-2})	0.53	0.16	0.13	0.07
Collembola				
number (10^5 m^{-2})	0.76	0.29	0.12	0.06
fresh weight (g m^{-2})	7.60	2.87	1.19	0.57
Diptera larvae				
number (10^5 m^{-2})	1.18	2.27	2.80	0.80
fresh weight (g m^{-2})	1.18	2.27	2.80	0.80

TABLE 10.2

Mean number (m^{-2}) of the macrofauna of forest ecosystems (data from Kitazawa, 1971)

Macrofauna	Subalpine coniferous forest	Temperate deciduous forest	Tropical highland forest	Tropical rain forest
Macrodecomposers				
Oligochaeta	18	17	–	0.7
Gastropoda	0.08	1.3	–	–
Crustacea	0.54	3.9	0.8	3.2
Diplopoda	5.1	3.7	3.0	2.3
Coleoptera larvae	7.5	8.5	1.0	0.7
Diptera larvae	5.9	–	0.8	0.2
Orthoptera	0.5	–	1.6	3.8
Apterygota	11.6	9.1	2.4	1.3
Total	49	45	9.2	12.2
Macropredators				
Chilopoda	5.2	24	1.2	1.0
Arachnoidea	7.2	16.6	4.0	6.7
Predatory Coleoptera	3.3	4.0	0.4	25
Hirudinea	0.4	–	–	–
Total	16	46	7.2	10.7
Total macrofauna	73	108	29.6	46.8

the fauna "the total biomass is largest in the temperate and subtropical ecosystems and is least in the tropical lowland rain forest." Respiration, on the other hand, is maximum in the subtropical forests (Fig. 10.2). These statements are supported by other observers, for example, Golley (1978). Presumably, the low biomass of soil fauna is due to the lack of substantial litter layers in tropical forests (Kitazawa, 1971).

As a consequence of the environmental conditions benefiting decay and leaching in tropical forests and the storage of nutrients in the living tissues of the flora and fauna, other portions of the decomposer system have evolved and assumed

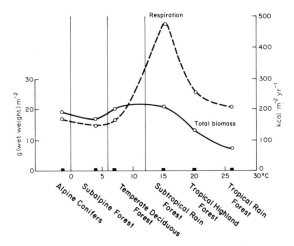

Fig. 10.2. The relationship between total biomass of soil fauna and respiration of soil fauna and type of ecosystem, as reported by Kitazawa (1971).

greater importance than the soil fauna. For example, the fungal populations can be significant in the recycling of nutrients from litter to roots (Chapter 9), as can be the bacteria.

Among the most important groups of organisms active in the physical and chemical reduction of plant material in tropical forests are the termites. Most species of termites are tropical or subtropical and all are social insects living in nests and colonies. They feed on decaying vegetation and wood, relying on cellulose as their main source of energy. Termites that feed on leaf litter usually belong to the Termitidae. These animals collect fresh litter and carry it to their nests. Other termites feed on wood. While a few types feed on living wood, most attack dead material. Other termites feed on fungi.

Termites obtain their energy from the digestion of cellulose, hemicelluloses and, in some cases, from lignin. Most of this digestion is made possible by symbiotic protozoa living in the digestive tract of the termite. The digestive capacity of these organisms can be quite high. Edwards (1974) cites data showing that over 90% of the cellulose, 60% of the hemicellulose and 3% of the lignin in wood was digested in experiments with *Kalotermes flavicollis*. Other species consume mineral soil, especially soil containing humus. I have observed in Zaire the boundary between the soil and parent rock depressed under termite mounds in deep cuts made for water canals. In this case the termites actively used the rock and transported it to the mound.

The nests of termites and the galleries from nests are often large and numerous. The Macrotermitinae in Africa and Indo-Malaya construct large mounds that form a conspicuous feature of the landscape in these forests. The mound may be 3 to 4 m in height and contain 1×10^5 to 24×10^5 kg ha^{-1} of soil (Wood and Sands, 1978), and cover up to 30% of the surface. These mounds are cemented with saliva of the termites; other nests and runways are cemented with excreta and/or plant material. These activities obviously have an impact on the ecosystem. Not only are large quantities of soil and vegetation moved physically changing the soil texture and water holding capacity but the chemistry of the system is also changed. Since the organic matter is collected from a wide area and is concentrated in the nest there is an increase in the nutrient content of the nest itself. Carbon, nitrogen, calcium, phosphorus, potassium and other elements have been shown to increase (Lee and Wood, 1971). Traditional farmers may plant crops on termite mounds to take advantage of these accumulations, as I have observed in Zaire.

Populations of termites vary widely depending upon the system. Table 10.3, modified from Wood and Sands (1978), suggests that the diversity of termites increases with moisture. The numbers and biomass fall below an upper limit of about 15 000 m^{-2} and 50 g m^{-2} (Wood and Sands, 1978 — see Table 10.4 for average forest data) for all types of ecosystems. Density and biomass in rain forests appear to fall below these upper limits.

Matsumoto (1976) has made an energetic study of termites in Malaysian rain forest. Live weight of these insects was 3.5 g m^{-2}, and they consumed annually 55.5 g m^{-2} of plant material. This is a small part of the litter production of the forest. Yet Maldague (1964) estimated in Zaire that termites might consume 570 g m^{-2} annually or about half the litterfall. Matsumoto (1978), at Pasoh forest in Malaysia, showed that termites consumed about 32% of the leaf litter falling on the forest floor (38.8 kg ha^{-1} week^{-1} consumed). Abe (1978) working in the same forest showed that wood also disappeared at a rapid rate (Table 10.5). In any case, termites by measure of their density, biomass, numbers of mounds or rates of consumption have an important impact on the decomposition in tropical forests. This impact can be in terms of reducing those parts of the system high in cellulose

TABLE 10.3

Diversity of termites in West African systems on a gradient of moisture from the most arid to the wet rain forest (from Wood and Sands, 1978)

Ecosystem	Area sampled (ha)	Total number of species	Numbers with feeding habit		
			soil	wood	grass, herbs
Sahel savanna	100	19	3	0	8
South Guinea savanna	7	23	8	2	10
Derived savanna	2700	34	13	3	11
Rain forest	1–5	43	31	8	2

TABLE 10.4

Density and biomass of termites in tropical forests (from Wood and Sands, 1978)

Forest	Nest type	Density ($N\ m^{-2}$)	Biomass ($g\ m^{-2}$)	Authority
Semideciduous	subterranean	3163	8.0	Wood and Johnson (unpubl.)
Riverine	subterranean and mound	1000	11.0	Maldague (1964)
Rain forest	subterranean	4450	–	Strickland (1944)
Rain forest	mound	87–104	0.1	Wiegert (1970)
Rain forest	mound	1330	3.4	Matsumoto (1976)

TABLE 10.5

Rate of disappearance in $1\frac{1}{2}$ years of wood from two tropical trees in west Malaysia (after Abe, 1978)

Species	Size of wood (cm)	% disappearance
Shorea parvifolia		
stem wood	(30–50)	14.5
large branch	(13–20)	49.8
medium branch	(6–13)	60.0
small branch	(3–6)	80.8
Ixonanthes icosandra		
medium branch	(6–13)	24.2
small branch	(3–6)	37.1

and lignin into less complex carbohydrates and other materials, in reducing materials down to CO_2, water and chemical ions, and to creating conditions for other decomposing organisms to invade and utilize dead material. Termite mounds may be invaded by tree roots which will directly use the nutrients available there. In other cases the stored nutrients become available when the nest is abandoned or destroyed by predators.

Ultimately the complexes of organic chemical constituents are broken down by the bacterial populations. The bacteria are poorly known in tropical forests and the ecological roles of bacteria are relatively poorly known in all ecosystems. It appears that this group of organisms is extremely varied and versatile. Some bacteria have enzyme systems which are specifically aimed at the decomposition of certain chemical bonds; others have enzymes with broad potential or can produce a variety of enzymes depending upon the available substrate. In tropical forests the species of trees have evolved a great diversity of biochemical systems which influence herbivory and also decomposition through the bacterial and other populations. Witkamp (1966) in a temperate forest found that the species of leaf was the dominant factor controlling microbial density on decomposing leaf litter and there is no reason to expect that this effect would be less important in tropical forests. Indeed, the effect should be even more significant in the tropics. These microbial populations are not restricted to the soil, of course; they are present through the ecosystem. Hatton and Rasmussen (1970) reported for El Verde, Puerto Rico, relatively large populations of fungi and bacteria in the air within the tropical forest.

Bacterial populations were most abundant at 15 m of height and were much greater than populations above the canopy.

The densities of bacteria are variable in space and time since they respond to substrate, moisture and other environmental factors as would any population. At El Verde, Witkamp (1970) found densities of bacteria of about 40×10^6 cm^{-3} soil in December, as compared with about 30×10^6 cm^{-3} in April, at the end of the dry period. Rambelli et al. (1977) suggest methods to obtain data on both the densities and the function of bacteria in tropical forest. In most forest studies this part of the flora is ignored.

It has been suggested (L. Biever, pers. comm.) that in some communities, even though the input of energy to the microbial population is very large and is well distributed over the year, the energy demands for nitrogen fixation by bacteria might also be large. This could mean that the actual energy available for decomposition by bacteria is limited. St. John (pers. comm.) has also pointed out that in phosphorus-deficient soils nitrogen may be abundant because the imbalance in phosphorus prevents its full utilization.

Harley (1975) postulated a connection between the photosynthate produced in the leaves and uptake by roots mediated through microorganisms. The fungi and other microorganisms transferring nutrients to the tree take up organic compounds from the roots, utilize these and also excrete them to bacterial populations in the soil. The movement of photosynthate from leaves to roots can take place in the matter of hours, in contrast to days and months for litterfall. This suggests that the decomposition system could be supplied by energy through these two routes and, therefore, actively and efficiently respond to inputs of nutrients and carbon and recycle these quickly.

Ever since Went and Stark (1968) drew attention to the role of fungi in tropical forests, suggesting that mycorrhizal fungi allow direct recycling of essential ions from decomposing litter to living roots, the fungi have been of special interest to tropical ecologists. Mycorrhizal fungi are a group which form symbiotic relationships with host plants. There are many species of mycorrhizal fungi and most vascular plants have obligate or facultative relationships with these fungi. Trappe and Fogel (1977), who reviewed the ecosystematic functions of mycorrhizae, state that only fourteen vascular plant families are regularly nonmycorrhizal. One plant may have tens of species of mycorrhizal fungi associated with it, and, indeed, on one rootlet several species may be observed.

Usually mycorrhizal fungi are subdivided into endo- and ecto-forms. The endomycorrhizae are an artificial grouping which includes those forms in which the fungus penetrates the hosts' cells. The vesicular–arbuscular form of endomycorrhizae is the most widely distributed form, but in tropical forests the orchidaceous form is also important. Unlike most mycorrhizae, the orchidaceous types are capable of decomposing organic matter. The ectomycorrhizae are characterized by a mantle of fungal tissue around the host rootlet and penetration of the fungus between the root cells. Ectomycorrhizae are characteristic of the root systems of many woody plant families. The biomass of these fungi can be very large in forests. For example, in temperate forests the upper 10 cm of soil may contain over 5000 kg of ectomycorrhizae per hectare dry weight (Trappe and Fogel, 1977). This was about 10% of the total root biomass.

Mycorrhizal fungi have a variety of positive impacts on the rhizosphere system and the growth of plants (Janos, 1975). The surface area of infected roots increases and the fungal hyphae grow out beyond the absorbing zone of the root itself. These hyphae function as extensions of the root system. The amount of hyphae can be high — Burgess and Nicholson (1961) estimated that 1 cm^3 of soil can contain 4 m of hyphae. Further, the hyphae can fuse with compatible hyphae from other roots from other plants, creating an underground network which can allow hosts sharing the same fungal systems to share water and nutrients. Infected roots have also been shown to live longer and to respire more actively.

The role of mycorrhizae in nutrient cycling has been mentioned in Chapter 9. In the tropical forest this role has been of special interest since nutrients could be readily lost via leaching. The mechanisms to conserve nutrients have evolved and been selected for in these forests and it appears that mycorrhizae are especially important. Went and Stark (1968) postulated a direct cycling of essential elements from decomposing matter, through fungi to tree roots. This hypothesis has been substantiated (to the degree possible in a rain forest environment

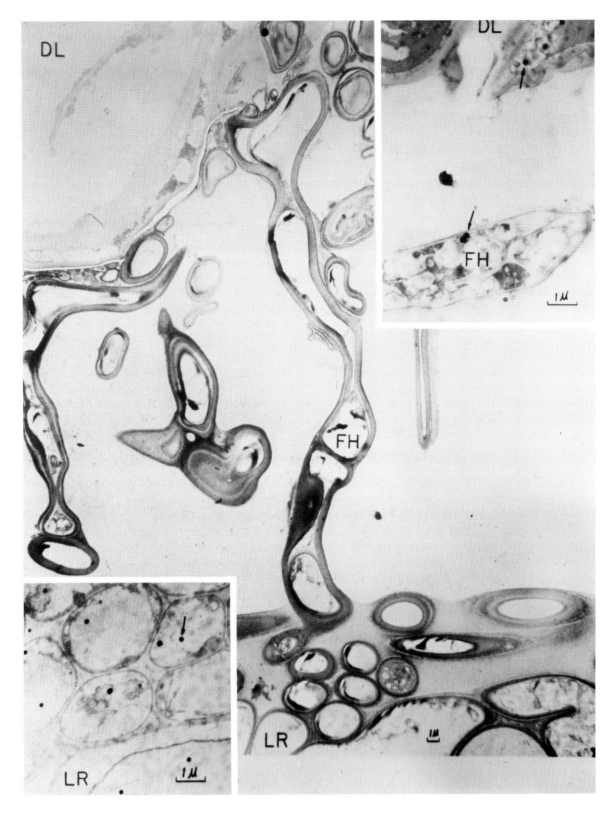

without controls, sterile soils, etc.) by scientists working at San Carlos de Rio Negro, Venezuela. Stark and Spratt (1977) found that on Oxisols over 35% of the roots formed surface mats on the soil and that over 90% of these roots contained endomycorrhizae. Herrera et al. (1978) isolated leaves containing radioactive phosphorus in the field in small growth chambers and exposed the root tip of a growing root associated with the mat of surface roots into the chamber. Eight weeks later the root, leaves and chambers were removed and the connection made of leaf, fungal hyphae and root were sectioned, stained, and counted. Complete connections formed between leaf and root (Fig. 10.3) and radioactivity occurred in leaf, hyphae and root. This experiment strongly suggests that phosphorus was directly transferred via the fungus to the root, although, of course, the evidence is circumstantial as bacteria were not eliminated from the chambers. Given the fact that mycorrhizae have the ability to take up, transfer, and store nutrients, that trees in the absence of mycorrhizal fungi grow poorly and may even be prevented from growing, and that these organisms are abundant in tropical forest ecosystems, it seems clear that they play an important role in the nutrient and carbon dynamics of the forest. Much greater attention needs to be paid to the fungi and bacteria because in tropical forests, unlike temperate forests, decomposition may be largely a bacteria–fungal mediated process and less a macro–microfaunal process. In all forests all of these elements play a role; in tropical forests the fungi are especially important.

CONCLUSIONS

Forest organisms tend to have finite life spans. Trees may survive for hundreds of years; small organisms live for days. At death these are decomposed into their chemical constituents which become part of the body of other organisms. In mature ecosystems the processes of mortality, decomposition, birth and growth are stabilized and in balance, so that there is no buildup of organic biomass nor a decline in biomass. This requires fit of the catabolic and anabolic parts of the system, both of which must also be flexible enough to operate in a constantly variable environment. We are impressed with the large diversity of tropical trees; we probably can be equally impressed with the diversity of decomposers and with the variety of the mechanisms to breakdown the myriad chemicals in the diverse flora. In tropical forests the differences in decomposition appear to be of degree, rather than of kind. The role of fungi and termites is more important than the macro- and micro-arthropods and earthworms in temperate forests. The fungi form a link between roots, litter and bacteria and improve the efficiency of transfer of nutrients, energy and water. They form a network which ties the ecosystem together beneath the ground surface, even to the extent of linking biological organisms that are genetically distinct. The termites address another character of tropical forests — very high biomass of wood. We have already seen how a high wood biomass can be adaptively advantageous to forest. However, the advantage could be a disadvantage when the trees die and fall to the ground. Termites are essential in this situation and together with their intestinal protozoa reduce the wood into materials that can be used and recycled. Further, the rather constant fall of litter is utilized by other termites, other macro- and micro-arthropods and fungi and converted relatively quickly to materials that can be recycled. Thus, in tropical forests there is seldom, except in prolonged dry periods, a time when litter and dead organic matter sits on the soil surface for any length of time.

Fig. 10.3. A photomicrograph of root (*LR*), litter (*DL*) and fungal hyphae (*FH*) of rain forest at San Carlos de Rio Negro. The upper inset shows radioactive phosphorus as black dots at the end of the arrows; the lower insert shows radioactivity in the root. Herrera et al. (1978) interpreted the photomicrograph as evidence of movement of phosphorus from the litter to the root, through the fungus.

REFERENCES

Abe, T., 1978. The role of termites in the breakdown of dead wood in the forest floor of Pasoh Study Area. *Malay Nat. J.*, 30(2): 391–404.

Bremner, J.M. and Blackmer, A.M., 1979. Effects of acetylene and soil water content on emission of nitrous oxide from soils. *Nature*, 280: 380–381.

Burgess, A. and Nicholson, D.F., 1961. The use of soil sections in studying the amount of fungal hyphae in soil. *Soil Sci.*, 92: 25–29.

Cole, C.V., Elliott, E.T., Hunt, H.W. and Coleman, D.C., 1978. Trophic interactions in soils as they affect energy and nutrient dynamics. V. Phosphorus transformations. *Microbial Ecol.*, 4: 381–387.

Edwards, C.A., 1974. Macroarthropods. In: C.H. Dickinson and G.J.F. Pugh (Editors), *Biology of Plant Litter Decomposition.* Academic Press, London, pp. 533–554.

Edwards, P.J., 1977. Studies of mineral cycling in a montane rain forest in New Guinea. II. The production and disappearance of litter. *J. Ecol.*, 65: 971–992.

Ellenberg, H., 1971. Nitrogen content, mineralization and cycling. Productivity of forest ecosystems. In: P. Duvigneaud (Editor), *Productivity of Forest Ecosystems. Proceedings of the Brussels Symposium 1969.* UNESCO, Paris, pp. 509–514.

Golley, F.B., McGinnis, J.T., Clements, R.G., Child, G.I. and Duever, M.J., 1975. *Mineral Cycling in a Tropical Moist Forest Ecosystem.* University of Georgia Press, Athens, Ga. 248 pp.

Golley, F.B., 1978. Insects as regulators of forest nutrient cycling. *Trop. Ecol.*, 18(2): 116–123.

Gosz, J.R., Likens, G.E. and Bormann, F.H., 1973. Nutrient release from decomposing leaf and branch litter in the Hubbard Brook Forest, New Hampshire. *Ecology*, 43: 173–191.

Harley, J.L., 1975. Problems of mycotrophy. In: F.E. Sanders, B. Mosse and P.B. Tinker (Editors). *Endomycorrhizas.* Academic Press, London, pp. 1–24.

Hatton, R.S. and Rasmussen, R.A., 1970. Microbial and chemical observations in a tropical rain forest. In: H.T. Odum and R.F. Pigeon (Editors), *A Tropical Rain Forest. A Study of Irradiation and Ecology at El Verde, Puerto Rico.* U.S. Atomic Energy Commission, Washington, D.C., pp. F43–F56.

Herrera, R., 1979. *Nutrient Distribution and Cycling in an Amazon Caatinga Forest on Spodosols in Southern Venezuela.* Thesis, University of Reading, Reading, 244 pp.

Herrera, R., Merida, T., Stark, N. and Jordan, C.F., 1978. Direct phosphorus transfer from leaf litter to roots. *Naturwissenschaften*, 65: 108–109.

Janos, D.P., 1975. Effects of vesicular–arbuscular mycorrhizae on lowland tropical rain forest trees. In: F.E. Sanders, B. Mosse and P.B. Tinker (Editors), *Endomycorrhizas.* Academic Press, London, pp. 437–446.

Jenny, H., Gessel, S.P. and Bingham, F.T., 1949. Comparative study of decomposition rates of organic matter in temperate and tropical regions. *Soil Sci.*, 68: 419–432.

Johnson, D.W., Cole, D.W., Gessel, S.P., Singer, M.J. and Minden, R.V., 1977. Carbonic acid leaching in a tropical, temperate, subalpine, and northern forest soil. *Arct. Alp. Res.*, 9: 329–343.

Jordan, C.F., Todd, R.L. and Escalante, G., 1979. Nitrogen conservation in a tropical rain forest. *Oecologia*, 39: 123–128.

Kitazawa, Y., 1971. Biological regionality of the soil fauna and its function in forest ecosystem types. In: P. Duvigneaud (Editor), *Productivity of Forest Ecosystems. Proceedings of the Brussels Symposium,* UNESCO, Paris, pp. 485–498.

Lee, K.G. and Wood, T.G., 1971. *Termites and Soils.* Academic Press, New York, N.Y., 250 pp.

Madge, D.S., 1965. Leaf fall and litter disappearance in a tropical forest. *Pedobiologica*, 5: 273–288.

Maldague, M.E., 1964. Importance des populations de termites dans les sols équatoriaux. *Trans. 8th Int. Congr. Soil Sci., Bucharest*, 3: 743–751.

Matsumoto, T., 1976. The role of termites in an equatorial rain forest ecosystem of West Malaysia. 1. Population density, biomass, carbon, nitrogen and calorific content and respiration rate. *Oecologia*, 22(2): 153–178.

Matsumoto, T., 1978. The role of termites in the decomposition of leaf litter on the forest floor of Pasoh study area. *Malay. Nat. J.*, 30: 405–413.

Meentemeyer, V., 1978. An approach to the biometeorology of decomposer organisms. *Int. J. Biometeorol.*, 22: 94–102.

Odum, H.T., Lugo, A., Cintron, G. and Jordan, C.F., 1970. Metabolism and evapotranspiration of some rain forest plants and soils. In: H.T. Odum and R.F. Pigeon (Editors), *A Tropical Rain Forest. A Study of Irradiation and Ecology at El Verde, Puerto Rico.* U.S. Atomic Energy Commission, Washington, D.C., pp. I103–I164.

Rambelli, A., Puppi, G., Bartoli, A., Maggi, O., Albonetti, S.G., Farrelli, C., Lunghini, D., Massain, G. and Riess, S., 1977. Aims and methods of microbiological studies in MAB-research projects. In: E.F. Brunig (Editor), *Transactions of the International MAB–IUFRO Workshop on Tropical Rainforest Ecosystems Research.* Hamburg–Reinbek, Chair of World Forestry, Spec. Rep., No. 1, pp. 227–232.

Sanchez, P.A., 1976. *Properties and Management of Soils in the Tropics.* Wiley and Sons, New York, N.Y., 618 pp.

Schlesinger, W.H., 1977. Carbon balance in terrestrial detritus. *Annu. Rev. Ecol. Syst.*, 8: 51–81.

Schulze, E.D., 1967. Soil respiration of tropical vegetation types. *Ecology*, 48: 652–653.

Stark, N. and Spratt, M., 1977. Root biomass and nutrient storage in rain forest oxisols near San Carlos de Rio Negro. *Trop. Ecol.*, 18: 1–9.

Trappe, J.M. and Fogel, R.D., 1977. Ecosystematic functions of mycorrhizae. In: *The Belowground Ecosystem. Range Sci. Dep. Sci. Ser.*, Color. State Univ., No. 26: 205–214.

Went, F.W. and Stark, N., 1968. Mycorrhiza. *Bioscience*, 18: 1035–1039.

Witkamp, M., 1966. Decomposition of leaf litter in relation to environmental conditions, microflora, and microbial respiration, *Ecology*, 47: 194–201.

Witkamp, M., 1970. Aspects of soil microflora in a gamma-irradiated rain forest. In: H.T. Odum and R.F. Pigeon (Editors), *A Tropical Rain Forest. A Study of Irradiation and Ecology at El Verde, Puerto Rico.* U.S. Atomic Energy Commission, Washington, D.C., pp. F29–F33.

Wood, T.G. and Sands, W.A., 1978. The role of termites in ecosystems. In: M.V. Brian (Editor), *Production Ecology of Ants and Termites.* Cambridge University Press, Cambridge, pp. 245–292.

Young, J.L. and Spycher, G., 1979. Water-dispersible soil organic-mineral particles: I. Carbon and nitrogen distribution. *Soil Sci. Soc. Am. J.*, 43: 324–328.

Chapter 11

FOOD WEBS: WHO EATS WHAT, WHY, HOW, AND WITH WHAT EFFECTS IN A TROPICAL FOREST?

DANIEL H. JANZEN

INTRODUCTION

In this essay I paint a picture rich in extrapolation and conjecture, held in place by very few data points and much guided by my personal unpublished experiences. But this is the state of the art. My essay is about the animals that feed for the most part on living things, or things they have just killed. I shall discuss the animals that eat living things under six simple headings, but actually these headings are used only because field biologists have specialized in these areas in their studies of animal feeding relationships. Whether they represent fairly discrete islands of interaction in the ecosystem remains to be seen.

EATERS OF VEGETATIVE PARTS

The folivores, herbivores, plant parasites, and leaf eaters of tropical forests feed on a food that differs in one fundamental way from that eaten by carnivores. Their food contains large quantities of species-specific chemical defenses and therefore the food species are for the most part not readily interchangeable even when in hand, mouth, or gut. The entire structure of interactions of plant eaters with their food is centered on that trait. Thus, the impact of herbivores on plants and on plant arrays must be measured in the (often instantaneously trivial) amount eaten *plus* the much greater cost to the plant of producing the traits that keep it from being eaten by most animals most of the time. In short, the impact of the herbivore array cannot be measured observationally by the size of its bites nor experimentally by its removal. Rather, removal experiments must be coupled with the impossible

task of allowing each individual plant to divert all of its huge herbivore defense budget to antiedaphic, competitive and reproductive effort. Second, since prey items are at best poorly interchangeable, the spatial and temporal patterns of the edible ones become extremely important to the consumer. And why stress these two universal truths in an essay on tropical forests and their herbivores? Because the statements are most universally true in tropical forests.

Patterns of herbivory on individual plants

A misconception common among extra-tropical biologists is that tropical forest trees do not suffer total defoliation (and that "outbreaks" of tropical defoliators do not occur). In tropical forests made up largely of seasonally deciduous trees, total defoliation of adult individuals is commonplace during the first one to three months of the rainy season (Janzen, 1981a). Major defoliation is less commonplace, but nevertheless occurs on the evergreen species within the deciduous forest and on the members of evergreen lowland tropical forests (e.g. Anderson, 1961). Within evergreen forests, complete or nearly complete defoliation is more common among the tree species in the early stages of succession than later. The animals that defoliate tropical trees are most commonly moth larvae (Lepidoptera), adult beetles (Coleoptera), leafcutter ants (Attini, neotropical only), Orthoptera, and various groups of Homoptera. It is my subjective impression that on a world-wide basis, moth larvae are the most common offenders, both in numbers of cases and species. Defoliation in a tropical forest is less conspicuous than in extratropical forests because the defoliators are usually sufficiently stenophagous that they attack only one species of tree among the tens to hundreds at a site, because the lost leaves are usually replaced within two to four weeks, and because the inter-specific synchrony of defoliation is not great. A common impact of total defoliation is the shedding of set flowers or fruits, or failure to sexually reproduce in the following cycle (e.g. Rockwood, 1973) as well as reduced vegetative growth. There appears to be strong intra-year variation in the species and the individuals of trees which are defoliated, though some species seem to be especially likely to be defoliated (e.g., *Bombacopsis quinatum* and *Enterolobium cyclocarpum* in the lowland deciduous forests of Guanacaste Province, Costa Rica). Shrubs and understorey plants, while of less interest to foresters, are also often defoliated by insects (e.g. Janzen, 1981a).

As spectacular as total defoliation may be, a much larger bite of the leafy material is taken by the literally thousands of species of herbivores in a tropical forest that eat holes and notches in leaves, bite off shoot apices, suck phloem and xylem fluid from roots, stems and leaves, roll leaves, mine in leaves, scrape epidermis off leaf surfaces, web up young shoots, cut off the occasional leaf to carry off and eat in some more secluded place, etc. Each of these behaviors is often specific to certain species of immature insects or to a particular vertebrate at a particular time. Leigh (1975) calculates that for the Barro Colorado Island (Panama) forest the amount of leafy machinery eaten per year by insects is about 12.5% and by vertebrates 2.4%. However, this is a very severe underestimate of the insects' impact because it does not measure parts removed by sucking, leaves and apices eaten in entirety, leaves so severely damaged that they are aborted, the tree's loss in competitive or edaphic status caused by resource diversion to vegetative repair, and finally and worst, the costs of preventing greater amounts of damage.

The details of how the bites are taken do matter. Leaving seasonal considerations aside, a bite taken from a leaf is most damaging about the time it is a fully expanded photosynthetic machine but has not yet begun to repay its production costs (perhaps the 2nd to 4th weeks of visible life) and least damaging at the time it is being dehisced in senescence. The most damaging time of herbivory for a leaf on a deciduous tree should be near the half-way time of

the leaf life span, as has been shown with extra-tropical crop plants (Chester, 1950). At this point in leaf age, there is no longer sufficient time to replace the lost leaf with a whole new leaf cycle, but the leaf has only just begun to repay the investment in its production.

A bite is not a bite is not a bite. A leaf roller may destroy much more of the leaf than it eats by greatly reducing its photosynthetic area. A leaf miner may do less damage than a chewer eating out the same amount because the miner does not produce such a large linear edge of opened leaf. A half gram of shoot tip eaten from the terminal axis may lower the competitive performance of a tree sapling more than the consumption of 10 kg of leaves (but see Harris, 1974). A 10% loss of seed material by drilling that mimics an insect attack caused a 30 to 50% reduction in seedling *Mucuna mutisiana* survival and shoot tip production in the face of severe herbivory (Janzen, 1976a). Even the distribution of bites should be of importance. For example, the role of inducible chemical defenses in deterring herbivores is recently getting much press (Ryan, 1978).

Apropos of this discussion, chemical defenses induced at the site of the bite may raise the fitness of the plant, not necessarily by reducing the percent of its foliage eaten but by causing the damage to be distributed in that pattern which least lowers the fitness of the plant (Janzen, 1979a). It seems likewise evident that the detailed distribution of a given amount of leaf removal (e.g., round holes, linear holes, marginal notches, a few big holes, many small holes, apical holes, distal holes, intervenation holes, etc.) will influence the impact of the herbivory on the host plant's fitness. We know nothing of this to date, but the combination of patterns offered by the fauna of insects in a tree species-rich tropical forest lends both realism and pertinence to the self-evident experiments.

One pattern of feeding seems to maximize the damage done to the plant, but it probably raises the fitness of the herbivore so much as to be selected for nevertheless. By far the bulk of tropical green tissue herbivory seems to occur between about sunset and midnight, that period in the 24 hour cycle when the nutrient content of green vegetation should be highest since it contains the day's photosynthate but has not yet translocated it or respired it, and that period when all the diurnal predators are blinded.

Ecosystem-level herbivory patterns

The overall quantity of leaf-eating, as measured by frass rain, caterpillar censuses, frequency of herbivore encounter, and appearance of leaf damage is highly seasonal in tropical forests. The longer and more well defined the dry season, the more concentrated the pulse of herbivory in the first one to three months of the following rainy season. One is left with the distinct impression that most of the leaf-eating insects in the habitat have a single generation of quite abundant larvae and adults at this time, and then either have a less abundant generation or very commonly remain dormant during the remainder of the rainy season. They then pass the dry season as active adults, migrants to a wetter area, or dormant eggs or pupae (and see Janzen 1973, 1976b). In evergreen tropical forests, if there is a sunnier and drier part of the year, as is usually the case, the peak of herbivory appears to occur during this time and immediately following it but is a gentler peak than in deciduous forests.

While it has never been measured, it is evident that there is severe supra-annual variation in the amount of herbivory in deciduous forests. For example, the first half of the 1977 and 1978 rainy seasons in Santa Rosa National Park (deciduous forest lowlands of Guanacaste Province, Costa Rica) were marked by extremely high general levels of herbivory and many species suffered total defoliation. In the rainy season of 1979, only one of the many previously severely defoliated species was again defoliated (*Enterolobium cyclocarpum*) and overall caterpillar densities were easily less than one tenth that of 1977 and 1978. A similar but less well documented situation appeared to occur in the lowland rain forests of Corcovado National Park (Costa Rica) in these three years.

There are conspicuous large differences in the amount of material eaten out of leaves in tree canopies in deciduous tropical forests as opposed to evergreen ones (and evergreen species in deciduous tropical forests; see Stanton, 1975). For example, in August 1979 there was a storm-produced tree fall of about 300 trees in Corcovado National Park. In clambering through the newly fallen crowns of at least 30 species of large trees I was struck by the presence of numerous crowns with no visible damage to their leaves and the fact that the others showed what would be deemed trivial damage as

compared to the badly shot-holed, gouged and otherwise bitten-up leaves of a normal deciduous forest canopy. Within the Santa Rosa National Park deciduous forest there are a number of large evergreen species (e.g., *Andira inermis, Brosimum alicastrum, Ficus goldmani, Hymenaea courbaril, Manilkara zapota, Mastichodendron capiri, Sloanea terniflora*). There are numerous species of leaf-eaters that feed on the crowns of these plants, but the overall amount removed is much smaller than that removed from deciduous neighbors. Even when these trees have their new leaf crops the defoliation is trivial. (These "evergreens" are not truly evergreen, but drop their leaves synchronously at the beginning or the end of the dry season and immediately grow a new crop as is commonplace for "evergreen' trees in deciduous tropical forests in general.)

Shifting away from the food itself, one is struck by the extreme host-specificity of many of the insects that eat foliage in tropical forests. The details are only now beginning to be documented in a number of ongoing studies; it is a reasonable guess that when the votes are in, at least half of the foliage-eating insects will have only one species of host plant and none will eat more than 10% of the species present (except for leaf-cutter ants). If this statement is true, there are three obvious conclusions. Distances between host plants in time and space in a species-rich tropical forest can influence the intensity of impact of the herbivores on those plants. Second, species richness of herbivores in a forest should be at least in part dependent on the species richness of the plants (e.g. Janzen, 1977). Third, it should be impossible to predict the effect on the forest of the addition or deletion of a herbivore without knowing a very great deal about the ecology of the interaction of that herbivore with its food.

However, comparatively euryphagous insects do occur. For example, to date I have recorded that the larvae of *Hylesia lineata* (Saturniidae) feed and develop to adults on 44 species of Santa Rosa National Park foliage in 17 plant families (in a flora of approximately 575 species of plants). This caterpillar eats and grows well on *Zuelania guidonia* (Flacourtiaceae), a tree that has at least 40% dry weight phenols in its foliage, and eats many other species of leaves known to be rich in phenolics. It appears that *H. lineata* larvae thrive on phenol-rich foods but grow comparatively slowly. Sphinx moth larvae (Sphingidae) are much more stenophagous (1–4 host plants per species in this forest) and a 3 to 4 g larva matures in 3 to 4 weeks. *H. lineata* larvae weigh 2 to 4 g at the time of pupation but require 7 to 10 weeks to attain this size. In short, *H. lineata* is probably getting very little food per bite or stomach-full but can eat many kinds of plants, while the more stenophagous leaf-eaters such as sphinx moth larvae get more food per bite but can eat many fewer species of plants. The Santa Rosa National Park deciduous forest occupied by *H. lineata* also contains a highly euryphagous arctiid moth larva (a "woolly bear" in the genus *Hypercompe*). It has none of its 17 known hosts in common with *H. lineata*.

To this point I have restricted my discussion by and large to insects, but vertebrates are trivial neither in their selective impact nor in their daily removal of leafy plant parts (Leigh, 1975; McKey et al., 1978; Rockwood and Glander, 1979). Anyone seriously interested in this question cannot start without first reading the symposium volume *The Ecology of Arboreal Folivores* (Montgomery, 1978). Perhaps one of the more dramatic but poorly documented examples of the impact of vertebrates is the ability of a few free-ranging cattle to deflect succession following a year of slash and burn agriculture in a small patch cut out of a neotropical forest. This must be occurring in Africa with native mammals and natural tree falls, and must have occurred in the neotropics before and during the Pleistocene (Janzen and Martin, 1981).

Tropical folivorous vertebrates are quite euryphagous in nearly all cases but like euryphagous insects, they are by no means unselective hay balers. A captive tapir in Costa Rica rejected the foliage of at least 55% species of deciduous forest plants out of 381 species offered. It rejected all but one (*Pterocarpus rohrii*) of 55 species of tree legumes, and ate all but one (*Trema micrantha*) of the fast-growing secondary succession trees with large non-aromatic leaves (Janzen, 1981b). Free-ranging Malayan tapirs are very selective feeders on tree sapling species (Williams and Petrides, 1980), as are the tapirs on Barro Colorado Island (Terwiliger, 1978). Howler monkeys and colobus monkeys are very selective in the plant species, ages, parts and quantities that they eat (Struhsaker, 1975; McKey et al., 1978; Rockwood and Glander,

1979). While Kenyan elephants and giraffes consume some apparently very nasty foliage such as that of ant-acacias (*Acacia drepanolobium*), they are conspicuous in their avoidance of other plants such as introduced *Tecoma stans*, various Euphorbiaceae and Amaryllidaceae.

The choosiness exhibited by free-ranging folivorous vertebrates is undoubtedly based on achieving the most acceptable mixture of nutrients, and secondary compounds given the state of the animal (juvenile, pregnant, migrating, overweight), exposure to predators while foraging, and capability of the gut microbial flora as generated by the content of previous meals (Freeland and Janzen, 1974). In short, the foraging forest rhino or colobus monkey is eking a living on a battlefield generated by millennia of plant–herbivore evolutionary and coevolutionary skirmishes. However, I suspect that the bulk of the chemical defense traits it encounters were evolved in response to herbivory by insects rather than vertebrates.

While the biomass of forest folivorous vertebrates is generally low compared to forest insects (which also have a much higher turnover rate and therefore are extracting more from the system per gram of animal biomass), there is no doubt that they exert their own selective pressure on certain species of plants and influence the structure of the vegetation (e.g. Oppenheimer and Lang, 1969; Mueller-Dombois, 1972; Spatz and Mueller-Dombois, 1973). I predict that palms would be rare in species and individuals in the Neotropics if we had free-ranging elephants. Tangles of vines highly edible to cattle are largely absent in African and Asian forests and this is probably due at least in part to the presence of large herbivorous mammals. Two- and three-toed sloths seem to attain the highest biomass of any neotropical arboreal folivore (Montgomery and Sunquist, 1978), but this is probably related to the fact that they have the lowest foliage intake per gram of animal of any mammal that subsists largely or entirely on leaves and that they eat the mature leaves of many species of forest trees.

The work done to date on the impact of the herbivore array, insect and vertebrate, makes it clear that the emphasis needs to be shifted from how many of what sizes (e.g., Eisenberg, 1978), to either detailed physiological studies of how much materials the different life forms and species need and use, or to detailed studies of what they as individuals and populations are actually harvesting in the forest and how the cessation or intensification of this harvest would influence the vegetation. In short, we need natural history of the animals and their guts, with emphasis on the effects on vegetation. The content of the recent symposium on arboreal folivores (Montgomery, 1978) makes this very clear.

EATERS OF SEEDS

I have no doubt that, per gram eaten, the seed predators have the largest impact on tropical forest structure of any animal life form. In absolute overall effect they also probably have the largest impact as well. Just as the consumers of living vegetative parts have to deal with an incredible mixture of nutrient and chemical defense qualities, so do the seed predators (Janzen, 1978a). In addition, the seed predators have to deal with a food type that is usually absent for most of the year, is often absent or highly fluctuating in density from year to year (Janzen, 1978b), may be superabundant when present, and much scarcer in space than are the adult trees (since many individual adult trees do not bear fruits in a given year).

Most tropical seed predators can be grouped into three life forms: those that eat developing embryos in the developing fruit, those that eat full-sized nearly mature seeds, and those that act as post-dispersal seed predators.

Predators on young embryos

Aside from the large folivorous vertebrates that sometimes eat young green fruits along with the foliage or deliberately pick immature green fruits out of foliage, predators on young embryos are generally moth larvae (Lepidoptera) and sucking bugs (Coreidae, Lygaeidae, Pentatomidae, Pyrrhocoridae). In the former case, the caterpillars mine through the ovaries or web inflorescences together and eat many flowers and young fruits (e.g., Bawa and Opler, 1978). In the latter case, the attacked seeds (in a multiple-seeded ovary) appear to have been physiologically aborted and are often censused as such rather than as victims of sucking bugs. This type of seed predation is perhaps the

mildest per seed killed because the parent plant has invested relatively little in fruit and seed at this stage, and because there is the possibility that it may be compensated for by the retention of other seeds or fruits that would have been aborted to tailor the fruit crop size to match food reserves or anticipated resource harvest. The moth larvae that eat very young seeds and fruits tend to be very stenophagous, but the bugs who play this game are often very euryphagous with respect to Latin binomials. They are avoiding most of a plant's unique chemical defenses by sucking from growing tissue, which is a tissue very likely to be similar among plant species (much as is the sapwood of tree trunks).

Predators on full-sized maturing seeds

Moth (Pyralidae) and beetle larvae (Bruchidae, Curculionidae, a few Cerambycidae) have specialized at eating full-sized maturing seeds while living inside them or their fruits (Janzen, 1980b), while squirrels, monkeys and parrots have specialized at eating them while living outside and moving from tree to tree (Emmons, 1975; McKey, 1978; Higgins, 1979). The insects tend to produce a single generation on a given seed crop, and then wait out the remainder of the year as active adults in the habitat. The amount of damage they do is generally related to the size of the seed crop (large seed crops may either swamp the ovipositional abilities of the arriving females or attract inordinate numbers of them), proximity of other seed crops in time and space (which may either dilute the number of arriving females or serve as a source for ovipositing females), and the suitability of the habitat in the vicinity of the seed crop for seed predator survival. The amount of damage done by the vertebrate seed predators involves these three parameters, but a fourth is also very important; the longer the immature but full-sized seeds are on the tree the more of them are eaten, thereby selecting strongly for rapid and synchronized seed and fruit maturation. That is to say, the functioning of predator satiation has a strong temporal component.

Predators on full-sized seeds have to deal with a wide array of seed secondary defensive compounds (Janzen, 1978a) and must have a wide variety of physiological and biochemical mechanisms for dealing with them (e.g., Rosenthal et al., 1976, 1977, 1978). In general they are highly stenophagous; for example, in a survey of seed-eating beetles in the deciduous forests in Guanacaste Province, Costa Rica, I found that of 110 species of beetle seed predators, 75% had only one host species, 13% had two, 8% had three and the maximum was eight in a flora of 975 plant species (Janzen, 1980b).

The vertebrate seed predators, on the other hand, are as euryphagous as their more folivorous relatives and seem to overcome seed defenses by having guts highly skilled at the necessary biochemistry and by being able to consume relatively small amounts of each species owing to the high nutrient content of the food (see especially McKey, 1978 on this point).

Pre-dispersal seed predators are relatively common and as a rough estimate attack a third to half of the species of seed crops in a lowland tropical forest on normal soil. In the deciduous forest study mentioned above, about 20% of all species of plants in the forest have pre-dispersal seed predation by insects and another 20 to 40% are attacked by some vertebrate. Percent seed predation within a crop is very difficult to determine unless very close watch is kept of the fruit and seed crop during its development. Immature fruits opened by vertebrates are often shed early and rotted away by the time the intact fruits fall or dehisce. Apparently intact seeds often have developing or dead insects inside of them (X-ray works well to detect these animals). Fruits with insects inside are often shed slightly earlier than are mature fruits and seeds, and if the sample is derived from this or early fallen fruits, a very misleading percent mortality may be obtained. Simultaneously, dispersal agents are often adept at removing the healthy fruits with intact seeds, which biases the sample percent mortality upwards in a crop of ripe nuts on or below the parent tree.

In short, pre-dispersal seed predation on nearly mature seeds reduces the size of the final seed crop and kills offspring on which maximum parental investment has been bestowed. Furthermore, the parent cannot replace the dead offspring with new ones even if it can physiologically perceive the death of its offspring, since fruits generally mature long after flowering occurs. I suspect that it is escape from both insect and vertebrate pre-dispersal (as well as post-dispersal) seed predators which is the driving selective pressure behind much of tropical

tree species' mast-seeding at supra-annual intervals (Janzen, 1974, 1976c, 1978b). It is therefore these animals which are in great part responsible for the highly pulsed input of seeds into many tropical forest habitats, a pulsation that should influence regeneration patterns and abundance of frugivores and other users of fruits and seeds. This pulsation also renders impossible the measurement of total harvestable productivity in a forest with any kind of study extending over only a year or two.

Post-dispersal seed predators

During and after seed dispersal the vertebrates become prominent as seed killers. Part of this seed predation is pure seed predation and part of it is the price paid for dispersal. Which interpretation is to be given to a given act of seed predation depends on the animal's species and state and on the species and location of seed under consideration. Baird's tapir (*Tapirus bairdii*) is a pure predator of *Mastichodendron capriri* seeds (by mastication), a 78% predator (by digestion) of *Enterolobium cyclocarpum* seeds, and apparently a pure disperser of fig seeds (Janzen, 1981c). Oil-birds are killers of the seeds in the fruits they feed to their nestlings, since these seeds are regurgitated to the floors of caves, but dispersers of the seeds (an unknown percent) that they consume and regurgitate while in flight in the forest (Snow, 1976). The agouti (*Dasyprocta*) is a predator on *Scheelea* palm nuts (seeds) but buries many for later consumption; some of these dispersed seeds are missed and become the recruitment into the palm population (Bradford and Smith, 1977). However, even this interaction may be only a remnant of a more complex Pleistocene one (Janzen and Martin, 1981).

Post-dispersal seed predators are of course confronted with the same seed chemicals as are the late pre-dispersal ones (though there may be some chemical changes as a seed matures) and may have to deal with a much harder seed coat or nut wall. However, the physical location of dispersed seeds is much more diffuse than that of the seed crop on the parent. The forest floor is constantly being searched by insect seed predators (sucking bugs, ovipositing beetles). These insects treat the seeds they find much as do the pre-dispersal seed predators but they will search until they exhaust the seed supply or the seeds escape by germination since a dispersed seed does not leave them behind. The bugs appear to be euryphagous within a set of closely related seeds, e.g., seeds of *Bombacopsis*, *Sterculia*, *Ceiba* and other Malvaceae and Sterculiaceae are preyed upon by Pyrrhocoridae (Janzen, 1972a), while legume seeds are preyed on by highly stenophagous beetles.

Peccaries (*Tayassu*) and forest-floor rodents are major predators on dispersed Neotropical forest tree seeds. The peccaries use odor and landmarks (such as the stumps around which agoutis have buried seeds) to locate seeds and nuts in the litter (Kiltie, 1981). Even extremely hard palm nuts are cracked by white-lipped peccaries (Kiltie, 1979). It is my impression that the large soft seeds enclosed in a very hard nut are usually poorly defended chemically (e.g., Malaysian *Lithocarpus*, African *Coula edulis*, Neotropical *Astryocaryum* and *Acrocomia* palm nuts).

While agoutis have received a great deal of attention as dispersers and killers of large seeds on the forest floor (e.g. Smythe, 1970) small heteromyid rodents, such as *Liomys salvini* in Guanacaste, Costa Rica, deciduous forests, are also impressively deadly. Captive *L. salvini*, weighing only 45 to 60 g, may consume as many as 15 to 20 newly germinated seeds of *Enterolobium cyclocarpum* per night to maintain their body weight. A *Liomys* will even keep itself alive by consuming 4 to 8 hard ungerminated 0.5 to 1.0 g *E. cyclocarpum* seeds per night and notching the remainder so that they will germinate for future meals (W. Hallwachs, pers. comm.).

The interaction between *L. salvini* and *E. cyclocarpum* illustrates well the behavioral complexity of prey location in this portion of the forest food web. *L. salvini* harvests *E. cyclocarpum* seeds directly from the fruits fallen below the parent tree. But these are the fruits that were not eaten by large mammals. Horses and cows are contemporary dispersal agents and digestive seed predators (and the horse is a Pleistocene one, see below) and defecate *E. cyclocarpum* seeds in a variety of habitats along with a huge odor cue, the pile of dung. *L. salvini* quickly seek out these piles and burrow through them after seeds. As many as six *Liomys* may arrive at one pile of horse dung the first night, and they may remove as many as 500 *E. cyclocarpum* seeds from a dung pile in one night. An *E. cyclocarpum* seed has three hopes: to be dumped in a habitat lacking *L. salvini* (e.g. in a river

by a tapir that ate the fruit; Janzen, 1981c), to be buried shallowly by the dung beetles (Scarabaeidae) as they go about their work, or to be cached by a *Liomys* that is shortly subsequently eaten by a predator (Janzen, unpubl.).

FLOWER VISITORS

The tropics are famous for the complexity and spectacular nature of their flower–visitor relationships, most of which are based on the animal providing outcrossing and the plant providing food. The bees (Hymenoptera) form a fairly distinct subset of the trophic web. These flying penises prey exclusively on pollen and drink nectar (sugar, protein- and/or oil-rich; and see Baker, 1978) and only connect directly with the trophic web by being prey for some predators and parasitoids and by being models in many mimicry systems. Also, as with other flower visitors, bees form a tight but diffuse connection with the general food web in that resources spent on them (production and strategic costs of flowers, nectar, pollen) are resources not available for defenses, repair of damage by herbivores, seed production, etc. They thereby constrict the size of the base of the food web that is used by consumers of other plant parts.

Most other flower visitors have at least one stage or time in their life when they feed on something quite different from flower nectar and/or pollen. *Heliconius* butterflies have larvae that are major parasites on *Passiflora* vines, the flowers of which are not visited by *Heliconius* (Gilbert, 1975). The *Glossophaga* bats that pollinate *Crescentia* flowers eat many insects (Howell and Burch, 1974; Heithaus et al., 1975) and are fig seed dispersers as well. Hummingbirds (Trochilidae) and sunbirds (Nectariniidae) are expert insect hawkers (Skead, 1967; Stiles, 1973; Gill and Wolf, 1975). Fig wasps (Agaontidae) that pollinate fig florets are also intense fig seed predators (Janzen, 1979b). *Polybia* wasps are intense predators on caterpillars and male ants yet visit flowers frequently for nectar. Being a system very poor in wind-pollinated species (i.e. cheap pollen flow between conspecifics standing shoulder to shoulder) tropical forests abound with complex systems for moving pollen via animals among widely dispersed individuals. However, the aspect of interest is not the actual food or its small cost to the total tree resource budget but rather the large influences that can be gained with such small expenditures of resources. For example, it is probable that fig trees are reliably outcrossed over distances of many kilometers and at extremely low densities of flowering individuals by releasing a pheromone that serves as a locator cue to the minute wasps that have just left a far distant conspecific (Janzen, 1979b). The amount of resource allocated to pheromones in a fig tree's budget is probably minute, yet this one trait may be in great part responsible for *Ficus* being one of the largest tropical tree genera (over 900 species), for *Ficus* occurring in almost every kind of tropical forest, and for *Ficus* being a common tree genus in most forest types around the tropics of the world (Janzen, 1979b). Certainly bats, birds, large moths and large bees move pollen over distances of 0.1 to 1 km or more (e.g., Janzen, 1971; Feinsinger, 1976, 1978; Frankie et al., 1976; Gould, 1978; Stiles, 1978) in return for a small fraction of the total plant budget. Furthermore, since the plant approximately controls the amount taken per unit photosynthate eaten, a much larger portion of the food web should be contributed by these animals than by consumers which generate large strategic losses, large insurance costs, and much literal waste. All three of these latter categories are losses to the plant yet support no part of the trophic pyramid.

There is another reason besides the dual trophic role of many species of flower visitors that interactions with flower visitors are one of the most interactive parts of tropical forest food webs. To the plants, flower visitors are a resource to be competed for. They therefore are one of the major causes of both synchronized flowering within species (e.g. Augsperger, 1978) and asynchronous flowering between species. Both these patterns should in turn strongly influence the availability of reproductive and vegetative resources to other consumers. Furthermore, since flower visitors are not under the complete evolutionary control of the trees, they may well prevent or constrain many of the imaginable patterns of tree behavior (as well as spatial distribution) in a tropical forest. Yet, dipterocarps seem to have solved the problem of synchronized outcrossing at many-year intervals even in a forest very rich in dipterocarps. They are pollinated by thrips (P.S. Ashton, pers. comm.), which presumably feed on some vegetative plant part during

the years of flower absence. Thrips are hardly more than animate wind. However, the chances of such a system arising to meet the needs of tree spacing and timing patterns in more normal tropical forests are much lower than are the chances of the evolution of more conventional plant–pollinator interactions.

SEED MOVERS

Seed movers, or dispersal agents are analogous in many ways to flower visitors. Many seeds are effectively contaminants of the disperser, stuck on the outside or imbedded in the digesta on the inside. Many of these are killed by being shed, regurgitated, or defecated in the wrong place, or by being digested as a minor part of the potential disperser's diet. Others are more deliberately carried off to be eaten at a later date but survive through errors of recovery by the owners (agoutis and *Liomys* mice are the bees of the forest seed world). Just as many tropical flowers are conspicuously engineered to keep out the bulk of the animals that would eat their nectar and pollen if they could gain entry, a given species of ripe fruit is undoubtedly designed by natural selection to be uninteresting or even distasteful to the majority of the frugivores in the habitat (Janzen, 1975). It should be designed to be attractive only to that set of seed and fruit consumers that, working in consort, generate the highest quality seed shadow for that parent tree. However, just as there are many flower visitors that get to a flower's rewards through the channels opened for the pollinators, fruit eaten by undesired animals is probably a major part of the fuel that runs the animal array of a tropical forest. For example. Howe and Vandekerckhove (1979) have found only one bird to be a likely high quality seed disperser for the deciduous forest shrub *Casearia corymbosa*, yet fourteen species of birds eat the fruit. Even the carnivores eat fruit — bats and birds that feed insects to their offspring and eat some themselves are often heavy fruit eaters as well. Even proper Carnivora such as jaguars, tayras, coatimundis, jackals, and tigers are heavy fruit eaters (just as are northern bears and foxes).

The numbers and species of vertebrates that subsist entirely or in large part on ripe fruits (with some green ones thrown in) vary enormously among tropical forest habitats. The rain forests of

Panama, perhaps most closely studied for primates, bats and birds (Hladik and Hladik, 1969; Karr 1976; Morrison, 1978) literally teem with frugivores while they are scarce in the Malaysian forests rich in Dipterocarpaceae on very poor soils (Janzen, 1980a). Yet the Indian–Southeast Asian–Australian tropics are (were) extremely rich in large fruit-pigeon numbers and species while the neotropics hardly have any; neotropical forest parrots (all Psittacidae) are very abundant in species and numbers primarily as predators on full-sized maturing seeds, while they are scarce in numbers and species in the Southeast Asian tropics. All of the large terrestrial vegetarian mammals in Africa eat many species of fruits, and disperse as well as prey on many species of seeds in the process; an analogous fauna is by and large missing from the neotropics after the Pleistocene megafaunal extinctions (Janzen and Martin, 1981).

Likewise, what they eat varies greatly among groups of frugivores. Small to medium-sized birds that eat many insects as well as fruits tend to be heavy consumers of small-seeded juicy fruits rich in sugars and vitamins; various fruit specialists of all sizes consume many species of fruits whose pulp is rich in oil and protein (McKey, 1975; McDiarmid et al., 1977). These seeds are often very large and are often regurgitated rather than passed all the way through the digestive tract. The large indehiscent relatively dry legumes and other fruits that are picked up off the forest floor by large mammals are very different in flavor and consistency from the large juicy fruits eaten by large forest primates. While one species of fig may be fed on by tens of species of birds, bats and mammals, another species only a few meters away may have its fruits eaten solely by squirrels.

Animate dispersers of seeds generate very different seed shadows than does wind, the wind that is such a prominent disperser of extra-tropical seeds (though there are many tropical wind-dispersed seeds as well). Animal-generated seed shadows tend to have large lacunae with no seeds and strong local peaks at resting places, sleeping places or other high concentrations of animals (e.g. Janzen et al., 1976). Such seed shadows can be attenuated in time far past the time when the mature fruits appeared on the tree, owing to the delay in passage through the animal gut. This delay may be as much as two weeks or more in a large vertebrate (Janzen, 1981c).

Seeds dispersed by animals may be especially conspicuous as when in piles of odoriferous dung, or especially cryptic as when buried individually by rodents. Animal-generated seed shadows often contain much heavier seeds than those dispersed by wind, and animals will orient the directions of their movement in response to many different variables rather than a single major direction as is often the case with a tropical wind-generated seed shadow.

The composite seed shadow generated by the entire forest is the base of the food chain for a large number of animals. In short, the forest supports these animals rather than a seedling lawn. When the animals are missing, as when a seed and seedling species is very well protected chemically (e.g. Rankin, 1978), the vertebrates have been hunted out (e.g., many African forests), the forest is on an island (e.g. Janzen, 1972b), or the vertebrates are largely missing because of low or too pulsed seed production (e.g. Janzen, 1974), the seedling lawns are truly impressive. In these cases the bulk of the plants die through intra-specific competition and a much greater and different form of nutrient flow enters the detritivores in the form of dead seedlings rather than as feces and carcasses of seed predators.

Fruit is a peculiar kind of food. Not only should it be engineered to be ignored by most of the animals except those that will put the seeds in the right place, it will have odd nutrient traits for the animals that should eat it. It must be rich in those chemical traits that make life difficult for microbes (Janzen, 1977). It should be rich in some nutrients and very poor in others; the optimal fruit will be an important yet small part of the diet of an animal who will deposit the seeds elsewhere while in search of its other resource needs. The worst fruit would be one that would allow the dispersal agent to sit in or near the parent tree and satisfy all of its dietary needs. Ironically, some fruit bats and figs may represent such a combination (Janzen, 1979b). If it were not for their need to roost in cavities, and (inexplicably) to carry the fruit away from the fig tree before eating it, bats would be terrible dispersal agents for the figs that they seem to be able to subsist on for long periods. Since humans are very fond of sugar, water and vitamin-rich fruits (even tending to call the others vegetables: avocados, eggplants, peppers), we have a fairly biased image of a tropical fruit as something that is rich in calories and water. A very large number of species of wild tropical fruits, however, is protein- and oil-rich and supports a set of birds that get the bulk of their food from these "foul-tasting" fruits [e.g., trogons, toucans, puff-birds, cotingas, oil-birds, bell-birds, manakins in the neotropics (McKey, 1975; Snow, 1976; McDiarmid et al., 1977)].

ANIMAL PARASITOIDS

In discussing whole tropical forest ecosystems, insect parasitoids (tachinid flies, parasitic Hymenoptera, etc.) would appear to be hardly more than a fine fuzz sprinkled across the upper reaches of the food web. The amount of nutrient and caloric resource they process is minute compared to the resource budget of a large tree. However, as with many seed-eaters, bud-biters and pollen carriers, the parasitoids have an enormous potential influence on which of the many potential players is on stage in a given tropical forest act. And since the players vary greatly in their contribution to the form of the overall ecosystem, this is not a trivial influence.

Tropical parasitoids have life cycles like those of extra-tropical ones. They lay their eggs on, in or near a host insect, the larvae develops on or in the host and eventually kills it, and the adult emerges shortly thereafter from a pupa or cocoon inside or near the debris from the dead host. As an adult, the insect is usually a flower visitor for nectar (and pollen?) while it searches for new hosts.

However, there is mounting evidence (Owen and Owen, 1974; Janzen, 1981d) that parasitoid species richness does not march ever upward as the species richness of the total pool of available prey rises in moving from extra-tropical to tropical regions of the earth. A theoretical explanation seems to be in order here. Parasitoids are numerically much less abundant than their hosts. As we move into the tropics, the increase in potential prey species richness is associated with a severe decline in the average density of a prey species. This means that the parasitoids must either exist at an even much lower density, become more euryphagous, or become more adept at prey location. All three undoubtedly occur, but one cannot expect all parasitoids to meet the challenge over evolutionary time. All three challenges mean that parasitoids should become progressively proportionately rarer

as the species richness of potential prey rises. Associated with this, for example, I have found that the greatest species richness of Ichneumonidae (a major hymenopterous parasitoid family) per unit area lies between about 37.5 and 42.5°N latitude in North America (Janzen, 1981d). I am finding that many species of potential prey (seed predator beetles in the Bruchidae and Curculionidae) seem to have no parasites in the lowland deciduous forests around Santa Rosa National Park (Janzen, 1980b).

We do not yet know enough of the interactions of tropical parasitoids with wild host populations to even guess the consequences of increased euryphagy and comparatively reduced parasitoid species richness with decrease in latitude. However, it should make one very wary of extrapolating from extra-tropical systems of parasitoid and host populations. It may well be that fluctuations of tropical host populations are much less influenced by parasitoids than is generally believed of their northern relatives. Likewise, it may well be that the future of biological control of crop insects in tropical systems lies more in manipulating the spatial and temporal juxtaposition of plants inedible and edible to the pest than in augmenting populations of parasitoids and arthropod predators.

CARNIVOROUS PREDATORS

The tropics are famous as a place of intensive and extensive predation by carnivores, leading to such things as large and exact mimicry complexes, amazing camouflage, elaborate escape behaviors, etc. (Robinson, 1969; Rettenmeyer, 1970; Andrews, 1979). From the viewpoint of food webs, however, this may mean little more than that there is less prey escape generated by unequal seasonal depression of predators and their various prey species than in extra-tropical areas. It may also mean that a given biomass of potential prey supports a smaller biomass of predators than does the same amount of prey in more northern areas. It is striking that tropical forests are particularly poor in those masses of highly edible prey that are so abundant in the spring in northern climates, and form the basis of the food web for so many northern predators. Aphids, large numbers of conspicuous and edible caterpillars and grasshoppers, masses of nesting birds, periodical cicadas, mayfly emergences, hordes of small rodents in peak years, passenger pigeons, salmon runs, etc., are prey types that are by and large missing from tropical forests. Termite swarms, at best an evening or two in duration, are about the only easily available and poorly protected analogue. Of course there is the odd year or place where caterpillars or grasshoppers, for example, are very abundant but these are very often highly distasteful insects and their location in time and space is highly unpredictable.

While it is difficult to ascertain the impact on the ecosystem of carnivore density heterogeneity among tropical habitats, it is certainly true that it exists. Small Caribbean islands are disproportionately rich in carnivorous insect groups (Janzen, 1973; Becker, 1975) and very poor in vertebrate predators. Presumably this is because the former are good at starving and the latter are poor at swimming. Africa contains conspicuously more species and biomass of predators on small animals such as snakes, lizards, mice, nesting birds, etc., than are found in comparable neotropical habitats. I have hypothesized that this is due to the living and dead large herbivores aiding in keeping the density of carnivores high in Africa (Janzen, 1976d), and have postulated that the greater predator density is responsible for the apparent lower density of lizards, snakes, bird nests, wasp nests, etc., as compared to similar neotropical habitats. Habitats with apparent low primary productivity, such as those growing on white sand soils in Asia, Africa and the neotropics, tend to have conspicuously reduced number and species richness of both carnivorous vertebrates and insects (as well as scavengers) (Janzen, 1980a).

It is certainly true that the tropics contain some extremely long food chains, but I suspect that this is brought out by the predictable presence of certain components of the system rather than the size of the base of the food pyramid. Furthermore, the long food chains in the tropics certainly cannot be thought of as standing on their own as populations subsisting free of the remainder of the food web.

In the following Central American food chain, it is obvious that there are as many lateral moves as vertical ones: sun to *Enterolobium cyclocarpum* fruits to *Liomys* mice to *Bothrops* viper to colubrid snake (Colubridae) to ocelot (*Felis pardalis*) to large boa. All four of the carnivores are taking prey from all potential levels of the food web except the plant (and even ocelots eat fruit).

INTEGRATION

Observers of ecosystems are fond of documenting how much energy or resource flows through the various linkages described in earlier pages, and how much accumulates at various points in the ecosystem. The driving emotion for such a query or documentation is easy to locate. It lies in the insatiable human, and very human, trait of really only caring about nature to the extent it yields resources that raise our fitness or that of our extended families. That is to say, ecosystem research is basically a harvest exercise. As such I find it totally uninteresting and therefore shall not waste space on harvest questions such as what is the productivity of the animals in a tropical forest, or what is the productivity of a tropical forest with and without its animals, or what is the standing crop of carnivores as compared to herbivores, etc.

However, ecosystem biologists do on occasion ask a question that is of more general interest as well. They ask things like what role do the parasitoids, the seed predators, the leaf eaters, etc. play in the ecosystem? Of course they play no role, but we can avoid that philosophical confrontation by asking what would happen in a forest were the fruit eaters, the flower visitors, the tapir killers, etc., to be magically removed or augmented. The answers will be of interest to both those who wish to harvest nature and to those who wish to understand her. In a real sense, I would like to ask what is the effect of a mutation that results in change in the relationships described or alluded to in the previous sections.

There are at least three ways to ask this question: logic, experiments, and observation of natural experiments. This is not the place for an essay on the relative merits of these three, rather it is my opinion that we know so little about the real world in tropical forests that logic is by far the poorest pathway and should be used only as a last resource. All the inference we can bring to bear may dictate that catastrophic disturbance and random colonization processes are adequate to "explain" the structure of tree species relationships in a tropical forest (Connell, 1978; Hubbell, 1979) but we will only know why *Enterolobium cyclocarpum* is a rare tree and found only in very select habitats adjacent to 300 other species of trees when we know the frequency distributions of what, how and when, destroys the thirty million large seeds, seedlings and saplings produced by the adult tree in its lifetime.

In short, then, what would be the effect of the removal of various subsets or all of the food web described in earlier sections on a tropical forest? Perhaps the most extreme case would be the removal of the herbivores that are parasitic and predaceous on plants. On a contemporary time scale, the absence of herbivores would lead to an immediate choking of the understorey with seedlings from the many surviving seeds and from the enlarged seed crops that come about due to no repairs and losses to leaf- and stem-eaters. This should result in more litter, more litter degraders, and intense competition among seedlings and between seedlings and the species of plants that normally pass their entire developmental cycle in the understorey (such is presently visible in Malaysian dipterocarp forest). Even a dying seedling takes up resources. The increased volume of roots and mycorrhizae, fed not so much by self-harvested resources as by seed reserves, should result in more thorough capture of minerals released by detritivores. The species composition of the understorey should change, since some of the usual residents will not be able to cope with the diffuse competition from the sudden influx of invaders. The species composition of the overstorey, whether from trees coming up in tree falls or from interstitial species insinuating their crowns into the canopy, should change rapidly as the numerical aspects of inter-specific competition change; species whose seeds and seedlings suffered no mortality from animals will suddenly have to endure many competitive bouts with species that previously they only rarely encountered. The increased density of seed shadows should result in the low probabilities of survival in this or that micro-habitat being multiplied by numbers of tries quite high enough to result in whole successes. All of this assumes the fairly unlikely case that the dispersal agents and the pollinators will be up to harvesting and moving this suddenly increased seed and pollen resource. Their failure, guaranteed to be heterogeneous in quality and quantity, will increase the difficulty of predicting the outcome in species

composition and relative abundances of the winners, though it will not necessarily make the system more stochastic.

Certain habitat-wide traits can be expected to change as well. The species richness of trees at a site should decrease because the increased number of reproductive tries and the increased intensity of trying should speed competitive bouts (and therefore speed the rate of arrival at equilibria) and should allow the best competitors for microhabitats to attain their maximum density as they will not be suffering from density-dependent disease and pest problems. The standing crop of adult plants on the site should probably not change except to the degree that reserves not needed for repair are channelled into vegetative growth rather than sexual reproduction. The poorer the habitat, the less of this type of change there should be, since the poorer the site the more of the budget must be going into vegetative parts of the plant. I would also expect a reduction in the finer kinds of variation in plant life form, since there are a smaller number of "best" kinds of life form if there is a smaller number of kinds of challenges facing the plants.

Over evolutionary time, the latter reduction should be even more intense. Non-biotic challenges and resources tend to be relatively monomorphic within a habitat and change little over evolutionary time compared to biotic challenges. Selection for the diversion of resources from repair, defense and sexual reproduction should result in a few supercompetitors for the homogeneous resources characterizing a habitat. It is not hard to envision thousands of square miles of *Phyllostachys* bamboo in a tropical Indian deciduous forest habitat or the same of *Brosimum utile* in a Costa Rican lowland rain forest, with each doing most of the replacement in the occasional tree falls as senescence occurs (much as is the case in some monospecific tropical forest stands today). At present we can only examine island floras for evidence to support this scenario, and none have been examined with this in mind.

On a less dramatic, and therefore more focused scale, the late Pleistocene extinction of much of the neotropical herbivorous megafauna (and its associated carnivores) was a true experiment over nearly evolutionary time in trophic ecology (Janzen and Martin, 1981). The seeds these animals used to disperse probably lay rotting in fruit, were eaten by small seed predators, or died as seedlings in competition with the parent tree. The parental tree species populations probably shrank in area and density to extinction or to those habitats where dispersal was minimally necessary. In a few cases, what had been trivial dispersal agents (e.g., perhaps agoutis with *Scheelea* palm seeds) became major ones. As the plants dependent on the large mammals dwindled in density and area of coverage, I expect that others took their place through expanding populations and occupation of new microhabitats. The understorey palms, so abundant in species and individuals in neotropical rain forests, are probably one such group of plants. Wind-dispersed species are probably others. The reduction in frequency of small tree falls trampled and browsed open repeatedly by proboscidians and other large forest herbivores would surely have had a depressant effect on vines and herbaceous upright plant species richness and density in mature forest. Moving up the food chain, it is easy to postulate that the same fauna of small carnivores, as is found today in Africa, with its postulated depressant effect on other small animals, would have occurred in the neotropics in the Pleistocene and its removal has led to the lizard-rich habitats we see today.

In yet another scenario, I can ask what would happen were I to hit the food pyramid at its very base, by reducing the substrate nutrient quality to that represented by silicon sand as is indeed found in the so-called "white sand and blackwater river" regions of the tropics today (Janzen, 1974). Throughout such forest we find the lavish displays of fruits and flowers, so common in many microhabitats on better tropical soils, to be largely absent; with them go the insects and small vertebrates that depend on them. But then, perhaps it is the other way round; dependency on other forms of pollination and dispersal take prominence as the overall level of food offered declines, leading to an ever-greater downward spiral. When such a forest is cleared by landslide, flood or other agent, the replacement rate is excruciatingly slow — peoples living in such areas regard a meter regrowth of early successional vegetation per year as phenomenally high. This means that the leaf-eaters from cows to caterpillars have slim pickings and what they pick is slow to be replaced.

Moving up the food chain in such a forest I expect the top levels to be worst hurt. Not surprisingly, scavengers should be few and especially proficient at surviving long fasts between meals. The aerial insect pickers should be scarce along with the foliage gleaners. Seed escape from the few seed-eaters present should be especially easy through satiation generated by high inter- and intra-specific synchrony of seed production at long intervals, long intervals being required to store enough reserves to make a large seed crop. Again, as with flowers and fruits, this should make life particularly difficult for the seed predators because even if there is a high average amount of food coming in, it comes at pulses too long for the animal machine to easily average it through fat storage, dormancy and migration (pigs seem to be about the best at all three).

But whence the pollinators for the large-scale flowerings that must accompany the large-scale seedings? Wind or wind-like organisms (animals that can subsist on other foods in between) will have to do it. But then again, cross-pollination may be of lesser importance in this land of reduced biotic challenge where the survival game is played by dormancy, excessive chemical defenses, slow growth rates, and edaphic specialization. Why edaphic specialization? If there is little or no escape from seed predators by distance movement, local timing and pattern, then it is by satiation, which by its very nature means that most seeds end up in the immediate vicinity of the parent. Here, then, there should be strong selection for a dispersal system that moves the seed just past the crown of the parent and into the area occupied on average by the soil type that supported the parent. Here the seedling will have to compete largely with sibs and conspecifics, and thinning will be achieved by crowding rather than intensive seed predation and herbivory. But if there is strong selection for competitive ability in the exact micro-habitat of one's parent, then the best genes to carry are likely to be those of individuals surviving close to your parent or even those of your parents. In losing the animal interaction we have lost a substantial fraction of the reason for continually trying out new combinations and for being open to receive those found successful by conspecifics.

This is not the place to discuss the various experiments that agricultural humans inflict on tropical forests. I have tried to outline some of the ways that the trophic web interacts with tropical forests and with itself. If there is any message to the agricultural experimenter it is that tropical vegetation and the animal interactions it contains tends to be highly tailored to the habitat. Predictions of outcomes have to be cast in percent yes and percent maybe and percent no. Pull the elephants out of a highland rain forest, a lowland rain forest and a lowland deciduous tropical forest and the species richness of trees may go down, stay the same and go up respectively. Put an irrigation ditch through a deciduous forest and the density of malvaceous seed predators will rise and the density of leguminous seed predators will fall. Put a 1-ha bean field in rain forest and the two may have virtually no insects in common after six months; do the same in deciduous forest and most insects in the bean field may also be found in the forest (in the rainy season, if there are any bean plants left). Superimposed on this stochastic heterogeneity, the best way to fulfil human highly idiosyncratic demands becomes virtually impossible to predict. For one society, the best replacement of its forest will be cattle ranches, for another a twenty species mixed plantation of cabinet-grade timber, and for a third simply a large sign introducing the world's finest museum of the organisms and interactions that produced *Homo sapiens* and all his friends and relations.

ACKNOWLEDGEMENTS

This study was supported by NSF DEB 77–04889 and the manuscript was constructively reviewed by W. Hallwachs.

REFERENCES

Anderson, J.A.R., 1961. Destruction of *Shorea albida* by an unidentified insect. *Emp. For. Rev.*, 40: 19–29.

Andrews, R.M., 1979. The lizard *Corytophanes cristatus*: an extreme "sit-and-wait" predator. *Biotropica* 11: 136–139.

Augsperger, C.K., 1978. *Reproductive Consequences of Flowering Synchrony in* Hybanthus prunifolius (*Violaceae*) *and Other Shrub Species of Panama.* Thesis, University of Michigan, Ann Arbor, Mich., 204 pp.

Baker, H.G., 1978. Chemical aspects of the pollination biology of woody plants in the tropics. In: P.B. Tomlinson and M.H. Zimmermann (Editors), *Tropical Trees as Living Systems.* Cambridge University Press, Cambridge, pp. 57–82.

Bawa, K.S. and Opler, P.A., 1978. Why are pistillate inflorescences of *Simarouba glauca* eaten less than staminate inflorescences? *Evolution*, 32: 673–676.

Becker, P., 1975. Island colonization by carnivorous and herbivorous coleoptera. *J. Anim. Ecol.*, 44: 893–906.

Bradford, D.F. and Smith, C.C., 1977. Seed predation and seed number in *Scheelea rostrata* palm fruits. *Ecology*, 58: 667–673.

Brown, L.N., 1972. Mating behavior and life habits of the sweetbay silk moth (*Callosamia carolina*). *Science*, 176: 73–75.

Chester, K.S., 1950. Plant disease losses: their appraisal and interpretation. *Plant Dis. Rep., Suppl.*, 193: 190–362.

Connell, J.H., 1978. Diversity in tropical rainforests of coral reefs. *Science*, 199: 1302–1310.

Eisenberg, J.F., 1978. The evolution of arboreal herbivores in the Class Mammalia. In: G.G. Montgomery (Editor), *The Ecology of Arboreal Folivores.* Smithsonian Institution Press, Washington, D.C., pp. 135–152.

Emmons, L., 1975. *Ecology and Behavior of African Rain Forest Squirrels.* Thesis, Cornell University, Ithaca, N.Y., 269 pp.

Feinsinger, P., 1976. Organization of a tropical guild of nectarivorous birds. *Ecol. Monogr.*, 46: 257–291.

Feinsinger, P., 1978. Ecological interactions between plants and hummingbirds in a successional tropical community. *Ecol. Monogr.*, 48: 269–287.

Frankie, G.W., Opler, P.A. and Bawa, K.S., 1976. Foraging behaviour of solitary bees: implications for outcrossing of a neotropical forest tree species. *J. Ecol.*, 64: 1049–1057.

Freeland, W.J. and Janzen, D.H., 1974. Strategies in herbivory by mammals: the role of plant secondary compounds. *Am. Nat.*, 108: 269–289.

Gilbert, L.E., 1975. Ecological consequences of a coevolved mutualism between butterflies and plants. In: L.E. Gilbert and P.H. Raven (Editors), *Coevolution of Animals and Plants.* University of Texas Press, Austin, Texas, pp. 210–240.

Gill, F.B. and Wolf, L.L., 1975. Economics of feeding territoriality in the golden-winged sunbird. *Ecology*, 56: 333–345.

Gould, E., 1978. Foraging behavior of Malaysian nectar-feeding bats. *Biotropica*, 10: 184–193.

Harris, P., 1974. A possible explanation of plant yield increases following insect damage. *Agro-ecosystems*, 1: 219–225.

Heithaus, R., Fleming, T. and Opler, P.A., 1975. Foraging patterns and resource utilization in seven species of bats in a seasonal tropical forest. *Ecology*, 56: 841–854.

Higgins, M.L., 1979. Intensity of seed predation on *Brosimum utile* by mealy parrots. *Biotropica*, 11: 80.

Hladik, A. and Hladik, C.M., 1969. Rapports trophiques entre végétation et primates dans la forêt de Barro Colorado (Panama). *Terre Vie*, 23: 25–117.

Howe, H.F. and Vandekerckhove, G.A., 1979. Fecundity and seed dispersal of a tropical tree. *Ecology*, 60: 180–189.

Howell, D.J. and Burch, D., 1974. Food habits of some Costa Rican bats. *Rev. Biol. Trop.*, 21: 281–294.

Hubbell, S.P., 1979. Tree dispersion, abundance, and diversity in a tropical dry forest. *Science*, 203: 1299–1309.

Janzen, D.H., 1971. Euglossine bees as long-distance pollinators of tropical plants. *Science*, 171: 203–205.

Janzen, D.H., 1972a. Escape in space by *Sterculia apetala* seeds from the bug *Dysdercus fasciatus* in a Costa Rican deciduous forest. *Ecology*, 53: 350–361.

Janzen, D.H., 1972b. Association of a rainforest palm and seed-eating beetles in Puerto Rico. *Ecology*, 53: 258–261.

Janzen, D.H., 1973. Sweep samples of tropical foliage insects: effects of seasons, vegetation types, elevation, time of day, and insularity. *Ecology*, 54: 687–708.

Janzen, D.H., 1974. Tropical blackwater rivers, animals, and mast fruiting by the Dipterocarpaceae. *Biotropica*, 6(2): 69–103.

Janzen, D.H., 1975. *Ecology of Plants in the Tropics*. Edward Arnold, London, 66 pp.

Janzen, D.H., 1976a. Reduction of *Mucuna andreana* (Leguminosae) seedling fitness by artificial seed damage. *Ecology*, 57: 826–828.

Janzen, D.H., 1976b. Sweep samples of tropical deciduous forest foliage-inhabiting insects: seasonal changes and interfield differences in adult bugs and beetles. *Rev. Biol. Trop.*, 24: 149–161.

Janzen, D.H., 1976c. Why bamboos wait so long to flower. *Annu. Rev. Ecol. Syst.*, 7: 347–391.

Janzen, D.H., 1976d. The depression of reptile biomass by large herbivores. *Am. Nat.*, 110: 371–400.

Janzen, D.H., Miller, G.A., Hackforth-Jones, J., Pond, M., Hooper, K. and Janos, D.P., 1976. Two Costa Rican bat-generated seed shadows of *Andira inermis* (Leguminosae). *Ecology*, 56: 1068–1075.

Janzen, D.H., 1977. Why are there so many species of insects? In: *Proc. XV Int. Congr. Entomol., Washington, D.C.*, 1976: 84–94.

Janzen, D.H., 1978a. The ecology and evolutionary biology of seed chemistry as related to seed predation. In: J.B. Harborne (Editor), *Biochemical Aspects of Plant and Animal Coevolution*. Academic Press, London, pp. 163–206.

Janzen, D.H., 1978b. Seeding patterns of tropical trees. In: P.B. Tomlinson and M.H. Zimmermann (Editors), *Tropical Trees as Living Systems*. Cambridge University Press, Cambridge, pp. 83–128.

Janzen, D.H., 1979a. New horizons in the biology of plant defenses. In: G.A. Rosenthal and D.H. Janzen (Editors), *Herbivores. Their Interaction with Secondary Plant Metabolites*. Academic Press, New York, N.Y., pp. 331–350.

Janzen, D.H., 1967b. How to be a fig. *Annu. Rev. Ecol. Syst.*, 10: 43–51.

Janzen, D.H., 1980a. Heterogeneity of potential food abundance for tropical small land birds. In: A. Keast and E.S. Morton (Editors), *Migrant Birds in the Neotropics*. Smithsonian Institution Press, Washington, D.C., pp. 545–552.

Janzen, D.H., 1980b. Specificity of seed-attacking beetles in a Costa Rican deciduous forest. *J. Ecol.*, 68: 929–952.

Janzen, D.H., 1981a. Patterns of herbivory in a tropical deciduous forest. *Biotropica*, in press.

Janzen, D.H., 1981b. Wild plant acceptability to a captive Costa Rican Baird's tapir. *Brenesia*, in press.

Janzen, D.H., 1981c. Digestive seed predation by a Costa Rican Baird's tapir. *Biotropica*, in press.

Janzen, D.H., 1981d. The peak in North American ichneumonid species richness lies between 38° and 42°N. *Ecology*, 62: 532–537.

Janzen, D.H. and Martin, P.S., 1981. Neotropical anachronisms: the fruits the mastodonts left behind. *Science*, in press.

Karr, J.R., 1976. Within and between habitat avian diversity in African and neotropical lowland habitats. *Ecol. Monogr.*, 46: 457–481.

Kiltie, R.A., 1979. *Seed Predation and Group Size in Rain Forest Peccaries*. Thesis, Princeton University, Princeton, N.J.

Kiltie, R.A., 1981. Distribution of palm fruits on a rain forest floor: why white-lipped peccaries forage near objects. *Biotropica*, in press.

Leigh, E.G., 1975. Structure and climate in tropical rain forest. *Annu. Rev. Ecol. Syst.*, 6: 67–85.

McDiarmid, R.W., Ricklefs, R.E. and Foster, M.S., 1977. Dispersal of *Stemmadenia donnell-smithii* (Apocynaceae) by birds. *Biotropica*, 9: 9–25.

McKey, D., 1975. The ecology of coevolved seed dispersal systems. In: L.E. Gilbert and P.H. Raven (Editors), *Coevolution of Animals and Plants*. University of Texas Press, Austin, Texas, pp. 158–191.

McKey, D., 1978. Soils, vegetation, and seed-eating by black colobus monkeys. In: G.G. Montgomery (Editor), *The Ecology of Arboreal Folivores*. Smithsonian Institution Press, Washington, D.C., pp. 423–437.

McKey, D., Waterman, P.G., Mbi, C.N., Gartlan, J.S. and Struhsaker, T.T., 1978. Phenolic content of vegetation in two African rainforests: ecological implications. *Science*, in press.

Montgomery, G.G. (Editor), 1978. *The Ecology of Arboreal Folivores*. Smithsonian Institution Press, Washington, D.C., 574 pp.

Montgomery, G.G. and Sunquist, M.E., 1978. Habitat selection and use by two-toed and three-toed sloths. In: G.G. Montgomery (Editor), *The Ecology of Arboreal Folivores*. Smithsonian Institution Press, Washington, D.C., pp. 329–359.

Morrison, D.W., 1978. Foraging ecology and energetics of the frugivorous bat *Artibeus jamaicensis*. *Ecology*, 59: 716–723.

Mueller-Dombois, D., 1972. Crown distortion and elephant distribution in the woody vegetations of Ruhuna National Park, Ceylon. *Ecology*, 53: 208–226.

Oppenheimer, J.R. and Lang, G.E., 1969. *Cebus* monkeys: effect on branching of gustavia trees. *Science*, 165: 187–188.

Owen, D.F. and Owen, J., 1974. Species diversity in temperate and tropical Ichneumonidae. *Nature*, 249: 583–584.

Rankin, J.M., 1978. *The Influence of Seed Predation and Plant Competition on Tree Species Abundances in Two Adjacent Tropical Rainforest Communities in Trinidad, West Indies*. Thesis, University of Michigan, Ann Arbor, Mich., 426 pp.

Rettenmeyer, C.W., 1970. Insect mimicry. *Annu. Rev. Entomol.*, 15: 43–74.

Robinson, M., 1969. Defenses against visually hunting predators. *Evol. Biol.*, 3: 225–259.

Rockwood, L.L., 1973. The effect of defoliation on seed production of six Costa Rican tree species. *Ecology*, 54: 1363–1369.

Rockwood, L.L. and Glander, K., 1979. Howling monkeys and leaf cutting ants: comparative foraging in a tropical deciduous forest. *Biotropica*, 11: 1–10.

Rosenthal, G.A., Dahlman, D.L. and Janzen, D.H., 1976. A

novel means for dealing with L-canavanine, a toxic meta-
bolite. *Science*, 192: 256–258.

Rosenthal, G.A., Janzen, D.H. and Dahlman, D.L., 1977.
Degradation and detoxification of canavanine by a specialized seed predator. *Science*, 196: 658–660.

Rosenthal, G.A., Dahlman, D.L. and Janzen, D.H., 1978. L-
canaline detoxification: a seed predator's biochemical
mechanism. *Science*, 202: 528–529.

Ryan, C.A., 1978. Proteinase inhibitors in plant leaves: a
biochemical model for pest-induced natural plant protection. *Trends Biochem. Sci.*, July: 148–150.

Skead, C.J., 1967. *The Sunbirds of Southern Africa*. A.A.
Balkema, Cape Town, 351 pp.

Smythe, N., 1970. The relationships between fruiting seasons
and seed dispersal in a neotropical forest. *Am. Nat.*, 104:
25–35.

Snow, D.W., 1976. *The Web of Adaptation: Bird Studies in the
American Tropics*. Quadrangle, New York, N.Y. 176 pp.

Spatz, G. and Mueller-Dombois, D., 1973. The influence of feral
goats on koa tree reproduction in Hawaii Volcanoes
National Park. *Ecology*, 54: 870–876.

Stanton, N., 1975. Herbivore pressure on two types of tropical
forests. *Biotropica*, 7: 8–11.

Stiles, F.G., 1973. Food supply and the annual cycle of the Anna
hummingbird. *Univ. Calif. Publ. Zool.*, 97: 1–109.

Stiles, G., 1978. Temporal organization of flowering among the
hummingbird foodplants of a tropical wet forest. *Biotropica*, 10: 194–210.

Struhsaker, T.T., 1975. *The Red Colobus Monkey*. University of
Chicago Press, Chicago, Ill., 311 pp.

Terwiliger, V.J., 1978. Natural history of Baird's tapir on Barro
Colorado Island, Panama Canal Zone. *Biotropica*, 10:
211–220.

Williams, K.D. and Petrides, G.A., 1980. Browse utilization,
feeding behavior and management of the Malayan tapir in
West Malaysia. *J. Wildl. Manage.*, 44: 489–494.

Chapter 12

REPRODUCTIVE BIOLOGY OF PLANTS IN TROPICAL FORESTS

H.G. BAKER, K.S. BAWA, G.W. FRANKIE, P.A. OPLER[1]

INTRODUCTION

The pollination of forest trees, lianas and vines, epiphytes, shrubs and herbs in tropical forests can involve all the usual interactions of plants with anthophilous animals to be seen in temperate regions, with the addition of pollination by bats. Also, by contrast to many temperate forest formations, wind pollination is uncommon as the selected mechanism (Whitehead, 1969) and self-pollination appears to be less common than reliance upon cross-pollination (Bawa, 1974, 1979). Similarly, the dispersal of seeds by wind is rather rare by comparison with the overwhelming frequency of fleshy fruits that are consumed by birds and mammals with subsequent regurgitation or defecation of the seeds by the animal at some distance from the parent plant (Van der Pijl, 1969; Janzen, 1975).

In other aspects of forest reproductive biology (including seedling establishment) there is the same increased emphasis on biotic interactions that is to be seen in pollination and seed dispersal. Consequently, our ultimate objective must be to place all of the reproductive considerations in an ecosystem context (Baker, 1979). However, this is being attempted only in a limited number of studies in the American, Asiatic and African tropics. Therefore, this chapter will contain a consideration of pollination and seed dispersal, under a variety of headings, in which individual species or groups of species are more often considered than are ecosystems; the syntheses and elucidation of emergent qualities as one moves from the individual level to a holistic treatment of ecosystems are largely unavailable as yet. This account will not make reference to all the available literature on individual species, however, because this is fragmentary and is scattered in a multitude of journals, some of which are not easily obtainable. Nevertheless, under each heading an attempt will be made to refer to a comprehensive review, as well as providing illustrative examples, often from the Central American forests with which the authors are most familiar.

SEED REPRODUCTION AND VEGETATIVE PROPAGATION

Trees and palms

Sometimes the proportion of viable seeds produced by a tropical forest tree is very low [e.g. 0.1% for *Endespermum* (*Dalbergia*) *malaccensis* (Fabaceae, Faboideae) and *Vernonia arborea* (Asteraceae)] (Ng in Whitmore, 1978). Nevertheless, seedlings of trees are seen frequently on the floors of wet forests at most times of the year, and in dry forests during the rainy season, at least. The distribution of such seedlings, and of saplings derived from them, has been the subject of considerable discussion and some investigation (the literature is summarized by Hubbell, 1979). Less obvious is the capacity of some of the trees to sprout from buds on underground stem tissue or the root system (Richards, 1952; Schnell, 1970; Janzen, 1975; Hartshorn, 1978). Both mechanisms of reproduction may be important in filling light gaps (see Hartshorn, 1978, for a discussion of regeneration in light gaps).

Sometimes fallen trees retain some contact with

---

[1] Names in alphabetical order.

their root systems, still embedded in the ground, and new "trees" (ramets) may spring up from dormant buds along the now horizontal trunk. An example is provided by *Pentaclethra macroloba* (Fabaceae, Mimosoideae) growing in wet soil at Finca La Selva, Costa Rica (H.G. Baker, pers. obs.; Hartshorn, 1972, 1978).

The notorious "strangler figs", as well as some other trees that begin their establishment as epiphytes are, of necessity, reproduced by seeds, probably conveyed by birds, bats, or non-volant mammals onto the branches of what will be the victim tree.

Palms, which usually lack means of vegetative propagation, must necessarily reproduce by seed each generation.

Little is known about the age at first flowering of tropical forest trees. One study (Ng, 1966) made on planted dipterocarps showed that many of these trees begin to flower and set seed before their thirtieth year.

Shrubs, tree ferns and bamboos

For most of the shrubs in tropical forests it is clear that the reproductive emphasis is on seed production. Although multiple stems may be developed, running rhizomes and the formation of new shoots from lateral roots may be less frequent than in temperate forests. Tree ferns, however, may show frequent multiplication by vegetative means (Schnell, 1970).

With bamboos, the situation is strikingly different. These oversized grasses are monocarpic (semelparous), with a long period of vegetative growth before flowering, which may last as long as 120 years in the Asiatic *Phyllostachys bambusoides* (McClure, 1966b; Janzen, 1976a, b). During this time, extensive rhizome and aerial shoot growth can produce an impenetrable thicket many meters across. It is usual for these plants to die after flowering and fruiting and be replaced by seedlings. Janzen (1976b) regards this delay of flowering (more or less synchronous within a species when it does occur), followed by prodigious caryopsis production, as an adaptation that allows the production and dispersal of these one-seeded fruits before seed predators can find them, feast upon them, and develop large populations.

In West African forests, dicotyledonous species

can form large thickets by the vegetative propagation of "air-layering," as in *Anthonota* (*Macrolobium*) *macrophylla* (Fabaceae, Faboideae) and *Scaphopetalum amoenum* (Sterculiaceae) (Longman and Jeník, 1974). Examples could also be quoted from each of the other continents.

Vines and lianas

Like the strangler figs, vines and lianas may develop from seeds that germinate on a branch or trunk of a tree that will ultimately support them. From this aerial origin, shoots or roots may descend to ground level. Other vines and lianas may germinate terrestrially and make their way upward (Richards, 1952; Schnell, 1970; Longman and Jeník, 1974; Whitmore, 1975). Because of the low chance of success in establishment of vines and lianas, seed formation on a lavish scale may be required. Nevertheless, established vines and lianas may be reestablished by sprouting of dormant buds (Janzen, 1975). This may have been one of the reasons for the successful utilization of neotropical forest-margin vines of the Fabaceae in the establishment of artificial pasture grasslands in the American and Australian tropics (Baker, 1978b).

Epiphytes and stem parasites

Epiphytes, by the nature of their habitat, are virtually restricted to seed or spore reproduction. This applies not only to the familiar herbaceous epiphytes (orchids, bromeliads, pteridophytes, etc.) and hemiparasites (mistletoes, etc.) but also to epiphytic shrubs and trees [e.g. species of *Clusia* (Hypericaceae) and *Blakea* (Melastomataceae)]. Reproduction by epiphytes is characteristically accomplished by the production of very large numbers of very small seeds (e.g. Piperaceae, Orchidaceae, Bromeliaceae, etc.) which may be distributed by wind or, more frequently, by birds and mammals that swallow and then regurgitate or defecate seeds that stick to the host tree's branches (Ridley, 1930; Schnell, 1970; Van der Pijl, 1972).

Herbs and root parasites

Opportunities for flowering and seed dispersal by the herbs of mature forest floors typically occur when a tree fall increases the illumination at ground level. Clearance by human agency also serves the same preparatory function. Otherwise, in the depths of the forest, vegetative spread and reproduction by rhizomatous growth are common [e.g. *Heliconia* (Musaceae), *Calathea* (Marantaceae), *Zingiber* (Zingiberaceae), etc.].

In the low light intensity of the forest floor, saprophytes and parasites have an advantage. Especially in the paleotropics, members of the Balanophoraceae are obligate parasites on the roots of woody plants. Such emphasis is put on vegetative reproduction here that, in the case of the African root parasite *Thonningia sanguinea*, which is dioecious, the occurrence together of the staminate and pistillate morphs is almost unknown (Bullock, 1948), so that propagation must take place almost exclusively by vegetative means.

SEED REPRODUCTION

Breeding systems

Research on breeding systems of tropical forest plants has focussed largely on forest trees and shrubs (East, 1940; Baker, 1959, 1976; Ashton, 1969, 1977; Styles, 1972; Bawa, 1974; Tomlinson, 1974; Bawa and Opler, 1975; Styles and Khosla, 1976; Soepadmo and Eow, 1977) and some tree-crop plants (Ferwerder and Wit, 1969; Purseglove, 1968; Baker, 1976; Simmonds, 1976). There are few data for forest herbs, except *Heliconia* (J. Kress, pers. comm., 1979) and Marantaceae (Kennedy, 1978). Lianas and epiphytes are almost uninvestigated.

The central issue in the discussion of tropical plant breeding systems has been the respective roles of inbreeding and outbreeding in the forests and their impacts on population differentiation and speciation (Baker, 1959; Fedorov, 1966; Ashton, 1969, 1977; Bawa, 1974, 1976). Consequently, the objective of most studies has been to determine whether most tropical forest plants are self- or cross-fertilized. It is important to note that this is distinct from determining whether or not the plants are self-incompatible. A self-compatible species may yet set most of its seed by cross-pollination. On the other hand, it should be stressed that even cross-pollination may amount to genetical inbreeding if it is between plants that have had a recent common ancestor. Thus, it becomes apparent that a range of

factors relating to pollinator behavior and its selection may be important in the evolution of breeding systems in tropical forest trees (Bawa and Opler, 1975; Frankie et al., 1976; Janzen, 1977a, b; Bawa, 1980; Bawa and Beach, 1981; Beach, 1981).

Geitononogamy and autogamy

The degrees of self- and cross-pollination in zoophilous plants depend to a considerable extent on the foraging activities of pollinators whose behavior is influenced by spatial and temporal variation of floral rewards (usually nectar and pollen). However, at a given moment, a large tree in the forest may bear hundreds of open flowers awaiting visitation by potential pollinators. Almost certainly most visitors to such a tree will visit many flowers before leaving the tree. Geitonogamy, the transfer of pollen from one flower to another on the same plant (with subsequent fertilization of the egg cells in the latter) is very likely to occur as a result of the pollinator's movements. Autogamy, the transfer of pollen from anthers to stigma in the same flower, followed by fertilization, may occur with or without pollinator assistance in such a tree. Genetically, the effects of geitonogamy and autogamy are the same, except for any rare case where different parts of the crown of a tree may diverge genetically through somatic mutation (Bawa, 1979).

Monoecism, the production of separate staminate and pistillate flowers on the same plant (as in many Meliaceae, Euphorbiaceae and Arecaceae), promotes outcrossing but still leaves open the possibility of geitonogamy. But, geitonogamy and autogamy may only *appear* to be possible if the functioning of "self" pollen on a stigma is prevented by a self-incompatibility mechanism. Although many tropical forest trees have self-incompatibility, this may not be complete, and it is therefore possible for self- and cross-fertilization to occur on the same tree, at the same time (Bawa, 1974; Gan et al., 1977).

For some tree species, there are conflicting reports as to the nature of the breeding system suggesting that this may vary between individuals or populations [cf. Opler et al. (1976a), for *Cordia alliodora* (Boraginaceae); and Valmajor et al. (1965), Baker (1970), and Soepadmo and Eow (1977), for *Durio zibethinus* (Bombacaceae)].

The extent of cross- or self-fertilization may also

depend upon climatic influences and upon pollinator availability, as well as the availability of conspecific trees within pollinator flight range. Consequently, for most forest trees it would be hard to measure the extent of outcrossing.

Outcrossing 1: Physical and timing mechanisms promoting outcrossing. In the large flowers of some trees of the Bombacaceae (e.g. *Ceiba acuminata*), the stigma, on a long exserted style, is held so far away from the anthers in an open flower that pollen could not be deposited on it without the intervention of appropriate animals. In the case of *C. acuminata* these are bats and hummingbirds (Baker et al., 1971). Such "physical" separation of anthers and stigma (technically, an example of herkogamy) increases the possibility of cross-pollination (or geitonogamy) and can be matched in many other tropical trees. A good example of herkogamy in a vine is provided by *Gloriosa superba* (Liliaceae).

Anther dehiscence and stigma receptivity can be separated in time (dichogamy) with either the release of pollen preceding stigma receptivity (protandry) or the reverse (protogyny). Protandry is particularly well-marked in the Fabaceae. Thus, in *Hymenaea courbaril* (Caesalpinioideae), in the neotropics, at anthesis in the early evening the anthers dehisce while the style remains coiled, with the stigma well-protected at the center of the coil. Later in the night, the style uncoils and a receptive stigma is presented (G.W. Frankie, pers. obs.).

In the tribe Gardenieae of the Rubiaceae, in a different kind of protandrous mechanism, the style elongates at anthesis, pushing like a piston between the introrsely dehiscing anthers and the pollen is presented to insect visitors on the unreceptive stigma. Later, when the pollen has been removed, the stigma becomes receptive to pollen brought in from elsewhere (Baker, 1958).

Where protandry involves relatively large flowers there is usually no synchronization between flowers on the same tree so that, although autogamy is prevented, geitonogamy is still possible. Where protandry is shown by species that have many small flowers aggregated into compact inflorescences, and functionally simulating large flowers, there may be synchrony within the inflorescence. Thus, in paleotropical and neotropical species of *Parkia* (Fabaceae, Mimosoideae), there is such synchrony. In *P. clappertoniana*, the tennis ball-sized spherical inflorescences have all the flowers in the staminate condition one night and all in the pistillate condition on a subsequent night (Baker and Harris, 1957). However, there is no synchrony between inflorescences and, once again, although autogamy is prevented, geitonogamy can occur when the bat pollinators make their rounds.

The inflorescence of *Parkia* shows an interesting division of labor between flowers, some of which function only as nectar-producers while the others are potential fruit-producers (Baker and Harris, 1957; Baker, 1978a).

Protogyny, which appears to be less frequent than protandry, may be a more effective mechanism for the promotion of outcrossing, because "foreign" pollen that reaches the stigma before the flower's own anthers dehisce will be favored in the pollen-tube race to the ovules, beating out any of the later released pollen even if the stigma should still be receptive at that time. Two well-studied examples of protogyny are provided by *Persea americana* (Lauraceae) and *Annona cherimolia* (Annonaceae) and, of course, by the highly specialized *Ficus* species (Moraceae) (McGregor, 1976).

Outcrossing 2: Incompatibility systems. Homomorphic self-incompatibility is found in most tropical trees that show this mechanism of avoiding autogamy *and* geitonogamy, but there are also heteromorphic (heterostylous) trees, shrubs, herbs and lianas in the tropical forests (East, 1940; Baker, 1958; Bawa, 1974; Arroyo, 1976; Opler et al., 1976a; Haber and Frankie, 1982).

In a dry, deciduous forest in Costa Rica, Bawa (1974) found 27 out of 34 hermaphrodite-flowered tree species to be self-incompatible as a result of bagging, selfing and crossing experiments. Arroyo (1976) and Zapata and Arroyo (1978) found a similar proportion of species to be self-incompatible in a lowland forest in Venezuela. Studies under way in lowland tropical rain forests in Malaya (Ashton, 1977) and wet forests in Costa Rica (Bawa, unpubl.) also indicate the presence of self-incompatibility in a high proportion of the trees. Further examples of individual species that show self-incompatibility have been put forward by East (1940), Purseglove (1968), Hedegart (1976), Mori and Kallunki (1976), Simmonds (1976), and Gan et al. (1977).

There have been very few determinations of the compatibility relations of forest shrubs, except for heterostylous and other Rubiaceae in West Africa (Baker, 1958) and in Costa Rica (Bawa and Beach, 1981) where self-incompatibility prevails, and for heterostylous (self-incompatible) and homostylous (self-compatible) species of *Cordia* (Boraginaceae) in the neotropics (Opler et al., 1976a). In a tropical lowland wet forest in Costa Rica, L. McDade (pers. comm., 1979) has found self-incompatibility in at least four species of *Aphelandra* (Acanthaceae), but J. Kress (pers. comm.) has determined that *Heliconia* (Musaceae) has both self-incompatible and self-compatible species. In the same forest, K. Grove (pers. comm., 1977) has found several herbs to be self-compatible.

Among lianas and vines, *Passiflora mucronata* has been found to be self-incompatible, and self-incompatibility seems to be frequent among climbers in the Bignoniaceae (Gentry, 1974a).

In many species, incompatibility barriers are either incomplete or break down easily (for example, see Baker, 1958; Lee, 1967; Purseglove, 1968, 1975; Bawa, 1974; Hedegart, 1976). In *Cordia alliodora* (Opler et al., 1976a) and *Luehea seemannii* (Haber and Frankie, 1982), there is experimental evidence that some trees are self-incompatible while others are self-compatible.

In tropical forests, it appears that the stage within the blooming period, as well as the age of the individual flower, may have a considerable effect on the integrity of the self-incompatibility system. For example, in *Byrsonima crassifolia* (Malpighiaceae), one of five trees used in experiments was initially found to be self-incompatible but, when the flowering period was nearly over, self-pollinated flowers produced fruits (Bawa, unpubl.). In *Piscidia carthagenensis* (Fabaceae, Faboideae), one day old artificially self-pollinated flowers did not set fruit, but two day old flowers set some. Trees of this species are usually cross-pollinated (Frankie and Haber, unpubl.). In *Luehea seemannii* (Tiliaceae), flowers that were self-pollinated 12–16 h after anthesis set more fruits than those pollinated within 2–4 h of anthesis (Haber and Frankie, 1982).

However, the frequency with which incompatibility systems break down, and the environmental factors which promote the breakdown, both need further study (cf. Baker, 1955, 1965a, 1974; Stebbins, 1957; Jain, 1976). Selfing tends to preserve existing genotypes; crossing promotes their recombination, so the breeding system of a tropical forest tree should be reflected in the structure of its populations and the variation between them. Studies of this kind of variation, which may well be made by electrophoresis of proteins in the cellular contents, are only just beginning to be made on tropical trees (cf. Gan et al., 1977).

Heteromorphic self-incompatibility systems are largely restricted to shrubs and small trees (e.g. Rubiaceae, Erythroxylaceae, Oxalidaceae, Boraginaceae) and may be missing from tall trees. Distyly is more common than tristyly in the forest plants, the latter being evidenced only in degraded form in *Averrhoa carambola* and *A. bilimbi* (Oxalidaceae) (Baker, unpubl.). In studies of two lowland forest ecosystems in Costa Rica, Bawa (unpubl.) found 2 to 3% of tree species in each ecosystem to be distylous.

In some tropical woody plants, heterostyly seems to have evolved into dioecism (Baker, 1958, 1959; Carlquist, 1966; Bawa and Opler, 1975, Opler et al., 1976a; Bawa, 1980). Thus, in *Mussaenda* spp. (Rubiaceae), choking of the corolla tube with hairs means that pollen is rarely picked up from the low anthers of long-styled plants and rarely put down on the stigmas of short-styled plants. Thus, the long-styled plants function as pistillate individuals and set seed, while the short-styled plants are functionally staminate (Baker, 1958, 1959). A similar picture may be seen in *Cordia* (Opler et al., 1976a). Consequently, observation of fruit-setting as well as detailed morphological study of flowers is necessary to ascertain whether they are functionally hermaphrodite (and heterostylous) or functionally unisexual.

In species with homomorphic self-incompatibility, the system appears usually to be of the gametophytically controlled type (Bawa, unpubl.), in contrast to the sporophytic control of the heteromorphic systems. Thus, in *Theobroma* (Sterculiaceae), the system has the unusual feature that pollen tubes from all pollinations grow equally fast to the embryo-sac and the differentiation between compatible and incompatible pollinations only becomes apparent when the male gametes of the latter fail to effect fertilization of the egg cell (Cope, 1962a). Cope (1962b) has shown that in an isolated population (and *Theobroma cacao* has a spotty distribution in Amazonian forest) derived self-compatible trees, which have greater fruitfulness, should ultimately displace those with self-incompatibility. However, there appears to be strong selective discrimination against self-compatible types (Purseglove, 1968) and, near the presumed center of origin of the species on the eastern slopes of the Andes, all clones so far examined have proved to be self-incompatible. On the other hand, the farther a collection is made from the center of origin, the greater is the proportion of self-compatible trees. Purseglove (1968) considers that this self-compatibility would help the spread of the species into new areas.

The presence of a self-incompatibility system in a plant does not negate entirely the possibility of genetical inbreeding, for this is not dependent upon self-fertilization alone; small effective population size due to a limited number of individuals from which pollen may be received, asynchronous flowering and limited seed dispersal, may all raise the level of inbreeding. Gene flow in time and space is difficult to monitor in tropical tree populations, and appropriate studies are still in their infancy. However, a recent study of trees in a Malayan rain forest indicates that genetic variance of seedlings decays rapidly as one moves away from a parent tree [*Shorea leprosula*, (Dipterocarpaceae), and *Xerospermum intermedium* (Sapindaceae)] (Gan et al., 1977). This conforms to Ashton's (1969) suggestion that trees in the humid tropics mostly exchange genes with their immediate neighbors within a "clump", although occasional exchange may also occur between members of different "clumps". For a demonstration that, at least in Costa Rican dry forest, trees may be clumped, see Hubbell (1979). Very recently, H.T. Chan (in Kavanagh, 1979) has shown that clumps of trees of Malaysian forest Dipterocarpaceae (which form because of limited seed dispersal) produce much more fruit than trees which are isolated as individuals.

Outcrossing 3: Monoecism and dioecism. Many tropical plants promote outcrossing by monoecism (e.g. many Meliaceae; Styles, 1972; Styles and Khosla, 1976) or render it obligate by dioecism (e.g. Caricaceae; Baker, 1976). The unisexual flowers of many monoecious taxa have well-developed, but non-functional, organs of the opposite sex, making it difficult to assess the nature of the sexuality from a casual examination of floral morphology. Thus,

following careful study, many species from tropical forests, described as hermaphrodite in old floras, have been found to produce functionally unisexual flowers (Styles, 1972; Bawa and Opler, 1975; Styles and Khosla, 1976; Bawa, unpubl.). The resemblance between the staminate and pistillate flowers (which contrasts with their striking difference in wind-pollinated temperate forest trees) is probably due to the necessity for both kinds of flowers to conform to the same "search image" formed by animal pollinators (insects, birds, bats) of these tropical trees.

Unisexuality of the flowers is more apparent in the woody species than in herbaceous taxa (including epiphytes). In a survey of the Barro Colorado Island flora, Croat (1978) reported the proportion of dioecious species in the flora (all life forms together) to be 9% (115 out of 1265 species). The same author (Croat, 1979) has made further analyses and shows that among the medium to large trees, 21% are dioecious and 15% are monoecious. The figures shrink to 7% and 12%, respectively, for small trees (and shrubs). Eight percent of scandent plants are dioecious and 12% are monoecious.

In their study of a dry forest in Guanacaste Province, Costa Rica, Bawa and Opler (1975) found 22% of the tree species to be dioecious. They quote 40% for a rain forest in Nigeria and 26% (including some dichogamous hermaphrodite species) for a lowland, mixed dipterocarp forest in central Sarawak (data from Jones, 1955, and Ashton, 1969, respectively). Clearly dioecism is more prevalent among trees of the tropics than in temperate regions, and probably more prevalent in large trees than in any other life-form. Reasons for this have been suggested by Bawa and Opler (1975), by Bawa (1980) and by Beach (1981).

Dioecious tropical trees show occasional variability in sex expression, which is manifested by one sex (usually the staminate) producing a few flowers that are hermaphrodite or, more rarely, of the opposite sex. Thus, in *Carica papaya*, there is a tendency for staminate trees, at the end of a flowering period, to produce hermaphrodite flowers from which seed-bearing fruits are formed. Seeds from these fruits give rise to both staminate and pistillate progeny, and the significance of this in maintaining the presence of both sexes in a local area has been examined by Baker (1976).

In some species of tropical forest trees, herma-

phrodite individuals, as well as pistillate and staminate ones, may occur on a regular basis [e.g.
Coccoloba padiformis (Polygonaceae)], or individual trees may vary in sexual state from time to
time. Some of these taxa are listed by Yampolsky
and Yampolsky (1922) as "polygamodioecious". In
the Barro Colorado Island (Panama) area, Croat
(1978) finds that there are 54 species (i.e. 4% of the
flora) in this condition. The adaptive significance of
such variation in sex expression is still obscure.

Dioecious tropical trees exhibit some sex-linked
dimorphism in reproductive traits such as the
number of flowers per inflorescence, flower size,
color and shape of the petals (most notably in
Carica, where the staminate flowers are gamope-
talous while the pistillate flowers are polypetalous),
in the amount of nectar produced, and in the degree
of herbivory on floral parts (Bawa and Opler, 1975,
1978; Baker, 1976). Bawa and Opler (1975) have
noted differences in the amounts of nectar secreted
by staminate and pistillate flowers, more often
greater in the pistillate flowers, but *Carica* spp.
show the complete opposite, for here the pistillate
flowers produce no nectar while the supply is good
in the staminate flowers (Baker, 1976). In the case
of *Carica* it is suggested that this keeps "dangerous"
flower visitors, such as hummingbirds (Trochilidae)
and *Trigona* bees, away from the pistillate flowers
where an easily damaged ovary fills the flower.
Successful pollination is carried out by moths that
visit the pistillate flowers by "mistake" in poor
light.

Baker (1978a) has shown that there may be
significant differences between pistillate and staminate trees of the same species in the ratio of sucrose
to hexoses in their floral nectars [e.g. in *Triplaris
americana* (Polygonaceae)]. The significance and
extent of such differences will only become evident
with further study.

Most tropical dioecious trees that have been
examined show biased sex ratios, with a large
majority favoring the staminate "sex" (Opler and
Bawa, 1978). In some other cases, only pistillate
plants are known (Tomlinson, 1974) and, here,
apomixis must be suspected.

Apomixis

Apomictic reproduction, usually involving
agamospermy (formation of embryos without sexual fusion) has been known for individual tropical

woody and herbaceous species since the nineteenth
century, the first record being due to Smith (1841),
who observed seed-setting by isolated pistillate
plants of the species now known as *Alchornea
ilicifolia* (Euphorbiaceae). Lists of species with one
or other of the apomictic mechanisms have been
published by Nygren (1954, 1967) and at least thirty
tropical genera (exclusive of grasses) are represented in these lists. The prevalent mechanism is
adventitious embryony, in contrast to apomixis in
those parts of the world where there is a short
growing season where dependence may be upon
diplospory or apospory, followed in each case by
diploid parthenogenesis (Baker, unpubl.). An illustration of the mechanism of adventitious embryony
in a tropical forest tree is presented for *Pachira
oleaginea* [now known as *Bombacopsis glabra*
(Bombacaceae)] by Baker (1960).

Eco-evolutionary explanations for this climate-
related difference will be considered elsewhere, but
it is notable that apomixis of any sort "freezes" the
heterozygosity (and, also the heterosis) that has
resulted from outcrossing in sexually reproducing
(amphimictic) ancestors. Consequently, the demonstration by Ashton (1977) and Kaur et al.
(1978) of a possible high level of apomixis in
Malayan climax forest trees, where amphimictic
reproduction might be difficult because of physical
separation of conspecific individuals, suggests that
the frequency of occurrence of this breeding system
should be investigated carefully in other tropical
forests.

S. Appanah (in Kavanagh, 1979) has found that
trees of the Dipterocarpaceae in Malaysia are
pollinated by thrips (Thysanoptera). These insects
are not numerous until a series of dipterocarp
species come into bloom. Then the thrips population increases enormously. However, the first tree
species in the flowering sequence, *Shorea macro-
ptera*, is faced with a paucity of thrips and it may be
significant that trees of this species are apomictic.

Pollination ecology (anthecology)

Initiation of flower formation and anthesis

Floral initiation involves two distinct phases: the
"induction" in a plant of a state of readiness to
produce flower buds (often controlled by photoperiod, along with appropriate temperatures), and
the "differentiation" of a previously vegetative

apex into a flower bud (Hillman, 1962; Salisbury, 1963). Anthesis (the opening of flowers) may follow directly or be delayed (bud dormancy).

The photoperiodic stimulus, if present, in tropical plants may come from a very slight change in the proportion of light to dark in the day length (McClelland, 1924; Bünning, 1948; Njoku, 1958; and others). But, whatever the triggering factors for "induction", "differentiation", or "anthesis" may be, most tropical plants flower discontinuously, with a tendency to flower at a particular season (Holttum, 1952; Daubenmire, 1972; Frankie et al., 1974; Opler et al., 1976b, 1980; Stiles, 1978; and other references in Frankie et al., 1974). A minority of plants in the moister habitats flower continuously, at least on a population basis, and these are most often encountered in pioneer seral communities in the wetter forest zones.

The breakage of flower bud dormancy leading to anthesis in tropical plants has been the subject of some debate, and it is likely that more than one kind of stimulus is involved. Fire (Hopkins, 1963), change of photoperiod (also Hopkins, 1963), temperature drops (Kerling, 1941; Holttum, 1952; Went, 1957), and removal of water stress (Alvim, 1960, 1964; Holdsworth, 1961; Daubenmire, 1972; Opler et al., 1976a; Alvim and Alvim, 1978), have all been reported or demonstrated to break dormancy. It appears that there are also endogenous rhythms involved, so that some tropical forest plants flower more than once a year (Holttum, 1952; Frankie et al., 1974; Opler et al., 1976a, 1980; Opler, 1981), while others grow for several to many years without flowering (including the bamboos already alluded to before). They, and some trees, are monocarpic (Foster, 1977). In Ghana, trees of the savanna ecotype of *Ceiba pentandra* (Bombacaceae) flower annually; large trees of the forest ecotype may remain vegetative for several years between flowering episodes (Baker, 1965b). Gentry (1974b) has surveyed flowering types in neotropical Bignoniaceae.

The following synchrony triggered by a sharp environmental stimulus such as a drought-ending tropical rain storm may be extremely important in maintaining intra-specific gene flow in the less common tree species. It also allows the temporal displacement of flowering by different species that would otherwise compete for the same specialized pollinators (Frankie, 1975; Opler et al., 1976a;

Frankie and Haber, in prep.). Stiles (1978) has shown that in a wet forest area (La Selva, Costa Rica), the sequence of flowering by hummingbird-pollinated species may be changed from year to year by climatic differences but that the continuity of the resource supply is maintained.

Anthesis usually occurs at a particular time of day or night for each flowering plant species and the full 24-h day may be exploited. In keeping with the warmth of tropical nights, forest plants show a higher proportion of nocturnally flowering species than in temperate regions, so that bats and moths have important roles to play as pollinators. The warmth is also reflected in the opening of such a characteristically diurnal flower as *Thevetia ovata* (Apocynaceae) in the pre-dawn darkness. Principally nocturnal plants, such as *Inga vera* (Fabaceae, Mimosoideae) open their flowers in mid-afternoon and they stay open all night; they may have a range of visitors from bees to bats (Salas, 1974). The flowers of some dioecious plants may represent a special case, as the staminate flowers may open several hours before the pistillate ones (Bawa and Opler, 1975).

The length of time during which a flower remains able to provide pollen or, more important, to receive it, varies greatly between species. Epiphytic orchids are famous for the length of time that their flowers remain fresh; an opposite extreme is presented by some *Passiflora* species whose flowers last only for a few hours and whose pollination is over in a few minutes after opening (Janzen, 1968). However, it is generally true that a single flower on a tropical tree usually lasts for about a day. Exceptions to this rule are provided by some of the protandrous and protogynous species whose flowers have androecia and gynaecia that are functional on different days (or nights). Some species have flowers that continue to contribute to the inflorescence's attractiveness even though they are "spent". An example is provided by *Lantana camara* (Verbenaceae) where the functioning flowers are yellow and the spent flowers, which are retained for a few days, are orange-red. A further example is provided by *Byrsonima crassifolia* (Malpighiaceae) with a similar color change.

Individual plants of monoecious species usually show a temporal separation in the anthesis of the staminate and pistillate flowers. Thus, Schmid (1970) found this to be true for the palm *Asterogyne martiana* in wet forest in Costa Rica. In *Cupania guatemalensis* (Sapindaceae), Bawa (1977) demonstrated that each individual plant has two separate, but brief, anthesis periods during which staminate flowers open and, between them, a longer period during which pistillate flowers are open.

Phenology and regularity of flowering

Periodic behavior of plants in tropical environments received little attention until recently (Holttum, 1952; Rees, 1964; McClure, 1966a; Gibbs and Leston, 1970; Nevling, 1971; Burger, 1974; Frankie et al., 1974; Opler et al., 1980). Some accounts of phenological events relevant to reproductive biology often occur as brief notes in large papers devoted to some other topic (e.g. Beard, 1946; Ducke and Black, 1953). Other information on specific phenological events can be found in floristic treatments (e.g. Allen, 1956; Little and Wadsworth, 1964; and, outstandingly, in Croat, 1978). Another source of phenological information is in papers dealing with species of economic importance (e.g. Broekmans, 1957; Rees, 1964; Lamb, 1966; Purseglove, 1968, 1975). In some studies, the data on periodicity of a small number of species have been pooled in an attempt to reflect general phenological trends in particular vegetation types (e.g. J.R. Baker and I. Baker, 1936; Hopkins, 1963; Daubenmire, 1972; various references in Richards, 1952).

More recently, efforts have been made to discern general community patterns in leafing, flowering and fruiting for many species of which particular forest types are composed. Studies have been made in Africa by Boaler (1966), in deciduous miombo woodland in Tanzania, and by Burger (1974) in four forest types in Ethiopia. In Asia, Ng (1977) has studied phenology in a dipterocarp forest in Malaya, with other studies in Malaya by Medway (1972) and in Sri Lanka by Koelmeyer (1959). In the neotropics, studies have been made in the semi-evergreen moist forest of Panama by Croat (1969, 1978) and by Foster (1974). In Costa Rica, phenological studies have been reported by Janzen (1967) in the dry forest, in moist forest by Fournier and Salas (1966), and in wet and dry forests by Frankie et al. (1974) for trees and Opler et al. (1980) for shrubs and treelets. Nevling (1971) studied the phenology of elfin forest in Puerto Rico, while Jackson (1978) investigated lower montane rain forest (technically just in the subtropics) in Brazil. With the exceptions of the work in Sri Lanka by Koelmeyer (1959) and in Malaya by Medway (1972), as well as the Costa Rica studies by us, these patterns are those found on a short-term basis only (usually about two years).

The analyses of Costa Rican forest tree phenology (Frankie et al., 1974) and of shrub and treelet phenology (Opler et al., 1980) may be summarized. In the wet forest (Finca La Selva), there were two apparent flowering peaks in the canopy species and three in the understorey. There was flowering in the two wet seasons as well as in the not-severe dry seasons, with little synchrony between the two layers. The shrubs of the wet forest showed multiple flowering more frequently, and their flowering could generally be described as "aseasonal". In the dry forest (Guanacaste), two peaks of flowering were visible in the trees; one extensive period during the long dry season and a second peak at the beginning of the rainy season. The dry forest shrubs, by contrast, showed only a major flowering peak in the early wet season, before being shaded by the leafing out of the deciduous trees. During the long dry season the shrubs tended to be in dormant condition, possibly because the drought is more severe for them than for deeper rooted trees. Riparian forest in Guanacaste tended to show intermediate phenological behavior of shrubs and trees, in keeping with an intermediate water supply situation.

In the wet forest, during each month of the year, substantial numbers of trees could be found bearing mature fruit, although there was a peak in the second dry season (August–October). In the dry forest, a peak in the production of mature fruit occurred in the latter part of the long dry season (with the result that seeds would be available on the forest floor at the onset of the rainy season). Shrubs in the dry forest evinced a bimodal fruiting pattern, with both mid-wet and mid-dry season peaks. Riparian forest in Guanacaste, intermediate in its moisture-availability picture between the wet and the dry forests, showed a generally intermediate phenological pattern.

In Panama, Barro Colorado Island is also intermediate, this time climatically, between the Costa Rican wet and dry forests, and phenological observations by Croat (1978) on plants of all life forms reveal that forest floor herbs reach the peak of their flowering early in the rainy season, and epiphytes mostly flower in mid- to late dry season. Vines have a more dispersed flowering pattern. Lianas reach a peak of flowering in the earlier part of the dry season; the peak for the larger trees comes later in the dry season. Shrub flowering peaks at the beginning of the rainy season. The fruiting seasons of these various life forms follow appropriately (herbs, midway to late in the rainy season; epiphytes chiefly in the late dry season; lianas also late in the dry season; trees show two peaks, at the beginning of the wet season and midway through it; shrubs in the wet season).

H.T. Chan (in Kavanagh, 1979) has found that, at Pasoh Forest Reserve, Malaysia, the trees of the Dipterocarpaceae show an overlapping sequence of flowering, with two to three weeks duration for each species, although fruit maturation and fall is concurrent. The sequence of flowering is related to the utilization of the same pollinators (thrips) by the various dipterocarp trees.

Efforts have been made to examine the phenological aspects of the interactions that take place between plants and animals at the community level, in the paleotropics by Putz (1979) and others, and in the neotropics by such investigators as Snow (1965), Janzen (1967), Smythe (1970), Gentry (1974b, 1976), Heithaus (1974, 1979), Stiles (1975, 1978), and Frankie (1975, 1976). Detailed studies of hummingbird ecology in relation to plant phenology have been made by Snow and Snow (1972), Feinsinger (1976, 1978), Stiles (1978) and Feinsinger and Colwell (1978). A series of papers by Frankie and Haber (in prep.) will characterize interactions between anthophilous visitors and the trees of the dry forests of Costa Rica (and, also, selected shrubs, lianas and vines). In the cases of large bees and hawkmoths, they will show that seasonal abundance of these insects is closely related to temporal and spatial patterns of floral resource availability.

The findings of Stiles (1978) are based on the study of flowering by 59 species of hummingbird-visited plants over a period of about four years in the wet forest of Finca La Selva, Costa Rica. Peaks of flower availability occurred in the dry and early wet seasons, flower shortage occurred in the wettest months of the year. However, together the different species of food plants cover the needs of the birds throughout the year. Interestingly, year-to-year

variation in rainfall caused some changes in the order in which the species flowered, but continuity was maintained.

In the future, we may expect general phenological studies to be spread over longer time periods, thereby giving more insight into the causes of variability of patterns from year to year, as well as the basic arrangement. This will also permit a greater understanding of the flowering and fruiting patterns of plants that do not flower each year. The triggers that bring on anthesis will be seen more clearly. Comparative studies of phenological patterns in disturbed and undisturbed habitats may be important in allowing us to manage tropical forests more appropriately, as well as to appreciate the interactions between the various organisms that inhabit them. Competitive interactions between plants in relation to their use of pollen and seed vectors (and the avoidance of this by temporal spacing) will be studied more intensively along the lines suggested by the work of Stiles (1975, 1978), Feinsinger (1978), Feinsinger and Colwell (1978) for pollinators, and by Foster (1974), Howe and Primack (1975), Howe (1977) and Howe and Estabrook (1977) for fruit dispersers.

Pollen vectors

(1) Wind pollination. Most pollination studies in tropical forests have been concerned with zoophilous plants and the animals connected with them, because the vast majority of tropical forest plants are animal-pollinated. Wind pollination is particularly rare in the wetter forests where the wide dispersion of conspecific individuals, added to the physical presence of unrelated trees in between, makes anemophily an inefficient system (Whitehead, 1969; Janzen, 1975). At ground level, lack of air movement may be an additional factor impeding wind pollination, and even the occasional grasses that are found here may be insect-pollinated to some extent (Soderstrom and Calderon, 1971; Karr, 1976).

Anemophily has been reported for some trees in deciduous forests bordering savannas where the unfavorable factors are at a minimum (Daubenmire, 1972; Bawa and Opler, 1975). Several tree species in the Moraceae in semi-deciduous forests of tropical Africa and Asia are also anemophilous (D. Leston, pers. comm., 1978; Corner, 1952), and so are some Rhizophoraceae in mangrove forests (Tomlinson et al., 1978). Wind pollination in a neotropical lowland evergreen (wet) forest has been reported recently by Bawa and Crisp (1980) for *Trophis involucrata* (Moraceae) and there are indications that there may be some others even in the understorey of Central American wet forests (Bawa, unpubl.). Some palms, including *Thrinax* spp., appear to be wind-pollinated (Uhl and Moore, 1977), but the once-prevalent belief that the Arecaceae as a whole are anemophilous has been shown to be incorrect (Schmid, 1970; Uhl and Moore, 1977).

The selective pressures responsible for the evolution of anemophily in occasional species in humid, evergreen forests are not obvious. Competition for pollinators and energetic constraints on the production of floral rewards and pollinator-attraction devices, may have selected in favor of wind pollination, for the understorey layer is not entirely windless and, in fact, too strong a wind is deleterious to efficient wind pollination. It is also possible that anemophily evolved in such families as the Moraceae and Arecaceae under different environmental conditions but has persisted after migration into the forest.

(2) Insect pollination. The wide range of anthophilous insects in tropical forests includes beetles, bees (with at least two distinguishable functional categories), wasps, moths (both sphingids and "settling moths"), butterflies, and various kinds of flies. However, most of the pollination-related information on these insect groups has been obtained from rather cursory observations. Surveys of pollination systems at the ecosystem level have been made almost exclusively in the neotropics, although recent work in Malaysia may redress the balance. Intensive studies of particular taxa are not very numerous, and experimental work is rare.

The syndromes of characters that adapt flowers to various insect pollinators in tropical forests are comparable to those of the temperate regions (cf. Van der Pijl, 1960–61; Baker and Hurd, 1968; Faegri and Van der Pijl, 1971, 1978). Some purely tropical correlations are notable, however. Thus, Bawa and Opler (1975) have pointed out that small white flowers with limited nectar supplies are characteristic of the relatively frequent dioecious tree species that are pollinated mostly by short-tongued bees. In *Cordia* (Boraginaceae), Opler et al. (1976a) found that the smallest-flowered species, *C. inermis*,

may have a list of insect flower visitors as much as 300 species long.

Janzen (1975) has pointed out that large proportions of the species and biomass of tropical bees are social, including such genera as *Apis*, *Trigona* and *Melipona*. However, they may have a less-than-proportional importance as pollinators, often being scavengers of pollen and nectar left over after pollination of the flower has taken place, or taking it from flowers where efficient pollination requires a nectar-collector. These social bees are also adept at cleaning the pollen on their bodies into pellets, so that less is carried from flower to flower in a pollinatory position (Janzen, 1975).

The large solitary bees are very important as pollinators of woody plants in the tropics. Studies of xylocopid bees in Southeast Asia were reported *in extenso* by Van der Pijl (1954). The fragrance-collecting male euglossine bees have been investigated by C.H. Dodson, R.L. Dressler and collaborators (summary in Dodson, 1975). Vogel (1968) also contributed significantly to the elucidation of the story. Traplining (that is, visiting a series of plants) by female euglossine bees was first described by Janzen (1971), who also pointed out that these bees appear to be capable of flights of as much as 23 km each day, so that the widespread dispersion of traplined flowering plants need not be an insuperable impediment to their cross-fertilization. The syndromes of characters of trapliners and of the plants they visit are described by Janzen (1971, 1974b).

Research by Frankie and Colville (1979) has shown that large bees of different species forage at different heights above ground in the dry forests of Costa Rica. Thus, by this means, nectar and pollen resource partitioning is achieved. The roles of territoriality and aggressive interactions between tropical forest bees are described by Dodson and Frymire (1961), Frankie and Baker (1974) and Frankie (1976). The influence of these instinctive reactions by the bees in promoting cross-pollination by displaced individuals is referred to in a later section. Also related to the promotion of cross-pollination is the suggestion by Gentry (1978) that "mass flowering" insect-pollinated species may expend energy in producing a surplus of pollinators and these, in turn, attract insectivorous birds that facilitate cross-pollination by scaring some of the insects away to other plants.

"Mass flowering," where the individual plant produces a large number of flowers over a short period of time, is most appropriate to canopy trees and lianas (e.g. *Tabebuia* and *Pterocarpus* in Central America) which show masses of color to animals that can fly above the forest canopy. This includes birds as well as large bees. By contrast, trees and shrubs under the canopy, as well as vines, some lianas and epiphytes may be better served by the "traplining" syndrome already described.

Comprehensive studies of insect pollination of the members of particular families are not yet as frequent as with temperate zone investigations. Notable are the investigations of the Bignoniaceae by Gentry (1974a) and of the Lecythidaceae by Prance (1976) and others. In both of these cases bees are responsible for most of the pollinatory activity.

Other Hymenoptera, particularly the various kinds of tropical wasps, play a larger role in pollination than is generally realized (see Faegri and Van der Pijl, 1978, pp. 107–109). It should be remembered that the extreme mutualism between *Ficus* species and their pollinators involves wasps of the Agaonidae (summaries in Ramirez, 1970; Galil and Eisikowitch, 1971). Ants, which are abundant in and on forest trees, may also be rare cross-pollinators.

Lepidoptera are frequent in the forests of the tropics, although not all of them are nectar-seekers. The strikingly colored, large butterflies of the genus *Morpho* feed on rotting fruit (Young, 1972). In Southeast Asia, Bänziger (1971) has described blood-sucking moths. Slightly less bizarre is the behavior of female butterflies of the genus *Heliconius*, described by Gilbert (1972, 1975). These butterflies take nectar from flowers and then collect a ball of pollen from staminate flowers of *Anguria* or *Gurania* vines (Cucurbitaceae), and, regurgitating nectar on to it, so that amino acids diffuse out into the nectar which is then imbibed by the butterfly. Very recently, DeVries (1979) has provided circumstantial evidence that butterflies in the genera *Parides* and *Battus* may do the same thing in Costa Rica. Other butterflies in tropical forests have more conventional nectar-collecting habits, and the same is true of "settling moths". The nectars of the flowers that these Lepidoptera visit are unusually rich in amino acids (see below) (Baker, 1978a).

Sphingid (hawk) moths are common in tropical forests after sunset. There is some evidence that, at lower elevations, a peak foraging activity may be reached in the early hours of the morning (W.A. Haber, G.W. Frankie and P.A. Opler, pers. obs.) but, in the cloud forest of Costa Rica activity is greatest at dusk and dawn. It is probable that the sphingids follow a "traplining" path in many cases, but this requires substantiation (however, see Linhart and Mendenhall, 1977).

The syndrome of hawkmoth flower characteristics is comparable with that amply described elsewhere for temperate plants (e.g. Van der Pijl, 1960–61; Baker and Hurd, 1968; Faegri and Van der Pijl, 1966, 1971, 1978), with the addition that some dingy-colored flowers with an unpleasant smell may also be attractive to moths (see below). Tropical hawkmoth flowers include some of the longest corolla tubes or spurs ever recorded, and these are matched by the lengths of the moths' proboscides. It is notable that the proboscis-length record holder, *Xanthopan morgani* f. *praedicta*, pollinates the epiphytic orchid *Angraecum sesquipedale* (which has a spur between 25 and 30 cm in length) in the forests of Madagascar.

As befits the claim that has been made for them to be the pioneers in insect pollination, beetles of various sorts are proportionately more important as pollinators in tropical forests than in temperate ones (cf. Van der Pijl, 1960–61, 1969; Gottsberger, 1974; etc.). Some of the tropical aroids may be highly specific in the beetles that they attract by their distinctive odors (e.g. *Amorphophallus titanum* and the large silphid beetle of the genus *Diamesus* that visits the inflorescences and is temporarily trapped; Faegri and Van der Pijl, 1978, p. 101).

However, Thien (1980), who has been investigating the pollination biology of "primitive" angiosperm trees, particularly in the forests of Southeast Asia and the islands in the Pacific Ocean, has concluded that various Diptera should receive more credit as pioneer pollinators. Probably, flies are more important as pollinators in tropical forests than has been generally realized; they are not esthetically attractive organisms and are not usually flower-specific, so they have been ignored by many casual observers. An example of this is the belated recognition of the role of syrphid flies in the pollination of the wet-forest palm *Asterogyne martiana* in Costa Rica (Schmid, 1970).

(3) Bird pollination. A useful summary of bird pollination literature is given by Faegri and Van der Pijl (1978, p. 123 seq.).

Trees and shrubs in neotropical forests may be pollinated by hummingbirds (Trochilidae) or by a variety of passerine (perching) birds (Passeriformes), including vireos (Vireonidae), warblers (Sylviidae), tanagers (Thraupidae), finches (Fringillidae), orioles (Oriolidae), blackbirds (Icteridae) and honeycreepers (Coerebidae) (Toledo, 1977). The last-named honeycreepers are the most likely to compete with hummingbirds for nectar from the forest flowers (Colwell et al., 1974). In Africa and Asia, acrobatic, non-hovering sunbirds (Nectariniidae) are very important as pollinators (Wolf, 1975; Faegri and Van der Pijl, 1978; etc.), in Asia they occur along with white-eyes (Zosteropidae). In the Indo-Malayan region, the honey-eaters (Meliphagidae) are involved; in Hawaii the Drepanididae feed on the nectar of forest trees (*Metrosideros*, *Sophora*, etc.). Rather different in their method of taking nectar (and, also, in their utilization of pollen as a protein-rich food source) are the Australian brush-tongued lorikeets (Trichoglossidae).

In Costa Rican wet forests, studies by Slud (1960), Linhart (1973), and Stiles (1975) have shown that, within the Trochilidae, male birds of many species defend feeding territories in forest clearings, etc., while the non-territorial "hermits" behave more like trapliners in the forest.

Toledo (1977) has pointed out for the rain forests of Vera Cruz, Mexico, that the hummingbirds tend to visit trees in the lower strata, as well as shrubs and herbs (the latter of considerable stature, such as *Heliconia* species). By contrast, the taller trees and more highly placed lianas tend to be visited by the perching birds. The perchers show most interest in nectar-feeding during periods of low fruit abundance and minimum insect availability. The same author (Toledo, 1975) reported on the variability through the year of nectar supplies to hummingbirds and the relation of this to their foraging and breeding behavior.

In a cloud forest area of Costa Rica, Feinsinger (1976, 1978) studied the foraging patterns of hummingbirds (mostly in disturbed communities) and related these to the patterns of nectar provision by the plants. Feinsinger and Colwell (1978) have related foraging behavior differences within and between species at different altitudes to concomitant changes in temperature, air density, and other factors.

Van der Pijl (1937) and Faegri and Van der Pijl (1978) have pointed to the differences in floral organization between paleotropical perching bird flowers and inflorescences, on one hand, and those of neotropical hummingbird flowers, on the other. Particularly, there is the provision of a standing place in the former, contrasting with the open space around the flower that can be occupied by a hovering hummingbird. This difference is also to be seen in a comparison between hummingbird and passerine bird-pollinated species of *Erythrina* in the neotropics (Cruden and Toledo, 1977).

Some ornithophilous tree species have unusually large cup-shaped flowers (e.g. *Spathodea campanulata*, Bignoniaceae, from the deciduous forests of West Africa, where these may be 10 cm in diameter and equally deep). These hold so much nectar (and rain water) that they can be used as drinking places by larger birds.

The rewards that are provided to visiting birds by tropical forest flowers are discussed in the next section. They may be produced year-round, thus feeding resident birds (cf. Stiles, 1978, for hummingbirds), or for part of the year, when they are used by migrant birds, which may move, on a seasonal basis, latitudinally or altitudinally (Janzen, 1975).

(4) Bats and other mammals as pollinators. The first notice of bats as pollinators in tropical forest areas appears to have been made by W. Burck, in the Buitenzorg (now Bogor) Botanic Garden, in 1892. From then until about 1954, relatively little attention was given to these crepuscular and nocturnal pollinators (except by Van der Pijl, 1936, in Southeast Asia). Since then, electronic flash photography and, still more recently, the utilization of image-intensifying, night-viewing devices as well as radio tracking instruments have made possible more frequent and detailed studies and have given us a true appreciation of the extent of this pollination system that is almost restricted to the tropics. Jaeger (1954), Baker and Harris (1957, 1959), Harris and Baker (1958, 1959), Carvalho (1960), Vogel (1958, 1968–69), Baker (1970, 1973), Ayensu (1974), Heithaus et al. (1974, 1975), Sazima and Sazima (1977, 1978), Lack (1978), and Gould (1977, 1978) are among those who have contributed examples and discussion of bat-pollination in tropical forests. A fine general review and discussion is provided by Start and Marshall (1976), who also include much first-hand data from Malaya.

Flower visitation by bats in the paleotropics is restricted to members of the suborder Megachiroptera (while the members of the suborder Microchiroptera are insectivorous there) (Baker and Harris, 1957; Vogel, 1968–69; Baker, 1973). However, the Megachiroptera did not spread to the neotropics and the Microchiroptera (which did) found a vacant niche in the tropical forests of the Americas and radiated into it (Baker, 1973). Sussman and Raven (1978) have suggested that flower visitation by non-volant forest mammals preceded bat pollination, and was largely replaced by bat pollination when the more effective flying mammals became available. If such was the case, the remnants of this older mammal involvement may still be seen in Madagascar, where lemurs may be pollen vectors, and in Australia, where marsupials are certainly involved (Morcombe, 1968, etc). Faegri and Van der Pijl (1978, p. 122) provide further examples of pollination by non-volant mammals.

Bat-pollinated plants in tropical forests are usually trees, lianas or, sometimes, epiphytes, with inflorescences or individual flowers that hang on stout peduncles or pedicels so that there is flying room for the bats clear of the foliage or branches. Examples are *Parkia clappertoniana* (Fabaceae, Mimosoideae) (Baker and Harris, 1957; Baker, 1978a) and *Mucuna andreana* (Fabaceae, Faboideae) (Baker, 1970). Alternatively, the flowers may be clustered near the tips of branches, so that a bat may land on the inflorescence and crawl over it, drinking nectar and eating pollen, as in *Ceiba pentandra* (Bombacaceae) (Harris and Baker, 1959; Baker, 1963). This arrangement is seen in bizarre form in the stiffly projecting inflorescence-rachises of *Oroxylum indicum* (Bignoniaceae) in Malaya (Gould, 1978). Some bat flowers are borne cauliflorously (e.g. *Crescentia* spp., Bignoniaceae). Many bat-pollinated trees flower in the leafless condition (which allows freer flying by the bats) and this may be part of the reason why bat pollination appears to be more frequent in dry forest areas than in the wet forests.

There are two quite different bat flower syn-

dromes (Faegri and Van der Pijl, 1978). Along with nocturnal anthesis, drab or whitish color, and a strong, rather sour odor, there may be either large-mouthed, sturdy single flowers (e.g. *Kigelia*, Bignoniaceae) or brush-type flowers (e.g. *Adansonia digitata*, Bombacaceae) or inflorescences (e.g. *Parkia clappertoniana*). A very large volume of rather dilute nectar is provided at night and pollen is also provided in substantial quantity, an important item because it forms the major supply of protein-building amino acids for many bats.

In collecting these rewards, bats may fly great distances. Start and Marshall (1976) found evidence that the megachiropteran *Eonycteris spelaea* may forage on the mangrove *Sonneratia alba* (Sonneratiaceae) at more than 38 km from its roost. *Macroglossus minimus* forages only on this mangrove and is restricted to roosting within 3 km of the food source. Gould (1977) has estimated that, also in Malaya, *Pteropus vampirus*, of the same suborder of bats, may fly long distances between its roost and trees of *Durio zibethinus*, in which it will forage. Foraging by Microchiroptera in the neotropics may also be over as much as 16 km (Janzen, 1975).

In the neotropics, small microchiropteran bats may forage singly, as with *Glossophaga soricina* on *Markea* sp. (Solanaceae) (reported in error as a species of the neighboring genus *Trianaea* in Baker, 1973), or in flocks, as in *Artibeus jamaicensis* on *Bauhinia pauletia* (Fabaceae, Faboideae; Heithaus et al., 1974). Sazima and Sazima (1977) noted that, in southeastern Brazil, *Phyllostomus discolor* may forage solitarily or in a group, depending upon the amounts of nectar available.

There is circumstantial evidence that foraging by some neotropical bats follows a traplining pattern (Baker, 1973; Heithaus et al., 1975; Sazima and Sazima, 1978). In the paleotropics, "opportunistic" feeding by megachiropteran bats at "mass flowering" trees may be more common (e.g. *Ceiba pentandra*, *Parkia clappertoniana*) (Baker, 1973), but Gould (1978) has demonstrated traplining by Megachiroptera, as well, in Malaya (see, also, Start and Marshall, 1976). Gould (1978) also claims evidence of territorial defense by *Eonycteris*.

Howell (1978) showed that bat-flower producing trees in Guanacaste (Costa Rica) produced flows of nectar at different times during the night, so that the bat visitors could be specialists for a certain amount of time and, therefore, probably more efficient cross-pollinators, yet generalists in acquiring their nourishment from a variety of sources. She also found evidence that the bats may carry the pollen of these different kinds of plants on different parts of the body, again increasing the efficiency of the bats as pollen vectors. Gould (1978) has shown that *Oroxylum indicum* and *Musa acuminata* may also "co-operate" in feeding the megachiropteran bat *Eonycteris spelaea* in Malaya.

The need for flowers or soft fruits to sustain a bat through the year is filled in the paleotropics by a procession of flowering and fruiting by unrelated species where this is permitted by the climate (Allen, 1939; Van der Pijl, 1969; Baker, 1973; Start and Marshall, 1976; Gould, 1978). In West Africa, *Eidolon helvum* may achieve this end by flock migration from flowering area to flowering area (Allen, 1939). The year-round behavior of neotropical flower- and fruit-visiting Microchiroptera has been considered by Heithaus et al. (1975). In this, *Carollia perspicillata* may sustain itself largely on fruit during the wet season while *Glossophaga soricina* may retain a nectarivorous propensity.

Attractants for pollinators

(1) Color. A great variety of colors and color patterns exist in tropical forests although a blaze of color may only be visible from above at certain times of the year, e.g. when *Cochlospermum* or *Tabebuia* crowns are in flower in the dry forests of Central America, or when *Warszewiczia* (Rubiaceae) is in flower in wetter forests. Red is the commonest color among bird-pollinated species (both hummingirds and passerines). Butterfly flowers range from white to yellow and pink (and, even, red) but are not blue. Moth flowers are usually pale in color, or white. Bee flowers may be almost any color, except that pure reds (to the human eye) are usually accompanied by ultraviolet reflection (invisible to us). Wasp flowers are often purplish-red.

Although most of the colors are associated with pollinator kinds in the same manner as in temperate regions, a few new correlations have been discovered (as well as those already referred to in bat-pollinated flowers). Thus, in wet and dry forests of Costa Rica, several moth-adapted species have pink, red or lavender-colored flowers instead of the white or cream color that is usually part of the moth-pollination syndrome (Haber, Frankie, Opler and Bawa, unpubl.). Examples from the dry forest include *Calliandra* spp. and *Pithecellobium saman* (both Fabaceae, Mimosoideae), *Hura crepitans* (Euphorbiaceae), *Schoepfia schreberi* (Olacaceae) and *Sloanea ternifolia* (Elaeocarpaceae). In the wet forest, *Guarea* spp. (Meliaceae), *Pithecellobium gigantifolium* and *P. catenatum* are representative. In West Africa, Harris and Baker (1958) saw and photographed sphingid moths visiting the deep purple flowers of *Kigelia africana* (Bignoniaceae).

Conversely, several wasp-pollinated tree species display cream-colored flowers instead of the usual purplish, fleshy textured corollas, e.g. *Casearia sylvestris* and *Xylosma* sp. (Flacourtiaceae), and *Karwinskia calderoni* and *Ziziphus guatemalensis* (Rhamnaceae) (Haber, Frankie, Opler and Bawa, unpubl.). Numerous other species with white or cream-colored flowers are pollinated by a combination of small bees and wasps (e.g. many *Cordia* species; Opler et al., 1976a).

More sophisticated studies of floral color and patterning that take into account ultraviolet reflectance or absorption, changes of color pattern with ageing of the flower, and the relation of these variables to the foraging patterns of flower visitors are still uncommon. Kevan (1978) has reviewed floral coloration in regard to anthecology. Barrows (1977) has studied the color change (from dark lavender to white) that occurs in flowers of *Pachyptera hymenaea* (Bignoniaceae) when pollen and nectar are no longer available, but the flowers still receive visits from bees while the stigma remains receptive, so the biological significance of the change is not clear. For many problems experiments may provide an answer. An indicator of what may be required is demonstrated by the experiments of Jones and Buchmann (1974) on *Caesalpinia eriostachys* and *Parkinsonia aculeata* (Fabaceae, Caesalpinioideae) on plants in nature. They showed that only one petal in the flower is ultraviolet absorbent and, by manipulation of the position of this petal (by surgery and reattachment), they demonstrated that the landing of the usual pollinatory bees can be disoriented.

Jones and Rich (1972) have drawn attention to a remarkable feature of the hummingbird pollination adaptation of *Columnea florida* (Gesneriaceae) in Costa Rica, where the birds are attracted by red spots on the leaves behind which the flowers are hidden. There is a similarity here to the bright red coloration of leaves and bracts in the vicinity of the flowers in many tropical euphorbias.

Future studies of flower coloration in the context of pollinator attraction may be undertaken on a family basis, such as those begun by Gentry (1974a) for the Bignoniaceae and by Prance and collaborators (Prance, 1976, etc.) for the Lecythidaceae.

(2) Scent of flowers. In tropical forests there is the usual association of a sweet scent with bee- and butterfly-pollinated flowers, and the usual absence of scent in bird-pollinated species. Aminoid odors are associated with beetle pollination, and fly-pollinated flowers (including the monstrous flowers of *Rafflesia*) have a familiar tendency to smell unpleasantly in the human nose. As Van der Pijl (1936) first pointed out, the smell of bat-pollinated flowers (as well as bat-distributed fruits) is usually rather sour, and has even been compared to the smell of the bats themselves. Moth-pollinated species usually have a sweet smell (as do their temperate relatives) but this cannot be relied upon because the sour scent of *Durio zibethinus* (Bombacaceae) flowers attracts moths as well as the expected bats (Baker, 1970). Flowers of the bat-pollinated *Kigelia africana*, in West Africa, have a foul smell (and a reddish-purple color) but they also attract moths as well as bats (Harris and Baker, 1958).

The work of C.H. Dodson, R.L. Dressler and their associates (summed up in Dodson, 1975) and of Vogel (1968) on the collection of scent substances from the petals of various tropical orchids by male euglossine bees has shown that characteristic combinations of "essential oils" are differentially attractive to bee species, so that there is assortative mating by the pollinia and stigmas of these orchids.

Overland (1960) has studied the endogenous rhythms involved in the opening and odor production of flowers of the nocturnally blooming *Cestrum nocturnum* (Solanaceae). Such endogenous rhythms, and their perfection into a 24-h cycle by environmental factors could be looked for with advantage in diurnal species as well. Salas (1974), reported that the nectar of *Inga vera* var. *spuria* (Fabaceae, Mimosoideae) is odorless when first produced (in late afternoon) and is attractive to a wide range of flower visitors. However, it becomes sour smelling after a couple of hours and, then, the flowers are visited by bats.

Rewards to flower visitors

(1) Nectar. (a) Chemistry of nectar. Chemical aspects of the pollination biology of woody plants in the tropics have been described by Baker (1978a), with emphasis on the chemistry of nectar. Nectars are now known to be much more than the sugar water of popular belief; nectars contain some or all of the following chemicals: sugars, proteins, amino acids, lipids, antioxidant organic acids, a variety of other nutritive organic substances in very small amounts, as well as other chemicals that may have a deterrent effect on some potential nectar-feeders (see section on deterrents below) (Baker and Baker, 1975; Baker, 1978a).

The energy-producing or tissue-building values of nectar depend upon the volume of nectar and the concentration in it of the chemicals in question (see below). There is some evidence from samples taken in the dry forest of Costa Rica that the concentration of sugars in nectar increases from the base to the apex of a tree (with a reverse gradient suggested for amino acids) (Baker, 1978a).

The ratios of sucrose to hexose sugars in nectars show a relationship to the nature of the pollinator, being high for hummingbird flowers and for moth flowers, but low for passerine bird-pollinated flowers and those pollinated by bats (Baker, 1978a; Baker and Baker, 1981). For butterfly flowers, the sucrose dominance is less clearly marked, and, for bee flowers, it is quite variable. Sometimes there is a strong phylogenetic constraint; nectars of the Asteraceae are usually hexose-dominated, those of the Ranunculaceae are sucrose-rich, irrespective of pollinator type (Baker and Baker, 1981).

The concentration of amino acids in nectar tends to be greater if nectar is the only (or the chief) source of protein-building material for the usual flower visitors than it is if the visitors have an abundant alternative (Baker, 1978a). In Costa Rica, settling moths, butterflies, and wasps (excepting some social wasps) depend upon nectar for their own nourishment, and the nectars of the flowers they visit have relatively high amino acid concentrations. The flower-visiting bats of the neotropics make use of fruit juices and pollen as sources of protein-building materials and consume some insects; the nectars they consume are weak in amino acids. Hummingbirds, particularly females at times of reproduction, are avid insect-eaters. Flowers could not possibly provide them with a significant alternative supply of protein-building materials, and they do not.

Nectars of woody tropical plants may contain from 2 to 24 detectable amino acids, according to the species concerned (Baker, 1978a). There is a more frequent representation of "non-protein" amino acids among floral nectars of tropical trees and lianas (55%) than in temperate plants (36%). If these amino acids have the toxic effect that they are believed to have when they occur in seeds (Rehr et al., 1973a, b), they may play a deterrent role to inappropriate flower visitors.

In 1969, Vogel pointed out that a number of South American plants, including members of the tropical forest family Malpighiaceae, produce drops of oil that are collected by certain anthophorine bees. The glands that exude these oils he called "elaiophors" and he suggested that this oil production is an *alternative* to nectar production. The bees, including those of the genus *Centris*, convey the oil to their nests where Vogel (1969, 1971, 1974) believes that it is mixed with pollen and used in feeding the larvae.

However, in 1973, Baker and Baker (1973, 1975) reported lipid-containing nectar — an aqueous liquid that contains lipids in suspension and also contains the usual sugars and amino acids, as well as other water-soluble substances — and it is suggested that Vogel's oil "alternative" to nectar is really a nectar that is extraordinarily rich in lipids. In lowland Costa Rican forests, lipid-containing nectars seem to be found most frequently in the trees. Among the trees and lianas, nectar lipids were found particularly frequently in the Caesalpinioideae and Bignoniaceae (Baker, 1978a).

Other substances in floral nectar, potentially important in the nutrition of flower visitors in the forests, include antioxidants (most notably ascorbic acid, vitamin C), and these are particularly often present in lipid-containing nectars, where they may prevent rancidity from developing (Baker and Baker, 1975). Also, they, like almost all the chemicals mentioned, may affect the "taste" of the nectar.

(b) Nectar volume and sugar concentration. The sugar concentrations of nectars from flowers adapted to different classes of flower visitors range widely (Fahn, 1949; Meeuse, 1961; Percival, 1965, 1974; Baker, 1975, 1977, 1978a; Cruden, 1979), while the volumes of nectars in flowers with different pollinatory adaptations ranges over several degrees of magnitude (Cruden et al., 1981; Opler, 1981). These two variables are inexorably linked, since the amount of sugar produced in nectar is a product of volume times concentration (the latter usually measured by refractometer in "sucrose equivalents"; Baker, 1975, 1977, 1978a; Cruden et al., 1981; Bolten et al., 1979).

Sugar concentrations of tropical forest nectars range from 5 to 80% (sucrose equivalents — as weight per total weight). In a series of determinations in the dry forest (in the dry season), it was found (Baker, 1978a) that hummingbird, sphingid moth and bat flower nectars had lower concentrations ($\bar{x} = 21\%$, 24% and 17%, respectively) than butterfly flower nectars ($\bar{x} = 29\%$) which, in turn, were less concentrated than that from settling moth, and bee flowers ($\bar{x} = 41\%$ and 46%, respectively). The low concentration of sugars in the hummingbird flower nectars may seem out of keeping with the high metabolic rates of these small birds, but at least three possible explanations have been put forward. Baker (1975) postulated that low viscosity is necessary to allow the quick uptake of nectar by hummingbirds, sphingids and bats which only spend brief periods at the flowers (and, in the case of the hummingbirds and sphingid moths the nectar must flow into a very narrow tube when being removed from the flower). Alternatively, it has been suggested by W.A. Calder (pers. comm., 1980) that a dilute nectar, taken up by the birds in large enough volume to satisfy their energy requirements, could be valuable because it relieves water stress that the birds might otherwise be under. This explanation may not be applicable in humid tropical forests. Thirdly, it is suggested by Bolten and Feinsinger (1978) that the exudation of a dilute nectar will discourage bees from "robbing" the flowers that need hummingbirds for successful pollination. However, the sugar concentrations in the nectars (from Trinidad) that they assume are too low for bees to bother with average 21.3%, which is not likely to be ignored by bees. Nevertheless, it is true that bees, wasps, butterflies and flies prefer and can deal with more concentrated nectar, and may even regurgitate liquid to dilute very concentrated nectar before ingesting it.

Nectar volume of tropical forest flowers usually increases concomitantly with floral biomass (Opler, 1981), although there are notable exceptions: for example, *Cochlospermum vitifolium* (Cochlospermaceae) and *Bixa orellana* (Bixaceae) in the neotropical dry forests have flowers as much as 7 cm in diameter but produce no nectar. Many small bee, butterfly, or fly flowers, such as some *Cordia* spp., produce less than a microliter of nectar in a day while, at the other extreme, the large flowers of the neotropical balsa tree (*Ochroma pyramidalis*, Bombacaceae) may produce 15 ml in the one night that they are open. In Asia, the staminate flowers of *Musa paradisiaca* (Musaceae) produce several milliliters during a single night (Fahn, 1949), while a single inflorescence of the West African *Parkia clappertoniana* can produce as much as 15 ml (which all runs into a common receptacle) in a night (Baker and Harris, 1957). *Ochroma*, *Musa* and *Parkia* are all pollinated by bats. Gould (1978) has some other figures for Malayan bat-pollinated flowers: *Oroxylum indicum*, 1.8 ml; *Durio zibethinus*, 0.36 ml; *Musa acuminata*, 0.63 ml.

The volume of nectar provided by the flowers is obviously related to the size of the flower visitors (Opler, 1981), and there is, not unexpectedly, an inverse correlation between nectar sugar concentration and volume of nectar provided; however, the sugar output, even in the face of dilution, is usually clearly greater in the flowers that provide voluminous nectar for relatively big birds, bats and moths.

In the Arctic, Hocking (1953, 1968) calculated the nectar sugar production per hectare of arctic tundra and has estimated what this can support in insect flight with rather surprising results, e.g. that one catkin of *Salix arctophila* (Salicaceae) provides for 950 "mosquito km" each day. It would be most helpful to have correspondingly quantitative data for tropical forests.

(2) Pollen. Pollen obtained by flower visitation is used nutritionally by beetles, by flies, by bees (for themselves and for their brood) and by bats, but apparently very rarely, if at all, by most flower-visiting birds (the lorikeets of Australia are exceptional in deliberately ingesting pollen; Churchill and Christensen, 1970). Gilbert (1972, 1975) has

shown that female butterflies of the genus *Heliconius* make use of pollen by collecting a sample of it from staminate flowers of the dioecious vines in the genera *Anguria* and *Gurania* (Cucurbitaceae) and regurgitating nectar on to it so that amino acids diffuse out into the nectar and are then inbibed by the butterfly. However, as yet, this phenomenon seems to be restricted to the neotropical forests where *Heliconius* lives (see, also, Dunlap-Pianka et al., 1977; DeVries, 1979).

Many flowers of forest plants are used by bees as sources of nectar and pollen, while some offer *only* pollen as a reward to visitors. In neotropical forests, notable examples are *Cochlospermum vitifolium* (Cochlospermaceae) among the trees, *Bixa orellana* (Bixaceae), *Solanum* spp. (Solanaceae) and many Melastomataceae among the shrubs. Nectarless *Cassia* spp. (Fabaceae, Caesalpinioideae) are to be found as all life forms from herbs to trees. All produce abundant pollen.

Nectarless flowers of members of the Annonaceae may be very attractive to beetles. By contrast, "advanced" nectarless flowers such as those of *Cassia* and *Swartzia* and the Melastomataceae are very closely adapted to pollen-collecting bees which are serviced by "feeding anthers", distinct from the "pollinating" anthers that deposit pollen on the body of the bee while it is feeding. In *Solanum*, the pollen escapes from the anthers through terminal pores and such pollen is "buzzed" from the anthers by bees that vibrate their bodies while in contact with the androecium and shake out the dust-like pollen.

Very little is known yet of the chemical composition of the pollen of tropical forest plants, but it is suggested by Howell (1974) that the pollen taken as food by bats may be especially rich in proteins, and this may be related to the low concentration of amino acids in bat flower nectar (Baker, 1977, 1978a). Much profitable work could be done in the general area of pollen chemistry of tropical forest plants and a start has been made on this recently (H.G. Baker and I. Baker, unpubl.).

(3) Other solid rewards. Solid "food bodies", providing nourishment for flower visitors with chewing mouthparts (and, possibly, deflecting the attention of those visitors away from the androecium and gynoecium), have been described for a number of tropical species. Thus, *Freycinetia arborea*

(Pandanaceae) feeds birds by its fleshy bracts in Southeast Asia. These birds, and rats which feed at the inflorescences in Hawaii, may be pollinators, as well as agents of destruction (Faegri and Van der Pijl, 1978).

Also, in the "trapping" inflorescences of some tropical Araceae, and even in the non-trapping *Amorphophallus variabilis*, the pollinatory beetles and other insects may consume solid matter produced at the bottom of the spathe. Many cases are known of the raising of a brood of beetles in the fleshy tissues of long-lived flowers, or more often, inflorescences (Faegri and Van der Pijl, 1978), but there is an unstable balance here between the advantages of pollination and the destruction of tissues.

Also falling within the category of solid rewards are the gall flowers inside a *Ficus* syconium, without which the complicated, obligatory life-cycle interaction between plant and agaonid wasp cannot be completed.

(4) Deception of flower visitors. In most plants, the advertisement of the existence of tangible rewards to flower visitors through the color, scent and shape of the flower is backed up by the provision of those rewards (usually nectar or pollen). However, deception is well-known in pollination biology, particularly in relation to insects with poorly developed discriminatory powers.

Partial deception certainly exists among tropical trees in those cases where staminate flowers of a monoecious or dioecious species provide a reward (nectar or pollen or both) while the pistillate flowers do not. The pistillate flowers must be visited "by mistake" by pollinators anticipating the same reward they get from staminate flowers (Baker, 1976). Examples of "mistake" pollination are provided by the species of *Carica* (Caricaceae), where the staminate flowers offer both pollen and nectar to a wide range of visitors (hummingbirds, bees, flies, butterflies and moths), but the pistillate flowers provide no reward, and are visited fleetingly by moths in the semi-darkness of the early evening. Other cases of "mistake" pollination are probably to be found elsewhere in tropical forests.

Clear cases of *total* deception, where no reward at all is provided, appear to be very rare at best among tropical trees, and it has been suggested (Baker, 1978a) that for a large tree the energy

outlay for flowering is so considerable that a small saving in not providing a reward to pollinators might be offset by the risk that the pollinators would not be deceived. Obviously, we need more information about the energy costs of providing rewards.

Deterrents to inappropriate flower visitors

(1) Physical deterrents. When flowers are adapted to particular pollinators, it is to be expected that there will be selection of features that reduce the availability of nectar and pollen to non-pollinators, or to those who would not be efficient as pollen vectors. In some cases, this is achieved by a change in floral morphology. Thus, butterfly and settling moth visitors to a hummingbird flower may be discouraged by lack of a standing platform in a tubular flower that is held horizontally. Conversely, a long, very narrow corolla-tube may suit Lepidoptera but discriminate against hummingbirds whose beaks require a broader tube. All long-tubed flowers protect their nectar from shorter-tongued bees, flies, beetles, etc., and a similar effect is produced by secreting the nectar into a spur. Crawling insects are often kept out of these tubes by an arrangement of hairs (e.g. *Mussaenda* spp., Rubiaceae, in the paleotropics; Baker, 1958).

Thoroughly illegitimate visitors, so-called nectar thieves, pierce the base of the corolla or the spurs or chew through unopened buds to obtain rich nectar or pollen rewards. Bees, beetles and hummingbirds (as well as other birds) may fall into this category; they play no role in pollination. Discouragement of such losses of the legitimate visitors' reward has sometimes been achieved by especially thick, clasping calyces or bracts (e.g. some Cucurbitaceae for the calyx, and many Acanthaceae for the bracts).

(2) Chemical deterrents. The chemistry of nectar is only beginning to be worked out, but it may be assumed that alkaloids, phenolics, glycosides and non-protein amino acids would be unpleasant or definitely toxic to some flower visitors. All have been found in the floral nectars of tropical forest plants (Baker and Baker, 1975; Baker, 1977, 1978a). A comparison of the proportions of floral nectars containing non-protein amino acids, alkaloids and phenolic substances, respectively, between samples from tropical forest species in Costa

Rica and samples from California and from the alpine tundra of the Colorado Rocky Mountains showed that the tropical nectars have a considerably higher proportion of each (Baker, 1977, 1978a).

Recently, there has been much controversy about whether or how tropical forest species keep their floral nectar from being taken by non-pollinating ants (Janzen, 1977c; Baker and Baker, 1978; Feinsinger and Swarm, 1978; Shubart and Anderson, 1978). It seems most likely that in some species a closed flower may "hide" nectar away from the ants while, in lesser frequency, there may be ant-repulsive chemicals in the nectar or in tissues adjacent to it (so that the nectar may be easily contaminated by these substances, W. Haber, pers. comm., 1979; see also Guerrant and Fiedler, 1981). Van der Pijl (1955), who noticed and demonstrated ant-repulsion by petals, mentioned especially odoriferous substances. However, in some cases, ants *do* enter the flowers and remove nectar.

Prevention of floral *tissue* destruction by herbivores by the presence of clusters of calcium oxalate crystals or an accumulation of tannins in appropriate parts of the flower is suggested by morphological and anatomical work of Uhl and Moore (1977) for several palm species.

(3) Biotic deterrents. The concept of the "ant guard" — ants that feed at extra-floral nectaries and protect flowers from the loss of their floral nectar to illegitimate flower visitors (most obviously those that would bore through the corolla to remove the nectar) — appears to have been introduced by Van der Pijl (1955). Substantiation of its efficacy in preserving the fecundity of the plants is provided by experimental studies by Keeler (1977) on *Ipomoea carnea* (Convolvulaceae), by Bentley (1977a) on *Bixa orellana* (Bixaceae), and by Schemske (1978) on *Costus woodsonii* (Zingiberaceae). Bentley (1977b) has reviewed the broader subject of protection of plants from various kinds of herbivores by ants.

Intra- and interspecific interactions between bees visiting tropical forest trees are receiving attention at present (Frankie et al., 1976; Frankie, 1976). These interactions vary from simple one-on-one aggressive encounters between individuals to mass activity involving groups of individuals (Frankie and Baker, 1974).

The one-on-one encounters, which often lead to one of the individuals being ejected from a flower and, occasionally, being pushed entirely off a plant, have been observed commonly among solitary bees of the Anthophorinae (especially *Centris* spp.) and Bombinae (some members of the Euglossinae) of the Central American tropics (Frankie, in prep.). Certain species of stingless (social) bees in the same forests are also known to display intra- and interspecific aggressive behavior (Johnson and Hubbell, 1974). In all these cases, the encounters are food-related and Johnson and Hubbell suggest that interspecific differences in aggression among coexisting stingless bees have determined differences in foraging behavior, at least on a short-term basis.

Some anthophilous insects are known to establish defended territories adjacent to floral resources in tropical forests, while those set up by male hummingbirds have been studied by Stiles and Wolf (1970), Linhart (1973) and Stiles (1975). This must reduce pollen flow between territories (cutting it out except for the cross-pollinatory activities of females and other intruders into the territory that remain for a short while before being chased away and trying their luck in another territory). Similar interactions have been observed in beetles (Frankie, 1976; Rauscher and Fowler, 1979) and in ants (G.W. Frankie, pers. obs.). Many observations of territoriality have been made on solitary bees (mostly Anthophoridae) in Central America (Frankie and Baker, 1974; Frankie, 1976, and unpubl.; Frankie et al., 1976) and in south America (Dodson and Frymire, 1961; Dodson, 1962, 1975).

In one study area in Costa Rican dry forest, Frankie (in prep.) observed that almost all tree species adapted for pollination by large bees (about 35 species) had one or more bee territories (mostly of *Centris* species). These appear to differ from the hummingbird territories in that they are related primarily to the mating behavior, but, again, they lead not only to frequent pollination *within* the territory, but also to occasional pollen transfer by displaced bees to other trees.

Foraging in groups by some "solitary" bees of the Anthophorinae has been observed in the dry forest in Costa Rica (Frankie and Baker, 1974; Frankie, 1976). Such foraging may cause a substantial stir among other non-grouped foraging bees to the point that they abandon given flower clusters and may move to other trees.

Gentry (1978) called attention to another type of aggresive interaction among flower visitors to mass-flowering species in the tropics. He observed that, along with anthophilous insects, insectivorous birds were also attracted to these large floral resources. The ensuing interaction between predators and prey resulted in the dispersal of the latter, who might carry pollen to another tree.

Certain tropical bees (mostly Anthophoridae) have been observed visiting some flowers on a plant but ignoring or only briefly touching others. Particularly where the presence or absence of nectar is not visible to an approaching bee, it is possible that an odorous mark left by a previous visitor is responsible in some cases. Recent temperate zone work with carpenter bees (*Xylocopa* spp.) on *Passiflora* (a genus that is well-represented in tropical forests) has shown that female bees mark flowers with a secretion from Dufour's gland (Frankie and Vinson, 1977; Vinson et al., 1978). Marked flowers can be recognized for up to fourteen minutes. Similar avoidance of flowers that appear to have been scent-marked has been observed with *Xylocopa gualanensis* females on *Passiflora pulchella* in the lowland dry forest of Costa Rica, and with males of *Epicharis* sp. on *Passiflora adenopoda* at a mid-elevation (1500 m) cloud forest (Frankie, unpubl.).

In the paleotropics, Burkill (1907) in India, and Van der Pijl (1954, and pers. comm., 1975) in Indonesia, have observed female xylocopid bees avoiding flowers that have been visited recently by themselves or other conspecific individuals.

Avoidance of recently visited flowers not only implies more efficient foraging by the insect but also may contribute to an increase in cross-pollination. This result may also be achieved, on a rather longer time scale, by changes in flower color (or of "nectar guides" in the flower) as a signal that further visits by anthophilous animals would be unrewarding (and possibly damaging to the plant). Such floral color changes may be seen, for example, in *Gloriosa superba* (Liliaceae) or some species of *Hibiscus* (Malvaceae).

SEED SETTING AND VOLUNTARY FRUIT SHEDDING

Flowering, even the production of hermaphrodite flowers, is not always followed by fruit and seed maturation in tropical forests. Thus, in *Hymenaea courbaril* (Fabaceae, Caesalpinioideae), although flowering may take place annually, fruit setting on a particular tree is abundant only in one year out of about five (Janzen, 1978a). In the intervening years, the plant functions primarily as a donor of male gametes. "Sub-adult" trees also act as pollen producers only, and the production of seed is also diminished in the forest relative to trees growing in the open (Janzen, 1978a).

Related to this is the common phenomenon of the shedding of developing fruits at some time before their maturation. This is particularly obvious where very large numbers of small flowers are produced, as in the subfamily Mimosoideae of the Fabaceae. For example, in *Parkia clappertoniana* in West Africa, there may be as many as 2000 potentially fertile flowers in a single inflorescence, but it is rare for more than four or five fruits to form from each inflorescence (Baker and Harris, 1957).

In the case of *Cassia grandis* (Fabaceae, Caesalpinioideae), in Central America, less than 1% of the flowers produce fruits (even in a "seed" year), and in intervening years few or none are formed. The seed crop takes a year or more to mature (Janzen, 1978a).

The length of time which fruits and their contained seeds take to mature on trees in tropical forests varies from a few days to a year, as in *Pithecellobium saman* and *Enterolobium cyclocarpum* (Fabaceae, Mimosoideae) (Janzen, 1978a).

Smythe (1970) made a careful study of the fruits and seeds that fell over a period of seventeen months in the forest on Barro Colorado Island (Panama). Small-seeded fruits matured in sequence throughout the year, so that the birds that feed on them were kept fully occupied, and competition for their services was minimized. Where the fruits contained large seeds, the chances of damage to the seeds by frugivorous animals (and by seed predators) was increased and, for them, synchronous fruiting within and between species had the advantage of "saturating the market", especially where scatter-hoarding animals, such as agoutis (*Dasyprocta punctata*) were involved. Caches of seeds that are forgotten may be able to germinate.

A striking feature of fruits produced by tropical forest trees is the usually rapid maturation up to a certain point, followed by a period of suspended development. An interesting case where differential speeds of ripening occurs in two species of the same tree genus is found in *Spondias* (Anacardiaceae) (Croat, 1974). *S. radlkoferi*, with fruits that are green and not sweet, contrasts with the probable ancestral species *S. mombin*, whose fruits are orange-colored and sweet. Where the species occur together on Barro Colorado Island, *S. mombin* matures its fruits in the early part of the rainy season, but *S. radlkoferi* takes longer to reach maturity and does so at a time (late in the rainy season) when there is a dearth of food for foraging mammals and so, despite its unattractive color and non-sweet taste, it is actively foraged by several species of monkeys and by agoutis.

Sequential ripening of fruit on a larger scale is shown by Snow (1965) for eighteen species of *Miconia* (Melastomataceae) in a single valley in Trinidad. His interpretation is that this has resulted from natural selection that has reduced competition for the attention of dispersal agents, in this case birds that eat the fruits and transport the seeds endozootically. However, this could also have been the indirect result of concomitantly spaced flowering periods.

SEED DISPERSAL

Methods of seed dispersal

Dispersal of seeds is an essential part of the reproductive process, and it has been the subject of study for as long as human beings have been concerned with agricultural, horticultural and forestry operations. For many tropical crop trees there has been selection for characters that *reduce* dispersal, as, for example, the selection (probably by West Africans) of trees of *Ceiba pentandra* with pods that do not split open at maturity, for which reason the kapok can be harvested easily (Baker, 1965b).

Where naturalists have been interested in wild plants, until recently they have measured the efficacy of seed dispersal by the likelihood that it will deposit a seed a long way from the parent plant. The more recent view is that, although long-distance dispersal may be important in increasing the range of a species, for most purposes dispersal that is enough to carry the seed to a germination point sufficiently far away from the parent plant to escape from competition with it (and to escape

from seed or seedling predators that may be centered on the parent plant) is most appropriate, for it will tend to land the seed in the same, or a similar, microhabitat to that of the parent. A review of pre-dispersal and post-dispersal seed predation is given by Janzen (1978a).

Consequently, we may expect to see the results of selection of mechanisms that carry most seeds to a moderate distance from the parent plant, with occasional seeds carried to a greater distance. Dispersal will not always be uniform in all directions and the area covered by the seed rain is often referred to as the "seed shadow", an unfortunate term because most "shadows", for example light shadows or rain shadows, refer to an absence of light and rain, respectively.

As a result of the forces against survival of seedlings very close to the parent trees, conspecific trees in a tropical forest may be expected to approximate a uniform dispersion, and evidence favoring this has been put forward by Janzen (1970) and by Connell (1971). It should be noted, however, that a very recent study of dry forest tree dispersions suggests that many species have more or less clumped distributions (Hubbell, 1979; see also Ashton, 1969).

The actual methods of seed dispersal in tropical forests may involve wind, water, or dispersal by fruit-eating or seed-eating birds or mammals. The fruits or seeds may be carried by the animal vectors directly from the tree, or fruits may fall to the ground and, splitting open there, enable the seeds to be dispersed secondarily by running animals. Especially unusual is the reported dispersal of Amazonian forest species by fish swallowing the seeds of riparian trees and vines as they fall into the water (Gottsberger, 1978). Some species of the fig genus *Ficus* (Moraceae) in Africa may suffer such heavy predation by lygaeid bugs (Hemiptera, Lygaeidae) that their distribution is restricted to the waterways where fruits may fall in moving water and be distributed to germination sites away from the predators (Slater, 1972). Other riparian species, in other families, owe their riverine distributions to the dispersal of their heavy seeds by floating in water (e.g., the liana *Entada scandens*, Fabaceae, Mimosoideae) (Ridley, 1930).

Much of the older literature on seed dispersal, including the dispersal of tropical forest trees, is summarized in H.N. Ridley's great book *The*

Dispersal of Plants Throughout the World, published in 1930. The tropical emphasis in this book stems from the experience of its author as Director of the Royal Botanic Gardens, Singapore. In 1972, L. van der Pijl produced his own review of the subject, again with a tropical emphasis based on his experience in Indonesia. Another investigator of tropical seed dispersal is E.J.H. Corner, also associated for many years with the botanical garden in Singapore, whose theoretical considerations of the subject crystallized in the "Durian theory" of flowering plant evolution (Corner, 1949, etc.).

However, more recently the quantitative and experimental work that is illuminating the subject is largely being carried out in the neotropics. Seed dispersal in tropical forests by birds has been mostly studied by ornithologists, particularly those interested in frugivorous birds (e.g., McDiarmid et al., 1977; Howe, 1977; Howe and Estabrook, 1977; Howe and VandeKerckhove, 1979; Cant, 1979). Studies have also been made of seed dispersal by bats in the paleotropics (e.g. Van der Pijl, 1957) and in the neotropics (e.g. Vásquez-Yanes et al., 1975; Heithaus et al., 1975; Janzen et al., 1976; Fleming et al., 1977; Janzen, 1978b). Seed dispersal by non-volant mammals has received less attention (see Van der Pijl, 1972).

In all these studies, there has been a limited amount of first-hand observation but, unlike the pollination of a flower, which may often be studied in all its phases within a few hours, tropical forest fruits may remain attached to the parent plant for months and then suddenly disappear. H.T. Chan (in Kavanagh, 1979) reported that Malaysian dipterocarps show staggered flowering but concurrent fruit fall. Ng and Loh (1974) measured the lengths of time between flowering and fruiting of 93 species of trees in Malaysian forests. These ranged from three weeks (*Pterocymbium javanicum*, Sterculiaceae) to eleven months (*Diospyros maingayi*, Ebenaceae). Thus, it becomes difficult to observe the agents of dispersal at work and, as a consequence, substitutes for first-hand observation have been sought.

.In 1957, Dansereau and Lems reviewed the literature on seed dispersal and introduced their system of classification based on the morphology of the diaspore (the unit of dispersal, be it a seed, a fruit, a part of a plant or even a whole plant) (Table 12.1). Although, for example, possession of a

TABLE 12.1

Classification of diaspore–dispersal systems in the scheme by Dansereau and Lems (1957)

Auxochore	diaspore planted by parent without disarticulation
Cyclochore	voluminous, air-filled diaspores (including tumbleweeds)
Pterochore[1]	diaspores with wing-like or saccate appendages
Pogonochore	diaspores with long hair-like or plumose appendages
Desmochore[1]	adhesive diaspores (spines, burrs, by glands)
Sarcochore[1]	diaspores with juicy or fleshy outer layers
Sporochore[2]	diaspores morphologically unspecialized, very light
Sclerochore[2]	diaspores morphologically unspecialized, moderate weight
Barochore[2]	diaspores morphologically unspecialized, very heavy
Ballochore	diaspores ejected or thrown off from parent

[1]Diaspores usually fruits; [2]Diaspores usually seeds.

fleshy fruit by a plant (a sarcochore) does not prove that it is dispersed by fruit-eating birds or mammals, the presence of many fleshy-fruited plants of various species in a community testifies to the importance of endozootic dispersal in that community, particularly if it coincides with a paucity of winged fruits or seeds (pterochores) or seeds invested in or provided with long hairs (pogonochores). Seeds or fruits provided with hooks or other means of attachment to fur or features (desmochores) will also testify to the importance of animal dispersal (in this case epizootic) in the community that contains them.

A convenient method of displaying the proportions of species with each kind of diaspore dispersal system is analogous to the "biological spectrum" by which Raunkiaer (1934) presented his analyses of life forms. Such dispersal spectra can be constructed for stands of forest or for layers (synusiae) within the forest.

Diaspore dispersal in primary forests

In the older literature, qualitative statements are made (Richards, 1952, pp. 93–94) that diaspore dispersal by wind is confined to some of the emergent and upper canopy trees. Schnell (1970, vol. 1, pp. 83–84) indicates that wind dispersal and animal dispersal are both to be seen in the big trees of tropical forests, while lesser trees may have heavy fruits (barochores) or fleshy ones (sarcochores), and are rarely anemochorous; wind dispersal is absent from the forest floor. However, occasional exceptions occur at every level, e.g., the big trees of the genus *Mimusops* (Sapotaceae) and some of the bigger members of the Lecythidaceae have barochores.

In Costa Rica, in the wet forest of La Selva, 71% of the canopy trees have sarcochores, while 18% have barochores, and only pterochores (10%) among the other diaspore categories are represented by more than 1% (Baker, Frankie and Opler, unpubl.). At the shrub level, the sarcochore percentage rises to 93% and ballochores come into the picture modestly (4%). At the herb level, only 73% of the species have sarcochores, the emphasis being shifted somewhat to epizootic (rather than endozootic) dispersal, with 18% desmochores and 9% ballochores (Baker, Frankie and Opler, unpubl.).

Hartshorn (1978), in effect, confirms these figures for La Selva, in reporting about 49% of the tree species to have bird-dispersed diaspores, while 13% are dispersed by bats, 3% by birds and bats, and 9% by wind. The remaining 26% are not categorized but, presumably, have heavy fruits that fall to the ground and break open, so that the seeds are secondarily dispersed by animals.

In tropical dry forests, the canopy is more likely to be broken, and winds are also able to penetrate more easily when the trees are leafless. Consequently, it is understandable that the proportions of wind-dispersed diaspores are higher. Baker, Frankie and Opler (unpubl.) found, in Guanacaste, Costa Rica, the following disposition for trees and palms: sarcochores only 49%, barochores 8%, pterochores 25%, pogonochores 5%, sclerochores 9% and ballochores 9%. At the shrub level, the sarcochore percentage rises to 61% and the diaspores that are appropriate for wind dispersal are correspondingly reduced. In the herb layer, the sarcochore percentage drops again to 40%, and sclerochores rate 20%, with the pterochores, pogonochores and sporochores (at 10% each) showing the importance of wind dispersal in these more open forests. Desmochores (also 10%) are better represented here than in the higher strata.

Diaspore dispersal and secondary forests

Richards (1952, p. 382) stated that, "It is ... a matter of common observation that the majority of the trees characteristic of young secondary forest have seeds or fruits well adapted for transport by wind or animals." In this, he was drawing attention to the absence of what we should now call barochores. He quotes as examples, in the neotropics, *Vismia guianensis* (Hypericaceae), distributed by birds and bats, while birds distribute the seeds of *Didymopanax morototoni* (Araliaceae), *Guazuma ulmifolia* (Sterculiaceae), *Miconia* spp. (Melastomataceae), and *Byrsonima* spp. (Malpighiaceae). In the West African secondary forests, *Musanga cecropioides* (Moraceae) is distributed by birds and bats (as is its neotropical counterpart *Cecropia*), while *Pycnanthus angolensis* (Myristicaceae) and *Macaranga barteri* (Euphorbiaceae) are bird-distributed. In Asia, *Melastoma malabathricum* (Melastomataceae) and species of *Macaranga*, *Mallotus* (Euphorbiaceae), *Trema* (Ulmaceae) and *Rhodamnia* and *Rhodomyrtus* (Myrtaceae) are dispersed by birds. Among the wind-dispersed secondary forest species are those of *Ochroma* (Bombacaceae) in the neotropics, *Ceiba* in both the neotropics and Africa, and *Alstonia* (Apocynaceae) and *Anthocephalus* (Rubiaceae) in Asia.

In Nigeria, Keay (1957) found wind-dispersed species of trees and lianas to be common only in the upper synusiae of a late secondary forest, with most of these species being shading-intolerant species relict from an early seral stage.

In two Costa Rican forest areas, however, the first plants to become reproductive in artificial clearings (although not necessarily the very first to arrive) had sclerochores with relatively light seed weight (Opler et al., 1977, 1980). These were rapidly succeeded by plants with other dispersal types, particularly sarcochores and, by the close of the study period (three years), the proportions of sclerochores had fallen to levels close to those of the adjacent mature forests, although the species represented were different.

Symington (1933) may have been the first to draw attention to the reservoir of viable secondary forest plant seeds in the soil of an undisturbed forest in Malaya. More recently, Budowski (1965, 1970), Guevara and Gómez-Pompa (1972) and Cheke et al. (1979) have made the same discovery for Central American, Mexican and Thai forests, respectively. Budowski (1965, 1970) has pointed out that the seeds of pioneers tend to require a light stimulus for germination, as well as good light while the seedlings grow into mature plants. Ultimately, they are either overtopped by trees of later seral stages or come to occupy positions as canopy trees or emergents in the mature forest. In Africa, *Musanga cecropioides* trees begin to die when aged between fifteen and twenty years and are unable to regenerate in their own shade (Ross, in Richards, 1952).

In light gaps, as opposed to clearings, in the wet forest of La Selva, Costa Rica, Hartshorn (1978) found that the majority of the species springing up in the gaps had seeds distributed by birds or bats. Herwitz (1979) has found, in the Corcovado National Park, Costa Rica, that regeneration in light gaps caused by the fall of a single tree may be mostly from seedlings or saplings already present in the undergrowth and surviving the falling of the tree.

Chemistry of seed reserves

Seeds contain food reserves (in endosperm or in the cotyledons) that will supply necessary energy and building materials to the embryo as germination occurs and the seed is converted into a seedling. In circumstances of poor light intensity, as is often the case in tropical forests, the seedling may not be able to produce adequate amounts of photosynthate until a considerable number of leaves have been expanded. In such a case, there must be a correspondingly larger provision of food materials in the seed which, in turn, must mean the selection of larger and heavier seeds.

Studies in temperate regions (Salisbury, 1942, for Great Britain; Baker, 1972, for California) have shown that the weights of individual seeds are greater for those species that germinate: (a) in heavy shade, (b) in circumstances of severe interplant competition, and (c) in circumstances where drought may prevail soon after germination. However, there must be a compromise between the provision of more abundant food reserves in the seed and the reduced number of seeds that this necessitates because of a limit on the availability of food substances to be incorporated in them. An additional "trade-off" is needed between size of seed and its dispersibility.

Janzen (1977d) has suggested that variation in weight between seeds on the same plant (in which the ratio of small to large may be 100% as in the case of *Mucuna andreana*, a vine of the Fabaceae, Faboideae) may be beneficial in that it spreads the seed "shadow" over a range of distances. Janzen (1970, etc.) had earlier pointed out that the numbers and weights of seeds produced by tropical forest plants may also be controlled by the activities of seed predators. Two alternative "strategies" have evolved that may overcome the predation. Small seeds may be produced in such large numbers that the seed predator population is inadequate to destroy all of them. This "strategy" will be particularly effective if the seeds are not produced at regular intervals (many forest trees), or are produced only at long intervals (e.g. bamboos). Alternatively, the plant may expend more energy on chemical defense of the seeds (by non-protein amino acids, as in *Mucuna andreana*, by alkaloids, cyanogenic glycosides, tannins, etc.). In the latter "strategy" there may be a limit on the amounts of defensive substances that can be produced and, for this reason, the numbers of seeds produced may be smaller than in the predator-satiation strategy. However, because there are fewer seeds, and they are chemically protected, they can be larger and contain more food reserves, so that they give the seedlings a better start in life. Nevertheless, there is always the possibility that one or more seed predator may evolve a means of detoxifying the chemical protectant and then being able to increase seed destruction.

The actual nature of energy-providing and tissue-building reserves in the seeds of tropical forest plants has been the subject of several analyses. For wet forests and dry forests in Costa Rica there is a relationship between seed weight and predominant storage reserve: for large seeds, this may be starch; for small seeds it is usually oil (the latter providing a more compact energy source) (Baker et al., in prep.). The small seeds of *Piper* spp. (Piperaceae) are anomalous in storing starch. Protein is always available and, of course, is particularly strongly represented in seeds of fabaceous (leguminous) plants.

The proportion of species with oil-storing seeds in samples from Costa Rican forest plants was 76% in trees and palms, 85% in shrubs and 91% in herbs. About 35% of all these species stored starch (in many cases in addition to oil). Almost all seeds contained enough protein to give positive results in crude tests with Millon's reagent.

There is also a linkage between oil as a seed reserve and phanerocotyly (otherwise known as epigeal germination), probably resulting from the fact that seed which germinates in phanerocotylar fashion is usually small compared to seed with cryptocotylar (hypogeal) germination.

SEEDLING ESTABLISHMENT

In reproductive biology, it is necessary to appreciate that seedling establishment is necessary if new genotypes are to be introduced into the forest structure (for it is obvious that persistence or spread through vegetative propagation will not do this).

Ng (1978) has discussed "strategies of establishment" in Malaysian rain forest trees. Large seeds with rapid, often epigeal germination suitable for establishing large seedlings with thick taproots in a shaded situation are most frequently found. This syndrome, characteristic of the great majority of trees, is opposed to the character set of a small percentage of "nomads" that tend to be found in clearings and at forest margins. These have smaller, more easily dispersible seeds with almost exclusively epigeal germination. The smaller diameter of the root that is formed enables them to establish seedlings in harder ground than can be exploited by the large-seeded forest species.

For the wet forest of La Selva, Costa Rica, Hartshorn (1978) estimated that the average time for the replacement of a tree is about 118 years. To provide this turnover there must be light gaps at appropriate intervals because Hartshorn found that 75 out of 104 canopy tree species examined are dependent upon light gaps for successful regeneration. Hartshorn (in Whitmore, 1978) reported that the proportion of species that depend on gaps for regeneration decreases as one moves down from the emergents and upper canopy through the understorey trees.

In the dry forest region of Guanacaste, in the same country, Hatheway and Baker (1970) observed that the big trees *Pithecellobium saman* and *Enterolobium cyclocarpum* (Fabaceae, Mimosoideae) appeared not to be maturing seedlings into saplings in the shade of the forest, but were doing so in a fully illuminated situation (which, also, was protected from grazing cattle).

Whitmore (1975, 1978) reported that in Southeast Asian forests, small gaps in a mature forest are filled by existing saplings or "suppressed" trees, while in big gaps there is a successional flora from seeds that are brought in or are already present in the soil.

Inherent dormancy of tree seeds appears to be rare in wet forest trees in West Africa. Any seeds that lie ungerminated in the soil of the forest floor only need a light stimulus to germinate (Longman, 1978). This has been the experience of Frankie, Baker and Opler (unpubl.) in wet forest in Costa Rica. Two papers by Ng (1973, 1975) give data on the germination rates of fresh seed of nearly 200 species of trees growing in Malaysian forests. "Rapid" (within twelve weeks of shedding), "intermediate" and "delayed" germinations were roughly in the proportions of 10:3:1 "which supports the popular belief that rapid germination is the predominant habit in Malaysian forests, but corrects the widespread notion that delayed germination is rare or impossible" (Ng, 1973, p. 54).

Experiments with the seeds of trees growing in the dry forests of Costa Rica showed that species of trees that matured their seeds in the wet season have evolved a dormancy mechanism that prevents germination of at least some of the seeds in the same wet season (Frankie et al., 1974). In the cases of *Casearia aculeata*, *Eugenia salamensis* var. *hiraeifolia* and *Spondias mombin*, the time necessary for 50% of the seeds to germinate was approximately 150 days. Such dormancy tends to ensure that seedlings will appear at such a time as will allow adequate root development before the onset of the short dry season (July through August) and the succeeding long dry season (late November to May).

SUMMARY REMARKS

This treatment of the reproductive biology of plants in tropical forests is not exhaustive of the published information, although it is hoped that a pathway into the literature thicket has been provided. It will be apparent that much work remains to be done before the individual relations of plants with dispersers of their pollen or seeds can be incorporated in what can truly be called an ecosystem study. However, we can see that, despite basic biological principles that apply in temperate and tropical forests alike, there are significant differences in detail and emphasis that result from a lesser seasonal differentiation of climate in tropical forests, and from a greater diversity of plants and animals (and the greater abundance of some of the latter, resulting in a narrowing of niches and an increase in biotic interactions). Improvements in our understanding of the reproductive biology of tropical forest plants will come about by the application of modern quantitative techniques of investigation and appropriate manipulation of ecosystem constituents (i.e. experimentation in addition to observation). Knowledge so gained may be vital in developing managerial plans for the relatively small amounts of tropical forest that seem likely to survive the ever-increasing impact of human population expansion.

ACKNOWLEDGEMENTS

The authors offer their thanks for financial support received from several grants provided by the National Science Foundation.

REFERENCES

Allen, G.M., 1939. *Bats*. Harvard University Press, Cambridge, Mass.

Allen, P.H., 1956. *The Rain forests of Golfo Dulce*. University of Florida Press, Gainesville, Fla.

Alvim, P. de T., 1960. Moisture stress as a requirement for flowering of coffee. *Science*, 132: 354.

Alvim, P. de T., 1964, Tree growth and periodicity in tropical climates. In: M.H. Zimmermann (Editor), *The Formation of Wood in Tropical Trees*. Academic Press, New York, N.Y., pp. 475–495.

Alvim, P. de T. and Alvim, R. 1978. Relation of climate to growth periodicity in tropical trees. In: P.B. Tomlinson and M.H. Zimmermann, (Editors), *Tropical Trees as Living Systems*. Cambridge University Press, Cambridge, pp. 445–464.

Arroyo, M.T.K., 1976. Geitonogamy in animal pollinated tropical angiosperms: A stimulus for the evolution of self-incompatibility. *Taxon*, 25: 543–548.

Ashton, P.S., 1969. Speciation among tropical forest trees: Some deductions in the light of recent evidence. *Biol. J. Linn. Soc.*, 1: 155–196.

Ashton, P.S., 1977. A contribution of rainforest research to evolutionary theory. *Ann. Mo. Bot. Gard.*, 64: 694–705.

Ashton, P.S., 1978. Crown characteristics of tropical trees. In: P.B. Tomlinson and M.H. Zimmermann (Editors), *Tropical Trees as Living Systems*. Cambridge University Press, Cambridge, pp. 591–616.

Ayensu, E.S., 1974. Plant and bat interactions in West Africa. *Ann. Mo. Bot. Gard.*, 61: 702–727.

Baker, H.G., 1955. Self compatibility and establishment after 'long-distance' dispersal. *Evolution*, 9: 347–348.

Baker, H.G., 1958. Studies in the reproductive biology of West African Rubiaceae. *J. W. Afr. Sci. Assoc.*, 4: 9–24.

Baker, H.G., 1959. Reproductive methods as factors in speciation in flowering plants. *Cold Spring Harbor Symp. Quant. Biol.*, 24: 177–191.

Baker, H.G., 1960. Apomixis and polyembryony in *Pachira oleaginea* Decne. (Bombacaceae). *Am. J. Bot.*, 47: 296–302.

Baker, H.G., 1963. Evolutionary mechanisms in pollination biology. *Science*, 139: 877–883.

Baker, H.G., 1965a. Characteristics and modes of origin of weeds. In: H.G. Baker and G.L. Stebbins (Editors), *The Genetics of Colonizing Species*. New York: Academic Press. New York, N.Y., pp. 147–171.

Baker, H.G., 1965b. The evolution of the cultivated kapok tree: A probable West African product. In: D. Brokensha (Editor), *Ecology and Economic Development in Tropical Africa*. Institute of International Studies, University of California, Berkeley, Calif., Res. Ser., No. 9: 185–216.

Baker, H.G., 1970. Two cases of bat pollination in Central America. *Rev. Biol. Trop.*, 17: 187–197.

Baker, H.G., 1972. Seed weight in relation to environmental conditions in California. *Ecology*, 53: 997–1010.

Baker, H.G., 1973. Evolutionary relationships between flowering plants and animals in American and African tropical forests. In: B.J. Meggers, E.S. Ayensu and W.D. Duckworth (Editors), *Tropical Forest Ecosystems in Africa and South America: A Comparative Review*, Smithsonian Institution Press, Washington, D.C., pp. 145–160.

Baker, H.G., 1974. The evolution of weeds. *Annu. Rev. Ecol. Syst.*, 5: 1–24.

Baker, H.G., 1975. Sugar concentrations in nectars from hummingbird flowers. *Biotropica*, 7: 37–41.

Baker, H.G., 1976. "Mistake" pollination as a reproductive system, with special reference to the Caricaceae. In: J. Burley and B.T. Styles (Editors), *Tropical Trees: Variation, Breeding and Conservation*. Academic Press, London, pp. 161–170.

Baker, H.G., 1977. Non-sugar constituents of nectar. *Apidologie*, 8: 349–356.

Baker, H.G., 1978a. Chemical aspects of the pollination of woody plants in the tropics. In: P.B. Tomlinson and M.H. Zimmermann (Editors), *Tropical Trees as Living Systems*. Cambridge University Press, Cambridge, pp. 57–82.

Baker, H.G., 1978b. Invasion and replacement in Californian and neotropical grasslands. In: J.R. Wilson (Editor), *Plant Relations in Pastures*. CSIRO, East Melbourne, Vic., pp. 268–284.

Baker, H.G., 1979. Anthecology: Old testament, New testament, Apocrypha. *N.Z. J. Bot.*, 17: 431–440.

Baker, H.G. and Baker, I., 1973. Some anthecological aspects of the evolution of nectar-producing flowers, particularly amino acid production in nectar. In: V.H. Heywood (Editor), *Taxonomy and Ecology* Academic Press, London, pp. 243–264.

Baker, H.G. and Baker, I., 1975. Studies of nectar-constitution and pollinator–plant coevolution. In: L.E. Gilbert and P.H. Raven (Editors), *Animal and Plant Coevolution*. University of Texas Press, Austin, Texas, pp. 100–140.

Baker, H.G. and Baker, I., 1978. Ants and flowers. *Biotropica*, 10: 80.

Baker, H.G. and Baker, I., 1981. Floral nectar constituents in relation to pollinator type. In: C.E. Jones and R.J. Little (Editors), *Handbook of Experimental Pollination Biology*. Van Nostrand–Reinhold, New York, N.Y., pp. 243–264.

Baker, H.G. and Harris, B.J., 1957. The pollination of *Parkia* by bats and its attendant evolutionary problems. *Evolution*, 11: 449–460.

Baker, H.G. and Harris, B.J., 1959. Bat pollination of the silk-cotton tree, *Ceiba pentandra* (L.) Gaertn. (*sensu lato*) in Ghana. *J. W. Afr. Sci. Assoc.*, 5: 1–9.

Baker, H.G. and Hurd, P.D., Jr., 1968. Intrafloral ecology. *Annu. Rev. Entomol.*, 13: 385–414.

Baker, H.G., Baker, I. and Opler, P.A., 1973. Stigmatic exudates and pollination. In: N.B.M. Brantjes and H.F. Linskens (Editors), *Pollination and Dispersal*. University of Nijmegen, Nijmegen, pp. 47–60.

Baker, H.G., Cruden, R.W. and Baker, I., 1971. Minor parasitism in pollination biology and its community function. The case of *Ceiba acuminata*. *Bioscience*, 21: 1127–1129.

Baker, J.R. and Baker, I., 1936. The seasons in a tropical rain-forest (New Hebrides). Part 2, Botany. *J. Linn. Soc. (Zool.)*, 39: 507–519.

Bänziger, H., 1971. Bloodsucking moths of Malaya. *Fauna*, 1: 4–16.

Barrows, E.M., 1977. Floral maturation and insect visitors of *Pachyptera hymenaea* (Bignoniaceae). *Biotropica*, 9: 133–134.

Bawa, K.S., 1974. Breeding systems of tree species of a lowland tropical community. *Evolution*, 28: 85–92.

Bawa, K.S., 1976. Breeding of tropical hardwoods: an evaluation of underlying bases, current status and future prospects. In: J. Burley and B.T. Styles (Editors), *Tropical Trees: Variation, Breeding and Conservation*. Academic Press, London, pp. 43–60.

Bawa, K.S., 1977. The reproductive biology of *Cupania guatemalensis* Radlk. (Sapindaceae). *Evolution*, 31: 52–63.

Bawa, K.S., 1979. Breeding systems of trees in a tropical lowland wet forest. *N.Z. J. Bot., Spec. Iss.*, 17: 521–524.

Bawa, K.S., 1980. Evolution of dioecy in flowering plants. *Annu. Rev. Ecol. Syst.*, 11: 15–40.

Bawa, K.S. and Beach, J.H., 1981. Evolution of sexual systems in flowering plants. *Am. Nat.*, in press.

Bawa, K.S. and Crisp, J.E., 1980. Wind pollination demonstrated in the understorey of a rain forest. *J. Ecol.*, 68: 871–876.

Bawa, K.S. and Opler, P.A., 1975. Dioecism in tropical trees. *Evolution*, 29: 167–179.

Bawa, K.S. and Opler, P.A., 1978. Why are pistillate inflorescences of *Simarouba glauca* eaten less than staminate inflorescences? *Evolution*, 32: 673–676.

Beach, J., 1981. Pollinator foraging and the evolution of dioecy. *Am. Nat.*, in press.

Beard, J., 1946. *The Natural Vegetation of Trinidad*. Oxford For. Mem. No. 20. Clarendon Press, Oxford.

Bentley, B.L., 1977a. The protective function of ants visiting the extrafloral nectaries of *Bixa orellana* (Bixaceae). *J. Ecol.*, 65: 27–38.

Bentley, B.L., 1977b. Extrafloral nectaries and protection by pugnacious bodyguards. *Annu. Rev. Ecol. Syst.*, 8: 407–428.

Boaler, S.B., 1966. Ecology of a miombo site, Lupa North Forest Reserve, Tanzania. II. Plant communities and seasonal variation in the vegetation. *J. Ecol.*, 54: 564–579.

Bolten, A.B. and Feinsinger, P. 1978. Why do hummingbird flowers secrete dilute nectar? *Biotropica*, 10: 307–309.

Bolten, A.B., Feinsinger, P., Baker, H.G. and Baker, I., 1979. On the calculation of sugar concentration in flower nectar. *Oecologia*, 41: 301–304.

Broekmans, A.F.M., 1957. Growth, flowering, and yield of the oil palm in Nigeria. *J. W. Afr. Inst. Oil Palm Res.*, 2: 187–220.

Budowski, G., 1965. Distribution of tropical American rainforest species in the light of successional processes. *Turrialba*, 15: 40–42.

Budowski, G., 1970. The distinction between old secondary and climax species in tropical Central American lowland forests. *Trop. Ecol.*, 11: 44–48.

Bullock, A.A., 1948. *Thonningia*. *Kew Bull.*, N.V., 1948: 363–367.

Bünning, E., 1948. Studien über Photoperiodizität in der Tropen. In: A.E. Murneck and R.O. Whyte (Editors), *Vernalisation and Photoperiodism*. Chronica Botanica Company, Waltham, Mass., pp. 161–164.

Burger, W.C., 1974. Flowering periodicity at four altitudinal levels in Eastern Ethiopia. *Biotropica*, 6: 38–42.

Burkill, I.H., 1907. Notes on the pollination of flowers in India. no. 1. *J. Asiatic Soc. Bengal*, 2: 511–514.

Cant, J.G.H., 1979. Dispersal of *Stemmadernia donnell-smithii* by birds and monkeys. *Biotropica*, 11: 122.

Carlquist, S., 1966. The biota of long distance dispersal. IV. Genetic systems in the flora of oceanic islands. *Evolution*, 20: 433–455.

Carvalho, C.T. de., 1960. Das visitas de morcegos às flores. *An. Acad. Bras. Cienc.*, 32: 359–377.

Cheke, A.S., Nanakorn, W. and Yankoses, C., 1979. Dormancy and dispersal of seeds of secondary forest species under the canopy of a primary tropical rain forest in northern Thailand. *Biotropica*, 11: 88–95.

Churchill, D.M. and Christensen, P., 1970. Observations on pollen harvesting by brush-tongued lorikeets. *Aust. J. Zool.*, 18: 427–437.

Colwell, R.K., Betts, B.J., Bunnell, P., Carpenter, F.L. and Feinsinger, P., 1974. Competition for the nectar of *Centropogon valerii* by the hummingbird *Colibri thalassinus* and the flower-piercer *Diglossa plumbea*, and its evolutionary implications. *Condor*, 76: 447–452.

Connell, J.H., 1971. On the role of natural enemies in preventing competitive exclusion in some marine animals and in rain forest trees. In: P.J. den Boer and G.R. Gradwell (Editors), *The Dynamics of Populations*. Adv. Study Inst. Dynamics Numbers Popul., Oosterbeek, pp. 298–312.

Cope, F.W., 1962a. The mechanism of pollen incompatibility in *Theobroma cacao* L. *Heredity*, 17: 157–182.

Cope, F.W., 1962b. The effects of incompatibility and compatibility on genotype proportions in *Theobroma cacao* L. *Heredity*, 17: 183–195.

Corner, E.J.H., 1949. The durian theory of the origin of the modern tree. *Ann. Bot., N.S.*, 13: 367–414.

Corner, E.J.H., 1952. *Wayside Trees of Malaya, 1.* Government Printing Office, Singapore.

Croat, T.B., 1969. Seasonal flower behavior in central Panama. *Ann. Mo. Bot. Gard.*, 56: 295–307.

Croat, T.B., 1974. A case for selection of delayed fruit maturation in *Spondias* (Anacardiaceae). *Biotropica*, 6: 135–137.

Croat, T.B., 1978. *Flora of Barro Colorado Island.* Stanford University Press, Stanford, Calif.

Croat, T.B., 1979. The sexuality of the Barro Colorado Island flora (Panama). *Phytologia*, 42: 319–348.

Cruden, R.W. and Toledo, V.M., 1977. Oriole pollination of *Erythrina brevifolia* (Leguminosae): Evidence for a polytypic view of ornithophily. *Plant. Syst. Evol.*, 126: 393–403.

Cruden, R.W., Hermann-Parker, S.M. and Peterson, S., 1981. Patterns of nectar production and plant–pollinator coevolution. In: B.L. Bentley and T.S. Elias (Editors), *The Biology of Nectaries.* Columbia University Press, New York, N.Y.

Dansereau, P. and Lems, K., 1957. The grading of dispersal types in plant communities and their ecological significance. *Contrib. Inst. Bot. Univ. Montréal*, No. 71.

Daubenmire, R., 1972. Phenology and other characteristics of tropical semi-deciduous forest in north-western Costa Rica. *J. Ecol.*, 60: 147–170.

DeVries, P.J., 1979. Pollen-feeding rainforest *Parides* and *Battus* butterflies in Costa Rica. *Biotropica*, 11: 237–238.

Dodson, C.H., 1962. The importance of pollination in the evolution of the orchids of tropical America. *Am. Orchid Soc. Bull.*, 31: 525–534; 641–649; 731–735.

Dodson, C.H., 1975. Coevolution of orchids and bees. In: L.E. Gilbert and P.H. Raven (Editors), *Coevolution of Animals and Plants.* University of Texas Press, Austin, Texas, pp. 91–99.

Dodson, C.H. and Frymire, G.P., 1961. Natural pollination of orchids. *Bull. Mo. Bot. Gard.*, 49: 133–152.

Ducke, A. and Black, G.A., 1953. Phytogeographical notes on the Brazilian Amazon. *Ann. Acad. Brasil. Cienc.*, 25: 1–46.

Dunlap-Pianka, H., Boggs, C.L. and Gilbert, L.E., 1977. Ovarian dynamics in heliconiine butterflies: Programmed senescence versus eternal youth. *Science*, 197: 487–490.

East, E.M., 1940. The distribution of self-sterility in the flowering plants. *Proc. Am. Philos. Soc.*, 82: 449–518.

Faegri, K. and Van der Pijl, L., 1966 (1971) (1978). *The Principles of Pollination Ecology.* Pergamon Press, London, (1st, 2nd and 3rd editions).

Fahn, A., 1949. Studies in the ecology of nectar secretion. *Palest. J. Bot.*, Jerusalem, 4: 207–224.

Fedorov, A.A., 1966. The structure of the tropical rain forest and speciation in the humid tropics. *J. Ecol.*, 54: 1–11.

Feinsinger, P., 1976. Organization of a tropical guild of nectarivorous birds. *Ecol. Monogr.*, 46: 257–291.

Feinsinger, P., 1978. Ecological interactions between plants and hummingbirds in a successional tropical community. *Ecol. Monogr.*, 48: 269–287.

Feinsinger, P. and Colwell, R.K., 1978. Community organization among Neotropical nectar-feeding birds. *Am. Zool.*, 18: 779–795.

Feinsinger, P. and Swarm, L.A., 1978. How common are ant-repellent nectars? *Biotropica*, 10: 238–239.

Ferwerder, F.P. and Wit, F. (Editors), 1969. *Outlines of Perennial Crop Breeding in the Tropics.* Veenman and Zonen, Wageningen.

Fleming, T.H., Heithaus, E.R. and Sawyer, W.B., 1977. An experimental analysis of the food location behavior of frugivorous bats. *Ecology*, 58: 619–627.

Foster, R., 1974. *Seasonality of Fruit Production and Seed Fall in a Tropical Forest Ecosystem in Panama.* Thesis, Duke University, Durham, N.C.

Foster, R., 1977. *Tachigalia versicolor* is a suicidal neotropical tree. *Nature*, 268: 624–626.

Fournier, L.A. and Salas, S., 1966. Algunas observaciones sobre la dinámica de la floración en el bosque tropical húmedo de Villa Colón. *Rev. Biol. Trop.*, 14: 75–85.

Frankie, G.W., 1975. Tropical forest phenology and pollinator–plant coevolution. In: L.E. Gilbert and P.H. Raven (Editors), *Coevolution of Animals and Plants.* University of Texas Press, Austin, Texas, pp. 192–219.

Frankie, G.W., 1976. Pollination of widely dispersed trees by animals in Central America, with an emphasis on bee pollination systems. In: J. Burley and B.T. Styles (Editors), *Tropical Trees: Variation, Breeding and Conservation.* Academic Press, London, pp. 151–160.

Frankie, G.W. and Baker, H.G., 1974. The importance of pollinator behavior in the reproductive biology of tropical trees. *An. Inst. Biol. Univ. Nac. Autón., Mexico,* 45 (*Ser. Bot.*): 1–10.

Frankie, G.W. and Coville, R., 1979. An experimental study on the foraging behavior of selected solitary bee species in the Costa Rican dry forest. *J. Kans. Entomol. Soc.*, 52: 591–602.

Frankie, G.W. and Vinson, S.B., 1977. Scent marking of passion flowers by females of *Xylocopa virginica texana* in Texas (Hymenoptera: Anthophoridae). *J. Kans. Entomol. Soc.*, 50: 613–625.

Frankie, G.W., Baker, H.G. and Opler, P.A., 1974. Comparative phenological studies of trees in tropical wet and dry forests in the lowlands of Costa Rica. *J. Ecol.*, 62: 881–919.

Frankie, G.W., Opler, P.A. and Bawa, K.S. 1976. Foraging behavior of solitary bees: Implications for outcrossing of a neotropical forest tree species. *J. Ecol.*, 64: 1049–1057.

Galil, J. and Eisikowitch, D., 1971. Studies on mutualistic symbiosis between syconia and sycophilous wasps in monoecious figs. *New Phytol.*, 70: 773–787.

Gan, Y.Y., Robertson, F.W., Ashton, P.S., Soepadmo, E. and Lee, D.W., 1977. Genetic variation in wild populations of rain forest trees. *Nature*, 269: 323.

Gentry, A.H., 1974a. Coevolutionary patterns in Central American Bignoniaceae. *Ann. Mo. Bot. Gard.*, 61: 728–759.

Gentry, A.H., 1974b. Flowering phenology and diversity in tropical Bignoniaceae. *Biotropica*, 6: 64–68.

Gentry, A.H., 1976. Bignoniaceae of southern Central America: Distribution and ecological specificity. *Biotropica*, 8: 117–131.

Gentry, A.H., 1978. Anti-pollinators for mass-flowering plants. *Biotropica* 10: 68–69.

Gibbs, D.G. and Leston, D., 1970. Insect phenology in a forest cocoa-farm locality in West Africa. *J. Appl. Ecol.*, 7: 519–548.

Gilbert, L.E., 1972. Pollen feeding and reproductive biology of *Heliconius* butterflies. *Proc. Natl. Acad. Sci.*, 69: 1403–1407.

Gilbert, L.E., 1975. Ecological consequences of a coevolved mutualism between butterflies and plants. In: L.E. Gilbert and P.H. Raven, (Editors), *Coevolution of Animals and Plants*. University of Texas Press, Austin, Texas, pp. 210–240.

Gottsberger, G., 1974. The structure and function of the primitive Angiosperm flower. *Acta Bot. Neerl.*, 23: 461–471.

Gottsberger, G., 1978. Seed dispersal by fish in the inundated regions of Humaitá, Amazonia. *Biotropica*, 10: 170–183.

Gould, E., 1977. Foraging behavior of *Pteropus vampirus* on the flowers of *Durio zibethinus*. *J. Malay. Nat.*, 30: 53–57.

Gould, E., 1978. Foraging behavior of Malaysian nectar-feeding bats. *Biotropica* 10: 184–192.

Guerrant, E.O., Jr. and Fiedler, P.L., 1981. Ants like nectar, but aren't so fond of flowers. *Biotropica*, in press.

Guevara, S.S. and Gómez-Pompa, A., 1972. Seeds from surface soils in a tropical region of Veracruz, Mexico. *J. Arnold Arb.*, 53: 312–335.

Haber, W.A. and Frankie, G.W., 1982. A comparative study of the reproductive biology of three *Luehea* species (Tiliaceae) in a neotropical dry forest. *Ecology*, in press.

Harris, B.J. and Baker, H.G., 1958. Pollination in *Kigelia africana* Benth. *J. W. Afr. Sci. Assoc.*, 4: 25–30.

Harris, B.J. and Baker, H.G., 1959. Pollination of flowers by bats in Ghana. *Nigerian Field*, 24: 151–159.

Hartshorn, G.S., 1972. *The Ecological Life History and Population Dynamics of* Pentaclethra macroloba, *a Tropical Wet Forest Dominant, and* Stryphnodendron excelsum, *an Occasional Associate*. Thesis, University of Washington, Seattle, Wash.

Hartshorn, G.S., 1978. Tree falls and tropical forest dynamics. In: P.B. Tomlinson and M.H. Zimmermann (Editors), *Tropical Trees as Living Systems*. Cambridge University Press, Cambridge. pp. 617–638.

Hatheway, W.H. and Baker, H.G., 1970. Reproductive strategies in *Pithecellobium* and *Enterolobium* — further information. *Evolution*, 24: 253–254.

Hedegart, T., 1976. Breeding systems, variation and genetic improvement of teak (*Tectona grandis* L.) In: J. Burley and B.T. Styles (Editors), *Tropical Trees: Variation, Breeding and Conservation*, Academic Press, London, pp. 109–124.

Heithaus, E.R., 1974. On the role of plant–pollinator interactions in determining community structure. *Ann. Mo. Bot. Gard.*, 61: 675–691.

Heithaus, E.R., 1979. Community structure of neotropical flower visiting bees and wasps: Diversity and phenology. *Ecology*, 60: 190–202.

Heithaus, E.R., Opler, P.A., and Baker, H.G., 1974. Bat activity and pollination of *Bauhinia pauletia*: Plant pollinator coevolution. *Ecology*, 55: 412–419.

Heithaus, E.R., Fleming, T.H. and Opler, P.A., 1975. Foraging patterns and resource utilization in seven species of bats in a seasonal tropical forest. *Ecology*, 56: 841–854.

Herwitz, S., 1979. *The Regeneration of Selected Tropical Wet Forest Tree Species in Corcovado National Park, Costa Rica*. Thesis, University of California, Berkeley, Calif.

Hillman, W.J., 1962. *The Physiology of Flowering*. Holt, Rinehart and Winston, New York, N.Y.

Hocking, B., 1953. The intrinsic range and speed of flight of insects. *Trans. R. Entomol. Soc., Lond.*, 104: 223–345.

Hocking, B., 1968. Insect-flower associations in the high Arctic with special reference to nectar. *Oikos*, 19: 359–387.

Holdsworth, M., 1961. The flowering of rain flowers. *J. W. Afr. Sci. Assoc.*, 7: 154–162.

Holttum, R.E., 1952. Evolutionary trends in an equatorial climate. *Soc. Exp. Biol. Symp.*, 7: 28–36.

Hopkins, B., 1963. The role of fire in promoting the sprouting of some savanna species. *J. W. Afr. Sci. Assoc.*, 7: 154–162.

Howe, H.F., 1977. Bird activity and seed dispersal of a tropical wet forest tree. *Ecology*, 58: 539–550.

Howe, H.F. and Estabrook, G.F., 1977. On intraspecific competition for avian dispersers in tropical trees. *Am. Nat.*, 111: 817–832.

Howe, H.F. and Primack, R.B., 1975. Differential seed dispersal by birds of the tree *Casearia nitida* (Flacourtiaceae). *Biotropica*, 7: 278–283.

Howe, H.F. and VandeKerckhove, G.A., 1979. Fecundity and seed dispersal of a tropical tree. *Ecology*, 60: 180–189.

Howell, D.J., 1974. Bats and pollen: Physiological aspects of the syndrome of chiropterophily. *Comp. Biochem. Physiol. A. Comp. Physiol.*, 48: 263–276.

Howell, D.J., 1977. Time sharing and body partitioning in bat-plant pollination systems. *Nature*, 270: 509–510.

Hubbell, S.P., 1979. Tree dispersion, abundance, and diversity in a tropical dry forest. *Science*, 203: 1299–1309.

Jackson, J.F., 1978. Seasonality of flowering and leaf-fall in a Brazilian subtropical lower montane moist forest. *Biotropica*, 10: 38–42.

Jaeger, P., 1954. Les aspects actuels du problème de la cheiropterogamie. *Bull. Inst. Fr. Afr. Noire, Sér. A*, 16: 796–821.

Jain, S.K., 1976. The evolution of inbreeding in plants. *Annu. Rev. Ecol. Syst.*, 7: 469–495.

Janzen, D.H., 1967. Synchronization of sexual reproduction of trees within the dry season in Central America. *Evolution*, 21: 620–637.

Janzen, D.H., 1968. Reproductive behavior in the Passifloraceae and some of its pollinators in Central America. *Behavior*, 32: 33–48.

Janzen, D.H., 1970. Herbivores and the number of tree species in tropical forests. *Am. Nat.*, 104: 501–528.

Janzen, D.H., 1971. Euglossine bees as long-distance pollinators of tropical plants. *Science*, 171: 203–205.

Janzen, D.H., 1974a. Tropical blackwater rivers, animals and mast fruiting by the Dipterocarpaceae. *Biotropica*, 6: 69–103.

Janzen, D.H., 1974b. The deflowering of Central America. *Nat. Hist.*, 83: 48–53.

Janzen, D.H., 1975. *Ecology of Plants in the Tropics*. Edward Arnold, London, 66 pp.

Janzen, D.H., 1976a. Why do bamboos wait so long to flower? *Annu. Rev. Ecol. Syst.*, 7: 347–391.

Janzen, D.H., 1976b. Why do bamboos wait so long to flower? In: J. Burley and B.T. Styles (Editors), *Tropical Trees: Variation, Breeding and Conservation*. Academic Press, London, pp. 179–188.

Janzen, D.H., 1977a. A note on optimal mate selection in plants. *Am. Nat.*, 111: 365–371.

Janzen, D.H., 1977b. Promising directions of study in tropical animal–plant interactions. *Ann. Mo. Bot. Gard.* 64: 706–736.

Janzen, D.H., 1977c. Why don't ants visit flowers? *Biotropica*, 9: 252.

Janzen, D.H., 1977d. Variation in seed size within a crop of Costa Rican *Mucuna andreana* (Leguminosae). *Am. J. Bot.*, 64: 347–349.

Janzen, D.H., 1978a. Seeding patterns of tropical trees. In: P.B. Tomlinson and M.H. Zimmermann (Editors), *Tropical Trees as Living Systems*. Cambridge University Press, Cambridge, pp. 83–128.

Janzen, D.H., 1978b. The size of a local peak in a seed shadow. *Biotropica* 10: 78.

Janzen, D.H., Miller, G.A., Hackforth-Jones, J., Pond, C.M., Hooper, K. and Janos, D., 1976. Two Costa Rican bat-generated seed shadows of *Andira inermis* (Leguminosae). *Ecology*, 57: 1060–1067.

Johnson, L.K. and Hubbell, S.P., 1974. Aggression and competition among stingless bees: Field studies. *Ecology*, 55: 120–127.

Jones, C.E. and Buchmann, S.L., 1974. Ultraviolet floral patterns as functional orientation cues in hymenopterous pollination systems. *Anim. Behav.*, 22: 481–485.

Jones, C.E. and Rich, P.V., 1972. Ornithophily and extrafloral color patterns in *Columnea florida* Morton (Gesneriaceae). *Bull. S. Calif. Acad. Sci.*, 71: 113–116.

Jones, E.W., 1955. Ecological studies on the rain forest of southern Nigeria. IV. The plateau forest of the Okomu Reserve. *J. Ecol.*, 43: 564–594.

Karr, J.R., 1976. An association between a grass (*Paspalum virgatum*) and moths. *Biotropica*, 8: 284–285.

Kaur, A., Ha, C.O., Jong, K., Sands, V.E., Chan, H.T., Soepadmo, E. and Ashton, P.S., 1978. Apomixis may be widespread among trees of the climax rainforest. *Nature* 271: 440–441.

Kavanagh, M., 1979. Flowering forests. *Nature*, 279: 374.

Keay, R.W.J., 1957. Wind-dispersed species in a Nigerian forest. *J. Ecol.*, 45: 471–478.

Keeler, K.H., 1977. The extrafloral nectaries of *Ipomoea carnea* (Convolvulaceae). *Am. J. Bot.*, 69: 1182–1188.

Kennedy, H., 1978. Systematics and pollination of the "closed-flowered" species of *Calathea* (Marantaceae). *Univ. Calif. Publ. Bot.*, 71: 1–90.

Kerling, L.C.P., 1941. The gregarious flowering of *Zephyranthes rosea* Lindl. *Ann. Bot. Gard. Buitenzorg*, 51: 1–42.

Kevan, P.G., 1978. Floral coloration, its colorimetric analysis and significance in anthecology. In: A.J. Richards (Editor), *The Pollination of Flowers by Insects. Linnean Soc. Symp. Ser.*, No. 6, pp. 51–78.

Koelmeyer, K.O., 1959. The periodicity of leaf change and flowering in the principal forest communities of Ceylon. *Ceylon For.*, 4: 157–189; 308–364.

Lack, A., 1978. The ecology of the flowers of the savanna tree *Maranthes polyandra* and their visitors, with particular reference to bats. *J. Ecol.*, 66: 287–296.

Lamb, B.F., 1966. *Mahogany of Tropical America: Its Ecology and Management*. University of Michigan Press, Ann Arbor, Mich.

Lee, H.Y., 1967. Studies in *Swietenia* (Meliaceae): Observations on the sexuality of the flowers. *J. Arnold Arb.*, 48: 101–104.

Linhart, Y.B., 1973. Ecological and behavioral determinants of pollen dispersal in hummingbird-pollinated *Heliconia*. *Am. Nat.*, 107: 511–523.

Linhart, Y.B. and Mendenhall, J.A., 1977. Pollen dispersal by hawkmoths. *Biotropica*, 9: 143.

Little, E.L., Jr. and Wadsworth, F.H., 1964. *Common Trees of Puerto Rico and the Virgin Islands*. U.S. Dep. Agric. Handbook, Washington, D.C., No. 249.

Longman, K.A., 1978. Control of shoot extension and dormancy; external and internal factors. In: P.B. Tomlinson and M.H. Zimmermann (Editors), *Tropical Trees as Living Systems*. Cambridge University Press, Cambridge, pp. 465–496.

Longman, K.A. and Jenik, J., 1974. *Tropical Forest and its Environment*. Longmans, London, 205 pp.

McClelland, T.B., 1924. The photoperiodism of *Tephrosia candida*. *J. Agric. Res.*, 28: 445–460.

McClure, H.E., 1966a. Flowering, fruiting and animals in the canopy of a tropical rain forest. *Malay. For.*, 29: 182–203.

McClure, H.E., 1966b. *The Bamboos*. Harvard University Press. Cambridge, Mass.

McDiarmid, R.W., Ricklefs, R.E. and Foster, M.S. 1977. Dispersal of *Stemmadenia donnell-smithii* (Apocynaceae) by birds. *Biotropica*, 9: 9–25.

McGregor, S.E., 1976. *Insect Pollination of Cultivated Crop Plants*. U.S. Dep. Agric. Washington, D.C., Handbook No. 496.

Medway, Lord, 1972. Phenology of tropical rain forest in Malaya. *Biol. J. Linn. Soc.*, 4: 117–146.

Meeuse, B.J.D., 1961. *The Story of Pollination*. Ronald Press, New York, N.Y.

Morcombe, M.K., 1968. *Australia's Western Wildflowers*. Landfall Press, Perth, W.A.

Mori, S. and Kallunki, J., 1976. Phenology and floral biology of *Gustavia superba* (Lecythidaceae) in central Panama. *Biotropica*, 8: 184–192.

Nevling, L.I., Jr. 1971. The ecology of an elfin forest in Puerto Rico, 16. The flowering cycle and an interpretation of its seasonality. *J. Arnold Arb.*, 52: 586–613.

Ng, F.S.P., 1966. Age at first flowering of dipterocarps. *Malay. For.*, 29: 290–295.

Ng, F.S.P., 1973. Germination of fresh seeds of Malaysian trees. *Malays. For.*, 36: 54–65.

Ng, F.S.P., 1975. Germination of fresh seeds of Malaysian trees. *Malays. For.*, 38: 171.

Ng, F.S.P., 1977. Gregarious flowering dipterocarps in Kepong 1976. *Malays. For.* 40: 126–137.

Ng, F.S.P., 1978. Strategies of establishment in Malayan forest trees. In: P.B. Tomlinson and M.H. Zimmermann

(Editors), *Tropical Trees as Living Systems*. Cambridge University Press, Cambridge, pp. 139–162.

Ng, F.S.P. and Loh, H.S., 1974. Flowering-to-fruiting periods of Malaysian trees. *Malays. For.*, 37: 127–132.

Njoku, E., 1958. The photoperiodic response of some Nigerian plants. *J. W. Afr. Sci. Assoc.*, 4: 99–111.

Nygren, A., 1954. Apomixis in the angiosperms. *Bot. Rev.*, 20: 577–649.

Nygren, A., 1967. Apomixis in the angiosperms. In: *Encyclopedia of Plant Physiology*, 18: 551–596.

Opler, P.A., 1979. Interaction of plant life history components as related to arboreal herbivory. In: G.G. Montgomery (Editor), *The Ecology of Arboreal Foliovores*. Smithsonian Institution Press, Washington, D.C.

Opler, P.A., 1981. Nectar production in a tropical ecosystem. In: B.L. Bentley and T.S. Elias (Editors), *Biology of Nectaries*. Columbia University Press, New York, N.Y.

Opler, P.A. and Bawa, K.S. 1978. Sex ratios in tropical trees. *Evolution*, 32: 812–821.

Opler, P.A., Baker, H.G. and Frankie, G.W., 1976a. Reproductive biology of some Costa Rican *Cordia* species (Boraginaceae). *Biotropica*, 7: 234–247.

Opler, P.A., Frankie, G.W. and Baker, H.G., 1976b. Rainfall as a factor in the release, timing and synchronization of anthesis by tropical trees and shrubs. *J. Biogeogr.*, 3: 231–236.

Opler, P.A., Baker, H.G. and Frankie, G.W., 1977. Recovery of tropical lowland forest ecosystems. In: J. Cairns, K.L. Dickson and E.E. Herricks, (Editors), *Recovery and Restoration of Damaged Ecosystems*. University Press of Virginia, Charlottesville, Va., pp. 399–421.

Opler, P.A., Frankie, G.W. and Baker, H.G., 1980. Comparative phenological studies of shrubs and treelets in wet and dry forests in the lowlands of Costa Rica. *J. Ecol.*, 68: 167–186.

Overland, L., 1960. Endogenous rhythm in opening and odor of flowers of *Cestrum nocturnum. Am. J. Bot.*, 47: 378–382.

Percival, M.S., 1965. *Floral Biology*. Pergamon Press, Oxford.

Percival, M.S. 1974. Floral ecology of coastal scrub on southeast Jamaica. *Biotropica* 6: 104–129.

Prance, G.T., 1976. The pollination and anthophore structure of some Amazonian Lecythidaceae. *Biotropica*, 8: 235–241.

Purseglove, J.W., 1968. *Tropical Crops: Dicotyledons*. Longmans, London, 2 vols.

Purseglove, J.W., 1975. *Tropical Crops: Monocotyledons* Longmans, London, 2 vols.

Putz, F.C., 1979. Aseasonality in Malaysian tree phenology. *Malays. For.*, 42: 1–24.

Ramirez, W.B., 1970. Taxonomical and biological studies of neotropical fig-wasps (Hymenoptera, Agaonidae). *Univ. Kans. Bull Sci.*, 49: 1–44.

Raunkiaer, C., 1934. *The Life Forms of Plants and Statistical Plant geography*. Clarendon Press, Oxford.

Rauscher, M.D. and Fowler, N.L., 1979. Intersexual aggression and nectar defense in *Chauliognathus distinguendus* (Coleoptera: Cantharidae). *Biotropica*, 11: 88–95.

Rees, A.R., 1964. Some observations on the flowering behavior of *Coffea rupestris* in southern Nigeria. *J. Ecol.*, 52: 1–7.

Rehr, S.S., Bell, E.A., Janzen, D.H. and Feeny, P.P., 1973a.

Insecticidal amino acids in legume seeds. *Biochem. Syst.*, 1: 63–67.

Rehr, S.S., Feeny, P.P. and Janzen, D.H., 1973b. *l*-dopa in legume seeds: A chemical barrier to insect attack. *Science*, 181: 81–82.

Richards, P.W., 1952. *The Tropical Rain Forest: An Ecological Study*. Cambridge University Press, Cambridge, 450 pp.

Ridley, H.N., 1930. *The Dispersal of Plants Throughout the World*. H.N. Reeve, Ashford.

Salas, S., 1974. *Analisis del Systema de Polinizacion de* Inga vera *subspecies* spuria. Thesis, University of Costa Rica.

Salisbury, E.J., 1942. *The Reproductive Capacity of Plants*. G. Bell and Sons, London.

Salisbury, F.B., 1963. *The Flowering Process*. Macmillan, New York, N.Y.

Sazima, I. and Sazima, M., 1977. Solitary and group foraging: two flower-visiting patterns of the lesser spear-nosed bat *Phyllostomus discolor. Biotropica*, 9: 213–215.

Sazima, M. and Sazima, I., 1978. Bat pollination of the passion flower, *Passiflora mucronata* in southeastern Brazil. *Biotropica*, 10: 100–109.

Schemske, D.W., 1978. A coevolved triad: *Costus woodsonii* (Zingiberaceae), its dipteran seed predator and ant mutualists. *Bull. Ecol. Soc. Am.*, 59: 89 (abstract).

Schmid, R., 1970. Notes on the reproductive biology of *Asterogyne martiana* (Palmae). *Principes*, 14: 3–9; 39–49.

Schnell, R., 1970. *Introduction à la Phytogéographie des Pays Tropicaux* Gauthier-Villars, Paris, 2 vols.

Schubart, H.O.R. and Anderson, A.B., 1978. Why don't ants visit flowers? A reply to D.H. Janzen. *Biotropica*, 10: 310–311.

Simmonds, N.W., 1976. *Evolution of Crop Plants*. Longmans, London.

Slater, J.A., 1972. Lygaeid bugs (Hemiptera: Lygaeidae) as seed predators of figs. *Biotropica*, 4: 145–151.

Slud, P., 1960. The birds of Finca "La Selva", Costa Rica: A tropical wet forest locality. *Bull. Am. Mus. Nat. Hist.*, 121: 49–148.

Smith, J., 1841. Notice of a plant which produces perfect seeds without any apparent action of pollen. *Trans. Linn. Soc.*, 18: 509–512.

Smythe, N., 1970. Relationships between fruiting seasons and seed dispersal methods in a neotropical forest. *Am. Nat.*, 104: 25–35.

Snow, B.K. and Snow, D.W., 1972. Feeding niches of hummingbirds in a Trinidad valley. *J. Anim. Ecol.*, 44: 451–485.

Snow, D.W., 1965. A possible selection factor in the evolution of fruiting seasons in a tropical forest. *Oikos*, 15: 274–281.

Soderstrom, T.R. and Calderon, C.E., 1971. Insect pollination in tropical forest grasses. *Biotropica*, 3: 1–16.

Soepadmo, E. and Eow, B.K., 1977, The reproductive biology of *Durio zibethinus* Murr. *Gard. Bull., Singapore*, 29: 25–32.

Start, A.N. and Marshall, A.G., 1976. Nectarivorous bats as pollinators of trees in West Malaysia. In: J. Burley and B.T. Styles (Editors) *Tropical Trees: Variation, Breeding and Conservation*. Academic Press, London, pp. 141–150.

Stebbins, G.L., 1957. Self-fertilization and population variability in the higher plants. *Am. Nat.*, 41: 337–354.

Stiles, F.G., 1975. Ecology, flowering phenology, and hummingbird pollination of some Costa Rican *Heliconia* species. *Ecology*, 56: 285–301.

Stiles, F.G., 1977. Co-adapted competitors: The flowering seasons of hummingbird pollinated plants in a tropical forest. *Science*, 198: 1177–1178.

Stiles, F.G., 1978. Temporal organization of flowering among the hummingbird foodplants of a tropical wet forest. *Biotropica*, 10: 194–210.

Stiles, F.G. and Wolf, L.L., 1970. Hummingbird territoriality at a tropical flowering tree. *Auk*, 87: 465–492.

Styles, B.T., 1972. The flower biology of the Meliaceae and its bearing on tree breeding. *Silvae Genet.*, 21: 175–182.

Styles, B.T. and Khosla, P.K., 1976. Cytology and reproductive biology of Meliaceae. In: J. Burley and B.T. Styles (Editors), *Tropical Trees: Variation, Breeding and Conservation*, Academic Press, London, pp. 61–68.

Sussman, R.W. and Raven, P.H., 1978. Pollination by lemurs and marsupials: An archaic coevolutionary system. *Science*, 200: 731–736.

Symington, C.F., 1933. The study of secondary growth on rain forest sites. *Malay. For.*, 2: 107–117.

Thien, L.B., 1980. Patterns of pollination in the primitive angiosperms. *Biotropica*, 12: 1–13.

Toledo, V.M., 1975. La estacionalidad de las flores utilizados por los Colibries de una selva tropical humida en México. *Biotropica*, 7: 63–70.

Toledo, V.M., 1977. Pollination of some rainforest plants by non-hovering birds in Veracruz, Mexico. *Biotropica* 9:262–267.

Tomlinson, P.B., 1974., Breeding mechanisms in trees native to tropical Florida — a morphological assessment. *J. Arnold Arb.*, 55: 260–290.

Tomlinson, P.B., 1977. Plant morphology and anatomy in the tropics — the need for integrated approaches. *Ann. Mo. bot. Gard.*, 64: 685–693.

Tomlinson, P.B. and Fawcett, P., 1972. Dioecism in *Citharexylum* (Verbenaceae). *J. Arnold Arbor.*, 53: 386–389.

Uhl, N.W. and Moore, H.E., 1977. Correlations of inflorescence, flower structure and floral anatomy with pollination in some palms. *Biotropica*, 9: 170–190.

Valmajor, R.V., Coronel, R.E. and Ramirez, D.A., 1965. Studies on floral biology, fruit set and fruit development in Durian. *Philipp. Agric.*, 47: 355–366.

Van der Pijl, L., 1936. Fledermäuse und Blumen. *Flora*, 131: 1–40.

Van der Pijl, L., 1937. Disharmony between Asiatic flower-birds and American bird-flowers. *Ann. Jard. Bot. Buitenzorg*, 48: 17–26.

Van der Pijl, L., 1954. *Xylocopa* and flowers in the tropics, I–III. *Proc. K. Ned. Acad. Wet.*, Ser. C, 57: 413–423; 541–562.

Van der Pijl, L., 1955. Some remarks on myrmecophytes. *Phytomorphology*, 5: 190–200.

Van der Pijl, L., 1957. Dispersal of plants by bats (Chiropterochory). *Acta Bot. Neerl.*, 6: 291–315.

Van der Pijl, L., 1960–61. Ecological aspects of flower evolution, I–II. *Evolution*, 14: 403–416; 15: 44–59.

Van der Pijl, L., 1969. Evolutionary action of tropical animals on the reproduction of plants. *Biol. J. Linn. Soc.*, 1: 85–92.

Van der Pijl, L., 1972. *Principles of Dispersal in Higher Plants.* Springer-Verlag, Berlin.

Vásquez-Yanes, C., Orozco, A., François, G. and Trejo, L., 1975. Observations on seed dispersal by bats in a tropical humid region in Veracruz, México. *Biotropica*, 7: 73–76.

Vinson, S.B., Frankie, G.W., Blum, M.S. and Wheeler, J.W., 1978. Isolation, identification and function of the Dufour gland secretion of *Xylocopa virginica texana* (Hymenoptera: Anthophoridae). *J. Chem. Ecol.*, 4: 315–323.

Vogel, S., 1958. Fledermausblumen in Südamerika. *Österr. Bot. Z.*, 105: 491–530.

Vogel, S., 1968. Scent organs of orchid flowers and their relation to insect pollination. *Proc. 5th World Orchid Conf., Long Beach, Calif.*, 1966: 253–259.

Vogel, S., 1968–9. Cheiropterophilie in der neotropischen Flora. I–III. *Flora*, 157: 562–602; 158: 185–222; 269–323.

Vogel, S., 1969. Flowers offering fatty oil instead of nectar. *Abstr. XI Int. Bot. Congr.*, p. 299.

Vogel, S., 1971. Ölproduzierende Blumen, die durch ölsammelnde Bienen bestaubt werden. *Naturwissenschaften*, 58: 58.

Vogel, S., 1974. Ölblumen und ölsammelnde Bienen. *Akad. Wiss. Lit., Mainz, Tropische und Subtropische Pflanzenwelt*, 7: 1–547.

Went, F.W., 1957. *Environmental Control of Plant Growth.* Chronica Botanica Company, Waltham. Mass.

Whitehead, D.R., 1969. Wind pollination in the angiosperms: Evolutionary and environmental considerations. *Evolution*, 23: 28–35.

Whitmore, T.C., 1975. *Tropical Rain Forests of the Far East.* Clarendon Press, Oxford, 281 pp.

Whitmore, T.C., 1978. Gaps in the forest canopy. In: P.B. Tomlinson and M.H. Zimmermann (Editors), *Tropical Trees as Living Systems.* Cambridge University Press, Cambridge. pp. 639–655.

Wolf, L.L., 1975. Energy intake and expenditure in a nectar-feeding sunbird. *Ecology*, 56: 92–104.

Yampolsky, C. and Yampolsky, H., 1922. Distribution of sex forms in the phanerogamic flora. *Bibl. Genet.*, 3: 1–62.

Young, A.M., 1972. Community ecology of some tropical rain forest butterflies. *Am. Midl. Nat.*, 87: 146–157.

Zapata, T.R. and Arroyo, M.T.K., 1978. Plant reproductive ecology of a secondary deciduous tropical forest in Venezuela. *Biotropica*, 10: 221–230.

Chapter 13

SUCCESSION

JOHN EWEL

AGENTS OF DISTURBANCE

Although the impact of people on tropical forests has never been greater than it is today, disturbance is not a new phenomenon to these ecosystems. Tropical forests have always been exposed to small-scale perturbations from tree falls (Hartshorn, 1978; Whitmore, 1978), herbivore outbreaks, and the movements and feeding activities of large mammals. Some coastal tropical forests at 10° to 20° latitude are regularly buffetted by cyclones (Webb, 1958; Wadsworth and Englerth, 1959; Whitmore, 1974; Lugo, 1978). Flooding, vulcanism, and earthquakes (Garwood et al., 1979) all exert their toll, assuring that tropical forests are continually disrupted. Because of the rapidity of weathering, and the preponderance of illites over the more stable kaolinites that would succeed them if weathering were to proceed further, landslides are extremely common in wet tropical mountains (Tricart, 1972).

Except for areas where tropical forests are regularly subjected to widespread devastation by hurricanes, earthquakes, and floods, successional communities probably occupied relatively little area during the course of recent evolution. Disturbed ecosystems were patches in a background matrix of mature forests. Today, however, the situation is fast becoming reversed. Rampant tropical deforestation, often followed by land abandonment and shifting land use patterns, is producing a situation in which mature tropical forests are predominantly islands against a background matrix of successional vegetation.

Some land use and colonization schemes turn out to have been inappropriate for the climate and soils where they are located. Many of these areas will not support permanent agriculture, so are allowed to revert to natural regrowth, as is occurring with some pastures in the neotropical lowlands. The net effect is a dramatic increase in fast-growing tropical second-growth vegetation.

Although the scale of devastation has changed, human-induced deforestation differs very little from that due to natural causes. Thus, the repair mechanisms already exist. The demise of mature forests, together with many of their specialized mature-phase species, has been accompanied by a dramatic increase in the successional vegetation. The ranges of many weedy generalists have expanded greatly, and today these species dominate the landscape throughout much of the tropics.

Shifting agriculture, especially as it is practised by land-hungry colonists seeking permanent farmlands, has long been recognized as a major cause of tropical deforestation. Logging is another major cause of disruption. Most humid tropical forests recover quickly from selective removal of high-grade timber, but logging roads often provide the accessibility that colonists are waiting for, so the logged forest never gets a chance to recover. Perhaps the most important cause of widespread tropical deforestation today is the establishment of huge monocultures such as rice, oil palm, pasture grasses, bananas, cacao, and rubber.

STRUCTURAL CHANGES

There are several general descriptions of tropical succession in the literature, but few have added much to the quarter-century-old concise overview of Richards (1955) or the exhaustive review by Budowski (1961). More recent contributions — and there have been many (e.g., see the Supplement on

Tropical Succession, *Biotropica*, 1980) — have emphasized specific findings on forest dynamics, plant reproduction, and nutrient cycling, plus succession in tropical environments other than the humid lowlands. Regional patterns are described in UNESCO (1978, chapter 9).

Succession in the wet tropical lowlands usually starts with rapid soil coverage by a mixture of weedy herbaceous plants and fast-growing vines. The distribution of these earliest colonizers seems to be due to chance distribution of seeds, both those in the soil and those dispersed onto the site immediately following disturbance. The importance of the pre-disturbance seed storage in the soil should not be underestimated, especially in areas where successional vegetation abounds. For example, we germinated 67 species from only 0.11 m² of soil (nearly 8000 individuals per m²) from an eight year old forest in Costa Rica (Ewel et al., 1981).

The pattern in the earliest stage of colonization is one of small patches, 2 to 30 m², dominated by single species. The distribution and size of the patches probably reflects seed dispersal rather than site differences, as most of these earliest colonizers seem to be able to occupy a broad range of sites. Diversity of this early, herbaceous stage is often very high. I have enumerated an average of more than 38 species on each of eight 18 m² plots in vegetation that was only three months old on Costa Rica's Osa Peninsula.

The initial herbaceous phase does not last long, except in the seasonally dry tropics where the process is arrested by the dry season and, in some cases, on a long-term basis by fires. Grasses are prominent successional components in the seasonally dry tropics.

In the humid lowlands the herbaceous plants usually die within a year. Vines that do not die grow up with the canopy, and woody pioneer species soon begin to dominate. These pioneer trees become established very early in the successional process; they can usually be found in the understorey of the herbaceous layer during the first few months following clearing. They grow up through the herb layer, and are first noticed as scattered emergents poking out of the top of the dense tangle of greenery beneath them. Some are covered by vines as they grow upward; others seem to escape the vines either by chance or by rapid growth, shed-

ding leaves and even branches as they grow; and still others (e.g. some *Cecropia* and *Musanga* spp.) support ant colonies that attack competitors. Vine control has long been recognized by tropical foresters as one of the most costly impediments to plantation establishment. Perhaps we could follow nature's example, and seek useful species that come equipped with their own biological control tools.

Within a few years, these fast-growing pioneer trees form a nearly closed canopy, often dominated by a single species. The vegetation changes from a mosaic of small, monospecific patches to a more uniform stand dominated by species tolerant of a broad range of site conditions. The lifespan of these pioneers is usually less than 25 years, and they survive by seed dispersal — usually wind or animal mediated — onto other, newly disturbed sites.

What happens after the demise of the pioneers is not quite so clear. Tree diversity increases, and the frequency and distribution of the species reflect a complex interaction of seed abundance, seed predation, competition, herbivory, and microsite differences. Budowski (1963, 1965, 1970) has enumerated twenty characteristics of early and late successional forests, and the tree species found therein; he has also compared them with mature forest. Some changes that occur have important economic implications. For example, growth rates of trees are highest in successional ecosystems, but wood densities are lower. The structurally "cheap", short-lived building blocks of successional ecosystems are later replaced by heftier materials — denser woods, tougher leaves — that are produced more slowly, but last longer.

The high net primary productivity of successional ecosystems supports large animal populations, although not the same species, usually, as the mature forests. Because of their high secondary productivity, patches of second growth are often favored hunting grounds of indigenous peoples (Linares, 1976). Most of the kinds of animals that thrive in successional habitats are "weedy" generalists, but that is not always the case. For example, in the subtropical Everglades of extreme southern Florida (U.S.A.), white-tailed deer are extremely abundant in succession on former farmlands. These deer, in turn, support numerous Florida panthers, one of the most endangered mammals in North America.

One difficulty is that tropical forest succession

has often been described as a process terminating in some well-defined end point: a mature forest composed of a diverse mixture of large-seeded, shade-tolerant plants (e.g., Richards, 1973, pp. 64–65). In spite of the pedagogic value of this heuristic model of the steady-state tropical forest, we must remind ourselves that it does not exist in nature: certainly not at the scale of a square kilometer, and probably not at the scale of a hectare.

Although there are great taxonomic differences among the successional floras of distinct biogeographic regions, the physiognomy of successional vegetation is remarkably homogeneous throughout the tropics. Furthermore, pantropical generalists such as *Trema*, *Ceiba*, and *Ficus* provide more floristic similarity among successional vegetations than among mature communities.

Plants typical of stressful tropical environments such as mangrove swamps, alpine communities, and semideserts often exhibit a high degree of ecological convergence. The same is true of successional species. One conspicuous example is the huge, palmately lobed leaves and low degree of branching characteristic of certain species of *Cecropia* (Americas), *Musanga* (Africa), and *Macaranga* (Asia). Such pioneers often form an even-aged canopy that dominates successional forests for up to twenty years, but, because they cannot reproduce in the understorey, they are dependent upon further forest disturbance for their survival.

STABILITY

It is convenient to consider ecosystem stability to have two components: resistance and resilience. Resistance, or the degree to which an ecosystem maintains itself in the face of forces that would change it, is not meaningful unless one specifies the type of outside changing force involved. For example, a lowland, moist tropical forest might be very resistant to physical changes such as high winds, but might be very susceptible to disturbance from a very modest decrease in temperature — much more so than would a boreal forest, for example.

Resilience may be an easier concept to deal with quantitatively. It can be measured as the rate at which an ecosystem returns to its initial, or pre-disturbance, condition. There are two ways to interpret succession as a measure of ecosystem resilience. The first is simply to measure the rate of change of a successional ecosystem. Thus, successional ecosystems that grow faster would be considered to be more resilient than those which grow more slowly. Another possibility is to measure the amount of structure accumulated in a successional ecosystem after a given time, and express that structure as a fraction of the amount of structure in the predisturbance, steady-state ecosystem.

The difference between these two interpretations of resilience might best be illustrated with an example. Suppose we have two steady-state ecosystems: a tropical dry forest in which the dominants average 20 m tall, and a lowland, wet forest in which the dominants average 60 m tall. Suppose that these two forests are felled and that the rate of regrowth is monitored. Further, suppose that, after five years, the dominant successional plants on the dry forest site are 10 m tall, while those on the wet forest site are 20 m tall. In one sense one might regard the wet forest ecosystem as more resilient because its successional vegetation is twice as tall as that on the dry forest site. On the other hand, one might regard the dry forest ecosystem as being more resilient because after only five years of regrowth its height is 50% of that of the original steady-state forest, whereas the height of the successional vegetation on the wet forest site is only 33% of its original steady-state value.

There is some evidence that, in the short term, tropical ecosystem resilience does indeed follow such patterns in wet and dry environments (Ewel, 1977). However, succession in dry tropical areas suffers repeated setbacks because of rainfall variability, so resilience in dry areas tends, in the longer term, to be lower by either measure: absolute rate of recovery, or relative rate of recovery. The least resilient tropical ecosystems of all may be those of high elevations. Tropical montane forests regrow extremely slowly, both on absolute and on relative scales (Ewel, 1980).

Fig. 13.1 is a model of ecosystem resilience. The x-axis is time; the y-axis is some measure of environmental quality, ranging from harsh to benevolent (e.g. dry to wet, cold to warm, infertile to fertile, etc.); and the z-axis is structure or maturity. Structure increases with maturity in the sense that Margalef (1968) uses maturity to describe both

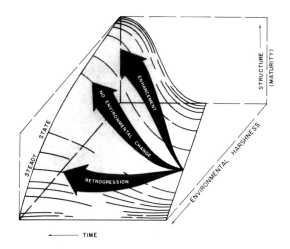

Fig. 13.1. Ecosystem resilience as a function of environmental quality and changes resulting from disturbance. See text.

short-term successional changes and evolutionary changes associated with environmental gradients.

The left-most plane of the figure represents the amount of structure in any ecosystem at maturity. In keeping with current ideas regarding the response of a steady-state ecosystem to increments of a potentially limiting factor, the curve of structure (=maturity) at steady state increases hyperbolically as environmental quality increases. Thus, it takes a greater increment of environmental quality to produce a given amount of increase in structure at steady state in a benevolent environment than it does in a harsh environment. At the harsh end of the spectrum, however, a small increase in environmental quality (or in some limiting factor) produces a substantial increase in the structure of the steady-state community.

Recovery of structure, or return to maturity, is shown in the figure as a sigmoid growth function. Other formulations might be better representations of certain responses, but the sigmoid curve is common to many kinds of growth measures, including biomass and leaf area development. Note that the time axis is compressed at the far end, i.e. in non-limiting environments. Almost all models that incorporate a measure of environmental resistance to regrowth produce responses indicating that recovery is slower — both relatively and absolutely — in harsh environments than in benevolent environments.

A steady-state ecosystem that is disrupted slides

from left to right along the curved surface illustrated in Fig. 13.1. As the system recovers, it can traverse three kinds of paths. First, it might recover by moving along the surface described as "no environmental change" in the figure. If it does, it will be more resilient than equally displaced systems located in harsher environments and less resilient than ecosystems in more benevolent environments.

Another possibility — and a common one in nature — is that the disruptive force, either natural or human-induced, reduces environmental quality. Landslides or volcanism that remove or cover nutrient-rich, mycorrhizae-laden surface soils are examples of natural events of this type. Some farming practices lead not only to vegetation destruction, but also to environmental degradation. Succession proceeds along the path labelled "retrogression". It is slower than the succession that might have occurred if the ecosystem had been subjected only to vegetation destruction, without concomitant degradation of the site. Furthermore, the new steady-state system may be less structured than the one that originally occupied the site. Return to the original condition must await amelioration of site conditions, a process that may occur extremely slowly.

Retrogression does not arise only from physical degradation of the site as a part of ecosystem disruption. Sometimes retrogression occurs as succession proceeds. One example is allelopathy, whereby one plant species releases substances into its surroundings that inhibit the growth, survival, or vigor of potential competitors. There has been relatively little work done on allelopathy in tropical succession (e.g., Gliessman, 1976, 1978), but there is no reason to think that allelopathy is less common in the tropics than in the temperate zone. Because many allelopathic substances are water-soluble, allelopathy may exert more control over succession in the dry tropics than in the wet tropics, where vast amounts might have to be excreted just to replace the amount leached away.

Another naturally mediated retrogression syndrome consists of colonization by successional species that are prone to fire. Repeated fires can lead to depletion of nitrogen and sulfur supplies, thus site degradation. A classic example from the tropics is *Imperata cylindrica*, the fire-adapted grass that often captures deforested sites in Malesia (*sensu* Whitmore, 1975), preventing their recolonization by tree species for decades, if not permanently (e.g. see Eussen and Wirjahardja, 1973).

Succession can proceed along a third, although less common route. This is the process of enhancement (see Fig. 13.1), whereby either the disruptive agent or the successional community improves environmental quality, such that the post-succession community is more structured than the predisturbance community. This can result from the deposition of nutrient-rich volcanic ash on top of an infertile soil; erosion of a highly weathered surface soil, exposing a more fertile subsoil; or farming practises that improve soil physical characteristics or fertility (Fig. 13.2). Enhancement is often biologically mediated, as when exotic plants are introduced onto species-depauperate islands. The resulting successional vegetation is often more

complex than the original system, although this is not always regarded as a desirable trait by ecologists. Ecosystem enhancement may be a more common phenomenon than we realize. This may partly reflect our conditioned response to regard natural disasters and human-induced change as environmental evils. Although degradation is the general rule, there are undoubtedly exceptions in which disruption of steady-state systems leads to environmental improvement and increased structural complexity.

Does the immense diversity and structural complexity of wet, tropical lowland forests automatically lead to fragility? Not necessarily. Although tropical forests are being destroyed at an alarming rate (Farnworth and Golley, 1974; Goodland and Irwin, 1975; Myers, 1979, 1980), the fragility of these ecosystems is a measure of the magnitude of

Fig. 13.2. An example of ecosystem structural enhancement after disturbance. The original, mature ecosystem (right) is a glade dominated by herbaceous plants. The successional community (left) follows farming that improves site quality, permitting invasion of the exotic tree *Schinus terebinthifolius*. Everglades National Park, Florida, U.S.A.

the destructive forces working against them, rather than an inherent property of the ecosystems themselves. When forests of the lowland humid tropics are subjected to large-scale disruption, recovery can be painfully slow. This is especially true if essential mycorrhizal fungus populations are destroyed (Janos, 1980) or if the seed sources needed for recolonization of mature-system species are removed from large areas (Gómez-Pompa et al., 1972). On the other hand, when disturbance is small scale, and comparable in frequency and magnitude to the kinds of disturbance that these tropical ecosystems evolved with, recovery is extremely rapid. Regrowth proceeds quickly, partly because of favorable conditions for plant growth, and partly because seeds of successional species are present in the soil (Keay, 1960; Guevara and Gómez-Pompa 1972; Liew, 1973; Kellman, 1974; Cheke et al., 1979) and are readily dispersed (Opler et al., 1980).

How does the resilience of wet, lowland tropical forests compare with that of other forests? If, in the simple model presented in Fig. 13.1, "maturity" is expressed as physical structure, such as biomass, then tropical ecosystems are probably as resilient as most others. If, however, the "maturity" axis incorporates not just any kind of high diversity, but diversity consisting of the same array of species that occupied the site prior to disturbance, then tropical lowland forests may be among the world's most fragile ecosystems. Although a denuded site may revegetate quickly, it will only return to the pre-disturbance floristic composition if nearby seed sources are left intact. When disruption is widespread the ability of the site to undergo succession is not necessarily impeded, but complete resilience — or return to the predisturbance floristic composition — may be lost completely. In that sense, tropical, lowland wet forests are indeed fragile — perhaps more so than their less diverse, and less "mature" temperate-zone counterparts.

In general, ecosystems in benevolent tropical environments, epitomized by the humid lowlands, are more resilient than ecosystems in cooler or drier environments. If, however, ecosystem retrogression or ecosystem enhancement occur, either as part of the disruptive process or as part of the recovery sequence, resilience is affected accordingly.

One useful guideline for tropical ecosystem manipulation might be to avoid any kind of disruption that would preclude eventual self-replacement of the original community. This guideline is admittedly a very conservative one, but until we know more about tropical forest ecosystems and their regeneration, and the long-term viability of the systems we are replacing them with, a cautious approach to change would seem to be in order.

REFERENCES

Budowski, G., 1961. *Studies on Forest Succession in Costa Rica and Panama.* Dissertation, School of Forestry, Yale University, New Haven, Conn., 189 pp.

Budowski, G., 1963. Forest succession in tropical lowlands. *Turrialba*, 13: 42–44.

Budowski, G., 1965. Distribution of tropical American rain forest species in the light of successional processes. *Turrialba*, 15: 40–42.

Budowski, G., 1970. The distinction between old secondary and climax species in tropical Central American lowland forests. *Trop. Ecol.*, 11: 44–48.

Cheke, A.S., Nanakorn, W. and Yankoses, C., 1979. Dormancy and dispersal of seeds of secondary forest species under the canopy of a primary tropical rain forest in northern Thailand. *Biotropica*, 11: 88–95.

Eussen, J.H. and Wirjahardja, S., 1973. Studies on an ilang-ilang (*Imperata cylindrica* (L.) Beauv.) vegetation. *Biotrop. Bull.*, 6: 1–24.

Ewel, J., 1977. Differences between wet and dry successional tropical ecosystems. *Geo-Eco-Trop*, 1: 103–117.

Ewel, J., 1980. Tropical succession: manifold routes to maturity. *Biotropica*, 12: 2–7.

Ewel, J., Berish, C., Brown, B., Price, N. and Raich, J., 1981. Slash and burn impacts on a Costa Rican wet forest site. *Ecology*, 62: 816–829.

Farnworth, E.G. and Golley, F.B. (Editors), 1974. *Fragile Ecosystems.* Springer-Verlag, Berlin, 258 pp.

Garwood, N., Janos, D.P. and Brokaw, N., 1979. Earthquake-caused landslides: a major disturbance to tropical forests. *Science*, 205: 997–999.

Gliessman, S.R., 1976. Allelopathy in a broad spectrum of environments as illustrated by bracken. *Bot. J. Linn. Soc.*, 73: 96–105.

Gliessman, S.R., 1978. Allelopathy as a potential mechanism of dominance in the humid tropics. *Trop. Ecol.*, 19: 200–208.

Gómez-Pompa, A., Vázquez-Yanes, C. and Guevara, S., 1972. The tropical rain forest: a nonrenewable resource. *Science*, 177: 762–765.

Goodland, R.J.A. and Irwin, H.S., 1975. *Amazon Jungle: Green Hell to Red Desert?* Elsevier, Amsterdam, 156 pp.

Guevara, S. and Gómez-Pompa, A., 1972. Seeds from surface soils in a tropical region of Veracruz, Mexico. *J. Arnold Arbor.*, 53: 312–335.

Hartshorn, G.S., 1978. Tree falls and tropical forest dynamics. In: P.B. Tomlinson and M.H. Zimmermann (Editors), *Tropical Trees as Living Systems.* Cambridge University Press, Cambridge, pp. 617–638.

Janos, D.P., 1980. Mycorrhizae influence tropical succession. *Biotropica*, 12: 56–64.

Keay, R.W.J., 1960. Seeds in forest soils. *Nig. For. Info. Bull., N.S.*, 4: 1–4.

Kellman, M.C., 1974. The viable weed seed content of some tropical agricultural soils. *J. Appl. Ecol.*, 11: 669–678.

Liew, T.C., 1973. Occurrence of seeds in virgin forest top soil with particular reference to secondary species in Sabah. *Malay. For.*, 36: 185–193.

Linares, O.F., 1976. "Garden hunting" in the American tropics. *Human Ecol.*, 4: 331–349.

Lugo, A.E., 1978. Stress and ecosystems. In: J.H. Thorp and J.W. Gibbons (Editors), *Energy and Environmental Stress in Aquatic Ecosystems*. USDOE Symp. Ser. (CONF – 771114). NTIS, Springfield, Va., pp. 62–101.

Margalef, R., 1968. *Perspectives in Ecological Theory*. University of Chicago Press, Chicago, Ill., 111 pp.

Myers, N., 1979. *The Sinking Ark*. Pergamon Press, New York, N.Y., 307 pp.

Myers, N., 1980. *Conversion of Tropical Moist Forests*. National Academy of Science, Washington, D.C., 205 pp.

Opler, P.A., Baker, H.G. and Frankie, G.W., 1980. Plant reproductive characteristics during secondary succession in neotropical lowland forest ecosystems. *Biotropica*, 12: 40–46.

Richards, P.W., 1955. The secondary succession in the tropical rain forest. *Sci. Progr.*, 43: 45–57.

Richards, P.W., 1973. The tropical rain forest. *Sci. Am.*, 229: 58–67.

Tricart, J., 1972. *The Landforms of the Humid Tropics, Forests and Savannas*. (Transl. by C.J. Kiewiet de Jonge.) St. Martin's Press, New York, N.Y., 306 pp.

UNESCO, 1978. *Tropical Forest Ecosystems, A State of Knowledge Report. Nat. Resour. Res.*, 14: 683 pp.

Wadsworth, F.H. and Englerth, G.H., 1959. Effects of the 1959 hurricane on forests in Puerto Rico. *Caribb. For.*, 20: 38–51.

Webb, L.J., 1958. Cyclones as an ecological factor in tropical lowland rain forests, north Queensland. *Aust. J. Bot.*, 6: 220–228.

Whitmore, T.C., 1974. *Change with Time and the Role of Cyclones in Tropical Rain Forest on Kolombangara, Solomon Islands*. Institute Paper No. 46, Commonwealth Forestry Institute, University of Oxford, 78 pp.

Whitmore, T.C., 1975. *Tropical Rain Forests of the Far East*. Clarendon Press, Oxford, 281 pp.

Whitmore, T.C., 1978. Gaps in the forest canopy. In: P.B. Tomlinson and M.H. Zimmermann (Editors), *Tropical Trees as Living Systems*. Cambridge University Press, Cambridge, pp. 639–655.

Chapter 14

ADAPTATIONS OF TROPICAL TREES TO MOISTURE STRESS

ERNESTO MEDINA

INTRODUCTION

A range of climatic types are found within the tropical belt that can be generally characterized by a relative homogeneous average monthly temperature (average decreasing with altitude) with seasonal patterns of rainfall distribution; the degree of rainfall seasonality varies with latitude and regulates vegetation phenology.

Rainfall distribution and potential evaporation determine the hydric gradient which results in the sequence tropical rain forest → evergreen seasonal forest → deciduous forest → thorn forest → thorn scrub → desert scrub, as described by Beard (1955) for American tropical lowland forests. Along this gradient tree height, density and forest complexity are progressively reduced and morpho-physiological adaptations to resist or avoid water stress are more frequent.

EVALUATION OF ENVIRONMENTAL ARIDITY

The aridity of a certain environment is best measured as the ratio of rainfall to potential evapotranspiration, or as the ratio between the energy equivalent to evaporate rainfall and the total amount of energy available for water evaporation (Troll, 1956; Flöhn in Walter, 1973). Those ratios require involved calculations of potential evapotranspiration or careful measurements of the energy balance at each site. A practical possibility based on standard measurements in weather stations would be the comparison between rainfall and potential evaporations as measured in Tank A (Walter and Medina, 1971) with the degree of climatic aridity measured as the difference between rainfall and Tank A evaporation ($R-E$).

The rainfall–evaporation pattern along a latitudinal transect in Venezuela is shown in Fig. 14.1. Stations selected are located in lowland areas, so that they differentiate mainly in the rainfall–evaporation regime and not in average temperature. $R-E$ figures are taken as potential water surplus when positive and potential water deficits when negative. We use the word potential because in many cases topographic features or soil water retention capacity modify actual water availability.

Fig. 14.1 shows clearly that Tank A evaporation changes drastically during the year, in an opposite pattern to rainfall. Potential evapotranspiration follows the same trend. Therefore, potential evapotranspiration in the tropics cannot be estimated simply from temperature data as has been extensively done in tropical America (Holdridge, 1947, 1959; Ewel and Madriz, 1968).

There are marked differences in the dry season estimated with climate diagrams (relation between average monthly temperature and rainfall in proportion 1:2) and $R-E$ values. The latter indicate a stronger aridity than the climate diagrams, a fact noticed when analysing climatic variability in the tropics on the basis of temperature and rainfall data (Walter and Medina, 1971).

Another aspect to be considered when assessing vegetation changes along aridity gradients is that vegetation is frequently modified by edaphic conditions. In those regions where oligotrophic soils predominate, other vegetation types appear, such as savannas in deciduous forest climate (Beard, 1944, 1955; Walter, 1973) or evergreen scrub in areas with $R-E$ indexes below -2000 mm (Loveless, 1961).

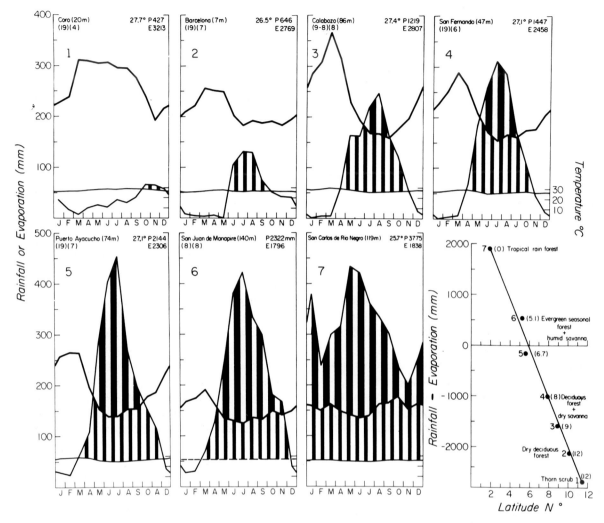

Fig. 14.1. Rainfall, Tank A evaporation and temperature data along a N–S transect in Venezuela. Thick line is Tank A evaporation, thin line is rainfall. Nearly horizontal line is temperature. Thin bars indicate humid period in climate diagram, thick bars indicate humid period after R–E index. Numbers in parentheses indicate dry months after the R–E index.

QUANTITATIVE EVALUATION OF PLANT WATER STRESS

Evaluation of water stress in plants can be obtained by looking at their water relations under natural conditions, i.e. ratios between water losses (transpiration) and water uptake (absorption); or measuring the water status in the whole plant or plant parts.

Measurements of transpiration under field conditions have proved to be very difficult because all methods available require a certain degree of disturbance of the natural energy environment of the plant. With a few exceptions, all transpiration measurements conducted on tropical trees used the Stocker rapid weighing method (Stocker, 1956). The procedure requires the detachment of the transpiring organ and its weighing at intervals of a few minutes. In spite of careful procedure, moving the leaf from natural environment to be weighed could result in completely wrong values. Furthermore, changes in the internal water status can have a strong influence in the transpiration of detached leaves. Such measurements therefore are subjected to severe criticisms (Franco and Magalhaẽs, 1965).

The development of diffusion porometers for the measurement of leaf conductance and devices for measurement of leaf temperature has allowed the evaluation of leaf properties in undisturbed natural conditions, such properties being intimately related to the energy interaction between the leaves and the surrounding atmosphere (for methodological details see Slavik, 1974).

Seasonal or daily variations in transpiration rates and leaf diffusive conductance can be used as indication of water stress, thus allowing detection of different behavior types within components of plant communities.

Direct measurement of water absorption in natural communities is not yet possible, but inferences can be made by measuring changes in soil water content in the roots' neighborhood.

Analyses of energy relationships between the leaves and surrounding environment have led to the development of models which are currently the best approach to evaluate adaptive behavior of higher plants to water utilization under natural conditions (Gates, 1968, 1975). Energy balance studies have resulted in relevant inferences to understand variation in leaf size and temperature regulation mechanisms which are applicable to tropical trees (Parkhurst and Loucks, 1972; Taylor, 1975).

The water status in the plant or plant tissues is measured as water potential (ψ) which indicates the difference between the water potential in analyzed tissue and that of pure water at the same temperature and pressure (Slatyer, 1967). The components of water potential in an ideal cell can be expressed as:

total water potential (ψ) = pressure (turgor) potential − osmotic potential (π) − matric potential (τ)

Total water potential and osmotic potentials are the most widely used parameters to evaluate plant water status in plants but the meaning and interpretation of each one under natural conditions may differ widely. While ψ is a direct indicator of water status in the plant, and minimum values of healthy leaves during periods of water stress could be taken as indicator of drought tolerance, π seems to reflect the water conditions in the habitat during prolonged periods. The postulated relationship of π with degree of plasma dehydration has served as a basis for explaining physiological behavior

and morphogenetic responses of drought-resistant plants (Walter, 1963a, b, 1964; Walter and Kreeb, 1970).

Minimum total water potentials and osmotic potentials are normally correlated when different plants and communities are compared, simply because minimal ψ is set by osmotic and matric potentials (Richter, 1976).

Variations of the pressure component of total water potential seem to have also important physiological consequences, mainly in regards to regulation of cell growth and leaf expansion (Hsiao, 1973; Oertli, 1976). Turgor pressure is conceived as a signal for regulation of cell sap concentration through a negative feedback mechanism (Cram, 1976); however, there are not enough measurements to evaluate its significance under natural conditions.

PHYSIOLOGICAL AND MORPHOLOGICAL ADAPTATIONS TO WATER STRESS

When considering plants from regions where water supply might restrict growth periodically, it is convenient to differentiate between drought-tolerant and drought-avoiding types (Parker, 1968; Levitt, 1972). The first group has a plasmatic tolerance to low total water potentials, and frequently to low osmotic potentials in their vacuolar sap. The second group presents several characteristics that allow them to overcome the water stress without reducing water potential to a great extent; for example, deep root systems which guarantee adequate water supply during dry periods, efficient stomata regulation of transpiration, or shedding of transpiring organs when water losses can not be recovered.

The main organ for energy exchange in any plant is the leaf, therefore its structure and function have been the object of detailed analysis in order to discover relations with limiting environmental parameters, mainly water supply. Analyses of leaf structure for xeromorphic features (leaf thickness, density of venation, stomata frequency and size, abundance of sclerenchyma and cutin, sunken stomata; Shields, 1950) have not always been successful in correlating leaf structure with environment. Frequently mesophytic leaf types dominate arid tropical environments, while sclerophylls are frequent in ecosystems with adequate supply of water during the whole year but with oligotrophic soils (Ferri, 1961; Medina, 1978).

Tropical trees do not present any peculiar characteristic regarding adaptations and responses to water stress, therefore they are amenable to a similar analysis of water stress adaptations of trees in any other region (e.g., Hsiao, 1973; Kozlowski, 1976).

Adaptations observed in tropical forest to water stress include: (a) increase in deciduous behavior, (b) dominance of microphylly and compound deciduous leaves, (c) greater development of underground organs and deeper root systems, (d) tolerance to low water potential and low osmotic potentials of the vacuolar sap in evergreens, (e) mechanisms for reducing amount of absorbed radiation as high degree of leaf inclination, leaf roughness and hairiness.

Phenology: evergreen vs deciduous tree types

Most climates in the tropics are seasonal in regards to rainfall distribution. The magnitude of the water deficits varies as shown in Fig. 14.1. On good soils the degree of water deficit during the dry season can be estimated by the proportion of deciduous, microphyllous to nanophyllous (*sensu* Raunkiaer) tree components as compared with evergreens.

Deciduous trees are defined as trees remaining leafless for a certain period of time (from days to months) during the dry season, and they can be considered to be drought-avoiders. Leaf shedding seems to be controlled mainly by drought, although photoperiod may be also involved (Daubenmire, 1972; Alvim and Alvim, 1978). Deciduousness has not been analyzed experimentally in great detail. Observations under natural conditions show that reinitiation of growth takes place generally shortly before the beginning of the rainy season, indicating that probably it is a rhythm triggered by day length and/or increasing night temperatures at the beginning of the wet season and not simply by water supply. Daubenmire (1972) measured strong reductions in stem diameter in deciduous trees due to loss of water accumulated in the stem.

The deciduous character of tropical trees may be facultative or obligate (Table 14.1). In the first type the duration of the leafless period is reduced as

water availability during the dry season increases, until new leaves are formed while shedding the old leaves. That means that leaf duration in facultative deciduous trees varies from approximately six to thirteen months, depending on the intensity of drought.

De Oliveira and Labouriau (1961) reported that trees from the deciduous dry thorn forest in northeast Brazil (caatinga), cultivated in the Botanical Garden of Rio de Janeiro, behave differently in relation to maintenance of leaf canopy. *Caesalpinia pyramidalis* and *Jatropha phyllacantha*, which are deciduous in their original habitat, become evergreen when cultivated with irrigation. *Spondias tuberosa* on the contrary, seems to be an obligate deciduous tree. Similar observations have been published for other trees by Daubenmire (1972) and Frankie et al. (1974). It is noteworthy that two other species of *Spondias* respond similarly in Costa Rica (Table 14.1).

There are but a few experimental studies on regulation of leaf shedding in tropical trees. Alvim and Alvim (1978) demonstrated that leaf shedding and flushing in the cacao tree are related to a sudden increase in water potential. Synchronization is effected by a period of drought followed by irrigation. Continuously irrigated plants do not show synchrony in bud burst. They showed also many examples of photoperiodic and thermoperiodic regulation of tree growth (flowering). In Manaus, at the Río Negro in the Amazon Basin, it has been also observed that flowering and probably leaf change is mainly associated with the dry, short dry season (Prance and Da Silva, 1975).

TABLE 14.1

Deciduous character of tropical trees from 1, De Oliveira and Labouriau (1961); 2, Schnetter (1971); 3, Daubenmire (1972); 4, Walter (1973); 5, Frankie et al. (1974)

Facultative deciduous		Obligate deciduous	
Caesalpinia pyramidalis	1	*Enterolobium cyclocarpum*	3
Prosopis juliflora	2	*Spondias tuberosa*	1
Jatropha phyllacantha	1	*Spondias mombin*	5
Hura crepitans	4	*Spondias purpurea*	3
Sterculia apetala	3	*Cordia alliodora*	5
Tectona grandis	4	*Tabebuia neochrysantha*	3
Genipa caruto	5	*Ceiba pentandra*	5
Ochroma pyramidalis	5		
Casearia arborea	5		

Clear differences in leaf shedding and flushing patterns can be observed in a wet forest at La Selva and a dry forest (deciduous) at Hacienda La Pacífica in Costa Rica (Frankie et al., 1974). Fig. 14.2 shows that peak flushing in the dry forest takes place at the beginning of the rainy season, and is easily differentiated from peak in leaf fall. In the wet forest at La Selva, the amount of trees which remain leafless for a certain period of time is considerably lower and most of them change leaves during the relatively short dry season. The amount of rainfall in the two areas is comparatively high. During 1969–70, 4000 to 5000 mm of rainfall was measured in La Selva and 1300 to 2200 mm in Hacienda La Pacífica (dry forest). The main difference between the two forests is that while in La Selva up to 45% of rainfall occurs from December to May, in the dry forest only a maximum of 17% falls during the same period. It is this seasonality that selects deciduous over evergreen trees.

Evergreen trees are dominant in humid forests without pronounced seasonality in water availability, but are also present in dry forests or can be even dominant in savannas (Eiten, 1972). The evergreen character has been associated with permanent water availability but also with poor soils (Loveless, 1961, 1962; Monk, 1966).

Leaf size, shape and inclination

Leaf size and shape are important in coupling leaves to the energy environment, because they regulate the interaction between leaf and wind and determine the thickness of the boundary layer. This boundary layer originates at the leaf surface as a consequence of slower air movement resulting from friction with the leaf surface, its thickness depending on wind velocity and leaf characteristic dimension (Taylor and Gates, 1970; Nobel, 1974; Taylor, 1975). Characteristic dimension controls the magnitude of the interaction between leaf surface and wind, and represents the transformation of actual leaf shape into an equivalent square surface whose convective heat exchange can be accurately calculated (Taylor, 1975). Leaf hairiness and surface undulation may be important, but their influence on characteristic leaf dimension has to be measured in each leaf.

Characteristic dimension affects leaf energy exchange mainly through convective heat exchange and boundary layer resistance to water vapor diffusion from the leaf. Under a given set of conditions bigger leaves tend to have a higher temperature and frequently lower transpiration rates.

Several authors have tried to explain the trend of reduction in leaf size from humid and/or shady habitats to dry and sunny habitats in terms of optimal water use efficiency, avoidance of extreme leaf temperatures or maximization of plant productivity (Parkhurst and Loucks, 1972; Taylor, 1975; Givnish and Vermeij, 1976).

Table 14.2 shows two examples of leaf size distribution (sensu Raunkiaer) among fully exposed trees in contrasting plant communities: an evergreen rain forest in Brazil (Cain et al., 1956) and an evergreen bushland in the arid coast at Port Henderson Hill in Jamaica (Loveless, 1961). It is clear that mesophyll leaves (approx. 20–180 cm^2) are dominant in the rain forest, while microphyllous leaves (2–20 cm^2) are dominant in the arid

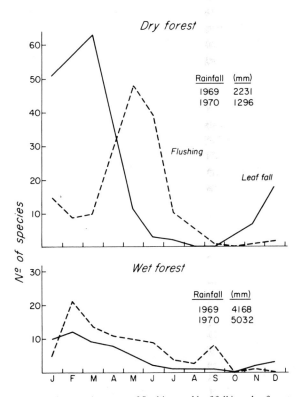

Fig. 14.2. Seasonal pattern of flushing and leaf fall in a dry forest (La Hacienda) and a wet forest (La Selva) in Costa Rica (included are only trees from the upper canopy) (redrawn from Frankie et al., 1974).

TABLE 14.2

Percentage distribution of leaf sizes (Raunkiaer size classes) in evergreen rainforest in Brazil (Cain et al., 1956) and evergreen bushland at Port Henderson Hill, Jamaica (Loveless, 1961)

	Rain forest macrophanerophytes	Bushland microphanerophytes
Number of species:	49	43
Macrophyll	2	–
Mesophyll	75	16
Microphyll	16	74
Nanophyll	2	7
Leptophyll	4	2

bushland. Small leaves tend to be better coupled to air temperature, because they allow an efficient heat exchange in high radiation, high temperature environments, which also may present frequent restrictions in water availability. In rain forest habitats, although upper leaves are exposed to high radiation and high air temperatures, availability of water allows efficient evaporative cooling. In many cases, however, even in humid habitats, short dry spells may be frequent. Those are more pronounced when soil water retention capacity is poor as in sandy soil areas.

It has been repeatedly observed, that upper leaves in the canopy of tropical trees show a pronounced inclination (Walter, 1973; Brunig, 1976). This leaf inclination effectively reduces absorbed radiation per unit leaf area, thus avoiding overheating (Medina et al., 1978) (Fig. 14.3). Reduction of absorbed radiation in a high radiation, high temperature environment decreases water requirements for evaporative cooling, allowing a more efficient water use under water stress.

The importance of energy balance in high temperature environment can be evaluated by heat resistance measurements. In tropical trees this

Fig. 14.3. Leaf inclination showed by tropical trees and shrubs. From left to right, upper row: *Heteropteris* sp., *Macairea rufescens*, *Rhodognaphalopsis discolor*; lower row; *Remigia involucrata*, *Clusia* sp., *Miconia* sp. These species are representative of the sclerophyllous *bana* vegetation on white sands along Rio Negro, Amazon Basin (Medina et al., 1978).

tolerance is around 45 to 50° (Ernst, 1971; Schnetter, 1971) and there is a certain variability with lower resistance found in natural humid forest (Biebl, 1964). Many compound leaves show leaflet movements associated with dark–light phases, but they can also be induced by water stress or high temperature. Ernst (1971) showed in *Brachystegia spicaeformis* that leaflets close during the day when surface temperatures surpass 32 to 34°C. Leaflet movement reduces illumination of the leaf by 50%, while maintaining a similar transpiration rate, thus effectively reducing temperature through evaporative cooling.

The proportion of compound leaves increases along humidity gradients, mainly due to increased amount of legumes with microphyllous, compound leaves (Givnish, 1978). Table 14.3 compiled by Givnish (1978) shows a marked increase in percentage of compound leaf species towards greater aridity. There is also a reduction of leaf length (as a measure of leaf size) from a subtropical moist forest to a dry tree veld. Givnish's interpretation is that possession of small leaves located along a deciduous rachis is probably advantageous in a seasonal dry environment.

Osmotic pressure of leaf cell sap in different tropical forests

Table 14.4 lists values of osmotic pressure of leaf cell sap from dominant species in different tropical forests, such as evergreen species from a dry coastal forest in Jamaica (after Loveless, 1961), a deciduous woodland dominated by legumes in south Central Africa (Ernst, 1971) and three evergreen communities in the Amazon Basin (upper Rio Negro) differing in species composition and soil characteristics (site description in Herrera, 1977).

Evergreen species of the dry forest show the highest values with a range from 18.2 to 43.5 bar. Leaf duration in this forest is around one year. The deciduous woodland, with an active canopy approximately of seven months has values which never are above 20 bar, even after the beginning of the dry season (Ernst and Walker, 1973). Leaves are shed during this period.

In the Rio Negro region, the three forest communities show a relatively equilibrated water balance as expressed by osmotic pressure of cell sap. Only in the *bana* site, an open sclerophyllous low forest, there is a tendency toward higher osmotic pressures during the relative dry season. Total water potentials of dominant trees and shrubs in this community are rarely below -14 bar (Medina et al., 1978). These tropical rain forest values are similar to those reported by Walter for Amani rain forest species (Walter, 1973).

Water potential, leaf diffusion resistance and leaf temperature

At the onset of the water stress two main behavior types can be differentiated: (a) plants that do not close their stomata and continue transpiring, therefore presenting a pronounced reduction of total leaf water potential, and (b) plants sensitive to water stress which close their stomata as soon as the water stress set in. In this case water potential is maintained within certain limits.

Stomatal closure also cuts CO_2 influx and under prolonged periods of water stress there is a net loss of carbohydrates. The plants normally shed their leaves and behave therefore as deciduous. This is probably the predominant mechanism in dry deciduous tropical forests.

The first group could be classified following

TABLE 14.3

Percentage of compound leaves and leaf size distribution of simple leaves in different forest types (from Givnish, 1978)

Habitat	Number of species		Species with simple leaves (%)			Compound leaves (%)
		Leaf length:	> 7.5 cm	2.5–7.5 cm	< 2.5 cm	
Moist sub-tropical forest	60		75	19	0	6
Mesophytic forest	150		32	47	3	18
Dry tree veld and scrub	500		11	34	13	42

TABLE 14.4

Osmotic pressure of leaf cell sap in tropical trees

Species	Osmotic pressure (bar)
DRY COASTAL FOREST (Harris and Lawrence, after Loveless, 1961)	
Capparis ferruginea	43.5
Cassia emarginata	23.9
Guaiacum officinale	32.3
Hypelate trifoliata	28.5
Piscidia piscipula	18.2
Sarcomphalus laurinus	19.8
DECIDUOUS WOODLAND (miombo) (after Ernst, 1971; rainy season)	
Uapaca kirkiana	7.6
Terminalia prunioides	10.0
Combretum molle	13.6
Piliostigma thonningii	10.1
Syzygium guineense	12.8
Julbernardia globiflora	14.2
Brachystegia spiciformis	14.9
Acacia vermicularis	15.1
Cussonia spicata	15.1
Brachystegia boehmii	15.3
Cassia abreviata	19.1
TROPICAL RAIN FOREST (short dry season)	
Lateritic non-flooded soils	
Caryocar cf. *brasiliense*	8.8
Licania cf. *fanshawei*	6.7
Ocotea sp.	10.6
Eperua purpurea	10.5
Podzolized flooded soils	
Micrandra spruceana	12.8
Manilkara sp.	11.7
Open sclerophyllous vegetation on sandy podzolized soils	
Rhodognaphalopsis discolor	10.7
Clusia sp.	11.2
Retiniphyllum concolor	12.2
Macairea rufescens	9.7
Remigia involucrata	8.7
Aspidosperma album	19.5
Mouriri uncitheca	13.9
Heteropteris sp.	10.6

Walter (1962) as euryhidric plants, indicating tolerance to drastic reductions of leaf water potential for extended periods. The second group can be described as stenohydrous. However, there are not enough measurements of water potential and osmotic potential of tropical trees to attempt a thorough analysis.

The striking differences in behavior of water potential under natural conditions are depicted in Fig. 14.4. Values belong to two contrasting forest

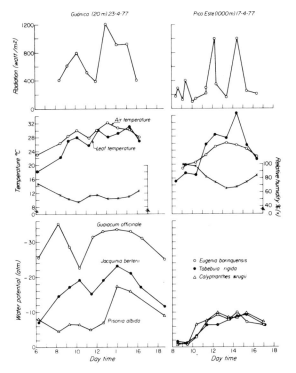

Fig. 14.4. Daily course of water potential and leaf temperature of selected trees in dry forest (Guánica) and a cloud forest (Pico Este) during the dry season in Puerto Rico (1 atm = 1.013 bar).

environments in Puerto Rico (Medina et al., unpubl.): the dry coastal forest in southern Puerto Rico (Guánica) and the elfin forest in the Luquillo Mountains (cloud forest). Values for water potential in the elfin forest were measured during an exceptional clear day, therefore peak light intensities similar to those in Guánica were measured. The three species measured in the elfin forest showed similar behavior. Average leaf temperatures were higher than air temperature, mainly because of low transpiration, although abundant water was available in the soil. This resulted in relatively high water potentials maintained throughout the day (−8 to −10 bar). In Guánica, the evergreen species *Guaiacum officinale* and *Jacquinia berterii* developed lower water potentials (−23 to −35 bar) indicating that they were actively losing water through transpiration. Daily variations of water potential also indicated that they were effectively pumping water from the soil, in spite of the fact that measurements were conducted during the dry season. Other species developed still lower water potentials, for example *Capparis* sp.

and *Coccoloba* sp., which were below −40 bar during most of the day.

Pisonia albida is an interesting example of the opposite behavior. Trees measured were beginning to develop new leaves, and were characterized by having relatively high water potentials (−5 to −7 bar) during most of the day; only during the afternoon going down to −17 bar. *P. albida* is a deciduous tree which remains leafless for several weeks. Development of new leaves before the onset of rains indicates that it should have water available, either in the soil or in the stem and roots, but also that periodicity of leaf shedding and flushing is not only regulated by water availability but also probably by photo- and thermoperiodicity as indicated earlier.

An interesting example of drought avoidance through root depth is given by the predominantly evergreen trees of South American savannas. Rawitscher and coworkers (1943, 1948) demonstrated that evergreen trees in the Brazilian Cerrados do not restrict transpiration during the dry season, in spite of leaf renewal during this period. They also observed that, sclerophyllous leaf structure notwithstanding, cuticular transpiration is relatively high. This again points to water availability during the whole year. In fact, Rawitscher et al. (1943) showed that in deep Cerrado soils, with a water table 17 to 19 m deep, there is water accumulated above it, corresponding to about three years rainfall.

Unfortunately most studies on transpiration of Cerrado plants have been conducted exclusively with detached leaves or twigs, which, without simultaneous measurements of leaf temperature, do not allow a complete evaluation of the results. One study, though, included quantitative measurements of stomatal aperture with a pressure porometer (Valio et al., 1966a, b), which gives figures proportional to leaf conductance (Alvim, 1964). Measurements were performed in *Terminalia argentea*, both during the dry and the rainy season. Redrawing Valio et al.'s results points out several important observations (Fig. 14.5). Maximal transpiration rate is similar in both seasons. The porometer values indicate however, that leaf conductance is considerably higher during the wet season, that there is an apparent stomatal closure at midday in both seasons not reflected in the transpiration curves, and also that stomata remain open

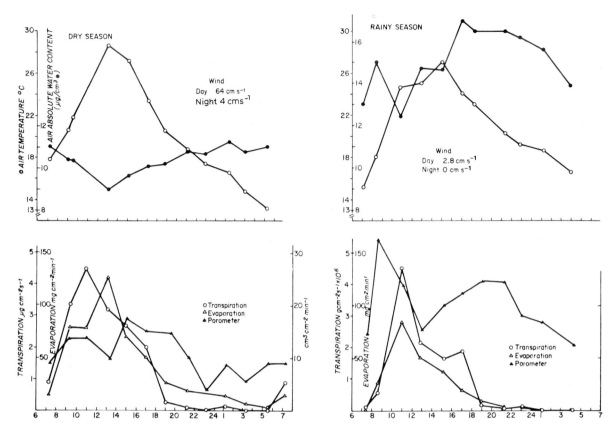

Fig. 14.5. Daily course of transpiration and leaf conductance in *Terminalia argentea* of Brazilian Cerrados during the dry and rainy season (redrawn from Valio et al., 1966a, b).

during the night. Similar transpiration rates in spite of different leaf conductances can be explained on the basis of different leaf temperatures, due to the fact that reduction in absolute air water content during the dry season is not enough to account for differences in leaf conductance. It could be predicted that in this species leaf temperature is higher during the dry season. Midday stomatal closure restricting transpiration seems to be widely spread in tropical trees independently of water availability in the soil. Vareschi (1960) and Foldats and Rutkis (1975) report similar behavior in *Curatella americana*, a typical tree of northern South American savannas. These stomatal responses may be related to the phenomenon of direct stomatal sensitivity to air humidity as described first by Schulze et al. (1972) for desert plants.

Sensitivity to water stress can also be measured through stomatal reactivity (Stocker, 1956; Alvim, 1960). Such measurements can be made with the rapid weighing of detached leaves or with porometers in attached leaves. Measurements on deciduous and evergreen savanna plants, deciduous trees from the dry forest of northeast Brazil and evergreen trees from the "Amazon caatinga" forest (Klinge et al., 1977) give the following general pattern (Ferri, 1944, 1953, 1961; Rawitscher, 1948; Ferri and Labouriau, 1952): evergreen trees with coriaceous leaves, generally deep rooted, present slow stomatal closure after detachment and relatively high cuticular transpiration, whereas deciduous, summer green trees have highly reactive stomata and very low cuticular transpiration. Deciduous trees therefore reduce transpiration losses very effectively during water stress.

It remains to be established what are the differences in minimum water potential that both leaf types can tolerate and which is the seasonal pattern of the osmotic pressure of the cell sap. It can be advanced, nevertheless, that evergreen trees are generally more drought-tolerant than deciduous trees, the sclerophyll leaf structure representing an important adaptation.

Structural and chemical differentiation of leaves in evergreen and deciduous trees

The sclerophyll leaf type common in many tropical trees ("megasclerophyll" leaf type of Richards, 1952) was considered to be primarily adapted to water stress, therefore it was expected that this leaf type would be positively selected in arid areas. This is clearly not the case. Trees with sclerophyllous leaves may be more tolerant to water stress (do not wilt and show relatively low water potentials and low osmotic potential of their vacuolar sap in arid areas), but not necessarily evolved in arid areas. In spite of their greater drought tolerance, they can not compete effectively with deciduous trees when the dry season is too long and the water table is out of root reach.

The sclerophyllous leaf structure of many tropical trees in widely different tropical climates is probably more related to nutritional conditions.

The hypothesis stating that nutritional deficiencies might be selecting sclerophyllous leaf types has been advanced by several authors (Arens, 1958; Loveless, 1961, 1962).

The degree of sclerophylly can be measured using the specific leaf area index (leaf area/leaf weight) (dimensional quotients of Stocker, 1956) and the leaf content of nitrogen and phosphorus. Table 14.5 shows that sclerophyllous leaves are thicker and present lower contents of nitrogen and phosphorus.

Differentiation of water and nutrient stresses under natural conditions may be difficult because frequently soil desiccation leads to reduction in nutrient transport to the roots. Sclerophyll trees are characterized by relatively slow growth, therefore being able to withstand prolonged dry periods without any nutrient supply at all. Deciduous trees, on the contrary, grow rapidly under favorable conditions, therefore having a higher requirement for nutrient supply. It is probable that leaf fall in deciduous trees is also related to reduced nutrient flow towards the root, but it is a matter that requires further investigation.

TABLE 14.5

Area/weight relationship and nitrogen and phosphorus content in leaves of evergreen and deciduous trees from savanna–deciduous forest ecosystems (data partially from Cuenca, 1976; and Montes and Medina, 1977)

	Area weight^{-1} (cm^2 g^{-1})	N (mg g^{-1})	P (mg g^{-1})
Evergreen			
Curatella americana	74	9.3	0.75
Byrsonima crassifolia	68	8.0	0.35
Palicourea rigida	65	8.7	–
Roupala complicata	53	8.4	–
Vochysia venezuelana	87	6.5	0.33
Xylopia aromatica	91	10.6	0.61
Deciduous			
Genipa caruto	104	18.0	0.99
Godmania macrocarpa	81	16.0	0.79
Cochlospermum vitifolium	131	10.5	1.24
Luehea candida	232	18.3	1.45
Randia aculeata	305	19.9	–
Pereskia guamacho	185	29.7	–

REFERENCES

Alvim, P. de T., 1960. Stomatal opening as practical indicator of moisture deficiency in Cacao. *Phyton*, 15: 79–89.

Alvim, P. de T., 1964. Tree growth periodicity in tropical climates. In: M.H. Zimmermann (Editor), *Formation of Wood in Forest Trees*. Academic Press, New York, N.Y., pp. 475–495.

Alvim, P. de T., 1965. A new type of porometer for measuring stomatal opening and its use in irrigation studies. In: F.E. Eckardt (Editor), *Methodology of Plant Eco-Physiology*. *Proceedings of the Montpellier Symposium*. UNESCO, Paris, pp. 325–330.

Alvim, P. de T. and Alvim, R., 1978. Relation of climate to growth periodicity in tropical trees. In: P.A. Tomlinson and M.H. Zimmermann (Editors), *Tropical Trees as Living Systems*. Cambridge University Press, Cambridge, pp. 445–464.

Arens, K., 1958. O Cerrado como vegetação oligotrofica. *Bol. Fac. Fil. Ciênc. Letr., Univ. S. Paulo.*, No. 224 (Bot. No. 15): 59–77.

Beard, J.S., 1944. Climax vegetation in Tropical America. *Ecology*, 25: 127–158.

Beard, J.S., 1955. The classification of Tropical American vegetation. *Ecology*, 36: 89–100.

Biebl, R., 1964. Temperaturresistenz tropischer Pflanzen auf Puerto Rico. *Protoplasma*, 59: 133–156.

Brunig, E.F., 1976. Tree forms in relation to environmental conditions: an ecological view point. In: M.G.R. Cannell and F.T. Last (Editors), *Tree Physiology and Yield Improvement*. Academic Press, New York, N.Y., pp. 139–156.

Cain, S.A., Castro, G.N. de O., Pires, J.M. and Da Silva, N.T., 1956. Application of some phytosociological techniques to Brazilian rain forest. *Am. J. Bot.*, 43: 911–941.

Cram, W.J., 1976. Negative feedback regulation of transport in cells. The maintenance of turgor, volume and nutrient supply. In: V. Lüttge and M.G. Pitman (Editors), *Encyclopedia of Plant Physiology IIa*. Springer-Verlag, Berlin, pp. 248–316.

Cuenca, G., 1976. *Balance nutricional de algunas leñosas de dos ecosistemas contrastantes: bosque nublado y bosque deciduo*. Thesis, Escuela de Biología, Universidad Central de Venezuela, Caracas, 137 pp.

Daubenmire, R., 1972. Phenology and other characteristics of tropical semi-deciduous forest in northwestern Costa Rica. *J. Ecol.*, 60: 147–170.

De Oliveira, J.G.B. and Labouriau, L.G., 1961. Transpiração de algumas plantas de Caatinga aclimatadas no Jardim Botanico do Rio de Janeiro. I. Comportamento de *Caesalpinia pyramidalis* Tull., de *Zizyphus joazeiro* Mart., de *Jatropha phyllacantha* Muell. Arg. e de *Spondias tuberosa* Arruda. *An. Acad. Bras. Ciênc.*, 33(3/4): 351–373.

Eiten, G., 1972. The Cerrado vegetation of Brazil. *Bot. Rev.*, 38: 201–341.

Ernst, W., 1971. Zur Ökologie der Miombo-Wälder. *Flora*, 160: 317–331.

Ernst, W. and Walker, B.H., 1973. Studies on the hydrature of trees in Miombo Woodland in Southern Central Africa. *J. Ecol.*, 61: 667–673.

Ewel, J.J. and Madriz, A., 1968. *Zonas de vida de Venezuela*. Ministerio de Agricultura y Cria. Sucre, Caracas, 264 pp.

Ferri, M.G., 1944. Transpiração de plantas permanentes dos "Cerrados". *Bol. Fac. Fil Ciênc. Letr., Univ. S. Paulo*, No. 41 (Bot. No. 4): 159–224.

Ferri, M.G., 1953. Water balance of plants from the "caatinga". II. Further information on transpirational and stomatal behavior. *Rev. Bras. Biol.*, 13: 237–244.

Ferri, M.G., 1960. Contribution to the knowledge of the ecology of the "Rio Negro Caatinga" (Amazon). *Bull. Res. Counc. Israel*, 8D: 195–208.

Ferri, M.G., 1961. Problems of water relations of some Brazilian vegetation types with special consideration of the concepts of xeromorphy and xerophytism. In: *Plant–water Relationships in Arid and Semi-arid Conditions. Madrid Symposium*. UNESCO, Paris, pp. 191–197.

Ferri, M.G. and Labouriau, L.G., 1952. Water balance of plants from the "caatinga". I. Transpiration of some of the most frequent species of the "caatinga" of Paulo Alfonzo (Bahia) in the rainy season. *Rev. Bras. Biol.*, 12: 301–312.

Foldats, E. and Rutkis, E., 1975. Ecological studies of chaparro (*Curatella americana* L.) and manteco (*Byrsonima crassifolia* H.B.K.) in Venezuela. *J. Biogeogr.*, 2: 159–178.

Franco, C.M. and Magalhaês, A.C., 1965. Techniques for the measurement of transpiration of individual plants. In: F.E. Eckardt (Editor), *Methodology of Plant Eco-Physiology*. *Proceedings of the Montpellier Symposium*. UNESCO, Paris, pp. 211–224.

Frankie, G.W., Baker, H.G. and Opler, P.A., 1974. Comparative phenological studies of trees in tropical wet and dry forests in lowlands of Costa Rica. *J. Ecol.*, 62: 881–919.

Gates, D.M., 1968. Transpiration and leaf temperature. *Annu. Rev. Plant Physiol.*, 19: 211–238.

Gates, D.M., 1975. Biophysical ecology. In: D.M. Gates and R.B. Schmerl (Editors), *Perspectives of Biophysical Ecology*. Ecological Studies, 12. Springer-Verlag, Berlin, pp. 1–28.

Givnish, T.J., 1978. Adaptive significance of compound leaves with particular reference to tropical trees. In: P.B. Tomlinson and M.H. Zimmerman (Editors), *Tropical Trees as Living Systems*. Cambridge University Press, Cambridge, pp. 351–380.

Givnish, T.J. and Vermeij, G.J., 1976. Sizes and shapes of liana leaves. *Am. Nat.*, 110(975): 743–778.

Herrera, R., 1977. Soil and terrain conditions in the International Amazon Project at San Carlos de Rio Negro, Venezuela: correlation with vegetation types. In: E. Brünig (Editor), *Transactions of the International MAB-IUFRO Workshop, Special Report*, 1: 182–188.

Holdridge, L., 1947. Determination of world plant formations from simple climatic data. *Science*, 105(2727): 367–368.

Holdridge, L., 1959. Simple method for determining evapotranspiration from temperature data. *Science*, 130(3375): 572.

Hsiao, T.C., 1973. Plant responses to water stress. *Annu. Rev. Plant Physiol.*, 24: 519–570.

Klinge, H., Medina, E. and Herrera, R., 1977. Studies on the ecology of Amazon Caatinga forest in southern Venezuela 1. General features. *Acta Cient. Venez.*, 28: 270–276.

Kozlowski, T.T., 1976. Water relations and tree improvement. In: M.G.R. Cannell and F.T. Last (Editors), *Tree Physiology and Yield Improvement*. Academic Press, New York, N.Y., pp. 307–328.

Levitt, J., 1972. *Responses of Plants to Environmental Stresses*. Academic Press, New York, N.Y., 697 pp.

Loveless, A.R., 1961. A nutritional interpretation of sclerophyll based on differences in the chemical composition of sclerophyllous and mesophytic leaves. *Ann. Bot.*, 25: 168–184.

Loveless, A.R., 1962. Further evidence to support a nutritional interpretation of sclerophylly. *Ann. Bot.*, 26: 547–561.

Medina, E., 1978. Significación eco-fisiológica del contenido foliar de nutrientes y el área foliar específica en ecosistemas tropicales. In: *Il Congreso Latinoamericano de Botánica, Brasilia*, p. 75.

Medina, E., Sobrado, M. and Herrera, R., 1978. Significance of leaf orientation for leaf temperature in an Amazonian sclerophyll vegetation. *Radiat. Environ. Biophys.*, 15: 131–140.

Monk, C.A., 1966. An ecological significance of evergreenness. *Ecology*, 47: 504–505.

Montes, R. and Medina, E., 1977. Seasonal changes in nutrient content of leaves of savanna trees with different ecological behavior. *Geo-Eco-Trop*, 1: 295–307.

Nobel, P.S., 1974. *Introduction to Biophysical Plant Physiology*. W.H. Freeman and Co., San Francisco, Calif., 488 pp.

Oertli, J.J., 1976. The states of water in the plant: theoretical consideration. In: O.L. Lange, L. Kappen and E.-D. Schulze (Editors), *Water and Plant Life*. Ecological Studies, 19. Springer-Verlag, Berlin, pp. 19–31.

Parker, J., 1968. Drought-resistance mechanisms. In: V.V. Kozlowski (Editor), *Water Deficits and Plant Growth*, 1. Academic Press, New York, N.Y., pp. 195–234.

Parkhurst, D.F. and Loucks, D.L., 1972. Optimal leaf size in relation to environment. *J. Ecol.*, 60: 505–537.

Prance, G.T. and Da Silva, M.F., 1975. *Arvores de Manaus*. INPA, Manaus.

Rachid, M., 1947. Transpiração e sistemas subterrâneos da vegetacão de verão nos campos cerrados de Emas. *Bol. Fac. Fil. Ciênc. Letr., Univ. S. Paulo*, No. 80 (Bot. No. 5): 1–139.

Rawitscher, F., 1948. The water economy of the vegetation of the "campos cerrados" in southern Brazil. *J. Ecol.*, 36: 237–268.

Rawitscher, F., Ferri, M.G. and Rachid, M., 1943. Profundidade de solos e vegetação em campos cerrados do Brasil meridional. *An. Acad. Bras. Ciênc.*, 15: 267–294.

Richards, P.W., 1952. *The Tropical Rain Forest, An Ecological Study*. Cambridge University Press, Cambridge, 450 pp.

Richter, H., 1976. The water status in the plant: experimental evidence. In: O.L. Lange, L. Kappen and E.-D. Schulze (Editors), *Water and Plant Life*. Ecological Studies, 19. Springer-Verlag, Berlin, pp. 42–58.

Schnetter, R., 1971. Untersuchungen zum Wärme- und Wasserhaushalt ausgewählter Pflanzenarten des Tropengebietes von Santa Marta (Kolumbien). *Beitr. Biol. Pflanz.*, 47: 155–213.

Shields, L.M., 1950. Leaf xeromorphy as related to physiological and structural influences. *Bot. Rev.*, 16: 399–447.

Schulze, E.-D., Lange, O.L., Buschbom, V., Kappen, L.A. and Evenari, M., 1972. Stomatal responses to changes in humidity in plants growing in the desert. *Planta*, 108: 259–270.

Slatyer, R.O., 1967. *Plant–Water Relationships*. Academic Press, London, 366 pp.

Slavik, B., 1974. *Methods of Studying Plant Water Relations*. Ecological Studies 9. Springer-Verlag, Berlin, 449 pp.

Stocker, O., 1956. Messmethoden der Transpiration. In: W. Ruhland (Editor), *Encyclopedia of Plant Physiology, III*. Springer-Verlag, Berlin, pp. 239–311.

Taylor, S.E., 1975. Optimal leaf form. In: D.M. Gates and R.B. Schmerl (Editors), *Perspectives in Biophysical Ecology*. Ecological Studies, 12. Springer-Verlag, Berlin, pp. 73–86.

Taylor, S.E. and Gates, D.M., 1970. Some field methods for obtaining meaningful leaf diffusion resistances and transpiration rates. *Oecol. Plant.*, 5: 105–113.

Troll, C., 1956. Das Wasser als pflanzengeographischen Faktor. In: W. Ruhland (Editor), *Encyclopedia of Plant Physiology, III*. Springer-Verlag, Berlin, pp. 750–786.

Valio, I.F.M., Moraes, B., Marques, M. and Cavalcante, P., 1966a. Sobre o balanço d'agua de *Terminalia argentea* Martius & Succ. nas condições do Cerrado, na estação seca. *An. Acad. Bras. Ciênc.*, 38(Suppl.): 243–260.

Valio, I.F.M., Moraes, V., Marques, M., Matos, M.E. and De Paula, J.E., 1966b. Sobre o balanço d'agua de *Terminalia argentea* Mart. & Succ. nas condições do Cerrado, na estação chuvosa. *An. Acad. Bras. Ciênc.*, 38(Suppl.): 227–290.

Vareschi, V., 1960. Observaciones sobre la transpiración de árboles llaneros durante la época de sequia. *Bol. Soc. Venez. Cienc. Nat.*, 21: 128–134.

Walter, H., 1962. *Einführung in die Phytologie, I. Grundlagen des Pflanzenlebens*. Eugen Ulmer Verlag, 4th ed., Stuttgart, 494 pp.

Walter, H., 1963a. Zur Klärung des spezifischen Wasserzustandes im Plasma und in der Zellwand bei der höheren Pflanzen und seine Bestimmung. Teil I. *Ber. Dtsch. Bot. Ges.*, 76: 40–53.

Walter, H., 1963b. Zur Klärung des spezifischen Wasserzustandes im Plasma und in der Zellwand bei der höheren Pflanzen und seine Bestimmung. Teil II. *Ber. Dtsch. Bot. Ges.*, 76: 54–71.

Walter, H., 1964. Zur Klärung des spezifischen Wasserzustandes im Plasma und in der Zellwand bei der höheren Pflanzen und seine Bestimmung. Teil III. *Ber. Dtsch. Bot. Ges.*, 78: 104–114.

Walter, H., 1973. *Vegetation der Erde, I. Die tropischen und subtropischen Zonen*. G. Fischer-Verlag, 3rd ed., Jena, 743 pp.

Walter, H. and Kreeb, K., 1970. Die Hydratation und Hydratur des Protoplasmas der Pflanzen und ihre Ökophysiologische Bedeutung. Protoplasmatologia II C 6. Springer-Verlag, Berlin, 306 pp.

Walter, H. and Medina, E., 1971. Caracterización climática de Venezuela sobre la base de climadiagramas de estaciones particulares. *Bol. Soc. Venez. Cienc. Nat.*, 29(119–120): 211–240.

Chapter 15

PHYSIOLOGICAL RESPONSES OF ANIMALS TO MOISTURE AND TEMPERATURE

HAROLD HEATWOLE

STATEMENT OF THE ENVIRONMENTAL PROBLEMS OF TROPICAL FOREST ANIMALS

The mild, relatively uniform temperatures and continuously abundant rainfall of tropical, lowland, non-seasonal rain forest constitute the most equable and seemingly favorable environment naturally occurring on the earth. Although high altitude tropical forests are cool, and even lowland ones lie along a moisture spectrum ranging from evenly distributed and plentiful rain to marked alternation of wet and dry seasons, most tropical forests experience less daily and seasonal fluctuation in temperature and moisture than do either forests at higher latitudes or tropical non-forested habitats.

One often intuitively views equable, mild environments as favorable and looks at the relatively slight fluctuations in temperature or moisture as inconsequential. This feeling is based on the unstated assumption that animals of a given broad taxon have similar responses to a given degree of environmental change. However, animals that have had a long history of adaptation to equable conditions may differ markedly from those that have adjusted evolutionarily to pronounced temporal change. One must remain alert to the possibility that a 0.5°C change in temperature may cover a greater proportion of the range of thermal adaptation of a lowland rain forest animal, and have more effect, than would a 5°C change for an animal adapted to a less equable environment. In the present section some information is presented on this topic which suggests a counter-conclusion for some taxa; for most no assessment is currently possible. Taxa may differ greatly in this regard.

As mentioned above, tropical forests exhibit a wide spectrum of degree of seasonality, and different degrees of adaptation to environmental variability occur among their faunas. In the present section, the major physiologic attributes of a variety of tropical forest taxa will be sketched and related to prevailing environments. A major emphasis will be placed upon the adaptive differences in seasonal versus non-seasonal forests.

In making such comparisons, it is difficult to lump all taxa into a single discussion as intertaxal differences in mode of life, or basic physiological restraints imposed by those modes of life, result in somewhat different adaptive responses by different groups. For example, reptiles and amphibians respond very differently to degree of seasonality in tropical forest. Although there are exceptions, amphibians as a group are moisture sensitive and the major single environmental parameter upon which their mode of life centers is availability of water. By contrast, reptiles encounter few water problems except in very arid environments, and they are primarily thermally oriented. Much of their daily behavior centers around exchanging heat with their environment and maintaining elevated body temperatures. Amphibians are usually more thermally passive and can generally maintain meaningful activity into a rather low temperature range. Accordingly, the two groups are influenced differently by environmental gradients. Number of species of reptiles decreases markedly along a decreasing temperature gradient from tropical lowlands upward into higher altitudes; amphibians are only slightly affected in the same range. By contrast, numbers of reptilian species are only slightly lowered as one proceeds from equable tropical forest to drier, more seasonal ones whereas amphibian species numbers are markedly reduced along the same continuum (review by Heatwole, 1981a).

Numbers of insect species and individuals differ markedly among different forest types. In tropical America, there is a strong reduction in number of species and individuals during the dry season in areas where the dry season is severe (Janzen, 1973). However, where the dry season is mild the numbers and species of insects actually appear to increase during the dry season. There are also altitudinal correlates with the highest insect densities occurring at intermediate elevations. Janzen (1973) postulates that the reason for this pattern is a higher harvestable productivity from the plant community at intermediate elevations because of lowered plant maintenance costs during cool nights.

A major difference among animals in terms of their modes of life is the source of their body heat. Endotherms (such as mammals and birds) produce the majority of their body heat by metabolic thermogenesis, resulting from the processing of energy taken in as food. Ectotherms (e.g., reptiles, amphibians, many invertebrates) depend primarily upon the external environment as their source of heat. The nature of thermoregulation, the rate of processing of energy, and the metabolic, respiratory and circulatory responses to temperature vary greatly between these two groups. In order to assess the variety of physiological responses to temperature and to compare different adaptive syndromes, it is important that the above groups of animals are treated separately. Consequently they are discussed in turn in the following paragraphs.

Of considerable importance is the response of an animal to unfavorably extreme conditions. Inasmuch as temperature varies widely among habitats, it is important to relate the tolerances of animals to conditions prevailing around them. For example, do species from equable habitats have different tolerance limits than those from fluctuating or more extreme environments? Can they adjust physiologically to the same extent over a short period of time? Do they have the same safety margins between prevailing conditions and potentially deleterious ones? When environments exceed tolerance limits or become unfavorable in some way, many animals seclude themselves in sheltered sites where they wait out the unfavorable period while living on stored energy reserves. How important is such a strategy to tropical forest animals,

and are there differences among different forest types? These topics require comparison among species from a variety of habitats.

Finally, even when conditions are not life-threatening directly, they may be inimical to reproduction and thus might pose problems for the indefinite continuance of the species. Species have evolved appropriate responses minimizing environmental hazards to successful breeding. These, known as "reproductive strategies", differ among environments and involve the timing and frequency of reproductive periods and the number and initial size of offspring. Comparison of reproductive strategies among taxonomically related species from different habitats and among taxonomically divergent species from the same habitat can provide insight into broad patterns of adaptive response. The above topics are all touched upon in the paragraphs below.

Not all topics are treated for all animal groups. The selection of type of animal discussed under each heading was dictated by (1) whether information was available on that topic for tropical forest species, (2) whether such information provided adaptive insights and in part by (3) the author's personal preferences and areas of expertise.

THERMOREGULATION

Birds and mammals

Avian and mammalian body temperatures mostly result from the balance between internal heat production and loss of heat from the body. As the external environment changes, the conditions influencing exchange between animal and its ambient are altered, and corresponding internal physiological adjustments may occur or behavioral responses brought to bear. Over a rather wide range of ambient temperatures (the so-called thermoneutral zone), the energy expended in making such adjustments is slight and the metabolic demands they impose are sufficiently small that no thermally imposed changes in metabolic rate are detectable. However, beyond the lower limits of the thermoneutral zone, there is a marked increase of oxygen consumption with decreasing environmental temperature (Fig. 15.1). The extra energy expended

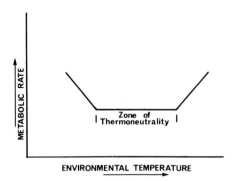

Fig. 15.1. Diagrammatic portrayal of the relation of metabolic rate and environmental temperature in an endotherm.

goes into increased thermogenesis which offsets the higher rates of heat loss in the cold. Other heat-producing mechanisms, for example shivering, also occur. These have their energetic cost and contribute to elevated metabolic rates. Similarly, beyond the upper end of the thermoneutral zone, the metabolic rate rises with increasing temperature and reflects the energetic expenditure on cooling mechanisms such as sweating or panting.

There are a number of factors that increase exchanges between animal and environment. Those that retard heat loss to a cool environment (and are consequently advantageous in cold conditions) may be quite a disadvantage in warmer climates. Some of the major factors involved in heat exchange will be discussed first and the characteristics of endotherms from tropical forests will be briefly contrasted with those of birds and mammals from thermally more extreme habitats.

Body size is a major factor influencing heat exchange. The smaller an animal is, the greater is its surface-to-volume ratio. Since heat production depends on volume, and heat exchange with the environment depends on the surface area through which that heat exchange occurs, small animals with their relatively large surface area tend to lose heat rapidly in a cool environment. High heat production is necessary to compensate for such heat losses and small endotherms accordingly have high metabolic rates and high energy requirements.

Insulation is another factor of importance. Hair or feathers trap air in interstitial spaces and reduce the conductance of the animal. The thickness and quality of the fur or feather covering influences its effectiveness as an insulator.

Avian and mammalian thermoregulation is an extremely complex phenomenon (for an extensive review see Whittow, 1970–1973). When subjected to heat or cold stress endotherms have a rich repertory of short-term thermoregulatory responses such as shivering, panting, sweating, body-licking, raising the hair or fluffing the feathers, and seeking favorable thermal environments (shade-seeking, use of environmental water for cooling, exposure to breezes, etc.). In addition there are various morphological adaptations which influence heat exchange in particular species (elephant ear, circulatory countercurrents between body and extremities, cephalic circulatory countercurrents in some ungulates, etc.).

Underlying this vast array of specific physiological mechanisms and behavioral responses, however, is a basic trichotomy in potential adaptive strategy. Homeotherms could: (1) reduce the temperature gradient between themselves and the environment, that is, adjust body temperatures more closely to that of the ambient as do some ectotherms; (2) alter their metabolic rate and hence their rate of heat production; or (3) maintain the same metabolic rate but alter rates of heat loss (Scholander, 1955). Of course combinations of the above are possible. The first option is sometimes employed in conjunction with option 2 in that, in the cold, hibernating mammals reduce body temperature and metabolic rate (Hudson, 1973). This combination is also employed, on a short-term basis, by small heterothermic birds and mammals as a means of conserving energy during periods of inactivity (e.g. Hudson, 1973; Calder and King, 1974). Also, the diurnal elevation in body temperature shown by a number of species of birds (Dawson and Hudson, 1970; Calder and King, 1974) reduces the temperature gradient between environment and body of birds in hot climates. However, body temperatures of most homeotherms from all climates are rather similar; where differences occur they are often phyletically, rather than climatically correlated (see below). Likewise, after adjustment for size, standard metabolic rates within the thermoneutral zone are much the same for a variety of species ranging from the Arctic to the Tropics (Scholander, 1955). Thus, options 1 and 2 are not a general mode of climatic adaptation among homeotherms (exceptions are noted below).

There may be some selective advantage in having a relatively high metabolic rate *per se*; consequently that rate may often be fixed by considerations other than climate, and adaptation to specific climates may of necessity follow other avenues. Option 3 is the avenue usually followed. In a comparison of arctic and tropical mammals and birds, Scholander (1950) and Scholander et al. (1950b) found that the lower limit of the thermoneutral zone differed markedly in ways correlating with climate. Arctic homeotherms could sustain much lower environmental temperatures before elevating their metabolism than could tropical ones (Fig. 15.2). These differences are related to the thickness and quality of the insulative covering (Scholander et al., 1950a).

There are some basic differences among different groups of homeotherms. Marsupials and monotremes have lower metabolic rates and heat production than do eutherians (Dawson, 1973). However, across a variety of environmental regimes, marsupials show a uniformity of metabolic rate. It would appear that they also tend to follow

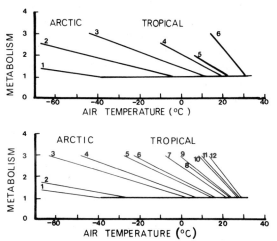

Fig. 15.2. Relation of metabolic rate to air temperature in some arctic and tropical birds (upper) and mammals (lower). Metabolism is expressed as multiples of basal metabolic rate, i.e. basal metabolism = 1. Arctic birds: *1* = Arctic gull (*Larus hyperboreas*); *2* = jay (*Perisoreus canadensis*); *3* = snowbunting (*Plectrophenax nivalis*). Tropical birds: *4* = manakin (*Pipra mentalis*); *5* = nighthawk (*Nyctidromus albicollis*); *6* = African vidua (*Vidua paradisea*). Arctic mammals: *1* = whitefox (*Alopex lagopus*); *2* = Eskimo dog pup (*Canis familiaris*); *3* = polar bear cub (*Thalarctos maritimus*); *4* = ground squirrel (*Citellus parryii*); *5* = lemming (*Dicrostonyx groenlandicus rubricatus*); *6* = weasel (*Mustela rixosa*). Tropical mammals: *7* = coati (*Nasua narica*); *8* = rat (*Proechimys semispinosus*); *9* = marmoset (*Leontocebus geoffroyi*); *10* = monkey (*Aotus trivirgatus*); *11* = raccoon (*Procyon cancrivorus*); *12* = sloth (*Choloepus hoffmanni*). Some parts of curves observed directly, others extrapolated. (After Scholander et al., 1950b.)

option 3 but at a somewhat lower metabolic level than do eutherians.

There are exceptions to the universal use of option 3 in climatic adaptation. Eutherian mammals and the marsupials each have exceptions that follow option 2. The best eutherian examples are the sloths which have rates of heat production well below those of most other eutherians. Other tropical forms such as armadillos and ant eaters also have low metabolic rates which may be a form of climatic adaptation although this characteristic has often been interpreted in phyletic rather than in ecological terms (Dawson, 1973).

The marsupial ecological equivalent of the sloth is the cuscus *Phalanger maculatus* (Dawson and Degabriele, 1973). This species has a basal metabolic rate equivalent to that of sloths but only 83% of that predicted for a marsupial its size. Like the sloth the cuscus has heavy fur and is well insulated.

In conclusion, most mammals adapt to thermal climatic differences in the degree they can dissipate heat. Tropical forest species differ from counterparts from colder climates primarily in terms of fur characteristics affecting heat loss, rather than in rate of heat production. Exceptions are the eutherian sloths and the marsupial cuscus of tropical forests which have heat production levels below those sustained by other mammals of equivalent size.

Reptiles

In contrast to mammals and birds, reptiles thermoregulate primarily by behavioral means. The types of behavior involved include basking, changing angle of orientation toward the sun's rays, altering the contours of the body to present a greater or lesser surface area to the sun, coiling (in snakes), burrowing, shade or water seeking, adjusting level of perching above a reflective substrate, changing time of daily activity period, and seeking warmer or cooler substrates (see reviews by Cloudsley-Thompson, 1971; and Heatwole, 1976). Despite this varied array of thermoregulatory behavior, physiological thermoregulation also occurs in reptiles, and between these two modes of control, body temperatures can often be maintained within rather precise limits. Although most diurnal reptiles thermoregulate, some aquatic forms, some secretive and burrowing species and some nocturnal thigmotherms are special cases which may be relatively passive to environmental temperatures. These are not considered in the following discussion which treats primarily diurnal heliotherms, especially lizards.

Metabolic rates are low in reptiles and consequently thermogenesis plays a minor role in thermoregulation in most species. However, in the large and active monitor lizards (*Varanus* spp.) it may account for a considerable proportion of the differences between heating and cooling rates (Bartholomew and Tucker, 1964), and some pythons use the heat of muscular contraction to control the temperature of eggs they brood (Vinegar et al., 1970; Van Mierop and Barnard, 1976). Panting is a common physiological means of thermoregulation in many lizards (Heatwole et al., 1973; Whitfield and Livezey, 1973).

In many species a variety of circulatory adjustments are also involved in thermoregulation (see White, 1976 for a review). Like mammals and birds, reptiles can constrict peripheral blood vessels and reduce circulation to areas contacting the external environment, or can dilate them and increase circulation. Furthermore, this effect is local and can proceed independently in different parts of the body. For example, in early morning a lizard basking in the sun on a cool rock can constrict the blood vessels in its ventral surface, thereby reducing blood flow to that region and lowering the conductive loss of heat to the rock. At the same time vasodilatation in the dorsum increases cutaneous blood flow in the back and enhances rate of uptake of heat from insolation.

Changes in heart rate and/or stroke volume alter rate of blood flow and hence heat transport, and are used by reptiles in thermoregulation.

The reptilian heart is considerably more versatile than that of homeotherms and has several features of importance to physiological thermoregulation. The incompletely divided ventricle permits alteration of the flow pattern of pulmonary and venous returns (i.e., oxygenated and unoxygenated bloods). Under some conditions, the two returns are kept completely separate and pulmonary venous blood is sent to the body, with the systemic return going to the lungs. However, shunting can occur that sends both systemic and pulmonary venous blood to the body, largely bypassing the pulmonary circuit. As long as respiratory demands are met, the extra flow of blood to the body resulting from the shunt can be used to enhance heat transport and influence thermoregulation.

Finally, circulatory countercurrents may influence regulation of the temperature of various parts of the body. Some lizards have alternate pathways of venous return from large blood sinuses in the head; one route passes through a countercurrent with the internal carotid artery (tending to maintain temperature differences between the head and body), whereas the other bypasses it (tending to produce uniformity in temperature between head and body). Action of a constrictor muscle around a blood vessel controls which route is predominantly used and probably is important in regulation of head–body temperature differences.

The control of at least some aspects of behavioral (e.g. seeking of cooler or warmer sites, changes in activity period) and physiological (e.g. panting) thermoregulation in reptiles seems to reside in the brain (probably hypothalamus). Brain control is modified by feedback from peripheral receptors, core receptors and pineal function as influenced by input from the parietal eye (Cabanac et al., 1967; Myhre and Hammel, 1969; Cabanac and Hammel, 1971; Templeton, 1971; Firth and Heatwole, 1976; Engbretson and Hutchison, 1976). Most aspects of both physiological and behavioral thermoregulation are related to the heliothermic habit.

Clearly reptilian thermoregulation can be a very complex phenomenon and in many habitats reptiles spend a great proportion of their active time thermoregulating. This is certainly true in areas of extreme and/or fluctuating environmental temperatures; most of the investigations of reptilian thermoregulation has centred around species from temperate areas, especially deserts. But what about in tropical forests, particularly the less seasonal ones, where shade is nearly uniform and temperatures are relatively mild and do not fluctuate widely? Do lizards thermoregulate there, or merely accept whatever temperatures are available in the naturally occurring range? Unfortunately, many of the studies of the thermal ecology of tropical reptiles have merely provided body temperatures and indicated how they differed from ambient ones and it is often difficult to assess the extent of thermoregulation. However, of the tropical diurnal terrestrial lizards and snakes for which at least a tentative assessment can be made, the majority seem to undergo some form of thermoregulation

(Inger, 1959; Wilhoft, 1961; Ruibal, 1961; Darevskii and Kadarsan, 1964; Hirth, 1964; Rand, 1964; Brattstrom, 1965; Heatwole, 1966; Rand and Rand, 1966; Brooks, 1968; Fitch, 1968, 1973c; Kennedy, 1968; McGinnis and Moore, 1969; Jenssen, 1970; Campbell, 1971; Clarke, 1973; Johnson, 1973; Huey and Webster, 1976; Fitch and Henderson, 1976). These species came from a number of different kinds of tropical forests and open tropical habitats and represented a variety of taxa; it can be concluded that thermoregulation is the norm. However, there were a few species that clearly were passive to temperature within the normal range of ambient values and exhibited no thermoregulatory behavior. Those are listed in Table 15.1. Two points are clear. One is that all of the species are from the genus *Anolis*. Although many other anoles have been shown to bask and carry out various other thermoregulatory activities, perhaps this taxon is prone toward thermal passivity. Since many members of this genus are continually in exposed situations (may even sleep on leaves of trees or shrubs) they must be able to operate at a wide range of temperatures and may not thermoregulate as precisely as species that have burrows or other retreats and which are active only during times of the day when they can regulate their temperature within narrow limits (Heatwole et al., 1969a).

The second point to be gleaned from Table 15.1 is that the thermally passive anoles fall into two distinct categories. Most of them are from heavily shaded forests or from montane forests characterized by frequent cloud or fog. In such forests patches of sunlight are rare and/or infrequent in time. Consequently the cost of thermoregulation would be high and may not warrant the required energy expenditure (Clarke, 1973; Huey and Webster, 1975, 1976). Huey (1974) applies this same argument to another iguanid genus, *Tropidurus*, which although not exhibiting the degree of thermal passivity of some anoles, nevertheless has one species (*T. albemarlensis*) which lives in an area characterized by frequent cloud, and which is relatively thermally passive.

Huey and Webster (1975) suggest that the ancestral condition is thermal passivity, with active thermoregulation by anoles from more open habitats being secondarily derived.

The second category of thermally passive anoles contains three species that are eurytopic and although inhabiting dense forest, they also occur in other more exposed habitats. Each of the three species represents the only anole occurring on its respective native island (a "solitary" species). Several theories have been advanced to account for such thermal passivity (Huey and Webster, 1975). If the traits of inhabiting forest and of being thermally passive are primitive in anoles as Huey and Webster (1975) suggest, then the solitary species on islands may have merely retained thermopassivity and become eurythermic as a by-product of occupying a wide number of habitats of varying thermal characteristics. The breadth of habitat selection was probably permitted by the absence of congeneric competitors. On islands where several species occurred, niche partitioning involved some species being restricted to particular habitats and

TABLE 15.1

Tropical lizard species which have been found to be thermally passive

Species	Habitat	Region	Authority
Anolis allogus	shade in denser parts of forest	Cuba	Ruibal (1961)
Anolis lucius	shade in denser parts of forest	Cuba	Ruibal (1961)
Anolis capito	moist, heavily shaded forest	Panama	Campbell (1971)
Anolis frenatus	tree-dwelling forest species	Panama	Campbell (1971)
Anolis tropidolepis	cloud forest	Costa Rica	Fitch (1972)
Anolis polylepis	wet forest	Costa Rica	Clarke (1973), Hertz (1974)
Anolis gundlachi	montane forest	Puerto Rico	Huey and Webster (1976)
Anolis oculatus	eurytopic: deeply shaded rain forest to fenceposts in open areas	Dominica	Brooks (1968), Ruibal and Philibosian (1970)
Anolis acutus	eurytopic lush forest to xeric scrub	St. Croix, Virgin Islands	McManus and Nellis (1973)
Anolis mamoratus	eurytopic	Guadeloupe	Huey and Webster (1975)

developing a corresponding stenothermy.

The second theory is that thermopassivity is a result of ecological release — that is, nearly the reverse of the above theory. The ecological release theory states that eurytopy reflects occupancy of a number of niches normally divided among several anole species on other islands. Occupancy of such a wide range of habitats with differing thermal characteristics would involve broadening of the range of thermal adaptation. Once such a broad spectrum of thermal adaptation was achieved, there would be little advantage in emphasizing any particular portion of it in particular habitats and these lizards would be correspondingly thermally passive.

Finally, thermopassivity in "solitary" anoles may have arisen from their social structure. Where congeners are absent and hence vacant niches available, aggressive interaction may force juveniles and females into ecological situations they would not otherwise meet. During its life an individual may pass through several thermal environments and eurythermy would be an advantage to such an animal.

In summary, thermoregulation seems to be the norm in open tropical habitats where the cost of basking is low. Thermopassivity may occur in densely shaded forests where cost of basking is high, or on islands with a solitary eurytopic anole species. In the latter case, thermopassivity may have been retained from a forest-dwelling ancestor or developed because of ecological release and/or habitat expansion arising from social factors.

There are also correlates between forest density and the thermoregulatory habit on an intraspecific level. For example, Huey and Webster (1976) showed that in closed forest, *Anolis cristatellus* from Puerto Rico was passive whereas in open habitats it basked.

It should be noted that the non-regulating habit is not obligatory in dense forests. Some species occupying the same habitat as the thermally passive ones listed in Table 15.1 did thermoregulate despite the presumed energetic difficulties involved.

In habitats which are structurally favorable for the carrying out of thermoregulation, thermal characteristics of the habitat may influence whether it does in fact occur. For example, *Anolis cupreus* basks in subtropical wet forest (where ambient temperatures are relatively low) but does not do so and is passive to a wide range of ambient tempera-

tures in tropical dry forest (Clarke, 1973; Fitch, 1973c).

Regulation of adult body temperature is not the only aspect of thermoregulation which must be considered. A proper thermal environment in the development of young is also important. Viviparity has been suggested to be one approach to the problem as thermoregulation by the adult might automatically result in control of the embryo's temperature as well. Viviparity is relatively uncommon among lizards in the tropics where temperatures are relatively equable and breeding seasons are long (Tinkle and Gibbons, 1977). However, at least one oviparous tropical reptile is known to control the temperature of the eggs outside. In the green iguana (*Iguana iguana*) temperatures very near 30°C are required for development; a high mortality occurs only a few degrees above and below this level (Licht and Moberly, 1965). Correspondingly, iguanas deposit their eggs in burrows in the ground at a depth which provides an appropriate temperature. Temperature measurements in nests in nature were 31 to 32°C (Rand, 1972).

Invertebrates

Terrestrial invertebrates, most of which are small and have relatively large surface areas, would not seem good candidates for physiological thermoregulation. However, a number of methods of temperature control are known among them. Terrestrial isopods, myriapods and some insects and arachnids have been reported to cool evaporatively at least for short periods (Warburg, 1965; Cloudsley-Thompson, 1970). Many insects warm the flight muscles to the temperature required for flight by isometric exercise or "shivering" (Heinrich, 1974). Some Odonata control heating and cooling by color change brought about by the migration of cytoplasmic granules in the hypodermal cells (O'Farrell, 1968). Desert tenebrionid beetles optimize body temperature through differential transmittance of different wave lengths. Near-infrared transmittance increases the percentage of radiation absorbed at times of low sun angle (promotes heating in morning and evening when visible and short-wave infrared radiations are attenuated). At midday, visible and ultraviolet radiation are absorbed by the insulated elytra, facilitating heat loss by convection (Henwood, 1975).

There are some tropical forest species that show a remarkable degree of physiological thermoregulation. Saturniid and sphingid moths maintain elevated thoracic temperatures during flight because of high heat production by flight muscles. Excess heat production can be dissipated by circulatory adjustments. Warm thoracic blood is circulated to the cooler, metabolically less active abdomen (Heinrich, 1970; Bartholomew and Epting, 1975). Two species of large beetles of the American tropics are endothermic, and in fact when active (but not flying) have metabolic rates equivalent to, or even higher than those of active mammals of the same size; these beetles can maintain metathoracic temperatures 5 to 7°C above ambient levels for many hours. When they fly, their temperature rises even higher (Bartholomew and Casey, 1977). It would seem that the large size (up to 4.1 g for *Stenodontes molarium*, Cerambycidae, and up to 6.3 g for *Strategus aloeus*, Scarabaeidae) of these beetles permits an unusual degree of physiological thermoregulation for an insect. They are primarily nocturnal and consequently cannot avail themselves of the avenues of behavioral thermoregulation available to diurnal heliotherms.

Despite the above examples, it would seem that behavioral responses are probably of more importance than physiological ones in most invertebrates (Cloudsley-Thompson, 1970). Some scorpions prevent overheating from warm substrates by stilting (elevating themselves off the ground by straightening the legs) (Alexander and Ewer, 1958). Some insects behaviorally regulate absorption of solar radiant energy, e.g. locusts and cicadas bask and the former posture in ways that control the angle of incidence of solar radiation (Cloudsley-Thompson, 1970; Heath et al., 1971). In tropical forests, however, invertebrates generally seem to employ more subtle and indirect means of temperature control. Selecting thermally favorable habitats or microhabitats is often the primary means of temperature regulation, although a combination of behavioral, morphological and physiological attributes may be synergistically involved. The Puerto Rican camaenid tree snails provide an example. Heatwole and Heatwole (1978) compared the thermal ecology of these snails from several forest types. The young snails of several species had lower temperature tolerances than did adults, and they correspondingly selected cooler microhabitats (under objects on the ground). The adults live in more exposed situations and during their diurnal inactive period often attach to the sides of tree trunks. When snails were heated to a certain temperature (the "falling point") they dropped off vertical surfaces, which in nature would put them into proximity of cooler conditions under litter or stones. This behavior can thus be looked upon as a means of temperature control in that unfavorably high body temperatures are avoided. Different species had different falling points, those from cooler montane forests or the more shaded lowland forests, had lower falling points than those from open forests or parkland, reflecting their respective differences in general thermal tolerances and prevailing body temperatures. Shell color also seemed to be important. Species from cool montane forests or heavily shaded lowland forest had dark shells, whereas those from more exposed situations had light colored shells. The single exception was *Polydontes acutangula* from montane rain forest, which had a white shell. This species lives on tree leaves and thus often was exposed to direct sunlight whereas other species from the same habitat occurred on shaded trunks. That the light color was effective in reducing absorption of solar energy was evidenced by the marked rise in body temperature of two snails in the sunlight immediately after their shells were painted black. Unpainted snails had no corresponding temperature change. All species in nature closely approached substrate and air temperatures in their vicinity but were below black-bulb temperatures. The light color of the more exposed species is probably necessary for maintaining such temperature relations.

P. acutangula had another unique characteristic. Its body was far too large to be accommodated in the shell and at high temperatures it had a high rate of evaporative loss. In its exposed microhabitat evaporative cooling may therefore have complemented the reflective shell in preventing overheating. In the montane rain forest where moisture is readily available, evaporative cooling would not be disadvantageous whereas in the hotter and drier forests it would be.

In summary, temperatures of these snails are influenced by: (1) a combination of habitat and microhabitat selection (which changes ontogenetically), (2) falling off of exposed vertical substrates at high levels of body temperature, (3) shell color and (4) perhaps evaporative cooling in one species.

The above example probably typifies the various ways that tropical invertebrates respond to the differing thermal environments of different forests. Each group will, of course, have its own syndrome of adaptive responses. Additional comparative ecological studies on a variety of taxa are badly needed.

A somewhat special case of thermoregulation is the control of microclimate exerted by some social insects. Temperature of the eggs in developing young in any species is regulated to a certain extent by the selection of oviposition site by the female. However, in some social insects a more active role is played by the adults (see reviews by Cloudsley-Thompson, 1970; and Wilson, 1971). Bees, ants and termites may raise nest temperature by metabolic heat production. Among some winged Hymenoptera the nest temperature is maintained remarkably constant by a combination of metabolic heat production, clustering, fanning, and use of water for evaporative cooling. Ants move brood from one part of the nest to another, or move them to entirely new nest sites and in this way keep the developing young at an appropriate temperature. Various social insects including winged Hymenoptera, ants and termites construct nests in ways that provide optimal microclimates. None of these thermoregulatory devices are unique to tropical forests and most are as characteristic of other habitats, if indeed not more so, and consequently they will not be dwelt upon further. However, one means of microclimatic control is a speciality of a tropical forest insect. The army ant, *Eciton hamatum*, was studied in mature seasonal evergreen forest in Panama by Jackson (1957). The ants are nomadic and form temporary bivouacs out of their own bodies. They cluster together and usually hang from some overhead support. The brood are kept in the interior of the bivouac. During the nomadic phase of 16 to 17 days, ants go on daily raiding expeditions for prey and in the evening move the bivouac to a new site; the brood are in the larval stage during this phase. Interspersed between such nomadic phases is a stationary phase of about 20 days during which raids are sporadic and the bivouac is kept at a single location; the young are in the pupal stage but with eggs being laid halfway through this phase. The temperature inside the bivouac is usually several degrees higher than

ambient level, shows less fluctuation, and departs somewhat from the ambient pattern of change. The temperature gradient was sharpest in early nomadic bivouacs.

TEMPERATURE TOLERANCES

Temperature tolerances of a variety of tropical animals have been measured. Usually tolerance levels correlate with the thermal conditions of the specific habitat, species from warmer habitats having higher tolerances than those from cooler ones. For example, Heatwole et al. (1965) studied the critical thermal maxima (CTMax) of two species of Puerto Rican tree frogs, both acclimated under the same conditions. *Eleutherodactylus richmondi*, which is restricted to cool rain forest at upper altitudes, did not tolerate as high a temperature as did *Eleutherodactylus coqui*, a more eurytopic and widespread species. Lowland populations of the latter species had higher temperature tolerances than did conspecific ones from montane rain forest.

There are fundamental differences in heat resistance among taxa of lizards, and to a certain extent thermal resistance follows phylogenetic lines rather than ecological ones. In the Australian fauna agamids are notably more resistant than scincids or pygopodids. Some genera of geckos are even less tolerant than most skinks, whereas other genera approach agamids in heat resistance (Licht et al., 1966). Nevertheless, there are ecological correlates. Within families or genera, temperature tolerance often relates to thermal characteristics of the habitat occupied, even among different tropical forest types. The American genus *Anolis* has been the most intensively studied of any tropical forest-inhabiting taxon. Ruibal (1961) found that in Cuba *Anolis allogus*, an inhabitant of shade in dense forests, begins to pant at about 30°C whereas *Anolis homolechis*, a dweller of clearings and forest edges, did not do so until about 36°C. Heatwole et al. (1969a) by contrast found that among four species of Puerto Rican anoles ranging in habitat from open lowland parkland to montane rain forest, and acclimated at the same constant temperature, there were no significant interspecific differences in panting threshold, all species having mean values between 30.2 and 39.7°C. However, the same species did show habitat-correlated differences in CTMax and lethal temperature, a finding later substantiated for the CTMax by Huey and Webster (1976) using three species, two of them the same as those included in the study of Heatwole et al. but adding one from xeric scrub. Ballinger et al. (1970) showed that among lowland Panamanian anoles two species from closed-canopy forest (*A. limifrons* and *A. frenatus*) and one from an ecotone between forest and grassland (*A. tropidogaster*) had similar CTMax's (33.4–35.7°C) and lethal temperatures (33.4–36.6°C) but these were lower than those of a grassland species (*A. auratus*: CTMax 34.4°C, lethal temperature 41.1°C).

Unfortunately, a comprehensive comparison of all the species of anoles studied cannot be made because of different methodologies and end points of thermal tolerance employed by different investigators; in some cases different studies gave different values for the same species. A particular cause of divergent results were differences in acclimation temperatures. Acclimation is known to influence thermal resistance in lizards generally and the CTMax of anoles specifically (Kour and Hutchison, 1970; Corn, 1971).

There are few data on temperature tolerances of tropical forest lizards and taxa other than anoles. Brattstrom (1971) measured the temperature tolerances of the skink *Tropidophorus queenslandiae*. This species inhabits tropical evergreen forest in northeastern Australia. Its tolerance was influenced by acclimation but, after accounting for acclimation effects, it was less resistant to heat than a number of species from the cool temperate coasts of southern Australia. *T. queenslandiae* inhabits wet soil and leaf litter and secretes itself under logs and rocks. Thus, its relatively low thermal tolerance reflects its cool equable microhabitat rather than the latitude of its geographic range.

Low temperature tolerance has seldom been studied in tropical forest lizards, probably because one tends to think of unfavorably low temperatures as never occurring in the lowland tropics. However, whether a given temperature is unfavorable or not depends on the characteristics of the species involved, rather than upon the temperature scale itself. McManus and Nellis (1973) indicated low tolerance of *Anolis acutus* from the Virgin Islands to temperatures below 20°C. Heatwole et al. (1969a) showed that Puerto Rican anoles had low survival at 11.5°C but that the species from the

cool, wetter forest at higher elevations had greater survival at low temperatures than did those from the lowlands. Similarly Gorman and Hillman (1977) kept *Anolis gundlachi* from Puerto Rican montane rain forest and *Anolis cristatellus* from more open, lowland habitats, at 16°C and high humidity for nineteen days with food supplied *ad libitum*. All the *A. gundlachi* survived, whereas the *A. cristatellus* all either died or lost weight. They concluded that *A. cristatellus* may be physiologically excluded from rain forest because of its intolerance to low temperatures.

Not all tropical forest animals show heat resistance correlated with the type of forest occupied. In the tree snail family Camaenidae in Puerto Rico, there is no consistent interspecific correlation between the thermal characteristics of the forest type occupied and lethal temperatures. As a result some of the snails from the hotter, more open lowland forests tended to operate at body temperatures closer to their stressful levels than did those from cooler upland ones (Heatwole and Heatwole, 1978).

Long-term survival at particular temperatures did differ among snail species, however. At moderate temperatures (30°C) *Caracolus carocollus* and *Caracolus marginella* had only slightly different survival times when deprived of food; both occur in warm, open lowland forests. Only the former also occurs in montane rain forest; it survived at low temperatures almost twice as long as the latter (Heatwole and Heatwole, 1978). This result is reminiscent of that reported above for lizards; perhaps *C. marginella* does not occur in the cool upland forests because of unfavorably low temperatures there.

It has long been known that, in animals generally, acclimation has a marked effect on temperature tolerances. However, few studies have compared the ranges through which the limits of tolerance can be shifted by acclimation in animals from different latitudes or types of habitat. Two papers by Brattstrom (1968, 1970) are notable exceptions and stand out as classics in their field. In the first paper, which dealt with a wide variety of species from the Americas, a result was obtained which was counter to that expected. Brattstrom's original working hypothesis was that "physiological adjustment would only have a selective advantage in the more variable temperate latitudes and that there would therefore be no requisite for a physiological adjustment in the uniform macro- and microclimate of the tropics". Brattstrom thus predicted "a broad range of adjustment in temperate forms and a narrow range in tropical forms". These expectations were not fulfilled and tropical forms did not have more narrow ranges of adjustment of heat tolerance than did temperate ones; the absolute values were often higher in tropical forms as expected on the basis of the elevated levels of temperature in the tropics, but the breadth of acclimation range was not correlated with latitude. Rather, species with restricted geographic ranges had narrow ranges of physiological adjustment, and widespread forms had broad adjustment ranges. In the second paper which dealt with Australian frogs, he obtained similar results, i.e. cryophilic species were more southern (higher latitudes) and thermophilic ones more northern (lower latitudes). Stenothermic and eurythermic frogs could occur at any latitude, the span of adjustment range again being related to the extent of geographic range. Species with restricted geographic ranges had poor ability to physiologically adjust, those with wide geographic ranges had wide ranges of adaptability.

The above pattern of acclimation is not restricted to frogs. Levins (1969) compared the acclimation of a tropical fruit fly (*Drosophila*) from a variety of habitats, including forests, in Puerto Rico. Broadniched eurytopic species, such as *D. melanogaster*, showed considerable flexibility and acclimated to different thermal conditions, but showed small genetic differences between populations from different localities. By contrast, none of the narrowniched species acclimated at all. Finally, *D. willistoni*, which is moderately broad-niched, neither acclimated nor showed interpopulation genetic variation; it was suggested that in the absence of physiological and genetic flexibility, this species avoids stress behaviorally.

Thus, it seems that, at least in the few groups tested, tropical species are no less able to adjust through a wide thermal range than are those from environments with greater environmental fluctuations in temperature. The crucial considerations seems to be extent of geographic range and niche breadth rather than latitude. Since only a few groups have been studied, however, it is essential to make wider comparisons.

WATER BALANCE

Water loss in reptiles

The mode of water balance in terrestrial reptiles is quite different from that of amphibians or mammals. Like birds, they primarily excrete uric acid or urate salts as the by-product of nitrogen metabolism. These relatively insoluble materials are excreted in a dry semi-solid form after water is reabsorbed via the cloaca (Schmidt-Nielson et al., 1963). Consequently, water losses accompanying nitrogen excretion are slight.

Most reptiles (unlike mammals) cannot produce urine with electrolyte concentrations hypertonic to the blood. However, species that live in areas of water scarcity or where environmental salt levels are high avoid excessive water loss potentially associated with ion excretion by (1) excreting excess ions in a concentrated brine from specialized extrarenal salt glands (Dunson, 1976), or (2) by tolerating accumulations of electrolytes in the tissues during periods of water shortage (Bradshaw, 1970). Furthermore, the reptilian integument is less pervious to evaporative water losses than is that of most amphibians or mammals (Chew and Dammann, 1961) and, contrary to mammals, evaporative losses via sweating do not occur; panting, however, is an avenue of thermoregulatory loss that is sustained by some lizards at high temperature (review by Heatwole et al., 1973).

The above characteristics collectively enable reptiles to conserve body water and maintain a greater independence from environmental moisture conditions than do more moisture-sensitive groups. However, within the reptiles there are varying degrees of adaptation to water scarcity and species from different habitats exhibit different levels of adaptation.

Evaporative water loss is highly sensitive to activity levels: the greater the activity the higher is the rate of water loss (Sexton and Heatwole, 1968; Heatwole and Veron, 1977). Consequently, it is necessary to either eliminate or evaluate the activity effect if one is validly comparing rates of loss among species. This can be done by comparisons of the standard rate of loss (SRL) — that is, the rate of loss of animals at zero activity (Sexton and Heatwole, 1968). This has seldom been achieved and, in the absence of precise data on activity levels of experimental animals, most interspecific comparisons must remain somewhat tentative.

Another factor of importance to evaporative water loss is body size, or more precisely the surface area : volume ratio determined by body size; other factors being equal, small reptiles would be expected to lose water more rapidly than larger ones.

Finally, environmental temperature and humidity affect evaporative losses (review by Heatwole, 1976). Different investigators have used different experimental conditions and hence studies are not always directly comparable. Despite all these difficulties, some useful conclusions can be drawn from existing literature. Understandably, reptiles from extremely dry habitats such as deserts have been studied more than those from tropical forests. There is, however, sufficient information on the latter to assess their capabilities.

Evaporative loss occurs via two routes, the respiratory surfaces and the skin. In many studies total evaporative loss was measured and no attempt made to compartmentalize it into the two components.

It is clear that there are large interspecific differences in rates of loss among reptiles. Generally, the rates of loss show size-related ecological correlates. Species from drier habitats tend to have lower rates of loss than those from wetter ones (Fig. 15.3). Such correlations are maintained when SRL's are compared and consequently the effect is related to more than merely activity differences among species from different types of habitat. For example, Sexton and Heatwole (1968) found that *Anolis limifrons* from tropical lowland rain forest had lower standard rates of loss than did *Anolis* (= *Norops*) *auratus* from open grassland of the

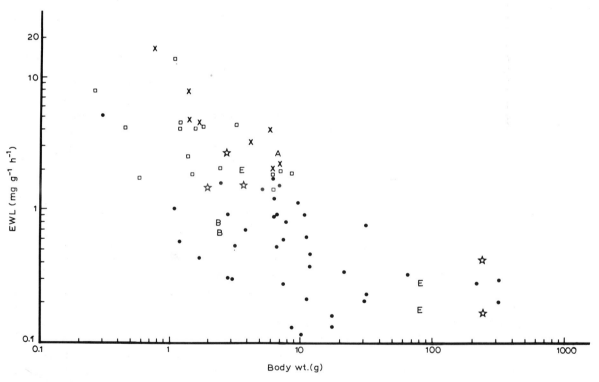

Fig. 15.3. Relation of mean total evaporative water loss (EWL) to body weight in lizards from a variety of habitats. Data either taken directly from, calculated from, or estimated from graphs in the references below. Where multiple temperatures were available, those nearest 25°C were graphed. Total range of test temperature was 20 to 27°C. Several studies employing only temperatures of 30°C or higher were excluded. Data from Sexton and Heatwole (1968), Cloudsley-Thompson (1970), Snyder (1971, 1975), Snyder and Weathers (1976), Duvdevani and Borut (1974), Heatwole (1976, data summary of literature on Australian species, p. 77), Heatwole and Veron (1977), Hillman and Gorman (1977), Hillman et al. (1979), and Leclair (1978). Dots represent species from tropical xeric scrub, temperate semi-arid to arid habitats, and desert. Squares represent species from tropical seasonal forest, woodlands, parks or grassland. Stars are species from temperate mesic woodland or open areas. X = species from moist tropical forest; A = a semi-aquatic species; B = temperate, burrowers; E = eurytopic species.

same general geographic area. Similarly, among the sphaerodactyline lizards, *Sphaerodactylus klauberi* from tropical montane rain forest had evaporative losses more than three times as high as those of *S. nicholsi townsendi* from nearby, rather xeric coastal areas (Heatwole and Veron, 1977).

Hillman et al. (1979) attempted to ascertain whether such differences were genetically based or whether they arose from acclimation of animals to different degrees of aridity. They compared different populations of two species of tropical eurytopic anoles, both of which occupied a variety of habitats from xeric scrub to rain forest. Those from dry habitats had lower rates of loss than those from more mesic ones. They also found that acclimation of animals under drier conditions resulted in a considerable lowering of their rates of evaporative loss although residual (presumed genetic) differences among populations remained. Since they did not measure SRL's (although they selected the lower values and hence those obtained when lizards were less active than at other times), it is not known to what extent acclimation influenced some physiological characteristic (skin permeability, metabolic or respiratory rate, etc.) and to what extent it may have reduced water loss by inducing lowered activity levels in the experimental animals.

Indeed, Stamps (1976) has shown that lizard activity decreases with increasing number of days since rain. However, it is likely that physiological processes are also involved, as Snyder (1971, 1975) has shown that respiration and water loss are closely related in lizards and has suggested that a reduced rate of respiratory metabolism has been a significant factor in saurian xeric adaptation. By contrast, Claussen (1967) found different rates of evaporative loss in two lizards with identical oxygen consumption rates. Thus, in different taxa of lizards activity and physiology may play different relative roles in water loss.

In conclusion, it appears that in continually moist, tropical forests (especially in cool montane rain forest) where replenishment of moisture is easy, and physical conditions of temperature and moisture do not favor rapid desiccation, lizards have not developed (or have lost) mechanisms for retarding evaporative losses. Species that come from tropical forests that are drier, even seasonally, have a greater resistance to evaporative losses, an adaptation that is carried still further in xeric regions, whether temperate or tropical.

Water loss in amphibians

Heatwole (in press) has recently reviewed the adaptive aspects of amphibian water balance. The details of that review are not repeated here but rather the major points are summarized and features of especial relevance to the amphibians of tropical forests discussed.

Most amphibians are ureotelic (excrete urea) and thus lack the renal water conserving mechanisms of the uricotelic birds and reptiles (but see below for exceptions). They cannot produce hypertonic urine and the mammalian renal mode of water conservation is consequently closed to them. Furthermore, amphibians sustain the highest evaporative rates of any terrestrial vertebrates. With a few exceptions (see below), evaporative loss through the skin is not subject to any effective direct physiological control and the skin exerts little or no resistance to evaporation. Consequently, rates of evaporative loss depend on the temperature, saturation deficit and speed of movement of the air around the animal and are greatly influenced by the animal's activity, metabolism and surface area to volume ratio. The last is determined in turn by body size and shape and the exposed surface area is influenced by posture.

In the absence of effective cutaneous control over evaporation, adaptation to dry habitats has proceeded along the pathways of: (1) behavioral adjustments; (2) increased rates of water uptake through the skin when water is available (amphibians never drink); (3) increased bladder volume with dilute urine being stored and subsequently reabsorbed in time of water scarcity; (4) enhanced ability to survive loss of body water (high vital limits; see below); and in the case of a few desert frogs (5) formation of a cocoon that retards water loss while the animal estivates underground. Not all these modes of adaptation are followed by all taxa and correlations with degree of dryness of the habitat occupied often holds up only within taxa such as the family but does not hold up between large taxa. Some adaptations are applicable only to species from quite arid regions; others occur in varying degrees in almost all amphibians.

Like many other amphibians, those from tropical

forests rely heavily on behavioral responses to maintain water balance. Selection of moist sites and nocturnality are two very common attributes. Regulation of the amount of activity is extremely important in view of the sensitivity of amphibian evaporative losses to activity level. Various species of tropical frogs adjust their level of activity to the degree of desiccation they have experienced. As fully hydrated frogs begin to dry out they progressively increase their activity until their body moisture content is about 60 to 69%; thereafter the activity level drops with further drying out (Heatwole and Newby, 1972). The early increase in activity probably results from escape or searching behavior. In other, non-tropical, species such behavior has been directly observed (Heatwole, 1960; Heatwole et al., 1971).

Although such activity temporarily results in increased rates of evaporation under natural conditions it would lead the animal to more favorable moisture conditions. However, when those conditions are not encountered (as in the laboratory experiments) further activity becomes maladaptive in that it hastens death by desiccation. It then becomes advantageous to remain quiet and increase the likelihood of surviving until the return of wet conditions.

Postural adjustment is another way of influencing rate of evaporative loss. An active frog undergoes a series of postural changes during locomotion which increases the exposed surface area momentarily. Extension of the limbs away from the body increases their exposed surface area and raising the venter off of the substrate exposes it to the air. In a eurytopic Puerto Rican tree frog, activity resulted in a three-fold increase in evaporative loss. The greatest single factor involved was posturally-induced surface area changes which accounted for 65% of the increase. Upset of the humidity gradient in the air next to the skin was responsible for an additional 15% of the increase and the remaining 20% to unidentified, possibly metabolic, factors (Heatwole et al., 1969b). Thus, the effect of activity on evaporative loss is primarily because of the surface area changes occurring during movement.

Amphibians can also reduce their effective surface area below that exposed during the normal resting posture. Salamanders coil (Heatwole, 1960) and frogs adopt a "water-conserving" posture in which they tuck their feet in close to the body and rest the entire venter including the throat and chin against the substrate; often the eyes are closed and depressed. This posture reduces the exposed surface to the minimum possible. I have noted this posture in two species of frogs (*Eleutherodactylus*) from tropical montane rain forest in Venezuela (Heatwole, 1963), and I have observed nearly identical behavior in frogs from the same type of habitat in Puerto Rico. It was employed at night when frogs were on exposed leaves during an unusually brisk breeze. Frogs from many habitats, tropical or otherwise, employ the water-conserving posture when experimentally desiccated, especially in the later stages of dehydration when activity levels are reduced.

In summary, when frogs being to dry out, they seek more favorable sites and as a result increase their activity. This behavior is expensive in terms of water loss and when a certain level of dehydration is reached, the animal reduces its water loss by decreasing its activity and adopting the water-conserving posture.

The above paragraphs provide a general outline of the modes of adaptation of most amphibians and of the behavioral means they use in keeping in water balance. There are, however, two exceptional genera which have adapted in different ways to a particular forest type. These will be treated now. These two genera, *Chiromantis* (from Africa) and *Phyllomedusa* (from South America) are ecologically equivalent but phylogenetically divergent (family Rhacophoridae and family Hylidae, respectively). Both are unusual in (1) excreting uric acid rather than urea and in (2) having evaporative losses equivalent to those of lizards of comparable size (Loveridge, 1970; Shoemaker et al., 1972; Shoemaker and McClanahan, 1975; Drewes et al., 1977). The mechanism of reducing evaporative loss is different in the two groups. In *Phyllomedusa* waterproofing lipids are secreted by integumental alveolar glands and the frogs wipe the secretions over the surface of the body with the feet (Blaylock et al., 1976) (Fig. 15.4). They also go into a deep torpor which would also tend to reduce evaporative loss. In *Chiromantis* the lipid glands and wiping behavior are absent, and waterproofing seems to be related in some way to the presence of specialized chromatophore units (Drewes et al., 1977).

Chiromantis and *Phyllomedusa* each have several species. All of those investigated so far have low

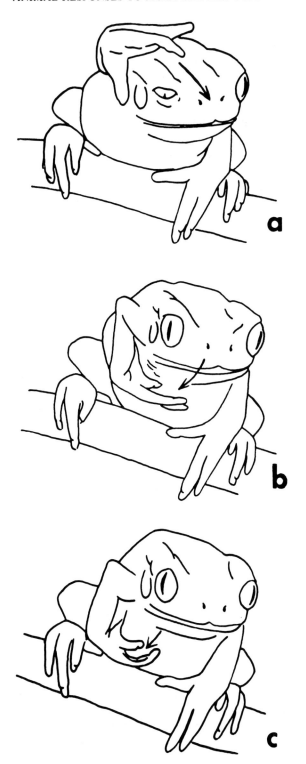

Fig. 15.4. *Phyllomedusa sauvagei* wiping lipid secretions over its body with the forelimbs. Drawings are in sequence with arrows indicating direction of movement. (From Blaylock et al., 1976.)

evaporative rates and produce uric acid. Both of these genera are tropical to subtropical and both are arboreal. *C. xerampelina* inhabits low veld savannas from Zululand to Kenya (Pienaar et al., 1976) and *C. petersi* occupies arid wooded steppe and subdesert steppe from lowland Ethiopia to north-central Tanzania (Drewes et al., 1977). Four species of *Phyllomedusa* occur in habitats ranging from "open forest" to "xerophytic open forest and brush" (Blaylock et al., 1976), although some species may occupy other habitats as well. Thus, the habitat in which uricotelic, waterproofed frogs have developed is tropical to subtropical xeric, open forest or scrub; only arboreal species in these habitats have developed such a unique water balance system. It appears that the combination of a relatively hot, dry environment accompanied by occupancy of a relatively exposed diurnal microhabitat (limbs of shrubs and trees in open forest or savanna) are the common ingredients in the evolution of uricotelism and relatively impervious integument in these remarkable frogs.

Cooler, moister or more densely shaded habitats would exert less selective pressure for the above adaptations even for arboreal frogs, and would have even less effect on more secretive forms. In this regard, the other genera in the subfamily Phyllomedusinae are interesting. In contrast to *Phyllomedusa*, *Agalynchnis* which inhabits humid tropical montane forests has high evaporative losses and like most anurans is primarily ureotelic. *Pachymedusa* is intermediate. It lives in dry Mexican forests but has relatively high evaporation rates, although it does have a few lipid glands in the skin; it is ureotelic (Shoemaker and McClanahan, 1975; Blaylock et al., 1976). A further difference is that *Phyllomedusa* does not rest in the water-conserving position during the day whereas *Agalynchnis* and *Pachymedusa* do (Blaylock et al., 1976). Thus, even in a single subfamily, there are major differences in excretion product and skin permeability which correlate with the degree of openness and the moisture characteristics of the tropical forests occupied.

Water loss in invertebrates

Some tropical forest invertebrates are extremely sensitive to evaporation and have exceptionally high rates of water loss. For example, some peripatus lose water at rates twice those sustained by earthworms and forty times those of cockroaches (Manton and Ramsay, 1937). However, most arthropods have cuticles more or less resistant to passage of water and/or means of closing off the respiratory passages to retard water loss from them (Edney, 1957) and are capable of greater conservation of water. Indeed, ticks and some insects are able to absorb moisture vapor from the air, even when the air is not saturated (Browning, 1954; Edney, 1966).

Snails also show varying degrees of ability to retard evaporative loss. At least in some species, and when the animals are inactive, the mantle has a remarkable resistance to desiccation, even at relative humidities as low as 1.5%. The superficial layer is hygroscopic and can actually gain water at high humidities. Machin (1972) proposes that the mantle has a superficial hygroscopic layer overlaying a deeper impermeable barrier. During activity when snails secrete water-rich mucus, evaporative rates are high. Thus, one way of retarding evaporative losses is to become inactive.

Some species can further reduce water loss during inactivity by secreting a chalky epiphragm across the opercular opening (see section on estivation). These are more often formed at low than at high humidities (Rokitka and Herreid, 1975a, b). These responses occur in a variety of snails from various habitats, including some tropical ones.

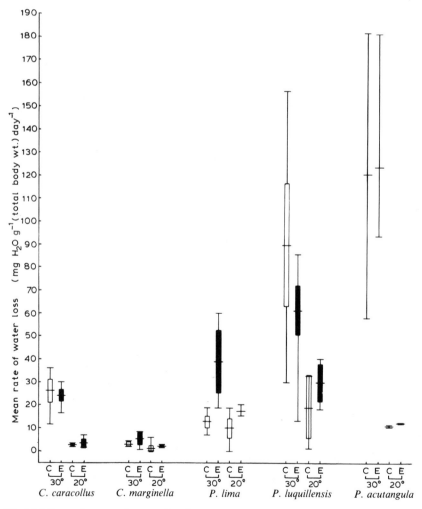

Fig. 15.5. Rates of evaporative water loss from some Puerto Rican snails (*Caracolus* spp. and *Polydontes* spp.) at different temperatures and at high humidities (open figures: C) and at low humidities (black figures: E). Vertical lines represent ranges, horizontal lines means, and rectangles two standard errors either side of the mean. (After Heatwole and Heatwole, 1978.)

Heatwole and Heatwole (1978) compared evaporative losses from various tropical camaenid snails from Puerto Rico. In most species evaporative losses were greater at elevated temperatures than at lower ones. Interspecific differences were not great at 20°C but those at 30°C were larger and reflected differences in habitat. *Polydontes luquillensis* and *P. acutangula*, both restricted to cool, moist montane rain forest, had higher evaporative losses than other species. *P. lima* and *Caracolus carocollus*, both of which occur over a wider altitudinal range (*P. lima* in open forest and parkland from lowlands to intermediate altitudes; *C. carocollus* from lowland closed forest to montane rain forest), had intermediate rates of evaporative loss, and the species that occurred only in open lowland forests and parks (*C. marginella*) had the lowest water losses of all (Heatwole and Heatwole, 1978) (Fig. 15.5). The rates of water loss were inversely proportional to survival times under the experimental conditions.

P. lima and *C. marginella* secrete epiphragms; the other species were not observed to do so (see section on estivation).

Thus, the ability of these various species to resist desiccation correlated with the moisture conditions and the openness of the different types of tropical forest occupied, and would seem to be adaptive.

TOLERANCES TO WATER LOSS

In the previous section, the rates of loss sustained by tropical forest animals were examined. However, evaporative rates tell only part of the story as the tolerance limits are also important. Even a low rate of loss would be significant for a species that could only tolerate loss of a small proportion of its body water. The same rate of loss would be less significant for an animal with greater tolerances.

The vital limit of water loss (VL) is a measure of desiccation tolerance. It is expressed as the percentage of the original fully hydrated weight that can be lost as water before death occurs.

Adjustment of the vital limit has certainly been one of the modes of adaptation of animals, including tropical forest forms. However, it has not been of universal importance. Among the reptiles there are closely related species from habitats of differing

aridity which have very similar vital limits. For example, Sexton and Heatwole (1968) found that the vital limit of a Panamanian tropical forest anole (*Anolis limifrons*) was not significantly different from that of a congener (*Anolis auratus*) from nearby open grassland. Similarly, among three tropical species of geckos of the genus *Sphaerodactylus*, ranging in habitat from xeric beaches and open forest to montane rain forest, mean vital limit did not differ by more than 1.3% (Heatwole and Veron, 1977; Leclair, 1978) (Table 15.2).

In other cases adaptive differences in vital limit are known. Munsey (1972) has pointed out that data from all lizard groups collectively show a weak correlation between habitat aridity and vital limit. The same can be concluded from the now more extensive data available (Table 15.2). Certainly, desert lizards have high vital limits compared to most other ones. The highest values known are from *Dipsosaurus dorsalis*, a desert species, and *Tarentola annularis*, a species from tropical Sudan. One of the lowest vital limits known is from a semi-aquatic skink (Table 15.2).

Tropical forest species are intermediate in value. Those from very moist forests such as montane rain forest have vital limits ranging from 19 to 27%. Species from more open habitats, including seasonal forest, have values between 20 and 30%. Finally, the eurytopic species and those from dry scrub have values of 25 to 32% (Table 15.2). Two tropical species which seem to have exceptionally high values were excluded from the above generalization. One of them (*Mabuya quinquetaeniatus*) has a vital limit exceeding 50%; this species occurs in a variety of open habitats in tropical Sudan and Egypt but is never far from moist situations. The second exception is *Anolis roquet salinei* with a vital limit of 37.8%. This species occupies tropical woodland in Martinique which is seasonally quite dry.

It can be concluded that there has been adaptive adjustment of the vital limit of water loss in reptiles, especially among desert species and some exceptional tropical ones, but that correlation of habitat aridity and vital limit is often rather weak. In many groups, especially those from tropical forests, adaptive adjustment of vital limit seems to have been relatively slight or even non-existent.

In amphibians there are often correlations between vital limit and dryness of the habitat, as long

TABLE 15.2

Vital limits of water loss in lizards from different habitats
[Data from Hall (1922) excluded as methods were too imprecise to provide meaningful results]

Species	Vital limit (%)	Habitat	Authority
IGUANIDAE			
Anolis gundlachi	20.0[a], 19.0[b]	tropical, montane rain forest	Hillman and Gorman (1977), Molinari-Teron (1969)
Anolis krugi	27.3[a], 24.5[b]	open edges of tropical montane rain forest	Hillman and Gorman (1977), Molinari-Teron (1969)
Anolis evermanni	25.2	tree trunks, tropical montane rain forest; canopy, tropical open lowland forest	Hillman and Gorman (1977)
Anolis limifrons	27.1	tropical lowland forest	Sexton and Heatwole (1968)
Anolis stratulus	25.2[a]	tropical open forest and parkland	Hillman and Gorman (1977)
Anolis distichus	29.7[a]	tropical open forest and parkland	Hillman and Gorman (1977)
Anolis cybotes	21.2[a]	tropical open forest and parkland	Hillman and Gorman (1977)
Anolis pulchellus	26.0, 20.0	tropical grassland	Hillman and Gorman (1977), Molinari-Teron (1969)
Anolis auratus	20.2	tropical grassland	Sexton and Heatwole (1968)
Anolis trinitatis	30.5[a]	tropical eurytopic	Hillman and Gorman (1977)
Anolis cristatellus	28.4–31.9[a,c]	tropical eurytopic	Hillman and Gorman (1977)
Anolis roquet salinei	37.8	tropical seasonally arid open forest	Leclair (1978)
Anolis cooki	28.5[a]	tropical xeric scrub	Hillman and Gorman (1977)
Anolis bonairensis	28.8[a]	tropical xeric scrub	Hillman and Gorman (1977)

(*continued on p. 257*)

as comparisons are made among closely related taxa (see review by Heatwole, in press). For example, in various families there is a progressive increase in vital limit in a series of genera or species graded from aquatic to semi-aquatic to terrestrial. The lowest vital limits known in frogs occur in species from rain forest (*Taudactylus diurnus*) or from streams (*Ascaphus truei*) and some of the highest ones occur in those from desert or semi-arid regions or exposed arboreal habitats.

In some cases, such correlations hold up even when different families are compared. However, at higher taxonomic levels than genus or family, ecological correlations often become less clear-cut or non-existent and are replaced by phyletic ones, e.g. salamanders generally have lower vital limits than anurans from comparable habitats. In some cases, quite anomalous situations occur. For example, *Eleutherodactylus* from tropical montane rain forest (Puerto Rico) has a higher vital limit than *Notaden bennetti* from semi-arid plains (Australia); both are leptodactylids.

Not much is known of the ecological correlates of vital limits in tropical snails. The Puerto Rican camaenids did not show any consistent relation of vital limit to degree of dryness of the habitat. It would seem that other adaptive avenues are used instead.

In contrasting the various modes of adaptation of three groups about which some assessment can be made (amphibians, lizards, snails) it is clear that environmental challenges have been met in somewhat different ways.

There is a variety of ways that animals can adapt

TABLE 15.2 (*continued*)

Species	Vital limit (%)	Habitat	Authority
IGUANIDAE (*continued*)			
Sceloporus occidentalis	38.7	temperate, semi-arid	Munsey (1972)
Callisaurus draconoides	45.7	desert	Munsey (1972)
Uma scoparia	48.4	desert	Munsey (1972)
Dipsosaurus dorsalis	50.2	desert	Munsey (1972)
SCINCIDAE			
Sphenomorphus quoyi	19.7	temperate, semi-aquatic	Heatwole and Veron (1977)
Mabuya quinquetaeniatus	*c.* 30	tropical, open areas	Cloudsley-Thompson (1965)
TEIIDAE			
Gymnophthalmus pleii	28.2	tropical, seasonally arid woodland	Leclair (1978)
Cnemidophorus tigris	44.9	temperate, eurytopic (mesic to desert)	Munsey (1972)
GEKKONIDAE (broad sense)			
Sphaerodactylus klauberi	24.3	tropical montane rain forest	Heatwole and Veron (1977)
Sphaerodactylus vincenti psammius	23.9	tropical, seasonally arid woodland	Leclair (1978)
Sphaerodactylus nicholsi townsendi	23.0	tropical, xeric sandy beaches	Heatwole and Veron (1977)
Hemidactylus mabouia	24.7	tropical xeric scrub, human dwellings	Heatwole and Veron (1977)
Tarentola annularis	> 50	tropical open areas, human dwellings	Cloudsley-Thompson (1965)

[a]Critical activity point, slightly lower than the vital limit.
[b]Corrected values from Heatwole and Veron who inadvertently reversed the figures for *A. krugi* and *A. gundlachi* in their review.
[c]The value of 28.4 from a population from an area of open parkland, the value of 31.9 from a population from an area of xeric scrub.

to different degrees of aridity and some of them have been discussed above. One of the major dichotomies is whether adaptation is via adjustment of the vital limit or via decreased skin permeability to evaporative loss; the two are not mutually exclusive. It is clear from the research reviewed in this section and the previous one, that lizards from habitats of different degrees of dryness often have different rates of evaporative loss. In addition, some taxa also show adaptive differences in vital limit. Thus, lizards have employed increased resistance to evaporation either alone or in conjunction with elevated tolerance limits.

By contrast, frogs have commonly developed adaptive differences in vital limit but in only two known genera has skin permeability been altered.

The limited information available on snails suggests that they tend to adapt via change in rates of loss rather than vital limit. More data are required for this group, however.

ESTIVATION

In equable tropical forests there is little need for seasonal inactivity. However, in seasonal tropical forests where thermal or hydric conditions may become harsh in the dry season, adaptations avoiding such environmental stress may be important. There are several possible strategies for avoiding seasonal environmental stress in forests with a marked dry season. One commonly used by invertebrates is to adjust the life history in such a way that during the most severe part of the year, the species is only represented by dormant, resistant stages (e.g. eggs). This is a widespread strategy used by arthropods in various seasonally fluctuating environments including temperate regions and deserts and is not unique to seasonal forests. Consequently it will not be treated further here.

A second strategy is to move out of the seasonal forest during the dry season and last out unfavorable periods in more equable environments. This seems to be a common response among tropical insects as Janzen (1973) found that in Costa Rica there was a marked reduction in numbers of species and individuals of insects during the dry season in areas where the dry season was severe; there was a strong movement of insects into moist refugia.

A third strategy is for the adult to go into dormancy in a secluded spot, i.e. to estivate. Although the lower vertebrates estivate in desert regions as a means of lasting out dry periods and hibernate over cold periods in temperate regions, dormancy does not seem to be such a common strategy among them in seasonal tropical forest. In contrast, some tropical forest snails do reduce activity under stressful conditions; the propensity or ability to do so seems to be related to the type of forest occupied. For example, Heatwole and Heatwole (1978) found that two species of Puerto Rican camaenid snails became dormant and secreted a chalky epiphragm which retarded evaporative loss especially at high temperatures and low humidities. These two species were from open, tropical lowland forest. Other species of the same family from moist, more equable forests did not display that response. In some species multiple epiphragms are secreted, the number increasing with duration of dormancy (Rokitka and Herreid, 1975a, b; Vander Laan, 1975); also species from dry habitats form thicker epiphragms than those from wetter ones (Machin, 1967).

REPRODUCTIVE STRATEGIES

Cyclicity

In temperate habitats breeding of vertebrates is strongly seasonal and correlated with the temporal change in temperature and availability of food. In the tropics, reproduction is often less restricted in time and may continue year-round in the more equable environments; when there is a pronounced

alternation of wet and dry seasons reproduction may be more cyclic.

Heatwole (in prep.) has reviewed the literature on reproductive cycles in amphibians in detail. The important conclusions are abstracted here. Where seasonal changes are regular and predictable, such as in temperate regions or the alternation of tropical wet and dry seasons, amphibian breeding periods tend to be brief and sharply defined, and to occur at the initiation of favorable environmental conditions. Hence, they are also regular and predictable. In more equable areas, breeding seasons tend to be longer and less sharply defined, in some cases continuing throughout the entire year. In areas where rainfall is scarce and unpredictable, amphibians breed whenever conditions are favorable; hence their reproductive periods are brief and sporadic. The equable tropical pattern contains species physiologically capable of breeding year-round; the irregular desert pattern, and perhaps some regular seasonal ones, probably include potentially continuous breeders which are inhibited part of the time by unfavorable environmental conditions. Many regular seasonal patterns are probably the result of seasonal genetic inability to produce gametes (an internal rhythm) coupled with behavioral responses permitting minor adjustments to weather conditions. It is suggested that the above sequence of types probably represents successive evolutionary stages in the adaptive radiation from equable to less stable environments. The intermediate stage (potentially continuous breeders, seasonally inhibited by environment) is probably the most successful in expanding its geographic range or ecologic amplitude; the obligate seasonal breeders are perhaps the least plastic.

Many reptilian reproductive cycles in the tropics show a strong correlation with the rainfall pattern. Licht and Gorman (1970) found that among Caribbean anoles egg production tended to decline with the advent of the dry season and increased abruptly with the beginning of a rainy season. The extent of the decline was correlated with the severity (e.g. duration) of the dry season. Although some species show relative independence from rainfall or respond to cues other than or in addition to rainfall, the earlier papers reviewed by Licht and Gorman (1970), and those which have appeared since (e.g., Sexton and Turner, 1971; Sexton et al., 1971; Fitch, 1973a; Fleming and Hooker, 1975) support the view that there is widespread dependence of egg production upon rainfall in tropical lizards and that reproductive cyclicity is adjusted accordingly.

Fitch (1973b) studied lizards from a number of forest types in Costa Rica. He arrayed the fourteen tropical species into four main reproductive categories that related to the seasonal moisture patterns of the different forests. Type 1 species had year-round reproduction and were confined to moist climates lacking seasonal contrasts. Type 2 species had year-round reproduction, but with the level of reproduction showing some seasonal variation; these species were confined to wet climates with moderate seasonal changes in moisture. Type 3 species divide their annual cycle into an extended breeding season and a non-breeding season of comparable length. Such species were characteristic of areas having a long dry season; reproduction occurred in the wet season. Finally, type 4 lizards have a relatively short annual reproductive season. This type was rare among tropical lizards but is characteristic of many temperate ones.

These interspecific differences have parallels on the intraspecific level. Sexton et al. (1963) and Heatwole and Sexton (1966) compared the reproductive cycle of a single species (*Anolis limifrons*) occurring in two parts of Panama with different intensities of dry season. The breeding season was less sharply defined in the zone with the more uniform rainfall than it was in the zone of greater seasonal disparity.

Reproductive cycles of birds have been extensively studied and have been reviewed by Immelmann (1971). He suggests that breeding patterns in different parts of the world are adaptations adjusting reproduction to the time of year when young can be raised most efficiently. He considered seasonal differences in availability of food to be the most important factor selecting for reproductive periodicity although he also indicated temporal differences in competition, predation, suitable nesting conditions, and climate as other ultimate selective forces. In temperate areas most species breed in spring or early summer, i.e., at a time of favorable food supply and temperature. In subtropical and tropical habitats there is a much greater heterogeneity of breeding seasons. Heavy rains may be directly harmful to nests, and inhabitants of lowland forest with very heavy annual precipitation

tend to concentrate breeding in the drier months. Most species from less humid regions with a regular alternation of wet and dry seasons tend to breed around the rainy season; where there are two wet and dry seasons some species nest in both wet seasons, others only in the longer of the two rainy periods. Some tropical species are continuous breeders. In some arid regions, breeding may be opportunistic, occurring irregularly whenever conditions are favorable.

There are a number of exceptions to the above generalizations, and the degree to which breeding is restricted seasonally varies rather widely.

The proximate factors controlling reproduction may be quite different from the ones actually exerting selective pressures. Endogenous rhythms are often involved but are influenced by environmental factors as well. Photoperiod is an important influence, especially on species that breed at high and middle latitudes. In tropical and arid areas rainfall seems to be one of the more important influences although Immelmann also implicated temperature, food supply, behavioral and social conditions, and a variety of other subsidiary factors.

Tropical mammals also show seasonality of breeding related to rainfall. Fleming (1973) reviewed the reproductive cycles of 45 species of mammals from the Panama Canal Zone. Reproductive activity was highest in the latter part of the dry season and lowest in the middle to late wet season. In many species initiation of reproductive activity seemed to be related to the cessation of heavy rains. These patterns resulted in young being produced or weaned when food resources were highest.

Among tropical forest snails reproductive cycle also seems to be related to the periodicity of rainfall. The African snail *Limicolaria martensiana* breeds at all months of the year but with two seasonal peaks associated with the two annual wet and dry seasons in such a way that the newly hatched snails appear during the wettest months (Owen, 1964). In the Cuban tree snail *Polymita muscarum* reproduction seems to be closely related to fluctuations of rainfall, and occurred at any time of year when weather was favorable (Díaz-Piferrer, 1962). In the Puerto Rican tree snail *Caracolus carocollus* populations from different forest types have different cycles. The reproductive period is such that the appearance of young coincides with favorably moist times of year but not during excessively wet periods (in wet montane rain forest) or excessively dry ones (in drier lowland forest) (Heatwole and Heatwole, 1978).

Strategies

There is great variability among animal species in terms of their reproductive habits. There are differences in the number of times reproduction occurs during a given season, in clutch size, degree of parental care of eggs, age and size at which sexual maturity is reached, and in length of reproductive life.

These attributes can be combined in various ways, the combination being known as the "reproductive strategy". Some features seem to occur together often and thus there are a few basic strategies that appear to be successful. A given strategy may be successful in one kind of environment but not in another. Specifying which reproductive characteristics have most often coevolved and identifying the adaptive significance of particular strategies are important aspects of modern ecology. In this section, those aspects of reproductive strategy applicable to tropical forest animals will be reviewed. Two groups have been examined more than others, birds and reptiles, and consequently the discussion will center around them. Other groups will be considered when appropriate.

Certain life history attributes have been shown to be associated. Tinkle (1969) has noted that characteristics which are likely to expose an animal to risk, such as high egg (or embryo) weight per clutch in relation to female body weight, conspicuous sexual coloration, elaborate courtship, aggressiveness and laying multiple clutches were more characteristic of early maturing, short-lived species than they were of late maturing, long-lived ones. He suggested that semelparous species with high juvenile and adult mortality must mature within a year and selection would favor almost any phenotype, even one exposed to considerable risk, that contributed to reproductive success. In long-lived species selection would favor individuals that took fewer risks even if it involved putting less energy and resources into reproduction each season.

In all cases, reproduction involves a risk and the number of times a species reproduces each year influences the probability of surviving to another season — that is, there is an inverse relationship between fecundity and mean annual adult survivorship. Consequently species living in the tropics and producing many clutches each year as a result of prolonged periods of favorable environmental conditions would have short life expectancies. There would be selection for early maturity.

In areas where, because of climatic limitation, only a single clutch could be produced each year, survival would be enhanced and selection would favor long life expectancy and other demographic characteristics associated with it. As life expectancy increased, a condition favorable for further restriction of per-season reproductive effort would be created, leading eventually to single broods per season or delayed maturity.

Viviparity and parental care are most often associated with late maturing single-brooded species. Tinkle hypothesized that the latter characteristics are more likely to evolve in temperate than in tropical areas, and that that was the reason viviparity and parental care were more frequent in temperate than tropical environments.

From the combination of empirical data and theoretical reasoning discussed above, Tinkle made several predictions relevant to the topic of this chapter. They were:

(1) In the tropics (or other areas with long periods favorable for reproduction) multiple clutches each season will be the rule.

(2) Species that produce multiple clutches or reproduce continuously (as in some parts of the tropics) will have short life expectancies, early maturity, and high reproductive risk.

(3) Single clutches during a reproductive season, delayed sexual maturity, viviparity and parental care will be characteristic of long-lived, single-brooded species from temperate or high altitude areas, or of tropical species where reproductive period is short because of a prolonged dry season.

In a later paper (Tinkle et al., 1970), these topics were treated in a more quantitative way. Two correlations were found when all available data were considered: clutch size increased with increased size at maturity; clutch size increased with increased age at first reproduction. However, the former correlation did not hold up when only tropical species were treated separately. Thus, clutch size in tropical species must be adjusted in different ways than in temperate ones. Tinkle et al. (1970) suggest that in tropical species: (1) because of more intensive intraspecific competition there may be greater selection for improved survivorship (e.g. larger egg size as their data suggest) rather than larger clutches; and/or (2) competition for food prevents the fat storage required for production of large clutches.

A computer clustering of various reproductive characteristics gave two clearly divided strategies (Fig. 15.6): (1) early maturing and multiple-brooded versus (2) late maturing and single-brooded. Viviparity was a subset of the latter strategy as almost all viviparous species produce one litter a year and have a late age at first reproduction. Strategy 1 contains species that are tropical (equable) or temperate (seasonal) in distribution, whereas strategy 2 contains primarily temperate species. Thus, the predictions of Tinkle's (1969) earlier paper for lizards seem to be fulfilled.

Later work on reproductive strategy has extended ideas on various aspects and have tested the

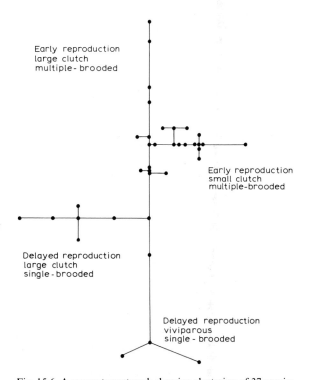

Fig. 15.6. A computer network showing clustering of 37 species of lizards by reproductive strategies. Each dot indicates one species. (Modified from Tinkle et al., 1970.)

Early reproduction large clutch multiple-brooded

Early reproduction small clutch multiple-brooded

Delayed reproduction large clutch single-brooded

Delayed reproduction viviparous single-brooded

generality of the conclusions of the two papers discussed above.

Tinkle and Gibbons (1977) have looked at viviparity in more detail and have extensively reviewed the literature on that topic. They point out that the number of viviparous species are most numerous at mid-latitudes, being reduced both in the tropics and in cold-temperate regions. However, the number of oviparous species is even more drastically reduced in cold-temperate regions and the *proportion* of viviparous species there is higher than elsewhere. Tinkle and Gibbons found no evidence that the developmental time was less in viviparous than in oviparous forms from the same latitude, nor that developmental time in the tropics was less than in temperate regions. However, the developmental time *inside the mother's body* is less in oviparous forms than in viviparous ones. Thus, where the season is sufficiently long for multiple clutches to occur, as in the tropics, viviparity would be a disadvantage as the extra time the young remain in the mother's body could be used instead to begin development of another clutch of eggs. Where only one clutch is possible anyway, this consideration would be less important. Thus, viviparity seems to be associated with reproductive strategy 2 (mostly temperate species) rather than strategy 1 (followed by most tropical species).

Shine and Berry (1978) carried these ideas a step further by pointing out that viviparity was no more closely correlated with low temperature than with various other environmental variables. They suggested that although live-bearing in reptiles may have evolved in cold areas and still may be favored there, environmental temperatures play little role in determining the relative success of viviparity under most climatic conditions and that subsequent radiation of live-bearers had little to do with cold.

Fitch (1973b) has supported many of the conclusions of Tinkle et al. (1970) but has questioned the generality of some of them. In a study of fifteen species from fourteen Costa Rican localities, he confirmed that most of the tropical lizards had relatively small clutches and low proportions of viviparous forms, and that early maturity and multiple brooding were common. However, he found that the correlation between female size and number of eggs per clutch did not hold up.

Finally, Maiorana (1976) has extended Tinkle's ideas by relating multiple-clutching to predation.

She suggests that if predation is a constant threat, laying fewer eggs as rapidly as they can be produced would result in a higher probable yield of young because (1) the eggs are less concentrated in time and space and therefore less subject to predation, and/or (2) because a lizard burdened with enough fat to produce a large clutch would be subject to greater predation risk. The first explanation would certainly require testing; it is counter to the idea that bursts of reproduction supersaturate the predator demand and result in increased survival (see Matthews, 1976).

The reproductive strategy of birds has been extensively studied, and Tinkle et al. (1970) have compared the avian and saurian conditions. Birds differ somewhat from lizards. They have a greater diversity of responses arising from such specializations as hole-nesting, colony formation, brood parasitism and cooperative rearing of young, and they show no consistent correlation between body size and clutch size. However, birds, like lizards, can be divided into two groups on the basis of age at first reproduction. Early maturing birds tend to lay large clutches (not always the case in lizards), have short developmental periods and low annual survivorship. Their nest sites are relatively accessible to predators and their rapid developmental rate permits replacing of clutches lost by predation.

The late maturing birds generally have small clutches, single broods per season, high annual adult survivorship and long developmental period. Their nests are in inaccessible places.

Both birds and mammals tend to have larger clutch or litter sizes in temperate regions than do their tropical relatives (Cody, 1971). A variety of hypotheses have been advanced to explain this phenomenon (see review by Maiorana, 1976). For birds they were: (1) greater day length during the breeding season at high latitudes provide a longer period to gather food for young; (2) increased predation in the tropics results in greater avoidance behavior by birds and concomitantly less time for gathering food for young; (3) increased nest predation makes it more worthwhile to have a greater number of nesting attempts per season, with fewer young at each one; and (4) continual coevolution of predator and prey in the tropics results in less food availability for birds. It is probable that a combination of factors is actually responsible. As Maiorana (1976) pointed out, empirical support for

some of these suggestions is lacking. It appears to be an area which in spite of large amounts of factual information, theoretical constructs have outstripped their empirical bases.

For mammals, the explanations were: (1) high mortality among small non-hibernating species in cold areas selects for compensatory increased litter size; and (2) the short activity season at high latitudes means that the number of possible litters per season are few and hence there is selection for larger litters for a given time.

Reproductive strategies among tropical tree snails show some similarities to those of vertebrates. For example, *Polydontes luquillensis* and *Polydontes acutangula* from relatively equable upland forest have shorter life spans than does the widespread *Caracolus carocollus*, which in addition to the above habitat also occurs in more seasonally variable forest (Heatwole and Heatwole, 1978).

REFERENCES

Alexander, A.J. and Ewer, D.W., 1958. Temperature adaptive behaviour in the scorpion, *Opisthophthalmus latimanus* Koch. *J. Exp. Biol.*, 35: 349–359.

Ballinger, R.E., Marion, K.R. and Sexton, O.J., 1970. Thermal ecology of the lizard, *Anolis limifrons*, with comparative notes on three additional Panamanian anoles. *Ecology*, 51: 246–254.

Bartholomew, G.A. and Casey, T.M., 1977. Endothermy during terrestrial activity in large beetles. *Science*, 195: 882–883.

Bartholomew, G.A. and Epting, R.J., 1975. Allometry of post-flight cooling rates in moths: a comparison with vertebrate homeotherms. *J. Exp. Biol.*, 63: 603–613.

Bartholomew, G.A. and Tucker, V.A., 1964. Size, body temperature, thermal conductance, oxygen consumption, and heart rate in Australian varanid lizards. *Physiol. Zool.*, 37: 341–354.

Blaylock, L.A., Ruibal, R. and Platt-Aloia, K., 1976. Skin structure and wiping behaviour of phyllomedusine frogs. *Copeia*, 1976: 283–295.

Bradshaw, S.D., 1970. Seasonal changes in the water and electrolyte metabolism of *Amphibolurus* lizards in the field. *Comp. Biochem. Physiol.*, 36: 689–718.

Brattstrom, B.H., 1965. Body temperatures of reptiles. *Am. Midl. Nat.*, 73: 376–422.

Brattstrom, B.H., 1968. Thermal acclimation in anuran amphibians as a function of latitude and altitude. *Comp. Biochem. Physiol.*, 24: 93–111.

Brattstrom, B.H., 1970. Thermal acclimation in Australian amphibians. *Comp. Biochem. Physiol.*, 35: 69–103.

Brattstrom, B.H., 1971. Critical thermal maxima of some Australian skinks. *Copeia*, 1971: 554–557.

Brooks, G.R., 1968. Body temperatures of three lizards from Dominica, West Indies. *Herpetologica*, 24: 209–214.

Browning, T.O., 1954. Water balance in the tick, *Ornithodoros moubata* Murray, with particular reference to the influence of carbon dioxide on the uptake and loss of water. *J. Exp. Biol.*, 31: 331–340.

Cabanac, H.P. and Hammel, H.T., 1971. Peripheral sensitivity and temperature regulation in *Tiliqua scincoides*. *Int. J. Biometeorol.*, 15: 239–243.

Cabanac, H.P., Hammel, H.T. and Hardy, J.D., 1967. *Tiliqua scincoides:* Temperature-sensitive units in lizard brain. *Science*, 158: 1050–1051.

Calder, W.A. and King, J.R., 1974. Thermal and caloric relations of birds. In: D.S. Farner and J.R. King (Editors), *Avian Biology, IV.* Academic Press, New York, N.Y., pp. 259–413.

Campbell, H.W., 1971. Observations on the thermal activity of some tropical lizards of the genus *Anolis* (Iguanidae). *Caribb. J. Sci.*, 11: 17–20.

Chew, R.M. and Dammann, A.E., 1961. Evaporative water loss of small vertebrates as measured with an infrared analyzer. *Science*, 133: 384–385.

Clarke, D.R., Jr., 1973. Temperature responses of three Costa Rican lizards (*Anolis*). *Caribb. J. Sci.*, 13: 199–206.

Claussen, D.L., 1967. Studies of water loss in two species of lizards. *Comp. Biochem. Physiol.*, 20: 115–130.

Cloudsley-Thompson, J.L., 1965. Rhythmic activity, temperature-tolerance, water-relations and mechanisms of heat death in a tropical skink and gecko. *J. Zool.*, 146: 55–69.

Cloudsley-Thompson, J.L., 1970. Terrestrial invertebrates. In: G.C. Whittow (Editor), *Comparative Physiology of Thermoregulation, I. Invertebrates and Nonmammalian Vertebrates.* Academic Press, New York, N.Y., pp. 15–77.

Cloudsley-Thompson, J.L., 1971. *The Temperature and Water Relations of Reptiles.* Merrow, Watford, 159 pp.

Cody, M.L., 1971. Ecological aspects of reproduction. In: D.S. Farner and J.R. King (Editors), *Avian Biology, I.* Academic Press, New York, N.Y., pp. 461–512.

Corn, M.J., 1971. Upper thermal limits and thermal preferenda for three sympatric species of *Anolis*. *J. Herpetol.*, 5: 17–21.

Darevskii, I.S. and Kadarsan, J., 1964. On the biology of the giant Indonesian monitor lizard (*Varanus komodoenses* Ouwens). *Zool. Zh.*, 43: 1355–1360. (English transl. Smithsonian Herpetological Information Services 1965.)

Dawson, T.J., 1973. "Primitive" mammals. In: G.C. Whittow (Editor), *Comparative Physiology of Thermoregulation, 3.* Academic Press, New York, N.Y., pp. 1–46.

Dawson, T.J. and Degabriele, R., 1973. The cuscus (*Phalanger maculatus*) — a marsupial sloth? *J. Comp. Physiol.*, 83: 41–50.

Dawson, W.R. and Hudson, J.W., 1970. Birds. In: G.C. Whittow (Editor), *Comparative Physiology of Thermoregulation, I. Invertebrates and Nonmammalian Vertebrates.* Academic Press, New York, N.Y., pp. 223–310.

Díaz-Piferrer, M., 1962. Reproduction of *Polymita muscarum* Lea, a Cuban tree snail. *Caribb. J. Sci.*, 2: 59–61.

Drewes, R.C., Hillman, S.S., Putnam, R.W. and Sokol, O.M., 1977. Water, nitrogen and ion balance in the African treefrog *Chiromantis petersi* Boulenger (Anura: Rhacophoridae), with comments on the structure of the integument. *J. Comp. Physiol.*, 116: 257–267.

Dunson, W.A., 1976. Salt glands in reptiles. In: C. Gans and W.R. Dawson (Editors), *Biology of the Reptilia, 5.* Academic Press, New York, N.Y., pp. 413–445.

Duvdevani, I. and Borut, A., 1974. Oxygen consumption and evaporative loss in four species of *Acanthodactylus* (Lacertidae). *Copeia*, 1974: 155–164.

Edney, E.B., 1957. *The Water Relations of Terrestrial Arthropods.* Cambridge Monographs in Experimental Biology 5. Cambridge University Press, London, 109 pp.

Edney, E.B., 1966. Absorption of water vapour from unsaturated air by *Arenivoga* sp. (Polyphagidae, Dictyoptera). *Comp. Biochem. Physiol.*, 19: 387–408.

Engbretson, G.A. and Hutchison, V.H., 1976. Parietalectomy and thermal selection in the lizard *Sceloporus magister*. *J. Exp. Zool.*, 198: 29–38.

Firth, B.T. and Heatwole, H., 1976. Panting thresholds of lizards: the role of the pineal complex in panting responses in an agamid, *Amphibolurus muricatus*. *Gen. Comp. Endocrinol.*, 29: 388–401.

Fitch, H.S., 1968. Temperature and behavior of some equatorial lizards. *Herpetologica*, 24: 35–38.

Fitch, H.S., 1972. Ecology of *Anolis tropidolepis* in Costa Rican Cloud Forest. *Herpetologica*, 28: 10–21.

Fitch, H.S., 1973a. A field study of Costa Rican lizards. *Univ. Kansas Sci. Bull.*, 50: 39–126.

Fitch, H.S., 1973b. Population structure and survivorship in some Costa Rican lizards. *Occas. Pap. Mus. Nat. Hist. Univ. Kansas*, No. 18: 1–41.

Fitch, H.S., 1973c. Observations on the population ecology of the Central American iguanid lizard *Anolis cupreus*. *Caribb. J. Sci.*, 13: 215–229.

Fitch, H.S. and Henderson, R.W., 1976. A field study of the rock anoles (Reptilia, Lacertilia, Iguanidae) of southern Mexico. *J. Herpetol.*, 10: 303–311.

Fleming, T.H., 1973. The reproductive cycles of 3 species of opossums and other mammals in the Panama Canal Zone. *J. Mammal.*, 54: 439–455.

Fleming, T.H. and Hooker, R.S., 1975. *Anolis cupreus:* The response of a lizard to tropical seasonality. *Ecology*, 56: 1243–1261.

Gorman, G.C. and Hillman, S., 1977. Physiological basis for climatic niche partitioning in two species of Puerto Rican *Anolis* (Reptilia, Lacertilia, Iguanidae). *J. Herpetol.*, 11: 337–340.

Hall, F.G., 1922. The vital limit of exsiccation of certain animals. *Biol. Bull.*, 42: 31–51.

Heath, J.E., Hanegan, J.L., Wilkin, P.J. and Heath, M.S., 1971. Adaptation of the thermal responses of insects. *Am. Zool.*, 11: 147–158.

Heatwole, H., 1960. Burrowing ability and behavioral responses to desiccation of the salamander, *Plethodon cinereus*. *Ecology*, 41: 661–668.

Heatwole, H., 1963. Ecologic segregation of two species of tropical frogs of the genus *Eleutherodactylus*. *Caribb. J. Sci.*, 3: 17–23.

Heatwole, H., 1966. Factors affecting orientation and habitat selection in some geckos. *Z. Tierpsychol.*, 23: 303–314.

Heatwole, H., 1976. *Reptile Ecology.* University of Queensland Press, St. Lucia, Qld., 178 pp.

Heatwole, H., 1979. Adaptations of amphibians to aridity. In:

H. Cogger (Editor), *Arid Australia. Proceedings of the Arid Lands Symposium.* Australian Museum, Sydney, Vic., in press.

Heatwole, H., 1981a. A review of structuring in herpetofaunal assemblages. In: N.J. Scott, Jr. (Editor), *Herpetological Communities*, in Press.

Heatwole, H., in prep. Activity — daily and seasonal. In: *Behavior of the Amphibia.*

Heatwole, H. and Heatwole, A., 1978. Ecology of the Puerto Rican camaenid tree-snails. *Malacologia*, 17: 241–315.

Heatwole, H. and Newby, R.C., 1972. Interaction of internal rhythm and loss of body water in influencing activity levels of amphibians. *Herpetologica*, 28: 156–161.

Heatwole, H. and Sexton, O.J., 1966. Herpetofaunal comparisons between two climatic zones in Panama. *Am. Midl. Nat.*, 75: 45–60.

Heatwole, H. and Veron, J.E.N., 1977. Vital limit and evaporative water loss in lizards (Reptilia, Lacertilia): a critique and new data. *J. Herpetol.*, 11: 341–348.

Heatwole, H., Mercado, N. and Ortiz, E., 1965. Comparison of critical thermal maxima of two species of Puerto Rican frogs of the genus *Eleutherodactylus*. *Physiol. Zool.*, 38: 1–8.

Heatwole, H., Lin, T.H., Villalón, E., Muñiz, A. and Matta, A., 1969a. Some aspects of the thermal ecology of Puerto Rican anoline lizards. *J. Herpetol.*, 3: 65–77.

Heatwole, H., Torres, F., Blasini de Austin, S. and Heatwole, A., 1969b. Studies on anuran water balance — I. Dynamics of evaporative water loss by the coqui, *Eleutherodactylus portoricensis*. *Comp. Biochem. Physiol.*, 28: 245–269.

Heatwole, H., Cameron, E. and Webb, G.J.W., 1971. Studies on anuran water balance — II. Desiccation in the Australian frog, *Notaden bennetti*. *Herpetologica*, 27: 365–378.

Heatwole, H., Firth, B.T. and Webb, G.J.W., 1973. Panting thresholds of lizards — I. Some methodological and internal influences on the panting threshold of an agamid, *Amphibolurus muricatus*. *Comp. Biochem. Physiol.*, 46A: 799–826.

Heinrich, B., 1970. Thoracic temperature stabilization by blood circulation in a free-flying moth. *Science*, 168: 580–582.

Heinrich, B., 1974. Thermoregulation in endothermic insects. *Science*, 185: 747–756.

Henwood, K., 1975. Infrared transmittance as an alternative thermal strategy in the desert beetle *Onymacris plana*. *Science*, 189: 993–994.

Hertz, P.E., 1974. Thermal passivity of a tropical lizard, *Anolis polylepis*. *J. Herpetol.*, 8: 323–327.

Hillman, S. and Gorman, G.C., 1977. Water loss, desiccation tolerance, and survival under desiccating conditions in 11 species of Caribbean *Anolis*. Evolutionary and ecological implications. *Oecologia*, 29: 105–116.

Hillman, S., Gorman, G.C. and Thomas, R., 1979. Water loss in *Anolis* lizards: evidence for acclimation and intraspecific differences along a habitat gradient. *Comp. Biochem. Physiol.*, 62A: 491–494.

Hirth, H.F., 1964. Temperature preferences of five species of neotropical lizards. *Herpetologica*, 20: 273–276.

Hudson, J.W., 1973. Torpidity in mammals. In: G.C. Whittow (editor), *Comparative Physiology of Thermoregulation, III. Special Aspects of Thermoregulation.* Academic Press, New York, N.Y., pp. 97–165.

Huey, R.B., 1974. Winter thermal ecology of the iguanid lizard *Tropidurus peruvianus*. *Copeia*, 1974: 149–155.

Huey, R.B. and Webster, T.P., 1975. Thermal biology of a solitary lizard: *Anolis marmoratus* of Guadeloupe, Lesser Antilles. *Ecology*, 56: 445–452.

Huey, R.B. and Webster, T.P., 1976. Thermal biology of *Anolis* lizards in a complex fauna: The *cristatellus* group on Puerto Rico. *Ecology*, 57: 985–994.

Immelmann, K., 1971. Ecological aspects of periodic reproduction. In: D.S. Farner and J.R. King (Editors), *Avian Biology*, I. Academic Press, New York, N.Y., pp. 341–389.

Inger, R.F., 1959. Temperature responses and ecological relations of two Bornean lizards. *Ecology*, 40: 127–136.

Jackson, W.B., 1957. Microclimatic patterns in the army ant bivouac. *Ecology*, 38: 276–285.

Janzen, D.H., 1973. Sweep samples of tropical foliage insects: effects of seasons, vegetation types, elevation, time of day, and insularity. *Ecology*, 54: 687–708.

Jenssen, T.A., 1970. The ethoecology of *Anolis nebulosus* (Sauria, Iguanidae). *J. Herpetol.*, 4: 1–38.

Johnson, C.R., 1973. Thermoregulation in pythons — II. Head-body temperature differences and thermal preferenda in Australian pythons. *Comp. Biochem. Physiol.*, 45A: 1065–1087.

Kennedy, J.P., 1968. Observations on the ecology and behavior of *Cnemidophorus guttatus* and *Cnemidophorus deppei* (Sauria, Teiidae) in southern Veracruz. *J. Herpetol.*, 2: 87–96.

Kour, E.L. and Hutchison, V.H., 1970. Critical thermal tolerances and heating and cooling rates of lizards from diverse habitats. *Copeia*, 1970: 219–229.

Leclair, R.J., 1978. Water loss and microhabitats in three sympatric species of lizards (Reptilia: Lacertilia) from Martinique, West Indies. *J. Herpetol.*, 12: 177–182.

Levins, R., 1969. Thermal acclimation and heat resistance in *Drosophila* species. *Am. Nat.*, 103: 483–499.

Licht, P. and Gorman, G.C., 1970. Reproductive and fat cycles in Caribbean *Anolis* lizards. *Univ. Calif. Publ. Zool.*, 95: 1–52.

Licht, P. and Moberly, W.R., 1965. Thermal requirements for embryonic development in the tropical lizard *Iguana iguana*. *Copeia*, 1965: 515–517.

Licht, P., Dawson, W.R. and Shoemaker, V.H., 1966. Heat resistance of some Australian lizards. *Copeia*, 1966: 162–169.

Loveridge, J.P., 1970. Observations on nitrogenous excretion and water relations of *Chiromantis xerampelina* (Amphibia, Anura). *Arnoldia*, 5: 1–6.

McGinnis, S.M. and Moore, R.G., 1969. Thermoregulation in the boa constrictor *Boa constrictor*. *Herpetologica*, 25: 38–45.

Machin, J., 1967. Structural adaptation for reducing water-loss in three species of terrestrial snail. *J. Zool.*, 152: 55–65.

Machin, J., 1972. Water exchange in the mantle of a terrestrial snail during periods of reduced evaporative loss. *J. Exp. Biol.*, 57: 103–111.

McManus, J.J. and Nellis, D.W., 1973. Temperature and metabolism of a tropical lizard, *Anolis acutus*. *Comp. Biochem. Physiol.*, 45A: 403–410.

Maiorana, V.C., 1976. Predation, submergent behavior, and tropical diversity. *Evol. Theory*, 1: 157–177.

Manton, S.M. and Ramsay, J.A., 1937. Studies on the Onychophora — III. The control of water loss in *Peripatopsis*. *J. Exp. Biol.*, 14: 470–472.

Matthews, E.G., 1976. *Insect Ecology*. University of Queensland Press, St. Lucia, Qld., 226 pp.

Molinari-Teron, J., 1969. *Comparison of Tolerance to Desiccation in Three Species of Anoline Lizards from Puerto Rico*. Thesis, University of Puerto Rico, Rio Piedras, 19 pp.

Munsey, L.D., 1972. Water loss in five species of lizards. *Comp. Biochem. Physiol.*, 43A: 781–794.

Myhre, K. and Hammel, H.T., 1969. Behavioral regulation of internal temperature in the lizard *Tiliqua scincoides*. *Am. J. Physiol.*, 217: 1490–1495.

O'Farrell, A.F., 1968. Physiological colour change and its significance in the biology of some Australian Odonata. *Proc. Int. Congr. Entomol.* (*Moscow 1968*), 1: 534.

Owen, D.F., 1964. Bimodal occurrence of breeding in an equatorial land snail. *Ecology*, 45: 862.

Pienaar, U. de V., Passmore, N.I. and Carruthers, V.C., 1976. *The Frogs of Kruger National Park*. Sigma Press, Pretoria, 91 pp.

Rand, A.S., 1964. Ecological distribution in anoline lizards of Puerto Rico. *Ecology*, 45: 745–752.

Rand, A.S., 1972. The temperatures of iguana nests and their relation to incubation optima and to nesting sites and season. *Herpetologica*, 28: 252–253.

Rand, A.S. and Rand, P.J., 1966. Aspects of the ecology of the iguanid lizard *Tropidurus torquatus* at Belém, Pará. *Smithson. Misc. Coll.*, 151: 1–16.

Rokitka, M.A. and Herreid II, C.F., 1975a. Position of epiphragms in the land snail *Otala lactea* (Müller). *Nautilus*, 89: 23–26.

Rokitka, M.A. and Herreid II, C.F., 1975b. Formation of epiphragms by the land snail *Otala lactea* (Müller) under various environmental conditions. *Nautilus*, 89: 27–32.

Ruibal, R., 1961. Thermal relations of five species of tropical lizards. *Evolution*, 15: 98–111.

Ruibal, R. and Philibosian, R., 1970. Eurythermy and niche expansion in lizards. *Copeia*, 1970: 645–653.

Schmidt-Nielsen, K., Borut, A., Lee, P. and Crawford, E., Jr., 1963. Nasal salt excretion and the possible function of the cloaca in water conservation. *Science*, 142: 1300–1301.

Scholander, P.F., 1950. Adaptation to cold in arctic and tropical mammals and birds in relation to body temperature, insulation and basal metabolic rate. *Biol. Bull.*, 99: 259–271.

Scholander, P.F., 1955. Evolution of climatic adaptation in homeotherms. *Evolution*, 9: 15–26.

Scholander, P.F., Walters, V., Hock, R. and Irving, L., 1950a. Body insulation of some arctic and tropical mammals and birds. *Biol. Bull.*, 99: 225–236.

Scholander, P.F., Hock, R., Walters, V., Johnson, F. and Irving, L., 1950b. Heat regulation in some arctic and tropical mammals and birds. *Biol. Bull.*, 99: 237–258.

Sexton, O.J. and Heatwole, H., 1968. An experimental investigation of habitat selection and water loss in some anoline lizards. *Ecology*, 49: 762–767.

Sexton, O.J. and Turner, O., 1971. The reproductive cycle of a neotropical lizard. *Ecology*, 52: 159–164.

Sexton, O.J., Heatwole, H.F. and Meseth, E., 1963. Seasonal population changes in the lizard, *Anolis limifrons*, in Panama. *Am. Midl. Nat.*, 69: 482–491.

Sexton, O.J., Ortleb, E.P., Hathaway, L.M., Ballinger, R.E. and Licht, P., 1971. Reproductive cycles of three species of anoline lizards from the isthmus of Panama. *Ecology*, 52: 201–215.

Shine, R. and Berry, J.F., 1978. Climatic correlates of live-bearing in squamate reptiles. *Oecologia*, 33: 261–268.

Shoemaker, V.H. and McClanahan, L.L., Jr., 1975. Evaporative water loss, nitrogen excretion, and osmoregulation in phyllomedusine frogs. *J. Comp. Physiol.*, 100: 331–345.

Shoemaker, V.H., Balding, D., Ruibal, R. and McClanahan, L.L., Jr., 1972. Uricotelism and low evaporative water loss in a South American frog. *Science*, 175: 1018–1020.

Snyder, G.K., 1971. Adaptive value of a reduced respiratory metabolism in a lizard, a unique case. *Respir. Physiol.*, 13: 90–101.

Snyder, G.K., 1975. Respiratory metabolism and evaporative loss in a small tropical lizard. *J. Comp. Physiol.*, 104: 13–18.

Snyder, G.K. and Weathers, W.W., 1976. Physiological responses to temperature in the tropical lizard, *Hemidactylus frenatus* (Sauria: Gekkonidae). *Herpetologica*. 33: 252–256.

Stamps, J.A., 1976. Rainfall, activity and social behaviour in the lizard, *Anolis aeneus*. *Anim. Behav.*, 24: 603–608.

Templeton, J.R., 1971. Periferal (*sic.*) and central control of panting in the desert iguana, *Dipsosaurus dorsalis*. *J. Physiol.*, 63: 439–442.

Tinkle, D.W., 1969. The concept of reproductive effort and its relation to the evolution of life histories of lizards. *Am. Nat.*, 103: 501–516.

Tinkle, D.W. and Gibbons, J.W., 1977. The distribution and evolution of viviparity in reptiles. *Misc. Publ. Mus. Zool. Univ. Mich.*, No. 154: 1–55.

Tinkle, D.W., Wilbur, H.M. and Tilley, S.G., 1970. Evolutionary strategies in lizard reproduction. *Evolution*, 24: 55–74.

Van der Laan, K., 1975. Aestivation in the land snail *Helminthoglypta arrosa* (Binney) (Pulmonata: Helicidae). *The Veliger*, 17: 360–368.

Van Mierop, L.H.S. and Barnard, S.M., 1976. Thermoregulation in a brooding female *Python molurus bivittatus* (Serpentes: Boidae). *Copeia*, 1976: 398–401.

Vinegar, A., Hutchison, V.H. and Dowling, H.G., 1970. Metabolism, energetics and thermoregulation during brooding of snakes of the genus *Python* (Reptilia: Boidae). *Zoologica*, 55: 19–50.

Warburg, M.R., 1965. Water relation and internal body temperature of isopods from mesic and xeric habitats. *Physiol. Zool.*, 38: 99–109.

White, F.N., 1976. Circulation. In: C. Gans and W.R. Dawson (Editors), *Biology of the Reptilia*. Academic Press, New York, N.Y., pp. 275–334.

Whitfield, C.L. and Livezey, R.L., 1973. Thermoregulatory patterns in lizards. *Physiol. Zool.*, 46: 285–296.

Whittow, G.C. (Editor), 1970–1973. *Comparative Physiology of Thermoregulation*. Academic Press, New York, N.Y., Vol. I 333 pp., Vol. II 410 pp., Vol. III 278 pp.

Wilhoft, D.C., 1961. Temperature responses in two tropical Australian skinks. *Herpetologica*, 17: 109–113.

Wilson, E.O., 1971. Social homeostasis and the superorganism. In: *The Insect Societies*. Harvard University Press, Cambridge, Mass., pp. 306–319.

Chapter 16

BEHAVIORAL ADAPTATIONS OF HIGHER VERTEBRATES TO TROPICAL FORESTS

JOHN F. EISENBERG

GENERAL ADAPTATIONS TO THE FOREST

A tropical forest varies in physiognomy depending on the stage of succession, soil type, soil porosity, elevation, latitude and rainfall pattern (Walter, 1973). The term tropical forest usually creates in the mind an image of a mature tropical evergreen forest growing under conditions of high rainfall and minimum annual variation in temperature. In mature forests of the preceding type, the tree crowns are often stratified with the tallest trees or emergents standing some 60 m in height. Lianas utilize the emergents as access routes to the sunlight and lianas may equal the trees in species diversity (Hladik, 1978). The mature tropical evergreen forests of the world have been elegantly portrayed by Corner (1954) and Richards (1952). Yet this physiognomic class of vegetation is one end of a continuum. Single rainfall peaks with drought conditions exceeding four months result in tropical forests which show pronounced periods of quiescence and with many species that are deciduous. All variations between evergreen tropical forests and obligate deciduous forests can be discerned (Dittus, 1977). In areas with high water tables or prolonged flooding, woody plants may be unable to survive during the rainy season. In northern South America vast tracts of palm savannas are the result of impeded vertical drainage (Beard, 1953). Pyrogenic savannas are also typical of those areas of the tropics which experience a single abrupt period of rainfall in the annual cycle (Walter, 1973).

The vertebrate faunas vary in composition within and between physiognomic classes of vegetation. Yet what we are concerned with here is the set of adaptations to the forest itself. In order to utilize the forest, higher vertebrates have had to adapt to conditions where most of the plant productivity is carried out many meters above the ground. Leaves and photosynthesis, blossoms and pollen, fruits and seeds are generally borne high above the earth, thus anatomical adaptations to facilitate tree crown feeding are of paramount importance.

Flight is a convenient mechanism for moving from shrub to tree crown and was first evolved by insects. In turn the reptiles evolved volant forms (e.g., Pterodactyla), followed by the birds (Aves) and mammals (Chiroptera). The Chiroptera exhibit their greatest diversity in the tropics as do the birds (Klopfer and McArthur, 1960; Fleming, 1973). Of course, the diversity of major taxa all seem to increase as one proceeds from the temperate zone to the tropics but the trend is most pronounced in the passerine birds (Slud, 1976) and the Chiroptera (McNab, 1971). While the reasons for this phenomenon may be the result of many factors, surely the volant vertebrates are able to make efficient use of the forest. Gliding vertebrates also reach an apex of diversity in the tropical forests. Malaya and Indonesia have a gliding frog (*Rhacophorus nigropalmatus*), a gliding snake (*Chrysopelea* sp.) and a gliding lizard (*Draco volans*). Among the sciurid subfamily Petauristinae (flying squirrels), the greatest diversity is found in the forests of Southeast Asia (Muul and Lim, 1978). The scaly tailed flying squirrels of the family Anomaluridae have convergently evolved in equatorial Africa while gliding ability has convergently evolved three times within the marsupial family Phalangeridae of Australasia (Eisenberg, 1978).

Evolution of feeding adaptations in tropical forests

The tropical forest with its multitude of tree and liana species provides an opportunity for feeding specializations almost unparalleled in any other biome. The vegetation is the fundament of the food chain and arthropods and terrestrial mollusks were among the first animal life forms to invade the forests. In dense, mature rain forests, the near constancy of temperature and humidity have encouraged adaptation and speciation among the Arthropoda to a fantastic degree (Bates, 1864; Wallace, 1869). Arthropod specializations for sap, leaf, pollen, and fruit feeding foreshadowed the evolution of similar feeding adaptations by the vertebrates. Plant defense mechanisms against arthropod predation resulted in the coevolution of arthropod feeding guilds and their plant prey (Feeny, 1975; Frankie, 1975). Plants and higher vertebrates have evolved similar inter-relationships (Montgomery and Sunquist, 1975; Smith, 1975).

Herbivory or feeding specializations for ingesting and processing leaves or foliaceous material is a rare condition among tropical, forest-adapted vertebrates. In the first place, in a mature tropical forest, most of the leafy material will be some distance above ground and, although terrestrial herbivores may browse or graze at the forest edge or in the clearings, the conspicuous lack of undergrowth in mature forests due to the shading effect of adult trees means that the bulk of the herbaceous material will be 20 to 30 m off the ground (Eisenberg and Lockhart, 1972). Thus, an exploitation of leaves in the forest requires arboreal adaptations or the power of flight.

Specializations among reptiles for feeding on leaves in trees is extremely rare (Rand, 1978). In fact, one of the most unique examples of arboreal herbivory among reptiles is to be found in the neotropics as exemplified by the common iguana, *Iguana iguana*. As Morton (1978) has outlined, arboreal folivory is a rare specialization among birds for the simple reason that the slow digestive processes associated with feeding on foliage means that a great deal of additional weight must be carried around in the form of half-digested material in the crop or intestines of the bird. Such excess weight is incompatible with the characteristic adaptation of birds, namely flight. Thus, specialization for leaf feeding in birds is quite rare, especially in birds that exploit tropical forests. Once again, the neotropics provide us with an example in the form of the hoatzin (*Opisthocomus hoazin*). On the other hand, among mammals, arboreal herbivory has

evolved independently in several lines, most conspicuously in the Marsupialia, Edentata, Rodentia and the Primates (see Montgomery, 1978).

Although the tropical evergreen forest provides a continuous source of leaves, the high species diversity of trees in tropical forests generally demand that a mammalian arboreal herbivore must be adapted to feed on a wide variety of leaf types. Since plants have developed chemical defenses against insect and vertebrate predators, mammalian digestive systems must be adapted to detoxify a wide range of chemicals (Freeland and Janzen, 1974; Janzen, 1978). Given that the problems of detoxification can be solved, foliage requires a great deal of pre-treatment to enhance its digestibility. Usually the leaf parts must be masticated and mixed with saliva thereby increasing the surface area and rendering it permeable to an aqueous medium which will contain either digestive enzymes or microbial symbionts which will assist in the digestive process. The digestion of structural carbohydrates such as cellulose by mammals requires the assist of microbial symbionts which either have as their primary site of fermentation the foregut or alternatively, the hindgut (Bauchop, 1978). If the animal in question is a hindgut fermenter, there will be a blind out-pouching near the junction of the large and small intestine referred to as a caecum, which is the primary site for microbial fermentation (Parra, 1978). The extensive modification of the digestive tract requires a rather prolonged period of natural selection to produce a species which is adapted for the efficient utilization of structural carbohydrate. If structural carbohydrate can be utilized ·and if the dental system is sufficiently adapted to finely masticate leaves, then in addition to an efficient source for energy, leaves are generally a potentially adequate protein resource for mammals (Hladik, 1978).

In order to derive energy from the digestion of leaves sufficient to meet the metabolic needs of the species and, given the slow rate of passage of the digesta in the gut necessary for efficient microbial fermentation, most arboreal herbivores tend to be of moderate size. In short, they cannot be too small or they would not be able to extract enough energy in a short enough time to meet the demands of heat loss (McNab, 1978). On the other hand, the species in question cannot be too large because of the mechanical problems inherent in efficient locomotion in trees where, after all, the leaves are. Thus, there seems to be lower and upper constraints on the size of vertebrate arboreal folivores and this fact to some extent limits the niche breadth (Eisenberg, 1978). Most species of vertebrates employ a mixed feeding strategy ingesting some leaves at certain seasons of the year, but depending on other plant parts for primary energy (Rudran, 1978).

Frugivory is generally defined as the use of those parts of a plant which are the various forms of the plant's reproducing body. Thus, in the broad sense, frugivory refers to a specialization for feeding on seeds, nuts and fleshy fruits. The nutritional content of fruits can vary. In soft fleshy fruits, carbohydrate may be quite high and fat and protein low (Du Boulay and Crawford, 1968). On the other hand, seeds are generally protein- and fat-rich. As an aid to seed dispersal, fleshy fruits have evolved as attractants to vertebrate frugivores thus ensuring that the seed encapsulated in the fleshy coat will be transported some distance from the parent tree (Smith, 1970; Smythe, 1970). When the plant co-evolves with animal seed dispersers in this fashion, the seed itself is generally protected with a tough coat ensuring that it passes through the digestive tract of the animal unharmed. In some cases, in fact, seeds will not germinate unless they have passed through the digestive tract of the dispersing animal (Hladik and Hladik, 1969). Where the timing of dispersal is important, plants often protect the seed by storing toxic substances in the pericarp making it unpalatable to the vertebrate disperser until the optimum time for potential germination whereupon the pericarp becomes tasty. We refer to this process as ripening.

Nuts, of course, have a hard coat which renders them free from certain forms of predation although rodents have evolved adaptations for opening the hard shell thus gaining access to the embryonic plant. Apparently this level of predation by rodents is offset by the rodents' tendency to scatter-hoard seeds, thus ensuring dispersal for the plant (Smythe, 1970). In the coevolution of the nut-producing tree and rodents, it would appear that the plant is willing to accept a certain amount of loss through predation by the rodents which still insures an adequate dispersal of its seed stock. Of course, some seed-producing plants still rely on the wind as a dispersing mechanism. Trees or tree-like plants in a rain forest that rely on wind as a dispersal

mechanism generally have several options open to them to prevent excessive predation on their seed crop. Since animals are of no assistance to them in the dispersal of seeds, then making the seeds either extremely small so that they are uneconomical for exploitation as a single source or coating the seed in such a way that it is unpalatable are viable alternatives. Still making a seed unpalatable to a predator involves a certain energetic cost. It would appear that the most adaptive strategy for most wind-dispersed seeds is to produce a huge crop suddenly which will sustain a certain load of predation but will never serve over the long term to support a predation load which would exterminate the seed crop (Janzen, 1976). Synchronized seeding and seeding at irregular intervals are viable options for seed plants relying on wind rather than vertebrates for the dispersal mechanism. Wind-borne seeds which are produced at restricted times of the year are still heavily preyed upon by birds and mammals. Mammals have the capacity of storing seeds in underground burrows or scatter-hoarding caches (Fleming, 1975). Birds, whether seed or fruit feeders, often have a mixed feeding strategy to accommodate the cycles of productivity. Birds are strongly tied to insectivorous feeding of young even though adults are chiefly frugivorous or granivorous (Morton, 1973).

With such a wide resource base provided by the plants of a tropical forest and given the long evolutionary history of terrestrial arthropods, it should not be surprising that insects have an "edge" over all other classes of animals in terms of efficiently exploiting by-products of plant metabolism. The abundance of adult forms of insects as well as their larval forms is to some extent seasonally dependent, depending ultimately on the plant cycles which sustain them. Insects provide an important food resource for other arthropods, arachnids, and of course vertebrates.

Specializations for insect feeding throughout the year or at the peak seasons of insect production are extremely common in the trophic patterns exhibited by vertebrates. Insectivory may in fact become obligate where the resource base of insects may be dependably exploited over a good portion of the annual cycle. The social insects belonging to the Orders Hymenoptera and Isoptera, which characteristically build complex permanent structures such as nests or hives, can be exploited consistently

throughout the annual cycle by specialized vertebrates. Such a specialized derivative of generalized
insect feeding is demonstrable when one examines
the mammalian taxa that have become obligate
myrmecophages. Of course, the history of exploitation of social insects by vertebrate myrmecophages such as anteaters (Lubin et al., 1977),
pangolins (Pages, 1970, 1976), and some species of
armadillos (Griffiths, 1968), has been so long that
they have coevolved as a predator–prey system,
with the defenses of the workers serving to offset
the adverse effects attendant on sustained predation by a vertebrate predator (Montgomery and
Lubin, 1977).

Myrmecophagous adaptations in mammals and
to a less specialized extent in birds are widespread
throughout the tropics, but once again it appears to
involve a narrow specialization and the degree of
species diversity is limited in any geographical area.
Myrmecophagous adaptations have coevolved between social insects and vertebrates on all major
continental land masses. In the neotropics it involves an adaptive radiation on the part of the
mammalian Edentata; in Africa, the same niche is
filled by the Tubulidentata and the Pholidota
(pangolins). In Southeast Asia, the pangolins fill the
niche as obligate myrmecophages and, in Australia,
the marsupial anteater *Myrmecobius* and the mono-
treme genera *Echidna* and *Zaglossus* preoccupy the
termite- and ant-feeding niche.

Feeding niches involving the indirect exploitation of plants such as feeding on nectar, gums
and resins with a concomitant high degree of
specialization have been convergently evolved on
all continental land masses. Nectar-feeding adaptations among birds are highly evolved in the Old
World sunbirds (Lack, 1971; Gill and Wolf, 1975)
and the New World hummingbirds (Calder, 1974).
Of course, nectar is supplemented by insect feeding
at times of the year when nectar production may be
low. Nectar feeding by mammals is generally preoccupied in the Old World by bats of the family
Pteropodidae (Start and Marshall, 1976) and in the
New World by the family Phyllostomatidae
(Wilson, 1973). In Australia, nectar feeding has
been exploited in a near obligate fashion by the
genus *Tarsipes* of the marsupial family Phalangeridae (Ride, 1970). Of course plants and animals
can coevolve if nectar feeding attracts animals to
not only feed but also act as pollen-dispersing

agents for the plant. Birds and mammals both serve
as pollen dispersal agents and complement the
activities of arthropods. Avian pollen dispersal is
common in the tropics for diurnal flowering plants
while bats may serve the same role at night (Fleming
et al., 1972; Start and Marshall, 1976; Gould, 1978).
In areas where the bat fauna may be depauperate an
ancient coevolved system of pollination may exist,
where lemurs (Madagascar), galagos (South Africa)
and phalangers (Australia) serve as the principal
nocturnal, vertebrate pollinators (Sussman and
Raven, 1978).

Feeding on sap, gums and resins from trees in a
supplemental mode is an exploitation system developed by a variety of invertebrates and vertebrates. Some vertebrates have become near obligate
gum and resin feeders. The niche appears to be
narrow and has been convergently occupied in
Australia by *Petaurus* of the Phalangeridae
(Collins, 1973), in Africa by the Lorisidae and
Galagidae (Charles-Dominique, 1977), and in
South America by certain species of the marmoset
genera *Callithrix* and *Cebuella* (Coimbra-Filho and
Mittermeier, 1977).

Of course, feeding on the bodies of other living
vertebrates or carnivory has become a third step in
the trophic chain exploited by many of the higher
vertebrates, and convergent carnivorous adaptations are widespread throughout when one compares the neotropics and the paleotropics.
Carnivory in birds often involves specializations for
feeding on large arboreal vertebrates. In South
America one finds the harpy eagle (*Harpia harpyja*)
specialized for feeding on monkeys, sloths, and the
lesser ant-eater. Parallel adaptations are found in
the Phillippines (*Pithecophaga jefferyi*), in Africa
(*Spizaetus coronatus*), and in Asia (*Aquila occi-
pitalus*). In mammals the top carnivores of tropical
forests are often strongly arboreal and the family
Felidae reaches its greatest diversity in the forested
region of Southeast Asia (Kleiman and Eisenberg,
1973).

Varying degrees of omnivory or alternate food
resource exploitation involving little specialization
for any one feeding mode is of course a strategy
open to vertebrates that are willing to forego the
efficiency of specialization for having alternate
food resources throughout the annual cycle. In
general, however, in the tropical rain forests of the
world, the bizarre specializations for procuring

plant parts high above the ground predominate as specializations if one were to compare the same sort of trophic adaptations with the temperate zone. In the vertebrates adaptations for arboreal folivory, great dependency on fruit, or the evolution of myrmecophagy are all feeding adaptations which tend to be strongly developed within the tropics and de-emphasized or absent as temperate-zone feeding strategies.

Behavioral thermoregulation

In considering adaptation to tropical environments, it would seem that thermoregulation would be of a low priority since one of the dominant themes stressed in the consideration of tropical environments is the constancy of temperature. Nothing could be farther from the truth, however, since as indicated in the previous sections the geographically defined tropics span a number of degrees of latitude on either side of the equator and involves both low and high elevation habitats. The annual temperature may vary significantly when areas within the geographically defined tropics are compared (Walter, 1973). On the other hand, it is true that in a multi-stratal, tropical, evergreen forest in the vicinity of the equator drastic changes in the ambient temperature at intermediate levels will be ameliorated by the effect of the forest structure itself. On the other hand, organisms adapted to working in the upper canopy and outside the protective shade can be subjected to extremes in temperature. In addition, climax tropical rain forests are usually rather humid and subjected to significant amounts of rainfall. Mammals and birds can become wet and, as a result, the insulation efficiency of fur and feathers can be decreased and significant heat loss can occur. Thus, thermoregulation is still somewhat of a problem, although surely not the same sort of problem that one would anticipate in the vicinity of the Arctic Circle.

Given that a species is adapted to a rather uniform high temperature, it does not follow that it is without problems in facing thermal differences in its environment. A large mammal, such as an elephant (e.g. *Elephas maximus*), may in fact suffer the reverse problem of finding it necessary to dissipate heat. Thus, utilization of shade, deploying its vascular circulation to the periphery of its body,

such as in its ears, and flapping the ears may serve to maintain its core body temperature within tolerable limits (McKay, 1973). If a large mammal, such as an elephant, were to forage continuously in direct sunlight without the ability to increase the radiation of heat from its body it would soon suffer thermal stress.

Ectothermic vertebrates, such as reptiles and amphibians, who cannot mobilize fat reserves in order to raise core body temperatures against an environment gradient, may become quite dependent on external heat sources for raising the body temperatures to levels compatible with sustained activity. Sunning behavior by reptiles in the tropics is as common an occurrence as it is in the temperate zones. Endothermic vertebrates, such as mammals and birds, may also employ behavioral means to regulate body temperatures. The three-toed sloth (*Bradypus infuscatus*) is able to carry on most of its metabolic processes with a core body temperature considerably lower than 38°C. Nevertheless, in spite of the fact that it is an endotherm, it makes use of environmental assistance in raising its core body temperature. Each morning in Panama, the studies of Montgomery and Sunquist (1978) clearly showed three-toed sloths move to tree crowns in order to make use of a solar "assistance" in raising body temperatures to a level which increases the efficiency of their digestive processes while minimizing the expenditure of their own stored fat reserves. Once core body temperatures have been raised to the appropriate level, the sloths will descend into the lower canopy thus maintaining an equilibrium temperature through behavioral means. Here, in fact, we have an endotherm utilizing external sources in a manner analogous to an ectotherm (such as a lizard) and thereby conserving energy. A detailed discussion of thermoregulation is presented in Chapter 15.

Humidity and rainfall

One unique problem that many tropical vertebrates must attempt to cope with is the problem of too much moisture. This is especially true of tropical evergreen forests where the rainfall is rather evenly spread throughout the annual cycle and may reach appreciable amounts with a concomitant high humidity. Indeed, if the porosity of the soil is poor and the water table is rather high, standing water may prevent the growth of woody vegetation and vast tracts of savanna are in fact the result of impeded vertical drainage for an extended period of time throughout each part of the annual cycle (Beard, 1953). It follows then that terrestrial vertebrates which cannot respire through their skins, such as most reptiles, mammals and birds, must seek out high ground or drown during seasons of excessive rainfall. Of course, arboreal vertebrates are spared this since trees, tree cavities, and shrubs may serve as refugia for them. In the event that climbing trees is not a viable alternative, then the animals are forced to forage on high ground during seasons of flooding.

Terrestrial vertebrates which must resort to high ground during flooding can thus be limited by the carrying capacity of the high ground during the flooding season and such a situation pertains over large areas of central Africa, South America and Southeast Asia. This in part may account for the reduced diversity with respect to terrestrial vertebrate fauna in these areas when compared with the diversity of arboreal or volant forms (Harrison, 1962). The selection of burrow sites in a tropical rain forest by fossorial vertebrates, such as mammals, is very often determined by the standing water table and the extent to which the water table fluctuates throughout the annual cycle. The texture of the soil for efficient burrowing is also important. Even given a habitat mosaic of different substrate types, the organisms in question may be unable to survive in the long term if there is not sufficient space to serve as a refugium during periods of excessive rainfall or flooding.

High humidity may be necessary for survival during the daily nesting phase of bats. Indeed roosting sites may be selected not only to minimize predation, but to maximize the ambient relative humidity at mid-day (Verschuren, 1957). Excessive humidity in birds and many mammals may be counteracted by periodically moving to tree crowns to dry out the pelage or feathers. After a rainstorm primates, squirrels and birds may expose themselves to the sun thereby drying out.

ADAPTATIONS TO STRONGLY SEASONAL FORESTS

Seasonality of plant productivity in the tropics

As indicated in previous sections, the geographically defined tropics not only include lands of varying relief but also a bewildering variety of soil types exhibiting varying degrees of permeability to rainfall (Sarmiento and Monasterio, 1975). Added to this is the fact that in vast regions of the geographically defined tropics the rainfall is strongly seasonal. Walter (1973), in his publication *The Vegetation of the Earth*, refers to "vegetation of the tropical summer-rain zone". Vast stretches of the tropics (world-wide) are characterized by a strong seasonal flux in the rainfall pattern. Such seasonality of rainfall involving excessive precipitation beyond that which the plants are capable of using for a period of some six months followed by varying drought periods between five and three months duration may impose a strict seasonality on plant productivity. Woody and herbaceous vegetation in such a habitat usually times its flowering, fruiting and flushing seasons around some overall adaptation to the availability or amount of water. During extreme seasonal drought periods when the evapotranspiration rate exceeds that required for efficient productivity of the plants, a period of vegetative quiescence occurs. It is during this time when alternate feeding strategies by frugivores, nectarivores, and insectivores must be employed to ensure survival (Morton, 1973). For vertebrates which are homeotherms, such periods can become critical.

Given a homeotherm, one adaptation to a seasonal scarcity of food is to reduce the metabolic rate and temporarily behave as if one were a poikilotherm. Valuable energy can be conserved and a minimum of energy is expended to maintain body temperature during torpor. Seasonal torpor on the part of tropical vertebrates is not uncommon in areas where sustained plant productivity is sharply demarcated. Torpor is exhibited by *Echidna* in the subtropics of Australia (Griffiths, 1968); by the dwarf lemurs *Microcebus murinus* and *Cheirogaleus major* as well as many tenrecine insectivores in Madagascar (Eisenberg and Gould, 1970; Russell, 1975); by armadillos of the genus *Dasypus* in the Neotropics (Eisentraut, 1960); and by some species of the neotropical genus *Marmosa* (Morrison and McNab, 1962).

An alternative to torpor available to volant forms such as birds and bats would involve a seasonal migration to areas more favorable for sustained productivity of the limiting resource, generally insects and fruits. Where such long-range movements are inefficient, as is the case with most small mammals, then the homeotherm must either enter torpor or rely on alternative strategies for exploitation. Of course, large vertebrates and even herbivores, such as the wildebeest (*Connochaetes taurinus*) in Africa, may accommodate themselves to changing productivity by traditional migratory movements (Lamprey, 1964; Leuthold, 1977). The wildebeest in East Africa are a primary example of this, since the movement patterns are rather predictable and are usually related to the productivity of new grasses. Their cyclic movement pattern in space parallels the shift in rainfall and the growth and abundance of new grass (Talbot and Talbot, 1963).

One way to adapt to food shortages without torpor is to be able to store sufficient body fat so that feeding demands are reduced during seasons of scarcity. To become fatted is a common adaptation among rodents which live in desert environments in the tropics or subtropics (Eisenberg, 1975). Fat storage is rather common among mammals on the island of Madagascar, in the tropics and subtropics, being exhibited by the primate genera *Microcebus* and *Cheirogaleus* (Petter-Rousseaux, 1974), the insectivore genera *Tenrec* and *Hemicentetes* (Eisenberg and Gould, 1970), and the carnivorous genus *Eupleres* (Albignac, 1973). On the continent of Australia, the subtropically adapted *Echidna* may also show fat storage (Griffiths, 1968) as do its myrmecophagous counterparts, the pangolins and aardvarks of the Ethiopian tropical regions (Pages, 1970).

Food caching on the part of homeothermic vertebrates is of course an alternative to fat deposition. Cases of food hoarding involving the storage of nuts and seeds are well known in the Rodentia. One of the better documented cases involves the scatter-hoarding activities of the caviomorph rodent genus *Dasyprocta*, as analyzed by Smythe (1978) in Panama. Definite periodicities in plant productivity demonstrated by Smythe (1970) are offset by the scatter-hoarding activities of *Dasyprocta*, which can then draw upon its scatter hoard during the six or seven weeks of reduced food

supply to sustain itself. Food caching is common among rodents, especially rodents adapted for feeding on seeds and nuts (Heaney and Thorington, 1978). Such hoarding activities are generally denied carnivores, insectivores, and folivores, not to mention nectar-feeding species.

Seasonal availability of water for vertebrate species which are dependent on a continuous source can become extremely limiting in areas of the tropics that experience sustained drought. Generally folivores are able to make up their water deficit from the moisture contained in plants. Other feeding adaptations are under more profound restrictions. Responses to predictable seasonal drought can involve again migratory movements on the part of tropical vertebrates. Migrations of elephants (*Elephas maximus*) may use traditional routes that allow daily drinking even under extremes of prolonged drought (McKay, 1973).

SPECIAL ADAPTATIONS TO HIGH SPECIES DIVERSITY AND LOW NUMERICAL DENSITY

Birds and mammals reach their maximum diversity in the tropics. MacArthur has presented data concerning the species richness of tropical birds. He furthermore suggests that tropical communities exhibit a lack of dominance (MacArthur, 1969). By this, he implied that no single species is extremely common but rather a uniformity of numerical density characterizes the stable tropical communities. Fleming (1975) presents an analysis of small mammal communities in the tropics, suggesting that dominance in these small mammal communities is extremely common. One or two species may account for from 65 to 94% of all small mammals trapped. O'Connell (1979) presents similar data on two small mammal communities in the northern neotropics.

The degree of numerical dominance expressed in a tropical community seems to be in part a function of two variables: (1) The amount of disturbance that the habitat has recently undergone. The data suggest that mature second growth situations show a bias toward strong numerical dominance by one or two species. (2) Climax conditions in tropical habitats which show marked seasonality may again show a tendency toward strong numerical dominance of one or two species. With tropical ungulate faunas, it is more difficult to demonstrate numerical dominance but, given their large size, it is often more convenient to express dominance in terms of total biomass. This is especially true of very large species such as elephants which may exhibit low numerical density but account for 25 to 40% of the total herbivore biomass in a given area. Eisenberg and McKay (1974) demonstrated that when a community of ungulates is considered in either African or Asian habitats, frequently one to four species account for 75% of the total biomass. Mature climax conditions, however, in tropical evergreen forests show a less pronounced dominance by ungulates. Given then that in mammal communities numerical dominance may be shown under certain conditions in the tropics (grasslands, early second growth, etc.), there still exists an amazing diversity of species for selected higher taxa. Consider the situation on Barro Colorado Island (Panama), where over 340 species of trees exist in 15 km² (Croat, 1978). With the exception of some clumps of palms (*Scheelia*), the forest is not characterized by stands of any single species. Many species seem to be over-dispersed. Now, if a form such as the three-toed sloth which is an obligate folivore were to specialize on a single species, it would have to move large distances from one tree to another and also crop only a small amount. If it were to crop extensively it would risk completely defoliating its food source. Montgomery and Sunquist (1975) have demonstrated that sloths do not over-crop their feeding trees, rather sloths exploit a tremendous variety of leaves, not only from trees but from the associated lianas in the crowns. Perhaps sloths exhibit a feeding diversity as an overall adaptation to toxins present in the leaves and by so diversifying their feeding habits reduce the risk of building up specific toxins to an appreciable extent. On the other hand, Montgomery and Sunquist (1978) have shown that each sloth has a tendency to use a modal feeding tree of a certain species and, although great diversity of feeding is shown, nevertheless a given sloth will usually have a given set of tree species for which it appears to be more specialized and, in fact, equipped to digest its leaves with greater efficiency. The intriguing results from Montgomery and Sunquist, however, are not only this dual pattern of modal feeding combined with diverse alternate feeding sources but that the feeding patterns of the sloths on Barro Colorado

are idiosyncratic. No two sloths, even if they be neighbors, necessarily show the same modal tree preferences. This suggests that sloths individually acquire the necessary bacterial symbionts to assist in breaking down leaves of those trees which they initially begin to utilize heavily. It further suggests that competition is thereby inadvertently reduced among the sloths of a given community.

Although diversity in feeding is shown by the three-toed sloth population on Barro Colorado Island, mammalian arboreal folivores can also show extreme specialization for a given tree species or set of species. In Australia, Eberhard (1978) has shown that the koala (*Phascolarctos cinereus*) can sustain itself on only three to four species of eucalyptus. In Ceylon the purple-faced langur (*Presbytis senex*) includes 70% of the foliage in its diet from a single species, *Adina cardifolia* (Hladik, 1978). Thus, even in situations of moderate forest diversity, extreme specialization can occur on the part of folivorous mammals. Of course such specialization would only be possible when the tree species in question tends to be abundant enough so that a population can sustain itself within a fixed home range without consistently defoliating their food trees. Perhaps the adaptation exhibited by the three-toed sloths on Barro Colorado Island is an adaptation to extreme over-dispersion of the tree species in the community.

With increasing species diversity in the tropics, it might be anticipated that closely related members of a given taxon would become extreme specialists in their feeding patterns as a result of natural selection through competition over thousands of years. It is true that in the tropics we often find many closely related species which are members of the same "guild", that is to say that, in the manner of procuring their food and in the type of food that they feed on, the guild members exhibit similarities in technique and preference. Very often guild members divide the resources by selecting prey of different size classes (Diamond, 1975; Karr and James, 1975). Alternatively, guild members may employ different food-seeking techniques although feeding on nearly identical prey items (Brown, 1975; Diamond, 1975). An example from mammals would include a consideration of myrmecophagous mammals in the tropics. In the New World tropics, the three true anteaters belonging to the family Myrmecophagidae prey on the social ants and termites. One genus, *Cyclopes*, is almost entirely arboreal. The genus *Tamandua* is both arboreal and terrestrial, whereas the giant anteater *Myrmecophaga* is completely terrestrial (Montgomery and Lubin, 1977). In a similar manner Pages (1970) has demonstrated how the pangolins of the order Pholidota have subdivided the foraging space in West Africa. These convergently evolved anteaters of the genus *Manis* have occupied the feeding niches in a manner closely paralleling that of the Myrmecophagidae in the New World tropics. *Manis longicaudata* is almost completely arboreal. *M. tricuspis* is scansorial whereas *M. gigantea* is strictly terrestrial.

Arboreal folivorous mammals often divide the feeding niches very finely. The sloths of the family Bradypodidae in the neotropics include two sympatric genera, *Bradypus* and *Choloepus*. *Choloepus* is strictly nocturnal whereas *Bradypus* is diurnal. *Bradypus* is an extreme obligate folivore whereas *Choloepus* subsists on fruits as well as leafy material. The feeding range for *Choloepus* is broader than that for *Bradypus* but their entirely different rhythms of activity help to reduce direct competition.

Very often when one examines primate communities and inspects the "folivore guild" in a given community, one finds a species which is an extreme obligate folivore and a second species less specialized for folivory and finally a third species which mixes its feeding patterns between fruit and leaves. This is the standard pattern for Southeast Asia with the guild *Presbytis obscurus*, *P. melalophus* and *Symphalangus syndactylus* (Curtin and Chivers, 1978). In Sri Lanka, *Presbytis senex* and *P. entellus* exhibit a similar subdivision of the resources, while in West Africa *Colobus guereza* and *C. badius* share the folivore niche in a manner analogous to the genus *Presbytis* on Ceylon.

Charles-Dominique (1975) has presented an elegant argument for the separation of the feeding niches in tropical habitats between the two grand classes of higher vertebrates: mammals and birds. This is especially true for those feeding specializations which converge, e.g. frugivory and aerial insectivory. It would appear that the bats have effectively held the nocturnal feeding niches from the birds and conversely the birds have diurnally preoccupied these niches and prevented the evolution of diurnal patterns on the part of the Chiroptera (see Charles-Dominique, 1975). Diversity within feeding guilds can not only lead to competition but also to forms of cooperation. The location of energy-rich "pockets" of food in a rain forest may be a formidable task [for example a single tree in fruit or a mass of army ants (*Eciton*) on the move]. Moynihan (1962) analyzed the phenomenon of mixed flock formation in birds and Morton (1973) suggested mixed flocks may improve the "fruit searching" strategy for flock members. In a similar manner mixed flocks of insectivorous birds may improve the odds of locating a foraging group of army ants which by their activities cause many cryptic insects to expose themselves to the birds (Willis, 1967).

Of course, mixed flocks or herds can be an adaptation to reduce predation by improving the probability of predator detection. Mixed herds of ungulates are likely to form when defense of transient resources (new grass) would be uneconomical.

A high diversity of species and a low numerical density for a given species prevails in climax tropical forests and can present problems in finding a mate during the breeding season. The problem is really not so different from that encountered by species in the temperate zone but perhaps magnified somewhat. Mechanisms for advertising location employing sound production or specific odors are prevalent among the arthropods and highly developed in the vertebrates. Many species of birds have convergently evolved mechanisms for advertising their presence through song or calls to prospective mates. In addition, one finds group displays by males apparently aiding in signal propagation and thus increasing the probability that females will be attracted to them. Such mating aggregations by males are termed leks. Generally only one male does most of the breeding during any given interval. Leks are traditional and have been evolved in the neotropical manikans (Foster, 1977) and in many species of the neotropical family Cottingidae (Gilliard, 1962). Calling in groups has also evolved in mammals. Recently Bradbury (1977) has analyzed the calling leks of the hammerhead bat (*Hypsignathus*) in West Africa.

One mechanism to reduce the energy expenditure in finding a mate would seem to be permanent pairing. Long-term monogamous pair bonds in tropical birds (Skutch, 1976) and tropical mammals are of widespread occurrence (see Kleiman, 1977). Long-term monogamous pairing, however, is only possible as a reproductive strategy if the potential life span of the prospective mate is long. For example, if a female were to live through only one season of reproduction and the male's sole task was to inseminate the female and he did not participate in any form of parental care, then it would be to the male's advantage to mate as many times as possible rather than to remain with the female. In order for selection to favor the male remaining with the female, either selection must provide for a division of labor between the male and the female, so that the increase in the male's investment of time increases the probability of the young's survival, or the male, by remaining near the female, must have a reasonable probability of mating subsequently through the years. Thus, by maintaining fidelity the male guarantees his reproductive success. Since many species of tropical birds and mammals appear to have an extended reproductive life over many years, it would appear that the monogamous pairing strategy is favored. Furthermore, in many tropical species of higher vertebrates, participation by the male in some form of parental care is not uncommon. The situation has been carefully analyzed for the birds by Skutch (1976) and for the Mammalia by Kleiman (1977).

REFERENCES

Albignac, R., 1973. *Faune de Madagascar, No. 36. Mammifères Carnivores.* O.R.S.T.O.M./C.N.R.S., Paris, 206 pp.

Bates, H.W., 1864. *The Naturalist on the River Amazons.* Murray, 2nd ed., London, 395 pp.

Bauchop, T., 1978. Digestion of leaves in vertebrate arboreal folivores. In: G.G. Montgomery (Editor), *The Ecology of Arboreal Folivores.* Smithsonian Institution Press, Washington, D.C., pp. 193–204.

Beard, J.S., 1953. The savanna vegetation of northern tropical America. *Ecol. Monogr.,* 23: 149–215.

Bradbury, J.W., 1977. Lek mating behavior in the Hammerheaded Bat. *Z. Tierpsychol.,* 45(3): 225–255.

Brown, J.H., 1975. Geographical ecology of desert rodents. In: M.S. Cody and J.M. Diamond (Editors), *Ecology and Evolution of Communities.* The Belknap Press of Harvard University Press, Cambridge, Mass., pp. 315–341.

Calder, W.A., III, 1974. Consequences of body size for avian energetics. In: R.A. Paynter, Jr. (Editor), *Avian Energetics.* Nuttall Ornithological Club, Cambridge, Mass., pp. 86–151.

Charles-Dominique, P., 1975. Nocturnality and diurnality: an ecological interpretation of these two modes of life by an analysis of the higher vertebrate fauna in tropical forest ecosystems. In: W.P. Luckett and F.S. Szalay (Editors), *Phylogeny of the Primates.* Plenum Press, New York, N.Y., pp. 69–88.

Charles-Dominique, P., 1977. *Ecology and Behaviour of Nocturnal Primates. Prosimians of Equatorial West Africa.* Columbia University Press, New York, N.Y., 277 pp.

Coimbra-Filho, A.F. and Mittermeier, R.A., 1977. Treegouging, exudate-eating and the "short-tusked" condition in *Callithrix* and *Cebuella.* In: D.G. Kleiman (Editor), *The Biology and Conservation of the Callithrichidae.* Smithsonian Institution Press, Washington, D.C., pp. 105–115.

Collins, L.R., 1973. *Monotremes and Marsupials: A Reference for Zoological Institutions.* Smithsonian Institution Press, Washington, D.C., Publ. No. 4888: 323 pp.

Corner, E.J.H., 1954. The evolution of tropical forests. In: J.S. Huxley, A.C. Hardy and E.B. Ford (Editors), *Evolution as a Process.* Allen and Unwin, London, pp. 34–46.

Croat, T.B., 1978. *Flora of Barro Colorado Island.* University of California Press, Stanford, Calif., 943 pp.

Curtin, S.H. and Chivers, D.J., 1978. Leaf-eating primates of Peninsular Malaysia, the siamang and the dusky leaf monkey. In G.G. Montgomery (Editor), *The Ecology of Arboreal Folivores.* Smithsonian Institution Press, Washington, D.C., pp. 441–464.

Diamond, J.M., 1975. Assembly of species communities. In: M.S. Cody and J.M. Diamond (Editors), *Ecology and Evolution of Communities.* The Belknap Press of Harvard University Press, Cambridge, Mass., pp. 342–444.

Dittus, W.P.J., 1977. The ecology of a semi-evergreen forest community in Sri Lanka. *Biotropica,* 9(4): 268–286.

Du Boulay, G.H. and Crawford, M.A., 1968. Nutritional bone disease in captive primates. In: M.A. Crawford (Editor), *Comparative Nutrition of Wild Animals.* Academic Press, London, pp. 223–236.

Eberhard, I., 1978. Ecology of the Koala, *Phascolarctos cinereus* (Goldfuss) (Marsupialia: Phascolorctidae) in Australia. In: G.G. Montgomery (Editor), *The Ecology of Arboreal Folivores.* Smithsonian Institution Press, Washington, D.C., pp. 315–328.

Eisenberg, J.F., 1975. Phylogeny, behavior and ecology in the Mammalia. In: P. Luckett and F. Szalay (Editors), *Phylogeny of the Primates: An Interdisciplinary Approach.* Plenum Press, New York, N.Y., pp. 47–68.

Eisenberg, J.F., 1978. The evolution of arboreal herbivores in the class Mammalia. In: G.G. Montgomery (Editor), *The Ecology of Arboreal Folivores.* Smithsonian Institution Press, Washington, D.C., pp. 135–152.

Eisenberg, J.F. and Gould., E., 1970. The tenrecs: A study in mammalian behavior and evolution. *Smithson. Contrib. Zool.,* 27: 1–137.

Eisenberg, J.F. and Lockhart, M., 1972. An ecological reconnaissance of Wilpattu National Park, Ceylon. *Smithson. Contrib. Zool.,* No. 101: 118 pp.

Eisenberg, J.F. and McKay, G., 1974. Comparison of ungulate adaptations in the New World and Old World tropical forests with special reference to Ceylon and the rainforests of Central America. In: V. Geist and F. Walther (Editors),

The Behaviour of Ungulates and Its Relation to Management, IUCN Publ., No. 24: 585–602.

Eisentraut, M., 1960. Heat regulation in primitive mammals and in tropical species. In: C.P. Lyman and A.R. Dawe (Editors), *Mammalian Hibernation. Bull. Mus. Comp. Zool.*, 124: 31–42.

Feeny, P., 1975. Biochemical coevolution between plants and their insect herbivores. In: L.E. Gilbert and P.H. Raven (Editors), *Coevolution of Animals and Plants*. University of Texas Press, Austin, Texas, pp. 3–19.

Fleming, T.H., 1973. Numbers of mammal species in North and Central American forest communities. *Ecology*, 54: 555–563.

Fleming, T.H., 1975. The role of small mammals in tropical ecosystems. In: F.B. Golley, K. Petrusewicz and L. Ryszkowski (Editors), *Small Mammals: Their Productivity and Population Dynamics*. Cambridge University Press, Cambridge, pp. 269–298.

Fleming, T.H., Hooper, E.T. and Wilson, D.E., 1972. Three Central American bat communities: structure, reproduction cycles, and movement patterns. *Ecology*, 53: 555–570.

Frankie, G.W., 1975. Tropical forest phenology and pollinator plant coevolution. In: L.E. Gilbert and P.H. Raven (Editors), *Coevolution of Animals and Plants*. University of Texas Press, Austin, Texas, pp. 192–209

Freeland, W.J. and Janzen, D.H., 1974. Strategies in herbivory by mammals: the role of plant secondary compounds. *Am. Nat.*, 108: 269–289.

Foster, M.S., 1977. Odd couples in manakins: a study of social organization and cooperative breeding in *Chiroxiphia linearis. Am. Nat.*, 111: 845–853.

Gill, F.B. and Wolf, L.L., 1975. Foraging strategies and energetics of East African sunbirds at mistletoe flowers. *Am. Nat.*, 109: 491–510.

Gilliard, E.T., 1962. On the breeding behaviour of the Cock-of-the-Rock (Aves: *Rupicola rupicola). Bull. Am. Mus. Nat. Hist.*, 124: 37–68.

Gould, E., 1978. The behavior of the moonrat, *Echinosorex gymnurus* and the pentail shrew, *Ptilocercus lowi* with comments on the behavior of other insectivora. *Z. Tierpsychol.*, 48: 1–27.

Griffiths, M., 1968. *Echidnas*. Pergamon Press, London, 192 pp.

Harrison, J.L., 1962. The distribution of feeding habits among animals in a tropical rainforest, *J. Anim. Ecol.*, 31: 53–64.

Heaney, L.R. and Thorington, R.W., 1978. Ecology of neotropical red-tailed squirrels, *Sciurus granatensis* in Panama. *J. Mammal.*, 59(4): 846–851.

Hladik, A., 1978. Distribution and composition of food for folivores. In: G.G. Montgomery (Editor), *The Ecology of Arboreal Folivores*. Smithsonian Institution Press, Washington, D.C., pp. 51–71.

Hladik, A. and Hladik, C.M., 1969. Rapports trophiques entre végétation et primates dans la forêt de Barro Colorado (Panama). *Terre Vie*, 1969: 25–117.

Hladik, C.M., 1978. Adaptive strategies of primates in relation to leaf-eating. In: G.G. Montgomery (Editor), *The Ecology of Arboreal Folivores*. Smithsonian Institution Press, Washington, D.C., pp. 373–396.

Janzen, D.H., 1976. Why do bamboos wait so long to flower? In:

J. Burley and B.T. Styles (Editors), *Tropical Trees*. Academic Press, London, pp. 135–139.

Janzen, D.H., 1978. Complications in interpreting the chemical defenses of trees against tropical arboreal plant-eating vertebrates. In: G.G. Montgomery (Editor), *The Ecology of Arboreal Folivores*. Smithsonian Institution Press, Washington, D.C., pp. 73–84.

Karr, J.R. and James, F.C., 1975. Eco-morphological configurations and convergent evolution in species and communities. In: M.S. Cody and J.M. Diamond (Editors), *Ecology and Evolution of Communities*. The Belknap Press of Harvard University Press, Cambridge, Mass., pp. 258–291.

Kleiman, D.G., 1977. Monogamy in mammals. *Q. Rev. Biol.*, 52: 39–69.

Kleiman, D.G. and Eisenberg, J.F., 1973. Comparisons of canid and felid social systems from an evolutionary perspective. *Anim. Behav.*, 21: 637–659.

Klopfer, P. and MacArthur, R.H., 1960. Niche size and faunal diversity. *Am. Nat.* 94: 293–300.

Knight, D.H., 1975. A phytosociological analysis of species-rich tropical forest on Barro Colorado Island, Panama. *Ecol. Monogr.*, 45: 259–284.

Lack, D., 1971. *Ecological Isolation in Birds*. Blackwell, London, 409 pp.

Lamprey, H.F., 1964. Estimation of the large mammal densities, biomass and energy exchange in the Tarangire game reserve and the Masoi Steppe in Tanganyika. *East Afr. Wildl. J.*, 2: 1–46.

Leuthold, W., 1977. *African Ungulates: A Comparative Review of Their Ethology and Behavioral Ecology*. Springer-Verlag, Berlin, 307 pp.

Lubin, Y., Montgomery G.G. and Young, O., 1977. Food resources of anteaters (Edentata: Myrmecophagidae). *Biotropica* 9(1): 26–34.

MacArthur, R.H., 1969. Patterns of communities in the tropics. *Biol. J. Linn. Soc.*, 1:19–30.

McKay, G., 1973. The ecology of the Asiatic elephant in southeastern Ceylon. *Smithson. Contrib. Zool.*, No. 125: 100 pp.

McNab, B.K., 1971. The structure of tropical bat faunas. *Ecology*, 52: 353–358.

McNab, B.K., 1978. Energetics of arboreal folivores: physiological problems and ecological consequences of feeding on an ubiquitous food supply. In: G.G. Montgomery (Editor), *The Ecology of Arboreal Folivores*. Smithsonian Institution Press, Washington, D.C., pp. 153–162.

Montgomery, G.G. (Editor), 1978. *The Ecology of Arboreal Folivores*. Smithsonian Institution Press, Washington, D.C., 574 pp.

Montgomery, G.G. and Lubin, Y.D., 1977. Prey influences on movements of Neotropical anteaters. In: R.L. Phillips and C. Jonkel (Editors), *Proceedings of the 1975 Predator Symposium*. Montana Forest and Conservation Experiment Station, University of Montana, Missoula, Mont., pp. 103–131.

Montgomery, G.G. and Sunquist, M.E., 1975. Impact of sloths on Neotropical forest, energy flow and nutrient cycling. In: F.B. Golley and E. Medina (Editors), *Tropical Ecological Systems: Trends in Terrestrial and Aquatic Research*. Springer-Verlag, Berlin, pp. 69–98.

Montgomery, G.G. and Sunquist, M.E., 1978. Habitat selection and use by two-toed and three-toed sloths. In: G.G. Montgomery (Editor), *The Ecology of Arboreal Folivores*. Smithsonian Institution Press, Washington, D.C., pp. 329–359.

Morrison, P.R. and McNab, B.K., 1962. Daily torpor in a Brazilian murine opossum (*Marmosa*). *Comp. Biochem. Physiol.*, 6: 57–68.

Morton, E.S., 1973. On the evolutionary advantages and disadvantages of fruit eating in tropical birds. *Am. Nat.*, 107: 8–22.

Morton, E.S., 1978. Avian arboreal folivores: why not? In: G.G. Montgomery (Editor), *The Ecology of Arboreal Folivores*. Smithsonian Institution Press, Washington, D.C., pp. 123–130.

Moynihan, M., 1962. The organization and probable evolutionary significance of some mixed species flocks of neotropical birds. *Smithson. Misc. Coll.*, No. 143: 1–140.

Muul, I. and Lim Boo Liat, 1978. Comparative morphology, food habits and ecology of some Malaysian arboreal rodents. In: G.G. Montgomery (Editor), *The Ecology of Arboreal Folivores*. Smithsonian Institution Press, Washington, D.C., pp. 361–369.

O'Connell, M.A., 1979. Ecology of didelphid marsupials from northern Venezuela. In: J.F. Eisenberg (Editor), *Studies on Vertebrate Zoology in the Northern Neotropics*. Smithsonian Institution, Washington, D.C., pp. 73–87.

Pages, E., 1970. Sur l'écologie et les adaptations de l'oryctérope et des pangolins sympatriques du Gabon. *Biol. Gabonica*, 6: 27–92.

Pages, E., 1976. Etude éco-éthologique de *Manis tricuspis* par radio-tracking. *Mammalia*, 39(4): 613–641.

Parra, R., 1978. Comparison of foregut and hindgut fermentation in herbivores. In: G.G. Montgomery (Editor), *The Ecology of Arboreal Folivores*. Smithsonian Institution Press, Washington, D.C., pp. 205–230.

Petter-Rousseaux, A., 1974. Photoperiod, sexual activity and body weight variations of *Microcebus murinus* (Miller 1777). In: G.A. Doyle and A.C. Walker (Editors), *Prosimian Biology*. Duckworth and Co., London, pp. 365–373.

Rand, A.S., 1978. Reptilian arboreal folivores. In: G.G. Montgomery (Editor), *The Ecology of Arboreal Folivores*. Smithsonian Institution Press, Washington, D.C., pp. 115–121.

Richards, P.W., 1952. *The Tropical Rain Forest: An Ecological Study*. Cambridge University Press, Cambridge, 450 pp.

Ride, W.D.L., 1970. *A Guide to the Native Mammals of Australia*. Oxford University Press, Oxford.

Rudran, R., 1978. Socioecology of the Blue Monkeys (*Cercopithecus mitis stuhlmanni*) of the Kibale Forest, Uganda. *Smithson. Contrib. Zool.*, No. 249: 88 pp.

Russell, R.J., 1975. Body temperatures and behavior of captive cheirogaleids. In: I. Tattersall and R.W. Sussman (Editors), *Lemur Biology*. Plenum Press, New York, N.Y., pp. 193–206.

Sarmiento, G. and Monasterio, M., 1975. A critical consideration of the environmental conditions associated with the occurrence of savanna ecosystems in tropical America. In: F.B. Golley and E. Medina (Editors), *Tropical Ecological Systems*. Springer-Verlag, Berlin, pp. 223–250.

Skutch, A.F., 1976. *Parent Birds and Their Young*. University of Texas Press, Austin, Texas, 503 pp.

Slud, P., 1976. Geographic and climatic relationships of avifaunas with special reference to comparative distribution in the neotropics. *Smithson. Contrib. Zool.*, No. 212: 149 pp.

Smith, C.C., 1970. The coevolution of pine squirrels (*Tamiasciurus*) and conifers. *Ecol. Monogr.*, 40: 349–371.

Smith, C.C., 1975. The coevolution of plants and seed predators. In: L.E. Gilbert and P.H. Raven (Editors), *Coevolution of Animals and Plants*. University of Texas Press, Austin, Texas, pp. 53–77.

Smythe, N., 1970. Relationships between fruiting seasons and seed dispersal methods in a Neotropical forest. *Am. Nat.*, 104: 25–35.

Smythe, N., 1978. The natural history of the Central American agouti (*Dasyprocta punctata*). *Smithson. Contrib. Zool.*, No. 257: 52 pp.

Start, A.N. and Marshall, A.G., 1976. Nectarivorous bats as pollinators of trees in West Malaysia. In: J. Burley and B.T. Styles (Editors), *Tropical Trees*. Academic Press, London, pp. 141–150.

Sussman, R.W. and Raven, P.H., 1978. Pollination by lemurs and marsupials: an archaic coevolutionary system. *Science*, 200: 731–736.

Talbot, L.M. and Talbot, M.H., 1963. The wildebeest in western Masailand, East Africa. *Wildl. Monogr.*, 12: 1–88.

Verschuren, J., 1957. *Ecologie, Biologie et Systématique des Chéiroptères, Exploration du Parc National de la Garamba*, No. 7. Institut des Parcs Nationaux du Congo Belge, Brussels, 473 pp.

Wallace, A.R., 1869. *The Malay Archipelago*. MacMillan, London, 638 pp.

Walter, H., 1973. *Vegetation of the Earth in Relation to Climate and Eco-physiological Conditions*. Springer-Verlag, Berlin.

Willis, E.O., 1967. The behavior of bicolored antbirds. *Univ. Calif. Publ. Zool.*, 79: 1–131.

Wilson, D.E., 1973. Bat faunas: A trophic comparison. *System. Zool.* 22: 14–29.

Chapter 17

PRODUCTION OF USABLE WOOD FROM TROPICAL FORESTS

FRANK H. WADSWORTH

INTRODUCTION

Native forests have been crucial to human habitation of the tropical zone. Forest products have housed, transported, defended, cured, fed, and cooked the food of diverse tropical peoples. The progress of civilization has increased human dependence on a growing variety of tropical forest benefits and products and per capita consumption of wood. Assurance of a continuing flow of these benefits and products for the increasing population of the tropics has become a concern of worldwide importance.

Nearly 80% of the wood harvested from the forests of the world's developing countries, a group almost congruent with those of the tropics, is used

for cooking fuel (Table 17.1). About two-thirds of the rest is sawlogs and veneer logs. From 1967 to 1977 the volume of all wood harvested for local use increased 2.6% annually, a rate about comparable to that of population growth. But the harvest of industrial wood alone, less than 20% of the total, increased nearly twice as rapidly.

Table 17.1 also indicates the growing importance of local consumption of forest products. The total volume consumed locally in 1977, about 1250 million m³, included 75% of the logs harvested, 87% of the sawnwood manufactured, 49% of the panels, and about all of the fuel-wood, pulpwood, pulp, and paper products. Fuelwood consumption rose only 2.1% annually, whereas that for logs rose 4.6%. Consumption of pulpwood from local forests

TABLE 17.1

Local consumption and exports of wood products from developing countries (from FAO, 1979)

Product	Apparent local consumption			Exports		
	1967 ($\times 10^6$)	1977 ($\times 10^6$)	annual change compounded (%)	1967 ($\times 10^6$)	1977 ($\times 10^6$)	annual change compounded (%)
Primary						
Fuel (m³)	838.4	1028.2	+2.1	0.9	0.7	−2.1
Industrial wood (m³)	148.3	226.4	+4.3	24.0	46.8	+6.9
logs	87.4	137.6	+4.6	23.5	44.9	+6.7
pulpwood	9.4	23.5	+9.6	0.3	0.8	+10.3
other	51.5	65.3	+2.4	0.2	1.1	+18.8
Total	986.7	1254.6	+2.6	24.9	47.5	+6.7
Secondary						
Sawnwood (m³)	40.9	59.6	+3.8	4.6	9.0	+6.9
Panels (m³)	2.5	6.4	+12.1	1.4	4.5	+12.4
Pulp (t)	2.5	5.4	+8.0	0.2	0.7	+13.3
Paper and board (t)	7.7	15.5	+7.3	0.3	0.6	+7.2

increased 9.6% annually, raising fiber use from 6 to 10% of all locally produced and consumed industrial wood.

Manufacture of secondary wood products locally is further evidence of the social and economic importance of the wood resources of these countries. The manufacture of sawnwood, including exports, increased at an annual rate of 4.2% during the 1967–77 period, whereas for panels it was 10.8% and for pulp and paper products 7.6%, all well above the rate of population increase.

Not only is consumption of local forest products rising within the developing countries, but some are relying increasingly on exports of such products as a source of foreign exchange. In 1977 about 3% of the total wood volume harvested was exported. Of the logs, however, 17% was exported, and of the sawnwood and panels, 21%. For almost all products, rates of exports during the 1967–77 period increased faster than rates of local use. Exports of logs, sawnwood, and paper products about doubled, while those of panels tripled. Exports of primary forest products in 1977 were valued at U.S. $2300 million. The annual 1967–1977 increase, in constant-dollar value, was 9%. For secondary products the 1977 export value was U.S. $13 500 million, and the constant-dollar annual increase during the previous ten years was 6%.

Nearly all of the forest products of the tropics come from forests produced by nature, not by human effort. With continuing deforestation future wood supplies must soon come from forests that are grown through human effort. The potentials for increasing production through management are explored in this chapter.

Most of the present and prospective wood resources of the tropics lie in the moist regions where

TABLE 17.2

The lands and forests of the moist tropics (from Sommer, 1976)

Region	Moist lands of the tropics	
	land ($\times 10^6$ km^2)	forested ($\times 10^6$ km^2)
Africa	3.6	1.8
America	8.0	5.1
Asia	4.4	2.5
Total	16.0	9.4

closed forests develop. Less than 60% of the tropical lands that once bore moist forests are still forested. Some of the deforested area might again become covered with productive forest (Table 17.2). Nevertheless, Sommer's (1976) study, based on 18% of the land area, indicates that net deforestation is taking place at a rate of 1.2% per year. The 1977 volume harvested (Table 17.1) is about 1% of Sommer's estimate of the growing stock (1.225×10^{11} m^3). Much of the deforestation is not accompanied by full utilization of the standing timber.

NATIVE FORESTS

Native forests, once logged for their merchantable trees, are not regarded as a highly productive potential source of wood for traditional products. To understand what may appear paradoxical in the midst of a warm humid climate one must look at the internal dynamics of forest ecosystems of the tropics.

Only a small part of the productivity of mixed tropical forest ecosystems is channelled toward the types of wood we have traditionally considered useful. This relationship is apparent in data from a wet tropical forest in Thailand (Table 17.3). The percentages presented in Table 17.3 are believed more indicative than absolute. The collection of such data is complex, and the precision of these has been seriously questioned by Whitmore (1975, pp. 94–97). Nevertheless, their broad relationships relevant to the purposes of this chapter appear useful.

The distribution of the phytomass shown in Table 17.3 is of basic significance. The stems, with nearly two-thirds of the biomass, are traditionally the most useful source of wood. In the forest studied by Kira (1969) branches account for about 38% of the stem biomass, roots about 14%, and leaves about 4%.

In sharp contrast to the biomass relationships is the allocation of productivity for the maintenance and growth of each component. Branches receive twice as much gross primary productivity as stems, leaves receive more than four times as much. In fact the growth of stems receives only 3.4% of the gross productive effort. Respiration expends 77% of the gross primary productivity, and an additional 19%

is used for sustaining the leaf and branch sub-systems. Basic limitations on wood increment in tropical moist forest have long been seen in the large crowns and low stand densities needed for rapid diameter growth (Dawkins, 1959, 1963). In Table 17.3 this relationship is apparently reflected in the high proportion of the production of the ecosystem that is spent in respiration and litterfall.

The allocation of tropical ecosystem productivity to stemwood is of less direct interest than recorded data on wood yields (Table 17.4). Those for un-treated forest are believed to refer to stands that are essentially in balance. In such forests increment is only enough to offset losses caused by occasional natural catastrophes.

The forests listed as silviculturally treated are only about as productive as the untreated forests (Table 17.4). A significant difference presumably exists, however, in the potential utility of the trees producing the increment. The maximum estimated

TABLE 17.3

Phytomass and dry-matter production in a tropical rain forest (from Kira, 1969)

Index	Stems (%)	Branches (%)	Leaves (%)	Roots (%)	Total (%)
Phytomass	63.6	24.7	2.5	9.2	100.0
Dry-matter fluxes					
1. Increase in living trees	3.4	1.3	0.1	0.5	5.3
2. Death of standing trees	0.6	0.2	0.0	0.2	1.0
3. Biomass increase (1–2)	2.8	1.1	0.1	0.3	4.3
4. Litter production	–	9.3	9.6	–	18.9
5. Net primary production (3+4)	2.8	10.4	9.7	0.3	23.2
6. Respiratory consumption	10.6	15.4	46.3	4.5	76.8
7. Gross primary production (5+6)	13.4	25.8	56.0	4.8	100.0

TABLE 17.4

Yields from tropical moist forests

Location	Mean annual wood increment[1]		Source
	m³ ha⁻¹	t ha⁻¹	
Untreated forest			
Africa		2.3–5.8	Huttel and Bernhard-Reversat (1975)
America	1.8–2.9	0.9–1.9	Huttel and Bernhard-Reversat (1975)
Asia–Pacific		3.7–4.5	Huttel and Bernhard-Reversat (1975)
Silviculturally treated[2]			
Africa			
Nigeria	4.2	2.7	Baur (1964)
General	1–2	0.6–1.3	Sommer (1976)
America			
Puerto Rico	3.3	1.7	Briscoe and Wadsworth (1970)
Trinidad	6.2	4.0	Baur (1964)
General	1–3	0.6–2.0	Sommer (1976)
Asia–Pacific			
Malaysia	2.2–4.2	1.4–2.7	Baur (1964)
Queensland	2.8	1.8	Baur (1964)
General	2–4	1.3–2.6	Sommer (1976)
Maximum		4–9	Dawkins (1967)

[1] Under bark; stemwood only. Weight in metric tons: mean specific gravity, green volume/ovendry weight = 0.65 (Huttel and Bernhard-Reversat, 1975), except 0.52 for Puerto Rico (Longwood, 1961).

[2] Structure and composition modified to increase free space around existing trees of species, size, and form selected as a future wood crop.

by Dawkins (1967) calls for an intensity of management not yet applied extensively.

Attainment of maximum usable wood production from natural tropical forests will call for additional silvicultural finesse. The discovery that the growth of individual trees is highly variable, even within species, and not always responsive to competition or silvicultural release as traditionally measured (Wadsworth, 1953; Lowe, 1966) suggests that more than mere tending of the "leading desirables" is needed. In the first place these must be selected by criteria such as early locational advantages (Lowe, 1966) or genetic efficiency in assimilation (Brunig, 1968). However, future reliance on natural regeneration precludes rapid genetic improvement and close control of tree location.

The limits of wood productivity of moist tropical forests (Table 17.4) appear to present a serious obstacle to meeting prospective demand for wood. We can reasonably assume that: (1) the extraction of wood from these forests will continue to rise as in the past decade (excluding one quarter of the fuelwood to be supplied by dry forests); (2) deforestation will continue at the $110\,000$ km^2 yr^{-1} rate estimated by Sommer (1976); and (3) a mean annual increment of 3 m^3 ha^{-1} may be achievable from these forests [despite the fact that at last count (FAO, 1963) only about 3% of them were even managed under working plans]. If so, then more than 40% of all moist forests standing today (3.8×10^6 km^2) would be required to sustain a yield at the level of even *current* wood use.

Future prospects are more disconcerting. By 1990 wood use will apparently increase to 1500 million m^3 annually, so 5 million km^2 of forest out of a dwindling 7.9 million km^2 would be needed. By the year 2000, with wood use probably rising to more than 2000 million m^3 annually, 6.8 million km^2 of forest, the entire area then remaining, would be required to sustain that level of production, sealing the fate of conflicting forest values.

TABLE 17.5

Yield data for selected tropical forest plantations

Species and location	Age (years)	Mean annual increment[1]		Source
		m^3 ha^{-1}	t ha^{-1}	
BROADLEAFS			(1–28)	
Gmelina arborea				
Malaysia	7–11	28–39	15–20	Freezaillah and Sandrasegeran (1966)
Philippines	8	34	17	Nañagas and Serma (1970)
Nigeria	8	28–33(o)	14–17	Sommer and Dow (1978)
Nigeria	15–17	19–29(o)	10–15	Sommer and Dow (1978)
Tectona grandis				
Cuba	14	10–16	7–11	Sommer and Dow (1978)
Nigeria	15–20	12–16	7–9	Horne (1961)
Panama	25	6	4	Wadsworth (1960)
Nigeria	48	6	3	Horne (1961)
Indonesia	50	7–18	5–12	Indonesia For. Res. Inst. (1975)
Nigeria	53–61	7–9	5–6	Renes (1977)
Swietenia macrophylla				
Nicaragua	9–13	3–9	1–4	Wadsworth (1960)
Puerto Rico	27	6	3	Wadsworth (1960)
Martinique	32	12	3	Wadsworth (1960)
Casuarina equisetifolia				
India	20	9	7	Ubhayakar (1953)
Eucalyptus saligna (upland)				
Brazil				
Site 1	11	49	28	Heinsdijk et al. (1965)
Site 5	11	43	8	Heinsdijk et al. (1965)

TABLE 17.5 (*continued*)

Species and location	Age (years)	Mean annual increment[1]		Source
		m³ha⁻¹	t ha⁻¹	
CONIFERS			(6–23)	
Araucaria cunninghamii (upland)				
Papua New Guinea	9	17	10	Papua New Guinea Dep. For. (1963)
Queensland	28	15	9	Higgins (1970)
Queensland	55	15	9	Hawkins and Muir (1968)
Cupressus lusitanica (upland)				
Venezuela	6	13	7	Schulz and Rodríguez (1967)
Colombia	15	11	6	Tschinkel (1972)
Uganda	22	32	16	Kingston and Kaumi (1972)
E. Africa	35	21	11	Paterson (1967)
Pinus caribaea				
Brazil	9–12	12–26	8–17	Sommer and Dow (1978)
Malaysia	10–12	17–25	11–16	Sommer and Dow (1978)
Surinam	12	17–24	11–16	Sommer and Dow (1978)
Puerto Rico (upland)	11–14	28–36[2]	18–23	Whitmore and Liegel (1980)
Cuba	14	26	17	Wadsworth (1960)
Tanzania	16	23	15	Sommer and Dow (1978)
Queensland, Australia	16	23	15	Sommer and Dow (1978)
Jamaica (upland)	20	21	14	Sommer and Dow (1978)
Fiji (upland)	26–27	25–28	16–18	Sommer and Dow (1978)
Pinus patula (upland)				
Uganda	13–15	10–20	6–11	Sommer and Dow (1978)
Tanzania	14–16	18–20	10–11	Willan (1964a,b), Wood (1964)
Malawi	15	20	11	Sommer and Dow (1978)
Uganda	20	23	13	Kingston (1970)
E. Africa	35	23	13	Paterson (1967)

[1]Under bark [unless marked (o)], generally to a 5 cm or 7.5 cm top. Conversions on the basis of green volume/ovendry weight specific gravities.
[2]Adjusted to under bark according to Voorhoeve (n.d.).

FOREST PLANTATIONS

Artificial forest regeneration provides an opportunity denied under natural regeneration to control precisely the species, genetic quality, and the spacing of trees at early age, all in the interest of high yields and quality. Tropical forest plantation yields under a variety of conditions are summarized in Table 17.5. Some of the results are averages for large planted areas. The plantations listed may be better than average, but most of the soils on which they have grown are too poor for or worn out by cultivated crops.

The common contention that forest plantations can produce significantly more usable wood than native forests seems supported by a direct comparison of Tables 17.4 and 17.5 (0.6–9 *vs* 1–28 t ha⁻¹ yr⁻¹). But such a direct comparison is crude. It does not take into consideration the fact that the plantation increment data exclude at least all stemwood below 7 cm in diameter. Were this additional volume included, the contrast would be still greater. However, no true comparison may be possible because the native forest is much older than the planted trees and therefore net productivity is less.

Marketable stemwood increment in forest plantations may be higher than that of mixed native forests because of less mortality, a greater proportion of the photosynthetic product going to stemwood, greater photosynthesis efficiency (fewer leaves and litterfall per unit of wood increment), or higher gross primary productivity (less respiration per unit of net primary productivity). Plantation mortality may be minimum, but it is not negligible. In fact, most of the plantations in Table 17.5 have been thinned, a practice that reduces gross productivity. In plantations of trees excurrent in form, stemwood may account for as much as 76% of the above-ground biomass (Kandya, 1973), compared to 64% in mixed forest (Kira, 1969). As to photosynthetic efficiency, rapid-growing plantation tree species may produce more mass, despite the low density of their woods, than averages for mixed forests.

How the yields of plantations compare to the maximum primary productivity by stable systems arising from centuries of evolution without catastrophe or human intervention is not apparent in the tabular data presented. The relevance of the level of primary productivity to that of usable wood, however, is apparently no greater than that of primary forest luxuriance to soil fertility in the tropics. Primary productivity, if Table 17.3 is indicative, may be composed 95% of respiration, leaves, and twigs that, however vital, are nevertheless but the bureaucracy that must be tolerated to achieve wood increment. Even if so-called "biomass" fuel from forests comes into vogue it seems certain that the extraction of only the stem and larger branches will be economically feasible. Ideally the small part of primary productivity that goes into wood increment should be maximized, relative to leaf surface and respiration.

In a 60-year-old deciduous mixed native forest and a 35-year-old plantation of *Shorea robusta* on the Gangetic plain of India (Table 17.6) stemwood again makes up 20% more of the stored phytomass of the forest plantation than it does of the native forest. Net primary productivity, production efficiency, and stemwood increment are two to three times those of the mixed forest. Yet, the plantation utilizes only about 70% as much nitrogen and 80% as much calcium per unit of net primary productivity as does the mixed forest.

The plantation, efficient as it may look in absolute terms, nevertheless consumes 30% more nitrogen and 40% more calcium than the mixed forest (Table 17.6). Because the supply of these and other nutrients is limited, the removal of such high yields raises questions about replenishment. In Portugal (FAO, 1955) the third successive coppice of *Eucalyptus globulus* yielded only 80% as much wood as the second. Part of this decline was attributed to progressive sprouting failures and part to soil impoverishment.

More light is shed on the nutrient requirements of two common plantation species by studies in India (Table 17.7). A 33-year-old teak plantation had a mean annual increment of 2.6 m³ ha⁻¹, whereas that of a 30-year-old pine plantation produced 2.3 m³ ha⁻¹. The wood and bark make up 94% of the above-ground phytomass of the teak and 90% of the pine. Only the wood and bark are cited in Table 17.7 because these are the components removed in the harvest.

The degree to which the findings presented in Table 17.7 are representative is not known, but the

TABLE 17.6

Shorea monoculture vs mixed deciduous forest (from Raman, 1975)

Index	Monoculture/mixed forest
Age	0.6
Net primary productivity	1.8
Net production efficiency	2.1
Mean annual stemwood biomass increment	2.9
Nitrogen	
Stored per unit of stemwood biomass	1.0
Current retention per year	1.3
Retention per unit of net primary productivity	0.7
Calcium	
Stored per unit of stemwood biomass	0.6
Current retention per year	1.4
Retention per unit of net primary productivity	0.8

TABLE 17.7

Major nutrients in plantation and bark (from Seth et al., 1963)

Parameter	N	P	K	Ca	Mg
Content of wood and bark (kg t^{-1})					
Tectona grandis	1.8	1.3	2.3	9.1	1.1
Pinus roxburghii	1.5	0.4	1.3	1.4	0.2
Proportion of above-ground nutrients (%)					
Tectona grandis	58	89	83	86	86
Pinus roxburghii	51	69	64	71	52
Mean annual retention (kg ha^{-1})					
Tectona grandis	4.3	3.3	5.7	22.4	2.8
Pinus roxburghii	3.1	0.9	2.7	2.9	0.4

more sharply defined relationships appear worthy of review.

The wood and bark of the teak is richer in nitrogen, phosphorus, potassium, calcium and magnesium than those of the pine. This is particularly true for phosphorus, calcium and magnesium. It is also apparent that the needles of the pine contain a larger proportion of the nutrients than do the leaves of the teak. Seth et al.'s (1963) study showed the bark to be consistently richer in these nutrients than the wood, a relationship that, in absolute terms, was more than offset by the fact that the wood of these plantations had four to five times more mass than the bark.

The mean annual retention gives an indication of the annual nutrient requirements for the production of wood and bark in these plantations (Table 17.7). The nutrients of the leaves, apparently smaller in quantity for each, are presumably largely recycled and so, except for accretion, do not constitute a comparable demand on outside sources.

The nutrient retention levels shown in Table 17.7 are meaningless unless related to the supplying power of appropriate sites. The supplying power of several Oxisols and Ultisols, the most extensive tropical groups (Aubert and Tavernier, 1972), has been measured in the uplands of Puerto Rico by progressive exhaustion of residual nutrients with several years of grass crops (Vicente-Chandler et al., 1974). For nitrogen the annual supplying power of the top 30 cm of three soils ranges between 90 and 120 kg ha^{-1}. The source of this nitrogen is not entirely clear. A substantial part is believed to come from the organic component in the soil (F. Abruña,

pers. comm., 1980). Edmisten (1970) concluded that under similar conditions in Puerto Rico the rainfall provides about 0.8 kg ha^{-1} of nitrogen per 1000 mm of precipitation. For the tropical moist region the annual rainfall is generally double that or more. Edmisten further concludes that nitrogen fixation within the natural forest system increases the gross amount arising from rainfall from 0.8 to 11.5 kg ha^{-1} per 1000 mm of rainfall. Although the plantations described in Table 17.7 may not possess as efficient a nitrogen trap as the native forest, they may well be more effective than grass in using the supplying power of soils, since their root systems can go much deeper than 30 cm.

The supplying power of phosphorus from tropical soils is generally a result of long accumulation and tight retention (Luse, 1970). Future needs for phosphorus could eventually prove to be a serious problem. However, wherever the residual from a natural forest ecosystem has decomposed (or burned) in place the stability of this nutrient, barring serious erosion, may suffice to meet the needs of several successive crops.

The supplying power of the other nutrients has been studied for five Oxisols and ten Ultisols of the moist uplands of Puerto Rico by Abruña et al. (1976; F. Abruña, pers. comm., 1980). These studies are also based on progressive exhaustion of each nutrient by four successive forage grass crops produced in an abundance of all nutrients except the one under study. For potassium the annual supplying power of these soils ranged between 50 and 90 kg ha^{-1}. For calcium it was 86 to 109, and for magnesium from 68 to 98 kg ha^{-1}.

To compare retention with supplying power the

TABLE 17.8

Annual nutrient supply and retention by high-yield plantations

Parameter	N (kg ha^{-1})	P (kg ha^{-1})	K (kg ha^{-1})	Ca (kg ha^{-1})	Mg (kg ha^{-1})
Soil supplying power[1]	90–120	?	50–90	86–109	68–98
Retention[2]					
Tectona	20	15	26	103	13
Pinus	16	5	14	15	2

[1]Sources: Vicente-Chandler et al. (1974), Abruña et al. (1976), F. Abruña (pers. comm., 1980).
[2]Retention data of Table 17.7 multiplied by 4.6 for *Tectona* and 5.2 for *Pinus*.

figures of Table 17.7 should be increased to correspond to the average annual yield level presumed for plantations, 12 m^3 ha^{-1} (Table 17.8). Plantations taking up nutrients corresponding to this increment rate may evidently be harvested repeatedly without serious deficiencies, with the possible exception of phosphorus. Despite any encouragement this analysis may provide, continuous and comprehensive monitoring of nutrient balances and any needed replenishment must become an integral part of high-yield forest plantation culture.

THE FUTURE OF TROPICAL WOOD PRODUCTION

The growing demand for wood in and from the tropics, along with intensifying competitive land-use pressures, calls for high-yield wood production on the most appropriate sites. The large, early, and readily marketable yields of forest plantations compete better for the land than any alternative timber production practice (Lowe, 1975). The arguments for intensive management have never been stronger.

TABLE 17.9

Land-use significance of forest plantation production ($\times 10^6$ km^2)

Proportion of future requirements[1] from forest plantations (%)	Projected use of tropical moist lands in year 2000[2]				
	timber production			other forest[5]	deforested[6]
	plantations[3]	native forest[4]	total		
12 (current)[7]	0.21	6.00	6.21	0.60	9.20
20	0.35	5.47	5.82	1.06	9.12
30	0.52	4.79	5.31	1.65	9.04
50	0.86	3.40	4.26	2.87	8.87
100	1.71	–	1.71	5.84	8.44

[1]Requirements in year 2000 based on current harvest rate (Table 17.1) for 75% of fuelwood (rest from dry forests) and all industrial wood, including exports, projected to 2000 at the 1967–77 annually compounded rates of increase, or 2050 million m^3 yr^{-1}.
[2]Adds to total 16 million km^2 (Table 17.2).
[3]Mean annual increment assumed at 12 m^3 ha^{-1}.
[4]Mean annual increment assumed at 3 m^3 ha^{-1}.
[5]Assuming half of plantations established on lands not now forested, these remaining native forests available for nature reserves, parks, watershed protection, or non-forest use.
[6]Deforestation presumed to continue at estimated current rate less half of the forest plantation area.
[7]Current plantation area and planting rates (from Persson, 1974): 80 000 km^2 and increasing 5000 km^2 yr^{-1}, or 210 000 km^2 in the year 2000.

An examination of the worldwide significance of heavier reliance on forest plantations in the tropics is presented in Table 17.9. We have already seen that reliance solely on native forests for future wood requirements is a blind alley. If concurrent forest plantings are maintained and new planting proceeds as currently estimated (Persson, 1974) they would cover about 1.3% of the land of the moist tropics by the year 2000. If their mean annual increment were $12 \text{ m}^3 \text{ ha}^{-1}$ they would then provide more than 12% of the requirements projected to that time. The rest, however, could only come from the productivity of the remaining moist forests. At their probable annual rate of yield under management ($3 \text{ m}^3 \text{ ha}^{-1}$) about 91% of those that had as yet been spared deforestation (at present rates) would be required to sustain the level of harvest then projected. Only 9% of the native forests would then be available for uses with which timber production interferes.

Table 17.9 shows the degree to which accelerated forest planting could reduce the area needed to produce future timber requirements. If instead of 12%, one half of the wood requirements in the year 2000 were produced in forest plantations, about 30% of the land now covered by native forests could be spared from timber production. It should be clear that if rising wood demands are to be met and significant areas of native tropical moist forests are to be preserved in natural condition or developed primarily for their values other than timber production, there must be (1) a prompt and rapid acceleration of forest planting on appropriate lands, with a special effort to use those already deforested, and (2) equally prompt protection and progressive management of extensive areas of native forests for their timber yields.

REFERENCES

Abruña, F., Vicente-Chandler, J., Figarella, J. and Silva, S., 1976. Potassium supplying power of the major ultisols and oxysols of Puerto Rico. *J. Agric. Univ. P. R.*, 60(1): 45–60.

Aubert, G. and Tavernier, R., 1972. Soil survey. In: *Soils of the Humid Tropics*. U.S. National Academy of Sciences, Washington, D.C., pp. 17–44.

Baur, G.N., 1964. *The Ecological Basis of Rainforest Management*. Government Printer, Canberra, A.C.T., 499 pp.

Briscoe, C.B. and Wadsworth, F.H., 1970. Stand structure and yield in the tabonuco forest of Puerto Rico. In: H.T. Odum and R.F. Pigeon (Editors), *A Tropical Rain Forest: A Study of Irradiation and Ecology at El Verde, Puerto Rico*. U.S. Atomic Energy Commission, Washington, D.C., pp. B79–B89.

Brunig, E.F., 1968. On the limits of vegetable productivity in the tropical rain forest and the boreal coniferous forest. *J. Indian Bot. Soc.*, 47(4): 314–332.

Dawkins, H.C., 1956. Rapid detection of aberrant girth increment of rain forest trees. *Empire For. Rev.*, 35(4): 449–454.

Dawkins, H.C., 1959. The volume increment of natural tropical high-forest and the limitations on its improvement. *Empire For. Rev.*, 38: 175–180.

Dawkins, H.C., 1963. Crown diameters: their relation to bole diameter in tropical forest trees. *Commonw. For. Rev.*, 42(4): 318–333.

Dawkins, H.C., 1964. The productivity of lowland tropical high forest and some comparisons with competitors. *J. Oxford Univ. For. Soc.*, 12: 15–18.

Dawkins, H.C., 1967. Wood production in tropical rain forest. *J. Ecol.*, 55: 20–21.

Edmisten, J., 1970. Preliminary studies of the nitrogen budget of a tropical rainforest. In: H.T. Odum and R.F. Pigeon (Editors), *A Tropical Rain Forest: A Study of Irradiation and Ecology at El Verde, Puerto Rico*. U.S. Atomic Energy Commission, Washington, D.C., pp H211–H215.

FAO, 1955. *Eucalyptus for Planting*. FAO, Rome, 403 pp.

FAO, 1963. *World Forest Inventory*. FAO, Rome, 113 pp.

FAO, 1979. *1977 Yearbook of Forest Products Statistics*. FAO, Rome, 462 pp.

Freezaillah, B.C.Y. and Sandrasegaran, K., 1966. Growth and yield of Yemane (*Gmelina arborea* Roxb.). *Malay. For.*, 29(3): 140–151.

Hawkins, P.J. and Muir, J.D., 1968. Aspects of management of plantations in tropical and subtropical Queensland. In: *9th British Commonwealth Forest Conference, India*, 34 pp.

Heinsdijk, D., Soares, R.O., Andel, S. and Ascoly, R.B., 1965. *Plantacoes de Eucaliptos no Brasil*. Bio. Set. Invent. Flor. Seçào Pesqu. Flor. Div. Silv. Brasil, No. 10: 69 pp.

Higgins, M.D., 1970. *Investigation into Geographic Variation in Hoop Pine*. Department of Forest, Brisbane, Qld.

Horne, J.E.M., 1961. Teak in Nigeria. *For. Dep. Nigeria, Inf. Bull.*, N.S., No. 16: 38 pp.

Huttel, Ch., and Bernhard-Reversat, F., 1975. Recherches sur l'écosystème de la forêt subéquatoriale de basse Côte-d'Ivoire. V Biomasse végétale et productivité primaire cycle de la matière organique. *Terre Vie*, 29: 203–228.

Indonesia Forest Research Institute, 1975. *Yield Table for Ten Industrial Wood Species*. Department of Forest, Jakarta.

Kandya, A.K., 1973. Notes on primary production of teak. *J. Indian Bot. Soc.*, 52: 40–44.

Kingston, B., 1970. *A Provisional Yield Table For Pinus patula Grown in Uganda and An Estimate of the Financial Rotation*. Dep. For., Kampala, Tech. Note, No. 166: 27 pp.

Kingston, B. and Kaumi. J.Y., 1972. *A Preliminary Yield Table For Cupressus lusitanica Grown in Plantations in Uganda*. Dep. For., Kampala, Tech. Note, No. 195: 18 pp.

Kira, T., 1969. Primary productivity of tropical rain forest. *Malays. For.*, 32(4): 375–384.

Longwood, F.R., 1961. *Puerto Rican Woods*. U.S. Dep. Agric., Washington, D.C., Agric. Handb. No. 205., 98 pp.

Lowe, R.G., 1966. Effect of competition on tree growth. In: *Papers 2nd Forest Conference Nigeria*, pp. 115–149.

Lowe, R.G., 1975. Nigerian experience with natural regeneration in tropical moist forest. In: *Tech. Conf. Tropical Moist Forest, FAO, Rome*, 12 pp.

Luse, R.A., 1970. The phosphorus cycle in a tropical rain forest. In: H.T. Odum and R.F. Pigeon (Editors), *A Tropical Rain Forest: A Study of Irradiation and Ecology at El Verde, Puerto Rico*. U.S. Atomic Energy Commission, Washington, D.C., pp. H161–H166.

Nañagas, F.V. and Serma, C.B., 1970. Preliminary study on the growth and development of *Gmelina arborea* in Canys 7, Minglanilla, Cebu. *Occas. Pap. Bur. For Philipp.*, No. 34: 12 pp.

Papua New Guinea, Dep. For., 1963. *Annual Report*. Department of Forestry, Port Moresby.

Paterson, D.N., 1967. Volume and value yields from East African exotic softwood crops in highland sites and fresh approach to East African silviculture. *E. Afr. Agric. For. Res. Org. For. Tech. Note, No.* 19: 22 pp.

Persson, R., 1974. *World Forest Resources*. Royal college of Forestry, Stockholm, Dep. For. Surv. Res. Note, No. 17, 24 pp.

Raman, S.S., 1975. Primary production and nutrient cycling in tropical deciduous forest ecosystem. *Trop. Ecol.*, 16: 140–146.

Renes, G.V.B., 1977. *An Investigation on Yield and Profitability of Teak Plantation in Southwest Nigeria*. UNDP/FAO For. Dev. Project, FAO, Rome.

Schulz, J.P. and Rodriguez, P., 1967. Establishment of yield plots in experimental plantations of *C. lusitanica* and *P. radiata* in the Venezuelan Andes. *Rev. For. Venez.*, 10(15): 21–45.

Seth, S.K., Kaul, O.N. and Gupta, A.C., 1963. Some observations on nutrition cycle and return of nutrients on plantations at New Forest. *Indian For.*, 89: 90–98.

Sommer, A., 1976. Attempt at an assessment of the world's tropical forests. *UnaSylva*, 28(112–113): 5–25.

Sommer, A. and Dow, T., 1978. *Compilation of Indicative Growth and Yield Data of Fast-Growing Exotic Tree Species Planted in Tropical and Subtropical Regions*. Document FO: MISC/78/11 Forest Resources Division, FAO, Rome.

Tschinkel, H., 1972. La clasificación de sitios y el crecimiento del *Cupressus lusitanica* en Antioquia, Colombia. *Rev. Fac. Nacl. Agron. Medellin*, 27(1): 3–30.

Ubhayakar, P.G., 1953. A note on coastal (fuelwood) plantations of *Casuarina equisetifolia* in North Kanara. *Indian For.*, 79(8): 446–452.

Vicente-Chandler, J., Abruña, F., Caro-Costas, R., Figarella, J., Silva, S. and Pearson, R.W., 1974. Intensive grassland management in the humid tropics of Puerto Rico. *Agric. Exp. Stn. Univ. P. R., Bull.* No. 233: 164 pp.

Voorhoeve, A.G., n.d. *Volume Tables*, Pinus caribaea *var.* hondurensis. Surinam Forest Service, Paramaribo, 31 pp.

Wadsworth, F.H., 1953. New observations of tree growth in tabonuco forest. *Caribb. For.*, 14(3/4): 106–111.

Wadsworth, F.H., 1960. Records of forest plantation growth in Mexico, the West Indies, and Central and South America. *Caribb. For.*, 21 (Suppl.): 400 pp.

Whitmore, J.L. and Liegel, L.H., 1980. Spacing trial of *Pinus caribaea* var. *hondurensis*. U.S. Dep. Agric. For. Serv. Res. Pap., South For. Exp. Stn., New Orleans, La., 8 pp.

Whitmore, T.C., 1975. *Tropical Rain Forests of the Far East*. Clarendon Press, Oxford, 282 pp.

Willan, R.L., 1964a. Trial plots, southern highlands. *For. Dep. Tanganyika, Tech. Note (Silviculture)*, No. 64.

Willan, R.L., 1964b. Trial plots — Sao Hill. *For. Dep. Tanganyika, Tech. Note (Silviculture)*, No. 66.

Wood, P.J., 1964. Trial plots. Northern and Kilimanjaro regions. *For. Dep. Tanganyika, Tech. Note (Silviculture)*, No. 70.

Chapter 18

CONVERSION RATES IN TROPICAL MOIST FORESTS

NORMAN MYERS

INTRODUCTION

As this volume makes clear, tropical moist forests are far richer, biotically speaking, than any other biome. At the same time, they are being degraded and destroyed more rapidly than any other biome. If present land-use trends and exploitation patterns persist — and they are likely to accelerate — large sectors of the biome are likely to become markedly modified, if not fundamentally transformed, during the course of the foreseeable future, i.e. the next three to five decades. In fact, many authoritative observers believe that by the end of the century many of the forests will have been reduced to impoverished remnants, if not eliminated altogether. This will represent a biological debacle to surpass virtually any other that has ever occurred since life's first emergence on the planet 3600 million years ago. It will mean the end of the greatest concentrations of species on earth, of the most complex and diverse ecosystems on earth, and of the most dynamic evolutionary processes on earth. On a planetary time scale, it will have happened in the twinkling of a geologic eye.

Thus it is worthwhile to document, in as much detail as is feasible within the scope of this chapter, the major rates of change.

Moreover, it is important to recognize that some forms of change are much more significant than others. Some, e.g. light logging, amount to only marginal disruption, from which a primary forest can generally recover within a matter of one or two decades. Other types of change, such as heavy logging, may not permit a primary forest to re-establish itself within less than one century. Still other forms of change, notably forest farming of more intensive type than the traditional extensive

style of shifting agriculture, may exert such continuous pressure on forest environments that local ecosystems receive no opportunity at all to start to restore themselves. In these senses, then, "change" can range from slight degrees of disruption to outright destruction of the primary forest — and, for the purposes of this chapter, as of this book as a whole, it is with the primary forest, as a uniquely rich and diversified ecosystem in its pristine state, that we need to be mainly concerned.

Given the many different types of change, with their varying levels of intensity, it is often inappropriate to talk about disruption, degradation, impoverishment, and destruction of primary forests. Instead, the author prefers to use the generic term "conversion", as a catch-all designation that covers all forms of change, with their quantitative and qualitative distinctions — though a necessary differentiation between distinct categories will be emphasized where necessary in this chapter.

PROBLEMS OF DOCUMENTATION

In view of the overall decline of the biome, it is urgently necessary to establish as much documentation as possible of actual rates of forest regression in as many countries as possible, especially in the sixteen countries that comprise 70 to 75% of the biome and in the ten countries that contain most of the richest type of tropical moist forest, viz. lowland rain forest. Because of the large areas involved, and the impenetrable nature of many tropical moist forests, most nations of the biome do not possess documentary evidence concerning their forests that amounts to much better than "informed estimates". True, these estimates are far better than nothing; they enable us to "get a handle" on the nature and scale of the challenge confronting those who wish to determine optimal ways to safeguard the biome for long-term sustainable uses of whatever kind (including preservation of selected localities). The great bulk of statistics, however, cannot be construed to represent other than "best-judgement assessments", and many of them are in effect "guesstimates".

For example, certain countries publish figures that are out-dated, on the grounds that they do not yet possess adequate survey capabilities to offer anything more worthwhile. Indonesia continues to state that its forest cover amounts to 1 220 000 km². This figure is at least twenty years old, and does not take into account the widespread logging, shifting cultivation, and transmigration programs that during the past two decades have accounted for large areas of undisturbed forest, possibly, as much as one-third of the entire extent, according to authorative on-the-ground observers (IDA Surveys during 1980). This discrepancy is all the more significant in that Indonesia could well encompass almost one-tenth of the biome.

In addition, certain countries do not distinguish in their statistical records between actual forest cover and "forest lands", the latter term being used to mean something like "public lands not alienated for specific purposes". As a result, official forest lands in, for instance, the Philippines include sizeable and long-established human communities, even urban settlements.

Thus, it is essential to recognize that many published estimates of forest cover are of doubtful validity. This reservation applies especially to·the ways in which these estimates are frequently used. For example, Zaire's forest cover is often stated to be around 1 million km² or more than 10% of the biome. Yet the most recent and far-ranging appraisal of Africa's forests (Persson, 1977) emphasizes that its best estimate for Zaire, based on 1972 information, derives from "poorly known data" with an accuracy level of plus or minus 40%. When Zaire is considered in conjunction with Indonesia (whose information gaps have been mentioned) and Brazil (whose statistical surveys have yet to be published), we find that as much as 5 million km², or well over half the entire biome, have yet to be documented in substantive fashion.

In these circumstances, there is need to adopt great caution with respect to estimates of conversion rates for most areas. In view of the widely variable categories of "information" that must be used in biome-wide surveys, a concise, overall statement of the present status of tropical moist forest is simply not possible. The same applies, only more so, for extrapolations for the future.

This chapter should be read, therefore, with these critical constraints constantly in mind. While compiling the statistical details, the author has been careful to avoid "bogus accuracy". Rather, he has frequently sought to describe the situation in many countries with what might be termed "precise imprecision".

Within the past two years or so, however, a number of countries have published results of comprehensive and systematic surveys, accomplished in the main through remote-sensing techniques. These reports provide substantive and authoritative data for forest cover. The two main countries in question are the Philippines and Thailand. The first of these features predominantly evergreen rain forest, the second almost entirely monsoonal deciduous forest, thus allowing a useful comparison to be drawn between two major distinctive forest ecotypes.

Each of these two countries finds that its forest cover is in fact far less than had been supposed as recently as the early 1970s. The Philippines now possesses only 38% forest cover as compared with former estimates of 57%, while Thailand now possesses only 25% as compared with 48%. Moreover, the forests of Thailand's eastern region, comprising over 15 000 km² in 1972, have been regressing at a rate of over 5% per year (Boonyobhas and Klankamsorn, 1976; Klankamsorn, 1978).

Several other countries, including a number of large ones and notably Brazil and Indonesia, have recently instituted comprehensive remote-sensing programs for their forest resources. They should be able to publish systematized results within the next 1 to 2 years. An interim report for northeastern Para in Brazil's eastern Amazonia reveals that an area of 35 612 km² has lost 28% of its forest cover within only five years (Tardin et al., 1979). These remote-sensing programs will greatly assist in achieving detailed evaluation of very extensive expanses of tropical moist forest.

MAIN AGENTS OF CONVERSION

Let us now take a brief look at some of the main agents of conversion[1].

The commercial exploiter of timber

A main reason why forests in all parts of the world are increasingly exploited, and sometimes over-exploited, is that more people want more wood. Wood serves many purposes. It is one of the first raw materials that a person uses, and it is likely to be his last. It plays a part in more activities of a modern economy than any other commodity. It serves a multitude of purposes as plywood, veneer, hardboard, particleboard, fiberboard and chipboard. It contributes to a number of beverages and foods (including alcohol and synthetic hamburgers), photographic film, explosives, and clothing including paper swimsuits.

Rough estimates suggest that the amount of wood cut worldwide in 1975 was well over 2500 million m³. Of this amount, around 43% was used as timber for construction needs, for panelling and for other "solid wood" purposes, 60% of it to meet the needs of the developed world; 10% was manufactured into pulp products, 85% for the developed world; and around 47% was used as fuel, over 80% of it to meet the needs of the developing world. If, as is likely, consumption of wood increases, there will be growing pressures for exploitation directed at the world's forests — and especially at those forests that have been relatively little exploited for wood to date, tropical moist forests. Although they contain about as much wood as their larger temperate counterparts, tropical moist forests contribute little more than one-tenth of the world's wood used for construction and for paperpulp.

In recent years, there has been a booming demand on the part of the developed world for the kind of timber that makes up over 90% of tropical moist forests — hardwood. In 1950, the developed world imported 4.2 million m³ of tropical hardwood timber; by 1973, the amount had grown to 53.3 million; and by 1980, it is likely to have reached 66 million, and by the year 2000 95 million (FAO, 1979). True, tropical regions use a lot of hardwood timber themselves, but the amount has little more than doubled since 1950, whereas developed-world imports have increased fourteen times, until the total has recently surpassed consumption by all tropical countries combined.

Because of the diversity of tree species in tropical moist forests, coupled with the reluctance of international timber markets to take more than a small proportion of wood types available, the commercial logger is inclined to aim for a highly selective harvest, taking a few choice specimens with disregard for what happens to the rest. Of Amazonia's 2500 tree species, only about 50 are widely exploited, even though as many as 400 are known to have commercial value. So when a patch of tropical moist forest is exploited, only a few trees, often fewer than 20 out of 400 per hectare, are taken. Yet the logging operation can leave many of the remaining trees injured beyond recovery, far more than would be the case in a temperate-zone forest. Tree crowns are often linked together with vines, lianas and other climbing plants, as many as 2000 per hectare, some of them 200 m long (Ewel and Conde, 1976). Commercial trees are often limited to those with the widest spreading crowns, as much as 15 m across; when one of these giants is felled, it is likely to cause several others to be broken or pulled down. Surveys in Southeast Asia reveal that average logging damages between one-third and two-thirds of residual trees (Tinal and Balenewan, 1974; Hadi and Suparto, 1977; Suparto et al., 1978). In addition, almost one-third of the ground may be left bare, in many instances with its soil impacted through heavy machinery. With greater care, the damage could be reduced by half — but less destructive exploitation would raise timber prices for the end-product consumer, and to that extent the consumer is implicitly involved in "mining" of the forests.

What is the overall impact of logging on tropical moist forests? It is difficult to arrive at any firm conclusion, due to the huge and dispersed areas involved, and due to the lack of systematic documentation on which to base a solid assessment. Nevertheless, for purposes of coming to grips with trends of declining forests, it is appropriate to come up with some kind of answer, even if little better than an "educated estimate". The amount of forest

---

[1] This review draws mainly on the reports of Myers (1979a and b), where field findings are set out in documented detail. The writer also acknowledges a number of previous reports, notably by Persson (1974, 1975, 1977), and by Sommer (1976).

in Southeast Asia that is newly affected each year currently amounts to between 10 000 and 27 000 km^2; in Latin America, 8000 to 25 000 km^2; and in Africa (mostly West Africa), 32 000 km^2. This makes a total for the tropics of 53 000 to 87 000 km^2. Moreover, these figures refer only to legal fellings of industrial timber; illegal fellings could swell the totals a good deal more (as in Indonesia and Thailand, where "timber poaching" is a great and growing problem).

Logging impact varies from area to area. In some localities, the consequence is only marginal modification, in other places it amounts to gross degradation of forest ecosystems. Although, as mentioned, research in Southeast Asia suggests that between one-third and two-thirds of residual trees are damaged beyond recovery, field reports from FAO staffers indicate that, for the tropics as a whole, one-tenth may be a more reasonable estimate. For purposes of present calculations, a figure of one-third is used — with the emphatic proviso that this is no more than an interim figure in the absence of anything more substantive, and used only to formulate a "working appraisal" of what is happening to tropical moist forests. In accord with these assumptions, timber exploitation could be occurring on somewhere between 17 700 and 29 000 km^2 of primary forests in the moist tropics each year.

The forest farmer

The commercial logger's impact is often grossly aggravated by what happens after he leaves his patch of forest. Along the timber tracks come subsistence peasants, able to penetrate deep into forest zones that have hitherto been closed to them. Clearing away more trees in order to plant their crops, they soon cause far more damage if not destruction than the lumberman ever did. Not only do forest farmers arrive in large numbers, they now tend to stay in their localities permanently.

Not that the forest farmer has always been detrimental to forest ecosystems. Before he became so numerous, he could generally operate as a shifting cultivator, practising a form of rotational agriculture that constituted sustainable use of forest environments. Due to increase in their numbers, shifting cultivators now make intensive as well as extensive use of forest ecosystems. Still more to the

point, these traditional farmers in certain countries are now being joined by huge communities of landless peasants who, due to lack of farming opportunity elsewhere, are moving into forest lands where they adopt a slash-and-burn style of agriculture that leaves little scope for regeneration of the natural forest.

These forest farmers have been estimated, in the mid-1970s, to total at least 140 million persons, or roughly 20 million families. If each family clears one hectare per year, this means they are accounting for some 200 000 km^2 of forest each year. True, a good number of these farmers exploit secondary forests; and in some sectors of primary forest, for example in Zaire, population density may still be low enough to permit sustainable use of the forest with prospect of eventual regeneration of primary vegetation. Roughly speaking, it is thought that 50 million cultivators in primary forests occupy at least 640 000 km^2, a Texas-sized area, while another 90 million cultivators in secondary forests occupy twice as much land, altogether accounting for over one-fifth of all tropical moist forests. According to a number of field studies, a minimum of 100 000 km^2 of forest are certainly eliminated each year, perhaps much more. The greatest loss occurs in Southeast Asia, where cultivators clear a minimum of 85 000 km^2 each year, adding to rather more than 1 million km^2 of formerly forested croplands in the region. Africa south of the Sahara is believed to have lost 1 million km^2 of moist forest to these cultivators even before modern development trends started after World War II; Africa's current loss is put at 40 000 km^2 per year, and as much as 400 000 km^2 of its moist forest lands may now be under this form of agriculture. A similar story applies in Latin America, though fewer details are available; all forms of expanding agriculture in Latin America, of which slash-and-burn cultivation is a major type, are thought to be accounting for 50 000 km^2 a year.

The figures above represent minimal estimates, prepared through order-of-magnitude reckonings. A further assessment can be arrived at through looking at the consequences of commercial logging, viz. the amount of forest accounted for by cultivators who move in after the logger has quit the scene. Field investigations in Ivory Coast indicate that for every 5 m^3 of logs removed by the timber exploiter, one hectare of forest disappears at the hands of the follow-on cultivator. What happens in Ivory Coast can be said to apply broadly in other parts of West Africa with their high-density populations; it is unlikely to apply in Congo, which, with an area similar to Ivory Coast's but with only one-seventh as many people, is under less pressure from spreading agriculturalists. Similar differentiation holds good for Southeast Asia and Amazonia.

To take a general overview, Africa in 1973 produced 31.2 million m^3 of logs, Southeast Asia 81 million, and Latin America 25.5 million. Together with smaller amounts elsewhere, this makes a total for the tropics of 149 million. Using the very rough rule of thumb developed in Ivory Coast, this could mean that, in the areas in question, 62 400, 162 000, 51 000 and 298 000 km^2 of forest were eliminated by slash-and-burn cultivators. The last figure, almost 300 000 km^2 for the tropics, compares with a minimal estimate of 100 000 km^2 through the preceding calculation. Because of differentiated impact, the figure of 300 000 km^2 is probably way too high, while 100 000 km^2, being a minimal conservative estimate, could be decidedly too low. For purposes of an overall appraisal of conversion trends, a figure of 200 000 km^2 is adopted here — albeit an estimate that is rough and ready in the extreme, but one that serves as a "reasonable working figure" for present purposes.

In short, the forest farmer as an agent of forest conversion could well be accounting for around one percent of the biome each year. Not that the problem lies entirely with him; without the catalytic role of the timber exploiter, the forest farmer would not be enabled to exert a fraction so much impact.

The future prospect could be still more detrimental to primary forests. Population growth rates in many countries of the biome are among the highest on earth. Unless economic development proceeds faster than hitherto (opening up opportunities for alternative forms of earning a living), it is possible that a large proportion of the population increase in these countries will cause the numbers of forest farmers to expand disproportionately. In other words, whereas overall population growth in the countries concerned may result in total numbers increasing by around two-thirds by the year 2000, the number of forest farmers could grow by at least 100% and conceivably by much more. True, these calculations are crude to a degree: they are advanced merely as a measure of population pressures that could overtake tropical moist forests during the foreseeable future.

The fuelwood gatherer

A further factor in conversion of tropical moist forests is demand for fuelwood. As already indicated, it is thought that almost half of all wood cut world-wide each year is used as fuel, with over four-fifths of it going to meet the needs of people in the developing world. (A few household surveys suggest that the amount of fuelwood actually cut could be $2\frac{1}{2}$ times as large as is "officially" estimated.) The situation has been grossly aggravated by the increase in oil prices, putting kerosene beyond the means of many households. To this extent, the oil-exporting countries bear a major though indirect responsibility for part of the exploitation pressures now directed at tropical moist forests.

On the basis of field reports, it is realistically reckoned that one person can obtain a sustainable supply of fuelwood from the equivalent of half a hectare of forest each year. More usually, however, in order to exploit supplies close to hand, as many as fifteen persons may be taking wood from one hectare — an excessively concentrated, and so unsustainable, rate of use. In large parts of the tropics, much wood is taken from secondary forests, scrub patches and village woodlots, rather than from virgin forests. For example, in Southeast Asia about one-third of the fuelwood comes from outside forests proper. In India it has been found that a village located inside or adjoining a forest meets its total fuelwood requirements from the forest; in areas within 10 km of forest boundaries, about 70% of the fuelwood comes from the forest; while beyond 10 km, the use of fuelwood from the forest steadily diminishes until at about 15 km it is almost nil (Mathur, 1975). A similar pattern of use is reported from a number of other countries.

However, this situation is changing in many parts of the developing world. When local supplies become exhausted, people start to look further afield. This trend is likely to accelerate: as human populations expand, many residual sources of fuelwood will become quickly subject to increasing over-exploitation, and they will disappear at ever more rapid rates. In addition, there are longer-range linkages. In a number of countries, large-scale commercialization of the fuelwood trade is directing exploitation pressures toward far-distant sources, as it becomes financially worthwhile for e.g. charcoal manufacturers to transport their supplies from forests in one part of a country to markets in another part of the country, sometimes hundreds of km away. This trend is already pronounced in Thailand: the Bangkok conurbation, with its five million inhabitants, derives much of its charcoal supplies from forests in remote northern sectors of the country (Lekagul and McNeely, 1978).

Of approximately 1000 million people living in the tropical moist forest biome (a very rough estimate, proposed only to gain a measure of the problem's dimensions), some 200 million people are believed to live within or on the fringes of forests. So far as can be ascertained, each of these people consumes an average of 0.5 to 1 m^3 of fuelwood per year. Let us suppose that at least one-fifth of fuelwood cut comes from primary forests. This means that fuelwood gathering affects around 25 000 km^2 of primary forests each year.

Assuming that human populations continue to expand, and that the remaining forests continue to be reduced (not only through exploitation for wood, but to make way for agriculture), residual tracts will become subject to increasing exploitation and over-exploitation. In some areas demand has already grown so great, and pressure on available supplies has become so acute, that it already costs as much to heat the cooking bowl as to fill it.

The cattle rancher

In Latin America, though not in Africa or Southeast Asia, a major agent of forest conversion is the cattle rancher. He clears away the forest completely, in order to establish grasslands. The pastures remain productive for six to ten years, then are taken over by scrub growth. The rancher does not usually mind since he can move on to another patch of forest and start again.

An increasing number of ranching enterprises in Latin America are foreign-owned. A U.S. consortium of Brescan-Swift-Armour-King Ranch holds around 720 km^2 in the eastern part of Brazilian Amazonia, with an investment of U.S. $6 million. Other multinational corporations in Brazilian Amazonia include Heublein, Sifco Industries and Twin Agricultural and Industrial Developers from the United States, Mitsui, Tsuzuki Spinning, and Nichimen and Grubo Bradesco from Japan, Liquigas from Italy, and George Markhof from Austria, among many more from industrialized nations. Investment on the part of the twelve largest enterprises totals U.S. $21 million, except for Volkswagen with U.S. $35 million. Volkswagen believes that although people may come to purchase fewer cars in the wake of the oil price increase, they will hardly be inclined to eat less beef. Volkswagen holds a concession of 1400 km^2 in the eastern Amazon, of which half is to be converted into pastureland. By mid-1976 the company had burned about 100 km^2 of forest, enough for a herd of 10 000 cattle. The eventual aim is to increase the grasslands to 700 km^2, to support 120 000 cattle.

To date, some 300 ranches have been established, with a cattle population of 6 million. This has entailed the elimination of 66 000 km^2 of forest. Virtually none of the timber felled has been disposed of as commercial wood, even though the marketable lumber could fetch U.S. $35 per m^3; the subsidized rancher does not find it worth his while to do other than douse herbicide onto the area to be cleared, then put a match to it. Result: an average of 50 m^3 of usable timber per hectare goes up in smoke, representing a total loss to date of U.S. $7700 million, or about $2\frac{1}{2}$ times as much per year as Amazonia's commercial sales of timber.

The rationale for cattle-raising is two-fold. First, due to Brazil's desire to assert its sovereignty over its vast and little-settled sector of Amazonia, the government seeks to develop the forest lands through whatever means may appear appropriate. Secondly, Brazil has an eye to the world's growing beef shortage. According to the Food and Agriculture Organization, world-wide demand for meat is projected to rise from 1970 to 1990 more rapidly than for other foods except fish. To meet this growing demand with its soaring prices, Brazil is determined to become one of the biggest beef exporters in the world. In 1973 the country possessed 95 million head of cattle, a total surpassed only by the Soviet Union and the United States. By 1980 Brazil hopes to have doubled its 1973 output of meat, and soon thereafter it aims to rank as the world's number one beef exporter.

However, raising beef in tropical forestlands is not so straightforward as it might seem. Stocking rates are low, a mere one animal per hectare. Steers take four years before they are ready for slaughter, at a weight of 450 kg. Soils quickly become exhausted of nutrients, and pastures feature poorer and poorer grass unless they receive ever-growing amounts of fertilizer. A few ranches in Brazilian Amazonia have already been abandoned and at least 200 look likely to become unprofitable after only five years. Due to a spreading problem of toxic weeds, some ranches have lost one-fifth of their cattle. Yet so compelling are the political considerations underpinning Brazil's urge to open up its sector of Amazonia that exceptional financial incentives are offered to attract cattle-ranching investors.

As the international beef trade grows, more countries of Latin America, notably Peru and Colombia, aim to convert portions of their Amazonian lowland forests into cattle ranches. Indeed, initiatives similar to those in Brazil, though not so expansive, are already being implemented in the Amazonian territories of Colombia and Peru, fostered in certain instances by the Inter-American Development Bank, the World Bank and UNDP. Bolivia hopes to open up its sparsely populated eastern region, an area larger than Spain, through an initiative on the part of the Anglo-Bolivian Land and Cattle Company, which plans to obtain financial support from Britain, the United States, German Federal Republic and France. Bolivia intends to sell off almost 1 million hectares of virgin forest, at a mere U.S. $42 per hectare, to 150 000 white settlers whom it hopes to attract from southern Africa.

In Central America, there has been a similar outburst of cattle ranching, though longer-standing and with greater emphasis on export markets — almost all the beef being despatched to the United States where (according to the Meat Importers Council of America) most of it makes its way into the hamburger and frankfurter trade. From the early 1960s, fast-food chains in the United States have boomed, until they grew in 1974 alone by 20%, or $2\frac{1}{2}$ times as fast as the restaurant industry overall (Dwoskin, 1975). As a consequence of this expansion, the trade has looked for additional supplies of meat, finding a source of cheap beef in Central America. The beef is "cheap" only in relation to supplies within the United States; beef grown in Montana, with high land and labour costs, is

almost four times as expensive as beef grown in Costa Rica (Lappe and Collins, 1977). Thus the price of a U.S. hamburger does not reflect the environmental costs of its production in Costa Rica. The American consumer, seeking a good-quality hamburger at "reasonable", i.e. non-inflationary, price, is not aware of the indirect consequences of his actions far away from his homeland. Nevertheless, he contributes — albeit unwittingly and certainly without wanton intent, but effectively and increasingly — to the elimination of forests in Central America. As the convenience-food trade in America continues boom, there will be, to quote Dr. Joseph A. Tosi of the Tropical Science Center in San José, Costa Rica, "A massive conversion of remaining lowland moist forest to low-productivity ranching operations".

Since 1950, the area of man-established pasturelands and the number of beef cattle in Central America have more than doubled (Dickinson, 1972; Parsons, 1976). This expansion has occurred almost entirely at the expense of natural forests, of which two-thirds have now been cleared. Costa Rica's pasturelands in 1950 covered 12.4% of the country, and expanded by 1973 to cover more than 25% — accounting for 16 000 km^2, or almost one-third of national territory. If the present clearing rate of 500 km^2 per year continues, the remaining tracts of primary forests will be finished by 1990.

Costa Rica's cattle herds, that in 1960 totalled slightly over 900 000, increased by 1976 to 1.9 million (Foreign Agricultural Service of U.S. Department of Agriculture, 1976). During the 1960s, beef production expanded by 92%. In the course of the same decade, however, local consumption of beef declined by 26%, to a mere 8 kg per head per year, almost all the extra output being exported. Costa Rica now exports around 45 million kg of beef per year, of which well over half goes to the United States, for a value of U.S. $34 million. In Central America as a whole, the average amount exported is one-third of all produced, but in Costa Rica it is two-thirds. This trade is of considerable benefit to the United States; it not only enables the American consumer to enjoy ample supplies of cheap beef, but it generates sizeable profits for the U.S. corporations involved, and it allows the country to put poor land back into its soil bank.

What, then, is the overall impact of cattle ranching on Latin America's tropical moist forests? We can form only a rough appraisal of the situation. According to best estimates of FAO, however, the period 1962 to 1985 is likely to see at least 325 000 km² of Latin America's tropical forests (an area the size of Norway or New Mexico) cleared for pasturelands (Brazil 125 000 and Colombia 66 000 km²). This works out at an average of just under 13 500 km² per year. Since the rate is likely to be greater at the end of the period than at the start, due to growing population pressures if nothing else, the figure for 1979 could well have reached 20 000 km² — a figure that is accepted for this review of conversion trends in tropical moist forests.

SUMMARY OF FOREST CONVERSION RATES

Conversion of tropical moist forests stems primarily from the commercial logger/follow-on cultivator combination, which is thought to be accounting, as a preliminary and very approximate calculation, for 200 000 km² per year. The fuelwood cutter could well be responsible for 25 000 km² a year, and the ranching entrepreneur (confined to Latin America) for 20 000 km². This makes a total of 245 000 km² per year. These figures do not include other agents of forest destruction, such as the commercial logger who over-exploits a patch of forest without being followed by the slash-and-burn cultivator; the cultivator who clears forest without any pioneering assistance from the logger; the plantation operator who replaces forest with monocultures of tree species such as eucalyptus, pines, rubber trees and oil palms; and others who eliminate the forest for various reasons, but whose impact is not on a scale to match the three main categories.

The total figure of 245 000 km² is way beyond the range of the best estimate hitherto available, that of FAO, viz. 120 000 to 170 000 km² (Sommer, 1976)[1]. But the figure of 245 000 km² is considered realistic on two grounds. First, the FAO data derive in many instances from trends documented in the early 1970s, if not before — since which time, exploitation patterns have accelerated markedly. Secondly, FAO calculations generally represent, for the sake of caution, minimal estimates. Of course, there is merit in caution when it is applied for the sake of accuracy. But to help us "get a

handle" on the problem of conversion of tropical forests, and thus establish the size of the problem we are grappling with, it is worthwhile to make an estimate of what we believe could be going on as well as what we know is going on. It is in this spirit that the figure of 245 000 km² is advanced.

Until more information is available, then, it is not unreasonable to suppose that the earth is losing around 670 km² of tropical moist forest a day, or an area the size of Wales or Massachusetts each month. This works out at a rate of 46 hectares per minute, to be compared with a figure of 20 hectares per minute derived from the 1976 estimate of FAO. Interestingly enough, the Director-General of FAO, Edouard Saouma, offered a figure of 30 hectares per minute at the World Forestry Congress organized by FAO in Jakarta, Indonesia, though he did not indicate how he arrived at this estimate.

DIFFERENTIATED CONVERSION RATES

A conversion rate of 245 000 km² per year means, in theory, that the entire biome of some 9.35 million km² (Sommer, 1976) could be eliminated within 38 years. Of course, the rate of conversion is likely to accelerate in many areas, and in hardly any areas is likely to decline. But it is facile to suppose that the future prospect for the biome will amount to a straight extrapolation of the present situation. Already, conversion trends are highly differentiated. This means that certain areas are undergoing conversion at rates fast enough to bring them

---

[1] FAO has recently produced a much more conservative set of data, suggesting that only half as much may be disappearing per year (Lanly and Clement, 1979). However, these recent calculations assume that forest exploited by a timber harvester remains forest, whether it is heavily or lightly logged; so forests exploited in this manner are not included in the FAO calculations. This author, by contrast, believes that the main concern of the scientist in tropical moist forests is with primary, i.e. undisturbed, forests; so forests that are subject to logging of any sort are here considered to be disrupted, thus converted from their original form. Moreover, the FAO assessment appears to play down the catalytic role of the commercial logger in opening up forests that would otherwise be closed, since impenetrable, to the forest farmer. By contrast, this writer's experience during the course of repeated visits to some 32 countries of the biome, is that the follow-on relationship between the logger and the farmer is a key factor contributing to accelerating rates of conversion of tropical moist forests.

to an end within less than one decade, whereas other areas could well remain little changed by the turn of the century. And yet others could show a reversal in the trend as rural populations move to cities and improve their standard of living. This differentiated pattern is clearly of critical importance to conservation plans, and it is dealt with in some detail in this concluding section to the chapter.

Virtually all lowland forests of the Philippines and Peninsular Malaysia seem likely to become logged over by 1990 at the latest, possibly a good deal earlier. Much the same applies to most parts of West Africa. Little could remain of Central America's moist forests within another ten years, probably less. Almost all of Indonesia's lowland forests have been scheduled for timber exploitation by the year 2000, and at least half by 1990. Extensive areas of Amazonia in Colombia and Peru could be claimed for cattle ranching and various forms of cultivator settlement by the end of the century; and something similar holds good for much of the eastern sector of Brazil's Amazonia.

By contrast, Central Africa features low human densities and abundant mineral resources. This reduces the incentive to liquidate "forest capital" in order to supply funding for various forms of economic development; hence there could well remain large expanses of little-disturbed forest by the end of the century. Similarly, the western portion of Brazil's Amazonia, because of its remoteness and perhumid climate, may undergo only moderate change.

In short, the overall outcome is likely to be extremely "patchy", both in terms of geographic areas and degree of conversion — ranging from marginal disruption to outright elimination.

A. Areas undergoing broad-scale conversion at rapid rates

(1) Most of the Philippines' lowland forests, predominantly rain forests, because of timber exploitation and forest farming; could be little left by 1990 if not earlier.

(2) Most of Peninsular Malaysia's lowland forests, almost all rain forests, due to timber exploitation and planned agriculture; could be little left by 1990 if not earlier.

(3) Much if not most of Indonesia's lowland forests, predominantly rain forests, due to timber exploitation, forest farming, and transmigration programs; could be little left in Sumatra and Sulawesi by 1990, in Kalimantan and most of the smaller islands by 1995, and in Irian Jaya by the year 2000.

(4) Much of Sumatra's and Sabah's lowland forests, almost all rain forests, due to timber exploitation; could be little left by the year 2000 if not earlier.

(5) Much if not most of Melanesia's lowland forests, due to timber exploitation and planned agriculture; could be little left by 1990.

(6) Most of Australia's lowland tropical forests, both rain forests and seasonal forests, due to timber exploitation and planned agriculture; could be little left by 1990 if not earlier.

(7) Much if not most of Thailand's forests, almost all seasonal forests, both lowland and upland, due to timber exploitation (especially illegal felling) and forest farming; could be little left by 1990 if not earlier.

(8) Much of Vietnam's forests, almost all seasonal forests, both lowland and upland, especially in the south, due to forest farming, timber exploitation, and immigration from the north; could be little left by 1990.

(9) Most of Bangladesh's forests, both lowland and upland, predominantly rain forests, due to timber exploitation, forest farming, and population pressure; could be little left by 1990 if not earlier.

(10) Much of India's forests, predominantly seasonal forests, mainly upland, due to forest farming and population pressure; could be little left by 1990.

(11) Much if not most of Sri Lanka's forests, predominantly rain forests, mostly upland, due to timber exploitation and forest farming; could be little left by 1990.

(12) Much if not most of Central America's forests, notably rain forests, both lowland and upland, due to forest farming, cattle raising, and timber exploitation; could be little left by 1990 if not earlier.

(13) Parts of Colombia's lowland rain forests on the borders of Amazonia, especially in Caqueta and Putumayo, due to colonist settlement and cattle raising; extensive tracts could be converted by 1990.

(14) Much of Ecuador's Pacific coast forests, mostly very wet and very rich rain forests, both

lowland and upland, due to plantation agriculture and some timber exploitation; could be widely converted by 1990.

(15) Parts of Brazil's eastern and southern sectors of Amazonia, lowland rain forests, notably in Para, Mato Grosso, and Rondônia; due to cattle raising, colonist settlement, and forest farming; appreciable tracts could be converted by 1990.

(16) Much if not most of West Africa's forests, mainly seasonal forests, due to timber exploitation and forest farming; could be little left by 1990 if not earlier.

(17) Much if not most of East Africa's relict montane forests, especially in northern Tanzania, mostly seasonal forests, due to timber exploitation, fuelwood cutting, and forest farming; could be little left by 1990.

(18) Much if not most of Madagascar's forests, especially rain forests, both lowland and upland, due to forest farming and timber exploitation; could be little left by 1990 if not earlier.

(19) Most if not virtually all of Brazil's Atlantic coast strip of moist forest, due to timber exploitation and cash-crop agriculture, notably sugarcane plantations; could be little left by 1990 if not a good deal earlier.

B. Areas undergoing moderate conversion at intermediate rates

(These areas cannot be so readily listed as those under A, since less is known about their present status and future prospects. The listing is deliberately conservative.)

(1) Much of Papua New Guinea's forests, mostly seasonal, both lowland and upland, due to timber exploitation and forest farming; extensive areas could be converted by the year 2000 if not earlier.

(2) Parts of Burma's lowland forests, almost all seasonal, due to forest farming and some timber exploitation; appreciable areas could be converted by the year 2000 if not earlier.

(3) Parts of Colombia's Pacific coast forests, very wet and very rich rain forests, both lowland and upland, due to timber exploitation; extensive sectors could be converted by 1990.

(4) Much of Ecuador's Amazonia forests, almost all rain forests, both lowland and upland, due to colonist settlement, forest farming, some planned agriculture, and also oil exploitation; appreciable

areas could be converted by 1990, and much more by the year 2000.

(5) Much of Peru's Amazonia forests, almost all rain forests, both lowland and upland, due to colonist settlement, forest farming, and some planned agriculture; appreciable areas could be converted by 1990, and much more by the year 2000.

(6) Parts of Brazil's Amazonia forests, lowland rain forests, notably in eastern Para, Amapa, Acre, sections of the TransAmazonica Highway system and of the *varzea* floodplains, and areas selected for timber exploitation, e.g., Tapajos River area, due to colonist settlement, forest farming, cattle raising, and timber exploitation; appreciable tracts could be converted by 1990.

(7) Parts of Cameroon's forests, both seasonal and rain forests, both lowland and upland, due to timber exploitation and forest farming; extensive areas could be converted by 1990.

C. Areas apparently undergoing little change

(Like B, these areas cannot be so readily listed as those under A, since less is known about their present status and future prospects. The listing is deliberately conservative, especially as concerns the long-term future.)

(1) Much of Brazil's western Amazonia, lowland rain forests, generally wetter and richer than eastern Amazonia; except for some timber extraction in limited areas, and some cultivation of varzea floodplains, exploitation of this huge zone could prove difficult in view of its unusually wet climate and distance from markets; it is reasonable to anticipate — so far as can be ascertained, and the point is stressed — that much of this vast tract of lowland rain forest could remain little changed for a good while to come possibly until the year 2000.

(2) Much of the forests of Guyana, Surinam and French Guiana, almost all rain forests, both lowland and upland; timber exploitation, at present very limited, may expand, but, because population pressures are low, there is little likelihood of widespread colonist settlement and forest farming. So it is reasonable to anticipate — with caveat as under Brazil above — that large areas may remain little changed for a good while to come, possibly until the year 2000.

(3) Much of the Zaire Basin, comprising Gabon, Congo and Zaire; some rain forest in Gabon,

remainder mainly seasonal, almost entirely low-land; population pressures are low, and there are abundant mineral resources on which to base national economic development; timber exploitation, primarily limited to Gabon and northern Congo, could expand; but in the main, it is reasonable to anticipate — with caveat as under Brazil above — that large areas may remain little changed for a good while to come, possibly until the year 2000.

In sum, the situation is highly differentiated — between and within the three main regions, also within some individual countries.

With respect to future trends, it seems plain that human population growth and economic aspirations, already factors of importance, will exert progressive pressures on tropical moist forests until their impact by the year 2000 could represent a colossal magnitude change from the present position. At the same time, it is necessary to bear in mind that exploitation patterns can alter. It would be a mistake to suppose that the future will amount to a simple extrapolation of the present situation. Some exploitation trends could reveal a geometric rather than an arithmetic progression, while others could decline in significance or even fade away as they are supplanted by innovative forms of exploitation. Other discontinuities could arise, such as shifts in consumer demand in the developed world for specialist hardwoods from the tropics, and in both developed-world and developing-world demands for paperpulp from mixed hardwoods from the tropics.

Exceptionally endangered areas

Certain sectors of the biome feature unusually rich forest ecosystems. These include localities with centers of species diversity and high levels of endemism. In a number of instances, these exceptionally rich forest tracts are experiencing exceptionally rapid conversion. They thus merit priority treatment.

The following areas could be considered for urgent attention, on the grounds that they offer exceptional scientific interest and they face exceptionally severe threat. The list is kept short in order to include only areas where the degree of urgency is acute. The list should not be considered to be exhaustive; and the ordering of items does not imply any kind of "merit ranking".

(a) Peninsular Malaysia's lowland rain forest, especially localities along the northwestern and eastern coasts with their high levels of endemism.

(b) Ecuador's Pacific coast rain forest bloc, extremely wet climatically and extremely rich biotically.

(c) Middle America's three rain forest blocs, the last remnants of a highly diversified biotic zone.

(d) Madagascar's eastern rain forests, with their very varied and species-rich communities, in which endemism for some groups of organisms reaches 75%.

(e) East Africa's relict montane forests, with their many endemics and a degree of sub-specific differentiation unknown elsewhere in Africa.

(f) Philippines' lowland rain forests, especially areas with high levels of plant and vertebrate endemism.

(g) Indonesia's lowland rain forests in Sumatra and Kalimantan, especially the wetter and presumably richer parts.

(h) Brazil's lowland rain forests in Amazonia where three reputed centres of diversity overlap with growth poles for economic development.

(i) Ecuador's and Peru's rain forests in the westernmost part of Amazonia, where the presumed Napo centre of diversity is located.

(j) Island groups of Melanesia, especially New Caledonia with its rich and distinctive rain forest flora.

(k) Sri Lanka's rain forest remnants, with their generally high levels of endemism.

(l) Ivory Coast's southwestern lowland forests, part of a postulated Pleistocene refuge with exceptionally rich stocks of endemics, notably mammals.

(m) Brazil's relict strip of Atlantic coast forest, already degraded virtually throughout its length and facing severe threat, despite its many endemic species (including certain tamarind monkeys).

REFERENCES

Boonyobhas, C. and Klankamsorn, B., 1976. *Application of ETS-I Imagery in Forestry*. National Research Council of Thailand, Bangkok, Tech. Rep. 760130.

Dickinson, J.C., 1972. Alternatives to monoculture in the humid tropics of Latin America. *Prof. Geogr.*, 24: 217–222.

Dwoskin, P.B., 1975. *Fast Food Franchises: Market Potentials for Agricultural Products in Foreign and Domestic Markets*. Department of Agriculture, Washington D.C., Econ. Res. Serv. No. 596.

Ewel, J. and Conde, L., 1976. *Potential Ecological Impact of Increased Intensity of Tropical Forest Utilization*. Forest Products Laboratory, Madison, Wis.

Food and Agriculture Organization, 1979. *Agriculture: Toward 2000*. FAO, Rome.

Foreign Agricultural Service of U.S. Dep. Agric., 1976. *Costa Rica: Agricultural Situation, and Livestock and Meat*. U.S. Department of Agriculture, Washington, D.C.

Hadi, S. and Suparto, R.S. (Editors), 1977. *Proceedings of Symposium on the Long-Term Effects of Logging in Southeast Asia*. Regional Center for Tropical Biology, Bogor.

Klankamsorn, B., 1978. Use of satellite imagery to assess forest deterioration in eastern Thailand. In: *Proceedings of 12th International Symposium on Remote Sensing of the Environment, Manilla, 1978, II*. Environmental Research Institute of Michigan, Ann Arbor, Mich., pp. 1299–1306.

Lanly, J.P. and Clement, J., 1979. *Present and Future Forest and Plantation Areas in the Tropics*. FAO, Rome, IO:MISC/79/1.

Lappe, F.M. and Collins, J., 1977. *Food First: Beyond the Myth of Scarcity*. Houghton Miflin, Boston, Mass.

Lekagul, B. and McNeely, J., 1978. Thailand launches extensive reafforestation program. *Tigerpaper*, 5(1): 9–13.

Mathur, R.S., 1975. Trends in the consumption of wood in India. *Indian For.*

Myers, N., 1979a. *The Sinking Ark*. Pergamon Press, New York, N.Y.

Myers, N., 1979b. *Conversion Rates in Tropical Moist Forests*. Report under Project of National Academy of Sciences, "Research Priorities in Tropical Biology". National Research Council, Washington, D.C., 205 pp.

Parsons, J.J., 1976. Forest to pasture: development or destruction? *Rev. Biol. Trop.*, 24(Suppl. 1): 121–138.

Persson, R., 1974. *World Forest Resources: Review of the World's Forest Resources in the Early 1970s*. Royal College of Forestry, Stockholm, Dep. For. Surv. Res. Note, No. 17.

Persson, R., 1975. *Forest Resources of Africa Part 1: Country Description*. Royal College of Forestry, Stockholm, Dep. For. Surv. Res. Note, No. 18.

Persson, R., 1977. *Forest Resources of Africa. Part II: Regional Analysis*. Royal College of Forestry, Stockholm, Dep. For. Surv. Res. Note, No. 22.

Sommer, A., 1976. Attempt at an assessment of the world's tropical moist forests. *UnaSylva*, 28(112/113): 5–24.

Suparto, R.S. and seven others (Editors), 1978. *Proceedings of Symposium on the Long-Term Effects of Logging in South-East Asia*. Regional Centre for Tropical Biology (BIOTROP), Bogor.

Tardin, A.T. and twelve others, 1979. *Levantamento de ares de desmatamento na Amazonia legal atraves de imagens do Satellite Landsat*. National Institute for Space Research (INPE), Sao Jose dos Campos, Report No. INPE–1411–NTE/142.

Tinal, U. and Balenewan, J.L., 1974. *A Study of Mechanical Logging Damage After Selective Cutting in the Lowland Dipterocarp Forest of East Kalimantan*. Regional Centre for Tropical Biology (BIOTROP), Bogor.

Chapter 19

PATTERNS OF RESOURCE USE AND HUMAN SETTLEMENT IN TROPICAL FORESTS

CHRISTINE PADOCH and ANDREW P. VAYDA

INTRODUCTION

Criticism of traditional resource use patterns in the tropics as wasteful and inefficient predominated in the literature in the past, but has given way in recent years to praise of the stability and conservativeness of these technologies. Such revised views of primitive man as conservator are not surprising and are at least partially justified. They reflect the realization that traditional resource users[1] usually allowed tropical forests to survive or at least to largely regenerate, whereas modern, fossil fuel-using man is expected to destroy these forests within the next century. However, in stressing the long-term persistence of traditional patterns, the "necessity" and universality of some techniques and the self-sufficiency and integrity of pre-modern resource use systems, commentators have done justice neither to the complexity nor the variability — temporal, spatial, and technological — of traditional human accommodations to tropical forests.

In this chapter we shall first review some of the conventional ways of viewing and classifying traditional resource use patterns, then point out some of the limitations of these familiar typologies, and finally discuss actual subsistence and settlement patterns in tropical forests, and comment on prospects for development of these areas.

In most broad discussions of indigenous resource use, some typology of food-getting technologies and/or of crops, crop types or crop assemblages, is meant to subsume the basic patterns of livelihood of all traditional groups. The division of technologies into hunting-gathering, shifting cultivation, and permanent-field cropping is probably most familiar and most commonly employed. These

three very broad divisions of the spectrum of traditional subsistence, often erroneously assumed to be a necessary evolutionary sequence, are used by anthropologists and geographers to designate different levels of intensity of land or resource use, as well as to differentiate levels of control and modification of forest environments. Observers have generally considered the following practices and patterns, technological and social, to be characteristic of these three very general types.

HUNTER-GATHERERS

Populations of hunter-gatherers ideally only harvest spontaneously occurring species and thus are thought to disturb their forest environments little. Of such groups employing no or minimal agriculture for their subsistence, only a very small number can be found in the humid tropics today. Near worldwide increases in population densities, government policies encouraging agricultural settlement of foragers, and extensive commercial exploitation of hunter-gatherers' habitats can all be cited as contributing to the almost total disappearance of non-agricultural peoples.

Observers of the few remaining populations of foragers have noted that small and variable social groupings, low areal densities, and considerable mobility of residence are typical of non-farmers (Steward, 1955; Turnbull, 1968; Lee, 1968). Research indicates that few tropical forest dwellers regularly aggregate in groups larger than fifty or so

---

[1]By "traditional" we mean pre-industrial or *not* fossil fuel using. We do not wish to imply that these systems have not changed over centuries, or are unchanging.

individuals, and these bands tend to vary both in composition and in geographical location throughout the year. The factors that make flexibility of residence and small groupings desirable or advantageous include the tropical forest's great diversity of species and wide dispersal of food sources, and the climatic and biotic conditions which limit successful food preservation.

The apparent necessity of at least limited nomadism among tropical hunter-gatherers should not, however, be considered evidence that the life of non-agriculturists in tropical regions is a constant, desperate struggle for existence. Recent research, although incomplete, points to a general pattern of largely adequate nutrition and few periods of significant hunger among such populations (Lee and DeVore, 1968; UNESCO, 1978). It is generally believed that tropical forest dwellers, like most other non-agricultural peoples, obtain far more of their nutritional needs through the harvesting of vegetable matter than through hunting of the largely arboreal and often elusive forest fauna. However, considerable investments of time and technical ingenuity in hunting characterize many groups.

The recognition that, in areas other than those at extreme latitudes, vegetable products predominate in the diet of foraging groups, has contributed to a general reassessment of previously widely held beliefs that the livelihood of non-farmers was usually precarious. Calling hunting-gathering groups in general the "original affluent society" as has been done by some anthropologists (e.g., Service, 1966; Lee and DeVore, 1968; Sahlins, 1972) may overstate the ease and reliability with which food can be acquired through foraging. Nevertheless, it may indeed be a more accurate characterization of hunter-gatherer life than the previously popular one of life in the "state of nature" as "nasty, brutish, and short".

SHIFTING CULTIVATORS

Far more important today as a method of resource use in tropical forested areas are the various forms of impermanent field agriculture called by researchers shifting cultivation, swidden, bush fallowing, or slash-and-burn, and by their practitioners *milpa* (Mexico and Central America),

ladang (Indonesia), *caingin* (Philippines), *citimene* (parts of Africa), and by many other local designations. In its various forms, shifting cultivation is believed to be employed by at least 240 million people (UNESCO, 1978, p. 469), principally in the humid tropics. Broadly viewed, shifting cultivation is a technology that during earlier historical periods was practiced in virtually every arable area of the earth, but today survives as a major food-getting method only in tropical regions. The persisting importance of this agricultural type in the lower latitudes has been attributed to various characteristics of both the tropical regions and of their inhabitants. Ignorance of proper agricultural techniques and avarice on the part of the cultivators were often cited in the past as reasons why tropical farmers appeared to use land wastefully. Swiddeners were observed to farm one area for a year or two, and then seemingly to "abandon" the supposedly "exhausted" area to invasion by weed species, only to go on to clear yet another plot, burn off the slashed vegetation, and plant crops in the ashes of this new temporary field.

Once the rather low average labor requirement per hectare farmed by shifting methods was determined, a low capacity for work among tropical populations, supposedly usually malnourished and weakened by parasitic diseases, was cited as a cause of the almost pan-tropical popularity of shifting cultivation (Gourou, 1953). The detailed study of shifting cultivation systems as well as of tropical soil and agronomic conditions has led gradually to a new perspective on this ancient farming method (e.g., DeSchlippe, 1956; Conklin, 1957, 1961; Nye and Greenland, 1960, Allan, 1965). Numerous investigations have shown that in many instances swiddening neither exhausts soil nutrients (Sanchez, 1972; Greenland, 1975), nor leads to excessive erosion (Kellman, 1969; Lal, 1974), nor does it reflect laziness or debility on the part of its practitioners. Increasingly, field investigations suggest that shifting cultivation is a way of farming particularly well suited to conditions often characteristic of humid tropical areas: rather infertile soils, a biotic store of nutrients, intense competition of weed species and attacks by pests and diseases, and unavailability of animal manures as well as of chemical fertilizers and pesticides. The practice of "rotating fields rather than crops", which is the most characteristic feature of shifting cultivation, is frequently although not necessarily accompanied by other patterns which have been identified as good agronomic practices for the particular conditions prevailing in the humid tropics. Among these practices are: intercropping of food, fiber and medicinal plants in diverse, multi-storied fields reminiscent of the forest they replace, little or no tillage of easily eroded tropical soils, and maintenance of cropping–fallow regimes that allow for periodic regeneration of woody growth in old fields and subsequent succession to forests.

Although almost invariably having much higher population densities than do foragers, swiddeners rarely live in permanent settlements of more than a few hundred; the land requirements per capita for this agricultural system are high. Much larger settlements would lead to the necessity of either shifting entire villages every few years or of traveling inconvenient distances to outlying fields; most prehistoric urban centers once believed to have been supported purely by shifting cultivation (see Dumond, 1961) are now thought to have relied heavily on more land-intensive forms of agriculture as well (Harrison and Turner, 1978). But land not in crops in any particular year is hardly considered by shifting cultivators to be useless or used up. Often it is being fallowed deliberately, to be again farmed after a period of years; and in the meantime, it serves as a source of wood and other materials for food, housing, fuel and other needs, as well as a habitat for wild or domesticated animals important in the diet or economy of the farmers.

PERMANENT-FIELD FARMERS

Most forms of agriculture other than the intermittent shifting cultivation should perhaps not be included in a discussion of the human use of tropical forests since these necessitate the permanent and widespread removal of forests. However, as will be discussed more fully below, permanent-field farmers are often also partial or periodic forest users or dwellers, and so a discussion of their resource use patterns is not excluded here. Often these more permanent or more land-intensive types of agriculture are combined with the other forms of subsistence discussed above, or are employed for only limited periods of time or are found on the edges of forested areas.

In several areas of the humid tropics, traditional food production systems are extremely high yielding and support populations of several hundred per square kilometer even after centuries of continuous use. Perhaps the most impressive of these agricultural types are systems for the cultivation of inundated rice in south and Southeast Asia. The great productivity and success of these systems rests largely on the maintenance of complex interactions between rice plants and irrigation waters containing both nitrogen-fixing blue-green algae and soil nutrients carried from the waters' source regions (Grist, 1965). The waters frequently also provide the farmers with a substantial animal protein supply in the form of fish. The great deltaic padi farming areas of Southeast Asia as well as the spectacular terracing and irrigation works of the Philippines, Indonesia, and Sri Lanka have long been counted among the greatest agricultural achievements of pre-industrial man. Less well-known but also highly and continuously productive are some dryland farming systems, such as the "banana cultures" of humid East Africa (Allan, 1965), where composting and manuring of ancient fields planted chiefly to varieties of bananas have allowed for their centuries-long continuous use. Intensive cultivation of tubers in Melanesia and Polynesia, often combined with some tree cropping, has supported very high population densities and permanent settlements on islands and in mountain valleys with limited room for population expansion (Brookfield and Hart, 1971; Barrau, 1958, 1961). Recent research has yielded evidence of intensive farming systems, previously little known and little appreciated, in several areas of pre-Hispanic Central and South America (Denevan, 1970; Denevan and Zucchi, 1978; Harrison and Turner, 1978). Maintaining effective control of soil moisture through irrigation and drainage, of slope through terracing and levelling of hills, and of soil fertility through composting and manuring, these systems were once widespread in many neotropical areas, but survive to the present day in only a few limited sites (Denevan, 1980).

OTHER TYPOLOGIES

The division of traditional resource use into three general types, hunting-gathering, shifting cultivation and permanent-field agriculture — the broadest of common typologies — can be of value: it does point out some very broad ecological, as well as social and demographic differences and similarities among tropical forest dwellers.

However, while useful for some needs and purposes, this typology — as obviously all typologies — fails to include information necessary for other purposes. Shifting cultivators in tropical forests, for instance, are said to be limited to "maximum" population densities which various authors have calculated to be as high as $400 \, \text{km}^{-2}$ (UNESCO, 1978) and as low as $10 \, \text{km}^{-2}$ (Gourou, 1953); shifting cultivators as a group have been highly praised as conservators and flatly condemned as destroyers. These apparent contradictions are not actually contradictions at all; neither are they evidence only of grave misperceptions on the part of observers. Rather, they are proof that a very broad spectrum of behavior has been included in the category of shifting cultivation. When such generalizations either lauding or condemning shifting agriculture lead to the formulation of policy, as they have often done in the past, and to consequent government action, their accuracy becomes important, and very broad generalizations usually cease to be useful.

Numerous reworkings and refinements of the very broad typology outlined above have been suggested, reflecting objections not only to the excessive generality of the scheme, but also to its failure to accommodate many "intermediate" types of resource use, and to what some observers believe is an inappropriate focus on intensity of land use (see Brookfield and Hart, 1971).

While hunting-gathering groups in tropical forests are now so few and remain so little studied that their technologies have rarely been further subdivided except in special cases like the division of the African Ituri Forest's pygmy populations into Mbuti net and spear hunters (Turnbull, 1968), the techniques of farming subsumed under the general categories of shifting and permanent-field cultivation have been further broken down in many ways.

Conklin, in a seminal work (1957), distinguished partial and integral systems of shifting cultivation, and subdivided each class further in two: partial systems into supplementary and incipient, integral into pioneer and established. This classification

system suggests important differences in traditional knowledge of methods of farming, in the importance of shifting cultivation to the local economies, and its integration with community culture, as well as differences in the use by farmers of previously felled as against unfelled forests. Each of these distinctions may be very important in evaluating a shifting cultivator group's impact on tropical forests, as well as the impact upon the group of any program aimed at changing the group's agricultural methods or altering its access to forested lands.

A similar identification of differing levels of skill, competence, and length of tradition, and allegedly of conservativeness of resource use, is inherent in Watters' (1971) scheme of dividing shifting cultivation into "traditional" systems and those "imposed by necessity". The former types are, according to Watters, generally stable and conservative of forest environments, whereas the latter are frequently devastating.

Far more refined and intricate, involving intersecting values of numerous criteria, are typologies suggested by Miracle (1967) for African systems, and Spencer (1966) for those of Southeast Asia. The latter classification, for instance, takes into account patterns of field shifts, of the farmers' residence, of tools and of crop type, and subdivides each of these criteria into several types.

A specific focus on principal crop types in tropical cultivation systems, particularly on the distinction between those cultigens that are vegetatively reproduced and those that reproduce by seeds, is the main feature of typologies particularly important to archeologists and other students of plant domestication and crop diffusion (e.g., Sauer, 1952; Spencer, 1966, ch. 6). While all researchers have stressed the almost universal practice among shifting cultivators of interplanting numerous crops, even shifting tropical agriculturists are often associated with a particular "staple" crop or "crop complex". Identification by principal cultigen may be somewhat more appropriate in classifying permanent-field cultivators, who more frequently isolate crops in fields, although they also rarely rely on one cultigen.

It is likely that most researchers appreciate the complexity and variability of permanent-field cultivation, having seen it frequently in their home midlatitudes. Therefore, extremely broad and supposedly universally applicable classifications of permanent-field agriculture in the tropics are encountered less frequently than are such classifications of more unfamiliar resource use techniques. Attempts at ordering localized agricultural systems tend to note differences between irrigated and rainfed farms, drained and dryland, terraced and unterraced, to draw distinctions in tools or cultivation methods (hoes, plows, etc.), or to classify by dominant crop or crop combination. Very specialized categorizations of, for instance, types of terracing (Spencer and Hale, 1961; Donkin, 1979), have also been done.

But rather than further subdividing and refining the usual, familiar classifications of resource use systems, some researchers have criticized the basis of all these typologies and have suggested that they do not necessarily highlight an exploitation system's most significant attributes, nor can they accommodate many systems. Among these critics, Brookfield (Brookfield and Hart, 1971) has suggested that a ranking of Melanesian cultivation systems according to the intensity of land use or their cultivation fallow ratio, as is usually done, is in many cases neither enlightening nor appropriate. He cites an example of a Melanesian group of cultivators who alter soil, slope and drainage by carefully terracing and irrigating fields, but then fallow them for extended periods of time (Brookfield, 1968), and argues that "the degree to which the ecosystem is modified by tillage, mounding, permanent clearance of forest, control of fallow cover, soil drainage and site drainage, irrigation and ponding, exclusion of livestock, weeding of the plot, prevention of erosion and deliberate fertilization" (Brookfield and Hart, 1971, p. 89), can all be as significant or even more significant than the cultivation/fallow ratio in classifying agricultural systems. Brookfield's typology of Melanesian systems, according to a very large number of attributes, is probably the most complete and sophisticated, if cumbersome, classification of traditional cultivation systems in the humid tropics (Brookfield and Hart, 1971).

Other systems, for instance, the tending of swamp padi in areas of Borneo where rice is planted in periodically flooded areas and tended with techniques largely identical to those used in swidden or shifting cultivation plots, except that the fields are rarely fallowed, also resist classification within the usual categories. In this, as in many other cases, the cropping/fallow ratio is not particularly useful in assessing either the cultivators' impact on the environment or their need for land. Other techniques often considered diagnostic of shifting cultivation systems, that is, burning of felled vegetation before cropping and allowing natural fallows to revegetate the land after it, are absent from some cultivation technologies that otherwise conform to classic descriptions of swidden systems. The Noanama' of Colombian high rainfall areas mulch rather than burn the slash that is cut (Eder, 1963), and Timor's Atoni, among other groups, replant fallows rather than allow natural succession to take place (Ormeling, 1956).

OTHER PROBLEMS IN CLASSIFICATION: IMPRECISE BOUNDARIES

Another traditional distinction between resource use systems is increasingly being questioned by researchers. This is the contrast between hunting-gathering or foraging and any form of cultivation. The two types of food-getting technology have been assumed to be easily distinguishable and also, as noted above, to be associated with greatly differing population densities, patterns of social organization, and radically different effects on the surrounding tropical forest environment.

Both recent archeological and ethnographic research into traditional subsistence have suggested that in many instances clear distinctions between agriculture and gathering cannot be made. Rather than there being a strict dichotomy between gathering and cultivating a continuum of resource use from the definitely gathered to the definitely cultivated, through varying degrees of "managed" resources, can in fact be detected (Bronson, 1975; Harris, 1977). For instance, according to Harris (1977), some Melanesian "hunter-gatherers" in pre-European times are believed to have relied heavily for their subsistence on the seeds of the palm-like cycad *Cycas media*. The cycads were not planted, but their productivity was probably enhanced by controlled and deliberate burning which cleared competing vegetation, stimulated asexual reproduction of the plant, and made harvesting of the seeds easier. Large stands of cycads on the Cape York Peninsula of Australia have been identified as probable artifacts of aboriginal manipulation —

although hardly cultivation — of this species. The food yield of some of those stands is alleged to compare favorably with the per area yields of some cultivated crops.

The distinction between gathering and agriculture is also blurred in the case of the sago eaters of Southeast Asia and the Pacific Islands, who cannot and do not distinguish between naturally occurring and planted stands of the sago palm (*Metroxylon sagu*), an important starch source in parts of the region (Tan, 1977; Ruddle et al., 1978). Likewise, economies based on the tapping of the lontar palm (*Borassus flabellifer*) as a food staple in the eastern islands of the Indonesian archipelago pose a classification problem. The very high population densities supported primarily by this technology (102 persons km^{-2} on the island of Savu) and the subsistence specialization and deliberate care of the palm make them hardly comparable to other hunting-gathering societies (Fox, 1977).

DIVERSITY OF SUBSISTENCE TECHNIQUES

However, no matter how elaborated or precise the classifications of resource use become or how well they accommodate "intermediate" types or variations, most conventional descriptions and reviews of traditional technologies still give an incomplete and misleading view of how people make a living, because they fail to mention the diversity of food-getting technologies used by each population. By assigning each group of traditional tropical forest dwellers to a particular category of resource users, most studies tend to obscure the fact that members of these groups rely simultaneously or serially on several different ways of exploiting resources.

For instance, the latest, and surely most convincing answers to long-debated questions concerning the subsistence of the pre-Colombian Mayas of Central America — did they depend on shifting cultivation or on tree crop cultivation, or on intensive farming? — are that they most probably depended on all of these technologies in varying measure at varying times (Harrison and Turner, 1978). Recent investigations suggest that shifting cultivation, both long and short fallow, of the typical Latin American crop mixes — corn, beans, squashes, etc. — was carried on by Mayans, as was

intensive farming of several types, including terraced dry-field cultivation, heavily intercropped house or kitchen gardens, cultivation of the *ramon* or breadnut tree (*Brosimum alicastrum*) in orchards near the houses, as well as tending of an array of other tree crops, vine crops, root crops and seed crops in extremely complex "artificial rain forests" (Wiseman, 1978). This last may have largely involved "managed" rather than strictly cultivated crops, resulting more from selective clearing and protected burning of natural forests than from clear-cutting and planting of desired plants. Dry-field Mayan farming was supplemented with several wet or periodically inundated varieties of agriculture, including the use of raised drained fields for subsistence crop cultivation in low-lying swampy areas, and of irrigated, continuously cropped dryland fields. Mayan diets doubtless also benefited significantly from the gathering of wild and tended forest plants and from hunting and fishing of both spontaneously occurring and somewhat "managed" animals and fish populations. It is probable that as population densities varied spatially and temporally, as climates grew wetter and drier, and as centralized control over Mayan food producers waxed and waned, the several food-getting technologies mentioned above changed in their relative importance. A great variety of subsistence sources was probably, however, available to most Mayan communities most of the time.

Information gathered in many other areas of the humid tropics confirms that the Mayan situation is not atypical. A review of archeological findings of several ancient Asian cities and high civilizations — among them Angkor, Prambanan, and Anuradhapura — shows that each was supported by a variety of agricultural technologies, including shifting cultivation, irrigated farming, and the intensive cultivation of dry land gardens (Bronson, 1978).

Often when no evidence of multiple farming techniques combined with other subsistence activities is mentioned in descriptions of forest-dwelling populations, the reason is an omission on the part of the ethnographer. Accustomed to associating a particular group with a particular type of subsistence activity, researchers often ignore or mention only very briefly subsidiary kinds of resource use. Among such frequently ignored or unnoticed food production technologies is the cultivation of a house or kitchen garden. An areally small, vegetatively and architecturally complex, and, to a mid-latitude observer, visually confusing production system, the kitchen garden, as recent research indicates, figures importantly in the subsistence of tropical populations on all continents. In Latin America it has been estimated that the Karinya of the Orinoco Basin derive 20% of their total subsistence needs from their house gardens (W.M. Denevan, pers. comm.). (This group, which exploits both forest and savanna environments, also cultivates four different kinds of dryland swiddens, three kinds of seasonally flooded permanently cropped fields and two types of ditched and drained fields in natural swamps.) In more densely settled areas of South America, the importance of house gardens is even greater. On the eastern slope of the Peruvian Andes, many of the residents of the town of Moyobamba gain more than half of their annual food needs from the complex, continuously cropped and harvested gardens surrounding their houses (W.M. Denevan, pers. comm.).

The continuing importance of gathering, as well as of hunting and fishing in the subsistence of agricultural peoples is also often unappreciated. Data on the use of spontaneously occurring species is certainly hard to gather and equally hard to find in ethnographies, but the few accounts that do include information on wild foods cite surprisingly high numbers of species used and high estimates of their dietary significance (see Blackwood, 1940; Barrau, 1962, and Morren, 1974, 1977, cited in UNESCO, 1978, p. 439; Dunn, 1975; Kunstadter, 1978). The agricultural Hanunoo of the southern Philippines, for instance, identify over 1000 uncultivated species of plants and use many of them. Many of these species probably are to some degree "managed" (Conklin, 1957). Field crops of shifting cultivators like the Iban of Sarawak tend to be seasonal. When the cultivated plant foods are unavailable, wild or "managed" plant species become most important; especially significant in the Iban diet are ferns of several genera, bamboo shoots, and the heart of a variety of palms. The pith of many palms, including sago, some planted but little cared for and some naturally occurring, also figure importantly in Bornean and other diets as "famine food", to be eaten when favored agricultural crops fail.

Even among Mexican peasants, seemingly long

and far removed from a hunting-gathering economy, gathering can be an important activity, primarily among the poor. The present-day reliance of farmers in Tlaxcala on many species of wild plants and animals — particularly aquatic species — has been alleged to be not unlike ancient Aztec exploitation patterns (Wilken, 1970).

At times the variety in resource use patterns has doubtless reflected variation in the forest environment. In Southeast Asia, for instance, low lying, swampy areas are traditionally cleared and cropped frequently, often annually, with wet rice; the water levels in the resulting fields are sometimes carefully controlled, sometimes not. Better drained hill slopes in the region are planted to more drought-tolerant hill rice varieties, and are usually fallowed longer than they are cropped. Variations in Melanesian agricultural systems often similarly follow environmental differences, with specialized crops and technologies particularly adapted to differing conditions of altitude, drainage, and soil type (Brookfield and Hart, 1971).

However, in many cases variations in resource use reflect not inherent natural differences between areas, but manmade differences. For instance, the planting of particular combinations of crops and use of particular tools often follows differing patterns of previous human use of sites. Crops that do well in virtually weed-free first-year swiddens often cannot withstand the vegetative competition in older fields. Thus, crop rotations are combined with natural fallows in many systems. The Azande pattern of farming, which includes the planting of numerous, intricate crop associations and variable crop successions is a well-documented example from the dry tropics of a pattern that is prevalent in the wet tropics as well (DeSchlippe, 1956).

Although infrequently noted by observers, it is probable that many tropical shifting cultivators vary the kinds of fields they plant each year — combining a first-year swidden with an older one; a hill-side one with a poorly drained one. Even if, as in the case of the Iban of Sarawak, much the same crop assemblage appears in each kind of field, the variation in labor requirements between the different kinds of fields, and their differing susceptibility to drought or failure because of an inadequate burn in clearing, make a variety of annual fields desirable (Padoch, 1978; Hatch, 1979).

Among other variables often related to differing

cultivation patterns are population density and distance from the farmer's residence or village. Fields nearer to homesteads and to larger population concentrations will tend to be cropped more frequently. The most intensive, continuously producing areas are usually the house or kitchen gardens immediately surrounding the homestead and frequently fertilized daily with household refuse (DeSchlippe, 1956; Netting, 1968).

Having noted the usual large variety in subsistence activities carried on by tropical forest populations, one is led to speculate as to the factors, other than environmental differences, responsible for the persistence of such complex patterns. Without discussing the topic at length here, we may mention, as factors that come immediately to mind, the desire to vary and spread out labor requirements, to hedge one's bets against any variations in weather, and to get a varied and thus probably more nutritionally complete diet.

However, the employment of a fixed, if varied, repertoire of agricultural and other subsistence techniques is not the traditional forest dweller's only way of coping with variation in environmental and social factors. Despite the conventional view of traditional technologies as centuries-old and immutable, flexibility and quick adjustment to both short-term fluctuations and to gradual, secular changes is probably more characteristic of such systems.

FLEXIBILITY AND CHANGE IN RESOURCE USE

The myth of totally unchanging pre-industrial foragers and farmers is immediately challenged when inventories of crops and collected products used by even the most remote groups are examined. All evidence points to frequent and quick acceptance of any opportunities to plant new species which are perceived to be useful. For instance, the early and widespread use of New World cultigens in the Old World, and vice versa, testifies to the eagerness of indigenous farmers to experiment; American maize has for centuries been a staple of many "conservative" African swiddeners, as well as an important crop of isolated tribesmen in Southeast Asia and Oceania; Old World rice is a dietary staple in many parts of the New World.

Among many peoples new planting material is deliberately sought whenever the farmer travels away from home (Brookfield and Hart, 1971; Padoch, 1978). As will be discussed at greater length below, new crops to be sold or bartered, and new uncultivated products gathered and sold to a changing market, are often among innovations eagerly accepted (Dunn, 1975; Pelzer, 1978). For example, within about a decade of the introduction of systematic rubber cultivation by colonialists in Southeast Asia, remote swiddeners in Sumatra and Borneo had planted the tree crops in their own fields (Pelzer, 1978). Clearly, traditional farmers and foragers can respond quickly and appropriately, not only to the stresses and vicissitudes their environments periodically offer, but to new opportunities as well (Vayda, 1979).

In adapting to changes in their environments, traditional forest populations will of course not only vary the products that they use, but also the subsistence techniques they employ, the amount of labor they expend, as well as any number of other social factors; and the sources of the changes that affect them are not invariably "outside" pressures or influences, but rather are frequently changes engendered by the traditional groups' own subsistence or other activities (see Boserup, 1965; Clarke, 1971; Street, 1969).

Not even forest-dwelling hunter-gatherers are the completely equilibrated, unchanging resource users they are commonly believed to be. A number of observers has recently argued that the environmental impact of small non-agricultural groups has been greatly understated, and that foraging activities have led to considerable change and selection of forest species (Harris, 1977; Rambo, 1978). Tropical forest hunter-gatherers have, no doubt, driven a few species to extinction and have influenced the numbers and range of many. Having caused change, they have then more or less successfully varied their activities in response to it.

The accuracy of our view of the processes of change among populations of foragers and shifting cultivators has doubtless been limited by both the inadequacy of histories and ethnographic accounts that are available, and by our preoccupation with the extremely rapid, often devastating changes of the last few decades. But the available historical and comparative studies of traditional tropical populations discredit the widely prevailing view that total social disorganization and breakdown of resource use systems in the face of overpowering modern economic and political forces are the only significant changes that groups of shifting cultivators and others have experienced over the last few centuries. Street, in an article arguing against prevailing "assumptions of technological and gastronomic stagnation" (1969, p. 104) among traditional groups, cites several examples to illustrate his point. Among the populations he mentions are the Kara of Lake Victoria, who, when faced with land shortage, abandoned their land extensive methods and turned to more intensive farming, including the use of manures, and a New Guinean people temporarily confined to a restricted area and unable to continue a shifting form of agriculture, who were observed to readily adopt a more land- and labor-intensive type.

A recently completed study of several upland communities in the Malaysian state of Sarawak (Borneo) also serves to show that flexibility and variability of resource use may be typical of a population of traditional shifting cultivators (Padoch, 1978). Iban farmers in several communities were observed to differ in their patterns of farming, in the cropping–fallow regimes their fields were subject to, in patterns of farm labor and of land tenure, as well as in the patterns and rates of emigration and expansion of the population. The ability of Iban to regulate growth of their own population by limiting fertility was also documented. These observed variations in resource use and other activities among the Iban showed both a propensity and ability of these "traditional" folk to expand and make use of available lands and resources, as well as an ability to use resources more sparingly and conservatively when altered circumstances made a change in behavior desirable.

Using historical and comparative data, other studies have confirmed that flexibility and change are not only not unknown or atypical of tropical forest societies, but that the direction of change in resource use among such groups is also variable. A sequence of land or resource use from less to more intensive, from hunting-gathering, through intermittent cropping to annual or even double cropping of areas is not a necessary sequence, and does not sum up the history of all or even most regions. Periods of disintensification of land use have alternated with periods of intensification in most areas.

Those tropical regions which in the last several centuries have experienced significant depopulation due to invasion, epidemics, and colonialism, most notably the American tropics, areas of Africa and the Pacific Islands, have recorded long histories of declines in the intensity of land use, histories illustrated by the many abandoned agricultural terraces, irrigation and drainage works still evident. Denevan (1980) reports that the larger part of the extensive systems of drained field cultivation once found in both tropical lowlands and uplands of South America were abandoned subsequent to European invasion and the ensuing depopulation of the continent. These once intensively cropped raised fields ceased to be farmed in traditional ways and were never revived or modernized. Similarly in Melanesia, Brookfield and Hart (1971, p. 122) have noted a "widespread retrogression in cultivation practices, a process which may by no means be at an end in Melanesia." On the islands of the New Hebrides, the Solomons and Fiji, previously important intensive cultivation practices have almost totally disappeared from the repertoire of traditional farmers.

While the two examples of disintensification cited above are surely more extreme and of longer duration than the changes in resource use that we suggest have occurred frequently, we have used them as examples because evidence of less dramatic changes, not involving visible earth works, is often difficult to confirm. Variations in the intensity of land and resource use are frequently very short-lived, reflecting a population's changing military fortunes, the passing effects of a natural disaster, market booms and busts, or other ephemeral factors. Increased pressures of whatever nature may lead a population to temporarily intensify its use of resources; a relaxation of those pressures may result in a rapid disintensification (Dumond, 1961; Bronson, 1972).

Researchers have suggested that even shifts from a predominantly agricultural to a mainly foraging resource use pattern have not been infrequent among tropical peoples, although solid evidence of such "retrogressions" may often be lacking. The suggestion is supported by the view widely held among researchers that foragers are usually not ignorant of agricultural techniques (Schrire, 1980). Frequently they do not farm because they do not perceive it as advantageous to their well-being to do so.

Observers of recent government-sponsored and spontaneous migrations of peoples from densely to sparsely settled tropical areas, have commented on the almost universal tendency — despite government discouragement — of such pioneers to adopt land-extensive, swiddening patterns of agriculture (Kartawinata et al., 1977; Kampto Utomo, 1975). Such modern examples of disintensification are surely similar to changes in resource use systems that have throughout history followed or accompanied changes in a variety of factors: variations in population structure and density, introduction or development of new crops, new techniques, and long- or short-term geophysical changes. Rather than an uneventful continuum, the history of most traditional groups is probably one of constant change; greater and lesser adjustments in resource use and population are made, with the result that, as Brookfield and Hart suggests for Melanesia, "a continual imbalance [is] ... maintained" (1971, p. 92), and new, always imperfect readjustments take the place of previous ones.

THE IMPORTANCE OF EXTERNAL TRADE

Just as the recent very rapid rate of change in resource exploitation worldwide has led many observers to overlook or understate the importance of pre-industrial changes in resource use, so also the dramatic increase of global economic interconnectedness and dependence of industrialized agriculture on materials from far beyond the consumers' home environs has led commentators to assume that traditional systems by contrast have always been totally self-contained and self-sufficient. While it cannot be denied that regional interdependence and trade were in most instances less crucial in the past than in the present, important and often extensive trade networks have long existed in most areas of the humid tropics, predating large cities and even agriculture.

Certainly in the forests of Southeast Asia, the totally isolated foraging group, harvesting only that which it consumed and subsisting purely on the fruits of its own localized environment, has hardly existed for millennia. Dunn (1975), using ethnographic descriptions of present-day Malayan aboriginal groups as well as historical accounts and archeological evidence, suggests that both today's

forest dwellers and their predecessors have long maintained a lively trade in forest produce. Trading relationships have always linked many, often diverse, inland groups, and exchanges with Malayan coastal peoples have probably steadily increased in importance since about 10 000 years before the present. Sometime between 5000 and 4000 B.P., Dunn estimates, an external commerce between Malayan traders and merchants from beyond the peninsula gained in importance. So for several thousands of years, the supposedly "isolated" Orang Asli of the Malay Peninsula — some predominantly hunter-gatherers, some shifting cultivators — have exported products of their surroundings, including rattans, damar, wild rubbers, camphor, and oils, to other parts of the Archipelago, to China and eventually to the West. Dunn's surveys indicate that collecting and sale of uncultivated forest products remains an important economic activity in present-day Malayan forest communities, and that the products obtained through trade are considered necessities by the Orang Asli.

Market trade carried on by populations often considered isolated and remote may have significant indirect as well as direct effects. Across the South China Sea from Malaya's Orang Asli, many shifting cultivators and foragers of Sarawak and Kalimantan (Borneo) have long participated in market trade, collecting and selling products of the island's high forests. Among hinterland groups engaged in the gathering and selling of "jungle produce" the previously mentioned Iban rank prominently. The very earliest Iban oral histories, going back many centuries, speak of the visits of traders to hardly accessible villages, and of the eagerness of mythical heroes to obtain brassware and ceramics manufactured in coastal areas or across the sea in China. The Iban indigenous legal system has for centuries rested on the systematic payment of fines in trade goods, and young Iban men have traditionally sought to prove their worth by making lengthy journeys and bringing back trade items, ceramics, brassware, and, more recently, firearms, outboard motors and money (Sandin, 1967; Freeman, 1970; Pringle, 1970; Padoch, 1978). Trade has always brought luxury items as well as some daily necessities into Iban households. But the Ibans' participation in market trade may be credited with a greater importance for the society than the actual flow of products might suggest. Field research (Padoch, 1978) indicates that the journeying and extended male absences — often several years at a time — associated with obtaining market goods, tend to relieve both short-term consumer pressure in some densely settled areas, and to keep down fertility and hence population growth [cf. similar patterns in African populations (Southall, 1967; Ghansah and Aryee, 1967) and in Melanesian groups (Maher, 1961)]. The items obtained through trade also allow for a higher population density in Iban areas than might have been locally supported; trade goods become especially important when poor agricultural yields locally reduce food supplies. Thus, market trade, the desire or need for non-local products, has played a more central role in patterns of Iban settlement and life than the relatively few trade goods traditionally visible around the house might indicate.

The Indonesian archipelago is also of course the homeland of travelers, traders and cash croppers far more famous and accomplished than the Iban or the Orang Asli. Groups such as the Buginese (Bugis) of southern Sulawesi (Celebes) have pioneered and colonized the coasts of many islands, traded and marauded over thousands of square kilometers of sea (Lineton, 1975). While the Buginese may be exceptional among traditional peoples in the extent of their traveling and trading operations, a long-standing and active involvement in trade is not at all atypical among the supposedly isolated and self-sufficient groups of the world's humid tropics. Today, forest-dwelling shifting cultivators, planting small patches of rubber, pepper, coffee, copra and benzoin, contribute a very significant percentage of Indonesia's export trade (Pelzer, 1978).

Close, often mutually dependent and occasionally exploitative relationships between tropical foragers and agriculturalists have been noted in many regions (Turnbull, 1968; Nicolaisen, 1976; Peterson, 1977, 1978), as have trading networks between coastal and interior regions, highlands and lowlands. The very extensive movement of goods and peoples through many altitudinal zones in the Andes has been investigated by several scholars (Murra, 1972; Orlove, 1977; Dillehay, 1979). Such "vertical" trade as well as seasonal movement of peoples throughout Andean regions continues to the present day.

A fuller recognition of the extent and importance of trade by pre-industrial groups not only calls into question generalizations concerning the self-sufficiency and integrity of such communities and further complicates the task of classification of groups. It also demonstrates the virtual impossibility of carrying out precise measurements of "carrying capacity" and relative stability of human groups and their particular ways of using resources, an activity once pursued by many researchers (Freeman, 1955; Conklin, 1959; Carneiro, 1961; Allan, 1965). Perhaps even more significantly, it suggests that the views long prevalent among development planners and others, that traditional rural folks have little experience with or interest in market trade, must be discounted, and explanations for the failure of some of these groups to enter the modern sector of the economy must be sought in factors other than ignorance or lack of interest (see Vayda, 1979; and the concept of the "wise rejector" put forward in Helleiner, 1975). And development efforts building upon, rather than completely replacing, traditional patterns of production and trade may accordingly be encouraged.

REFERENCES

Allan, 1965. The African Husbandman. Barnes and Noble, New York, N.Y.

Barrau, J., 1958. Subsistence agriculture in Melanesia. Bernice P. Bishop Mus. Bull., 219.

Barrau, J., 1961. Subsistence agriculture in Polynesia and Micronesia. Bernice P. Bishop Mus. Bull., 223.

Barrau, J., 1962. Les plantes alimentaires de l'Océanie, origines, distribution et usages. Musée Colonial de la Faculté des Sciences, Marseille.

Blackwood, B., 1940. Use of plants among the Kukukuku of Southeast Central New Guinea. In: Proceedings of 6th Pacific Science Congress.

Boserup, E., 1965. The Conditions of Agricultural Growth. Aldine, Chicago, Ill.

Bronson, B., 1972. Farm labor and the evolution of food production. In: B. Spooner (Editor), Population Growth: Anthropological Implications. MIT Press, Cambridge, Mass., pp. 190–218.

Bronson, B., 1975. The earliest farming: demography as cause and consequence. In: S. Polgar (Editor), Population, Ecology and Social Evolution. Mouton, The Hague., pp. 53–78.

Bronson, B., 1978. Angkor, Anuradhapura, Prambanan, Tikal: Maya subsistence in an Asian perspective. In: P.D. Harrison and B.L. Turner (Editors), Pre-Hispanic Maya Agriculture.

University of New Mexico Press, Albuquerque, N.M., pp. 255–300.

Brookfield, H.C., 1968. New directions in the study of agricultural systems in tropical areas. In: E.T. Drake (Editor), *Evolution and Environment*. Yale University Press, New Haven, Conn., pp. 413–439.

Brookfield, H.C. and Hart, D., 1971. *Melanesia: A Geographical Interpretation of an Island World*. Methuen, London.

Carneiro, R. L., 1961. Slash-and-burn cultivation among the Kuikuru and its implications for cultural development in the Amazon Basin. *Antropologica, Suppl.*, 2: 47–67.

Clarke, W.C., 1971. *Place and People: An Ecology of a New Guinean Community*. University of California, Berkeley, Calif.

Conklin, H.C., 1957. *Hanunoo Agriculture*. FAO, Rome.

Conklin, H.C., 1959. Shifting cultivation and succession to grassland climax. In: *Proceedings of Ninth Pacific Science Congress*, 7: 60–62.

Conklin, H.C., 1961. The study of shifting cultivation. *Curr. Anthropol.*, 2(1): 27–61.

Denevan, W.M., 1970. Aboriginal drained field cultivation in the Americas. *Science*, 169: 647–654.

Denevan, W.M., 1980. Traditional agricultural resource management in Latin America. In: G. Klee (Editor), *World Systems of Traditional Resource Managment*. V.H. Winston and Sons, Washington, D.C., pp. 235–245.

Denevan, W.M. and Zucchi, A., 1978. Ridged-field excavations in the Central Orinoco Llanos, Venezuela. In: D.L. Browman (Editor), *Advances in Andean Archeology*. Mouton, The Hague.

DeSchlippe, P., 1956. *Shifting Cultivation in Africa: The Zande System of Agriculture*. Routledge and Kegan Paul, London.

Dillehay, T.D., 1979. Pre-hispanic resource sharing in the Central Andes. *Science*, 204: 24–31.

Donkin, R.A., 1979. *Agricultural Terracing in the Aboriginal New World*. Viking Fund Publications in Anthropology, No. 56. University of Arizona Press, Tucson, Ariz.

Dumond, D.E., 1961. Swidden agriculture and the rise of Maya civilization. *Southwestern J. Anthropol.*, 17: 301–316.

Dunn, F.L., 1975. Rain-forest collectors and traders: A study of resource utilization in modern and ancient Malaya. *Malays. Branch R. Asiatic Soc., Monogr.*, No. 5.

Eder, H.W., 1963. *El Rio y El Monte*. ONR Report. Department of Geography, University of California, Berkeley, Calif.

Fox, J.J., 1977. *Harvest of the Palm: Ecological Change in Eastern Indonesia*. Harvard University Press, Cambridge, Mass.

Freeman, J.D., 1955. *Iban Agriculture: A Report on the Shifting Cultivation of Hill Rice by the Iban of Sarawak*. H.M.S.O., London.

Freeman, J.D., 1970. *Report on the Iban*. Athlone Press, London.

Ghansah, D.K. and Aryee, A.F., 1967. The demographic and social effects of migration in Ghana. In: *Proceedings of the World Population Conference, Belgrade, 1965*, 4. United Nations, New York, N.Y., pp. 199–201.

Gourou, P., 1953. *The Tropical World*. Longmans and Green, London.

Greenland, D.J., 1975. Bringing the green revolution to the shifting cultivator. *Science*, 190: 841–844.

Grist, D.H., 1965. *Rice*. Longman, London, 4th ed.

Harris, D.R., 1977. Subsistence strategies across Torres Strait. In: J. Allen, J. Golson and R. Jones (Editors), *Sunda and Sahul: Prehistoric Studies in Southeast Asia, Melanesia and Australia*. Academic Press, London, pp. 421–463.

Harrison, P.D. and Turner II, B.L. (Editors), 1978. *Pre-Hispanic Maya Agriculture*. University of New Mexico Press, Albuquerque, N.M.

Hatch, T., 1980. Shifting cultivation in Sarawak: past, present and future. In: J.I. Furtado (Editor), *Tropical Ecology and Development. Proc. Fifth Int. Symp. Tropical Ecology, 1979, Kuala Lumpur*, pp. 483–496.

Helleiner, G.K., 1975. Smallholder decision making: tropical African evidence. In: L.G. Reynolds (Editor), *Agriculture in Development Theory*. Yale University Press, New Haven, Conn., pp. 27–52.

Kampto Utomo, 1975. *Masyarakat Transmigran Spontan Didaerah Wai Sekampung (Lampung)*. Gadjah Mada University Press, Yogyakarta.

Kartawinata, K., Vayda, A.P. and Wirakusumah, R.S., 1977. East Kalimantan and the Man and Biosphere Program. *Berita Ilmu Pengetahuan dan Teknologi (Jakarta)*, 21(2): 16–27 (reprinted in *Borneo Res. Bull.*, April 1978).

Kellman, M.C., 1969. Some environmental components of shifting cultivation in upland mindanao. *J. Trop. Geogr.*, 28: 40–56.

Kunstadter, P., 1978. Ecological modification and adaptation: an ethnobotanical view of Lua' Swiddeners in northwestern Thailand. In: R. Ford (Editor), *The Nature and Status of Ethnobotany*. Museum of Anthropology, Ann Arbor, Mich., pp. 169–200.

Lal, R., 1974. Soil Erosion and Shifting Cultivation. In: *FAO/SIDA/ARCN Regional Seminar on Shifting Cultivation and Soil Conservation in Africa (Ibadan)*. FAO, Rome.

Lee, R.B., 1968. What hunters do for a living, or how to make out on scarce resources. In: R.B. Lee and I. De Vore (Editors), *Man the Hunter*. Aldine, Chicago, Ill., pp. 30–48.

Lee, R.B. and DeVore, I. (Editors), 1968. *Man the Hunter*. Aldine, Chicago, Ill.

Lineton, J., 1975. Pasompe' Ugi': Bugis Migrants and Wanderers. *Archipel*, 10: 173–201.

Maher, R.F., 1961. *New Men of Papua: A Study in Culture Change*. University of Wisconsin Press, Madison, Wis.

Miracle, M.P., 1967. *Agriculture in the Congo Basin*. University of Wisconsin Press, Madison, Wis.

Morren, G.E.B., 1974. *Settlement Strategies and Hunting in a New Guinea Society*. Dissertation, Columbia University, New York, N.Y. (unpublished).

Morren, G.E.B., 1977. From hunting to herding: pigs and the control of energy in montane New Guinea. In: T.P. Bayliss-Smith and R.G.A. Feachem (Editors), *Subsistence and Survival: Rural Ecology in the Pacific*. Academic Press, London, pp. 273–315.

Murra, J., 1972. El "control vertical" de un maximo de pisos ecologicos en la economia de las sociedades Andinas. In: J. Murra (Editor), *Visita de la Provincia de Leon de Huanuco en 1562*. Universidad Nacional Hermilio Valdizan, Huanaco.

Netting, R. McC., 1968. *Hill Farmers of Nigeria: Cultural*

Ecology of the Kofyar of the Jos Plateau. University of Washington Press, Seattle, Wash.

Nicolaisen, J., 1976. The Penan of Sarawak. *Folk*, 18: 205–236.

Nye, D.H. and Greenland, D.J., 1960. *The Soil Under Shifting Cultivation.* Commonwealth Agriculture Bureau, Harpenden.

Orlove, B.S., 1977. Integration through production: The use of zonation in Espinar. *Am. Ethnol.*, 4(1): 84–101.

Ormeling, F.J., 1956. *The Timor Problem.* Wolters, Groningen.

Padoch, C., 1978. *Migration and Its Alternatives Among the Iban of Sarawak.* Dissertation, Columbia University, New York, N.Y. (unpublished).

Pelzer, K.J., 1978. Swidden cultivation in Southeast Asia: historical, ecological, and economic perspectives. In: P. Kunstadter, E.C. Chapman and S. Sabhasri (Editors), *Farmers in the Forest.* University Press of Hawaii, Honolulu, Hawaii, pp. 271–286.

Peterson, J.T., 1977. The merits of margins. In: W. Wood (Editor), *Cultural-ecological perspectives on Southeast Asia.* Ohio University Center for International Studies, Athens, Ohio, pp. 48–62.

Peterson, J.T., 1978. The Ecology of Social Boundaries: Agta Foragers of the Phillipines. *Ill. Stud. Anthropol.*, 11.

Pringle, R., 1970. *Rajahs and Rebels. The Ibans of Sarawak Under Brooke Rule, 1841–1941.* Cornell University Press, Ithaca, New York.

Rambo, A.T., 1978. Primitive Man's Impact on Genetic Resources of the Malaysian Tropical Rain Forest. In: *SARRAO (Malaysia) Workshop on Genetic Resources of Plants, Animals and Microorganisms, Kuala Lumpur.*

Ruddle, K., Johnson, D., Townsend, P.K. and Rees, J.D., 1978. *Palm Sago: A Tropical Starch from Marginal Lands.* University Press of Hawaii, Honolulu, Hawaii.

Sahlins, M.D., 1972. *Stone Age Economics.* Aldine, Chicago, Ill.

Sanchez, P.A., 1972. Soil management under shifting cultivation. In: P.A. Sanchez (Editor), *A Review of Soils Research in Tropical Latin America.* North Carolina State University, Raleigh, N.C.

Sandin, B., 1967. *The Sea Dayaks of Borneo Before White Rajah Rule.* Michigan State University Press, East Lansing, Mich.

Sauer, C.O., 1952. *Agricultural Origins and Dispersals.* American Geographical Society, New York, N.Y.

Schrire, C., 1980. An inquiry into the evolutionary status and apparent identity of San hunter-gatherers. *Human Ecol.*, 8(1): 9–32.

Service, E.R., 1966. *The Hunters.* Prentice-Hall, Englewood Cliffs, N.J.

Southall, A., 1967. The demographic and social effects of migration on the populations of East Africa. In: *Proceedings of the World Population Conference, Belgrade, 1965, 4.* United Nations, New York, N.Y., pp. 235–238.

Spencer, J.E., 1966. *Shifting Cultivation in Southeastern Asia.* University of California Press, Berkeley, Calif.

Spencer, J.E. and Hale, G.A., 1961. The origin, nature and distribution of agricultural terracing. *Pac. Viewpoint*, 2: 1–40.

Steward, J., 1955. *Theory of Culture Change.* University of Illinois Press, Urbana, Ill.

Street, J.M., 1969. An evaluation of the concept of carrying capacity. *Prof. Geogr.*, 21(2): 104–107.

Tan, K. (Editor), 1977. *Papers of the First International Sago Symposium, Kuching, 1976.* Kemajuan Kanji Sdn. Bhd, Kuala Lumpur.

Turnbull, C.M., 1968. The importance of flux in two hunting societies. In: R.B. Lee and I. DeVore (Editors), *Man the Hunter.* Aldine, Chicago, Ill., pp. 132–137.

UNESCO, 1978. *Tropical Forest Ecosystems: A State-of-Knowledge Report. Prepared by UNESCO, UNEP and FAO. Nat. Resour. Res.*, 14: 683 pp.

Vayda, A.P., 1979. Human ecology and economic development in Kalimantan and Sumatra. *Borneo Res. Bull.*, 11: 23–32.

Watters, R.F., 1971. *Shifting Cultivation in Latin America.* FAO, Rome.

Wilken, G.C., 1970. The ecology of gathering in a Mexican farming region. *Econ. Bot.*, 24(3): 286–295.

Wiseman, F.M., 1978. Agricultural and historical ecology of the Maya lowlands. In: P.D. Harrison and B.L. Turner (Editors), *Pre-Hispanic Maya Agriculture.* University of New Mexico Press, Albuquerque, N.M., pp. 63–115.

Chapter 20

DISEASE-CAUSING ORGANISMS: COMPONENTS OF TROPICAL FOREST ECOSYSTEMS

THOMAS M. YUILL

Human activity in the tropical rain forest goes through a series of stages, each with its particular impact on the forest ecosystem, and each with its own risk of disease for man and his domestic animals. Man first enters the forest as a hunter or gatherer. Next, valuable timber trees may be cut, and people begin to live in the forest in longer-term camps. Settlers enter, make small openings in the forest to plant crops and establish pastures. This process continues, openings coalesce until only islands of the original forest, or perhaps no forest at all, remain. Settlement of forests may be impeded by diseases of humans or domestic animals. The attempted colonization of the Uruma area in 1954–55 by Okinawan settlers is an example of impacts of health-related problems on settlement schemes. The colony was established in a forested region on a tributary of the Amazon River in Nuflo de Chavez Province of Bolivia (Schaeffer et al., 1959). Some 400 healthy people, including men, women and children, arrived in August–September, 1954. "Jungle fevers" struck in late October, and the first fatal case soon occurred. The outbreak continued until the colony was abandoned the following July, and involved approximately half of the settlers. Fifteen people died. However, much of the settlement of tropical forests is done by individuals acting independently, rather than through officially organized and sponsored groups. Circumstances of illness and even death in people on isolated farms, remote from rural health centers, are likely to be superficially described or may not be reported at all. Thus, the impact of disease under these circumstances is difficult to assess. Unlike the striking epidemic of acute disease in the Uruma Forest settlers, a variety of sporadic illness such as fevers, colds, diarrhea due to a wide range of infectious

and parasitic organisms, are likely to occur. With the exception of diarrhea in young children, most of these episodes do not end in death, but many are very debilitating, and interfere significantly with the work efficiency of the afflicted individuals.

PARASITIC AND INFECTIOUS ORGANISMS

Parasitic and infectious organisms of vertebrates are every bit as real a part of the tropical forest biotic community as are the vertebrates that sustain them or the arthropods that may transmit them. Some of these organisms may be strictly parasitic, requiring living hosts for harborage, multiplication and dissemination. Others may be facultative, passing part of their lives as parasites. In either case, severe disease is an unusual event. It is not in the parasite's best interests to interfere significantly with the host population on which it depends. In nearly all host–parasite relationships of long standing, there has been sufficient time for selection of resistant hosts, and for attenuated (mild) strains of the infectious or parasitic organism. Catastrophic disease may occur when: (1) a host and parasite come into contact for the first time, and there has been no opportunity for selective adaptation of hosts and parasite; (2) host populations change, with numbers of susceptible individuals increasing, thus facilitating transmission of large numbers (a large "dose") of the parasite; or (3) the host defenses are compromised by malnutrition, advanced age, adverse environmental conditions, or other stressors. However, human activity does lead to changes in the size and structure of populations in and around tropical rain forests, and otherwise innocuous organisms have caused serious human and animal disease problems as a result.

Requirements for transmission and survival

The successful parasitic or infectious organism must be able to become established in or on its host, multiply, leave its host, and survive until the next host is encountered. Some parasitic organisms must end up in precisely the right tissue to initiate infection. Others are not so exacting; practically any tissue will do. The assault on the new host may be launched via a variety of routes. The organisms may float through the air, in aerosolized droplets and be inhaled. The droplet size will determine the depth of penetration of the respiratory tract, which may be critical for the initiation of infection. Parrot fever, for example, must be in tiny, deeply penetrating droplets to reach the tissue in which multiplication can begin (Burkhart and Page, 1971). If it gets stuck to mucous membranes higher up in the bronchioles, it cannot infect. Other parasitic organisms gain entry via the oral route, in contaminated food and water. Many parasites are transmitted up food chains. The intermediate stages of many parasites are found in the tissues of primary consumers. Predation of the consumer passes the parasites along to their new hosts, in which the adult stage is reached. Eggs or larvae pass out of the predator, contaminate the food supply of the primary consumer species, which ingest the parasites, completing the cycle. Still other organisms may be passed from host to host through sexual activity. The efficiency of venereal transmission will be influenced by the size, composition and stability of most breeding groups, and by breeding behavior and physiology of the host species. Some parasitic and infectious organisms are transported to the host by vertebrate or invertebrate vectors, which inject the organisms into the host when they bite. Entry into the host can also be gained by penetration of intact skin, or via the eyes by droplets, insect transport, or by the host's own grooming activity. *Dermatobia hominis*, the neotropical bot or "nuche", has a remarkable system of host seeking. The gravid female fly captures mosquitoes or biting flies and deposits her eggs on them. When these mosquitoes or flies feed on large mammals (including humans), the body warmth induces the eggs to hatch, and the larvae quickly penetrate the skin and undergo larval development as subcutaneous parasites until they reach a length of 18–24 mm, then they leave their boil-like pouches, fall to the ground and pupate in the soil (James, 1947). Exit of infectious and parasitic agents from the host employs these same routes; departure may be accomplished via feces, urine, respiratory or genital secretions, or biting arthropods.

Once out of the host, the infectious organism must be able to withstand a hostile environment, including such factors as drying, high temperatures, acid or alkaline pH, and ultraviolet rays. Parasites may have thick-walled eggs, or resistant cyst forms. Other parasites pass part of their developmental cycle as larvae outside of the host. These larvae move over limited distances, and seek out favorable microclimates while they await the arrival of new hosts. Ectoparasitic arthropods, especially flying insects, are relatively mobile, and can quickly seek out microclimates that are more favorable for survival. Bacteria may develop highly durable spores. Anthrax (*Bacillus anthracis*) spores in soil, for example, may remain infectious for their vertebrate hosts for decades, under a truly amazing range of environmental conditions. Some arthropod-borne viruses, such as yellow fever or equine encephalomyelitis viruses, are extremely fragile, and perish within a few hours outside of their host's or vector's cells, at tropical temperatures. However, in the normal course of their transmission cycles, they are not exposed to a hostile environment. These viruses go directly from their mammalian hosts into the vector mosquitoes, multiply, and then are inoculated into new mammalian hosts by bite. Temperature also can influence the relationship of the infectious organism and its insect vector. An increase in mean ambient temperature from 18° to 37°C shortens the extrinsic incubation period (time from ingestion of the infectious agent, development or multiplication in the vector, until transmission is possible) of yellow fever virus in *Aedes aegypti* from 36 to 4 days (Bres, 1976). Similarly, human malaria (*Plasmodium vivax*) requires 55 days to develop fully in anopheline mosquitoes at 16°C, 7 days at 28°C, but 32°C is detrimental to parasite development. Plague transmission halts when ambient temperatures exceed 27.5°C, because the plague bacillus (*Yersinia pestis*) cannot multiply sufficiently to block the gut of the flea vector to produce the voracious feeding behavior by the flea necessary to effectively spread this disease.

Life is simple for some infectious and parasitic

organisms. They have no sexual or complex developmental phases in their life cycle. Leptospires are a good example — they infect and multiply in their vertebrate host, pass out of the host with the urine, survive in surface water (assuming tolerable pH and other conditions), and infect the next vertebrate host that steps in their puddle or stream by penetration through the skin. Metazoan and protozoan parasites have more complicated life cycles, in which certain phases are accomplished in very specific host or vector tissues, and other stages may be as free-living forms, away from host or vector. If the host–parasite relationship is one of long-standing, the number of invading organisms small, and the host defenses normal, little overt disease may result. If these conditions are not met, the specific tissues for which the invading organism has affinity may be damaged, and disease will occur. Occasionally parasitic or infectious organisms blunder into host species in which normal development or subsequent escape is not possible. In many instances, these invading organisms are quickly eliminated by the defences of the aberrant, dead-end host. At other times, severe disease may result in the dead-end host. Visceral larval migrans is a good example. In this case the larvae of nematode parasites may wander throughout the body, damaging host tissue in the process, and causing blindness, brain and other nervous tissue damage.

Survival in a diverse ecosystem

Survival of infectious or parasitic organisms in any ecosystem depends on successful transmission to new susceptible hosts. The tropical rain forest presents some unique problems for parasite survival. Parasitic and infectious organisms employ two strategies for survival in tropical rain forests where host species diversity is great, but population densities of any given vertebrate species are low. They can be generalists, infecting many species of vertebrates, and perhaps be transmitted by a variety of vectors, or they can be specialists, confined to a limited number of host and vector species. A classical neotropical generalist is *Trypanosoma cruzi*, the protozoan parasite that causes Chagas disease in man (Zeledon, 1974; Arean, 1976). Approximately 150 mammal species are reservoirs, including such diverse forms as opossums, armadillos,

raccoons, skunks, and man. *T. cruzi* is transmitted by several species of Triatominae (cone-nosed or kissing bugs), including 12 of the 92 species in the New World. The generalists have an additional advantage if they infect vertebrates with high biotic potential and rapid rates of population turnover, so that old, immune cohorts are quickly replaced by new susceptible individuals. Rodents fit into this host category. Sylvan Venezuelan equine encephalitis virus is transmitted by several *Culex* (*Melanoconion*) species of mosquitoes to tropical swamp and forest rodents. Rodent population dynamics are such that the virus can be maintained indefinitely in geographically restricted foci.

Infectious and parasitic organisms that are specialists (occur in just one or a few taxa) survive in diverse tropical ecosystems by movement or by persisting in the host, vector or environment. Sylvan yellow fever is the classic example of movement. The virus is transmitted in the forest canopy among monkeys by *Haemagogus* spp. and *Sabethes* spp. mosquitoes in the neotropics, and by *Aedes africanus* in Africa (Johnson, 1975). Yellow fever produces an infection in primates that lasts but a few days, after which the monkey either dies or rapidly recovers and is immune for life. Yellow fever virus cannot persist indefinitely in one small area, sustained by a few primate troops. Monkey populations are small, individuals are long-lived and birth rates are low. There simply are not enough susceptible individuals present to support continuous transmission of the virus within the troop and the epidemic quickly "burns out". The result is that sylvan yellow fever occurs in wandering foci, sometimes over very extensive areas. For example, sylvan yellow fever progressed slowly up Central America in the early 1950s, apparently starting in northeast Colombia and ending in northern Guatemala (Trapido and Galindo, 1956).

In contrast to short, acute infection produced by yellow fever virus, other infectious and parasitic agents establish persistent infections, and accomplish transmission in the face of low host population density by means of a long period of infectivity. Parasitic protozoa and metazoa that inhabit the gastrointestinal tract are good examples of persistently infecting organisms. They live for many months to years, and produce thousands to millions of eggs or cysts. The eggs or cysts are resistant to adverse environmental conditions, and may remain viable for long periods of time. Thus, a single host can distribute an enormous number of eggs or cysts about its territory during its lifetime. If even one-thousandth of one percent of these eggs or cysts find their way into the next host, the parasite population can be sustained in the host population. These persistently infecting organisms seldom cause significant disease in their normal hosts. However, in host species with which the parasitic or infectious organisms have not had contact, and no selective processes have operated, severe disease and death may occur, as in the case of Bolivian hemorrhagic fever and Lassa fever both of which caused alarming epidemics when people first came in contact with these rodent viruses. Other organisms may produce short-term acute infection, but persist for long periods of time in the environment. Viable anthrax spores survive for decades in the soil. Other organisms may persist in their vectors for a long time. Kyasanur Forest disease virus produces acute infection in vertebrates, but tick vectors, although infected with the virus, are apparently not affected adversely and may live many months. The ticks are capable of transmitting the virus to the next generation through the egg (Singh et al., 1968).

DISEASE OF MAN AND ANIMALS IN THE FOREST

Man as a casual intruder

Entry of man into the forest, as a hunter, gatherer or even transient just passing through, exposes him to the risk of infection. The classical example is sylvan yellow fever (YF) in the neotropical rain forest (Boshell, 1957). While the primary transmission cycle goes on in the forest canopy (Fig. 20.1), our woodcutter, walking along the forest floor, can pass beneath the focus of transmission in the canopy unaware, except perhaps for the presence of dead howler monkeys, that anything is going on. He may get into trouble, however, when he cuts a tree, bringing the canopy down to ground level, along with infected mosquitoes that bite him. Because the woodcutter is apt to live in remote, rural areas, far from medical facilities, he likely is not vaccinated. Yellow fever still poses a major threat to the public health — not from the scattered cases that occur almost annually in the

Fig. 20.1. Sylvan (monkey) yellow fever is carried to rural and urban areas by individuals who become infected in the forest. The disease may reach epidemic proportions when the virus is spread from person to person by *Aedes aegypti* mosquitoes. (Drawing by Linda Bunkfeldt.)

forests of South America — but from the still present risk of urban "yellow jack". The forest is connected to villages, towns and cities by our woodcutter. The urban YF vector *Aedes aegypti* recently has reinvaded much of urban and rural South and Central America from which it had formerly been controlled (Pan American Health Organization, 1979). In many areas, vaccination programs have not been thorough. When our woodcutter goes to town while he is incubating the infection, or in the early stages of the disease, there is a significant possibility that an explosive epidemic of yellow jack may result among non-immunized residents of the area.

The hunter or gatherer is also at risk to other infectious and parasitic diseases. His risk is dependent on where he is, when he is there, and what he is doing. Individuals who venture into the forest in South America may develop mucocutaneous leishmaniasis (*espundia*) when *Lutzomyia* spp. sandflies transmit the organism (*Leishmania braziliensis*) from forest rodent reservoirs. This disease causes spreading, disfiguring open skin ulcers. Central American chicle gatherers may contract another form of cutaneous leishmaniasis (chiclero ulcer) when they enter the forests during the rainy season (Fig. 20.2) and are bitten by *Lutzomyia flaviscutellata* sandflies carrying the organism (*Leishmania mexicana*) from *Ototylomys* spp. and other forest rodents (Biagi, 1976). The prolonged epidemic of severe fever that caused the failure of the Okinawan settlement in Bolivia was caused, in

Fig. 20.2. The parasite that causes mucocutaneous leishmaniasis is transmitted between tropical rain forest rodents by sandflies. Humans become infected when they enter the forest and are bitten by these flies. (Drawing by Linda Bunkfeldt.)

part, by insect-transmitted Uruma virus (Schaeffer et al., 1959). Risk of infection by certain diseases may vary within the forest itself. If our hunter-gatherer camps near wet areas (streams, rivers, ponds, lakes, swamps) in the neotropics he may be exposed to *Culex* (*Melanoconion*) spp. mosquitoes carrying the sylvan form of Venezuelan equine encephalitis that is maintained in forest rodents and possibly marsupials (Yuill, 1979). This virus causes severe, acute fever in humans. If the setting is grassy openings in the south Asian dipterocarp forest, the intruder may contract scrub typhus, when *Leptotrombidium* chiggers transmit *Rickettsia tsutsugamushi* from their normal rat (*Rattus* spp.) hosts (Wisseman and Traub, 1976). Scrub typhus also causes acute fever, rash and may terminate in encephalitis and death in severe cases. The probability of infection is related to the amount of time spent in the areas where the infectious and parasitic agents occur. Pygmies in the Congo spend more time in the forests than do members of other tribes. The pygmies have significantly higher prevalence of monkey roundworms (*Strongyloides fulleborni*) than do other tribesmembers (Nelson, 1972). Probability of acquiring infection in the forest may

vary seasonally. Populations of arthropod vectors may vary dramatically between wet and dry seasons. Amount of water, flow and physiochemical characteristics may profoundly influence persistence of viable *Leptospira* spp. in the environment (Diesch and Ellinghausen, 1975). The kind of human activity in the forest also influences risk of infection. Individuals capturing parrots and other psittacine birds may contract parrot fever (*Chlamydia psittaci*), although the risk is greater to animal dealers who keep large numbers of birds under stressful conditions (Schachter, 1975). Although yellow fever does not occur on the Indian Subcontinent woodcutters in Mysore State, India, do risk infection with another life-threatening virus, Kyasanur Forest disease (KFD) (Work, 1958). This severe febrile disease, with hemorrhage, appeared suddenly in 1957, and persists in widening foci.

The effects of casual intrusion do not stop at the forest edge. As mentioned above, the infected woodsman may spread yellow fever to villages, towns and cities. The aminal collector may ship captive parrots that are carriers of parrot fever to urban centers. Newcastle disease, capable of causing explosive, fatal disease in domestic poultry, has been spread similarly via movement of captive wild tropical birds in international commerce (Lancaster and Alexander, 1975). Psittacines from neotropical forests and mynah birds from Southeast Asia spread Newcastle disease virus to poultry in Florida and California (Fig. 20.3). Control of the California outbreak cost over U.S. $62 million. These outbreaks have resulted in more strict con-

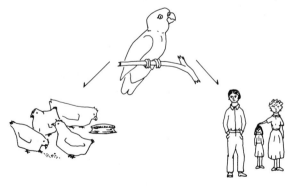

Fig. 20.3. Captive parrots can spread parrot fever to humans, and Newcastle disease to domestic poultry. (Drawing by Linda Bunkfeldt.)

trol and testing of wild birds imported from tropical areas around the world. Also, the consequences of tropical diseases of man may become apparent in temperate zone cities thousands of kilometers from the rain forest. African green monkeys (*Ceropithicus aethiops*) were collected from Ugandan forests and shipped alive to European medical laboratories for preparation of kidney cell cultures. In a single epidemic in 1967, humans in contact with these monkeys in German and Yugoslavian laboratories developed a generalized disease with headache, nausea, rash, severe hemorrhage, pneumonitis, pancreatitis and hepatitis. Some of these workers spread the disease to other people with whom they were in contact. There were 31 cases with seven deaths from this disease, subsequently shown to be caused by a previously unrecognized agent, Marburg virus (Kissling, 1975; Work, 1976).

Disease spread to domestic animals in the forest

The casual human intruder into the forest is likely to be accompanied by dogs, and possibly horses. Intensified human activity in the forest has a corresponding increase in the numbers and kinds of domesticated animals. The beginning of agricultural or forestry activity requires draft animals (equines, oxen, elephants) and food animals (poultry, pigs, and perhaps, goats). Large ruminants usually arrive much later on the scene, since they require extensive pastures. Animal health authorities seldom worry about these animals; their numbers are too small and dispersed for effective disease surveillance. Thus, there are no statistics on which an assessment of economic impact can be based. However, the presence of infectious and parasitic organisms capable of infecting domestic animals in the forest is well documented. Dogs and pigs are apt to acquire *Salmonella* spp. infection by eating feces, drinking fecally contaminated water, or consuming offal of wild animals fed to them by their hunter owners. Rabies, present in various wild mammals in the tropics throughout the world, is an ever-present threat to unvaccinated hunting dogs. Infected dogs may pass both of these diseases to their owners. Horses, mules and donkeys in neotropical forests may be infected by mosquito-transmitted eastern or western equine encephalitis virus, develop severe central nervous system in-

fection and die or be rendered unfit for work. Poultry may contract Newcastle disease or other avian maladies from wild birds with which they are in contact.

Introducing new diseases into forest ecosystems

Human and animal health officials are usually concerned about the spread of diseases that are maintained in nature, in the forest, to rural or urban areas. There is reason for concern about diseases not present in forested areas becoming established there when people and their domestic animals arrive on the scene. If one were to single out the disease one would least like to see introduced into the forest ecosystem, it would be human malaria, not for the risk to indigenous fauna, but because of the adverse effect that this disease can have on all people that follow, and the difficulty and expense in controlling it once introduced. Until recently, malaria was by far the most important infectious disease of man (McGregor, 1976). Even now, it remains a serious and sometimes resurgent problem in the tropics around the world, as developing countries have had difficulty maintaining costly control programs, and as drug-resistant strains of the organisms and insecticide-resistant strains of the mosquito vector have emerged. The vector genus, *Anopheles*, is widespread and ecologically versatile. More than sixty species have been shown to be effective vectors in different parts of the world. There is a high degree of probability that there is an efficient vector of human malaria in any given tropical rain forest in the world (Young, 1976). A few examples follow. In the neotropics, *A. albimanus* breeds in brackish, stagnant or freshwater lakes and pools, *A. p. pseudopunctipennis* occurs in clear pools and mountain streams, and *A. bellator* and *A. cruzii* breed in bromeliad epiphytes. In Africa, *A. funestus* is found in clear water swamps, streams and lakes, *A. gambiae* breeds in pools, *A. melas* occurs in brackish water of mangrove swamps and coastal streams. In tropical Asia, *A. culicifacies* is found in a wide variety of larval habitats from fresh to brackish water, *A. minimus* breeds in slow streams and springs, *A. balabacensis* breeds both in the forest canopy and in shady pools on the ground, and *A. umbrosus* is found in mangrove swamps and in dense forest.

There are a wide variety of disease-causing agents

of potential importance to man and livestock that could be introduced into tropical forest ecosystems by infected people or domestic animals and maintained there. Both yellow fever and rabies are generally believed to have been introduced into the neotropics from Africa and Europe, although there is some evidence to suggest that both were present before the Spanish Conquest. Other organisms with a broad host range, such as many *Salmonella* spp., *Leptospira* serotypes and many arthropod-borne viruses, have potential for introduction into the biotic community, but studies to document this chance type of occurrence have not been done.

DISEASE CONSEQUENCES OF FOREST PERTURBATION

Conversion of forested areas to agricultural use simplifies the ecosystem; species diversity is reduced and population densities of the species that remain, or are introduced, increase. Some of the vertebrates and arthropod vectors that were present originally may be able to capitalize on the changes, and will increase their numbers. New species arrive, including man, his domestic animals, and exotic camp followers such as rats (*Rattus* spp.), mice (*Mus musculus*), and a variety of arthropods, frequently including *Aedes aegypti*. The emerging agroecosystems may favor transmission of infectious and parasitic organisms endemic in the area, or of newly introduced disease-causing agents.

Crops may attract wild vertebrates that bring diseases that are transmissible to man. In Africa, green monkeys (*Cercopithecus aethiops* and *C. nictitans*) raid farms located near the forest. *Aedes simpsoni* mosquitoes breed in water that collects in the leaf axils of bananas and other plants, and the adult mosquitoes feed on people and monkeys. If the raiding monkeys are infected with yellow fever, the virus can be transmitted by mosquito bite from monkeys to the people residing on the farm, and subsequently from person to mosquito to person (Taufflieb et al., 1971). Other infectious agents may be continuously present in the area, but cause no disease in people or domestic animals until a large population of susceptible hosts is established. In Southeast Asia, Japanese encephalitis may be transmitted among many wild vertebrate species by rice-field breeding *Culex* spp. mosquitoes, with little

human infection. Pigs can serve as amplifying hosts, and establishment of swine populations in endemic areas may increase virus transmission, with resultant transmission to people. Disease then occurs in both humans and swine (Bendell, 1970).

Risk of infection can be increased when agricultural activities begin, or terminate. When tropical forest is converted to rice culture, incidence of leptospirosis in rice rats may increase, with up to 50% of the rats excreting the organism in their urine. Perturbation following swidden agriculture can have effects on disease transmission even after the settlers have moved on. In Malaysia, abandoned aboriginal villages harbored large rodent populations because of abundant food and shelter for the rodents. These rodents had high incidence of leptospirosis. Transient people passing through or camping in the old villages frequently contracted leptospirosis from water contaminated with rat urine. Although the organism can penetrate intact skin, skin lesions from leech wounds facilitated entry of the leptospires (McCrumb et al., 1957).

Increased agricultural activity also increases the opportunity for invasion by opportunistic organisms that are not normally infectious. Repeated contact with soil in the humid neotropics can result in paracoccidioidomycosis — a severe fungus infection of lungs, mucous membranes and lymph nodes caused by *Paracoccidioides brasiliensis* (Restrepo et al., 1970).

Agricultural activity can also reduce human disease. In Africa, river blindness caused by *Oncocerca volvulus* infection prevents settlement of some valleys. People dwelling in certain forests have severe parasitisms, many parasitic nodules, acquire infection at an early age and have high prevalence of river blindness. This parasite is transmitted by the black fly *Simulium damnosum*. Clearing of the forests, probably coupled with changes in the quality of the water in which the black flies breed, has reduced vector populations, and decreased the transmission rates of the parasite and river blindness (Rodger, 1977).

Conversion of forests to grazing lands may also create situations favorable for disease transmission. Populations of disease-carrying native vertebrates may increase dramatically. Prior to the development of the cattle industry, vampire bat (*Desmodus rotundus*) populations were probably significantly limited by the availability of large mammal hosts from which to obtain blood meals. Vampire bats are now common throughout cattle raising areas in the lowland neotropics, and transmit rabies to horses and especially to cattle. Before the initiation of vampire control programs, annual cattle losses were estimated at one million head (Linhart, 1975).

The establishment of large populations of exotic susceptible grazing animals, in this instance horses, mules and asses, can result in explosive epidemics of infectious agents already present in the area. In low-land Colombia and Venezuela, forests were cleared, pastures were established, and equine populations expanded. Venezuelan equine encephalitis virus, an ecologically versatile agent, became adapted to this agroecosystem. The virus can be efficiently transmitted by many mosquito species, several of which feed avidly on horses and some also feed on man. The first massive epidemics occurred in the 1930s, and have recurred at irregular intervals since. The last major epidemic apparently jumped from Ecuador to Guatemala, spread through Central America to Costa Rica, and northward through Mexico to the lower Rio Grande River Valley of Texas. Mortality rates in horses are high; up to 80% of the animals that are infected may die, and survivors may be so incapacitated that they are unable to work. Mortality has been much lower in humans (approximately 0.5% of those infected died, mostly children) than that in horses, but some epidemics have been so severe and widespread that tens of thousands of people were ill, overfilling available hospital space, and hundreds died (Pan American Health Organization, 1972).

The transition from forest to pasture can also cause increases in arthropod vectors that transmit diseases. Increased cattle grazing in the Kyasanur Forest of India was deemed responsible for a corresponding increase in *Haemaphysalis spinigera* ticks, with "spill-over" of Kyasanur Forest disease virus transmission from its normal rodent tick cycle to monkeys resident in the forest, and people that entered the forest to tend cattle or cut wood (Work, 1958). In other areas, biting fly (tabanid) populations may increase during the forest–pasture transition. If the pasture is near riverine marshes, or lakes and swamps in the neotropics, the tabanids may transmit equine trypanosomiasis, or "mal de caderas" from native capybara (*Hydrochoerus* spp.) and infected cattle to horses. This disease, caused by *Trypanosoma equinum*, causes fever, hind quar-

ter weakness, and may terminate in death in four to five months (Bruner and Gillespie, 1973).

The particular mix of people, insects, and microbes that occur when a variety of habitats are juxtaposed at the forest edge may create some unique disease problems. The failure of the Uruma colony in Bolivia was essentially a simple forest edge phenomenon — Uruma virus, and probably the other agents that caused the severe jungle fevers, spilled over from the forest fauna into the susceptible population residing in the clearing.

More complex effects of infectious and parasitic disease on human populations, agricultural practices and, in turn, on plant and wild animal communities is illustrated by trypanosomiasis in the Lake Victoria area of Uganda (Ford, 1970). At the turn of the century, Soga tribesmen lived in savanna and areas of savanna–forest transition. Extensive banana areas were established in the settlements, and agricultural clearings extended from the populous lake shore and savanna areas, into the forested areas. A sleeping sickness epidemic, caused by *Trypanasoma gambiense*, began in 1901. By the time the survivors were evacuated from the area in 1908, 200 000 of the original 300 000 inhabitants were dead. The trypanosome was transmitted by the tsetse fly (*Glossina fuscipes*) capable of persisting in riverine and lacustrine forest remnants. The abandoned banana gardens gave way to mixed forest–savanna, and large game mammals, reservoirs of cattle trypanosomiasis, moved into the area. Human populations increased following the sleeping sickness epidemic, and farms were re-established in the former epidemic area. Cattle populations also expanded, but stabilized in the late 1930s, and then declined for ten years due to cattle trypanosomiasis. At this time, there was another, but smaller, outbreak of human sleeping sickness, as people moved into the hill areas away from the lake, and came in contact with *G. pallidipes* and *G. brevipalpis* tsetses in forest and thicket patches. An infected human introduced the disease into the area, and over 2000 people were infected, of whom 10% died. Drugs to control cattle trypanosomiasis were introduced into the area in the early 1950s, and the cattle population expanded again, with substantial encroachment into forest and savanna areas, and a corresponding decrease in tsetse fly habitat. Interestingly, there was a third, but very small outbreak of human sleeping sickness from 1954 to 1957. Sufficient forest remained to sustain populations of *G. fuscipes* at the forest edge. Introduction of outboard motors and nylon fish nets promoted fishing, and resulted in an increase in the proportion of the population frequenting the tsetse habitat.

FUTURE

The future of tropical forests is clear — human activity will continue to modify them, and unchanged areas will become smaller and more scarce. The open questions are where the changes will occur, and at what rate. The disease consequences of future forest modifications are not altogether predictable either. Will entirely new diseases spring up? They may, just as they have in the recent past with the sudden appearance of two tropical rodent-borne hemorrhagic fevers of man, Bolivian hemorrhagic fever in the Bolivian Amazon River headwaters, and Lassa fever in West Africa. We should be prepared to see dramatic spread of tropical diseases, due to rapid transport of humans and animals, as appeared to be the case with epidemic Venezuelan equine encephalitis, and was certainly the case following jet plane transport of a Lassa fever patient and of Newcastle disease-carrying captive birds to the United States. Not only is the physical structure of tropical forests changing, so is their chemical composition, as substances associated with industrial and agricultural processes find their way into the forest via air and water. The impacts that chemical intrusion may have on disease ecology in and around tropical forest ecosystems have not been determined, but certainly bear watching. The changes that surely will occur in tropical forests do not justify relaxing our guard against recognized old diseases. Efficient malaria vectors are present in the tropical forests around the world, and only require contact with infected individuals to begin transmission. All the elements necessary for a major yellow fever outbreak are present in many parts of the New World, and just await input of the virus into the system.

REFERENCES

Arean, V.M., 1976. American trypanosomiasis. In: G.W. Hunter, J.C. Swartzwelder and D.F. Clyde (Editors), *Tropical Medicine*. Saunders, Philadelphia, Penn., pp. 440–450.

Bendell, P.E.J., 1970. Japanese encephalitis in Sarawak: Studies on mosquito behavior in Land Dayak village. *Trans. R. Soc. Trop. Med. Hyg.*, 64: 497–502.

Biagi, F., 1976. Cutaneous and mucocutaneous leishmaniasis. In: G.W. Hunter, J.C. Swartzwelder and D.F. Clyde (Editors), *Tropical Medicine*. Saunders, Philadelphia, Penn., pp. 440–450.

Boshell, J., 1957. Marche de la fièvre jaune sylvatique vers les régions du nordouest de l'Amérique centrale. *Bull. W.H.O.*, 16: 431–436.

Bres, P., 1976. Arbovirus infections. In: R. Cruickshank, K.L. Standard and H.B.L. Russell (Editors), *Epidemiology and Community Health in Warm Climate Countries*. Churchill Livingstone, New York, N.Y., pp. 145–159.

Bruner, D.W. and Gillespie, J.H., 1973. *Hagan's Infectious Diseases of Domesticated Animals*. Cornell University Press, Ithaca, N.Y., 6th ed., 1385 pp.

Burkhart, R.L. and Page, L.A., 1971. Chlamydiosis (ornithosis-psittacosis). In: J.W. Davis, R.C. Anderson, L. Karstad and D.O. Trainer (Editors), *Infectious and Parasitic Diseases of Wild Birds*. Iowa State University Press, Ames, Iowa, pp. 118–140.

Diesch, S.L. and Ellinghausen, H.C., 1975. Leptospirosis. In: W.T. Hubbert, W.F. McCulloch and P.R. Schnurrenberger (Editors), *Diseases Transmitted from Animals to Man*. Thomas, Springfield, Ill., pp. 436–462.

Ford, J., 1970. Interactions between human societies and various trypanosome–tsetse–wild fauna complexes. In: J.P. Garlick and R.W.J. Keay (Editors), *Human Ecology in the Tropics*. Pergamon Press, London, pp. 81–97.

James, M.T., 1947. The flies that cause myiasis in man. *U.S. Dep. Agric. Misc. Publ.*, No. 631.

Johnson, K.M., 1975. Yellow fever. In: W.T. Hubbert, W.F. McCulloch and P.R. Schnurrenberger (Editors), *Diseases Transmitted from Animals to Man*. Thomas, Springfield, Ill., pp. 929–938.

Kissling, R.F., 1975. Marburg virus. In: W.T. Hubbert, W.F. McCulloch and P.R. Schnurrenberger (Editors), *Diseases Transmitted from Animals to Man*. Thomas, Springfield, Ill., pp. 866–870.

Lancaster, J.E. and Alexander, D.J., 1975. Newcastle disease virus and spread. *Can. Dep. Agric. Monogr.* No. 11.

Linhart, S.B., 1975. Biology and control of vampire bats. In: G.M. Baer (Editor), *The Natural History of Rabies, II*. Academic Press, New York, N.Y., pp. 221–239.

McCrumb, F.R., Jr., Stockhard, L., Robinson, C.R., Turner, L.H., Levis, D.G., Maisey, C.W., Kelleher, M.F., Gleiser, A. and Smadel, J.E., 1957. Leptospirosis in Malaya. I. Sporadic cases among military and civilian personnel. *Am. J. Trop. Med. Hyg.*, 6: 238–256.

McGregor, I.A., 1976. Epidemiology and control of malaria. In: R. Cruickshank, K.L. Standard and H.B.L. Russell (Editors), *Epidemiology and Community Health in Warm Countries*. Churchill Livingstone, New York, N.Y., pp. 208–222.

Nelson, G.S., 1972. Human behaviour in the transmission of parasitic diseases. In: E.U. Canning and C.A. Wright

(Editors), *Behavioural Aspects of Parasite Transmission.*
Academic Press, London, pp. 109–122.

Pan American Health Organization, 1972. Venezuelan equine
encephalitis. *Pan Am. Health Organ. Sci. Publ.*, No. 243:
416 pp.

Pan American Health Organization, 1979. Dengue in the
Caribbean, 1977. *Pan Am. Health Organ. Sci. Publ.*, No.
375: 186 pp.

Restrepo, A., Robledo, M., Gutierrez, F., Sanclemente, M.,
Castaneda, E. and Calle, G., 1970. Paracoccidioidomycosis
(South American blastomycosis). *Am. J. Trop. Med Hyg.*,
19: 68–76.

Rodger, F.C. (Editor), 1977. *Oncocerciasis in Zaire*. Pergamon
Press, London, 195 pp.

Schachter, J., 1975. Psittacosis. In: W.T. Hubbert, W.F.
McCulloch and P.R. Schnurrenberger (Editors), *Diseases
Transmitted from Animals to Man*. Thomas, Springfield,
Ill., pp. 369–381.

Schaeffer, M., Gajudsek, D.C., Brown-Lema, A. and
Eichenwald, H., 1959. Epidemic jungle fevers among
Okinawan colonists in the Bolivian rain forest. I.
Epidemiology. *Am. J. Trop. Med. Hyg.*, 8: 372–396.

Singh, K.R.P., Goverdhan, M.K. and Bhat, H.R., 1968.
Transovarial transmission of Kyasanur Forest disease virus
to small mammals by *Ixodes petauristae*, *I. ceylonensis* and
Haemaphysalis spinigera. *Ind. J. Med. Res.*, 56: 594–609.

Taufflieb, R., Robin, Y. and Cornet, M., 1971. Le virus amaril et
la faune sauvage en Afrique. *Cah. O.R.S.T.O.M., Sér.
Entomol. Méd. Parasitol.*, 9: 351–371.

Trapido, H. and Galindo, P., 1956. Parasitological reviews: The
epidemiology of yellow fever in Middle America. *Exp.
Parasitol.*, 5: 285–323.

Wisseman, C.L. and Traub, R., 1976. Scrub typhus (chigger-
borne rickettsiosis). In: G.W. Hunter, J.C. Swartzwelder
and D.F. Clyde (Editors), *Tropical Medicine*. Saunders,
Philadelphia, Penn., pp. 125–130.

Work, T.H., 1958. Russian spring–summer virus in India.
Kyasanur Forest disease. *Progr. Med. Virol.*, 1: 248–279.

Work, T.H., 1976. Exotic virus diseases. In: G.W. Hunter, J.C.
Swartzwelder and D.F. Clyde (Editors), *Tropical Medicine*.
Saunders, Philadelphia, Penn., pp. 1–56.

Young, M.D., 1976. Malaria. In: G.W. Hunter, J.C. Swartzwelder
and D.F. Clyde (Editors), *Tropical Medicine*. Saunders,
Philadelphia, Penn., pp. 353–396.

Yuill, T.M., 1979. Mosquito- and other diptera-borne arboviral
infections (excluding yellow fever and dengue). In: W.T.
Hubbert, W.F. McCulloch and P.R. Schnurrenberger
(Editors), *Update on the Zoonoses*. Iowa State University
Press, Ames, Iowa, in press.

Zeledon, R. 1974. Epidemiology, modes of transmission and
reservoir hosts of Chagas disease. In: *Trypanosomiasis and
Leishmaniasis*, *Ciba Foundation Symposium 20*. Elsevier,
Amsterdam, pp. 51–77.

Chapter 21

CONSERVATION OF RAIN FORESTS FOR SCIENTIFIC RESEARCH, FOR WILDLIFE CONSERVATION, AND FOR RECREATION AND TOURISM

NORMAN MYERS

INTRODUCTION

In no other biogeographic zone is there a more pressing need to establish protected areas than in the tropical rain forest biome.

Ecologically, tropical rain forests are among the most complex of ecosystems, matched or possibly surpassed only by coral reefs. Biotically, they are among the richest areas on earth, comprising some 20–40% of earth's stock of species, or somewhere between one and five million species. Despite their "biological treasure-house" character, however, tropical rain forests are less protected than is the case for virtually any other biome. To date, a mere 2% or so of the biome has been set aside as parks or reserves, and many of these areas amount to little more than markings on a map, with few substantive safeguards on the ground. Ecologists and biogeographers suggest that a good 10%, and possibly as much as 20%, of the biome needs to be designated as parks and reserves, if we are to adequately respond to the challenge of preserving representative samples of the biome's ecosystems.

Moreover, tropical rain forests are being disrupted and degraded, if not destroyed outright, at a rate that may leave most of them in severely impoverished state by the end of the century or shortly thereafter (Myers, 1979a, 1980; Persson, 1974, 1975; Sommer, 1976; UNESCO, 1978). Thus, there is an urgent premium on setting aside as many protected areas as possible, to preserve intact ecosystems in inviolate form.

So great is the pressure to exploit remaining rain forests, however, that it is worthwhile to spell out some preservation objectives. A list of objectives, itemizing the goods and services that are supplied through protected areas, can serve as a "pres-ervation rationale" to balance against incentives to exploit rain forests for conventional products such as timber. A "shopping list" of objectives would include the following:

(1) The preservation of rain forests' exceptional diversity, through the setting aside of both unique and representative networks of sample ecosystems.

(2) The preservation of sufficiently large rain forest areas to allow some of the foremost evolutionary processes on earth to continue undisturbed.

(3) The safeguarding of rain forests' regulatory functions for biosphere functions, notably in terms of climatic stability at local, regional and global levels.

(4) As a consequence of 1 to 3 above, the supply of both unique and representative ecosystems for purposes of scientific research, whether basic theoretical research or applied utilitarian research.

(5) As a corollary and extension of 4 above, the supply of both unique and representative ecosystems for purposes of benchmark and monitoring studies, in order that land-use planners can derive and evaluate environmentally sound management of rain forest resources.

(6) The conservation of wildlife in all its variety, both qualitative and quantitative.

(7) The conservation of genetic resources and gene pools of wild species of animals and plants, both among and within species, in order to perpetuate the biotic base of rain forest ecosystems, and to supply materials for modern agriculture, medicine and pharmaceuticals, and industrial processes.

(8) The conservation of wildlands, for purposes similar to 6 and 7 above.

(9) The safeguarding of watershed processes, in

325

order to avoid flooding, soil erosion, and other degradations of hydrological systems.

(10) The provision of undisturbed forest areas for recreation, including tourism, through enjoyment of nature, together with related activities of leisure-time and educational types.

This constitutes an extensive list of preservation objectives — though it is by no means exhaustive, nor are the items ranked in priority order.

Since it is beyond the scope of this chapter to consider each item in detail, they are reviewed here under three broad headings, viz. scientific research, wildlife conservation, and recreation and tourism.

SCIENTIFIC RESEARCH

So scanty is our understanding of tropical rain forests (Richards, 1973; Farnworth and Golley, 1974; Golley and Medina, 1975; Adisoemarto and Brunig, 1979), that to date we know more about certain sectors of the moon's surface than we do about much of the rain forest biome. For example, as this volume shows, we have limited knowledge of the structure and dynamics of only a few rain forest ecosystems. Indeed, it is not going too far to say that we have scarcely begun to describe the ecological patterns displayed by the great majority of tropical organisms.

But what little we do know suggests that a number of basic biological questions can best, or only, be resolved through research in tropical rain forests — and that among these topics are key issues of evolutionary processes, speciation, adaptation, and community interactions. If we do not, within the virtually immediate future, establish enough scientific preserves to serve as sites for long-term research, it is possible that fundamental factors of biology will remain beyond our comprehension forever.

Moreover, rain forest research will not only help to resolve core questions of theoretical biology. It will also help us to push ahead with applied science, thus enabling us to gain a grasp of the factors that underlie sustained-yield productivity in the moist tropics — including, notably, agricultural ecosystems. For example, if we could better understand the plant/animal relationships, and especially their coevolutionary relationships, we would learn much of importance for modern crop husbandry.

Something the same applies to studies of flowering and fruiting phenology, and of processes and conditions of seed germination. In addition, we could learn much of relevance to timber exploitation, if we could advance beyond our primitive understanding of growth patterns and competitive adaptability of commercial tree species — all of which factors would help to ensure adequate regeneration of rain forest communities after the timber harvester has finished his work.

Primary and secondary forests

Scientific research along these lines can generally be conducted only in primary forest ecosystems. That is to say, it is limited to forest tracts that have not been disturbed through modern forms of exploitation. Even light logging, removing a mere $10 \, m^3$ of timber per hectare, can cause disruption from which the original forest will not recover for at least one and possibly several decades; while heavy logging, removing at least $60 \, m^3 \, ha^{-1}$, and sometimes twice as much, can leave behing a fundamentally modified forest that may need more than one century to restore itself. In the main, then, only primary forest serves the needs of the research scientist — with all that implies for siting of parks and reserves.

This is not to say, however, that secondary forests cannot sometimes meet the needs of science. We need to know, for example, how far secondary forests, with their varying degrees of man-caused disruption, can pass through a predictable series of seral stages, at different rates according to local conditions (climatic and edaphic factors, etc.) as they proceed on their way toward primary status again. Likewise, we need to know how far secondary forests, with their generally smaller numbers of tree species and their simplified communities, can serve man's needs for timber and other forest products.

In the main, however, it is primary forests that are the focus of the scientist's attention, since they alone reveal how rain forest ecosystems function with all their pristine complexity and diversity. Furthermore, it is only primary forests that offer benchmark criteria by which we can measure the nature and consequences of man's intervention in forest ecosystems for his own benefit.

Which sectors to preserve?

Today's scientists face the challenge of advising on which fragments of tropical rain forests shall be safeguarded for them to investigate in the future, while watching the rest be swiftly swept away as a result of mis-use and over-use of forest resources. So: which sectors of the biome shall scientists recommend for preservation, as sites for their research?

This agonizing question is all the more difficult to answer in that, with regard to most of the biome, we have only vague ideas about what would constitute "representative networks of preserves". What, for example, do we mean when we speak of "rain forest formations" in each of the three main regions, viz. tropical Latin America, tropical Africa and Southeast Asia? How do we define these formations, how numerous are they, what is their distribution, their subdivisions? So preliminary is our inventory of the biome, that we are far from having covered all the main forest types, possibly leaving significant formations or subdivisions of formations still to be identified.

True, in certain parts of the biome, we have achieved a moderate grasp of the situation. In Amazonia, it is now thought that there are at least eight main phytogeographical zones, or "plant regions", that have their characteristic floral communities, and hence their distinctive faunal communities too (Prance, 1977). In Southeast Asia, a number of forest types have been identified and defined, though a biogeographical account of their location and extent is still very far from complete (Whitmore, 1975). In tropical Africa, with its main surviving tract of rain forest confined to the Zaire Basin, we have only rudimentary ideas of where boundary lines lie between different forest formations and biogeographic zones.

Centres of diversity and Pleistocene refugia

Conversely, the crucial question of "Where should scientific preserves be sited?" can be partially answered through some recent documentation of "centres of diversity". Certain patches of rain forest feature exceptional concentrations of species, many of them endemics; and these areas may coincide with the so-called Pleistocene refugia that survived during times of greatest climatic

dryness and greatest contraction of the forests during the late Pleistocene (McArthur and Wilson, 1967; Terborgh, 1974; Diamond, 1975; Myers, 1979b; Prance, 1981). According to the "forest refugia" theory, the forests of Amazonia and of tropical Africa underwent a series of climatic fluctuations during the late Pleistocene; sometimes the regions were as wet as they are now, while at other times rainfall was much less, causing extensive sectors of the forest to disappear for a period. (Southeast Asia, by contrast, does not appear to have undergone such profound changes, since its archipelago, lying in a maritime rather than a continental setting, proved less prone to desiccation.) The cycle of advance and retreat of lowland rain forests in Amazonia and tropical Africa probably occurred at least twice during the late Pleistocene, and perhaps four times. During the dry phases, forest species were confined to a number of isolated patches of wet or moist forest, from which surviving species could later re-colonize the expanding spread of forest when wetter times returned.

To the extent that the "forest refugia" theory is correct (certain scientists believe the supposed refugias are artifacts of localized research), these areas are likely to harbour a richer diversity of species than virtually any other areas of the biome. If these areas thus constitute concentrations of species, with high levels of endemism, they clearly deserve priority for preservation. When we "lock away" one of these localities as a park or a reserve, we derive a better return per dollar investment than would probably be the case for much larger areas elsewhere. However, because of the disagreement with the refugia concept, scientists would do well to take a broader view when they advise park planners on where to locate sites for research.

Preserves already established

How far have we in fact progressed with establishment of preserves for scientific research? The answer must be that we have scarcely advanced beyond the starting line. True, there is Barro Colorado Island in the Panama Canal Zone, and Finca La Selva in Costa Rica, together with a handful of other long-established scientific areas elsewhere. As compared with the size of the challenge, however, there is a long way to go. Indeed, the scientific community can be characterized as less than energetic in its efforts to tackle the problem, at least until the 1970s. Only recently have major research programmes, such as the International Biological Programme (IBP) and UNESCO's Man and the Biosphere Programme (MAB) begun to investigate the full potential of tropical rain forests as living laboratories and education centres (UNESCO, 1973, 1974, 1978).

Since IBP has now been completed, whereas MAB is an on-going programme, it is appropriate here to describe the latter initiative in more detail. In essence, MAB aims to protect selected natural areas that are representative of the world's major ecosystems with emphasis, as an urgent priority, on the tropics; and it seeks to achieve this goal through establishment of Biosphere Reserves. To spell out the defined objectives of Biosphere Reserves, they are intended "To conserve for present and future use the diversity and integrity of biotic communities of plants and animals within natural ecosystems, and to safeguard the genetic diversity of species on which their continuing evolution depends; to provide areas for ecological and environmental research, including, particularly, baseline studies, within and adjacent to these reserves; (and) to provide facilities for education and training." MAB considers that tropical forests, together with savanna grasslands, coastal ecosystems and islands, constitute a zone that critically deserves more effective conservation — and indeed many scientists believe that no biome deserves greater priority than tropical rain forests.

The Biosphere Reserves Project focuses on ecosystems that have unique or special interest and ecosystems that are representative of biomes. Biosphere Reserves may include man-modified landscapes, thus serving the important goal of enabling scientists to compare and contrast disturbed forests with primary forests, and thus to evaluate the optimal ways for man to intervene in tropical rain forests.

Regrettably, the MAB Project has established very few Biosphere Reserves in tropical rain forests as yet — one in Ivory Coast, one in eastern Borneo, one in Papua New Guinea and about ten others scattered throughout the biome. As mentioned, parks and reserves of conventional types comprise only 2% of all tropical rain forests, very few of them featuring any kind of scientific facility.

WILDLIFE CONSERVATION

The wildlife of tropical rain forests, like the rain forests themselves, can be considered as part of the "global natural heritage". Insofar as they therefore constitute a heritage for all humankind, they deserve protection for all people — whether people in rain forest countries or elsewhere — now and forever.

True, we must not forget that these tropical rain forests and their wildlife constitute, at the same time, natural resources over which the developing countries concerned exercise national sovereignty. This constraint has important implications for conservation policies and programmes, which wildlife supporters outside tropical forest countries must remember. Nevertheless, wildlife supporters in, say, North America and Europe can express a legitimate interest in tropical rain forests and their wildlife, as integral parts of the global ecosystem. Just as scientists, wildlife enthusiasts, and other citizens of Brazil, Indonesia and Zaire can express concern about ecosystems in southern Florida, the Rhine Valley and Lake Baikal (all ecosystems with their own intrinsic value, and all facing environmental threats), so tropical rain forests, with their exceptionally rich wildlife communities, can be construed as part of the planetary patrimony, of value to the entire community of nations.

Species richness

Tropical rain forests harbour a greater abundance and variety of species, in both quantitative and qualitative senses, than are to be found elsewhere. For example, rough estimates for the biome amount to some 40% of the planet's overall stock of species (Lowe-McConnell, 1969; Raven et al., 1971; Meggers et al., 1973; Raup et al., 1973; Raven, 1974, 1976; Myers, 1976, 1979a). Were tropical rain forests to continue to be destroyed at present estimated rates (see Chapter 18), this could lead to the elimination of at least one-quarter and possibly one-third of all species — somewhere between half a million and several million species. This would be a marked impoverishment not only for the biome and for the tropical countries in question, but for the whole of humankind. It would be a far greater loss of species than has ever occurred in a single spasm of extinction at any stage in the entire 3600 million years since life first emerged on earth; and it would represent a profound shift in the course of evolution.

This leads us to a difficult question: how many protected areas, of what size and where located, do we need to conserve this remarkable array of wildlife? Fortunately there are now some insights from the recently developed theory that is partly related to the theory of Pleistocene refuges, and partly to the theory of island biogeography.

In essence, this theory postulates that, under the influence of natural processes, wildland habitats tend to become fragmented, resulting in a patchwork pattern of island-like ecological enclaves. The process has been grossly compounded by man's activities, which reduce the size of ecological fragments and cause them to become increasingly isolated from each other. In these relict habitats, communities of species exist in balance with the carrying capacity of the life support system in question: the larger the area and the less it is isolated, the greater the number of species "at equilibrium" (Terborgh, 1974; Cody and Diamond, 1975; Diamond, 1975; Simberloff and Abele, 1976).

All this has critical implications for planning of protected areas. When a park is set aside, it is virtually certain to become an island of intact "nature" in a sea of man-dominated, and hence alien, environments; and the species living there will decline from the number supported by the area when it was part of a "continent", to the number it can support as an island. The total number of species will steadily fall until it reaches a new equilibrium. The key questions are, how great will the decline be, and are some species more susceptible to elimination than others? In turn, this leads to two practical considerations: what can we do to amend the process, and how can we make the conservation of species and habitats in protected areas as efficient as possible?

It is possible to estimate the likely losses in "park islands" by looking at what has happened when geographical islands have appeared under natural circumstances, as when a continental area has become submerged and has left behind a series of islands. Studies on island archipelagoes of the New Guinea Shelf, the Caribbean, and the Adriatic, and off the coast of California reveal that the highest extinction rates have occurred on small islands with rare species. Lack's investigations (1976) in the West Indies have suggested that larger islands, by virtue of their greater variety of habitats, are ecologically richer, and tend to support more bird species than smaller islands. However, the work of Simberloff and Abele (1977) in Florida indicates that for certain categories of species which have small size, notably insects, spiders and other arthropods, relatively small islands are sufficient area for preservation of species diversity. The findings of island biogeography generally suggest that, if 90% of an original habitat becomes grossly disrupted, and the remaining 10% is protected as a park, we can expect to save no more than about half of the species restricted to that particular area. Soon after the preserve is established, "equilibration" (the extinction process) will occur more rapidly than later on. Conversely, if the size of a protected area can be increased ten times, the number of species with the prospect of long-term survival may well be doubled. As a rough rule of thumb, arithmetic loss of space appears to lead to geometric decline in the value of the remaining space.

Now that biogeographers and ecologists can make rough estimates of extinction rates for the most vulnerable categories of species, notably mammals and birds, they can determine what minimal sizes are required to keep extinction rates "reasonably low". For example, Terborgh (1974) proposes that, if the aim is to keep the extinction rate of a community of bird species at less than 1% per century, then we need to think in terms of a preserve of at least 2500 km^2. Most parks and reserves in tropical rain forests are smaller than this area.

The theories of Pleistocene refugia and island biogeography as applied to park planning in Amazonia

Let us see how the combined theories of Pleistocene refugia and island biogeography work out for conservation in Amazonia. Since the region is reputed to contain at least one million species (Prance, 1977, 1981), it will need an extensive network of protected areas to safeguard a representative array of ecosystems. According to the theoretical calculations described earlier, preserving 1% of Amazonia's forests might correspond, very roughly, to saving 25% of its species; and 10% should correspond to saving 50%. So 20%, chosen extremely carefully for habitat coverage, might make a reasonably sound job of safeguarding a large part of the spectrum of species in Amazonia.

Approaching the challenge of Amazonia conservation from the standpoint of this related theory of Pleistocene refugia, recent research suggests that Amazonia features some sixteen centres of species diversity, all of which deserve priority conservation (Prance, 1977). In addition, as we have already seen, there are eight phytogeographical zones in Amazonia, zones that likewise require urgent protection through a representative system of parks and reserves.

Translating these calculations into conservation programmes works out somewhat as follows, according to Wetterberg et al. (1976). Suppose each of the eight phytogeographical subdivisions merits three protected areas, each area measuring 2590 km^2. Then this would amount to 62 160 km^2. A number of smaller parks and reserves would also be required, in order to protect centres of diversity, restricted-range species, unique microhabitats, and exceptional localities such as turtle- and bird-nesting areas. Three such additional areas in each subdivision, measuring 1000 km^2 each, would amount to 24 000 km^2. Each protected area would need a buffer zone around its perimeter, to hold off artificial disturbances from outside; if each such strip were 10 km wide, the total area involved would be 98 460 km^2. All this makes for an overall total of just under 185 000 km^2, or an area almost four-fifths the size of Great Britain or the entire state of Nebraska or South Dakota.

The Brazilian government has accepted this strategy in principle — which represents a fine advance for conservation. But to date, Brazil has established only two major parks in the region, the Amazonas National Park of approximately 10 000 km^2 and the 22 000 km^2 Rio Negro National Park. Regrettably, these two giant parks contain only one of the Pleistocene refugia, and only fragments of the vegetation formations that are now designated as priorities for conservation.

Large as the total proposed area may appear to be, it amounts to only 5% of Brazil's sector of Amazonia. Therein could lie a crucial limitation for the conservation strategy. Although the plan takes account of the theory of Pleistocene refugia, it does not seem to take much heed of the theory of island biogeography. And it is hard to see how, for

purposes of park planning, the one theory is much use without the other. As indicated earlier, conservationists may need to think in terms of preserving 20% of Amazonia in order to safeguard the region's stock of species. Furthermore, Brazil's strategy postulates no criteria for "minimum critical size" of each of the areas in question, half of which amount to around 1000 km^2; according to the theory of island biogeography, any preserve in the tropical rain forests that is less than 2500 km^2 could turn out to be too small for its purpose.

Worse still — though Brazil's conservation planners can do little about this — four of the presumed Pleistocene refugia fall entirely within those parts of the Amazon Basin that Brazil has designated as growth poles for intensive development through cattle ranching and smallholder cultivation, while major parts of other high-priority conservation foci overlap with development areas. If any one of these refuges was to be eliminated, a large number of species would probably go with it. Fortunately, Brazil's President Joao Baptista Figueriedo, speaking of future development for Amazonia, has stressed the need for "preservation of ecological equilibrium", to which protected areas of forest are "indispensable".

What of other parts of Amazonia? Peru has established two parks in its sector of the region, the 15 000 km^2 Manu Park and the 14 000 km^2 Pacaya–Samiria Park. Venezuela has expanded its Canaima Park to 30 000 km^2, and has declared another four new parks. Surinam, although a small country, has set an exceptional example in placing a large part of its forest under protected status. Colombia, with a huge zone of relatively undisturbed Amazon forest, states that it is planning several new parks. Major advances as these initiatives are, they are far from enough for a forest tract of over 5 million km^2.

In addition to the fact that only limited areas of the rain forest biome have hitherto been set aside, there is a further — and potentially critical — reservation. According to a number of Brazilian scientists, there could be little purpose in setting aside as much as 20% of Amazonia's rain forest were the remaining 80 percent to be developed. Because of hydrological and climatic repercussions arising from broad-scale deforestation, the consequences to developed and undeveloped lands could be severe. According to recent research by

Salati et al. (1978) and Molion (1976), the Amazon rain forest cycles a vast amount of moisture within its system; in fact, less than half of the region's rainfall drains away through rivers into the sea, the rest being returned to the atmosphere through trees and other plants via evapotranspiration. In other words, the region derives much of its moisture from within its own boundaries, as well as from external sources such as the Atlantic Ocean. When a substantial sector of the rain forest is eliminated, evapotranspiration could be critically curtailed. In turn, this could mean a steadily desiccating ecosystem which would increase with each reduction of the forest expanse.

In these circumstances, it could be a risky strategy for conservationists to confine their efforts to supposed Pleistocene refuges and other concentrations of species, in conjunction with a planning framework derived from island biogeography. No matter how carefully a network of protected areas might be designed, they could, were the remainder of the forest to be steadily destroyed, eventually become drier, leaving mere remnants of the uniquely rich biotas they were intended to preserve.

Secondary forest forms of wildlife

It is important to note that most of the wildlife of tropical rain forests is adapted to primary forests, and cannot prosper, or even survive, in secondary forests. For example, 90% of non-flying Malaysian mammals derive from primary forests, and 65% of them depend upon forest areas for their habitats; similarly 70% of 660 breeding bird species of the Sunda Shelf region — the western sector of insular Southeast Asia — are forest species; while 96% of Borneo's amphibians are found only in primary forests (Inger, 1967; Medway and Wells, 1971; Medway, 1981). But not all rain forest wildlife favours primary forests. In certain parts of the Sunda Shelf region, many if not most of the large herbivorous mammals and their predators actually depend for their food supplies on secondary forests, viz. on abandoned fields of shifting cultivators and on forest edges (Lekagul and McNeely, 1978). One species of wild cattle, *Bos gaurus*, in the Kuala Lumpat area has disappeared at least partly because the area has become so effectively protected that no new forest clearings are allowed. Insofar, then, as man is a long-term ecological factor in

tropical rain forests, some protected areas which allow human disturbance at traditional, or ecologically sound, level are essential if good populations of the entire spectrum of Southeast Asian wildlife are to be maintained.

So much for consideration of the scale of park networks needed to protect the spectrum of species in tropical rain forests. A further key question remains. How large do parks have to be to safeguard genetic diversity within species as well as among species? In other words, how do we determine minimal areas to protect gene pools for each individual species? Again, we can offer only preliminary answers to this basic question. To consider a few examples, wild fruit trees in Malaysia's lowland rain forest occur at low densities; a sample survey of 676 hectares reveals that few species feature more than 24 individual trees per 100 hectares, while 11 out of 18 species have fewer than 13 trees per hectare. So if each species requires 10 000 trees to provide an adequate gene pool, sizeable areas will have to be set aside to cater for these species (Whitmore, 1975). In the same region, hornbills that possibly require minimal populations of 5000 individuals to ensure adequate gene pools, will need between 2000 and 10 000 km^2, and monkeys with similar-sized populations will need anywhere from 250 to over 3000 km^2 (Medway and Wells, 1971; Medway, 1981). If a tiger population could survive with as few as 400 individuals, the area required to support them may have to be as large as 40 000 km^2.

RECREATION AND TOURISM

It is sometimes suggested that recreation and tourism represent a rationale for developing countries to set aside forest areas as parks and reserves. The argument runs somewhat as follows. Recreation on the part of local people, and tourism on the part of people from further afield (generally overseas), can be big business. The Luquillo National Forest in Puerto Rico attracts over one million local people each year; while international tourism ranks among the world's fastest-growing economic sectors. So, on the face of it, recreation and tourism should offer justification for designating tracts of rain forest as "off limits" to development.

Disadvantages of rain forests as sites for visitors

Regrettably, the theory does not work out so well in practice for tropical rain forests. The Luquillo National Forest is very much the exception. It is located close to a large concentration of local people. Most rain forest parks, by contrast, are far removed from centres of population. More important still, tropical rain forests have yet to demonstrate their capacity to attract international tourists in their droves. Savannah parks in Africa, with their throngs of easily visible wildlife, are a different case altogether. Americans and other developed-world citizens are willing to spend large sums of money to have a chance to view prides of lions, herds of giraffes and armies of wildebeest at close quarters. Tropical rain forests do not feature nearly so many of these touristically attractive animals: Gorillas, orangutans, tigers, and rhinos are creatures with plenty of "charisma", but they are exceptionally difficult to trace in rain forests, and still more difficult to approach close enough to inspect through a camera lens. Despite good interpretive facilities in a few rain forest parks, visitors are little interested in the abundant and diversified plant life of rain forests, let alone their myriad insects. Even the best tourist infrastructure, in terms of viewing trucks, saltlicks, waterholes, and similar measures, to help tourists and wild creatures to view each other at short range, seem little able to pull in tourists in sufficient numbers to make parks a paying proposition as compared with alternative forms of usage for rain forests. More arrangements such as the famous Tigertops could probably assist. But in the main, tropical rain forests as sites for floods of visitors have yet to be successful.

Conservation areas and multiple use

Fortunately, recreation and tourism can be combined with other types of rain forest utilization. A patch of forest set aside ostensibly to attract visitors can serve several other purposes, for example, for preservation of genetic reservoirs, safeguarding of watershed systems, regulation of local climate, etc. While certain of these complementary forms of "utilization" may appear to conflict with the strict "no exploitation" philosophy of parks and reserves, there need be no significant conflict in actual operation. Indeed, rain forest managers can now employ an extensive "conservation toolbox" with several categories of landuse — of which parks and reserves are only one category. According to the International Union for Conservation of Nature and Natural Resources (1978), there are at least ten types of conservation areas, ranging from Strict Nature Reserves to Multiple-Use Management Areas, each type being based on the objectives for which the area is to be managed. Thus a patch of rain forest that is set aside for recreation and tourism but in fact reveals little capacity to attract visitors, can serve several other purposes at the same time. So conservationists need not be too purist in their commitment to the pristine concept of parks and reserves; rather they might look at the idea of "conservation zones" that protect other resources besides "wildland amenities". For example, there seems to be no practical reason why a patch of rain forest should not be subject to selective exploitation, e.g. through gathering of wild foods (honey, rodents, etc.), a few highly specialist types of timber (e.g. rosewood), and germplasm for agriculture, at the same time that they offer a variety of biological experiences to visitors. Taken together, these different forms of rain forest utilization provide land managers and decision makers with a broad set of managerial options for forest land management. In this direction may lie the best prospect for long-term protection of rain forest tracts in relatively undisturbed form. Indeed, there could even be a danger that the high-prestige concept of parks may, in the rain forest biome, be accorded excessive emphasis, leaving other areas, at least equally important, in neglect. Conversely, there is a major advantage in having a number of conservation landuse categories in the biome: each nation can design a system of protected areas that meets its own needs, including responsibility for protection of irreplaceable resources and contribution to local development on a sustainable basis.

PRESENT POSITION AND FUTURE PROSPECTS

As we have seen, tropical rain forests to date feature all too few protected areas. Worse still, many of these protected areas are faring badly in the face of economic pressures to put them to more useful-seeming purposes.

In Southeast Asia, and especially in lowland forest zones, parks and reserves now come under attack of many kinds. In Sumatra, two parks have been violated by logging operations, a nature reserve has been given out for timber concessions, a sawmill has been built on the edge of the Gunung Leuser Reserve, and forests supposedly protected as hydrological reserves are being exploited for various purposes. In east Kalimantan (Borneo), one-third of the 2000-km^2 Kutai Reserve has been taken for logging. In Malaysia the 5000-km^2 Taman Nagara Park is subject to threat by logging interests that eye the Malaysian $1800 million worth of timber within its borders, and something similar applies to the 2000-km^2 Endau Rompin Park. In many protected areas of the Philippines, there is much hunting and intensive collecting of fuelwood, while shifting cultivators seem to operate with impunity, and certain localities even feature townships; the 73 000-ha Mount Apo National Park in Mindanao, southern Philippines, contains several endemic species, plus a concentration of the extremely endangered monkey-eating eagle (now re-named the Philippines eagle), yet the park may well be reduced to 13 790 ha, the rest being given over to logging and settlement. Many other instances could be cited to indicate how protected areas often fail to withstand economic pressures. The process seems likely to grow critical for rain forest conservation in the years ahead, unless protection policies and practices can better integrate these areas with their socioeconomic environments.

At the same time, it is heartening to hear that several countries have recently set aside an impressive array of parks and reserves — impressive, that is, as compared with previous situations, marginally significant compared with what is required. Peru hopes to protect almost 55 000 km^2 of its 650 000 km^2 of rain forest by 1980; several areas are to be established after the pattern of the Manu National Park, that incorporates the drainage of an entire tributary river system. As mentioned, Brazil hopes to set aside 175 000 km^2 of its sector of Amazonia. Indonesia plans to expand its parks and reserves from 36 000 to 100 000 km^2 by 1983. Zaire proposes to increase its network from 78 130 km^2 to 351 000 km^2, or 15% of the country, by 1980.

If the latter "big three" countries of the tropical rain forest biome follow through with their plans, their protected areas will amount altogether to 626 000 km^2, or an area almost the size of Spain and Portugal put together, or Texas, representing well over 7% of the entire biome. This will be highly encouraging, even if far short of the minimum 10 to 20% of the biome postulated by the theory of island biogeography.

REFERENCES

Adisoemarto, S. and Brunig, E.F. (Editors), 1979. *Transactions of the Second International MAB-IUFRO Workshop on Tropical Rainforest Ecosystems Research*. Chair of World Forestry, University of Hamburg, Hamburg, Reinbek, Spec. Rep. No. 2.

Cody, M.L. and Diamond, J.M. (Editors), 1975. *Ecology and Evolution of Communities*. Belknap Press of Harvard University Press, Cambridge, Mass.

Diamond, J.M., 1975. The island dilemma: lessons of modern biogeographic studies for the design of natural preserves. *Biol. Conserv.*, 7: 129–146.

Farnworth, F.G. and Golley, F.B. (Editors), 1974. *Fragile Ecosystems*. Springer-Verlag, Berlin.

Golley, F.B. and Medina, E. (Editors), 1975. *Tropical Ecological Systems*. Springer-Verlag, Berlin.

Inger, R.F., 1967. Annual reproductive patterns of lizards from a Bornean rain forest. *Ecology*, 47(6): 1007–1021.

Lack, D., 1976. *Island Biology*. Studies in Ecology, 3. Blackwell, Oxford.

Lekagul, B. and McNeely, J.A., 1978. *Mammals of Thailand*. Thailand Conservation Society, Bangkok.

Lowe-McConnell, R.H. (Editor), 1969. *Speciation in Tropical Environments*. Academic Press, New York, N.Y., 248 pp.

MacArthur, R.H. and Wilson, E.O., 1967. *The Theory of Island Biogeography*. Princeton University Press, Princeton, N.J., 203 pp.

Medway, Lord, 1981. Gene pools for forest species in peninsular Malaysia. In: *Proceedings of Eighth World Forestry Congress*. FAO, Rome, in press.

Medway, Lord and Wells, D.R., 1971. Diversity and density of birds and mammals at Kuala Lumpur Pahang. *Malay. Nat. J.*, 24: 238–247.

Meggers, B.J., Ayensu, E.S. and Duckworth, W.D. (Editors), 1973. *Tropical Forest Ecosystems in Africa and South America: A Comparative Review*. Smithsonian Press, Washington, D.C.

Myers, N., 1976. An expanded approach to the problem of disappearing species. *Science*, 193: 198–202.

Myers, N., 1979a. *The Sinking Ark*. Pergamon Press, New York, N.Y., 307 pp.

Myers, N., 1979b. Islands of conservation. *New Sci.*, 83(1169): 600–602.

Myers, N., 1980. *Report on Survey of Conversion Rates in Tropical Moist Forests*. National Research Council, Washington, D.C., 205 pp.

Molion, L.C.B., 1976. *A Climatonic Study of the Energy and Moisture Fluxes of the Amazonas Basin with considerations of Deforestation Effects.* Dissertation, University of Wisconsin, Madison, Wis.

Persson, R., 1974. *World Forest Resources.* Royal College of Forestry, Stockholm, Dep. For. Res. Note, No. 17.

Persson, R., 1975. *Forest Resources of Africa.* Royal College of Forestry, Stockholm, Dep. For. Res. Note, No. 18.

Prance, G.T., 1977. The phytogeographic subdivisions of Amazonia and their influence on the selection of biological reserves. In: G.T. Prance and T.S. Elias (Editors), *Extinction is Forever.* New York Botanical Garden, Bronx, N.Y., pp. 195–213.

Prance, G.T. (Editor), 1981. *The Model for Biological Diversification in the Tropics.* Columbia University Press, New York, N.Y.

Raup, D.M., Gould, S.J., Schopf, T.J.M. and Simberloff, D.S., 1973. Stochastic models of phylogeny and the evolution of diversity. *J. Geol.,* 81(5): 525–542.

Raven, P.H., 1974. Trends, priorities and needs in systematic and evolutionary biology. *Syst. Zool.,* 23: 416–439.

Raven, P.H., 1976. The destruction of the tropics. *Frontiers,* 40: 22–23.

Raven, P.H., Berlin, B. and Breedlove, D.E., 1971. The origins of taxonomy. *Science,* 174: 1210–1213.

Richards, P.W., 1973. The tropical rain forest. *Sci. Am.,* 229(6): 58–68.

Simberloff, D.S. and Abele, L.G., 1976. Island biogeography theory and conservation practice. *Science,* 191: 285–286.

Salati, E., Dall'olio, A., Matsui, E. and Gat, J.R., 1978. *Recycling of Water in the Amazon Basin: An Isotopic Study.* Division of Environmental Science, Centro de Energia Nuclear na Agricultura, Piracicaba.

Sommer, A., 1976. Attempt at an assessment of the world's tropical moist forest. *UnaSylva,* 28(112/113): 5–24.

Terborgh, J.W., 1974. Preservation of natural diversity: the problem of extinction-prone species. *BioScience,* 24: 715–722.

UNESCO, 1973. *Report of Expert Panel on Project No. 8, Conservation of Natural Areas and of the Genetic Material They Contain.* MAB Report Series No. 12. UNESCO, Paris, 64 pp.

UNESCO, 1974. *Report of Task Force on Criteria and Guidelines for the Choice and Establishment of Biosphere Reserves.* MAB Report Series No. 22. UNESCO, Paris, 61 pp.

UNESCO, 1978. *Tropical Forest Ecosystems: A State-of-Knowledge Report. Nat. Resour. Res.,* 14: 683 pp.

Wetterberg, G.B., Padua, M.T.J., De Castro, C.S. and De Vasconcelos, J.M.C., 1976. *An Analysis of Nature Conservation Priorities in the Amazon.* Instituto Brasileiro de Desenvolvimento Florestal, Brasilia.

Whitmore, T.C., 1975. *Tropical Rain Forests of the Far East.* Clarendon Press, Oxford, 282 pp.

Chapter 22

ECODEVELOPMENT

FRANK B. GOLLEY

INTRODUCTION

The term ecodevelopment was coined by Maurice F. Strong, the first Executive Director of the United Nations Environmental Program (UNEP, 1976) and is defined as development of a locality taking the fullest sustainable advantage of that locality's physical, biological and cultural resources. Ecodevelopment planning is constrained by the ability to harmonize changes in cultural, economic and ecological factors to ensure that the real, basic needs of people are meant on a sustained basis. One of the basic strategies of ecodevelopment is to increase national and local self reliance. Another is to fit development within the history and culture of the local people because, once the basic needs of food, clothing and shelter are met, the other improvements in life's quality depend upon subjective evaluations.

Ecodevelopment schemes are being organized in many parts of the world under UNEP encouragement and in many cases these involve tropical forest landscapes. It is appropriate to end a book on tropical forest ecosystem structure and function with a consideration of ecodevelopment patterns for tropical forests.

The word development itself has attained wide usage since the 1950s. In its economic and political sense it means change, growth, expansion, progress. The direction of development has sometimes been assumed to be toward the social-cultural and economic characteristics of the countries of North America and Europe. Indeed, these countries are called developed, while those with other characteristics are labelled developing countries. The contrast developed–developing misleads, of course. Few, if any, nations or peoples support a concept of

a steady state. Rather, all seek to develop, change, grow and expand in ways appropriate to that culture. This means that developed nations or regions are strong competitors for resources with developing nations or regions. Ecodevelopment shifts the focus from this broad competitive dichotomy toward different objectives. Raymond Dassman, in a recent conference, stated that these objectives were (1) a focus on the basic, real needs of the people, (2) emphasis on self reliance, and (3) development recognizing the symbiotic relationship between man and the natural world. In this chapter we will consider how the knowledge on tropical forest ecosystem structure and function may help in realizing these objectives of ecodevelopment in tropical forest landscapes.

CULTURAL CONTROL

While this volume has focused mainly on the biological attributes of tropical forests, the cultural and social characteristics of people are of equal significance when we move from a pure ecological analysis toward an applied analysis. Culture expresses the adaptation of a human group to its environment in terms of its history, biological and social characteristics and mythology. Culture represents the group's unique view of the world and it controls the actions of the individuals making up the group so that they share recognizable traits and patterns of behavior.

The culture of forest dwellers who live within tropical forests differs in significant ways from nonforest dwellers, regardless of whether these latter peoples are residents of tropical, temperate or arctic countries. As we have seen in Chapter 19, forest people have adapted to and depend upon the forest environment. They can satisfy their basic biological needs from the forest. While the forest peoples differ greatly in social-cultural patterns, they share a complex knowledge of the forest plant and animal species. Classification of plants, animals and ecological communities are based on practical and religious utility, and in many cases are very similar to the classification schemes of biological taxonomists.

Nonforest people also have their own cultural attitudes about tropical forests. Forests are damp, dark places, dense with vegetation, containing dangerous animals and disease. The removal of forest so that one can see and feel the sun gives the nonforest dweller a feeling of progress. Removal of enough forest so that one can see neighbors is even more progressive. Destruction and removal of the forest is absolutely destructive to the culture of the forest people because their very existence is tied to the environment of trees and associated life. Removal of forest is a positive, or at least a neutral, act to the nonforest dweller. It creates some money and jobs immediately and in the longer run it converts a landscape that is unusable and dangerous into one that is familiar.

In cultural terms humans must convert another human or a natural object into something recognizable before they can communicate with and use it. Nonforest people find it exceedingly difficult to deal with natural forest, rather they convert it to managed forest, plantations or agricultural fields. While the arguments for such conversion are couched in social-economic terms, they are always the social-economic terms appropriate to nonforest, agricultural urban cultures. The exploitation of tropical forests is fundamentally a battle between forest and nonforest cultures and with the energy and material sources to provide the chainsaws, bulldozers, guns and helicopters the nonforest cultures must inevitably win the battle unless the terms of modern cultures change.

The inability to appreciate the value of natural forest is characteristic of tropical farmers, agriculturalists and urban dwellers, as well as bureaucracies and lumber corporations. In fact, the ability to relate to the problem of the forest dweller probably is most characteristic of people whose culture includes a deep humanitarian element and who are sufficiently distant from the tropical forest environment to be able to view it in an abstract sense. The deep ecology movement (Naess, 1974) seeks to encourage a more tolerant, caring and ecological culture for man which could provide a bridge between urban dweller, forest man and the natural world. Ecodevelopment includes deep ecology only peripherally at present.

PRINCIPLES OF STRUCTURE AND FUNCTION APPLIED

In the preceding chapters a number of ecological principles of tropical forest structure and function have been presented and discussed. In this section I want to identify certain principles which have special significance to ecodevelopment. A thorough discussion of the application of ecological principles to development has been presented by Dasmann et al. (1973).

The first principle concerns the organization of ecosystems. Each ecosystem can be subdivided into components, each of which can be treated as an individual system (Fig. 22.1). Each ecosystem can also be considered as a component of a larger or more complex system. Thus, ecosystems can be arranged in a hierarchy of systems, ranging from a tropical forest landscape with forests, swamps, mountains, rivers and lakes, to tropical forest plant and animal populations. The significance of this principle of hierarchical organization is that all the systems are coupled together and interrelated. An action in one system may have an impact or many impacts in the other systems of the hierarchy. Thus, development activities in the forest can influence the river systems associated with forests.

The second principle involves the flow of energy or power in ecological systems. Odum and Pinkerton (1955) have stated that systems which maximize energy flow have a greater competitive advantage than systems which maximize their efficiency of power use. The maximum energy output theorem helps to explain the relationship between regions and people in tropical forests. If there is a reason to control the pattern of competitive relationships it is necessary to monitor and regulate power or energy flow.

The third principle also is concerned with energy flow. An increase in energy input to a system will result in an increase in system organization. This

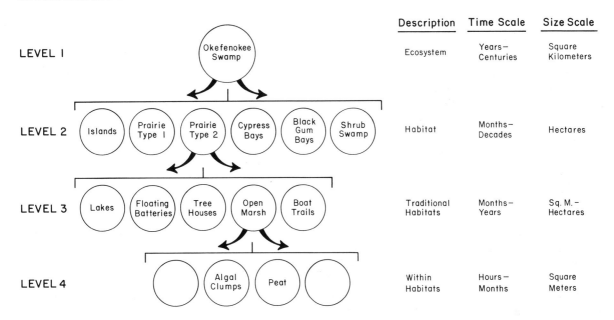

Fig. 22.1. Hierarchical model of the Okeefenokee swamp ecosystem, showing four levels of different size and with different time scales of response. (Drawn from unpublished report by B. Patten, Institute of Ecology, University of Georgia, Athens, Ga., U.S.A.)

relationship holds to a point where the organization is optimum. Further energy input can result in system disturbance and a loss of organization. Ecological succession illustrates this principle in tropical forests. The numbers of species increase with succession, as do the number of connections between species. These relationships are described by various measures of species diversity. In mature, old forests the numbers either stabilize or decrease. Thus, ecodevelopment needs to consider the relation between energy input by development and the desired level of organization of the system. Since these relationships are poorly understood, development may need to be preceded by research to demonstrate the form of expected relationship (e.g. Norman, 1978).

The fourth principle concerns limits to ecological rate processes. All such processes can be described by a performance curve (Fig. 22.2), which shows that the process may increase with change in input only to a point. At this point the relation of input to output is optimum. Further input results in a decline in the output. The optimum represents the limit to performance for that particular input. Fertilizer amendments to soil in relation to crop production illustrate this principle. In ecosystems the performance curves are more complicated since

many inputs and outputs are linked together. Development can only proceed so far until the optimum conditions are exceeded. This is a different type of limit than that described by Liebig's Law of the Minimum — the essential element in minimum supply limits growth. Instead, this principle states that given ever-increasing inputs (great wealth, aid, discovery of resources) optimum development may be exceeded and the system performance upset. Too little and too much are both dangers in ecodevelopment.

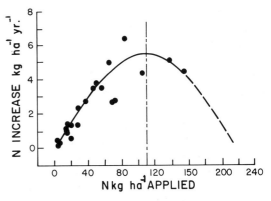

Fig. 22.2. The relationship of nitrogen increase in a crop of maize to the nitrogen applied as fertilizer (Data from Institute of Ecology, University of Georgia, Athens, Ga., U.S.A.).

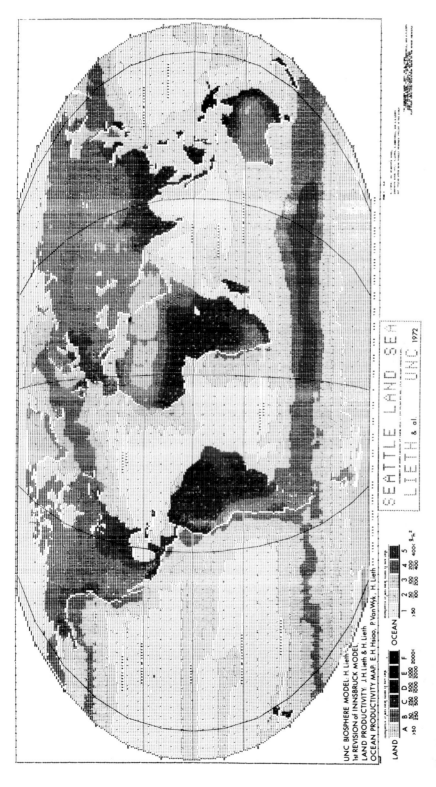

Fig. 22.3. Distribution of net primary production over the biosphere. (From H. Lieth.)

The final principle pertinent here involves the geography of resource distribution. In all systems we find that resources are distributed in patches and aggregations. This is because the earth is a sphere and receives energy unequally over its surface and is also a planet with an ever-changing surface. Tectonic plate movement, uplift, volcanism, erosion, and other geologic forces create heterogeneity of ore deposits, soils, topography and so on. Patches where resources are available in excess or in the proper proportions may have abundant populations. Patches where resources are limited have less abundance. While unequal distribution of resources can be overcome by redistribution of resources, the costs of redistribution decrease the total resources available. Fig. 22.3 illustrates the distribution of one of these resources, primary production on the earth. Tropical forest regions have generally high production rates of natural vegetation.

MEETING THE BASIC, REAL NEEDS OF PEOPLE

According to Bennett (1976), "much human behavior is devoted to reordering phenomena to avoid a random or entropic state. This proposition balances the recurrent tendency to make stability or, at least, homeostasis the normative basis of theory in human phenomena or to apply concepts appropriate mainly to nonhuman realms to the much more dynamic human realm." The real, basic needs of people may not be simply the biological or physical–chemical needs but include satisfaction of the human need to organize, reorder and understand in a logical and mythical sense the world around them. We understand rather clearly the biological needs of humans. For example, the data on human nutritional requirements are well known. However, we do not understand how social-cultural factors influence biological needs.

Further, the needs for people must be referenced to the social-ecological hierarchy. If we are referring to the people living within tropical forest, the problem revolves around providing protection for an adequate area of forest, to meet their annual and generational needs. If we refer to the people of the region or a nation, ecodevelopment will have a different form than it would for agricultural people, the urban population or people generally. Seldom is it possible to solve all of these needs with one plan.

Rather, actions and needs conflict and methods of identifying the basis of conflict and resolving conflict are necessary.

In most development processes this set of actions is generalized. For example, there may be first a comparison of the rates of production, food consumption, nutritional status, or population growth between nations and regions. These comparisons lead to the conclusion that one region has less or more than another, which provides a basis for initiation of activities to equalize the differences. The needs of people in a broad region are defined in terms of the conditions of people in another region, without taking into account the geography of resources and population. Discussion of the cultural reasons for these patterns are beyond the scope of this chapter. Nevertheless, there is abundant experience that operation on general objectives does not meet specific needs (Paddock and Paddock, 1973). Rather, ecodevelopment needs must be identified and generated at the local level by the people themselves. Further, it must be accepted that the needs will vary from people to people and place to place, may conflict with the needs perceived by scientists and technologists, may be contradictory, and may reflect more the need to reorder the environment than to cause directional change.

However, recognizing that need is a culturally determined factor, we can examine briefly the biological and physical factors underlying human life in the forested tropics. The human populations are distributed quite unequally over the face of the earth and the rates of increase of population are disproportionately larger in the tropical areas (Table 22.1). Population, in turn, creates demands upon the soil, forests, mines, and oceans. Since tropical regions do not have the same proportions of the landscape in tilled area (Table 22.2), to satisfy equal food demand per capita in tropical and temperate areas requires higher yield per acre in tropical agriculture. While intensive agricultural systems in the tropics do produce extremely high yields (for example, three crops of rice and other species may be obtained per year in China, the Phillippines and elsewhere), the intensive hand labor required for this production is not culturally acceptable in many parts of the tropics.

An alternative is to maintain a culturally acceptable agricultural technique and increase the quan-

TABLE 22.1

Percentage increases in population and energy consumption per capita between 1950 and 1970

	Population (%)	Energy per person (%)
World	46	57
Africa	59	73
North America	38	43
Latin America	75	122
Asia	52	197
Europe	18	96
Oceania	54	54

Source: United Nations.

TABLE 22.2

World land use, 1966 (in millions of km²)

	Total	Tilled	Pasture	Forest	Other[1]
Europe	4.9	1.5	0.9	1.4	1.1
U.S.S.R.	22.4	2.3	3.7	9.1	7.3
Asia	27.8	4.5	4.5	5.2	13.7
Africa	30.2	2.3	7.0	6.0	15.0
North America	22.4	2.6	3.7	8.2	7.9
South America	17.8	0.8	4.1	9.4	3.5
Oceania	8.5	0.4	4.6	0.8	2.7
Total[2]	134.2	14.3	23.6	40.2	51.2
Percentage	100%	10.6%	21.3%	29.9%	38.2%

[1]Deserts, wasteland, built-on land, glaciers, wetlands.
[2]Less Antarctica.

tity of land by cutting forest and converting it to food production landscapes. This process is going on rapidly throughout the world. In some cases the process is spontaneous with shifting cultivators or small cattle men (Heckadon, 1977) opening up the forest. In other cases, governments actively settle farmers in forests. While farmers have an understanding of the forest components leading to adequate farm sites (Golley et al., 1971), they do not understand the scale of operation needed to produce an adequate livelihood for their family plus the surplus to support the infrastructure of a frontier and a settled area. As small farmers fail and move deeper into the forest, successful small farmers and larger landowners buy up the land and convert it to profitable and culturally acceptable agricultural systems. In the neotropics these often are cattle ranches, producing meat for markets in

temperate regions (Table 22.3 gives an example of this process in Central America).

Eventually these strategies must change. The basic productive power of most regions or nations is agriculture. Until agricultural production is adequate, other production sectors are unstable. This is especially true when other production sectors are based on nonrenewable resources such as mature tropical forest, oil, copper, tin and other materials. When these resources are extracted and processed they are gone forever — they should, therefore, be husbanded carefully and command high prices because of their rarity. The Chinese have shown that with intensive hand labor and highly motivated social systems very poor landscapes can be transformed into agricultural lands producing a surplus. Such intensive systems exist or did exist in most tropical areas. For example, in the Mesoamerican region of the neotropics a very intensive agricultural system developed which utilized swamp lands and lake borders. Mounds of soil and vegetation are used as fields, water weeds trap nutrients and serve as fertilizer and mulch (Lot et al., 1978) and the muds under the water between fields are used for fertilizer and soil amendments. In Mexico these systems are called *chinampas* and are under investigation as a modern system for intensive crop production (Gómez-Pompa, 1978). It is likely that intensive use of present agricultural lands could provide adequate food to satisfy tropical population demands, without converting more forest to fields. However, this possibility does not fit the cultural attitudes of nonforest, cattle-loving people who consider hand labor and close attention to soil, water and plants as the mark of a peasantry

TABLE 22.3

Increase in pasture acreage and per capita beef consumption (Parsons, 1976) in selected Central American nations

Country	Percent increase in pasture acreage 1960–1970	Per capita beef consumption (kg)	
		1959–63 (aver.)	1972
Panama	43%	19	23.5
Nicaragua	48%	13	15
Costa Rica	62%	12	8.5
Honduras	–	7	6.5
El Salvador	–	7.5	5.5

or a farmer — both words pejorative in the vocabulary of many peoples in both the tropical and temperate world.

Can the forest provide a solution to meeting the basic, real needs of the people? We have seen in Chapters 8 and 17 that forests can be highly productive of wood products. Of course, mature forest is not growing or increasing in size, therefore production replaces death only and harvest of mature forest is much like tapping an oil well. To replace a mature forest requires hundreds of years and thus the forest is not a renewable resource in human terms. Mature forest can be converted into or replaced by production forest, however. And these production forests can supply wood products, biomass energy, fire wood and other products such as wild game. The translation of wood products into satisfaction of the demands of a tropical population could theoretically be adequate. Yet I know of no case where lumber and mill workers have such incomes that they can obtain material benefits equal to urban industrial workers or white-collar workers. However, these differences may be controlled by culturally determined attitudes toward the value of labor and not the production of the resources.

Finally, forests are also discussed as sources of special products and as the source of future products (gene pools). It is often true that forest people know most, if not all, of the forest species and have practical or ceremonial and ritual uses for most of the forest plants and animals. The high diversity of tropical forests is imitated in the traditional home gardens and agricultural plots of tropical farmers (Terra, 1954, 1958). However, I know of no economic evaluation of the potential value of forest as a source of new products. Production of subsidiary products, other than wood, is usually of minor economic importance (Moraes, 1974) (Table 22.4).

Clearly, the amount of information necessary to evaluate the ability of the resource base to meet the basic, real needs of the population is inadequate. In most cases surveys of known resources are non-existent or out of date. Trained cadres of scientists and engineers are unavailable for research, the infrastructure for research is inadequate, and the research that is done is directed toward irrelevant topics. Tropical countries, as well as temperate countries, need to devise mechanisms to direct and support research, surveys and technology and yet retain the flexibility to pursue new and unimaginable ends.

SELF RELIANCE

The importance of self reliance may best be explained by considering a society, region, or nation as a box. This means that the boundaries to the system can be defined and that the internal details of the system are not taken into account initially. This system receives a variety of inputs from its environment, such as water, nutrients from the soil, oil, iron and so on. It also may receive inputs from other systems through trade, aid, migration and other exchanges. The system produces outputs which similarly may go to the environment and to other societies.

A self-reliant system depends mainly upon inputs from its environment to alter, improve or change its internal order within the box. It minimizes inputs from other systems. Of course, no system is closed. Since the earth is geographically heterogenous, all systems must exchange resources and products to obtain the necessary mix of materials for modern life. Thus, most governments are preoccupied with regulating the inputs and outputs to a nation to obtain balance and to allow for internal change or growth. Clearly as the ratio of inputs (or outputs) from the system environment to the inputs from other systems becomes smaller, the central control

TABLE 22.4

Main agricultural and extractive plant products from Amazonia, 1972 (from Moraes, 1974)

Products	Worth (Cr$1000)	Area (1000 ha)	%Needs covered
Timber	180 000	3000	export
Meat (beef cattle)	128 226	4600	50[1]
Black pepper	50 800	10	export
Manioc	46 500	122	100
Rubber	44 300	extractive	export
Milk	39 700	37	20
Jute (plus urena)	37 800	24	export
Rice	28 300	106	80
Brazil nuts	19 700	extractive	export
Maize	15 600	75	50
Cowpea (plus beans)	12 800	19	80

[1]Prices are beyond the reach of lower income population.

required to negotiate and deal with other different, often hostile, societies becomes greater. Self reliance shifts the attention internally by reducing the need for inputs from other societies and focuses on the system's ability to order, reorder and control the conversion of inputs to outputs within its own cultural and historical conditions. Presumably a self-reliant system would emphasize planning and research and de-emphasize communication and trade with other systems.

A major task in building a self-reliant system is to construct and maintain adequate storages of essential materials so that oscillations in the environment cannot disturb the balance. In the tropical forest we have observed how the large biomass of tree trunks, branches, and roots act as storages to buffer changes in nutrient flux (Chapter 9). Similar storages are required in human systems but they are difficult to operate since there is a continuous pressure from population growth and population demand to use the stores. If the stores are used then the population must bear the brunt of adaptation to changes in input–outputs. This is less difficult for societies able to accept mortality as a balancing force than one which seeks to ban mortality and regulate natality instead.

In a self-reliant society the quality of life or standard of living of the inhabitants will depend upon the way that resources are allocated among the members of the society and the level of the resource base. This means that two societies with vastly different resource bases may have the same average standard of living or societies with same resource bases may have vastly different standards of living. These patterns are culturally determined. Ecodevelopment does not express an opinion on which pattern is best, rather it seeks to make clear alternative patterns so that a society can recognize options and accept limits in a realistic way.

In tropical forest landscapes forestry and agriculture clearly are the major economic activities and should be carried out to provide food, shelter and clothing for the inhabitants, plus a surplus for storage and for exchange. In such societies, as in temperate societies, these farmers and foresters should be among the best paid and most respected occupations. The value of their labor should be sufficient to provide them a high standard of living, with adequate opportunity for education, for medical treatment and care, for care of the elderly, for

entertainment and recreation, and to provide the motivation for optimum food and forest production. They should not support urban workers with cheap food and products based on extremely long hours, hard labor, intermittent employment, and denial of education, medical and social-recreation opportunities. Many societies have their priorities backward by placing all emphasis on the city and industry. Urban and industrial development must be balanced with agricultural–forest development or cities become clogged by migrating unemployed agricultural workers and industrial growth is difficult. Yet in most cultures agricultural and forest workers are among the lowest on the social hierarchy and urban workers are vastly better off than their rural counterparts.

Industrial development, especially that concerned with processing agricultural and forest products should be decentralized and placed in the rural areas where it can take advantage of excess labor or seasonal labor and is near the point of production. In this case a transport net of canals, railroads and highways are needed to distribute products.

Heavy industry which will depend upon mines and imported material must be centrally located where it has a labor force, where the economic equation is favorable and where the outputs of wastes do not destroy the environment. In all countries examples can be found where industrial wastes destroy the self reliance of that country in food, forest or aquatic production. Ecodevelopment shows that these are not either/or patterns but that it is possible to plan to have both industry and undisturbed waters and lands.

SYMBIOTIC PLANNING

Ecodevelopment recognizes that man is a biological–ecological being and ultimately depends upon the ecosystems in which he lives. While man alters and creates ecosystems, these are linked to the natural ecosystems and natural environments which provides a variety of services to man free of direct economic expense. These services include processing of wastes, providing clean air and water, and furnishing flexibility and stability. It is impossible to bring all of these forces under man's direct control, but it is not clear what proportion of the earth's land and waters can be altered before the services are irreversibly disrupted.

The tropical forest remains today as one of the world's last large areas of intact forest. The forest is important in controlling the rate at which water reenters the atmosphere and runs off the soil to rivers. One forest area, the Amazon, produces over 20% of the world's fresh water entering the oceans. There is some evidence that climate can be altered by removal of forest and by industrialization as in other regions (Bryson and Baerreis, 1967; Changnon, 1968). Thus, preservation of the tropical forest, or at least large parts of it, is a defensible position, although it is clear that tropical nations should receive some benefits from the world community if they are so public spirited as to forgo development of forested regions.

It is more likely for ecodevelopment planning to seek a compromise situation, where some of the landscape is transformed into agricultural land and forest plantations on suitable sites and natural tropical forest is preserved for forest dwellers, for sight seeing, for recreation, for control of water runoff and research. For example, Malaysia has developed a series of rain forest national parks (*Malayan Nature Journal*, 1971) which conserve tropical forest *per se*. Many other countries, most notably Costa Rica whose former President Daniel Oduber received several international conservation awards for park establishment, have also developed viable tropical park systems. The Malaysia parks are large and furnish a variety of experiences for visitors, ranging from simple walks to see plants and animals, to arduous trails where young people can mount expeditions and explore the natural heritage of their nation. In one, Taman Negara, a nature camp is operated for school children, who live for a week exposed directly to the rain forest. There is no better way to teach urban and rural children appreciation for the forest than to give them this type of experience. In fact, probably an ability to understand the ecological principles underlying forest and land–water management probably can only be taught in this way — otherwise the urban dweller is susceptible to the argument that man is the master of all nature.

Preserved tropical forest areas have a variety of values — historical, religious, social-cultural, biological and ecological. But the question of their size and shape is more difficult to answer

(Chapter 21). Some of the animals in tropical forests roam over vast expanses of territory and if these animals are to be included in the park or reserve their ranges must be determined and all required habitats identified. It is not sufficient to draw lines on maps based on rivers, roads or political jurisdictions. Also some tropical forest animals, especially some of the birds, have limited ability to move over unsuitable habitat. For this reason such isolated patches of reserves have smaller faunas of these species than patches connected by corridors of forest where migration between patches can occur (Terborgh, 1975). These few examples are sufficient to show how complicated the preservation of parks and reserves can be.

As mentioned in Chapter 21, UNESCO's Man and Biosphere Program (MAB) has emphasized setting up preserves of tropical forest in their biosphere reserve program. Biosphere reserves are to be centers for research into the ecology of tropical forest and some of the data presented in this volume comes from MAB research projects. Ecosystem research, such as that supported and encouraged by MAB, is difficult because it requires teams of scientists each focusing on an important part of the forest structure and function yet contributing to the whole objective of the study. Typically modern science is reductionistic, individualistic and competitive. While ecosystem research retains individual creativity, it is synthetic since all contribute to the overall objectives which are encapsulated in the initial hypotheses and the ecosystem models. I believe that it is this type of scientific research that will be most useful in ecodevelopment.

Finally, the symbiotic aspect of ecodevelopment also involves a religious or philosophical component. All major religions have statements on the ethical relation of man to man. Ecodevelopment extends these ethical statements to man and other beings, including ecosystems. Man has a responsibility to act ethically toward other animals, plants, and landscapes (Blackstone, 1974). Forest man expresses his relationship to the tropical forest in terms of direct mutual dependence since he lives within the forest daily and is an extension of the forest so that it penetrates his being. Modern man is separated from nature by ecosystems of his own invention. These are linked to and depend upon the natural systems and modern man must be able to visualize and appreciate these linkages and take a more global view in order to appreciate his dependence and responsibility to forests and waters. He obtains this appreciation through education, mass communication, and visits to parks and reserves. If he can express this more general, more abstract dependence and responsibility in an ethical code then there is a basis for ecodevelopment. The sage can find statements in the holy books of all peoples which express this ethical relation of man to nature — however, these statements have been given less attention than those concerned with relations of man to man. A balanced ethic of man to nature, man to man is more appropriate to the modern predicament.

REFERENCES

Bennett, J.W., 1976. Anticipation, adaptation, and the concept of culture in anthropology. *Science*, 192 (4242): 847–853.

Blackstone, W.T. (Editor), 1974. *Philosophy and Environmental Crisis*. University of Georgia Press, Athens, Ga., 140 pp.

Bryson, R.A. and Baerreis, D.A., 1967. Possibilities of major climatic modification and their implications: Northwest India, a case for study. *Bull. Am. Meteorol. Soc.*, 48(3): 136–142.

Changnon, S.A., Jr., 1968. The LaPorte weather anomaly — fact or fiction? *Bull. Am. Meteorol. Soc.*, 49(1): 4–11.

Dasmann, R.F., Multon, J.P. and Freeman, P.H., 1973. *Ecological Principles for Economic Development*. Wiley and Sons, New York, N.Y., 252 pp.

Golley, F.B., Olien, M.D. and Hoy, D.R., 1971. Cognized environments of San Carlos Valley settlers. *Rev. Geogr.*, 74: 33–50.

Gómez-Pompa, A., 1978. An old answer to the future. *Mazingira*, 5: 50–55.

Heckadon, S., 1977. Dinamica social de la cultura del potrero en Panama. In: R. Torres de Araus (Editor), *Actas del IV Symposium Internacional de Ecologia Tropical, Panama*, III, pp. 797–817.

Karr, J.R., 1978. Man and wildlife in the tropics: past, present, and future. In: *Wildlife and People*. Purdue University, West Lafayette, Ind., pp. 120–139.

Lot, A., Novelo, A. and Quiros, A., 1978. The Chinampa: Agricultural system that utilizes aquatic plants. In: *Eighteenth Annual Meeting Aquatic Plant Management Society*, Florida.

Malayan Nature Journal, 1971. The national parks of Malaysia. *Malay. Nat. J.*, 24(3/4): 111–262.

Moraes, V.H.F., 1974. Case study for Brazil. In: G.M. Dalen and C.R. Tipton (Editors), *Environmental Accomplishments to Date: A Reason for Hope*. Battelle Memorial Institute, Columbus, Ohio, pp. 27–32.

Naess, A., 1974. The ecopolitical frontier: a case study. *Intecol Bull.*, 5: 18–26.

Norman, M.J.T., 1978. Energy inputs and outputs of subsistence cropping systems in the tropics. *Agroecosystems*, 4: 355–366.

Odum, H.T. and Pinkerton, R.C., 1955. Time's speed regulator: the optimum efficiency for maximum power output in physical and biological systems. *Am. Sci.*, 43(2): 331–343.

Paddock, W. and Paddock, E., 1973. *We Don't Know How*. Iowa State University Press, Ames, Iowa, 331 pp.

Parsons, J.J., 1976. Forest to pasture: development or destruction? *Rev. Biol. Trop.*, 24(Suppl. 1): 121–138.

Terborgh, J., 1975. Faunal equilibria and the design of wildlife preserve. In: F.B. Golley and E. Medina (Editors), *Tropical Ecological Systems, Trends in Terrestrial and Aquatic Research*. Springer-Verlag, Berlin, pp. 369–380.

Terra, G.J.A., 1954. Mixed garden horticulture in Java. *Malay. J. Trop. Geogr.*, 3: 33–43.

Terra, G.J.A., 1958. Farm systems in Southeast Asia. *Neth. J. Agric. Sci.*, 6(4): 157–190.

UNEP, 1976. *Ecodevelopment. Report of the Governing Council. Fourth Session, Nairobi*. UNEP/GC/80.

United Nations Statistical Office, 1954. *Statistical Yearbook 1953*. United Nations Publ. Serv., New York, N.Y.

United Nations Statistical Office, 1972. *Statistical Yearbook 1971*. United Nations Publ. Service, New York, N.Y.

SYSTEMATIC LIST OF GENERA[1]

MONERA (PROKARYOTA)

BACTERIA

Bacillus
Chlamydia
Leptospira
Rickettsia
Salmonella
Yersinia

PLANTS

FUNGI

ŻYGOMYCOTINA
Endogonaceae
Endogone

PINOPHYTA (GYMNOSPERMAE)

Araucariaceae
Agathis
Araucaria
Cupressaceae
Cupressus
Cycadaceae
Cycas
Pinaceae
Pinus
Podocarpaceae
Dacrydium
Podocarpus

MAGNOLIOPHYTA (ANGIOSPERMAE)

LILIOPSIDA
(MONOCOTYLEDONES)

Amaryllidaceae
Araceae
Amorphophallus
Arecaceae
Acrocomia
Asterogyne
Astrocaryum
Borassus
Cocos
Corypha
Eugeissona
Hyphaene
Metroxylon
Scheelea

Thrinax
Bambusaceae
Bambusa
Oxytenanthera
Phyllostachys
Bromeliaceae
Costaceae
Costus
Cyclanthaceae
Heliconiaceae
Heliconia
Liliaceae
Gloriosa
Marantaceae
Calathea
Musaceae
Musa
Orchidaceae
Angraecum
Pandanaceae
Freycinetia
Microdesmis
Pandanus
Poaceae
Imperata
Saccharum
Spartina
Zingiberaceae
Zingiber

MAGNOLIOPSIDA
(DICOTYLEDONES)

Acanthaceae
Aphelandra
Aceraceae
Acer
Anacardiaceae
Mangifera
Schinus
Spondias
Trichoscypha
Anisophylleaceae
Combretocarpus
Annonaceae
Annona
Polyalthia
Xylopia
Apocynaceae
Alstonia
Aspidosperma
Thevetia
Araliaceae
Cussonia
Didymopanax

Asteraceae
Vernonia
Averrhoaceae
Averrhoa
Avicenniaceae
Avicennia
Balanophoraceae
Thonningia
Betulaceae
Alnus
Betula
Bignoniaceae
Crescentia
Godmania
Kigelia
Oroxylum
Pachyptera
Spathodea
Tabebuia
Tecoma
Bixaceae
Bixa
Bombacaceae
Adansonia
Bombacopsis
Cavanillesia
Ceiba
Durio
Ochroma
Pachira
Rhodognaphalopsis
Bonnetiaceae
Ploiarium
Boraginaceae
Burseraceae
Aucoumea
Dacryodes
Protium
Santiria
Cactaceae
Pereskia
Caesalpiniaceae
Brachystegia
Caesalpinia
Cassia
Copaifera
Delonix
Dimorphandra
Eperua
Hymenaea
Julbernardia
Koompassia
Macrolobium
Mora
Parkinsonia
Piliostigma
Swartzia
Capparidaceae
Capparis
Caricaceae
Carica
Caryocaraceae
Caryocar
Casuarinaceae

Casuarina
Gymnostoma
Chrysobalanaceae
Licania
Parinari
Clusiaceae
Calophyllum
Clusia
Cratoxylon
Vismia
Cochlospermaceae
Cochlospermum
Combretaceae
Combretum
Laguncularia
Terminalia
Convolvulaceae
Ipomoea
Cucurbitaceae
Anguria
Gurania
Cunoniaceae
Dilleniaceae
Curatella
Dipterocarpaceae
Cotylelobium
Dipterocarpus
Dryobalanops
Hopea
Shorea
Upuna
Vatica
Ebenaceae
Diospyros
Ehretiaceae
Cordia
Elaeocarpaceae
Sloanea
Ericaceae
Erythroxylaceae
Euphorbiaceae
Alchornea
Drypetes
Hevea
Hura
Jatropha
Macaranga
Mallotus
Micranda
Fabaceae
Andira
Anthonota
Baphia
Bauhinia
Endespermum
Erythrina
Mucuna
Piscidia
Pterocarpus
Robinia
Sophora
Fagaceae
Castanea
Fagus

---

[1] The taxonomic relationships of all genera of plants and animals are shown. Genera are listed alphabetically under families, arranged into phyla and subphyla; orders are included in the animal kingdom.

MAGNOLIOPSIDA (continued)

Lithocarpus
Nothofagus
Quercus
Flacourtiaceae
 Casearia
 Scottellia
 Xylosma
 Zuelania
Gesneriaceae
 Columnea
Guttiferae (Hypericaceae)
Ixonanthaceae
 Ixonanthes
Juglandaceae
 Engelhardtia
Lamiaceae
 Persea
Lauraceae
 Eusideroxylon
 Ocotea
Lecythidaceae
 Couroupita
 Eschweilera
Loganiaceae
 Fagraea
Magnoliaceae
 Liriodendron
Malpighiaceae
 Byrsonima
 Heteropteris
Malvaceae
 Gossypium
 Hibiscus
Melastomataceae
 Blakea
 Macairea
 Melastoma
 Miconia
Meliaceae
 Carapa
 Guarea
 Swietenia
Memecylaceae
 Memecylon
 Mouriri
Mimosaceae
 Acacia
 Calliandra
 Entada
 Enterolobium
 Inga
 Parkia
 Pentaclethra
 Piptadeniastrum
 Pithecellobium
 Prosopis
 Samanea
Moraceae
 Artocarpus
 Brosimum
 Castilla
 Ficus
 Trophis
Myristicaceae
 Pycnanthus
Myrsinaceae
Myrtaceae
 Calypthranthes
 Eucalyptus
 Eugenia
 Metrosideros
 Rhodamnia
 Rhodomyrtus

Syzygium
Tristania
Whiteodendron
Nauclaceae
 Adina
 Anthocephalus
Nyctaginaceae
 Bougainvillea
 Pisonia
Olacaceae
 Coula
 Minquartia
 Schoepfia
 Strombosia
Oleaceae
 Fraxinus
Passifloraceae
 Passiflora
Piperaceae
 Piper
Polygonaceae
 Coccoloba
 Triplaris
Proteaceae
 Grevillea
 Roupala
Rafflesiaceae
 Rafflesia
Rhamnaceae
 Karwinskia
 Sarcomphalus (Ziziphus)
 Ziziphus
Rhizophoraceae
 Rhizophora
Rubiaceae
 Coffea
 Corynanthe
 Genipa
 Massularia
 Mussaenda
 Palicourea
 Randia
 Remigia
 Retiniphyllum
 Warszewiczia
Salicaceae
 Populus
 Salix
Sapindaceae
 Cupania
 Hypelate
 Xerospermum
Sapotaceae
 Chrysophyllum
 Manilkara
 Mastichodendron
 Mimusops
 Nemaluma
 Omphalocarpon
 Palaquium
Solanaceae
 Cestrum
 Markea
 Solanum
 Trianaea
Sonneratiaceae
 Sonneratia
Sterculiaceae
 Cola
 Guazuma
 Pterocymbium
 Scaphopetalum
 Sterculia
 Theobroma
Strychnaceae

Strychnos
Tetramelaceae
 Octomeles
Theophrastaceae
 Jacquinia
Thymelaeaceae
 Gonystylus
Tiliaceae
 Luehea
 Tilia
Uapacaceae
 Uapaca
Ulmaceae
 Trema
Urticaceae
 Cecropia
 Musanga
Verbenaceae
 Gmelina
 Lantana
 Tectona
Violaceae
 Rinorea
Vochysiaceae
 Vochysia
Zygophyllaceae
 Guaiacum

ANIMALS

PROTOZOA

 Leishmania
 Paracoccidioides
 Plasmodium
 Trypanosoma

ASCHELMINTHES

NEMATODA
 Oncocerca
 Strongyloides

ANNELIDA

OLIGOCHAETA
 Enchytraeidae
HIRUDINEA

MOLLUSCA

GASTROPODA
 Caracolus
 Limicolaria
 Polydontes
 Polymita

ARTHROPODA

ARACHNIDA (ARACHNOIDEA)
Acarina (Acari)
 Haemaphysalis
 Leptotrombidium

COLLEMBOLA

CRUSTACEA
Isopoda

INSECTA

Coleoptera
 Brenthidae
 Bruchidae
 Buprestidae

Cerambycidae
 Stenodontes
Cetoniidae
Curculionidae
Lucanidae
Scarabaeidae
 Strategus
Scolytidae
Silphidae
 Diamesus
Tenebrionidae
Diptera
 Culicidae
 Aedes
 Anopheles
 Culex
 Haemagogus
 Sabethes
 Cuterebridae
 Dermatobia
 Drosophilidae
 Drosophila
 Glossinidae
 Glossina
 Pschychodidae
 Lutzomiya
 Simulidae
 Simulium
 Tachinidae
Hemiptera
 Aphididae
 Coreidae
 Fulgoridae
 Lygaeidae
 Membracidae
 Pentatomidae
 Pyrrhocoridae
Homoptera
Hymenoptera
 Agaontidae
 Anthophoridae
 Apis
 Centris
 Epicharis
 Melipona
 Trigona
 Formicidae
 Atta
 Eciton
 Ichneumonidae
 Vespidae
 Polybia
 Xylocopidae
 Xylocopa
Isoptera
 Kalotermitidae
 Kalotermes
 Rhinotermitidae
 Coptotermes
 Parrhinotermes
 Schedorhitermes
 Termitidae
 Amitermitinae
 Amitermes
 Microcerotermes
 Macrotermitinae
 Macrotermes
 Microtermes
 Odontotermes
 Nasutitermitinae
 Bulbitermes
 Hospitalitermes
 Lacessitermes
 Longipeditermes
 Nasutitermes

INSECTA (*continued*)

Termitinae
Dicuspiditermes
Homallotermes
Pericapritermes
Procapritermes
Termes
Lepidoptera
Arctiidae
Hypercompe
Heliconiidae
Heliconius
Lycaenidae
Mimacraea
Pseudaletis
Morphidae
Morpho
Nymphalidae
Acraea
Papilionidae
Battus
Parides
Pyralidae
Saturniidae
Hylesia
Sphingidae
Xanthopan
Neuroptera
Odonata
Orthoptera
Acridinae
Symphyta
Thysanoptera

MYRIAPODA
Chilopoda
Diplopoda

CHORDATA

AMPHIBIA
Salientia
Ascaphidae
Ascaphus
Taudactylus
Hylidae
Agalynchnis
Phyllomedusa
Leptodactylidae
Eleutherodactylus
Notaden
Rhacophoridae
Chiromantis
Rhacophorus

REPTILIA
Squamata
Agamidae
Draco
Amphisbaenidae
Colubridae
Crotalidae
Bothrops
Gekkonidae

Hemidactylus
Sphaerodactylus
Tarentola
Iguanidae
Anolis
Callisaurus
Dipsosaurus
Iguana
Sceloporus
Tropidurus
Uma
Natricidae
Chrysopelea
Scincidae
Mabuya
Sphenomorphus
Tropidophorus
Teiidae
Cnemidophorus
Gymnophthalmus
Varanidae
Varanus

AVES
Apodiformes
Trochilidae
Charadriiformes
Laridae
Larus
Falconiformes
Accipitridae
Aquila
Harpia
Nyctidromus
Pithecophaga
Spizaetus
Galliformes
Megapodiidae
Crax
Opisthocomidae
Opisthocomus
Passeriformes
Coerebidae
Corvidae
Perisoreus
Drepanididae
Fringillidae
Plectrophenax
Icteridae
Meliphagidae
Nectariniidae
Oriolidae
Pipridae
Pipra
Ploceidae
Vidua
Thraupidae
Sylviidae
Vireonidae
Zosteropidae
Psittaciformes
Psittacidae
Trichoglossidae

MAMMALIA
Artiodactyla

Bovidae
Bos
Cephalophus
Connochaetes
Neotragus
Tayassuidae
Tayassu
Tragulidae
Hyemoschus
Carnivora
Canidae
Alopex
Canis
Felidae
Felis
Mustelidae
Mustela
Procyonidae
Nasua
Procyon
Ursidae
Thalarctos
Viverridae
Eupleres
Chiroptera
Desmodontidae
Desmodus
Nycteridae
Eonycteris
Phyllostomatidae
Artibeus
Carollia
Glossophaga
Phyllostomus
Pteropodidae
Eidolon
Hypsignathus
Macroglossus
Pteropus
Edentata
Bradypodidae
Bradypus
Choloepus
Dasypodidae
Dasypus
Myrmecophagidae
Cyclopes
Myrmecophaga
Tamandua
Insectivora
Tenrecidae
Hemicentetes
Tenrec
Marsupialia
Dasyuridae
Myrmecobius
Didelphidae
Marmosa
Macropodidae
Dendrolagus
Petauridae
Petaurus
Phalangeridae
Phalanger
Phascolarctidae
Phascolarctos

Tarsipedidae
Tarsipes
Monotremata
Tachyglossidae
Echidna
Zaglossus
Perissodactyla
Tapiridae
Tapirus
Pholidota
Manidae
Manis
Primates
Callithricidae
Aotus
Callithrix
Cebuella
Leontocebus
Cercopithecidae
Cercopithecus
Macaca
Colobidae
Colobus
Presbytis
Hylobatidae
Hylobates
Lemuridae
Arctocebus
Cheirogalus
Euoticus
Galago
Microcebus
Perodicticus
Lorisidae
Galago
Pongidae
Symphalangus
Proboscidea
Elephantidae
Elephas
Rodentia
Anomaluridae
Dasyproctidae
Dasyprocta
Heteromyidae
Liomys
Hydrochoeridae
Hydrochoerus
Microtidae
Dicrostonyx
Muridae
Mus
Ototylomus
Proechimys
Rattus
Sciuridae
Aethiosciurus
Citellus
Epixerus
Funisciurus
Heliosciurus
Myosciurus
Protoxerus
Tubulidentata
Orycteropodidae
Orycteropus

AUTHOR INDEX[1]

Aaltonen, V.T., 120, *132*
Abbott, W., 99, *115*
Abe, T., 79, 83, *89*, 161, 162, *165*
Abele, L.G., 329, *334*
Abelson, P.H., 118, *132*
Abruña, F., 285, 286, *287*, *288*
Addor, E.E., 52, *73*
Addy, N.D., 127, *134*
Adiosoemarto, S., 326, *333*
Adlard, P.G., 64, *73*
Aellen, V., 78
Albignac, R., 78, 273, *276*
Albonetti, S.G., *166*
Alder, D., 64, *73*, *74*
Alexander, A.J., 246, *262*
Alexander, D.J., *323*
Alexandre, J., 99
Allan, W., 302, *311*
Allen, G.M., 197, *209*
Allen, L.H., *134*
Allen, P.H., 191, *209*
Alvim, P. de T., 21, *26*, 190, *209*, 228, 233, 234, *236*
Alvim, R., 190, *209*, 228, *236*
Alway, F.J., 121, *132*
Ambroes, P., *133*
Amobi, C.C., 21, *26*
Andel, S., *287*
Anderson, A.B., 202, *214*
Anderson, J.A.R., 52, 58, *73*, 167, *180*
Andersson, F., 120, *132*
Andersson, S.O., 120, *132*
Andrews, R.M., 176, *180*
Apasuti, C., 75
Arean, V.M., 317, *323*
Arens, K., 235, *236*
Armstrong, J.S., 75
Arroyo, M.T.K., 186, *209*, 215
Art, H.W., 130, *132*
Aryee, A.F., 311, *312*
Ascoly, R.B., *287*
Ashton, P.S., 10, *26*, 29, 31, 39, *43*, *44*, 49, 50, 51, 52, 53, 58, *73*, 174, 185, 186, 188, 189, 204, *209*, *211*, *213*
Aubert, G., 285, *287*
Aubréville, A., 29, 30, *43*
Augspurger, C.K., 174, *180*
Ausmus, B.S., 142, *156*
Austin, M.P., 29, 38, 39, *44*

Axelrod, D.I., 6, *8*
Ayensu, E.S., 195, *209*, *333*

Baerreis, D.A., 343, *344*
Baker, H.G., 173, *180*, 183–190, 193–204, 206–208, *209–213*, 223, 226
Baker, I., 191, 198, 199, 201, 202, *209*, *210*
Baker, J.R., 191
Balding, D., *265*
Balenewan, J.L., 291, *300*
Ballinger, R.E., 248, *262*, 265
Bandhu, D., 123, *132*
Bandola-Ciolczyk, E., *134*
Bänziger, H., 195, *210*
Barnard, S.M., 243, *265*
Barrau, J., 303, 307, *311*
Barrett, R., *28*
Barrows, E.M., 197, *210*
Bartholomew, G.A., 243, 246, *262*
Bartoli, A., *166*
Bates, H.W., 7, 78, *89*, 94, *99*, 268, *276*
Bauchop, T., 268, *276*
Baumgartner, A., 49, *73*
Baur, G.N., 281, *287*
Bawa, K.S., 171, *180*, 183, 185, 186, 188–193, 197, *210*, *211*, *213*
Beach, J., 185, 188, *210*
Beard, J.S., 191, *210*, 225, *236*, 267, 272, *276*
Becker, P., 177, *180*
Beebe, W., 78, *89*
Bell, A.D., 9, 17, 19, *26*, *27*
Bell, E.A., *214*
Bellier, G., 78
Bendell, P.E.J., 321, *323*
Bennett, J.W., 339, *344*
Benson, C.W., 78, *89*
Bentley, B.L., 202, *210*
Berish, C., *222*
Berlin, B., *334*
Bernhard-Reversat, F., 29, 30, *44*, 45, 68, *73*, 105, *114*, 124, *132*, 138, 140, 141, *154*, 281, *287*
Berry, J.F., 261, *265*
Best, G.R., 141, *154*

Betts, B.J., *210*
Bhat, H.R., *324*
Biagi, F., 318, *323*
Biebl, R., 231, *236*
Biever, L., 163
Bingham, F.T., 133, *166*
Black, C., 127, 129, *132*
Black, G.A., 38, 39, 41, *44*, *46*, 196, *211*
Blackmer, A.M., 159, *165*
Blackstone, W.T., 343, *344*
Blackwood, B., 307, *311*
Blasini de Austin, S., *264*
Blaylock, L.A., 252, 253, *262*
Blommers-Schlösser, R., 78
Blow, F.E., 122, *132*
Blum, M.S., *215*
Boaler, S.B., 191, *210*
Boggs, C.L., *211*
Bolten, A.B., 199, *210*
Bonaccorso, F., 81, 85, *89*, 90
Bonnevie-Svendsen, C., 120
Boonyobhas, C., 290, *299*
Bormann, F.H., 21, *26*, *134*, *136*, 139, *154*, *166*
Borut, A., 263, *265*
Boserup, E., 308, *311*
Boshell, J., 318, *323*
Botkin, D.B., 118, *136*
Boulay, G.H. du, *see* Du Boulay, G.H.
Bourgeron, P.S., 29, 32, 33, 34, 37, 38, 39, 42, *44*
Bourlière, F., 79, *89*, 98, *99*
Bouxin, G., 29, 38, 39, 41, *44*
Bowen, H.J.M., 104, 109, *114*
Boysen-Jensen, P., 120, *132*
Bradburg, J.W., 275, *276*
Bradford, D.F., 172, *180*
Bradshaw, S.D., 249, *262*
Brattstrom, B.H., 244, 248, *262*
Bray, J.R., 119–124, 126, *132*
Breedlove, D.E., *334*
Breitsprecher, A., 21, *26*
Bremner, J.M., 159, *165*
Bres, P., 316, *323*
Briscoe, C.B., 281, *287*
Broekmans, A.F.M., 191, *210*
Brokaw, N., *222*
Bronson, B., 305, 306, 309, *311*

SYSTEMATIC INDEX[1]

[1] In this index, no attempt has been made, for larger taxonomic entities, to list all the pages where subordinate taxa are mentioned. These may be found by use of the Systematic List of Genera (pp. 345–347). For some major groupings, more detailed entries will be found in the General Index.

GENERAL INDEX